MW01166849

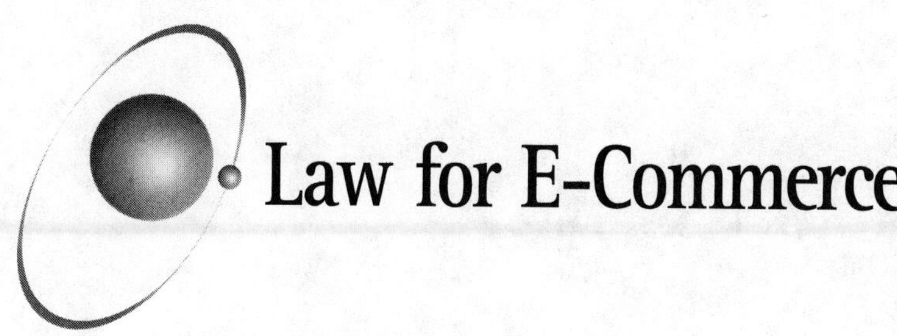
Law for E-Commerce

Law for E-Commerce

Roger LeRoy Miller
Institute for University Studies
Arlington, Texas

Gaylord A. Jentz
Herbert D. Kelleher Emeritus Professor in Business Law
University of Texas at Austin

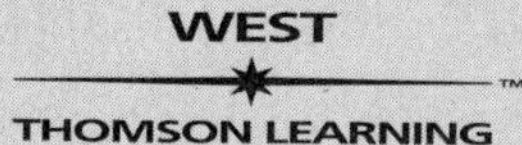

Australia · Canada · Mexico · Singapore · Spain · United Kingdom · United States

VICE PRESIDENT AND PUBLISHER: **Jack Calhoun**
SENIOR ACQUISITIONS EDITOR: **Rob Dewey**
SENIOR DEVELOPMENTAL EDITOR: **Jan Lamar**
PRODUCTION MANAGER: **Bill Stryker**
MANUFACTURING COORDINATOR: **Sandee Milewski**
MARKETING MANAGER: **Nicole Moore**
INTERNAL DESIGN: **Bill Stryker**
COMPOSITOR: **Parkwood Composition Service**
PRINTER: **West Group**
COVER DESIGN: **Paul Neff Design, Cincinnati**
COVER ILLUSTRATION: **Henk Dawson/Dawson 3D, Inc.**

Printed in the United States of America
1 2 3 4 5 04 03 02 01

Library of Congress Cataloging-in-Publication Data

Law for e-commerce/ Roger LeRoy Miller, Gaylord A. Jentz.
p. cm.
Includes bibliographic references and index.
ISBN 0-324-13159-3 (text)
ISBN 0-324-12279-9 (package)
1. Business law—United States 2. Electronic commerce—Law and legislation—United States. I. Jentz, Gaylord A. II. Title
KF889.3 .M53 2002
343.7309'944—dc21

2001035511

Contents in Brief

Contents

APPENDICES

Preface

The world of e-commerce is new, expanding, and increasingly important. Doing business online has led to dramatic improvements in efficiency in numerous industries. The ability to communicate in written form at virtually zero cost to anyone located anywhere in the world and at any time has speeded up the process of globalization. To some extent, the importance of e-commerce cannot be measured by the value of the annual transactions consummated online. This number is impressive—measuring in the many billions of dollars and growing rapidly—but it doesn't tell the full story, for e-commerce is now pervasive. It affects management, marketing, human resources, finance, accounting/taxation, and economics.

Currently, our legal system is struggling to keep up with the changes occurring in the online world. Never before has the law had to be adapted so quickly to new business practices. Yet in the last few years, a body of law for e-commerce has been evolving, as old law is adapted to the online world and new legislation is passed. Today's student and businessperson alike must have at least a passing knowledge of how the law is being applied in the online world—not only to understand the intersection of law and e-commerce, but also to be able to fully utilize the benefits of e-commerce.

At the outset, we must emphasize that the basic principles of law do not change simply because we are entering the online legal environment. To be sure, Congress and state legislatures are enacting new laws that specifically address certain problems in the online environment. Yet for the most part, old principles of law are being adapted and applied to new problems generated by evolving technology. Consequently, the basics of our legal environment are a necessary starting point for understanding law for e-commerce.

The Organization of This Book

Because the basic foundations of the law provide the framework for the study of law for e-commerce, Unit One of this text (the first six chapters) is, in effect, a mini-course in our legal environment. Chapter 1 presents a straightforward introduction to law. In Chapters 2 and 3, dispute resolution is examined in detail, including the resolution of disputes over domain names. In Chapter 4, we examine torts and crimes—civil and criminal wrongs. These wrongs take on a special significance when they occur in cyberspace. As you might expect, a thorough understanding of intellectual property is critical for understanding law for e-commerce. Chapters 5 and 6 deal with the legal protection available for intellectual property (including patents, copyrights, trademarks, cyber marks, and trade secrets) in both the offline and online environments.

The remaining chapters of this text examine law for e-commerce as it relates to management, marketing, human resources, finance, accounting/taxation, and economics. We strongly believe that a wide variety of students taking basic and advanced courses in these six disciplines will benefit not only from a basic introduction to the online legal environment but also from a study of law for e-commerce relating specifically to their specialized areas of study. Consequently, we offer this text in six additional modularized editions. Each of these streamlined editions includes Chapters 1 through 6, or the core chapters, plus two chapters relating to a particular discipline. Each module includes a full set of appendices.

A Companion Web Site

Instructors and students can access the companion Web site for *Law for E-Commerce* at http://lec.westbuslaw.com. The Web site offers Internet Applications (consisting of Internet activities for every chapter in this text), Instructor Resources, Student Resources, Court Case Updates, a "Talk to the Author" feature, and other useful resources.

Special Features

We have included in this text two special features, one focusing on controversial issues in the online world and the other offering guidelines on some aspect of e-commerce. Each chapter contains one or more of these features, which we describe here.

CONTROVERSIAL ISSUES IN THE ONLINE WORLD Not surprisingly, because e-commerce is so new, controversies abound with respect to how the law should be applied to the online world. In features titled *Controversial Issues in the Online World,* we look at the most pressing and exciting of these controversies. Here are just a few of the topics discussed in these features:

- Electronic Filing and Privacy Issues (Chapter 2).
- Is Virtual Pornography a Crime? (Chapter 4).
- Code-Cracking Software for DVDs Online—The Courts Speak (Chapter 5).

Each *Controversial Issues* feature concludes with a question "For Critical Analysis."

E-GUIDELINES Because so much business is now being conducted online, students and businesspersons alike can benefit from certain guidelines relating to e-commerce. Thus, most of the chapters in the text include a special *E-Guidelines* feature. Some examples are:

- ODR Guidelines for E-Commerce (Chapter 2).
- The Protection of Privacy Rights in Cyberspace (Chapter 4).
- Copyright Protection in a Digital Age (Chapter 5).

Each of the *E-Guidelines* features ends with a checklist that offers a series of practical tips for businesspersons.

An Effective Case Format

Even those business students and businesspersons who are not familiar with the law can profit from seeing how the courts reason through legal issues. The best way to do so is to actually read what the courts (judges) have said. Thus, in every chapter we present three to six actual court cases, each of which contains excerpts from the court's opinion. The cases are numbered sequentially for easy referencing in class discussions, homework assignments, and examinations.

Each case is presented in a special format, which begins with the case title and citation (including parallel citations). Whenever possible, we also include a URL, just below the case citation, that can be used to access the case online. Whenever a URL is presented, a footnote to the URL explains how students can navigate the site accessed to find the specific case. Following the citations for the case, we present sections giving the background and facts of the case, excerpts from the court opinion showing the court's reasoning on the issue, and the decision and remedy in the case.

In addition, many of the cases are preceded by a *Company Profile,* which provides background information on a party to the case, or a *Historical and Social [or other] Setting.* Each case concludes with a *For Critical Analysis* question that invites the reader to consider further one of the issues touched on in the case or some related issue, such as the ethical implications of the court's decision.

Other Special Features of This Text

We believe that the best way to learn is to have a text that contains a complete set of pedagogical devices. *Law for E-Commerce* is such a text. We list here the special pedagogical devices we use:

- **Concepts Covered**—These are key learning objectives that give the reader an overall view of what lies ahead.
- **In-Margin Definitions of Key Legal Terms**—Terminology is one of the biggest stumbling blocks in learning law concepts. Key legal and technological terms are described not only in the text but also in the margin.
- **In-Margin *On the Web* Features**—Whenever appropriate, a specific link to a relevant Web page is given.
- **Exhibits**—When appropriate, an exhibit is presented to further illustrate a point. For example, in Chapter 3, exhibits illustrate the extent to which the Internet is used for online shopping, the number of Internet-related consumer complaints, the number of these complaints that are resolved through online dispute resolution, and so on. Chapter 4 includes an exhibit illustrating how the same act can lead to a tort lawsuit as well as a criminal prosecution. An exhibit in Chapter 5 summarizes the various forms of intellectual property.
- **Terms and Concepts**—At the end of each chapter, we present a list of all important terms and concepts that were boldfaced and defined in the margins within the chapter. Any reader who has doubts about the meaning of a term or concept can turn to the referenced page number in this list for the term's definition.
- **Questions and Case Problems**—Every chapter ends with a full set of questions and case problems that instructors can assign. Each case problem is fol-

lowed by the full case title and citation so that readers who wish to do so can examine the entire court opinion.

Appendices

Many readers will want to keep *Law for E-Commerce* as a reference book. Consequently, we provide a full set of appendices appropriate for the online legal world. They include:

Appendix A: **Digital Millennium Copyright Act of 1998 (Excerpts)**

Appendix B: **ICANN's Uniform Domain Name Dispute-Resolution Policy (Excerpts)**

Appendix C: **Anticybersquatting Consumer Protection Act of 1999 (Excerpts)**

Appendix D: **Federal Trademark Dilution Act of 1995 (Excerpts)**

Appendix E: **Uniform Electronic Transactions Act (Excerpts)**

Appendix F: **Uniform Computer Information Transactions Act (Excerpts)**

Appendix G: **Electronic Signatures in Global and National Commerce Act of 2000 (Excerpts)**

Appendix H: **Internet Tax Freedom Act of 1998 (Excerpts)**

A Full Set of Supplements

Instructors using this text can order a full set of supplements. These supplements include a comprehensive *Instructor's Manual with Test Bank* and an *Answers Manual*. The *Answers Manual* presents suggested answers to the hypothetical questions in the *Questions and Case Problems* section at the end of each chapter, as well as the court's conclusion and reasoning for the actual case problems presented in that section.

A number of other supplements are also available, including the following:

- *Handbook of Landmark Cases and Statutes in Business Law.*
- *Handbook on Critical Thinking and Writing.*
- *A Guide to Personal Law.*
- Westlaw®.
- Court TV®.
- *CNN® Legal Issues* Update Video.
- *Business Law: The Game.*
- *Quicken® Business Lawyer®* 2000 CD-ROM and Applications.
- *Black's Handbook of Basic Law Terms.*
- *The New York Times Guide to Business Law and Legal Environment.*
- InfoTrac® College Edition.

Acknowledgments

In preparing this text, we were the fortunate recipients of an incredibly skilled and dedicated editorial, production, and printing and manufacturing team at West. In particular, we wish to thank Rob Dewey and Jan Lamar for their guidance and helpful advice during each stage of the project. We owe a lasting debt of gratitude to our production manager, Bill Stryker, for his impressive design and his amazing ability to turn around quickly our materials. We are also indebted to Peggy Buskey for her work on the companion Web site and to Nicole Moore for her marketing skills.

Numerous other individuals helped us to create an up-to-date, error-free book in a brief span of time. We particularly thank William Eric Hollowell, who provided much of the necessary research, and Lavina Leed Miller, who coordinated the project and provided editorial and research assistance from the outset of the project through its final stages. We were fortunate to have the copyediting and proofreading services of Suzie Franklin DeFazio. We also thank Roxie Lee for her proofreading and other assistance, which helped us to meet our ambitious publishing schedule, and Sue Jasin of K&M Consulting for her contributions to the project.

More than any other subject in the field of law and the legal environment, law for e-commerce is changing rapidly. Instructors, students, and businesspersons who have comments about additional topics that we should include in future editions should write us directly. We value all such comments and will take them to heart when we start the second edition of this text.

Roger LeRoy Miller
Gaylord Jentz

DEDICATION

To Nello,
Your tireless efforts at helping me reach
excellence go beyond friendship.
I'll never attain your level,
but I'll look better while trying.
Thanks.

–R.L.M.

To my wife, JoAnn; my children, Kathy,
Gary, Lori, and Rory; and my grandchildren,
Erin, Megan, Eric, Emily, Michelle, Javier,
Carmen, and Steve.

–G.A.J.

The Online Legal Environment

Contents

CHAPTER 1
Introduction to Law

Concepts Covered

After reading this chapter, you should be able to:

1. Explain what is generally meant by the term *law*.
2. Describe the origins and importance of the common law tradition.
3. Identify the four major sources of American law.
4. List some important classifications of law.
5. Define what is meant by the term *cyberlaw*.

"The law is of as much interest to the layman as it is to the lawyer."

Lord Balfour, 1848–1930
(British prime minister, 1902–1905)

One of the most important functions of law in any society is to provide stability, predictability, and continuity so that people can be sure of how to order their affairs. If any society is to survive, its members must be able to determine what is legally right and legally wrong. They must know what sanctions will be imposed on them if they commit wrongful acts. If they suffer harm as a result of others' wrongful acts, they need to know how they can seek redress. By setting forth the rights, obligations, and privileges of residents, the law enables individuals to go about their business with confidence and a certain degree of predictability. The stability and predictability created by the law provide an essential framework for all civilized activities, including business activities.

In this introductory chapter, we first look at the nature of law and then examine the foundation and fundamental characteristics of the American legal system. We next describe the basic sources of American law and some general classifications of law. We conclude with a discussion of how the electronic environment of cyberspace is altering the traditional American legal landscape. Finally, in a special appendix to this chapter, we offer practical guidance on several topics, including how to find the sources of law discussed in this chapter (and referred to throughout the text) and how to read and understand court opinions.

Section 1 WHAT IS LAW?

LAW
A body of enforceable rules governing relationships among individuals and between individuals and their society.

There have been and will continue to be different definitions of law. Although the definitions of law vary in their particulars, they all are based on the general observation that, at a minimum, law consists of *enforceable rules governing relationships among individuals and between individuals and their society.* These "enforceable rules" may consist of unwritten principles of behavior established by a nomadic tribe. They may be set forth in a law code, such as the Code of

Hammurabi in ancient Babylon or the law code of one of today's European nations. They may consist of written laws and court decisions created by modern legislative and judicial bodies, as in the United States. Regardless of how such rules are created, they all have one thing in common: they establish rights, duties, and privileges that are consistent with the values and beliefs of their society or its ruling group.

Because of our common law tradition (which will be discussed shortly), the courts—and thus the personal views and philosophies of judges—play a paramount role in the American legal system. This is particularly true of the United States Supreme Court, which has the final say on how a particular law or legal principle should be interpreted and applied. Indeed, Oliver Wendell Holmes, Jr., once stated that law was a set of rules that allowed one to predict how a court would resolve a particular dispute—"the prophecies [predictions] of what the courts will do in fact, and nothing more pretentious, are what I mean by the law."

Clearly, judges are not free to decide cases solely on the basis of their personal philosophical views or their opinions on the issues before the court. A judge's function is not to make the laws—that is the function of the legislative branch of government—but to interpret and apply them. From a practical point of view, however, the courts play a significant role in defining what the law is. This is because laws enacted by legislative bodies tend to be expressed in general terms. Judges thus have some flexibility in interpreting and applying the law. It is because of this flexibility that different courts can, and often do, arrive at different conclusions in cases that involve nearly identical issues, facts, and applicable laws. This flexibility also means that each judge's unique personality, legal philosophy, set of values, and intellectual attributes frame, to some extent, the judicial decision-making process.

SECTION 2 THE COMMON LAW TRADITION

Because of our colonial heritage, much of American law is based on the English legal system, which originated in medieval England and continued to evolve in the following centuries. A knowledge of this system is necessary for an understanding of the American legal system today.

Early English Courts

The origins of the English legal system—and thus the U.S. legal system as well—date back to 1066, when the Normans conquered England. William the Conqueror and his successors began the process of unifying the country under their rule. One of the means they used to this end was the establishment of the king's courts, or *curiae regis*. Before the Norman Conquest, disputes had been settled according to the local legal customs and traditions in various regions of the country. The king's courts sought to establish a uniform set of customs for the country as a whole. What evolved in these courts was the beginning of the **common law**—a body of general rules that prescribed social conduct and applied throughout the entire English realm.

COMMON LAW
That body of law developed from custom or judicial decisions in English and U.S. courts, not attributable to a legislature.

REMEDY
The relief given to an innocent party to enforce a right or compensate for the violation of a right.

COURTS OF LAW AND REMEDIES AT LAW In the early English king's courts, the kinds of **remedies** (the legal means to recover a right or redress a wrong)

COURT OF LAW
A court in which the only remedies that could be granted were things of value, such as money damages. In the early English king's courts, courts of law were distinct from courts of equity.

REMEDY AT LAW
A remedy available in a court of law. Money damages are awarded as a remedy at law.

DAMAGES
Money sought as a remedy by a party whose legal interests have been injured.

COURT OF EQUITY
A court that decides controversies and administers justice according to the rules, principles, and precedents of equity.

REMEDY IN EQUITY
A remedy allowed by courts in situations where remedies at law are not appropriate. Remedies in equity are based on settled rules of fairness, justice, and honesty, and include injunction, specific performance, rescission and restitution, and reformation.

EQUITABLE MAXIMS
General propositions or principles of law that have to do with fairness (equity).

that could be granted were severely restricted. If one person wronged another in some way, the king's courts could award as compensation one or more of the following: (1) land, (2) items of value, or (3) money. The courts that awarded this compensation became known as **courts of law,** and the three remedies were called **remedies at law.** (Today, the remedy at law normally takes the form of money **damages**—money given to a party whose legal interests have been injured.) Even though the system introduced uniformity in the settling of disputes, when a complaining party wanted a remedy other than economic compensation, the courts of law could do nothing, so "no remedy, no right."

COURTS OF EQUITY AND REMEDIES IN EQUITY Equity is a branch of law, founded on what might be described as notions of justice and fair dealing, that seeks to supply a remedy when no adequate remedy at law is available. When individuals could not obtain an adequate remedy in a court of law because of strict technicalities, they petitioned the king for relief. Most of these petitions were decided by an adviser to the king, called a *chancellor,* who was said to be the "keeper of the king's conscience." When the chancellor thought that the claims were fair, new and unique remedies were granted. Eventually, formal chancery courts, or **courts of equity,** were established.

The remedies granted by equity courts became known as **remedies in equity,** or equitable remedies. These remedies include *specific performance* (ordering a party to perform an agreement as promised), an *injunction* (ordering a party to cease engaging in a specific activity or to undo some wrong or injury), and *rescission* (the cancellation of a contractual obligation). As a general rule, today's courts, like the early English courts, will not grant equitable remedies unless the remedy at law—money damages—is inadequate.

In fashioning appropriate remedies, judges often were (and continue to be) guided by so-called **equitable maxims**—propositions or general statements of equitable rules. Exhibit 1–1 lists some important equitable maxims. The last maxim listed in that exhibit—"Equity aids the vigilant, not those who rest on their rights"—merits special attention. It has become known as the equitable doc-

Exhibit 1–1 Equitable Maxims

1. *Whoever seeks equity must do equity.* (Anyone who wishes to be treated fairly must treat others fairly.)
2. *Where there is equal equity, the law must prevail.* (The law will determine the outcome of a controversy in which the merits of both sides are equal.)
3. *One seeking the aid of an equity court must come to the court with clean hands.* (Plaintiffs must have acted fairly and honestly.)
4. *Equity will not suffer a wrong to be without a remedy.* (Equitable relief will be awarded when there is a right to relief and there is no adequate remedy at law.)
5. *Equity regards substance rather than form.* (Equity is more concerned with fairness and justice than with legal technicalities.)
6. *Equity aids the vigilant, not those who rest on their rights.* (Equity will not help those who neglect their rights for an unreasonable period of time.)

trine of **laches** (a term derived from the Latin *laxus,* meaning "lax" or "negligent"), and it can be used as a defense. A **defense** is an argument raised by the **defendant** (the party being sued) indicating why the **plaintiff** (the suing party) should not obtain the remedy sought. (Note that in equity proceedings, the party bringing a lawsuit is called the **petitioner,** and the party being sued is referred to as the **respondent.**)

The doctrine of laches arose to encourage people to bring lawsuits while the evidence was fresh. What constitutes a reasonable time, of course, varies according to the circumstances of the case. Time periods for different types of cases are now usually fixed by **statutes of limitations.** After the time allowed under a statute of limitations has expired, no action can be brought, no matter how strong the case was originally.

LACHES
The equitable doctrine that bars a party's right to legal action if the party has neglected for an unreasonable length of time to act on his or her rights.

DEFENSE
That which a defendant offers and alleges in an action or suit as a reason why the plaintiff should not recover or establish what he or she seeks.

DEFENDANT
One against whom a lawsuit is brought; the accused person in a criminal proceeding.

PLAINTIFF
One who initiates a lawsuit.

PETITIONER
In equity practice, a party that initiates a lawsuit.

RESPONDENT
In equity practice, the party who answers a bill or other proceeding.

STATUTE OF LIMITATIONS
A federal or state statute setting the maximum time period during which a certain action can be brought or certain rights enforced.

Legal and Equitable Remedies Today

The establishment of courts of equity in medieval England resulted in two distinct court systems: courts of law and courts of equity. The systems had different sets of judges and granted different types of remedies. Parties who sought legal remedies, or remedies at law, would bring their claims before courts of law. Parties seeking equitable relief, or remedies in equity, would bring their claims before courts of equity. During the nineteenth century, however, most states in the United States adopted rules of procedure that resulted in combined courts of law and equity—although some states, such as Arkansas, still retain the distinction. A party now may request both legal and equitable remedies in the same action, and the trial court judge may grant either or both forms of relief.

The distinction between legal and equitable remedies remains relevant to students of business law, however, because these remedies differ. To seek the proper remedy for a wrong, one must know what remedies are available. Additionally, certain vestiges of the procedures used when there were separate courts of law and equity still exist. For example, a party has the right to demand a jury trial in an action at law, but not in an action in equity. In the old courts of equity, the chancellor heard both sides of an issue and decided what should be done. Juries were considered inappropriate. In actions at law, however, juries participated in determining the outcome of cases, including the amount of damages to be awarded. Exhibit 1–2 summarizes the procedural differences (applicable in most states) between an action at law and an action in equity.

Exhibit 1–2 Procedural Differences between an Action at Law and an Action in Equity

Procedure	Action at Law	Action in Equity
Initiation of lawsuit	By filing a complaint	By filing a petition
Parties	Plaintiff and defendant	Petitioner and respondent
Decision	By jury or judge	By judge (no jury)
Result	Judgment	Decree
Remedy	Monetary damages	Injunction, specific performance, or rescission

The Doctrine of *Stare Decisis*

One of the unique features of the common law is that it is *judge-made* law. The body of principles and doctrines that form the common law emerged over time as judges decided actual legal controversies.

PRECEDENT
A court decision that furnishes an example or authority for deciding subsequent cases involving identical or similar facts.

REPORTER
A publication in which court cases are published, or reported.

CASE PRECEDENTS AND CASE REPORTERS When possible, judges attempted to be consistent and to base their decisions on the principles suggested by earlier cases. They sought to decide similar cases in a similar way and considered new cases with care, because they knew that their decisions would make new law. Each interpretation became part of the law on the subject and served as a legal **precedent**—that is, a decision that furnished an example or authority for deciding subsequent cases involving similar legal principles.

By the early fourteenth century, portions of the most important decisions of each year were being gathered together and recorded in *Year Books,* which became useful references for lawyers and judges. In the sixteenth century, the *Year Books* were discontinued, and other forms of case publication became available. Today, cases are published, or "reported," in volumes called **reporters,** or *reports.* We describe today's case reporting system in detail later in this chapter.

STARE DECISIS
A common law doctrine under which judges are obligated to follow the precedents established in prior decisions.

STARE DECISIS* AND THE COMMON LAW TRADITION** The practice of deciding new cases with reference to former decisions, or precedents, became a cornerstone of the English and American judicial systems. The practice forms a doctrine called ***stare decisis[1] (a Latin phrase meaning "to stand on decided cases"). Under this doctrine, judges are obligated to follow the precedents established within their jurisdictions.

For example, suppose that the lower state courts in California have reached conflicting conclusions on whether drivers are liable for accidents they cause while merging into freeway traffic, even though the drivers looked and did not see any oncoming traffic and even though witnesses (passengers in their cars) testified to that effect. To settle the law on this issue, the California Supreme Court decides to review a case involving this fact pattern. The court rules that in such a situation, the driver who is merging into traffic is liable for any accidents caused by the driver's failure to yield to freeway traffic—regardless of whether the driver looked carefully and did not see an approaching vehicle.

BINDING AUTHORITY
Any source of law that a court must follow when deciding a case. Binding authorities include constitutions, statutes, and regulations that govern the issue being decided, as well as court decisions that are controlling precedents within the jurisdiction.

The California Supreme Court's decision on this matter will influence the outcome of all future cases on this issue brought before the California state courts. Similarly, a decision on a given question by the United States Supreme Court (the nation's highest court) is binding on all courts. Case precedents, as well as statutes and other laws that must be followed, are referred to as **binding authorities.** (Nonbinding legal authorities on which judges may rely for guidance, such as precedents established in other jurisdictions, are referred to as *persuasive authorities.*)

The doctrine of *stare decisis* helps the courts to be efficient, because if other courts have carefully analyzed a similar case, their legal reasoning and opinions can serve as guides. *Stare decisis* also makes the law stable and predictable. If the law on a given subject is well settled, someone bringing a case

1. Prononunced *ster*-ay dih-*si*-ses.

to court can usually rely on the court to make a decision based on what the law has been in the past.

DEPARTURES FROM PRECEDENT Although courts are obligated to follow precedents, sometimes a court will depart from the rule of precedent if it decides that the precedent should no longer be followed. If a court decides that a ruling precedent is simply incorrect or that technological or social changes have rendered the precedent inapplicable, the court might rule contrary to the precedent. Cases that overturn precedent often receive a great deal of publicity.[2]

Note that judges have some flexibility in applying precedents. For example, a trial court may avoid applying a Supreme Court precedent by arguing that the facts of the case before the court are distinguishable from the facts in the Supreme Court case—therefore, the Supreme Court's ruling on the issue does not apply to the case before the court.

WHEN THERE IS NO PRECEDENT Occasionally, cases come before the courts for which no precedents exist. Such cases, called *cases of first impression*, often result when new practices or technological developments in society create new types of legal disputes. In the last several years, for example, the courts have had to deal with disputes involving transactions conducted via the Internet. When existing laws governing free speech, pornography, fraud, jurisdiction, and other areas were drafted, cyberspace did not exist. Although new laws are being created to govern such disputes, in the meantime the courts have to decide, on a case-by-case basis, what rules should be applied.

Generally, in deciding cases of first impression, courts consider a number of factors, including persuasive authorities (such as cases from other jurisdictions, if there are any), legal principles and policies underlying previous court decisions or existing statutes, fairness, social values and customs, **public policy** (governmental policy based on widely held societal values), and data and concepts drawn from the social sciences. Which of these sources is chosen or receives the greatest emphasis depends on the nature of the case being considered and the particular judge or judges hearing the case. As mentioned previously, judges are not free to decide cases on the basis of their own personal views. In cases of first impression, as in all cases, judges must have legal reasons for ruling as they do on particular issues. When a court issues a written opinion on a case (we discuss court opinions in the appendix that follows this chapter), the opinion normally contains a carefully reasoned argument justifying the decision.

PUBLIC POLICY
A government policy based on widely held societal values and (usually) expressed or implied in laws or regulations.

Stare Decisis and Legal Reasoning

LEGAL REASONING
The process of reasoning by which a judge harmonizes his or her decision with the judicial decisions of previous cases.

Legal reasoning is the reasoning process used by judges in deciding what law applies to a given dispute and then applying that law to the specific facts or

2. For example, when the United States Supreme Court held in the 1950s that racial segregation in the public schools was unconstitutional, it expressly overturned a Supreme Court precedent upholding the constitutionality of "separate-but-equal" segregation. The Supreme Court's departure from precedent received a tremendous amount of publicity as people began to realize the ramifications of this change in the law. See *Brown v. Board of Education of Topeka*, 347 U.S. 483, 74 S.Ct. 686, 98 L.Ed. 873 (1954). (Legal citations are explained in a special appendix following this chapter.)

circumstances of the case. Through the use of legal reasoning, judges harmonize their decisions with those that have been made before, as required by the doctrine of *stare decisis.*

Students of business law also engage in legal reasoning. For example, you may be asked to provide answers for some of the case problems that appear at the end of every chapter in this text. Each problem describes the facts of a particular dispute and the legal question at issue. If you are assigned a case problem, you will be asked to determine how a court would answer that question and why. In other words, you will need to give legal reasons for whatever conclusion you reach. We look here at the basic steps involved in legal reasoning and then describe some forms of reasoning commonly used by the courts in making their decisions.

BASIC STEPS IN LEGAL REASONING At times, the legal arguments set forth in court opinions are relatively simple and brief. At other times, the arguments are complex and lengthy. Regardless of the brevity or length of a legal argument, however, the basic steps of the legal reasoning process remain the same in all cases. These steps, which you also can follow when analyzing cases and case problems, form what is commonly referred to as the *IRAC method* of legal reasoning. IRAC is an acronym comprised of the first letters of the following words: Issue, Rule, Application, and Conclusion. To apply the IRAC method, you would ask the following questions:

1. *What are the key facts and issues?* For example, suppose that a plaintiff comes before the court claiming *assault* (a wrongful and intentional action, or tort, in which one person makes another fearful of immediate physical harm). The plaintiff claims that the defendant threatened her while she was sleeping. Although the plaintiff was unaware that she was being threatened, her roommate heard the defendant make the threat. The legal issue, or question, raised by these facts is whether the defendant's actions constitute the tort of assault, given that the plaintiff was not aware of those actions at the time they occurred.

2. *What rules of law apply to the case?* A rule of law may be a rule stated by the courts in previous decisions, a state or federal statute, or a state or federal administrative agency regulation. In our hypothetical case, the plaintiff **alleges** (claims) that the defendant committed a tort. Therefore, the applicable law is the common law of torts—specifically, tort law governing assault (see Chapter 4 for more detail on torts). Case precedents involving similar facts and issues thus would be relevant. Often, more than one rule of law will be applicable to a case.

ALLEGE
To state, recite, assert, or charge.

3. *How do the rules of law apply to the particular facts and circumstances of this case?* This step is often the most difficult one, because each case presents a unique set of facts, circumstances, and parties. Although there may be similar cases, no two cases are ever identical in all respects. Normally, judges (and lawyers and law students) try to find **cases on point**—previously decided cases that are as similar as possible to the one under consideration. This is a difficult, but important, step.

CASE ON POINT
A previous case involving factual circumstances and issues that are similar to the case before the court.

4. *What conclusion should be drawn?* This step normally presents few problems. Usually, the conclusion is evident if the previous three steps have been followed carefully.

FORMS OF LEGAL REASONING Judges use many types of reasoning when following the third step of the legal reasoning process—applying the law to the facts of a particular case. Three common forms of reasoning are deductive reasoning, linear reasoning, and reasoning by analogy.

Deductive Reasoning. Deductive reasoning is sometimes called syllogistic reasoning because it employs a **syllogism**—a logical relationship involving a major premise, a minor premise, and a conclusion. For example, consider the hypothetical case presented earlier, in which the plaintiff alleged that the defendant committed assault by threatening her while she was sleeping. The judge might point out that "under the common law of torts, an individual must be *aware* of a threat of danger for the threat to constitute civil assault" (major premise); "the plaintiff in this case was unaware of the threat at the time it occurred" (minor premise); and "therefore, the circumstances do not amount to a civil assault" (conclusion).

SYLLOGISM
A form of deductive reasoning consisting of a major premise, a minor premise, and a conclusion.

Linear Reasoning. A second important form of legal reasoning that is commonly employed might be thought of as "linear" reasoning, because it proceeds from one point to another, with the final point being the conclusion. An analogy will help make this form of reasoning clear. Imagine a knotted rope, with each knot tying together separate pieces of rope to form a tight length. As a whole, the rope represents a linear progression of thought logically connecting various points, with the last point, or knot, representing the conclusion. For example, suppose that a tenant in an apartment building sues the landlord for damages for an injury resulting from an allegedly dimly lit stairway. The court may engage in a reasoning process involving the following "pieces of rope":

1. The landlord, who was on the premises the evening the injury occurred, testifies that none of the other nine tenants who used the stairway that night complained about the lights.
2. The fact that none of the tenants complained is the same as if they had said the lighting was sufficient.
3. That there were no complaints does not prove that the lighting was sufficient, but it proves that the landlord had no reason to believe that it was not.
4. The landlord's belief was reasonable, because no one complained.
5. Therefore, the landlord acted reasonably and was not negligent in respect to the lighting in the stairway.

On the basis of this reasoning, the court concludes that the tenant is not entitled to compensation on the basis of the stairway's lighting.

Reasoning by Analogy. Another important type of reasoning that judges use in deciding cases is reasoning by *analogy.* To reason by **analogy** is to compare the facts in the case at hand to the facts in other cases and, to the extent that the patterns are similar, to apply the same rule of law to the present case. To the extent that the facts are unique, or "distinguishable," different rules may apply. For example, in case A, it is held that a driver who crosses a highway's center line is negligent. In case B, a driver crosses the line to avoid hitting a child. In determining whether case A's rule applies in case B, a judge would consider the reasons for the decision in case A and whether case B is sufficiently similar for those reasons to apply. If the judge holds that B's driver is not liable, that judge must indicate why case A's rule does not apply to the facts presented in case B.

ANALOGY
In logical reasoning, an assumption that if two things are similar in some respects, they will be similar in other respects also. Often used in legal reasoning to infer the appropriate application of legal principles in a case being decided by referring to previous cases involving different facts but considered to come within the policy underlying the rule.

There Is No One "Right" Answer

Many persons believe that there is one "right" answer to every legal question. In most situations involving a legal controversy, however, there is no single correct result. Good arguments can often be made to support either side of a legal controversy. Quite often, a case does not present the situation of a "good" person suing a "bad" person. In many cases, both parties have acted in good faith in some measure or have acted in bad faith to some degree.

Additionally, as already mentioned, each judge has his or her own personal beliefs and philosophy, which shape, at least to some extent, the process of legal reasoning. What this means is that the outcome of a particular lawsuit before a court can never be predicted with absolute certainty. In fact, in some cases, even though the weight of the law would seem to favor one party's position, judges, through creative legal reasoning, have found ways to rule in favor of the other party in the interests of preventing injustice.

CONCEPT SUMMARY 1.1—THE COMMON LAW TRADITION

SOURCE	DESCRIPTION
Origins of the Common Law	The American legal system is based on the common law tradition, which originated in medieval England. Following the conquest of England in 1066 by William the Conqueror, king's courts were established throughout England, and the common law was developed in these courts.
Legal and Equitable Remedies	The distinction between remedies at law (money or items of value, such as land) and remedies in equity (including specific performance, injunction, and rescission of a contractual obligation) originated in the early English courts of law and courts of equity, respectively.
Case Precedents and the Doctrine of *Stare Decisis*	In the king's courts, judges attempted to make their decisions consistent with previous decisions, called precedents. This practice gave rise to the doctrine of *stare decisis*. This doctrine, which became a cornerstone of the common law tradition, obligates judges to abide by precedents established in their jurisdictions.
***Stare Decisis* and Legal Reasoning**	Legal reasoning refers to the reasoning process used by judges in applying the law to the facts and issues of specific cases. Legal reasoning involves becoming familiar with the key facts of a case, identifying the relevant legal rules, linking those rules to the facts, and forming a conclusion. In linking the legal rules to the facts of a case, judges may use deductive reasoning, linear reasoning, or reasoning by analogy.

SECTION 3 SOURCES OF AMERICAN LAW

There are numerous sources of American law. *Primary sources of law,* or sources that establish the law, include the following:

1. The U.S. Constitution and the constitutions of the various states.
2. Statutory law—including laws passed by Congress, state legislatures, or local governing bodies.

3. Regulations created by administrative agencies, such as the Food and Drug Administration.

4. Case law and common law doctrines.

We describe each of these important sources of law in the following pages.

Secondary sources of law are books and articles that summarize and clarify the primary sources of law. Examples are legal encyclopedias, treatises, articles in law reviews, and compilations of law, such as the *Restatements of the Law* (which will be discussed shortly). Courts often refer to secondary sources of law for guidance in interpreting and applying the primary sources of law discussed here.

On the Web

You can access many of the sources of law discussed in this chapter at the FindLaw Web site, which is probably the most comprehensive source of free legal information on the Internet, at **http://www.findlaw.com**.

Constitutional Law

The federal government and the states have separate written constitutions that set forth the general organization, powers, and limits of their respective governments. **Constitutional law** is the law as expressed in these constitutions.

CONSTITUTIONAL LAW
Law that is based on the U.S. Constitution and the constitutions of the various states.

According to Article VI of the U.S. Constitution, the Constitution is the supreme law of the land. As such, it is the basis of all law in the United States. A law in violation of the Constitution, if challenged, will be declared unconstitutional and will not be enforced, no matter what its source.

The Tenth Amendment to the U.S. Constitution reserves all powers not granted to the federal government to the states. Each state in the union has its own constitution. Unless it conflicts with the U.S. Constitution or a federal law, a state constitution is supreme within the state's borders.

Statutory Law

Laws enacted by legislative bodies at any level of government, such as the statutes passed by Congress or by state legislatures, make up the body of law generally referred to as **statutory law.** When a legislature passes a statute, that statute ultimately is included in the federal code of laws or the relevant state code of laws (these codes are discussed later in this chapter).

STATUTORY LAW
The body of law enacted by legislative bodies (as opposed to constitutional law, administrative law, or case law).

Statutory law also includes local **ordinances**—statutes (laws, rules, or orders) passed by municipal or county governing units to govern matters not covered by federal or state law. Ordinances commonly have to do with city or county land use (zoning ordinances), building and safety codes, and other matters affecting the local unit.

ORDINANCE
A law passed by a local governing unit, such as a municipality or a county.

A federal statute, of course, applies to all states. A state statute, in contrast, applies only within the state's borders. State laws thus may vary from state to state. No federal statute may violate the U.S. Constitution, and no state statute or local ordinance may violate the U.S. Constitution or the relevant state constitution.

UNIFORM LAWS The differences among state laws were particularly notable in the 1800s, when conflicting state statutes frequently made trade and commerce among the states very difficult. To counter these problems, in 1892 a group of legal scholars and lawyers formed the National Conference of Commissioners on Uniform State Laws (NCCUSL) to draft **uniform laws,** or model laws, for the states to consider adopting. The NCCUSL still exists today and continues to issue uniform laws.

UNIFORM LAW
A model law created by the National Conference of Commissioners on Uniform State Laws and/or the American Law Institute for the states to consider adopting. If the state adopts the law, it becomes statutory law in that state. Each state has the option of adopting or rejecting all or part of a uniform law.

The Library of Congress offers extensive links to state and federal government resources at **http://www.loc.gov**.

Each state has the option of adopting or rejecting a uniform law. *Only if a state legislature adopts a uniform law does that law become part of the statutory law of that state.* Note that a state legislature may adopt all or part of a uniform law as it is written, or the legislature may rewrite the law however the legislature wishes. Hence, even when a uniform law is said to have been adopted in many states, those states' laws may not be entirely "uniform."

The earliest uniform law, the Uniform Negotiable Instruments Law, had been completed by 1896 and adopted in every state by the early 1920s (although not all states used exactly the same wording). Over the following decades, other acts were drawn up in a similar manner. In all, over two hundred uniform acts have been issued by the NCCUSL since its inception. The most ambitious uniform act of all, however, was the Uniform Commercial Code.

THE UNIFORM COMMERCIAL CODE The Uniform Commercial Code (UCC), which was created through the joint efforts of the NCCUSL and the American Law Institute,[3] was first issued in 1952. The UCC has been adopted in all fifty states,[4] the District of Columbia, and the Virgin Islands. The UCC facilitates commerce among the states by providing a uniform, yet flexible, set of rules governing commercial transactions. The UCC assures businesspersons that their contracts, if validly entered into, normally will be enforced.

ADMINISTRATIVE LAW The body of law created by administrative agencies (in the form of rules, regulations, orders, and decisions) in order to carry out their duties and responsibilities.

ADMINISTRATIVE AGENCY A federal or state government agency established to perform a specific function. Administrative agencies are authorized by legislative acts to make and enforce rules to administer and enforce the acts.

EXECUTIVE AGENCY An administrative agency within the executive branch of government. At the federal level, executive agencies are those within the cabinet departments.

INDEPENDENT REGULATORY AGENCY An administrative agency that is not considered part of the government's executive branch and is not subject to the authority of the president. Independent agency officials cannot be removed without cause.

Administrative Law

An important source of American law is **administrative law**—which consists of the rules, orders, and decisions of administrative agencies. An **administrative agency** is a federal, state, or local government agency established to perform a specific function. Administrative law and procedures constitute a dominant element in the regulatory environment of business. Rules issued by various administrative agencies now affect virtually every aspect of a business's operation, including the firm's capital structure and financing, its hiring and firing procedures, its relations with employees and unions, and the way it manufactures and markets its products.

FEDERAL AGENCIES At the national level, numerous **executive agencies** exist within the cabinet departments of the executive branch. The Food and Drug Administration, for example, is an agency within the Department of Health and Human Services. Executive agencies are subject to the authority of the president, who has the power to appoint and remove officers of federal agencies. There are also major **independent regulatory agencies** at the federal level, such as the Federal Trade Commission, the Securities and Exchange Commission, and the Federal Communications Commission. Although these agencies are part of the executive branch of government, the president's power is less pronounced in regard to them because their officers serve for fixed terms and cannot be removed without just cause.

3. This institute was formed in the 1920s and consists of practicing attorneys, legal scholars, and judges.

4. Louisiana has not adopted Articles 2 and 2A (covering contracts for the sale and lease of goods), however.

STATE AND LOCAL AGENCIES There are administrative agencies at the state and local levels as well. Commonly, a state agency (such as a state pollution-control agency) is created as a parallel to a federal agency (such as the Environmental Protection Agency). Just as federal statutes take precedence over conflicting state statutes, so federal agency regulations take precedence over conflicting state regulations. Increasingly, administrative agencies at all levels of government are delivering services via the Internet—see this chapter's *E-Guidelines* feature on the next page for a discussion of this development.

Case Law and Common Law Doctrines

As is evident from the earlier discussion of the common law tradition, another basic source of American law consists of the rules of law announced in court decisions. These rules of law include interpretations of constitutional provisions, of statutes enacted by legislatures, and of regulations created by administrative agencies. Today, this body of law is referred to variously as the common law, judge-made law, or **case law**.

CASE LAW
The rules of law announced in court decisions. Case law includes the aggregate of reported cases that interpret judicial precedents, statutes, regulations, and constitutional provisions.

THE RELATIONSHIP BETWEEN THE COMMON LAW AND STATUTORY LAW Common law doctrines and principles govern all areas not covered by statutory or administrative law. In a dispute concerning a particular employment practice, for example, if a statute regulates that practice, the statute will apply rather than the common law doctrine that applied prior to the enactment of the statute.

Even though the body of statutory law has expanded greatly since the beginning of this nation, thus narrowing the applicability of common law doctrines, there is a significant overlap between statutory law and the common law. For example, many statutes essentially codify existing common law rules, and thus the courts, in interpreting these statutes, often rely on the common law as a guide to what the legislators intended.

Additionally, how the courts interpret a particular statute determines how that statute will be applied. If you wanted to learn about the coverage and applicability of a particular statute, for example, you would, of course, need to locate the statute and study it. You would also need to see how the courts in your jurisdiction have interpreted the statute—in other words, what precedents have been established in regard to that statute. Often, the applicability of a newly enacted statute does not become clear until a body of case law develops to clarify how, when, and to whom the statute applies.

Restatements of the Law. The American Law Institute (ALI) has drafted and published compilations of the common law called *Restatements of the Law,* which generally summarize the common law rules followed by most states. There are *Restatements of the Law* in the areas of contracts, torts, agency, trusts, property, restitution, security, judgments, and conflict of laws. The *Restatements,* like other secondary sources of law, do not in themselves have the force of law but are an important source of legal analysis and opinion on which judges often rely in making their decisions.

Many of the *Restatements* are now in their second or third editions. For example, the ALI has recently published the first volume of the third edition of

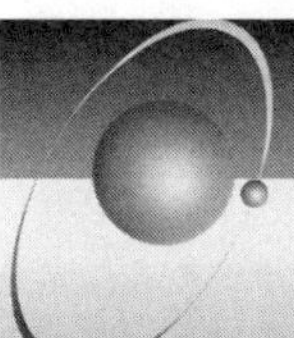

E-Guidelines

Accessing Government Agencies on the Web

Most large cities and all of the agencies of the federal government offer information and assistance via the Internet. Today, most local governments have Web sites on which they list public meeting schedules, post public documents, and offer other services to their citizens. Americans can also access virtually all state and national government agencies online. Among other things, they can find information on state and national parks, the rules for naturalization and immigration, and decisions rendered by state and federal courts.

EZ Government on the Web

Due to security issues and the high level of technology required, far fewer interactive applications are available to citizens at government agency Web sites than can be found in the world of e-commerce. Nevertheless, their number is growing. Increasingly, state and local government agencies are allowing citizens to use the Internet for a variety of transactions, such as paying for parking tickets or renewing driver's licenses. In Riverside, California, tax bills are payable through the Internet. In Atlanta, citizens can pay parking tickets, renew their driver's licenses, and obtain building permits by going online. In Maryland, some professionals can renew their licenses by visiting a state government site.

In 2000, the federal government launched an interactive Web site (Pay.gov) that will allow Americans to conduct any number of transactions online. These transactions will include applying for passports, paying off student loans, and filing forms with the Immigration and Naturalization Service.

The federal government also maintains FirstGov.gov, a Web site designed to serve as a gateway to all government information on the Internet. For example, from this site, users can conduct research at the Library of Congress or track a National Aeronautics and Space Administration (NASA) mission. Also, through this portal, users can interact with agencies online to conduct such business as applying for student loans, tracking Social Security benefits, and administering government contracts.

Online Government Is Less Costly

Today, businesses and individuals conduct transactions worth about $600 billion with federal, state, and local governments each year. A tiny fraction—less than 1 percent—of these funds changes hands over the Internet. That amount will increase sharply over the next decade, providing a number of benefits to taxpayers. Besides being more convenient, a "virtual government" will be less costly. The state of Maryland, for example, saved $1.6 million when 40 percent of its 250,000 professionals renewed their licenses online. Arizona saves $5 every time a citizen renews her or his vehicle registration via the Internet. Eventually, those savings are passed on to the taxpayer.

CHECKLIST

- ☑ Bookmark (set Favorites) FirstGov.gov and other important government Web sites.
- ☑ Before you physically go to a government agency or even call it, check the appropriate Web site to see if you can accomplish your task online.
- ☑ See if you can sign up for an e-mailing list with the government agencies with which you have the most contact.

the *Restatement of the Law of Torts.* References to second or third editions of the *Restatements* often identify the specific edition in parentheses. For example, a reference to the second edition of the *Restatement of the Law of Contracts* may read simply the *Restatement (Second) of Contracts.*

CONCEPT SUMMARY 1.2—SOURCES OF AMERICAN LAW

SOURCE	DESCRIPTION
Constitutional Law	The law as expressed in the U.S. Constitution and the state constitutions. The U.S. Constitution is the supreme law of the land. State constitutions are supreme within state borders to the extent that they do not violate a clause of the U.S. Constitution or a federal law.
Statutory Law	Laws (statutes and ordinances) created by federal, state, and local legislatures and governing bodies. None of these laws may violate the U.S. Constitution or the relevant state constitution. Uniform statutes, when adopted by a state, become statutory law in that state.
Administrative Law	The rules, orders, and decisions of federal or state government administrative agencies.
Case Law and Common Law Doctrines	Judge-made law, including interpretations of constitutional provisions, of statutes enacted by legislatures, and of regulations created by administrative agencies. The common law—the doctrines and principles embodied in case law—governs all areas not covered by statutory or administrative law.

SECTION 4 CLASSIFICATIONS OF LAW

Because the body of law is so large, one must break it down by some means of classification. A number of classification systems have been devised. For example, one classification system divides law into substantive law and procedural law. **Substantive law** consists of all laws that define, describe, regulate, and create legal rights and obligations. **Procedural law** consists of all laws that establish the methods of enforcing the rights established by substantive law.

Another classification system divides law into civil law and criminal law. **Civil law** is concerned with the duties that exist among persons or between citizens and their governments, excluding the duty not to commit crimes. Typically, in a civil case, a private party sues another private party (although the government can also sue a party for a civil law violation) to make that other party comply with a duty or pay for the damage caused by failure to comply with a duty. Much of the law that we discuss in this text is civil law. The whole body of tort law (see Chapter 4), for example, is civil law, as is the law governing contracts.

Criminal law, in contrast, is concerned with wrongs committed *against the public as a whole*. Criminal acts are defined and prohibited by local, state, or federal government statutes and prosecuted by public officials, such as a district attorney (D.A.), on behalf of the state, not by their victims or other private parties.

Other classification systems divide law into federal law and state law, private law (dealing with relationships among private entities) and public law (addressing the relationship between persons and their governments), national law and international law, and so on.

SUBSTANTIVE LAW
Law that defines the rights and duties of individuals with respect to each other, as opposed to procedural law, which defines the manner in which these rights and duties may be enforced.

PROCEDURAL LAW
Rules that define the manner in which the rights and duties of individuals may be enforced.

CIVIL LAW
The branch of law dealing with the definition and enforcement of all private or public rights, as opposed to criminal matters.

CRIMINAL LAW
Law that defines and governs actions that constitute crimes. Generally, criminal law has to do with wrongful actions committed against society for which society demands redress.

The Virtual Law Library Index, created and maintained by the Indiana University School of Law, provides an index of legal sources categorized by subject at **http://www.law.indiana.edu**.

CYBERLAW
An informal term that refers to all laws governing electronic communications and transactions, particularly those conducted via the Internet.

SECTION 5 E-COMMERCE AND THE LAW

Increasingly, traditional laws are being adapted and applied to new legal issues stemming from the use of a new medium—the Internet—to conduct business transactions. Additionally, new laws are being created to deal specifically with such issues. Frequently, people use the term **cyberlaw** to designate the emerging body of law (consisting of court decisions, newly enacted or amended statutes, and so on) that governs cyberspace transactions. Cyberlaw is not really a classification of law; rather, it is an informal term used to describe how traditional classifications of law, such as civil law and criminal law, are being applied to online activities.

Anyone preparing to enter today's business world will find it useful to know how old and new laws are being applied to activities conducted online, such as advertising, contracting, banking, filing documents with the courts or government agencies, employment relations, and a variety of other transactions. For that reason, this text is devoted entirely to this topic. Special features throughout the text also focus on how technology, and particularly the use of the Internet, is transforming the business world.

TERMS AND CONCEPTS

QUESTIONS AND CASE PROBLEMS

1–1. Statutory versus Common Law. How does statutory law come into existence? How does it differ from the common law? If statutory law conflicts with the common law, which law will govern?

1–2. Reading Citations. Assume that you want to read the entire court opinion in the case of *Millennium Enterprises, Inc. v. Millennium Music, LP,* 33 F.Supp.2d 907 (D.Or. 1999). The case considers whether a South Carolina business firm could be sued in Oregon based on the circumstance that its Web site could be accessed in Oregon. Read the section entitled "Finding Case Law" in the appendix that follows this chapter, and then explain specifically where you would find the court's opinion.

1–3. Sources of American Law. This chapter discussed a number of sources of American law. Which source of law takes priority in the following situations, and why?

(a) A federal statute conflicts with the U.S. Constitution.
(b) A federal statute conflicts with a state constitutional provision.
(c) A state statute conflicts with the common law of that state.
(d) A state constitutional amendment conflicts with the U.S. Constitution.

1–4. *Stare Decisis.* In the text of this chapter, we stated that the doctrine of *stare decisis* "became a cornerstone of the English and American judicial systems." What does *stare decisis* mean, and why has this doctrine been so fundamental to the development of our legal tradition?

1–5. Court Opinions. Look at the appendix that follows this chapter, which discusses court opinions. What is the difference between a concurring opinion and a majority opinion? Between a concurring opinion and a dissenting opinion? Why do judges and justices write concurring and dissenting opinions, given the fact that these opinions will not affect the outcome of the case at hand, which has already been decided by majority vote?

1–6. Common Law versus Statutory Law. Courts can overturn precedents and thus change the common law. Should judges have the same authority to overrule statutory law? Explain.

1–7. *Stare Decisis.* "The judge's role is not to make the law but to uphold and apply the law." Do you agree or disagree with this statement? Discuss fully the reasons for your answer.

WEB EXERCISES

This text's Web site also offers online research exercises. These exercises will help you find and analyze specific types of legal information available at designated Web sites. To access these exercises, go to this book's Web site at **http://lec.westbuslaw.com** and click on "Internet Applications." When that page opens, select the relevant chapter to find the Web exercise or exercises relating to topics in that chapter. The following exercise will direct you to some of the important sources of law discussed in Chapter 1:

Activity 1–1: Internet Sources of Law

CHAPTER 1 Appendix

The Bluebook: A Uniform System of Citation offers detailed information on the format for citations to legal sources at **http://www.law.cornell.edu/citation/citation.table.html**.

SECTION 1 FINDING AND ANALYZING THE LAW

The statutes, agency regulations, and case law referred to in this text establish the rights and duties of businesspersons engaged in various types of activities. The cases presented in the following chapters provide you with concise, real-life illustrations of how the courts interpret and apply these laws. Because of the importance of knowing how to find statutory, administrative, and case law, this appendix offers a brief introduction to how these laws are published and to the legal "shorthand" employed (in citations) when referencing these legal sources.

SECTION 2 FINDING STATUTORY AND ADMINISTRATIVE LAW

When Congress passes laws, they are collected in a publication titled *United States Statutes at Large*. When state legislatures pass laws, they are collected in similar state publications. Most frequently, however, laws are referred to in their codified form–that is, the form in which they appear in the federal and state codes.

In these codes, laws are compiled by subject. The *United States Code* (U.S.C.) arranges all existing federal laws of a public and permanent nature by subject. Each of the fifty subjects into which the U.S.C. arranges the laws is given a title and a title number. For example, laws relating to commerce and trade are collected in Title 15, "Commerce and Trade." Titles are subdivided by sections. A citation to the U.S.C. includes title and section numbers. Thus, a reference to "15 U.S.C. Section 1" means that the statute can be found in Section 1 of Title 15. ("Section" may also be designated by the symbol §, and "Sections," by §§.) Sometimes a citation includes the abbreviation *et seq.*, as in "15 U.S.C. Sections 1 *et seq.*" The term is an abbreviated form of *et sequitur,* which in Latin means "and the following"; when used in a citation, it refers to sections that concern the same subject as the numbered section and follow it in sequence.

State codes follow the U.S.C. pattern of arranging law by subject. They may be called codes, revisions, compilations, consolidations, general statutes, or statutes, depending on the preferences of the states. In some codes, subjects are designated by number. In others, they are designated by name. For example, "13 Pennsylvania Consolidated Statutes Section 1101" means that the statute can be found in Title 13, Section 1101, of the Pennsylvania code. "California Commercial Code Section 1101" means the statute can be found under the subject heading "Commercial Code" of the California code in Section 1101. Abbreviations may be used. For example, "13 Pennsylvania Consolidated

Statutes Section 1101" may be abbreviated "13 Pa. C.S. §1101," and "California Commercial Code Section 1101" may be abbreviated "Cal. Com. Code §1101."

Commercial publications of these laws and regulations are available and are widely used. For example, West Group publishes the *United States Code Annotated* (U.S.C.A.). The U.S.C.A. contains the complete text of laws included in the U.S.C., plus notes on court decisions that interpret and apply specific sections of the statutes, as well as the text of presidential proclamations and executive orders. The U.S.C.A. also includes research aids, such as cross-references to related statutes, historical notes, and library references. A citation to the U.S.C.A. is similar to a citation to the U.S.C.: "15 U.S.C.A. Section 1."

Rules and regulations adopted by federal administrative agencies are initially published in the *Federal Register,* a daily publication of the U.S. government. Later, they are incorporated into the *Code of Federal Regulations* (C.F.R.). Like the U.S.C., the C.F.R. is divided into fifty titles. Rules within each title are assigned section numbers. A full citation to the C.F.R. includes title and section numbers. For example, a reference to "17 C.F.R. Section 230.504" means that the rule can be found in Section 230.504 of Title 17.

SECTION 3 FINDING CASE LAW

To understand how to read citations to court cases, we need first to look briefly at the court system. As will be discussed in Chapter 2, there are two types of courts in the United States, federal courts and state courts. Both the federal and state court systems consist of several levels, or tiers, of courts.

Trial courts, in which evidence is presented and testimony given, are on the bottom tier (which also includes lower courts handling specialized issues). Decisions from a trial court can be appealed to a higher court, commonly an intermediate *court of appeals,* or an *appellate court.* Decisions from these intermediate courts of appeals may be appealed to an even higher court, such as a state supreme court or the United States Supreme Court.

When reading the cases presented in this text, you will note that most of the state court cases are from state appellate courts. This is because most state trial court opinions are not published. Except in New York and a few other states that publish selected opinions of their trial courts, decisions from the state trial courts are merely filed in the office of the clerk of the court, where they are available for public inspection. Many of the federal trial (district) courts do publish their opinions, however, and you will find that several of the cases set forth in this book are from these courts, as well as the federal appellate courts.

State Court Decisions

Written decisions of the state appellate, or reviewing, courts are published and distributed in volumes called *Reports,* which are numbered consecutively, and collectively referred to as reporters.

Decisions of the appellate courts of a particular state are found in the reporters of that state. A few states–including those with intermediate appellate courts, such as California, Illinois, and New York–have more than one reporter for opinions given by their courts.

Additionally, state court opinions appear in regional units of the National Reporter System, published by West Group. Most lawyers and libraries have the West reporters because they report cases more quickly, and are distributed more widely, than the state-published reporters. In fact, many states have eliminated their own reporters in favor of West's National Reporter System. The National Reporter System divides the states into the following geographical areas: *Atlantic* (A. or A.2d), *South Eastern* (S.E. or S.E.2d), *South Western* (S.W. or S.W.2d), *North Western* (N.W. or N.W.2d), *North Eastern* (N.E. or N.E.2d), *Southern* (So. or So.2d), and *Pacific* (P. or P.2d). (The *2d* in the preceding abbreviations refers to *Second Series.* In the near future, the designation *3d,* for *Third Series,* will be used for some of the regional reporters.) The states included in each of these regional divisions are indicated in Exhibit 1A–1, which illustrates West's National Reporter System.

After an appellate decision has been published, it is normally referred to (cited) by the name of the case (called the *style* of the case); the volume, name, and page of the state's official reporter (if different from West's National Reporter System); the volume, unit, and page number of the National Reporter; and the volume, name, and page number of any other selected reporter. (Citing a reporter by volume number, name, and page number, in that order, is common to all citations; often, as in this book, the year the decision was made will be included in parentheses, just following the citations to reporters.) When more than one reporter is cited for the same case, each reference is called a *parallel citation.*[5]

For example, consider the following case citation: *Crews v. Hollenbach,* 126 Md.App. 609, 730 A.2d 742 (1999). We see that the opinion in this case may be found in Volume 126 of the official *Maryland Appellate Reports,* on page 609. The parallel citation is to Volume 730 of the *Atlantic Reporter, Second Series,* page 742. In reprinting appellate opinions in this text, in addition to the reporter, we give the name of the court hearing the case and the year of the court's decision. Citations to state court decisions are explained in Exhibit 1A–2 on page 22.

Federal Court Decisions

The Center for Information Law and Policy, a joint project by Villanova Law School and the Illinois Institute of Technology's Chicago-Kent College of Law, provides access to numerous legal resources, including opinions from the federal appellate courts. Go to **http://www.clip.org**.

Federal district (trial) court decisions are published unofficially in West's *Federal Supplement* (F.Supp. or F.Supp.2d), and opinions from the circuit courts of appeals are reported unofficially in West's *Federal Reporter* (F., F.2d, or F.3d). Cases concerning federal bankruptcy law are published unofficially in West's *Bankruptcy Reporter* (Bankr.).

The official edition of all decisions of the United States Supreme Court for which there are written opinions is the *United States Reports* (U.S.), which is published by the federal government. The series includes reports of Supreme Court cases dating from the August term of 1791, although many of the Supreme Court's decisions were not reported in the early volumes.

5. Note that Wisconsin recently adopted a "public-domain citation system" in which the format is somewhat different. For example, a Wisconsin Supreme Court decision might be designated "2000 WI 40," meaning that the case was decided in the year 2000 by the Wisconsin Supreme Court and was the fortieth decision issued by that court during that year. (Parallel citations to the *Wisconsin Reports* and West's *North Western Reporter* are still required when citing Wisconsin cases, but they must follow the public-domain citation.)

Exhibit 1A–1 National Reporter System—Regional/Federal

Regional Reporters	Coverage Beginning	Coverage
Atlantic Reporter (A. or A.2d)	1885	Connecticut, Delaware, Maine, Maryland, New Hampshire, New Jersey, Pennsylvania, Rhode Island, Vermont, and District of Columbia.
North Eastern Reporter (N.E. or N.E.2d)	1885	Illinois, Indiana, Massachusetts, New York, and Ohio.
North Western Reporter (N.W. or N.W.2d)	1879	Iowa, Michigan, Minnesota, Nebraska, North Dakota, South Dakota, and Wisconsin.
Pacific Reporter (P. or P.2d)	1883	Alaska, Arizona, California, Colorado, Hawaii, Idaho, Kansas, Montana, Nevada, New Mexico, Oklahoma, Oregon, Utah, Washington, and Wyoming.
South Eastern Reporter (S.E. or S.E.2d)	1887	Georgia, North Carolina, South Carolina, Virginia, and West Virginia.
South Western Reporter (S.W. or S.W.2d)	1886	Arkansas, Kentucky, Missouri, Tennessee, and Texas.
Southern Reporter (So. or So.2d)	1887	Alabama, Florida, Louisiana, and Mississippi.
Federal Reporters		
Federal Reporter (F., F.2d, or F.3d)	1880	U.S. Circuit Court from 1880 to 1912; U.S. Commerce Court from 1911 to 1913; U.S. District Courts from 1880 to 1932; U.S. Court of Claims (now called U.S. Court of Federal Claims) from 1929 to 1932 and since 1960; U.S. Court of Appeals since 1891; U.S. Court of Customs and Patent Appeals since 1929; and U.S. Emergency Court of Appeals since 1943.
Federal Supplement (F.Supp. or F.Supp.2d)	1932	U.S. Court of Claims from 1932 to 1960; U.S. District Courts since 1932; and U.S. Customs Court since 1956.
Federal Rules Decisions (F.R.D.)	1939	U.S. District Courts involving the Federal Rules of Civil Procedure since 1939 and Federal Rules of Criminal Procedure since 1946.
Supreme Court Reporter (S.Ct.)	1882	U.S. Supreme Court since the October term of 1882.
Bankruptcy Reporter (Bankr.)	1980	Bankruptcy decisions of U.S. Bankruptcy Courts, U.S. District Courts, U.S. Courts of Appeals, and U.S. Supreme Court.
Military Justice Reporter (M.J.)	1978	U.S. Court of Military Appeals and Courts of Military Review for the Army, Navy, Air Force, and Coast Guard.

NATIONAL REPORTER SYSTEM MAP

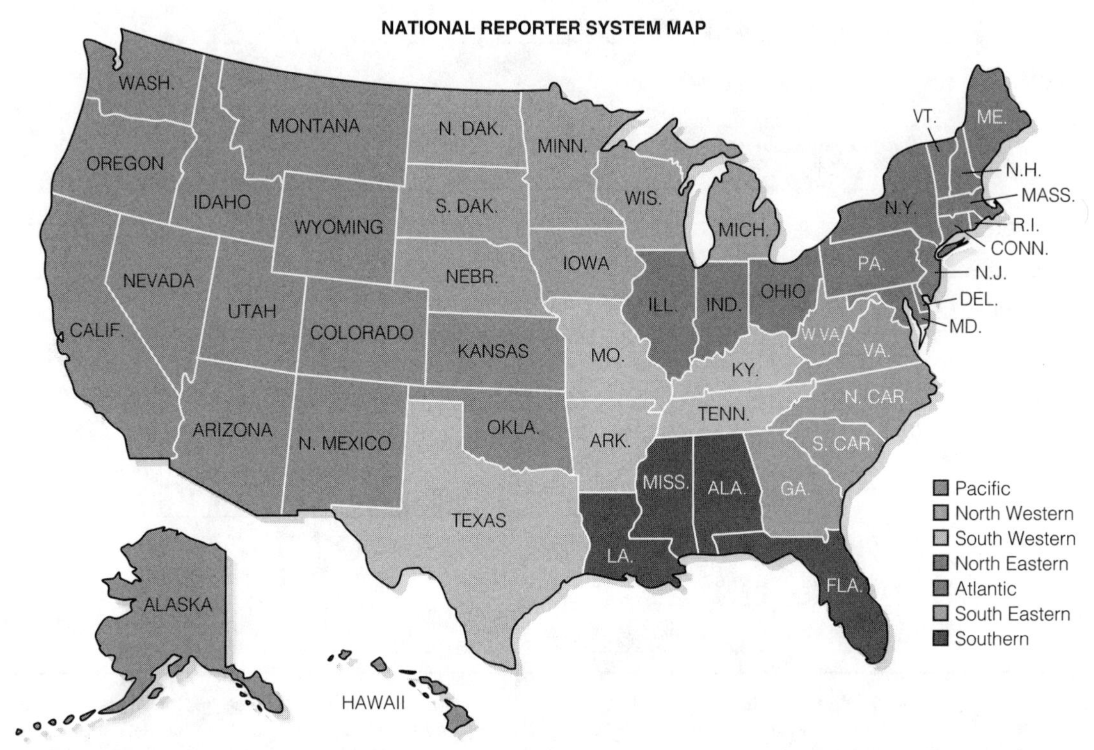

Exhibit 1A–2 How to Read Citations

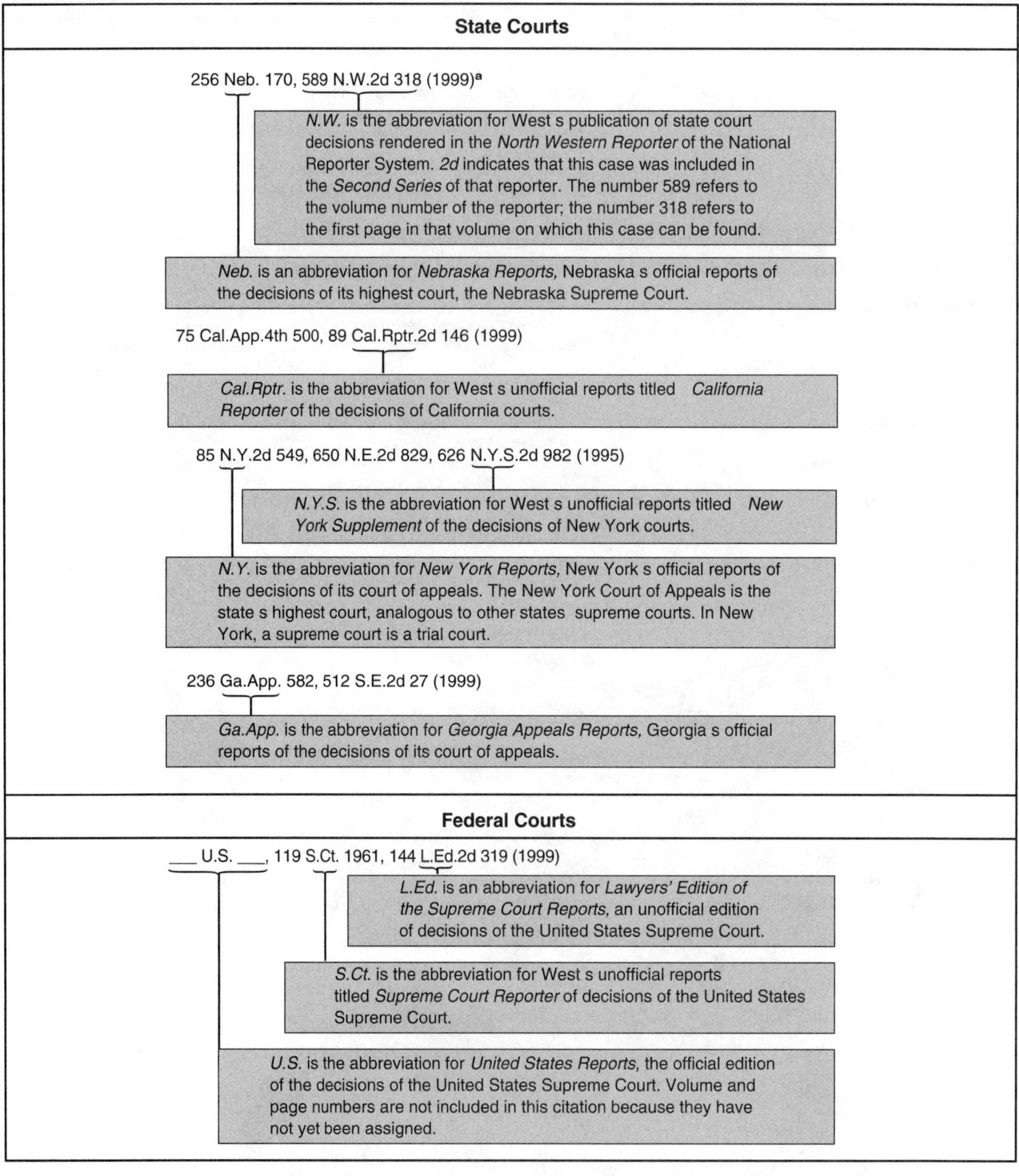

a.°°The case names have been deleted from these citations to emphasize the publications. It should be kept in mind, however that the name of a case is as important as the specific numbers of the volumes in which it is found. If a citation is incorrect, the correct citation may be found in a publication s index of case names. The date of a case is also important because, in addition to providing a check on error in citations, the value of a recent case as an authority is likely to be greater than that of an earlier case.

State Courts
256 Neb. 170, 589 N.W.2d 318 (1999)[a]
N.W. is the abbreviation for West s publication of state court decisions rendered in the North Western Reporter of the National Reporter System. 2d indicates that this case was included in the Second Series of that reporter. The number 589 refers to the volume number of the reporter; the number 318 refers to the first page in that volume on which this case can be found.
Neb. is an abbreviation for Nebraska Reports, Nebraska s official reports of the decisions of its highest court, the Nebraska Supreme Court.
75 Cal.App.4th 500, 89 Cal.Rptr.2d 146 (1999)
Cal.Rptr. is the abbreviation for West s unofficial reports titled California Reporter of the decisions of California courts.
85 N.Y.2d 549, 650 N.E.2d 829, 626 N.Y.S.2d 982 (1995)
N.Y.S. is the abbreviation for West s unofficial reports titled New York Supplement of the decisions of New York courts.
N.Y. is the abbreviation for New York Reports, New York s official reports of the decisions of its court of appeals. The New York Court of Appeals is the state s highest court, analogous to other states supreme courts. In New York, a supreme court is a trial court.
236 Ga.App. 582, 512 S.E.2d 27 (1999)
Ga.App. is the abbreviation for Georgia Appeals Reports, Georgia s official reports of the decisions of its court of appeals.
Federal Courts
___ U.S. ___, 119 S.Ct. 1961, 144 L.Ed.2d 319 (1999)
L.Ed. is an abbreviation for Lawyers' Edition of the Supreme Court Reports, an unofficial edition of decisions of the United States Supreme Court.
S.Ct. is the abbreviation for West s unofficial reports titled Supreme Court Reporter of decisions of the United States Supreme Court.
U.S. is the abbreviation for United States Reports, the official edition of the decisions of the United States Supreme Court. Volume and page numbers are not included in this citation because they have not yet been assigned.

Exhibit 1A–2 How to Read Citations (Continued)

Federal Courts (continued)

177 F.3d 114 (2d Cir. 1999)

2d Cir. is an abbreviation denoting that this case was decided in the United States Court of Appeals for the Second Circuit.

38 F.Supp.2d 1233 (D.Colo. 1999)

D.Colo. is an abbreviation indicating that the United States District Court for the District of Colorado decided this case.

English Courts

9 Exch. 341, 156 Eng.Rep. 145 (1854)

Eng.Rep. is an abbreviation for *English Reports, Full Reprint,* a series of reports containing selected decisions made in English courts between 1378 and 1865.

Exch. is an abbreviation for *English Exchequer Reports,* which included the original reports of cases decided in England s Court of Exchequer.

Statutory and Other Citations

18 U.S.C. Section 1961(1)(A)

U.S.C. denotes *United States Code,* the codification of *United States Statutes at Large.* The number 18 refers to the statute s U.S.C. title number and 1961 to its section number within that title. The number 1 refers to a subsection within the section and the letter A to a subdivision within the subsection.

UCC 2—206(1)(b)

UCC is an abbreviation for *Uniform Commercial Code.* The first number 2 is a reference to an article of the UCC and 206 to a section within that article. The number 1 refers to a subsection within the section and the letter b to a subdivision within the subsection.

Restatement (Second) of Contracts, Section 162

Restatement (Second) of Contracts refers to the second edition of the American Law Institute s *Restatement of the Law of Contracts.* The number 162 refers to a specific section.

17 C.F.R. Section 230.505

C.F.R. is an abbreviation for *Code of Federal Regulations,* a compilation of federal administrative regulations. The number 17 designates the regulation s title number, and 230.505 designates a specific section within that title.

Exhibit 1A–2 How to Read Citations (Continued)

Westlaw® Citations

2001 WL 12345

WL is an abbreviation for Westlaw®. The number 2001 is the year of the document that can be found with this citation in the Westlaw® database. The number 12345 is a number assigned to a specific document. A higher number indicates that a document was added to the Westlaw® database later in the year.

Uniform Resource Locators[b]

www.westlaw.com

The suffix *com* is the top-level domain (TLD) for this Web site. The TLD *com* is an abbreviation for "commercial," which means that a for-profit entity hosts (maintains or supports) this Web site.

westlaw is the host name—the part of the domain name selected by the organization that registered the name. In this case, West Group registered the name. This Internet site is the Westlaw database on the Web.

www is an abbreviation for "World Wide Web." The Web is a system of Internet servers[c] that support documents formatted in *HTML* (hypertext markup language). HTML supports links to text, graphics, and audio and video files.

www.uscourts.gov

This is the "Federal Judiciary Home Page." The host is the Administrative Office of the U.S. Courts. The TLD *gov* is an abbreviation for "government." This Web site includes information and links from, and about, the federal courts.

www.law.cornell.edu/index.html

This part of a URL points to a Web page or file at a specific location within the host's domain. This page, at this Web site, is a menu with links to documents within the domain and to other Internet resources.

This is the host name for a Web site that contains the Internet publications of the Legal Information Institute (LII), which is a part of Cornell Law School. The LII site includes a variety of legal materials and links to other legal resources on the Internet. The TLD *edu* is an abbreviation for "educational institution" (a school or a university).

www.ipl.org/ref/RR

RR is an abbreviation for this Web site's "Ready Reference Collection," which contains links to a variety of Internet resources.

ref is an abbreviation for "Internet Public Library Reference Center," which is a map of the topics into which the links at this Web site have been categorized.

ipl is an abbreviation for Internet Public Library, which is an online service that provides reference resources and links to other information services on the Web. The IPL is supported chiefly by the School of Information at the University of Michigan. The TLD *org* is an abbreviation for "organization (nonprofit)."

b. The basic form for a URL is "service://hostname/path." The Internet service for all of the URLs in this text is *http* (hypertext transfer protocol). Most Web browsers will add this prefix automatically when a user enters a host name or a hostname/path.

c. A *server* is hardware that manages the resources on a network. For example, a network server is a computer that manages the traffic on the network, and a print server is a computer that manages one or more printers.

Unofficial editions of Supreme Court cases include West's *Supreme Court Reporter* (S.Ct.), which includes cases dating from the Court's term in October 1882; and the *Lawyers' Edition of the Supreme Court Reports* (L.Ed or L.Ed.2d), published by the Lawyers Cooperative Publishing Company (now a part of West Group). The latter contains many of the decisions not reported in the early volumes of the *United States Reports.*

Sample citations for federal court decisions are also listed and explained in Exhibit 1A–2.

Old Case Law

On a few occasions, this text cites opinions from old, classic cases dating to the nineteenth century or earlier; some of these are from the English courts. The citations to these cases appear not to conform to the descriptions given above, because the reporters in which they were published were often known by the name of the person who compiled the reporter and have since been replaced.

Case Digests and Legal Encyclopedias

The body of American case law consists of over five million decisions, to which more than forty thousand decisions are added each year. Because judicial decisions are published in chronological order, finding relevant precedents would be a Herculean task if it were not for secondary sources of law that classify decisions according to subject. Two important "finding tools" that are helpful when researching case law are case digests, such as West's *American Digest System;* and legal encyclopedias, such as *American Jurisprudence, Second Edition,* and *Corpus Juris Secundum,* both published by West Group.

SECTION 4 HOW TO READ AND UNDERSTAND CASE LAW

The decisions made by the courts establish the boundaries of the law as it applies to business firms and business relationships. It thus is essential that businesspersons know how to read and understand case law. The cases that we present in this text have been condensed from the full text of the courts' opinions—that is, in each case we have summarized the background and facts, as well as the court's decision and remedy, in our own words and have included only selected portions of the court's opinion ("in the language of the court"). For those who wish to review court cases to perform research projects or to gain additional legal information, however, the following sections will provide useful insights into how to read and understand case law.

The Legal Information Institute (LII) at Cornell Law School, which offers extensive information about U.S. law, is also a good starting point for legal research. The URL for this site is **http://www.law.cornell.edu**.

Case Titles

The title of a case, such as *Adams v. Jones,* indicates the names of the parties to the lawsuit. The *v.* in the case title stands for *versus,* which means "against." In the trial court, Adams was the plaintiff—the person who filed the suit. Jones was the defendant. If the case is appealed, however, the appellate court will sometimes place the name of the party appealing the decision first, so that the case may be called *Jones v. Adams* if Jones is appealing. Because some appellate courts retain the trial court order of names, it is often impossible to distinguish the plaintiff from the defendant in the title of a reported appellate court decision. You must carefully read the facts of each case to identify the parties. Otherwise, the discussion by the appellate court will be difficult to understand.

Terminology

The following terms, phrases, and abbreviations are frequently encountered in court opinions and legal publications. Because it is important to understand what is meant by these terms, phrases, and abbreviations, we define and discuss them here.

PARTIES TO LAWSUITS As mentioned previously, the party initiating a lawsuit is referred to as the *plaintiff* or *petitioner,* depending on the nature of the action, and the party against whom a lawsuit is brought is the *defendant* or *respondent.* Lawsuits frequently involve more than one plaintiff and/or defendant. When a case is appealed from its original court or jurisdiction to another court or jurisdiction, the party appealing the case is called the *appellant.* The *appellee* is the party against whom the appeal is taken. (In some appellate courts, the party appealing a case is referred to as the *petitioner,* and the party against whom the suit is brought or appealed is called the *respondent.*)

JUDGES AND JUSTICES The terms *judge* and *justice* are usually synonymous and represent two designations given to judges in various courts. All members of the United States Supreme Court, for example, are referred to as justices, and justice is the formal title usually given to judges of appellate courts, although this is not always the case. In New York, a *justice* is a judge of the trial court (which is called the Supreme Court), and a member of the Court of Appeals (the state's highest court) is called a *judge.* The term *justice* is commonly abbreviated to J., and *justices,* to JJ. A Supreme Court case might refer to Justice Kennedy as Kennedy, J., or to Chief Justice Rehnquist as Rehnquist, C.J.

DECISIONS AND OPINIONS Most decisions reached by reviewing, or appellate, courts are explained in written *opinions.* The opinion contains the court's reasons for its decision, the rules of law that apply, and the judgment.

When all judges or justices unanimously agree on an opinion, the opinion is written for the entire court and can be deemed a *unanimous opinion.* When there is not a unanimous opinion, a *majority opinion* is written; it outlines the views of the majority of the judges or justices deciding the case. If a judge agrees, or concurs, with the majority's decision, but for different reasons, that judge may write a *concurring opinion.* A *dissenting opinion* is written by one or more judges who disagree with the majority's decision. The dissenting opinion is important because it may form the basis of the arguments used years later in overruling the precedential majority opinion.

Occasionally, a court issues a *per curiam* opinion. *Per curiam* is a Latin phrase meaning "of the court." In *per curiam* opinions, there is no indication of which judge or justice authored the opinion. This term may also be used for an announcement of a court's disposition of a case that is not accompanied by a written opinion. Sometimes, the cases presented in this text are *en banc* decisions. When an appellate court reviews a case *en banc*, which is a French term (derived from a Latin term) for "in the bench," generally all of the judges sitting on the bench of that court review the case.

A Sample Court Case

To illustrate the various elements contained in a court opinion, we present an annotated court opinion in Exhibit 1A–3, beginning on the next page. The opinion is from an actual case that the U.S. Court of Appeals for the Second Circuit decided in 2000. Federal Express Corporation initiated the lawsuit against Federal Espresso, Inc., and others, claiming in part that the name "Federal Espresso" infringed on the Federal Express trademark. The court denied the plaintiff's request for a *preliminary injunction* (an injunction granted at the beginning of a suit to restrain the defendant from doing some act, the right to which is in dispute). Thus, the issue before the appellate court was whether the trial court erred in refusing to grant the injunction.

You will note that triple asterisks (* * *) and quadruple asterisks (* * * *) frequently appear in the opinion. The triple asterisks indicate that we have deleted a few words or sentences from the opinion for the sake of readability or brevity. Quadruple asterisks mean that an entire paragraph (or more) has been omitted. Additionally, when the opinion cites another case or legal source, the citation to the case or other source has been omitted to save space and to improve the flow of the text. These editorial practices are continued in the other court opinions presented in this text. In addition, whenever we present a court opinion that includes a term or phrase that may not be readily understandable, a bracketed definition or paraphrase has been added.

Knowing how to read and understand court opinions and the legal reasoning used by the courts is an essential step in undertaking accurate legal research. Yet a further step is "briefing," or summarizing, the case. Legal researchers routinely brief cases by reducing the texts of the opinions to their essential elements.

EXHIBIT 1A–3 A Sample Court Case

FEDERAL EXPRESS CORP. v.
FEDERAL ESPRESSO, INC.
United States Court of Appeals, Second Circuit, 2000.
201 F.3d 168.

This line gives the name of the judge who authored the opinion of the court.

KEARSE, Circuit Judge.

* * * *

The court divides the opinion into three parts, headed by roman numerals. The first part of the opinion summarizes the factual background of the case.

I. BACKGROUND

* * * Federal Express, incorporated in 1972, invented the overnight shipping business. It has used the name "Federal Express" since 1973. * * * Federal Express currently has 140,000 employees, ships 2.9 million packages per day, and has annual revenues of more than $11 billion.

Federal Express provides service in at least 210 countries * * *.

* * * *

In March 1994, defendants Anna Dobbs ("Dobbs") and David J. Ruston, her brother, formed a business called New York Espresso in Syracuse, New York, for the wholesale distribution of commercial espresso machines. In April 1994, Dobbs, her husband defendant John Dobbs, and Ruston decided to change the name of the business from New York Espresso to "Federal Espresso." * * *

* * * [I]n November 1995, Dobbs opened a coffee shop, called "Federal Espresso," [in] Syracuse * * *.

* * * *

Defendants opened a second store * * * in August 1997. * * *

* * * Federal Express commenced the present action in August 1997. It principally asserted claims of * * * **trademark infringement** * * * and claims of **dilution** of the distinctive quality of its famous mark * * *; and it moved for a preliminary injunction.

* * * [T]he **district court denied the motion** * * *.

* * * *

The unauthorized use or imitation of another's trademark.

A doctrine that protects a trademark from infringement by another party even when there is no competition or likelihood of confusion, such as when products are dissimilar.

A federal trial court in which a lawsuit is initiated.

The decision of the trial court, from which the appeal was taken.

The second major section of the opinion analyzes the issue before the court.

II. DISCUSSION

* * * [A] party seeking a preliminary injunction must demonstrate (1) the likelihood of **irreparable injury** in the absence of such an injunction, and (2) * * * likelihood of success on the **merits** * * *.

* * * *

* * * The hallmark of [trademark] infringement * * * is **likelihood of confusion.**

A wrong of a repeated and continuing nature for which damages are difficult to estimate.

The substance, elements, or grounds of a cause of action.

Likelihood of confusion occurs when a substantial number of ordinarily prudent purchasers are likely to be misled or confused as to the source of a product.

EXHIBIT 1A–3 A Sample Court Case (Continued)

A *presumption* is an assumption of fact that the law requires to be made from another fact.

To make apparent or clear, by evidence; to prove.

* * * [P]roof of a likelihood of confusion would create a **presumption** of irreparable harm, and thus a plaintiff would not need to prove such harm independently. By the same token, however, if the plaintiff does not **show** likelihood of success on the merits, it cannot obtain a preliminary injunction without making an independent showing of likely irreparable harm.

As to Federal Express's claims of trademark infringement, we have no difficulty with the district court's ruling that Federal Express did not show likelihood of confusion and hence did not show that it was likely to succeed on the merits of those claims. * * * Accordingly, since Federal Express did not make any independent showing of likelihood of irreparable harm, the trademark infringement claims did not **warrant** the granting of a preliminary injunction.

To justify or call for; to deserve.

* * * *

The type of dilution pertinent to the present case is "blurring," a process that may occur where the defendant uses or modifies the plaintiff's trademark to identify the defendant's goods and services, raising the possibility that the mark will lose its ability to serve as a unique identifier of the plaintiff's product. * * *

* * * *

* * * Here, * * * the principal products—coffee and overnight delivery service—are dissimilar; there would seem to be little likelihood of confusion; and while Federal Express is a vast organization, operating in 210 countries, employing 140,000 persons, and grossing more than $11 billion annually, defendants are three individuals with two stores in Syracuse. * * * The court was entitled to conclude, given these facts and the tiny extent of the overlap among customers of Federal Express and Federal Espresso, that dilution was not **imminent** and that a preliminary injunction was not needed.

Impending; near at hand; on the point of happening.

* * * *

The final section of the opinion, in which the court gives its order.

III. CONCLUSION

* * * The order of the district court denying a preliminary injunction is affirmed.

CHAPTER 2

Resolution of Disputes

Concepts Covered

After reading this chapter, you should be able to:

1. Explain the concepts of jurisdiction and venue.
2. State the requirements for federal jurisdiction.
3. Identify the basic components of the federal and state court systems.
4. Compare and contrast the functions of trial courts and appellate courts.
5. Discuss various ways in which disputes can be resolved outside the court system.

"The Judicial Department comes home in its effects to every man's fireside: it passes on his property, his reputation, his life, his all."

John Marshall, 1755–1835
(Chief Justice of the United States Supreme Court, 1801–1835)

As Chief Justice John Marshall observed in the chapter-opening quotation, ultimately, we are all affected by what the courts say and do. This is particularly true in the business world—nearly every businessperson will likely face a lawsuit at some time in his or her career. It is thus important for anyone involved in business to have an understanding of the American court systems, as well as the various methods of dispute resolution that can be pursued outside the courts.

Today in the United States there are fifty-two court systems—one for each of the fifty states, one for the District of Columbia, and a federal system. Keep in mind that the federal courts are not superior to the state courts; they are simply an independent system of courts, which derives its authority from Article III, Section 2, of the U.S. Constitution. By the power given to it under Article I of the U.S. Constitution, Congress has extended the federal court system beyond the boundaries of the United States to U.S. territories such as Guam, the Virgin Islands, and Puerto Rico.[1] As we shall see, the United States Supreme Court is the final controlling voice over all of these fifty-two systems, at least when questions of federal law are involved.

In this chapter, after examining the judiciary's general role in the American governmental scheme, we discuss some basic requirements that must be met before a party may bring a lawsuit before a particular court. We then look at the court systems of the United States in some detail. We conclude the chapter with an overview of some alternative methods of settling disputes.

---

1. In Guam and the Virgin Islands, territorial courts serve as both federal courts and state courts; in Puerto Rico, they serve only as federal courts.

SECTION 1 THE JUDICIARY'S ROLE IN AMERICAN GOVERNMENT

As you learned in Chapter 1, the body of American law includes the federal and state constitutions, statutes passed by legislative bodies, administrative law, and the case decisions and legal principles that form the common law. These laws would be meaningless, however, without the courts to interpret and apply them. This is the essential role of the judiciary–the courts–in the American governmental system: to interpret the laws and apply them to specific situations.

Checks and Balances in the American Governmental System

The federal form of government established by the U.S. Constitution divided governing powers among three branches of government–the legislative, executive, and judicial branches–each of which has a different function. The legislative branch makes the laws, the executive branch implements the laws, and the judicial branch interprets the laws.

Additionally, the Constitution established a system of *checks and balances* through which each branch of the government can check the actions of the other branches. For example, Congress can enact laws, but the president has veto power over congressional acts. The president can sign treaties with other nations, but treaties do not become effective until Congress (the Senate) ratifies them. The Supreme Court, as the final interpreter of the meaning of the U.S. Constitution, has the power to declare acts of the legislative and executive branches unconstitutional, but the president appoints the justices of the Supreme Court, with the advice and consent of the Senate.

Judicial Review

When the Supreme Court (or other courts) declare acts of the executive or legislative branches of government unconstitutional, they are exercising their power of **judicial review.**[2] The power of judicial review enables the judicial branch to act as a check on the other two branches of government, which, as mentioned, is in line with the checks and balances system established by the U.S. Constitution.

JUDICIAL REVIEW
The process by which courts decide on the constitutionality of legislative enactments and actions of the executive branch.

The power of judicial review is not mentioned in the Constitution (although many constitutional scholars conclude that the founders intended the judiciary to have this power). Rather, this power was established by the United States Supreme Court in 1803 by its decision in *Marbury v. Madison,*[3] in which the Supreme Court stated, "It is emphatically the province and duty of the Judicial Department to say what the law is. . . . If two laws conflict with each other, the courts must decide on the operation of each. . . . So if the law be in opposition to the Constitution . . . [t]he Court must determine which of these conflicting

2. In a broad sense, judicial review occurs whenever a court "reviews" a case or legal proceeding–as when an appellate court reviews a lower court's decision. When referring to the judiciary's role in American government, however, the term *judicial review* is used to indicate the power of the judiciary to decide whether the actions of the other two branches of government do or do not violate the Constitution.

3. 5 U.S. (1 Cranch) 137, 2 L.Ed. 60 (1803).

rules governs the case. This is the very essence of judicial duty." Since the *Marbury v. Madison* decision, the power of judicial review has remained unchallenged. Today, this power is exercised by both federal and state courts.

SECTION 2 BASIC JUDICIAL REQUIREMENTS

Before a lawsuit can be brought before a court, certain requirements must be met. These requirements relate to jurisdiction, venue, and standing to sue. We examine each of these important concepts here.

Jurisdiction

JURISDICTION
The authority of a court to hear and decide a specific action.

In Latin, *juris* means "law," and *diction* means "to speak." Thus, "the power to speak the law" is the literal meaning of the term **jurisdiction.** Before any court can hear a case, it must have jurisdiction over the person against whom the suit is brought or jurisdiction over the property involved in a lawsuit. The court must also have jurisdiction over the subject matter. Keep in mind throughout this discussion of jurisdiction that we are talking about jurisdiction over the *defendant* in a lawsuit.

***IN PERSONAM* JURISDICTION**
Court jurisdiction over the "person" involved in a legal action; personal jurisdiction.

LONG ARM STATUTE
A state statute that permits a state to obtain personal jurisdiction over nonresident defendants. A defendant must have "minimum contacts" with that state for the statute to apply.

JURISDICTION OVER PERSONS Generally, a particular court can exercise ***in personam* jurisdiction** (personal jurisdiction) over residents of a certain geographical area. A state trial court, for example, normally has jurisdictional authority over residents of a particular area of the state, such as a county or district. A state's highest court (often called the state supreme court)[4] has jurisdictional authority over all residents within the state.

In some cases, under the authority of a state **long arm statute,** a court can exercise personal jurisdiction over nonresident defendants as well. Before a court can exercise jurisdiction over a nonresident defendant under a long arm statute, though, it must be demonstrated that the defendant had sufficient contacts, or *minimum contacts,* with the state to justify the jurisdiction.[5] For example, if an individual has committed a wrong within the state, such as injuring someone in an automobile accident or selling defective goods, a court can usually exercise jurisdiction even if the person causing the harm is located in another state. Similarly, a state may exercise personal jurisdiction over a nonresident defendant who is sued for breaching a contract that was formed within the state.

In regard to corporations,[6] the minimum-contacts requirement is usually met if the corporation does business within the state, advertises or sells its products within the state, or places its goods into the "stream of commerce" with the intent that the goods be sold in the state. Suppose that a business incorporated under the laws of Maine and headquartered in that state has a branch office or manufacturing plant in Georgia. Does this corporation have sufficient contacts

4. As will be discussed shortly, a state's highest court is often referred to as the state supreme court, but there are exceptions. For example, in New York the supreme court is a trial court.

5. The minimum-contacts standard was established in *International Shoe Co. v. State of Washington,* 326 U.S. 310, 66 S.Ct. 154, 90 L.Ed. 95 (1945).

6. In the eyes of the law, corporations are "legal persons"—entities that can sue and be sued.

with the state of Georgia to allow a Georgia court to exercise jurisdiction over the corporation? Yes, it does. If the Maine corporation advertises and sells its products in Georgia, or places goods within the stream of commerce with the expectation that the goods will be purchased by Georgia residents, those activities may also suffice to meet the minimum-contacts requirement.

In the following case, the issue was whether phone calls and letters constituted sufficient minimum contacts to give a court jurisdiction over a nonresident defendant.

CASE 2.1 Cole v. Mileti

United States Court of Appeals, Sixth Circuit, 1998.
133 F.3d 433.
http://www.law.emory.edu/6circuit/jan98/index.html[a]

HISTORICAL AND ECONOMIC SETTING *A movie production company is expensive to operate. Over the two to five years it can take to produce a film, there are many expenses, including maintaining an office and hiring professionals of all kinds. Newcomers to the industry make many of the same mistakes that are the pitfalls of all businesses. For a novice producer or investor, there is the uncertainty of not knowing what to do and the danger of being outnegotiated by those who prey on a novice's ignorance. Finally, once a film is made, there is the audience, which may not choose to see it.*

BACKGROUND AND FACTS Nick Mileti, a resident of California, co-produced a movie called *Streamers* and organized a corporation, Streamers International Distributors, Inc., to distribute the film. Joseph Cole, a resident of Ohio, bought two hundred shares of Streamers stock. Cole also lent the firm $475,000, which he borrowed from Equitable Bank of Baltimore. The film was unsuccessful. Mileti agreed to repay Cole's loan in a contract arranged through phone calls and correspondence between California and Ohio. When Mileti did not repay the loan, the bank sued Cole, who in turn filed a suit against Mileti in a federal district court in Ohio. The court entered a judgment against Mileti. He appealed to the U.S. Court of Appeals for the Sixth Circuit, arguing in part that the district court's exercise of jurisdiction over him was unfair.[b]

a. This page, which is part of the Web site of the Emory University School of Law, lists the published opinions of the U.S. Court of Appeals for the Sixth Circuit for January 1998. Scroll down the list of cases to the *Cole* case. To access the opinion, click on the case name.

b. As will be discussed shortly, federal courts can exercise jurisdiction over disputes between parties living in different states. This is called *diversity-of-citizenship* jurisdiction. When a federal court exercises diversity jurisdiction, the court normally applies the law of the state in which the court sits—in this case, the law of Ohio.

IN THE LANGUAGE OF THE COURT. . .
MERRITT, Circuit Judge.

* * * *

* * * [There is] a three-part test to determine whether specific jurisdiction exists over a nonresident defendant like Mileti. First, the defendant must purposefully avail himself of the privilege of conducting activities within the forum state [the state in which the court sits]; second, the cause of action must arise from the defendant's activities there; and third, the acts of the defendant or consequences caused by the defendant must have a substantial enough connection with the forum state to make its exercise of jurisdiction over the defendant fundamentally fair.

If, as here, a nonresident defendant transacts business by negotiating and executing a contract via telephone calls and letters to an Ohio resident, then

CASE 2.1–Continued

the defendant has purposefully availed himself of the forum by creating a continuing obligation in Ohio. Furthermore, if the cause of action is for breach of that contract, as it is here, then the cause of action naturally arises from the defendant's activities in Ohio. Finally, when we find that a defendant like Mileti purposefully availed himself of the forum and that the cause of action arose directly from that contact, we presume the specific assertion of personal jurisdiction was proper.

DECISION AND REMEDY The U.S. Court of Appeals for the Sixth Circuit held that the district court could exercise personal jurisdiction over Mileti. The appellate court reasoned that a federal district court in Ohio can exercise personal jurisdiction over a resident of California who does business in Ohio via phone calls and letters.

FOR CRITICAL ANALYSIS–Economic Consideration *Why might a defendant prefer to be sued in one state rather than in another?*

***IN REM* JURISDICTION**
Court jurisdiction over a defendant's property.

JURISDICTION OVER PROPERTY A court can also exercise jurisdiction over property that is located within its boundaries. This kind of jurisdiction is known as ***in rem* jurisdiction**, or "jurisdiction over the thing." For example, suppose a dispute arises over the ownership of a boat in dry dock in Fort Lauderdale, Florida. The boat is owned by an Ohio resident, over whom a Florida court normally cannot exercise personal jurisdiction. The other party to the dispute is a resident of Nebraska. In this situation, a lawsuit concerning the boat could be brought in a Florida state court on the basis of the court's *in rem* jurisdiction.

PROBATE COURT
A state court of limited jurisdiction that conducts proceedings relating to the settlement of a deceased person's estate.

BANKRUPTCY COURT
A federal court of limited jurisdiction that handles only bankruptcy proceedings. Bankruptcy proceedings are governed by federal bankruptcy law.

JURISDICTION OVER SUBJECT MATTER Jurisdiction over subject matter is a limitation on the types of cases a court can hear. In both the federal and state court systems, there are courts of *general* (unlimited) *jurisdiction* and courts of *limited jurisdiction*. A court of general jurisdiction can decide cases involving a broad array of issues. An example of a court of general jurisdiction is a state trial court or federal district court. An example of a state court of limited jurisdiction is a probate court. **Probate courts** are state courts that handle only matters relating to the transfer of a person's assets and obligations after that person's death, including issues relating to the custody and guardianship of children. An example of a federal court of limited subject-matter jurisdiction is a bankruptcy court. **Bankruptcy courts** handle only bankruptcy proceedings, which are governed by federal bankruptcy law.

A court's jurisdiction over subject matter is usually defined in the statute or constitution creating the court. In both the federal and state court systems, a court's subject-matter jurisdiction can be limited not only by the subject of the lawsuit but also by how much money is in controversy, whether the case is a felony (a more serious type of crime) or a misdemeanor (a less serious type of crime), or whether the proceeding is a trial or an appeal.

ORIGINAL AND APPELLATE JURISDICTION The distinction between courts of original jurisdiction and courts of appellate jurisdiction normally lies in whether the case is being heard for the first time. Courts having original jurisdiction are courts of the first instance, or trial courts—that is, courts in which lawsuits begin, trials take place, and evidence is presented. In the federal court system, the *district courts* are trial courts. In the various state court systems, the trial courts are known by different names, as will be discussed shortly.

The key point here is that normally, any court having original jurisdiction is known as a trial court. Courts having appellate jurisdiction act as reviewing courts, or appellate courts. In general, cases can be brought before appellate courts only on appeal from an order or a judgment of a trial court or other lower court.

JURISDICTION OF THE FEDERAL COURTS Because the federal government is a government of limited powers, the jurisdiction of the federal courts is limited. Article III of the U.S. Constitution establishes the boundaries of federal judicial power. Section 2 of Article III states that "[t]he judicial Power shall extend to all Cases, in Law and Equity, arising under this Constitution, the Laws of the United States, and Treaties made, or which shall be made, under their Authority." In effect, this clause means that whenever a plaintiff's cause of action is based—at least in part—on the U.S. Constitution, a treaty, or a federal law, a **federal question** arises, and the case comes under the judicial authority of the federal courts. Any lawsuit involving a federal question can originate in a federal court. People who claim that their constitutional rights have been violated can begin their suits in a federal court.

FEDERAL QUESTION
A question that pertains to the U.S. Constitution, acts of Congress, or treaties. A federal question provides a basis for federal jurisdiction.

Federal district courts can also exercise original jurisdiction over cases involving **diversity of citizenship.** This term applies whenever a federal court has jurisdiction over a case that does not involve a question of federal law. The most common type of diversity jurisdiction has two requirements:[7] (1) the plaintiff and defendant must be residents of different states, and (2) the dollar amount in controversy must exceed $75,000. For purposes of diversity jurisdiction, a corporation is a citizen of both the state in which it is incorporated and the state in which its principal place of business is located. A case involving diversity of citizenship can be filed in the appropriate federal district court. If the case starts in a state court, it can sometimes be transferred, or "removed," to a federal court. A large percentage of the cases filed in federal courts each year are based on diversity of citizenship.

DIVERSITY OF CITIZENSHIP
Under Article III, Section 2, of the Constitution, a basis for federal court jurisdiction over a lawsuit between citizens of different states if the amount in controversy is more than $75,000.

Note that in a case based on a federal question, a federal court will apply federal law. In a case based on diversity of citizenship, however, a federal court will apply the relevant state law (which is often the law of the state in which the court sits).

EXCLUSIVE VERSUS CONCURRENT JURISDICTION When both federal and state courts have the power to hear a case, as is true in suits involving diversity of citizenship, **concurrent jurisdiction** exists. When cases can be tried only in federal courts or only in state courts, **exclusive jurisdiction** exists. Federal courts have exclusive jurisdiction in cases involving federal crimes, bankruptcy, patents, and copyrights; in suits against the United States; and in some areas of

CONCURRENT JURISDICTION
Jurisdiction that exists when two different courts have the power to hear a case. For example, some cases can be heard in either a federal or a state court.

EXCLUSIVE JURISDICTION
Jurisdiction that exists when a case can be heard only in a particular court or type of court, such as a federal court or a state court.

7. Diversity jurisdiction also exists in cases between (1) a foreign country and citizens of a state or of different states and (2) citizens of a state and citizens or subjects of a foreign country. These bases for diversity jurisdiction are less commonly used.

admiralty law (law governing transportation on the seas and ocean waters). The states also have exclusive jurisdiction in certain subject matters—for example, divorce and adoption.

Concept Summary 2.1—Jurisdiction

Type of Jurisdiction	Description
Personal/Property	Exists when a defendant or a defendant's property is located within the territorial boundaries within which a court has the right and power to decide cases. Jurisdiction may be exercised over out-of-state defendants under state long arm statutes.
Subject Matter	Limits the court's jurisdictional authority to particular types of cases. 1. *Limited jurisdiction*—Exists when a court is limited to a specific subject matter, such as probate or divorce. 2. *General jurisdiction*—Exists when a court can hear cases involving a broad array of issues.
Original	Exists with courts that have the authority to hear a case for the first time (trial courts).
Appellate	Exists with courts of appeal and review; generally, appellate courts do not have original jurisdiction.
Federal	Arises in the following situations: 1. When a federal question is involved (when the plaintiff's cause of action is based at least in part on the U.S. Constitution, a treaty, or a federal law). 2. In diversity-of-citizenship cases between citizens of different states when the amount in controversy exceeds $75,000. (Diversity jurisdiction also exists in cases between a foreign country and citizens of a state or of different states and in cases between citizens of a state and citizens or subjects of a foreign country.)
Concurrent	Exists when both federal and state courts have authority to hear the same case.
Exclusive	Exists when only state courts or only federal courts have authority to hear a case.

Venue

VENUE
The geographical district in which an action is tried and from which the jury is selected.

Jurisdiction has to do with whether a court has authority to hear a case involving specific persons, property, or subject matter. **Venue**[8] is concerned with the most appropriate geographic location for a trial. For example, two state courts (or two federal courts) may have the authority to exercise jurisdiction over a case, but it may be more appropriate or convenient to hear the case in one court than in the other.

Basically, the concept of venue reflects the policy that a court trying a suit should be in the geographical neighborhood (usually the county) in which the incident leading to the lawsuit occurred or in which the parties involved in the

8. Pronounced *ven*-yoo.

lawsuit reside. Pretrial publicity or other factors, though, may require a change of venue to another community, especially in criminal cases in which the defendant's right to a fair and impartial jury has been impaired.

For example, a change of venue from Oklahoma City to Denver, Colorado, was ordered for the trials of Timothy McVeigh and Terry Nichols after they had been indicted in connection with the 1995 bombing of the federal building in Oklahoma City. As a result of the bombing, more than 160 persons were killed, and hundreds of others were wounded. In view of these circumstances, it was felt that to hold the trial in Oklahoma City could prejudice the rights of the defendants to a fair trial.

Standing to Sue

In order to bring a lawsuit before a court, a party must have **standing to sue,** or a sufficient "stake" in a matter to justify seeking relief through the court system. In other words, a party must have a legally protected and tangible interest at stake in the litigation in order to have standing. The party bringing the lawsuit must have suffered a harm or been threatened with a harm by the action about which he or she has complained. In some circumstances, a person can have standing to sue on behalf of another person. For example, suppose that a child suffers serious injuries as a result of a defectively manufactured toy. Because the child is a minor, a lawsuit can be brought on his or her behalf by another person, such as the child's parent or legal guardian.

STANDING TO SUE
The requirement that an individual must have a sufficient stake in a controversy before he or she can bring a lawsuit. The plaintiff must demonstrate that he or she either has been injured or threatened with injury.

Standing to sue also requires that the controversy at issue be a **justiciable**[9] **controversy**—a controversy that is real and substantial, as opposed to hypothetical or academic. For instance, in the above example, the child's parent could not sue the toy manufacturer merely on the ground that the toy was defective. The issue would become justiciable only if the child had actually been injured due to the defect in the toy as marketed. In other words, the parent normally could not ask the court to determine what damages *might* be obtained if the child had been injured, because this would be merely a hypothetical question.

JUSTICIABLE CONTROVERSY
A controversy that is not hypothetical or academic but real and substantial; a requirement that must be satisfied before a court will hear a case.

Meeting standing requirements is not always easy. In the following case, for example, an environmental organization sued a company for allegedly discharging pollutants into waterways beyond the amount allowed by the Environmental Protection Agency. At issue in the case was whether the organization had standing to sue under federal environmental laws.

9. Pronounced jus-*tish*-a-bul.

CASE 2.2 Friends of the Earth, Inc. v. Crown Central Petroleum Corp.

United States Court of Appeals,
Fifth Circuit, 1996.
95 F.3d 358.
http://www.ca5.uscourts.gov/oparchdt.cfm?Year-1996[a]

a. This is a page within the Web site of the U.S. Courts of the Fifth Judicial Circuit. Click on "1996." When the link opens, click on "September." When that link opens, click on "September 3." From the list of cases that appears, click on the case name to access the opinion.

BACKGROUND AND FACTS Crown Central Petroleum Corporation does business as La Gloria Oil & Gas Company. Under a permit issued by the Environmental Protection Agency (EPA), La Gloria's oil refinery discharges storm-water run-off into Black Fork Creek. Black Fork Creek flows into Prairie Creek, which flows into the Neches River, which flows into Lake Palestine eighteen miles downstream. Friends of the Earth,

CASE 2.2—Continued

Inc. (FOE), is a not-for-profit corporation dedicated to the protection of the environment. FOE filed a suit in a federal district court against La Gloria under the Federal Water Pollution Control Act.[b] FOE claimed that La Gloria had violated its EPA permit and that this conduct had directly affected "the health, economic, recreational, aesthetic and environmental interests of FOE's members" who used the lake. La Gloria filed a motion for summary judgment, arguing that FOE lacked standing to bring the suit. The court granted the motion, and FOE appealed.

b. 33 U.S.C. Sections 1251–1387.

IN THE LANGUAGE OF THE COURT. . .
PATRICK E. HIGGINBOTHAM, Circuit Judge:

* * * *

To demonstrate that FOE's members have standing, FOE must show that * * * the injury is "fairly traceable" to the defendant's actions * * * .

* * * *

* * * FOE offered no competent evidence that La Gloria's discharges have made their way to Lake Palestine or would otherwise affect Lake Palestine. * * * FOE and its members relied solely on the truism that water flows downstream and inferred therefrom that any injury suffered downstream is "fairly traceable" to unlawful discharges upstream. At some point this common sense observation becomes little more than surmise [conjecture]. At that point certainly the requirements [for standing] are not met.

DECISION AND REMEDY The U.S. Court of Appeals for the Fifth Circuit affirmed the lower court's decision. FOE lacked standing to bring a suit against La Gloria.

FOR CRITICAL ANALYSIS–Social Consideration *What might result if the courts did not impose the requirement of standing to sue?*

Procedural Rules

Both the federal and the state courts have established procedural rules that shape the litigation process. All civil trials held in federal district courts are governed by the Federal Rules of Civil Procedure. Each state also has rules of civil procedure that apply to all courts within that state. In addition, each court has its own local rules of procedure that supplement the federal or state rules.

Generally, these rules are designed to protect the rights and interests of the parties, to ensure that the litigation proceeds in a fair and orderly manner, and to identify the issues that must be decided by the court—thus saving court time and costs. Court decisions may also apply to trial procedures. For example, the United States Supreme Court has held that parties' attorneys cannot discriminate against prospective jurors on the basis of race or gender. Some lower courts have held that people cannot be excluded from juries because of their sexual orientation or religion.

The parties must comply with procedural rules and with any orders given by the judge during the conduct of the litigation. When a party does not follow a court's order, the court can cite him or her for contempt. A party who commits *civil* contempt (failing to comply with a court's order for the benefit of another party to the proceeding) can be taken into custody, fined, or both, until the party complies with the court's order. A party who commits *criminal* contempt (obstructing the administration of justice or disrespecting the court) also can be taken into custody and fined but cannot avoid punishment by complying with a previous order.

SECTION 3 THE STATE AND FEDERAL COURT SYSTEMS

As mentioned earlier in this chapter, each state has its own court system. Additionally, there is a system of federal courts. Although no two state court systems are exactly the same, the left-hand side of Exhibit 2–1 illustrates the basic organizational framework characteristic of the court systems in many states. The exhibit also shows how the federal court system is structured. We turn now to an examination of these court systems, beginning with the state courts.

State Court Systems

Typically a state court system includes several levels, or tiers, of courts. As indicated in Exhibit 2–1, state courts may include (1) trial courts of limited jurisdiction, (2) trial courts of general jurisdiction, (3) intermediate appellate courts, and (4) the state's highest court (often called the state supreme court). Judges in the state court system are usually elected by the voters for specified terms.

On the Web
The National Center for State Courts (NCSC) offers links to the Web pages of all state courts at **http://www.ncsc.dni.us/court/sites/courts.htm**.

Generally, any person who is a party to a lawsuit has the opportunity to plead the case before a trial court and then, if he or she loses, before at least one level of appellate court. Finally, if a federal statute or federal constitutional issue is involved in the decision of a state supreme court, that decision may be further appealed to the United States Supreme Court.

EXHIBIT 2–1 The State and Federal Court Systems

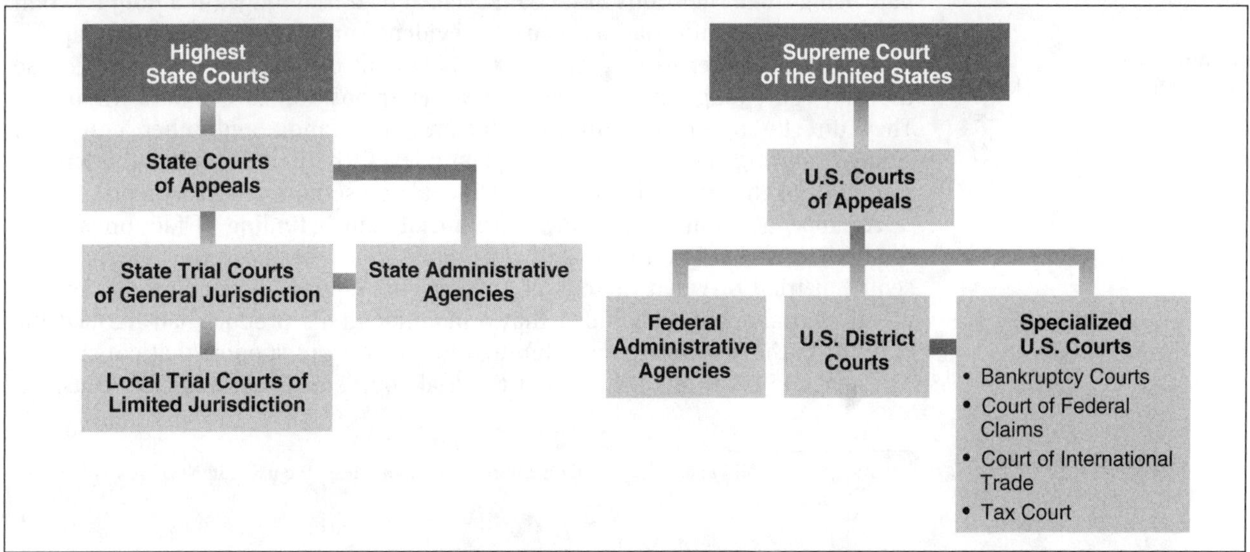

TRIAL COURTS Trial courts are exactly what their name implies—courts in which trials are held and testimony taken. State trial courts have either general or limited jurisdiction. Trial courts that have general jurisdiction as to subject matter may be called county, district, superior, or circuit courts.[10] State trial courts of general jurisdiction have jurisdiction over a wide variety of subjects, including both civil disputes and criminal prosecutions. In some states, trial courts of general jurisdiction may hear appeals from courts of limited jurisdiction.

SMALL CLAIMS COURTS
Special courts in which parties may litigate small claims (usually, claims involving $5,000 or less). Attorneys are not required in small claims courts, and in many states attorneys are not allowed to represent the parties.

Courts of limited jurisdiction as to subject matter are often called special inferior trial courts or minor judiciary courts. **Small claims courts** are inferior trial courts that hear only civil cases involving claims of less than a certain amount, such as $5,000 (the amount varies from state to state). Suits brought in small claims courts are generally conducted informally, and lawyers are not required. In a minority of states, lawyers are not even allowed to represent people in small claims courts for most purposes. Decisions of small claims courts may be appealed to a state trial court of general jurisdiction.

Other courts of limited jurisdiction include domestic relations courts, which handle only divorce actions and child custody cases; local municipal courts, which mainly handle traffic cases; and probate courts, as mentioned earlier.

COURTS OF APPEALS Every state has at least one court of appeals (appellate court, or reviewing court). A court of appeals may be an intermediate appellate court or the state's highest court. About three-fourths of the states have intermediate appellate courts. Generally, courts of appeals do not conduct new trials, in which evidence is submitted to the court and witnesses are examined. Rather, an appellate court panel of three or more judges reviews the record of the case on appeal, which includes a transcript of the trial proceedings, and then determines whether the trial court committed an error.

QUESTION OF LAW
In a lawsuit, an issue involving the application or interpretation of a law; therefore, the judge, and not the jury, decides the issue.

QUESTION OF FACT
In a lawsuit, an issue involving a factual dispute that can only be decided by a judge (or, in a jury trial, a jury).

Appellate courts look at questions of law and procedure. Usually, they do not look at questions of fact. A **question of law** is a question concerning the application or interpretation of the law, on which only a judge, not a jury, can rule. A **question of fact** is a question about what really happened in regard to the dispute being tried. Questions of fact are decided by a trial judge (in a nonjury trial) or by a jury (in a jury trial) based on the evidence presented. Normally, an appellate court will defer to the trial court's judgment on questions of fact because the trial court judge and jury were in a better position to evaluate testimony. They directly observed witnesses' gestures, demeanor, and other nonverbal behavior during the trial. At the appellate level, the judges review the written transcript of the trial, which does not include these nonverbal elements.

An appellate court will tamper with a trial court's finding of fact only when the finding is clearly erroneous (that is, when it is contrary to the evidence presented at trial) or when there is no evidence to support the finding. For example, if at trial a jury concluded that a manufacturer's product had harmed the plaintiff but no evidence was submitted to the court to support that conclusion, the appellate court might hold that the trial court's decision was erroneous.

---

10. The name in Ohio and Pennsylvania is Court of Common Pleas; the name in New York is Supreme Court, Trial Division.

STATE SUPREME (HIGHEST) COURTS The highest state courts usually are called simply supreme courts, but they may be designated by other names. For example, in both New York and Maryland, the highest state court is called the court of appeals. In Maine and Massachusetts, the highest court is labeled the supreme judicial court. In West Virginia, the highest state court is the supreme court of appeals. The decisions of each state's highest court on all questions of state law are final. Only when issues of federal law are involved can a decision made by a state's highest court be overruled by the United States Supreme Court.

The Federal Court System

The federal court system is basically a three-tiered model consisting of (1) U.S. district courts (trial courts of general jurisdiction) and various courts of limited jurisdiction, (2) U.S. courts of appeals (intermediate courts of appeals), and (3) the United States Supreme Court.

The Web site for the federal courts offers information on the federal court system and links to all federal courts at **http://www.uscourts.gov**.

Unlike state court judges, who are usually elected, federal court judges—including the justices of the Supreme Court—are appointed by the president of the United States, subject to confirmation by the U.S. Senate. Article III of the Constitution states that federal judges "hold their offices during good Behaviour." In effect, this means that federal judges have lifetime appointments. Although they can be impeached (removed from office) for misconduct, this is rarely done. In the entire history of the United States, only seven federal judges have been removed from office through impeachment proceedings.

U.S. DISTRICT COURTS At the federal level, the equivalent of a state trial court of general jurisdiction is the district court. U.S. district courts have original jurisdiction in federal matters, and federal cases typically originate in district courts. There are other federal courts with original, but special (or limited), jurisdiction, such as the federal bankruptcy courts and others shown earlier in Exhibit 2–1.

There is at least one federal district court in every state. The number of judicial districts can vary over time, primarily owing to population changes and corresponding changes in caseloads. Currently, there are ninety-four federal judicial districts. Exhibit 2–2 on the next page shows the boundaries of U.S. district courts, as well as the U.S. courts of appeals (discussed next).

U.S. COURTS OF APPEALS In the federal court system, there are thirteen U.S. courts of appeals—referred to as U.S. circuit courts of appeals. Twelve of the federal courts of appeals (including the Court of Appeals for the D.C. Circuit) hear appeals from the federal district courts located within their respective judicial "circuits," or geographical boundaries (shown in Exhibit 2–2). The court of appeals for the thirteenth circuit, called the Federal Circuit, has national appellate jurisdiction over certain types of cases, such as cases involving patent law and those in which the U.S. government is a defendant. The decisions of a circuit court of appeals are binding on all courts within the circuit court's jurisdiction and are final in most cases, but appeal to the United States Supreme Court is possible.

EXHIBIT 2–2 U.S. District Courts and Courts of Appeals

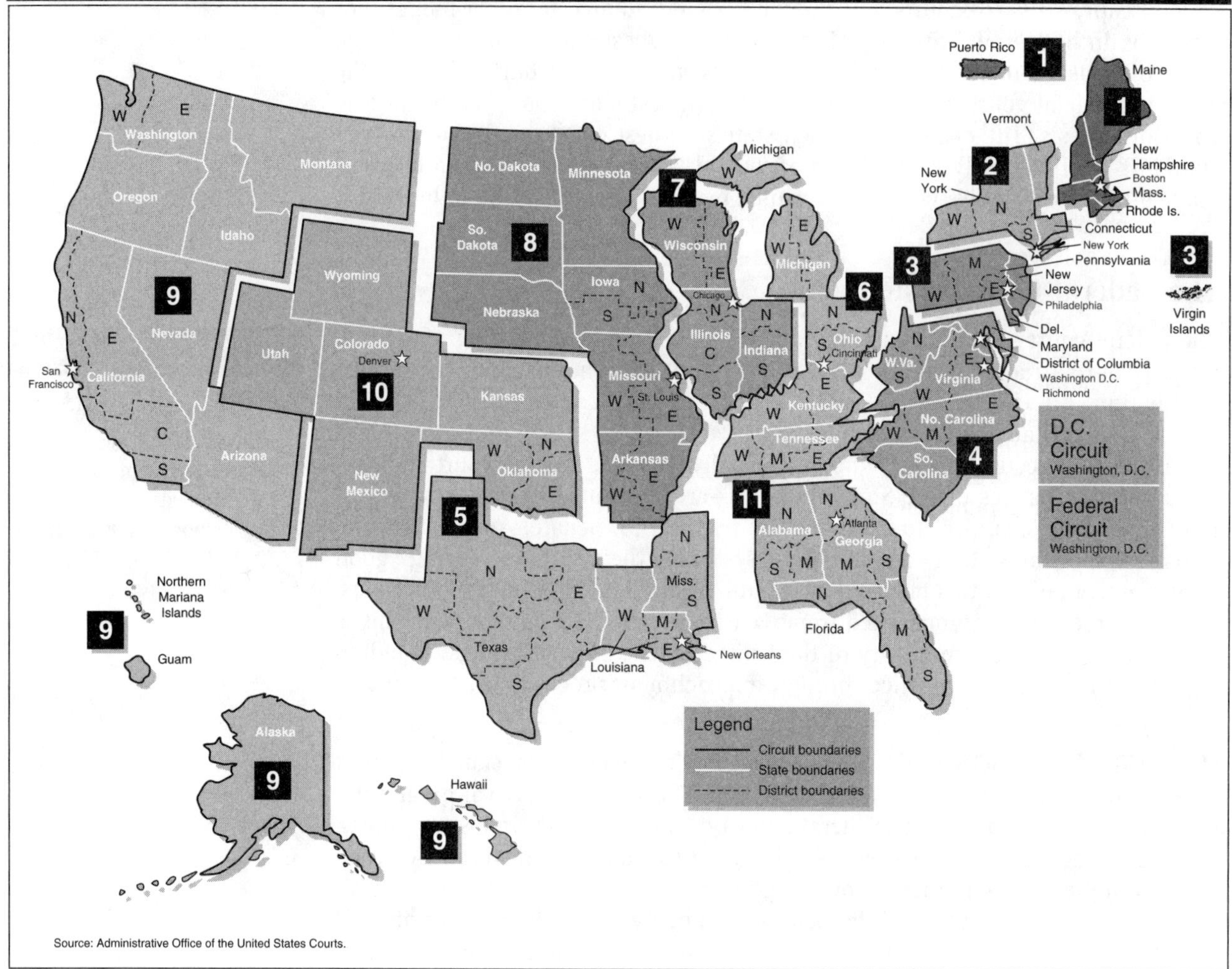

Source: Administrative Office of the United States Courts.

UNITED STATES SUPREME COURT At the highest level in the three-tiered federal court system is the United States Supreme Court. According to the language of Article III of the U.S. Constitution, there is only one national Supreme Court. All other courts in the federal system are considered "inferior." Congress is empowered to create other inferior courts as it deems necessary. The inferior courts that Congress has created include the second tier in our model—the U.S. circuit courts of appeals—as well as the district courts and the various federal courts of limited, or specialized, jurisdiction.

The United States Supreme Court consists of nine justices. Although the Supreme Court has original, or trial, jurisdiction in rare instances (set forth in Article III, Section 2), most of its work is as an appeals court. The Supreme Court can review any case decided by any of the federal courts of appeals, and it also has appellate authority over cases involving federal questions that have been decided in the state courts. The Supreme Court is the final arbiter of the Constitution and federal law.

On the Web

For information on the justices of the United States Supreme Court, links to opinions they have authored, and other information about the Supreme Court, go to **http://oyez.nwu.edu**.

HOW CASES REACH THE SUPREME COURT To bring a case before the Supreme Court, a party requests the Court to issue a writ of *certiorari*. A **writ of *certiorari***[11] is an order issued by the Supreme Court to a lower court requiring the latter to send it the record of the case for review. The Court will not issue a writ unless at least four of the nine justices approve of it. This is referred to as the **rule of four.**

WRIT OF *CERTIORARI*
A writ from a higher court asking the lower court for the record of a case.

RULE OF FOUR
A rule of the United States Supreme Court under which the Court will not issue a writ of *certiorari* unless at least four justices approve of the decision to issue the writ.

Whether the Court will issue a writ of *certiorari* is entirely within its discretion. The Court is not required to issue one, and most petitions for writs are denied. (Thousands of cases are filed with the Supreme Court each year, yet it hears, on average, less than one hundred of these cases.[12]) A denial is not a decision on the merits of a case, nor does it indicate agreement with the lower court's opinion. Furthermore, denial of the writ has no value as a precedent. A denial of the writ simply means that the decision of the lower court remains the law within that court's jurisdiction.

Typically, the petitions granted by the Court involve cases that raise important constitutional questions or cases that conflict with other state or federal court decisions. For example, if federal appellate courts are rendering conflicting or inconsistent opinions on an important issue, such as how a particular federal statute should be applied to a specific factual situation, the Supreme Court may agree to review a case involving that issue. The Court can then render a definitive opinion on the matter, thus clarifying the law for the lower courts.

On the Web

Decisions of the United States Supreme Court are published online at **http://supremecourtus.gov**. You can locate decisions of the U.S. courts of appeals by going to **http://www.uscourts.gov**, which provides links to the Web sites of all of the U.S. courts of appeals.

11. Pronounced sur-shee-uh-*rah*-ree.

12. From the mid-1950s through the early 1990s, the Supreme Court reviewed more cases per year than it has in the last few years. In the Court's 1982–1983 term, for example, the Court issued written opinions in 151 cases. In contrast, during the Court's 1999–2000 term, the Court issued written opinions in only 73 cases.

CONCEPT SUMMARY 2.2—TYPES OF COURTS

COURT	DESCRIPTION
Trial Courts	Trial courts are courts of original jurisdiction in which actions are initiated. 1. *State courts*—Courts of general jurisdiction can hear any case that has not been specifically designated for another court; courts of limited jurisdiction include domestic relations courts, probate courts, municipal courts, small claims courts, and others. 2. *Federal courts*—The federal district court is the equivalent of the state trial court. Federal courts of limited jurisdiction include the bankruptcy court and others shown in Exhibit 2–1 on page 39.

CONCEPT SUMMARY 2.2—TYPES OF COURTS (continued)

COURT	DESCRIPTION
Intermediate Appellate Courts	Courts of appeals are reviewing courts; generally, appellate courts do not have original jurisdiction. About three-fourths of the states have intermediate appellate courts; in the federal court system, the U.S. circuit courts of appeals are the intermediate appellate courts.
Supreme Court	The highest state court is that state's supreme court, although it may be called by some other name. Appeal from state supreme courts to the United States Supreme Court is possible only if a federal question is involved. The United States Supreme Court is the highest court in the federal court system and the final arbiter of the Constitution and federal law.

SECTION 4 TECHNOLOGY AND THE COURTS

As in other areas of the law, adapting traditional judicial concepts, such as jurisdictional requirements, to an online world has not been easy for the courts. At the same time, technological developments, including the Internet, promise to relieve the courts of several burdens—including overloaded dockets (schedules), mountains of paperwork, and bulging record-keeping facilities. In this section, we first look at how the courts have been applying traditional jurisdictional concepts to the cyber world. We then discuss some of the ways in which technology is transforming certain judicial procedures and the implications of technology for the courts in the future.

Jurisdiction in Cyberspace

The Internet's capacity to bypass political and geographic boundaries undercuts the traditional basis for a court to assert personal jurisdiction. This basis includes a party's contacts with a court's geographic jurisdiction. For a court to compel a defendant to come before it, there must be at least minimum contacts—the presence of a salesperson within the state, for example. Are there sufficient minimum contacts if the only connection to a jurisdiction is an ad on the Web originating from a remote location?

Consider an example. Adam lives in Florida. Carol, who lives in New York and has never been to Florida or done business with anyone in Florida, advertises her business on the Web. Carol's home page has received hundreds of "hits" by residents of Florida. Adam files a suit against Carol in a Florida state court. Can the court compel Carol to appear?

On the one hand, it could be argued that Carol knows (or should know) that her Web site could be accessed by residents of Florida, and by advertising her business on the Web, she should reasonably expect to be called into court there. If this reasoning is applied, then setting up a Web site could subject the owner to a suit anywhere that the site can be accessed. Some courts have upheld exercises of jurisdiction on the basis of the accessibility of a Web page.[13]

---

13. See, for example, *Minnesota v. Granite Gates Resorts, Inc.*, 568 N.W.2d 715 (Minn.App. 1997), aff'd 576 N.W.2d 747 (Minn. 1998).

On the other hand, it could be argued that it is not possible for Carol to set up a Web page that excludes residents of Florida (or of any other specific jurisdiction). With this in mind, it would seem unreasonable and unfair to subject Carol to the possible personal jurisdiction of every court in the United States and maybe the world. For this reason, some courts have concluded that without more, a presence on the Web is not enough to support jurisdiction over nonresident defendants.[14]

Recently, a new standard has started to become generally accepted for evaluating the exercise of jurisdiction based on contacts over the Internet. This standard is a "sliding scale." On this scale, a court's exercise of personal jurisdiction depends on the amount of business that an individual or firm transacts over the Internet. The standard is explained more fully in the following case.

14. See, for example, *Weber v. Jolly Hotels*, 977 F.Supp. 327 (D.N.J. 1997).

CASE 2.3 Zippo Manufacturing Co. v. Zippo Dot Com, Inc.

United States District Court,
Western District of Pennsylvania, 1997.
952 F.Supp. 1119.
http://zeus.bna.com/e-law/cases/zippo.html[a]

HISTORICAL AND TECHNOLOGICAL SETTING *In a case decided before 1960, the United States Supreme Court noted that "[a]s technological progress has increased the flow of commerce between States, the need for jurisdiction has undergone a similar increase."*[b] *Twenty-seven years later, the Court observed that jurisdiction could not be avoided "merely because the defendant did not physically enter the forum state [the state in which a lawsuit is initiated]. * * * [I]t is an inescapable fact of modern commercial life that a substantial amount of commercial business is transacted solely by mail and wire communications across state lines."*[c]

a. This is a page in the "Electronic Commerce & Law Report" library.
b. *Hanson v. Denckla*, 357 U.S. 235, 78 S.Ct. 1228, 2 L.Ed.2d 1283 (1958).
c. *Burger King Corp. v. Rudzewicz*, 471 U.S. 462, 105 S.Ct. 2174, 85 L.Ed.2d 528 (1985).

BACKGROUND AND FACTS Zippo Manufacturing Company (ZMC) makes, among other things, "Zippo" lighters. Zippo Dot Com, Inc. (ZDC), operates a Web page and an Internet subscription news service. ZDC has the exclusive right to use the domain names "zippo.com," "zippo.net," and "zipponews.com." ZMC is based in Pennsylvania. ZDC is based in California, and its contacts with Pennsylvania have occurred almost exclusively over the Internet. Two percent of its subscribers (3,000 of 140,000) are Pennsylvania residents who contracted over the Internet to receive its service. Also, ZDC has agreements with seven Internet service providers in Pennsylvania to permit their subscribers to access the service. ZMC filed a suit in a federal district court against ZDC, alleging trademark infringement and other claims, based on ZDC's use of the word "Zippo." ZDC filed a motion to dismiss for lack of personal jurisdiction.

IN THE LANGUAGE OF THE COURT. . .
McLAUGHLIN, District Judge.

* * * *

* * * *[T]he likelihood that personal jurisdiction can be constitutionally exercised is directly proportionate to the nature and quality of commercial activity that an entity conducts over the Internet.* * * * At one end of the spectrum are situations where a defendant clearly does business over the Internet. If the

CASE 2.3–Continued

defendant enters into contracts with residents of a foreign jurisdiction that involve the knowing and repeated transmission of computer files over the Internet, personal jurisdiction is proper. At the opposite end are situations where a defendant has simply posted information on an Internet Web site which is accessible to users in foreign jurisdictions. A passive Web site that does little more than make information available to those who are interested in it is not grounds for the exercise of personal jurisdiction. The middle ground is occupied by interactive Web sites where a user can exchange information with the host computer. In these cases, the exercise of jurisdiction is determined by examining the level of interactivity and commercial nature of the exchange of information that occurs on the Web site. [Emphasis added.]

* * * *

* * * We are being asked to determine whether [ZDC's] conducting of electronic commerce with Pennsylvania residents constitutes * * * doing business in Pennsylvania. We conclude that it does. [ZDC] has contracted with approximately 3,000 individuals and seven Internet access providers in Pennsylvania. The intended object of these transactions has been the downloading of the electronic messages that form the basis of this suit in Pennsylvania.

DECISION AND REMEDY The court held that it has jurisdiction over parties that conduct substantial business in its jurisdiction exclusively over the Internet. The court concluded that ZDC fits this description and denied the motion to dismiss.

FOR CRITICAL ANALYSIS–Technological Consideration *Is the court in this case applying traditional jurisdictional rules to cyberspace or creating new rules? Explain.*

Electronic Filing

Numerous documents may have to be filed with the court during the pretrial phase of litigation. During and after the trial, other documents may need to be filed. Additionally, these documents must be made available to the other party or parties involved in the lawsuit. As just mentioned, one of the promises of today's communications technology, and particularly the Internet, is that it will help to reduce the mountains of paperwork typically involved in litigation.

A number of courts have taken steps to reduce the burden of paperwork involved in litigation by allowing parties to a lawsuit to file court documents electronically. Filing documents with a court by electronic means may involve transferring the documents over the Internet, such as through an e-mail system, or delivering them to the court on a computer disk or CD-ROM.

ELECTRONIC FILING IN THE FEDERAL COURTS The federal court system first experimented with an electronic filing system in January 1996, in an asbestos case heard by the U.S. District Court for the Northern District of Ohio. In the same year, the Federal Rules of Civil Procedure were amended to change the definition of *filing* so that it permits the filing of papers by electronic means.

Currently, a number of federal courts permit attorneys to file documents electronically in certain types of cases. At last count, more than 130,000 documents in approximately 10,000 cases had been filed electronically in federal courts. The Administrative Office of the U.S. Courts has recently announced that it is considering the possibility of permitting electronic filing in all U.S. district courts on a nationwide basis. (For a discussion of some of the implications of nationwide electronic filing, see the *Controversial Issues* feature on page 48.)

STATE AND LOCAL EXPERIMENTS WITH ELECTRONIC FILING State and local courts also are setting up electronic court filing systems. Since late 1997, the Pima County, Arizona, court system has been accepting pleadings via e-mail. In 1998, the supreme court of the state of Washington also began to accept online filings of litigation documents. In addition, electronic filing projects are being developed in other states, including Kansas, Virginia, Utah, and Michigan. Notably, the judicial branch of the state of Colorado recently decided to implement the first statewide court e-filing system in the United States. When implementation is complete, an Internet-based service will allow all Colorado civil courts to accept legal filings electronically. In California, Florida, and a few other states, some court clerks offer docket information and other searchable databases online.

THERE ARE STILL HURDLES TO OVERCOME Although electronic filing provides many benefits, there are numerous hurdles to overcome on the road to this "paperless" future. These hurdles involve both technological and human factors. For one thing, electronic filing typically is permissible only in cases specifically approved by the court and (usually) only if all parties involved in the case agree to the procedure. The parties' agreement to electronic filing is important because if certain hardware or software is required, one party may bear more of a burden, in terms of time and cost, than the other.

For example, in one case, an appellant filed a brief (an attorney's written argument supporting his or her client's position in a case) on a CD-ROM using an Internet browser interface. Every citation was in the form of a hyperlink. The brief also contained the entire trial record, including a transcript, and an audio-video appendix with deposition testimony. The federal court of appeals refused to accept the brief because the other party to the lawsuit did not have the equipment to "read" it and access the hypertext links included on the CD-ROM. In its written opinion, the court emphasized that although it did not wish to discourage electronic filing, it did not seem fair to impose such a burden on the other party.[15]

Software and hardware incompatibilities also pose problems. For example, when a state trial court judge in Mississippi was about to try a lawsuit brought by thousands of plaintiffs against twelve corporate defendants, the judge ordered the parties to file their documents electronically. The parties were to use specially designed software called LawPlus. Problems immediately surfaced. First, LawPlus used a proprietary system that relied on Microsoft Word, while practically all of the law firms involved used WordPerfect. As a result, the attorneys encountered constant problems with document conversion. Second, the

15. *Yukiyo, Ltd. v. Watanabe,* 111 F.3d 883 (Fed.Cir. 1997).

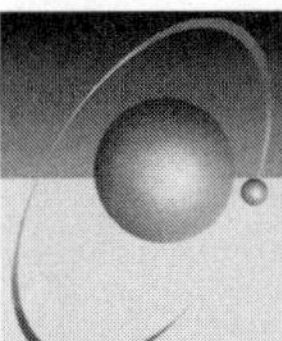

Controversial Issues in the Online World

Electronic Filing and Privacy Issues

The amount of paper used in documents submitted to the courts in any one year is staggering. Not surprisingly, the courts are moving in the direction of requiring documents to be filed electronically—via CD-ROMs or the Internet. Electronic filing eliminates the "paper chase" that occurs in all court systems. Such filing also reduces (but does not eliminate) the possibility of lost court papers.

Since the latter part of the 1990s, the Administrative Office of the U.S. Courts has been experimenting with electronic filing. A pilot project involved nine U.S. district courts. The experiment appears to be working so well that the Administrative Office of the U.S. Courts is now considering the possibility of expanding the program to all of the ninety-four U.S. district courts by 2003. No doubt the efficiency resulting from the electronic filing of court documents will save the courts (and thus taxpayers) large sums of money. The controversy surrounding electronic filing, though, has nothing to do with its efficiency or cost-saving features. Rather, it has to do with the privacy of the parties involved.

Realize that most appellate court decisions—decisions of state appellate courts, state supreme courts, U.S. appellate courts, and the United States Supreme Court—are now online. At issue here is what the effects might be of putting all federal trial (district) court decisions online.

Paper Filing and Practical Obscurity

Traditionally, all court documents relating to proceedings in federal trial courts (and state trial courts) have been filed in the traditional way—via hard-copy documents delivered to the relevant court, which enters them into its records. Most of these records are public, meaning that anyone can access them if they wish to do so. Yet from a practical point of view, how many people access these records? The answer is, only persons who are strongly motivated to access them—because to obtain them, a person must go to the relevant courthouse in person and request to see the documents.

If you live in California, for example, and are curious about a lawsuit occurring in a trial court in Mississippi, you would have to travel to Mississippi to obtain the documents that have been filed in the lawsuit. Furthermore, even if you go to Mississippi, you may not know where to look in the myriad documents filed in a particular lawsuit for certain types of information, such as a defendant's bill-paying history or a defendant's medical records. The fact that very few court filings are viewed by others is simply an indication of how difficult—and costly—it is to access these filings. By default, therefore, the parties to lawsuits traditionally have been assured that the information filed in court documents will not be widely disseminated (unless a party happens to

system was modem based and very slow. Ultimately, LawPlus was abandoned, and the parties went back to using paper.[16]

No doubt, ways to overcome these technological difficulties will be found in the coming years. Currently, for example, the Administrative Office of the U.S. Courts is looking for a new electronic database-management system that will be set up in most federal courts and provide some uniformity. The system will provide electronic filing and document-management capabilities, as well as case management features (details about cases that normally would be in paper files, appointment books, accounting systems, and personal computers).

16. For a discussion of this problem and other technological challenges faced by the judge in this case, see Wendy R. Leibowitz, "Courts in Tech Trenches," *The National Law Journal,* April 19, 1999, p. A25.

Controversial Issues in the Online World, Continued

be a well-known company such as Microsoft Corporation and the media inquire into the matter). In sum, although technically court documents are public, from a practical perspective they remain obscure, protected from unrestricted viewing.

Electronic Filing—How Will It Affect Privacy?

This "practical obscurity," as lawyers call it, may soon disappear, at least with federal district court decisions, if electronic filing becomes the norm. Electronic filing opens up all federal trial court documents to anyone with an Internet connection and a Web browser. Utilizing special software, called "data-mining" software, anyone can go online and within just a few minutes access information from dozens of courts. This means that there are now serious privacy issues at stake in nationwide electronic filing. Presumably, there is a possibility for abuse by those who use data-mining technology to acquire information on individuals' private lives.

The Choices Ahead

The choices facing the administrators of the federal judicial system are relatively limited. The first choice is to maintain the status quo, thereby limiting the types of privacy problems that will arise. Another choice is to exclude from public view on the federal court Web sites documents that are not necessary to an understanding of the determination of cases at hand. Yet another choice would be to allow attorneys filing such documents to request which part of a document should be "sealed" from public view.

Finally, there might be two levels of public access: (1) the current access associated with paper documents and applied only to paper documents, and (2) limited access to those documents when they are online. Criminal cases, for example, might routinely have more limited accessibility than civil cases. Another area for limited accessibility might be bankruptcy records.

You can be sure, though, that the controversy over electronic filing will continue. You can also be sure that any restrictions on electronic filings will be met with lawsuits under the Freedom of Information Act of 1966—an act that requires the federal government to disclose certain records to "any person" on request.

FOR CRITICAL ANALYSIS

Do you see anything wrong with posting online all court documents? After all, if someone has violated the law, shouldn't that fact be publicized as widely as possible? Can you think of any circumstances in which the electronic filing of court documents might not be in the best interests of society? Explain your answer.

Courts Online

Most courts today have sites on the Web. Of course, it is up to each court to decide what to make available at its site. Some courts display only the names of court personnel and office phone numbers. Others add court rules and forms. Some include judicial decisions, although generally the sites do not feature archives of old decisions. Instead, the time within which decisions are available online is limited. For example, California keeps opinions online for only sixty days.

Appellate court decisions are often posted online immediately after they are rendered. Recent decisions of the U.S. courts of appeals, for example, are available online at their Web sites. The United States Supreme Court has also launched an official Web site on which the Court publishes its opinions immediately after they are announced to the public. (These Web sites are listed elsewhere in this chapter in the *On the Web* features.)

Toward a Virtual Courtroom

Someday, we may see the use of "virtual" courtrooms, in which judicial proceedings take place only on the Internet. The parties to a case could meet online to make their arguments and present their evidence. This might be done with e-mail submissions, through video cameras, in designated "chat" rooms, at closed sites, or through the use of other Internet facilities. These courtrooms could be efficient and economical. We might also see the use of virtual lawyers, judges, and juries—and possibly the replacement of court personnel with computers or software.

The Internet may also be used in other ways by the courts. In a groundbreaking decision in early 2001, for example, a Florida county court granted "virtual" visitation rights in a couple's divorce proceeding. Although the court granted custody rights to the father of the couple's ten-year-old daughter, the court also ordered each parent to buy a computer and a videoconferencing system so that the mother could "visit" with her child via the Internet at any time.[17]

SECTION 5 ALTERNATIVE DISPUTE RESOLUTION

ALTERNATIVE DISPUTE RESOLUTION (ADR)
The resolution of disputes in ways other than those involved in the traditional judicial process. Negotiation, mediation, and arbitration are forms of ADR.

LITIGATION
The process of resolving a dispute through the court system.

Alternative dispute resolution (ADR) refers to the various methods by which disputes are settled outside the court system. Typically, to save time and money for all parties involved, attorneys advise their clients to attempt a settlement before resorting to **litigation**—the process of resolving a dispute through the court system. Frequently, a settlement is achieved after a lawsuit has been initiated and pretrial investigations undertaken, but before a trial takes place. At this point, the parties and their attorneys have an opportunity to assess the evidence and attempt a settlement based on the relative strengths or weaknesses of their positions. Most civil lawsuits (about 95 percent) are settled before they go to trial.

ADR offers many advantages to disputing parties. Litigating even the simplest complaint is costly, and because of the backlog of cases pending in many courts, it may sometimes be several years before a case is actually tried. ADR, in contrast, usually entails fewer costs and allows disputes to be resolved relatively quickly. ADR also offers the advantage of privacy. Court proceedings are public, whereas ADR allows the parties to come together privately and work out an agreement. Another advantage of ADR is its flexibility. Normally, the parties themselves can control how the dispute will be settled, what procedures will be used, and whether the decision reached (either by the parties themselves or by a neutral third party) will be legally binding or nonbinding. ADR also offers advantages for the courts. To ease the burden on the courts and reduce costs, both the state and federal court systems have implemented programs that encourage or even require some form of ADR prior to trial.

Methods of ADR range from neighbors sitting down over a cup of coffee in an attempt to work out their differences to huge multinational corporations agreeing to resolve a dispute through a formal hearing before a panel of experts. Some of the most commonly used methods of ADR include negotiation, mediation, and arbitration.

---

17. For a discussion of this case, see Shelley Emling, "After the Divorce, Internet Visits?" *Austin American-Statesman,* January 30, 2001, pp. A1 and A10.

Negotiation

One of the simplest forms of ADR is **negotiation,** a process in which the parties attempt to settle their dispute informally, with or without attorneys to represent them. Typically, during the pretrial stages of litigation, the parties and/or their attorneys may meet informally one or more times to see if a mutually satisfactory agreement can be reached. In some courts, pretrial negotiation is mandatory. In these courts, before parties may proceed to trial, they must first meet with each other and attempt to negotiate a settlement. Only if the parties cannot reach an agreement will the court decide the issue. In other courts, negotiation is one of a menu of ADR options that the parties may (or must, in some cases and in some courts) pursue prior to trial.

NEGOTIATION
A process in which parties attempt to settle their dispute without going to court, with or without attorneys to represent them.

In working out a mutually satisfactory agreement, disputing parties often find it helpful to have the input of a neutral (unbiased) third party. In the traditional negotiation process, however, attorneys act as advocates for their clients, which means that they put their clients' interests first. In recent years, to facilitate negotiation, various forms of what might be called "assisted negotiation" have been employed. Forms of ADR associated with the negotiation process include minitrials, early neutral case evaluation, summary jury trials, and conciliation.

MINI-TRIALS A **mini-trial** is a private proceeding in which each party's attorney briefly argues the party's case before the other party. Typically, a neutral third party, who acts as an adviser and an expert in the area being disputed, is also present. If the parties fail to reach an agreement, the adviser renders an opinion as to how a court would likely decide the issue. The proceeding assists the parties in determining whether they should negotiate a settlement of the dispute or take it to court.

MINI-TRIAL
A private proceeding in which each party to a dispute argues its position before the other side and vice versa. A neutral third party may be present and act as an adviser if the parties fail to reach an agreement.

EARLY NEUTRAL CASE EVALUATION In **early neutral case evaluation,** the parties select a neutral third party (generally an expert in the subject matter of the dispute) to evaluate their respective positions. The parties explain their points of view to the case evaluator however they wish. The case evaluator then assesses the strengths and weaknesses of the parties' positions, and this evaluation forms the basis for negotiating a settlement.

EARLY NEUTRAL CASE EVALUATION
A form of alternative dispute resolution in which a neutral third party evaluates the strengths and weakness of the disputing parties' positions; the evaluator's opinion forms the basis for negotiating a settlement.

SUMMARY JURY TRIALS A form of ADR that has been successfully employed in the federal court system is the **summary jury trial (SJT).** In an SJT, which occurs after a lawsuit has been initiated but before the trial, the litigants present their arguments and evidence to a jury. The jury then renders a verdict. The jury's verdict, however, is not binding. Rather, it serves as a guide to both sides in reaching an agreement during the mandatory negotiations that immediately follow the trial. Because no witnesses are called, the SJT is much speedier than a regular trial, and frequently the parties are able to settle their dispute without resorting to an actual trial. If no settlement is reached, both sides have the right to a full trial later.

SUMMARY JURY TRIAL (SJT)
A method of settling disputes in which a trial is held, but the jury's verdict is not binding. The verdict acts only as a guide to both sides in reaching an agreement during the mandatory negotiations that immediately follow the summary jury trial.

CONCILIATION Disputes may also be resolved in a friendly, nonadversarial manner through **conciliation,** in which a third party assists parties to a dispute in reconciling their differences. The conciliator helps to schedule negotiating

CONCILIATION
A form of alternative dispute resolution in which the parties reach an agreement themselves with the help of a neutral third party, called a conciliator, who facilitates the negotiations.

sessions and carries offers back and forth between the parties when they refuse to face each other in direct negotiations. Technically, conciliators are not to recommend solutions. In practice, however, they often do. In contrast, a mediator is expected to propose solutions.

Mediation

MEDIATION
A method of settling disputes outside of court by using the services of a neutral third party, called a mediator. The mediator acts as a communicating agent between the parties and suggests ways in which the parties can resolve their dispute.

One of the oldest forms of ADR is mediation. In the **mediation** process, the parties themselves attempt to negotiate an agreement, but with the assistance of a neutral third party, called a mediator. The mediator need not be a lawyer. The mediator may be a single person, such as a paralegal, an attorney, or a volunteer from the community. Alternatively, a panel of mediators may be used. Usually, a mediator charges a fee, which can be split between the parties. Mediation is essentially a form of assisted negotiation, but one in which the mediator plays a more active role than the neutral third parties in negotiation-associated forms of ADR.

As with negotiation, some courts may encourage or require the parties to undertake mediation prior to a trial. Some states offer mediation as the only ADR method that may (or must) be undertaken before proceeding to trial. Florida, for example, has a comprehensive statewide mediation program to facilitate pretrial settlements.

THE MEDIATOR'S ROLE The mediator's role is basically to help the parties evaluate their positions and clarify the issues on which they do and do not agree. A mediator will try to discern what the parties' real interests are, as opposed to the stances that the parties have put forward. This is often done by holding private sessions with each party, in which the mediator learns what information the parties are unwilling to disclose to each other. Through joint and individual sessions with the parties, the mediator obtains information to assess realistically the alternative ways in which the dispute might be resolved. The mediator then proposes a solution, or alternative solutions, including what compromises will be necessary to reach an agreement.

THE ADVANTAGES OF MEDIATION Unlike litigation (and, to a certain extent, negotiation), mediation is not adversarial in nature. Rather, a mediator tries to find common grounds on which an agreement can be based. Therefore, the process tends to reduce antagonism between the disputants and to allow them to resume their former relationship. For this reason, mediation is often the preferred form of ADR for business disputes involving parties who either must or would like to continue an ongoing relationship. For example, business partners may be able to work out their differences through mediation more satisfactorily than through other forms of ADR or through litigation. Mediation is also beneficial in settling differences between employers and employees or other parties involved in long-term relationships.

ARBITRATION
The settling of a dispute by submitting it to a disinterested third party (other than a court), who renders a decision. The decision may or may not be legally binding.

Arbitration

A more formal method of alternative dispute resolution is **arbitration**, in which an arbitrator (a neutral third party or a panel of experts) hears a dispute and renders a decision. The key difference between arbitration and the forms of ADR just discussed is that in arbitration, the third party's decision may be legally binding on the parties.

Many courts, in both the federal and state court systems, require the pretrial arbitration of disputes. Often, arbitration is required only in cases in which the dollar amount in controversy is under a specified threshold amount. For example, courts in several federal districts require pretrial arbitration in cases involving less than $100,000. In Hawaii, all disputes involving less than $150,000 must be arbitrated. When pretrial arbitration is mandated by a court, normally the arbitrator's decision is not legally binding. If either of the parties is not satisfied with the decision, the court will try the case.

THE ARBITRATION PROCESS In some respects, formal arbitration resembles a trial, although usually the procedural rules are much less restrictive than those governing litigation. In the typical hearing format, the parties present opening arguments to the arbitrator and state what remedies should or should not be granted. Next, evidence is presented, and witnesses may be called and examined by both sides. The arbitrator then renders a decision, called an **award.**

AWARD
In the context of arbitration, the arbitrator's decision.

An arbitrator's award is usually the final word on the matter. Although the parties may appeal an arbitrator's decision, a court's review of the decision will be much more restricted in scope than an appellate court's review of a trial court's decision. The general view is that because the parties were free to frame the issues and set the powers of the arbitrator at the outset, they cannot complain about the results. The award will only be set aside if the arbitrator's conduct or "bad faith" substantially prejudiced the rights of one of the parties, if the award violates an established public policy, or if the arbitrator exceeded his or her powers (by arbitrating issues that the parties did not agree to submit to arbitration).

ARBITRATION CLAUSES AND STATUTES Virtually any commercial matter can be submitted to arbitration. Frequently, parties include an **arbitration clause** in a contract specifying that any dispute arising under the contract will be resolved through arbitration rather than through the court system. Parties can also agree to arbitrate a dispute after it arises.

ARBITRATION CLAUSE
A clause in a contract that provides that, in the event of a dispute, the parties will submit the dispute to arbitration rather than litigate the dispute in court.

Most states have statutes (often based in part on the Uniform Arbitration Act of 1955) under which arbitration clauses will be enforced, and some state statutes compel arbitration of certain types of disputes, such as those involving public employees. At the federal level, the Federal Arbitration Act (FAA), enacted in 1925, enforces arbitration clauses in contracts involving maritime activity and interstate commerce—activities that the federal government has the authority to regulate through legislation.

ARBITRABILITY When a dispute arises as to whether the parties to a contract with an arbitration clause have agreed to submit a particular matter to arbitration, one party may file suit to compel arbitration. The court before which the suit is brought will not decide the basic controversy but must decide the issue of *arbitrability*—that is, whether the matter is one that must be resolved through arbitration.

Even when a claim involves a violation of a statute passed to protect a certain class of people, a court may determine that the parties must nonetheless abide by their agreement to arbitrate the dispute. Usually, a court will allow the claim to be arbitrated if the court, in interpreting the statute, can find no legislative intent to the contrary.

In one important case, the United States Supreme Court held that a claim brought under the Age Discrimination in Employment Act (ADEA) of 1967 could be subject to compulsory arbitration. The plaintiff in the case, Robert Gilmer, had been discharged from his employment at the age of sixty-two. Gilmer sued his employer, claiming that he was a victim of age discrimination. The employer argued that Gilmer had to submit the dispute to arbitration because he had agreed, as part of a required registration application to be a securities representative with the New York Stock Exchange, to arbitrate "any dispute, claim, or controversy" relating to his employment. The Supreme Court held that Gilmer, by agreeing to arbitrate any dispute, had waived his right to sue.[18]

Note that Gilmer had waived his *own* rights in a broadly worded arbitration clause. In the following case, the Supreme Court addressed the question of whether a union, in an equally broadly worded arbitration clause, can waive the rights of the employees whom it represents.

---

[18] *Gilmer v. Interstate/Johnson Lane Corp.*, 500 U.S. 20, 111 S.Ct. 1647, 114 L.Ed.2d 26 (1991).

CASE 2.4 Wright v. Universal Maritime Service Corp.

Supreme Court of the United States, 1998.
525 U.S. 70,
119 S.Ct. 391,
142 L.Ed.2d 361.
http://supct.law.cornell.edu/supct/html/97-889.ZS.html[a]

BACKGROUND AND FACTS Ceasar Wright was a longshoreman and a member of the International Longshoremen's Association (ILA). The ILA supplies workers to Universal Maritime Service Corporation and other members of the South Carolina Stevedores Association (SCSA). A collective bargaining agreement (CBA) between the ILA and the SCSA provided for the arbitration of "matters under dispute" in one clause and "all matters affecting wages, hours, and other terms and conditions of employment" in another. Still another clause stated that "[a]nything not contained in this Agreement shall not be construed as being part of this Agreement." Wright suffered a job-related injury that resulted in a disability. When a physician approved Wright's return to work, the SCSA members refused to hire him because of the disability. Wright filed a suit in a federal district court against Universal and others, on the ground that they had discriminated against him in violation of the Americans with Disabilities Act (ADA) of 1990. The defendants argued that the suit should be dismissed because Wright had not submitted his claim to arbitration. The district court ruled in the defendants' favor, and the U.S. Court of Appeals for the Fourth Circuit affirmed this ruling. Wright appealed to the United States Supreme Court.

a. This page is part of the Supreme Court Collection of cases maintained by the Legal Information Institute, which is part of Cornell Law School.

IN THE LANGUAGE OF THE COURT. . .

Justice *SCALIA* delivered the opinion of the Court.

* * * *

* * * In [a previous case] we stated that a union could waive its officers' statutory right * * * to be free of antiunion discrimination, but we held that such a waiver must be *clear and unmistakable*. * * * [Emphasis added.]

* * * [T]he right to a federal judicial forum is of sufficient importance to be protected against a less-than-explicit union waiver in a CBA. The CBA in this case does not meet that standard. Its arbitration clause is very general, providing for arbitration of "[m]atters under dispute"—which could be understood to mean matters in dispute under the contract. And the remainder of the contract contains no explicit incorporation of statutory antidiscrimination requirements. The Fourth Circuit relied upon the fact that the equivalently broad arbitration clause in *Gilmer v. Interstate/Johnson Lane Corp.*—applying to "any dispute, claim or controversy"—was held to embrace federal statutory claims. But *Gilmer* involved an individual's waiver of his own rights, rather than a union's waiver of the rights of represented employees—and hence the "clear and unmistakable" standard was not applicable.

* * * *

We hold that the collective-bargaining agreement in this case does not contain a clear and unmistakable waiver of the covered employees' rights to a judicial forum for federal claims of employment discrimination. We do not reach the question whether such a waiver would be enforceable.

DECISION AND REMEDY The Supreme Court held that the arbitration clause in the CBA did not clearly waive the union members' right to have a court rule on federal claims of employment discrimination. Thus, Wright was not required to submit his claim to arbitration. The Court did not decide whether such a waiver would be enforceable if it were clear. The Court vacated (voided, or annuled) the judgment of the lower court and remanded the case.

FOR CRITICAL ANALYSIS–Ethical Consideration *Does compulsory arbitration contradict the public policy enunciated in statues specifically designed to protect employees' rights, such as the right to be free from discrimination?*

Providers of ADR Services

ADR services are provided by both government agencies and private organizations. A major provider of ADR services is the **American Arbitration Association (AAA).** Most of the largest law firms in the nation are members of this nonprofit association. Founded in 1926, the AAA now handles over ninety thousand claims a year in its numerous offices around the country. Cases brought before the AAA are heard by an expert or a panel of experts in the area relating to the dispute and are usually settled quickly. Generally, about half of the panel members are lawyers. To cover its costs, the AAA charges a fee, paid by the party filing the claim. In addition, each party to the dispute pays a specified amount for each hearing day, as well as a special additional fee in cases involving personal injuries or property loss.

AMERICAN ARBITRATION ASSOCIATION (AAA)
The major organization offering arbitration services in the United States.

Hundreds of for-profit firms around the country also provide dispute-resolution services. Typically, these firms hire retired judges to conduct arbitration hearings or otherwise assist parties in settling their disputes. The leading firm in this relatively new private system of justice is JAMS/Endispute, which is based in Santa Ana, California. Private ADR firms normally allow the parties to decide

For information on alternative dispute resolution, go to the American Arbitration Association's Web site at **http://www.adr.org**.

on the date of the hearing, the presiding judge, whether the judge's decision will be legally binding, and the site of the hearing—which may be a conference room, a law school office, or a leased courtroom. The judges follow procedures similar to those of the federal courts and use similar rules. Usually, each party to the dispute pays a filing fee and a designated fee for a hearing session or conference.

There are also international organizations, such as the International Chamber of Commerce, that provide forums for the arbitration of disputes between parties to international contracts.

Finally, a growing number of firms are offering dispute-resolution services online. See Chapter 3 for a discussion of this latest development in ADR.

Concept Summary 2.3—Alternative Dispute Resolution (ADR)

Type of ADR	Description
Negotiation	The parties come together, with or without attorneys to represent them, and try to reach a settlement. Traditionally, no third party was involved in the process. Today, several forms of "assisted negotiation"—negotiation involving a neutral (unbiased) third party—are used, including mini-trials, early neutral case evaluation, and (in some federal courts) summary jury trials, or SJTs. The opinion of the third party (or "jury," in an SJT) forms the basis for negotiating a settlement.
Mediation	The parties themselves reach an agreement with the help of a third party, called a mediator, who plays an active role in settling the dispute. The mediator tries to discover and assess the real causes of the dispute (through discussions with the parties individually and jointly), assists the parties in evaluating their positions, and proposes possible solutions. Mediation is usually the preferred method of ADR in cases involving ongoing or long-term relationships.
Arbitration	In this more formal method of ADR, the parties submit their dispute to a neutral third party, the arbitrator, who renders a decision. The decision is binding unless the parties (or a court, in court-related arbitration) specify otherwise. Arbitration awards may be appealed to a court, but only in special circumstances (such as if the award is contrary to public policy) will a court set aside an arbitrator's award. If there is a question concerning the arbitrability of a certain type of claim, a court must decide the issue.

Terms and Concepts

alternative dispute resolution (ADR) 50
American Arbitration Association (AAA) 55
arbitration 52
arbitration clause 53
award 53
bankruptcy court 34
conciliation 51
concurrent jurisdiction 35
diversity of citizenship 35
early neutral case evaluation 51
exclusive jurisdiction 35
federal question 35
in personam jurisdiction 32
in rem jurisdiction 34
judicial review 31
jurisdiction 32
justiciable controversy 37
litigation 50

QUESTIONS AND CASE PROBLEMS

2–1. Arbitration. In an arbitration proceeding, the arbitrator need not be a judge or even a lawyer. How, then, can the arbitrator's decision have the force of law and be binding on the parties involved?

2–2. Courts of Appeals. The defendant in a lawsuit is appealing the trial court's decision in favor of the plaintiff. On appeal, the defendant claims that the evidence presented at trial to support the plaintiff's claim was so scanty that no reasonable jury could have found for the plaintiff. Therefore, argues the defendant, the appellate court should reverse the trial court's decision. May an appellate court ever reverse a trial court's findings with respect to questions of fact? Discuss fully.

2–3. Courts of Appeals. Appellate courts normally see only written transcripts of trial proceedings when they are reviewing cases. Today, in some states, videotapes are being used as the official trial reports. If the use of videotapes as official reports continues, will this alter the appellate process? Should it? Discuss fully.

2–4. Jurisdiction. Marya Callais, a citizen of Florida, was walking one day near a busy street in Tallahassee, Florida, when a large crate flew off a passing truck and hit her, resulting in numerous injuries. She incurred a great deal of pain and suffering, plus significant medical expenses, and she could not work for six months. She wants to sue the trucking firm for $300,000 in damages. The firm's headquarters are in Georgia, although the company does business in Florida. In what court might Callais bring suit—a Florida state court, a Georgia state court, or a federal court? What factors might influence her decision?

2–5. Arbitration. Randall Fris worked as a seaman on an Exxon Shipping Co. oil tanker for eight years without incident. One night, he boarded the ship for duty while intoxicated, in violation of company policy. This policy also allowed Exxon to discharge employees who were intoxicated and thus unfit for work. Exxon discharged Fris. Under a contract with Fris's union, the discharge was submitted to arbitration. The arbitrators ordered Exxon to reinstate Fris on an oil tanker. Exxon filed a suit against the union, challenging the award as contrary to public policy, which opposes having intoxicated persons operate seagoing vessels. Can a court set aside an arbitration award on the ground (legal basis) that the award violates public policy? Should the court set aside the award in this case? Explain. [*Exxon Shipping Co. v. Exxon Seamen's Union,* 11 F.3d 1189 (3d Cir. 1993)]

2–6. Jurisdiction. Cybersell, Inc., is an Arizona corporation (Cybersell AZ) that provides Internet marketing services. Cybersell AZ applied with the U.S. Patent and Trademark Office (USPTO) to register "Cybersell" as a service mark. Before the application was granted, unrelated parties formed Cybersell, Inc., a Florida corporation (Cybersell FL), to provide consulting services for marketing on the Internet. Cybersell FL put up a Web site using the name "Cybersell," but its interactivity was limited to taking a surfer's name and address. No one in Arizona contacted Cybersell FL, or even hit on its Web page, before the USPTO granted Cybersell AZ's service mark application. Cybersell AZ then told Cybersell FL to stop using "Cybersell" and filed a suit in a federal district court in Arizona against Cybersell FL, alleging, among other things, trademark infringement. Cybersell FL filed a motion to dismiss for lack of jurisdiction. How should the court rule? Why? [*Cybersell, Inc., an Arizona Corporation v. Cybersell, Inc., a Florida Corporation,* 130 F.3d 414 (9th Cir. 1997)]

2–7. Standing. Blue Cross and Blue Shield insurance companies (the Blues) provide 68 million Americans with health-care protection. The Blues have paid billions of dollars for care attributable to illnesses related to tobacco use. In an attempt to recover some of this amount, the Blues filed a suit in a federal district court against tobacco companies and others, alleging fraud, among other things. The Blues claimed that beginning in 1953, the defendants conspired to addict millions of Americans, including members of Blue Cross and Blue Shield plans, to cigarettes and other tobacco products. The conspiracy involved misrepresentation about the safety of nicotine and its addictive properties, marketing efforts targeting children, and agreements not to produce or market safer cigarettes. The success of the defendants caused lung, throat, and other cancers, as well as heart disease, stroke, emphysema, and other illnesses. The defendants asked the court to dismiss the case on the ground that the plaintiffs did not have standing to sue. Do the Blues have standing in this case? Why or why not? [*Blue Cross and Blue Shield of New Jersey, Inc. v. Philip Morris, Inc.*, 36 F.Supp.2d 560 (E.D.N.Y. 1999)]

WEB EXERCISES

Go to **http://lec.westbuslaw.com**, the Web site that accompanies this text. Select "Internet Applications," and then click on "Chapter 2." There you will find the following Internet research exercises that you can perform to learn more about alternative dispute resolution and the judiciary's role in American government:

Activity 2–1: Alternative Dispute Resolution

Activity 2–2: The Judiciary's Role in American Government

Chapter 3

E-Commerce and Dispute Resolution

Concepts Covered

After reading this chapter, you should be able to:

1. State the types of disputes that are classified as "e-commerce disputes."
2. Discuss the role and function of the Internet Corporation for Assigned Names and Numbers (ICANN) in settling e-commerce disputes.
3. Indicate what legal principles apply in the online resolution of most disputes.
4. Identify online dispute-resolution (ODR) services available to resolve small- and medium-sized business claims.
5. Summarize some of the advantages and disadvantages of online dispute resolution.

"[C]ompanies looking to profit from this growing marketplace need to learn to avoid the pitfalls of protracted court battles that can last years and cost billions."

William Slate II, 1946–
(President, American Arbitration Association, 1994–)

In Chapter 2, we discussed the courts' assertion of personal jurisdiction over disputes arising in cyberspace and the traditional methods of resolving disputes outside the judicial process (alternative dispute resolution, or ADR). In this chapter, we discuss the types of disputes that most commonly arise in e-commerce and some of the methods for their resolution without using the judicial process. E-commerce can include any business transaction that occurs in cyberspace, whether it involves a sale from business to business (B2B) or one from business to consumer (B2C).

E-COMMERCE
A business transaction that occurs in cyberspace.

For B2B and B2C transactions, cyberspace offers buyers convenient marketplace accessibility twenty-four hours a day, seven days a week (24/7), and gives sellers access to an enormous customer base. The number of Americans who use the Internet and the number of those who shopped online during a recent business quarter are shown in Exhibit 3–1 on page 60. This situation presents challenges, however. For example, buyers must be confident that they have access to effective resolution procedures for problems arising in e-commerce. There are difficulties with resolving such problems. These include language and cultural differences, and the obstacles that occur when a buyer and a seller are in separate, distant locations. When litigation is the only choice, it can be complicated by questions concerning the applicable law and the enforcement of a judgment.

EXHIBIT 3–1 Shopping Online

Ninety million Americans used the Internet in the third business quarter of 2000.

Sixty million Americans shopped online during the third business quarter of 2000.

Complying with the laws of all possible jurisdictions and being subject to potential lawsuits in all possible courts increase the cost of doing business in cyberspace. Businesses and consumers desire the continued growth of the new marketplace; they simply want to avoid the difficulties inherent in resolving problems arising out of online transactions.

SECTION 1 E-COMMERCE DISPUTES

E-COMMERCE DISPUTE
A dispute that arises from business conducted in cyberspace.

Any dispute that arises in e-commerce can be classified as an **e-commerce dispute.** This chapter focuses on the most common of these disputes: disagreements over the rights to domain names and disagreements over the quality of goods sold via the Internet. The second type of dispute includes complaints related to auction Web sites. These complaints make up more than half of the cyberspace complaints that the Federal Trade Commission (FTC) receives. Exhibit 3–2 on page 61 compares the total number of Internet-related consumer complaints with the number of online auction–related complaints that the FTC received in a recent year. According to at least one survey, as many as 40 percent of online consumers have experienced problems with at least one e-commerce transaction.

Considering the potentially large number of e-commerce disputes, why aren't the courts overwhelmed with such cases? Part of the answer is that many of these disputes, even those concerning domain names, involve small amounts of money and parties in distant locations. To settle these conflicts, it is now possible to use **online dispute resolution (ODR)**. These alternative forums are helping to identify and develop rules that may ultimately become a code of conduct for all of those, regardless of jurisdiction, who do business in cyberspace. Exhibit 3–3 illustrates how ODR fits into the universe of "all e-commerce disputes."

As mentioned, the focus in this chapter is on the two most common types of e-commerce disputes. Realize, though, that other types of disputes are expected to become more numerous as commerce is increasingly conducted over the Internet. Already, B2B commerce is expanding at a rapid pace. Consider that an estimated $1.2 trillion was spent in B2B commerce in 2001, and this amount is expected to quadruple by 2004. As both B2B and B2C commerce continues to grow, disputes relating to e-transactions will inevitably increase. Significantly, the American Arbitration Association (AAA), which, as mentioned in Chapter 2, is a leading provider of dispute-resolution services, recently announced that it has developed a new B2B e-commerce dispute-management protocol. The goal of the AAA is to facilitate both the development of global standards for businesses participating in B2B commerce and the use of technology in settling e-commerce disputes.

EXHIBIT 3–2 Internet-Related Consumer Complaints

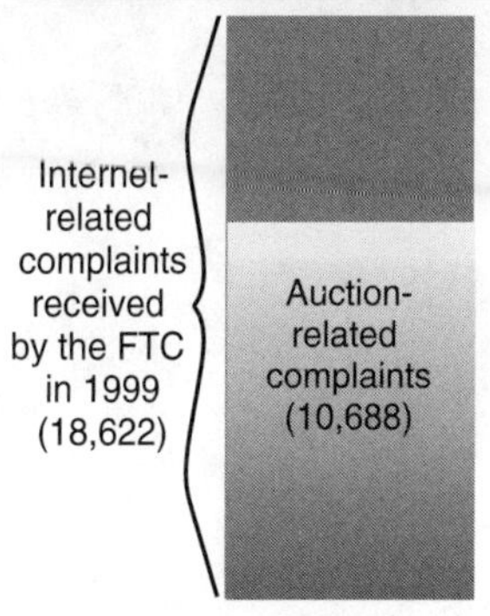

ONLINE DISPUTE RESOLUTION (ODR)
The resolution of a dispute in cyberspace. Cyberspace is the online world within which computer-based networks operate.

SECTION 2 ONLINE RESOLUTION OF DOMAIN NAME DISPUTES

A **domain name** is part of an Internet address, such as "westlaw.com." The top level domain (TLD) is the part of the name to the right of the period and represents the type of entity that operates the site (for example, "com" is an abbreviation

DOMAIN NAME
The last part of an Internet address, such as "westlaw.com." The top level (the part of the name to the right of the period) represents the type of entity that operates the site ("com" is an abbreviation for "commercial"). The second level (the part of the name to the left of the period) is chosen by the entity.

EXHIBIT 3–3 Online Dispute Resolution

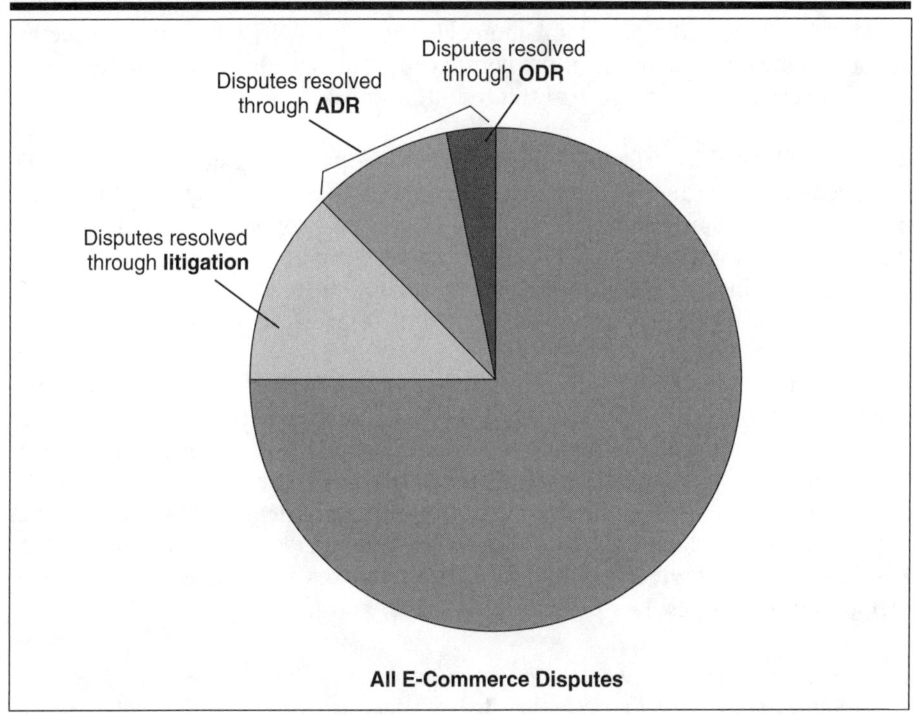

for "commercial"). The second level (the part of the name to the left of the period) is chosen by the business entity or individual registering the domain name.

Disputes that have arisen over the use of the same, or similar, domain names have involved parties' attempts to profit from the goodwill of a competitor, to sell pornography, to offer for sale another party's domain name, and to otherwise *infringe on* (use without authorization) others' trademarks. As you will read in Chapter 6, a *trademark* is a distinctive mark affixed to goods to identify the goods and their origins. A *service mark* is a distinctive mark used in the sale or advertising of services. A *trade name,* such as the name of a business, can also be protected under trademark law if the business's name is the same as its trademarked product. Once established, the owner of a mark is entitled to its exclusive use.

In the real world, one business can often use the same name as another without causing any conflict, particularly if the businesses are small, their goods or services are different, and the areas within which they do business are separate. In the online world, however, there is only one area of business–cyberspace. Thus, disputes between parties over which one has the right to use a particular domain name have become common. The problem is, because cyberspace is international in scope, litigating such disputes can be exceedingly cumbersome and costly. As a result, new ways of settling such disputes have been devised and are being implemented. At the forefront of this development is the Internet Corporation for Assigned Names and Numbers (ICANN).

Internet Corporation for Assigned Names and Numbers

The Web site of the Internet Corporation for Assigned Names and Numbers (ICANN) can be found at **http://www.icann.com**.

The Internet Corporation for Assigned Names and Numbers (ICANN) is a nonprofit corporation that the federal government set up to oversee the distribution of domain names. We will look more closely at ICANN's role in overseeing domain names in Chapter 6, in the context of trademark law. Here, we examine ICANN's services with respect to the resolution of domain name disputes.[1]

ICANN'S SERVICES To obtain relief from a party engaged in trademark infringement, a mark's owner was at one time limited primarily to filing a suit in a court with appropriate jurisdiction. ICANN began operating an online arbitration system on January 1, 2000, to resolve domain name disputes. Now, if trademark infringement involves a domain name, instead of, or in addition to, filing a suit, a party may submit a complaint to an ICANN–approved dispute-resolution provider.

PANEL
An arbitrator, or arbitrators, appointed to make a decision in a dispute-resolution proceeding.

ICANN refers to these dispute-resolution proceedings as *administrative proceedings* and to the arbitrator, or arbitrators, as the **panel.** To initiate an administrative proceeding, the complainant chooses one of four services that ICANN has approved: the National Arbitration Forum, eResolution, the World Intellectual Property Organization Arbitration and Mediation Center (WIPO Center, discussed later in this chapter), or the CPR Institute for Dispute Resolution. Each service appoints its own arbitrators to a panel. The panelists include former judges, law professors, lawyers, and nonlawyers.

1. See ICANN's Uniform Domain Name Dispute Resolution Policy at http://www.icann.org/udrp/udrp-policy-24oct99.htm. This policy is also discussed below.

What is the legal effect of a decision and order in a dispute resolved by one of these services? That was the question in the following case.

CASE 3.1 Weber-Stephen Products Co. v. Armitage Hardware and Building Supply, Inc.

United States District Court,
Northern District of Illinois, 2000.
__ F.Supp.2d __.

BACKGROUND AND FACTS Armitage Hardware and Building Supply, Inc., owned a number of domain names. Weber-Stephen Products Company believed that the names included Weber-Stephen's registered trademarks and service marks and that Armitage was using these marks in a deceptive, confusing, and misleading manner, intentionally and in bad faith. Weber-Stephen initiated an administrative proceeding with the WIPO Center, one of the ICANN–approved dispute-resolution providers. Weber-Stephen asked a WIPO Center panel to resolve the issue of whether Armitage was using its domain names in bad faith. Weber-Stephen also asked that Armitage's domain names either be transferred to Weber-Stephen or be canceled. The next day, Weber-Stephen filed a suit in a federal district court against Armitage, alleging violations of the law, including trademark infringement. In response, Armitage asked the court to declare the WIPO Center proceeding nonbinding and stay (postpone) the suit or, if the proceeding was ruled to be binding, to stay that proceeding to consider whether Armitage could be compelled to participate. (Recall that under the Federal Arbitration Act, when an arbitrator's decision is binding, a court's review of that decision is more limited than if the decision is nonbinding.)

IN THE LANGUAGE OF THE COURT. . .
ASPEN, Chief J. [Judge.]

* * * *

No federal court has yet considered the legal effect of a WIPO proceeding. However, the ICANN [Uniform Domain Name Dispute Resolution Policy, discussed later in this chapter] and its accompanying rules do contemplate the possibility of parallel proceedings in federal court. First, the Policy provides that ICANN will cancel or transfer domain name registrations upon "our receipt of an order from a court * * * of competent jurisdiction, requiring such action * * * ." Also, the procedural rules governing the Policy provide that if legal proceedings are initiated prior to or during an administrative proceeding with regard to a domain name dispute that is the subject of the administrative complaint, the panel has the discretion to decide whether to suspend or terminate the administrative proceeding or whether to proceed and make a decision. And the language of the Policy suggests that the administrative panels' decisions are not intended to be binding on federal courts. For example, under the heading "Availability of Court Proceedings," the ICANN Policy provides:

> * * * [If we receive] official documentation (such as a copy of a complaint, file-stamped by the clerk of the court) that you have commenced a lawsuit against the complainant in a jurisdiction to which the complainant has submitted * * * , we will not implement the Administrative Panel's decision, and we will take no further action, until we receive (i) evidence satisfactory to us of a resolution between the parties; (ii) evidence satisfactory to us that your lawsuit has been dismissed or withdrawn; or (iii) a copy of an order

CASE 3.1–Continued

> from such court dismissing your lawsuit or ordering that you do not have the right to continue to use your domain name.

Furthermore, Armitage's counsel sent an e-mail inquiry to <domain.disputes@wipo.int>, and the response from the WIPO Arbitration and Mediation Center said that the administrative panel's determination would be binding on the registrar[a] of the domain name, but that "[t]his decision is not binding upon a court, and a court may give appropriate weight to the Administrative Panel's decision." * * *

We conclude that this Court is not bound by the outcome of the ICANN administrative proceedings. But at this time we decline to determine the precise standard by which we would review the panel's decision, and what degree of deference [respect, willingness to abide by] (if any) we would give that decision. Neither the ICANN Policy nor its governing rules dictate to courts what weight should be given to a panel's decision, and the WIPO e-mail message stating that "a court may give appropriate weight to the Administrative Panel's decision" confirms the breadth of our discretion.

Because both parties to this case have adequate avenues of recourse should they be unhappy with the administrative panel's imminent decision, we find no need to stay the pending ICANN administrative action. Instead, we hereby stay this case pending the outcome of those proceedings.

a. A *registrar* is the entity through which a company or individual registers a domain name.

DECISION AND REMEDY The court held that the outcome of an ICANN administrative proceeding was not binding on the court, but it did not decide to what extent it would defer to the WIPO Center panel's decision. The court stayed its own proceedings until the panel issued its decision.

FOR CRITICAL ANALYSIS–Economic Consideration *Sometimes, a party establishes a domain name as an address for a Web site before the name's owner can take legal action. When this occurs and the owner files a suit, it may be some time before the dispute is resolved in court. Is there anything the owner might do in the meantime to prevent the other party from profiting from—or harming—the reputation and goodwill associated with the owner's mark?*

ICANN'S DISPUTE-RESOLUTION PROCEDURE All of ICANN's approved dispute-resolution providers follow ICANN's prescribed procedure.[2] As indicated in Exhibit 3–4 on page 69, a complaint is filed with one of the four approved services, and the party against whom the complaint is made is given the opportunity to file an answer. Both the complaint and the answer are submitted online, although hard copies are also delivered to the provider. A decision is issued, also online, in sixty days or less. The decision may be appealed to a court.

2. See ICANN's Rules for Uniform Domain Name Dispute Resolution Policy at http://www.icann.org/udrp/udrp-rules-24oct99.htm.

ICANN's Uniform Domain Name Dispute Resolution Policy includes three elements that must be proved to have a domain name transferred or cancelled. These elements are:

1. The challenged domain name must be identical or confusingly similar to a trademark or service mark in which the complainant has rights.

2. The party against whom the complaint is made must have no rights or legitimate interests in the domain name.

3. The challenged domain name must be registered and be used in bad faith.[3]

The issue in the following case was whether those elements were proved.

3. ICANN's Uniform Domain Name Dispute Resolution Policy Rule 4(a).

CASE 3.2 Blue Max Technology v. Compudigital Industries

National Arbitration Forum, 2000.
Claim No. FA0007000095107.
http://www.icann.org/udrp/proceedings-list-name.htm[a]

BACKGROUND AND FACTS In 1969, International Instrumentation, Inc., began manufacturing computer-related products under the brand name "Blue Max" and registered this name as a trademark. Over the next twenty-five years, the product name came to have more widespread recognition than the company name. For this reason, in 1998 the firm reincorporated itself under the name Blue Max Technology. Blue Max uses the domain name "bluemax.net" to promote its services on the Internet. Compudigital Industries registered the domain name "bluemax.com" in 1996. In early 1999, Compudigital used this name to link users to a test Web page for an auction site that was under construction. Before the end of the year, Compudigital stopped using the name completely. Blue Max contacted Compudigital and was told that the firm was not using, and did not plan to use, the name. Blue Max offered up to $10,000 for the name. Compudigital refused the offer and forced Blue Max into a bidding war with another party. Blue Max filed a complaint with the National Arbitration Forum (NAF), an ICANN–approved dispute-resolution provider. Despite notices sent by mail, e-mail, and fax, Compudigital did not respond. Blue Max asked the NAF Panel to order the domain name "bluemax.com" transferred to Blue Max.

a. This Web site is maintained by ICANN. Scroll down the "Domain Name" column to "bluemax.com." In the corresponding box in the "Status/Panel Decision" column, click on "Name transfer" to access this decision.

IN THE LANGUAGE OF THE PANEL. . .
Honorable[b] James A. *CARMODY*, as Panelist.

* * * *

* * * [T]he ICANN Uniform Domain Name Dispute Resolution Policy ("Policy") directs that the complainant must prove each of the following three elements to support a claim that a domain name should be cancelled or transferred:

Identical and/or Confusingly Similar

The Complainant [Blue Max] has * * * rights in the mark BLUE MAX. The Respondent's [Compudigital's] domain name is identical to the Complainant's mark.

Rights or Legitimate Interests

* * * *

b. "Honorable" is a title of courtesy for an official or a judge. In this case, James Carmody is a retired judge.

CASE 3.2—Continued

The domain name in question is not a mark by which the Respondent is commonly known. Rather, the Respondent is associated with the domain name Compudigital Industries. The Respondent has * * * not argued that it is using the domain name in connection with a bona fide offering of goods and services or is making a legitimate noncommercial or fair use of the site. Failure to respond to the Complaint permits the inference that the use of the Complainant's mark is misleading and Respondent has no rights or legitimate interests in the domain name in question.

Registration and Use in Bad Faith

* * * *

The Respondent used the domain name to attract users to the auction site prior to 1999. Attracting users to a website or other on-line location by creating a likelihood of confusion with the Complainant's mark as to the source of the website is evidence of bad faith registration and use.

The Respondent also is now passively holding the domain name without use. The Respondent * * * admitted that the domain name was not in use and was not to be used in the immediate future. This is evidence of bad faith.

The Respondent used the domain name for a profit by offering it for sale to the Complainant and the Complainant's competitors for valuable consideration in excess of out-of-pocket expenses.

Based on the above, the panel concludes that the Respondent registered and used the domain name in bad faith.

* * * *

Having established all three elements * * * , it is the decision of the panel that the requested relief be granted.

Accordingly, for all of the foregoing reasons, it is ordered that the domain name, "BLUEMAX.COM" be transferred from the Respondent to the Complainant.

DECISION AND REMEDY The NAF Panel concluded that Blue Max established all of the elements under ICANN's policy to have a domain name transferred or cancelled. The panel ordered the name "bluemax.com" transferred to Blue Max.

FOR CRITICAL ANALYSIS—Ethical Consideration *"Proving bad faith in the registration and use of a domain name is impossible to do because determining whether someone acts in good or bad faith is ultimately a subjective decision." Do you agree with this statement? Why or why not? Were the criteria that the panel used to decide this case subjective or objective in nature?*

World Intellectual Property Organization Arbitration and Mediation Center

The World Intellectual Property Organization Arbitration and Mediation Center (WIPO Center) is part of the International Bureau of the World Intellectual Property Organization. Since 1994, the WIPO Center has arbitrated and mediated international commercial disputes between private parties. The WIPO Center focuses particularly on the resolution of disputes involving cyberspace and e-commerce. This includes disputes that arise from the use of domain names and other conflicts involving intellectual property.

The WIPO Center offers four dispute-resolution services. Each has different advantages and legal effects.

1. *Arbitration* is the WIPO Center's service in which the outcome is binding on the parties. There may be one arbitrator or a team of arbitrators. Once a party agrees to arbitration, he or she cannot unilaterally withdraw.

2. *Expedited arbitration* is a speedier, less expensive form of arbitration, with a single arbitrator and condensed proceedings.

3. *Mediation* involves a neutral third party who helps the disputing parties to resolve their differences but who cannot impose a settlement. Any party may withdraw at any time.

4. *Mediation followed by arbitration* requires the parties to attempt a resolution through mediation within a certain time. If no settlement is reached, either party can refer the dispute to arbitration for a binding decision.

The WIPO Center is an ICANN–approved service and follows ICANN's dispute-resolution procedure and policy when they apply. The following AT&T proceeding illustrates the WIPO Center's application of the ICANN rules.

Information about the World Intellectual Property Organization Arbitration and Mediation Center (WIPO Center) can be found at **http://arbiter.wipo.int/center/index.html**.

CASE 3.3 AT&T Corp. v. Alamuddin

World Intellectual Property Organization Arbitration and Mediation Center, 2000.
Case No. D2000-0249.
http://www.icann.org/udrp/proceedings-list-name.htm[a]

COMPANY PROFILE *For more than a century, AT&T Corporation (**http://www.att.com**) has created, provided, distributed, advertised, and sold telecommunications and related goods and services in the United States and abroad. Today, these goods and services include Internet access, e-mail, and Web hosting services. AT&T serves more than 80 million customers—consumers, businesses, and governments—with more than 150,000 employees and annual revenue of more than $64 billion. AT&T operates the world's largest, most sophisticated communications network and has one of the largest digital wireless networks in North America.*

BACKGROUND AND FACTS AT&T owns the trademarks "AT&T" and "ATT" (as in "1 800 Call ATT"), and invests money and effort to advertise and promote them. AT&T's registered domain names, including "ATT.com," "ATT.net," and "ATTWIRELESS.com," use these trademarks. In 1998, Tala Alamuddin, a British citizen living in Singapore, registered the domain name "ATT2000.com." At that address, Alamuddin set up a Web site that stated, "This URL is for sale." When contacted by AT&T, Alamuddin said that if the corporation wanted "ATT2000.com," it would have to pay for it. AT&T filed a complaint against Alamuddin with the WIPO Center, asking for the transfer of "ATT2000.com." AT&T argued in part that the domain name was confusingly similar to its trademarks and that Alamuddin showed bad faith in attempting to sell the name. Alamuddin responded in part that she originally planned the Web site to sell Asian clothing and other items related to the millennium, and that she bought supplies and made contacts toward this end, but that she dropped this plan when she accepted a full-time job. She claimed that "ATT2000" signified her given name ("Tala") and the new millennium ("2000"). AT&T asserted that this claim "defies credibility."

a. Scroll down the "Domain Name" column to "att2000.com." In the corresponding box in the "Status/Panel Decision" column, click on "Name transfer" to access this decision.

CASE 3.3–Continued

IN THE LANGUAGE OF THE PANEL. . .

Hon. Sir Ian *BARKER* Q.C. [Queen's Counsel, a special type of attorney in the United Kingdom], Presiding Panelist.

* * * *

The Panel finds no evidence that the Respondent [Alamuddin], before receiving notice of the dispute, used or demonstrably prepared to use the domain name in connection with a bona fide offering of services without intent for commercial gain. The Respondent claims that she had purchased stock and made contacts, yet she has provided no supporting documents. She no longer wishes to conduct an Internet mail-order business in Asian clothing and curios. She wants to retain the name, but gives no reason why. There is no evidence that she is known by the domain name. The submission that ATT somehow reflects her given name of Tala is pathetic. The Panel therefore decides that the Respondent has no rights or legitimate interests in respect of the domain name.

* * * *

The Internet is a worldwide institution and persons accessing any website can come from any country. It must be assumed that some hits on the Respondent's website could come from persons living in countries where there is a registered AT&T mark (which include the United Kingdom). These persons could easily have had dealings with the Complainant [AT&T] or its websites or else have encountered AT&T, which is inevitable for anyone who has lived in the United States, even as a visitor. They could easily conclude that the domain site had something to do with the Complainant's operations in the year 2000. Geographical destinations can be irrelevant to users of the Internet.

There is evidence that the Respondent offered to sell the domain name to the Complainant "as part of an acceptable cash settlement." Many cases decided by WIPO Center panels have concluded that such behaviour constitutes use of the Complainant's mark in bad faith. * * *

The Panel accordingly determines that the Respondent has registered and used the Complainant's mark in bad faith.

* * * *

The Panel has determined that, under [ICANN's Uniform Domain Name Dispute Resolution] Policy, the Complainant has proved its case. Accordingly, the Complainant is entitled to the limited relief which this Panel is empowered to give.

DECISION AND REMEDY The WIPO Center panel decided that "ATT2000.com" was confusingly similar to AT&T's trademarks, and that Alamuddin had no legitimate rights in the name, which she was using in bad faith. The panel ordered a transfer of the name to AT&T.

FOR CRITICAL ANALYSIS–ECONOMIC CONSIDERATION *Suppose that the "ATT" in "ATT2000.com" did represent Alamuddin's business name, that she was actually using the Web site to market products, and that there was no evidence of bad faith in her use of the domain name. Is there anything AT&T could do in this situation to prevent Alamuddin's use of the name?*

SECTION 3 ONLINE RESOLUTION OF OTHER DISPUTES

With the growth of e-commerce has come an increase in the number of disputes that traditional court systems were not designed to handle. Businesses and their customers are located in all parts of the world, and do business with little regard for geographic and jurisdictional boundaries. Transactions take place rapidly. Personal contact is minimal, and when a mistake or a misunderstanding occurs, resolving the dispute can be time consuming and expensive.

The Internet provides new opportunities for the resolution of these disputes. As one example, consider **newsgroups.** Newsgroups are discussion groups to which participants go to post and read messages. A dispute that, in the real world, could be resolved only through litigation, or even not at all, may be resolved inexpensively and quickly within the virtual world of the newsgroup with or without the assistance of others, by parties who do not need to meet face to face. Newsgroups and other Internet capabilities make cyberspace a unique vehicle for dispute resolution.

When a dispute develops for which outside help is needed, there are an increasing number of Web sites that offer it. These alternatives may be best for resolving small- to medium-sized business liability claims, which may not be worth the expense of litigation or traditional methods of alternative dispute resolution. In most of the online forums, there is no automatic application of the law of any specific jurisdiction. Instead, results are often based on general, universal legal principles.

EXHIBIT 3–4 Steps in an ICANN Dispute-Resolution Proceeding

Dispute arises over a domain name

Party files a complaint with an ICANN–approved dispute-resolution service provider, and a panel is chosen to decide the dispute

Opposing party is contacted by the panel and given the opportunity to file a response

Panel considers the parties' arguments, requests further statements or documents, and issues a decision

Appeal, if any, is filed with a court

Steps, if necessary, are taken to implement the decision

Negotiation Services

CyberSettle.com. Inc., clickNsettle.com, U.S. Settlement Corp. (ussettle.com), and other Web-based firms offer online forums for negotiating monetary settlements through blind bidding. These services are useful for, among other parties, insurance companies and their claimants to work out settlements.

An online negotiation service does not evaluate the merits of a claim that is submitted to it. Instead, the parties to a dispute may agree to submit offers that, if they fall within a previously agreed range, will end the dispute, and the parties will split the difference. Software filters, and keeps secret, offers that are not within the range. If there is no agreed-on range, typically an offer includes a deadline within which the other party must respond before the offer expires. The parties can drop the negotiations at any time.

Such cyber resolution of disputes, or e-resolution, is generally more practical than litigating. Notice is by e-mail. Password-protected access is possible twenty-four hours a day, seven days a week (24/7). Fees are sometimes nominal and otherwise low (often 2 percent to 4 percent, or less, of the disputed amount).

NEWSGROUP
A discussion group operated according to certain Internet formats and rules. Like a bulletin board, a newsgroup is a location to which participants go to read and post messages.

Mediation Providers

Mediation providers have also tried resolving disputes online. Most notable have been the efforts of eBay, a Web-based auction site, to provide mediation services for its sellers and buyers whose transactions result in disputes. In general, online mediation is the same as offline mediation, except that the parties never see each other. Everything is done via e-mail.

ONLINE OMBUDS OFFICE To test the capability of an online service to mediate disputes among its customers, eBay initiated a pilot program with the Online Ombuds Office (OOO). A dissatisfied customer could request the service through eBay's Web page. Most of the disputes involved goods that were not received, were damaged in transit, or were not what the buyer expected.

To learn more about negotiation services available on the Web, go to **http://clicknsettle.com** and **http://cybersettle.com**.

The Center for Information Technology and Dispute Resolution of the University of Massachusetts runs the OOO. The OOO works with the World Organization of Webmasters to resolve online disputes involving its members. Another of the OOO's services has been to mediate online domain name disputes. The OOO has also resolved disputes among newsgroup participants, business competitors, and Internet service providers and their customers.

SQUARETRADE At the end of the OOO pilot program, eBay continued its mediation services with SquareTrade, another online mediation provider. SquareTrade resolves, currently for no charge, disputes involving $100 or more between eBay customers. The mediators try to do more than offer opinions, attempting to negotiate a settlement.

SquareTrade also resolves disputes among other parties. SquareTrade uses Web-based software that walks participants through a five-step e-resolution process. A complaint is filed, and the other party is notified. Negotiation between the parties occurs on a secure page within SquareTrade's Web site. The parties may consult a mediator. The case is resolved. The entire process takes as little as ten to fourteen days, and there is no fee unless the parties use a mediator.

Other Web firms—for example, Resolution Forum, Inc., discussed later in this chapter—offer similar services and often offer other forms of dispute resolution as well. As with offline methods of dispute resolution, any party may appeal to a court at any time.

Arbitration Programs

A number of companies offer online arbitration programs. As explained earlier in this chapter, among the conflicts that these firms arbitrate are domain name disputes. Any e-commerce dispute may be appropriate for arbitration, however. Companies that offer online arbitration programs include Resolution Forum, Inc., and the Virtual Magistrate Project. The American Arbitration Association is now in the process of launching technology-based arbitration services as well.

RESOLUTION FORUM, INC. Resolution Forum, Inc. (RFI) is a nonprofit organization associated with the Center for Legal Responsibility at South Texas College of Law. RFI offers arbitration services through its CAN-WIN conferencing system. Using standard browser software and an RFI password, the parties to a dispute access an online conference room. When multiple parties are involved, private communications and breakout sessions are possible via private messaging facilities. RFI also offers mediation services.

VIRTUAL MAGISTRATE PROJECT The Virtual Magistrate Project (VMAG) is affiliated with the American Arbitration Association, Chicago-Kent College of Law, Cyberspace Law Institute, National Center for Automated Information Research, and other organizations. VMAG offers arbitration for disputes involving users of online systems; victims of wrongful messages, postings, and files; and system operators subject to complaints or similar demands. VMAG arbitrates intellectual property, personal property, real property, and tort disputes related to online contracts.

VMAG attempts to resolve a dispute within seventy-two hours. A complaint is submitted online and reviewed for appropriateness. Proceedings occur in a password-protected online newsgroup setting. Private e-mail among the participants is possible. A VMAG arbitrator's decision is issued in a written opinion. A party may appeal the outcome to a court.

Unlike offline arbitration, in which the results are usually kept private, a VMAG arbitrator's decision is made public. This may include the messages, postings, and other parts of the file of a case. This material is available through a Web site maintained by the Center for Law and Information Policy at Villanova Law School.

Other Methods of Online Dispute Resolution

Other methods of online dispute resolution (ODR) have begun to emerge. The more innovative services combine characteristics of traditional forms of dispute resolution, including the judicial system, with qualities of cyberspace forums. These hybrid programs illustrate the current state of dispute-resolution techniques and indicate the direction toward which they may eventually evolve.

For example, iCourthouse offers ODR by jury. Unlike juries in the judicial system, however, iCourthouse juries consist of volunteers who choose whether they want to serve and which cases, and how many, they want to decide. The jury is free to the parties with the dispute.

iCourthouse can be found at **http://www.i-courthouse.com**.

To initiate a case, a party registers, files his or her claim, and receives a case number and a password. This party and his or her opponent post their arguments and submit their evidence, which can include audio and video media. Jurors review the evidence, ask questions, make comments, and render their verdicts. The parties are given a verdict summary that includes the jurors' comments about the case.

For a fee, the parties can select their jurors, which can be any number the parties choose. The jurors deliberate in a chat room where the parties and their attorneys "listen in." Unless otherwise agreed, all decisions are nonbinding and the parties can still go to court. According to iCourthouse, however, no one has.

SECTION 4 THE FUTURE OF E-COMMERCE DISPUTE RESOLUTION

The evolving methods of online dispute resolution (ODR) provide a glimpse at the future of e-commerce dispute resolution. These methods were among the topics at a seminar hosted by the U.S. Department of Commerce and the Federal Trade Commission in June 2000.[4] During the seminar, a group of U.S. companies involved heavily in e-commerce set forth, for those who do business in cyberspace, new guidelines that included proposals for the resolution of e-commerce disputes. These proposals are discussed in this chapter's *E-Guidelines* feature.

As explained in this chapter, ODR approaches traditional conflict resolution in innovative ways. These innovations illustrate how all methods of dispute resolution can change to make efficient use of the speed and intelligence available in the technology of cyberspace. For this change to take place, however, the advantages of ODR must come to outweigh the disadvantages.

---

4. For more information about this workshop, go to the International Trade Administration's Web site at http://www.ita.doc.gov or to the FTC's Web site at http://www.ftc.gov.

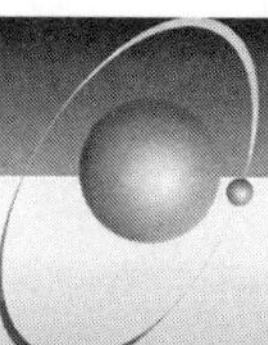

E-Guidelines

ODR Guidelines for E-Commerce

The International Trade Administration, an agency of the U.S. Department of Commerce, and the Federal Trade Commission (FTC) sponsored a public workshop in June 2000 titled "Alternative Dispute Resolution for Consumer Transactions in the Borderless Online Marketplace." The participants reviewed the use of, and the developments, obstacles, and issues associated with, alternative dispute resolution (ADR) and online dispute resolution (ODR) in e-commerce.

The Electronic Commerce and Consumer Protection Group

On the first day of the June 2000 workshop, a consortium of seven U.S. companies with an important stake in e-commerce proposed its own *Guidelines for Merchant-to-Consumer Transactions* in cyberspace. The companies that issued the proposals included America Online, Inc., AT&T Corporation, Dell Computer Corporation, International Business Machines Corporation (IBM), Microsoft Corporation, Network Solutions, Inc., and Time Warner, Inc. These firms called themselves the Electronic Commerce and Consumer Protection Group (the Group).

The Group's Guidelines

The group's voluntary guidelines focused on protection for consumers who make purchases online. The guidelines included the following:

1. Consumers should have a prompt, easy, and effective way to contact merchants.
2. Merchants should not engage in deceptive, fraudulent, or misleading practices.
3. Merchants should provide consumers with the opportunity to review their transactions before the transactions become binding. Merchants should also employ return and refund policies.
4. Merchants should make "reasonable efforts" to ensure the security of consumer information and adopt privacy policies that are consistent with existing industry standards and legal requirements.
5. Third party ODR should be implemented, but it should be nonbinding to avoid undercutting consumers' existing legal rights.

The primary emphasis was on the proposal for ODR. "The goal is to resolve [e-commerce disputes] in a manner that reflects that the monetary value of these disputes, while important to individual consumers, is often small in amount," the Group stated. "Therefore, traditional court-based solutions, including small claims courts, particularly for people who live in different countries, are by and large impractical."

The Group recognized that ODR would reduce the costs and complications for both consumers and businesses. In turn, this should foster competition among businesses and lead to additional choices for consumers.

The Group hopes that its guidelines lead to a permanent framework for consumer protection and the growth of e-commerce. The guidelines are available online at **http://www.ecommercegroup.org/guidelines.htm**.

CHECKLIST

☑ Businesses should favor the adoption of these guidelines. If widely employed, they would likely reduce some of the uncertainty in e-commerce and increase consumers' willingness to buy online.

☑ These guidelines have been criticized. They do not apply to online auctions, they do not encourage limits on consumer liability (such as those that apply in cases of credit-card fraud), they require that consumers use ODR before going to court, and they do not require that merchants be bound by any ODR results.

The Advantages of ODR

Online dispute resolution (ODR) has some advantages over more traditional forms of dispute resolution. For instance, the use of computers makes ODR faster, more convenient, and more efficient. Access to ODR services is possible on a 24/7 basis. The results are easily publicized. ICANN, for example, posts all of its decisions online. The cost is low compared to the higher expense of litigation (which, in a domain name dispute, for example, can be more than $50,000). In fact, ODR is often free.

The Internet's low cost and speed of communication make it easier for parties to negotiate a resolution without the use of a third party. The low cost also makes this form of dispute resolution attractive to those with low-value disputes, such as those arising from transactions in Web auctions. Eventually, government agencies and other entities that deal with large numbers of disputes may turn to ODR as an effective vehicle for resolving those conflicts.

The Disadvantages of ODR

There are disadvantages to ODR. For instance, ODR is not yet widely accepted. Also, efficiency, speed, and low cost could be an obstacle to a party who wants to wear out his or her opponent in a long, expensive, contentious battle.

There are no sheriffs to execute ODR judgments, which means that, unlike the orders in cases decided by courts, the results in cases decided in extrajudicial, online forums are not directly enforceable. There are also issues of jurisdiction, which have not been completely resolved. For example, should cyberspace have its own jurisdiction, or should it link to the physical locations of the parties?

Finally, current technology has some drawbacks. E-mail is not sufficient for resolving all types of disputes. Software for smoother and more visual interaction than presently available needs to be developed.

TERMS AND CONCEPTS

domain name 61
e-commerce 59
e-commerce dispute 61
newsgroup 69
online dispute resolution (ODR) 61
panel 62

QUESTIONS AND CASE PROBLEMS

3–1. Domain Names. Urban Sport, Inc., is a nationally renowned manufacturer and retailer of clothing and other items under its "Urban Sport" trademark. Urban Sport registered the mark with the U.S. Patent and Trademark Office in 1990. Urban Sport's e-commerce business is located at **http://www.urbansports.com**. In 1996, Frank registered thirty domain names, including "urbansport.com" and other names that contain the registered trademarks of other entities, with Network Solutions, Inc. Frank used the names to funnel Internet traffic to his Web site at **http://www.names-for-sale.com**, where he offered to sell each of the names to the highest bidder. Urban Sport filed a complaint with the National Arbitration Forum (NAF), seeking to have the "urbansport.com" name transferred to the firm. What standards will the NAF apply in considering Urban Sport's case? What should the NAF decide, and why?

3–2. Online Dispute Resolution. On a Web-based auction site, Beth advertises a laptop computer for sale "as is" to the highest bidder. After a brief online discussion with Beth about the qualities of the computer, Adam submits a bid. Adam's bid is the highest offer, and Beth ships the computer to him, insured and packed in bubble wrap and packing peanuts. Ten days later, Adam begins sending e-mail complaints to Beth about an inadequate processor, insufficient memory, and a cracked case. He threatens to complain about the deal in every chat room on the Web unless she refunds his money. Which ODR forum is the most appropriate for resolving the dispute between Beth and Adam, and why? What might be a good resolution of this dispute?

3–3. Online Dispute Resolution. Which method of ODR would be most appropriate for resolving each of the following disputes, and why?

(a) An ad for Local Network Systems Design, Inc., in the city telephone directory is in the wrong classification and the publisher refuses to fix it.
(b) A former employee of Standard Personnel Corp. claims that the company wrongfully fired her.
(c) American Bicycle Co.'s landlord postpones repairing a leaky roof, which causes American Bicycle to lose some of its merchandise in a storm.

3–4. Online Dispute Resolution. Reliable Accounting & Payroll Service contracts with Superior Contractors Corp. to build an office building. Superior subcontracts the telephone wiring to Town Electricians, Inc. Reliable contracts separately with Town Electricians to include computer network wiring in the new building. Before Town Electricians finishes its part of the job, Reliable pays Superior, and Superior pays the subcontractor. Town Electricians goes out of business. Reliable wants Superior to either finish the wiring or make good the amount that Reliable paid to Town Electricians. Superior refuses. Reliable submits a description of the situation to iCourthouse. Describe the process by which this dispute would be resolved on iCourthouse. What are the advantages and disadvantages of this type of dispute resolution?

3–5. Domain Names. BroadBridge Media, L.L.C., sells an Internet-based system through which a client can control its customer's use of the content on a compact disc (CD). BroadBridge's technology converts and compresses analog audio information into digital information and burns it onto a CD. A customer accesses the CD by going to a particular Web site and downloading certain information. Before 2000, BroadBridge distributed more than 4.5 million compact discs under the trademark "HyperCD," and the domain name and e-mail address "hypercd.com." HyperCD was registered as a trademark with the U.S. Patent and Trademark Office in 1997, but BroadBridge failed to renew its domain name and e-mail registration, which lapsed on March 1, 2000. Three weeks later, Creation Technologies, Inc. (CTI), which was developing similar technology, registered "hypercd.com" as a domain name. BroadBridge offered to pay CTI up to $7,000 for its transfer of the name back to BroadBridge, but CTI refused to accept less than $46,000. BroadBridge filed a complaint with ICANN and, two days later, a suit in a federal district court, against CTI. CTI responded to the suit in part by arguing that filing a complaint with ICANN prohibits the filing of a suit. Is CTI correct? How should the court rule? [*BroadBridge Media, L.L.C. v. Hypercd.com,* 106 F.Supp.2d 505 (S.D.N.Y. 2000)]

3–6. Domain Names. Pure Color contracted with Sabin and Associates for Sabin to design and sell a Web site to Pure Color with the domain name "PURECOLOR.COM" for $7,500. As part of the deal, Sabin promised to transfer that name to Pure Color and gave the firm a signed "Domain Name Assignment Agreement." When Pure Color contacted Network Solutions, Inc., the registrar refused to transfer the name because the agreement was not notarized. Meanwhile, Sabin, which had not finished the work for Pure Color, disappeared—its phone was disconnected and its mail went unanswered—but the incomplete Web site remained on the Internet. Pure Color obtained a different domain name and a new Web site, and filed a complaint with the National Arbitration Forum. Pure Color contended that Sabin "highjacked" the PURECOLOR.COM domain name, which was identical to Pure Color's trademark. Pure Color asked that the name be transferred to the complainant. What should the arbitrator decide, and why? [*Pure Color v. Sabin and Associates,* NAF Case No. FA0006000095009 (2000)]

3–7. Domain Names. Gordon Sumner is a musician, who since at least 1978 has been known professionally as "Sting." Sumner has used that name worldwide in recording music and performing concerts. In 1995, Michael Urvan registered the domain name "sting.com" with Network Solutions, Inc., and linked the name to various Web sites, most of which were under construction. When contacted by Sumner, Urvan offered to sell the name for $25,000. Sumner filed a complaint with the World Intellectual Property Organization Arbitration and Mediation Center (WIPO Center), asking that the name be transferred to him or that Urvan's registration be canceled. Sumner asserted that the name "Sting" was synonymous in the public mind with his activities as a musician. Urvan responded that there were twenty registered trademarks with the word "sting," none of which were owned by Sumner. Urvan added that the word "sting" is a common word, that he was not Sumner's competitor, and that there was no confusion between him and Sumner. In whose favor should the WIPO Center rule, and why? [*Sumner v. Urvan,* WIPO Case No. D2000-0596 (2000)]

WEB EXERCISES

Go **http://lec.westbuslaw.com**, the Web site that accompanies this text. Select "Internet Applications," and then click on "Chapter 3." There you will find the following Internet research exercise that you can perform to learn more about online dispute resolution:

Activity 3–1: Online Dispute Resolution

CHAPTER 4
Cyber Torts and Crimes

Concepts Covered

After reading this chapter, you should be able to:

1. Explain how torts and crimes differ.
2. Identify the elements of many torts, including those arising in cyberspace.
3. Describe some of the crimes that affect business, including crimes occurring in cyberspace.
4. State the essential elements of criminal liability.
5. Summarize some of the defenses to crimes.

"Tort more or less means 'wrong' . . . . One of my friends [in law school] said that Torts is the course which proves that your mother was right."

Scott Turow, 1949–
(American lawyer and author)

As Scott Turow's statement in the chapter-opening quotation indicates, **torts** are wrongful actions.[1] Through tort law, society compensates those who have suffered injuries as a result of the wrongful conduct of others. The basic purpose of tort law is to provide remedies for the invasion of various *protected interests.* Society recognizes an interest in personal physical safety, and tort law provides remedies for acts that cause physical injury or that interfere with physical security and freedom of movement. Society recognizes an interest in protecting property, and tort law provides remedies for acts that cause destruction or damage to property. Society also recognizes an interest in protecting certain intangible interests, such as personal privacy, family relations, reputation, and dignity, and tort law provides remedies for invasion of these interests.

TORT
A civil wrong not arising from a breach of contract. A breach of a legal duty that proximately causes harm or injury to another.

CRIME
A wrong against society proclaimed in a statute and, if committed, punishable by society through fines and/or imprisonment—and, in some cases, death.

Of course, torts are not the only kinds of wrongful acts that exist in the law. Crimes also involve wrongs. A **crime** can be defined as a wrong against society proclaimed in a statute and punishable by a fine and/or imprisonment—or, in some cases, death. Because crimes are *offenses against society as a whole,* they are prosecuted by a public official, such as a district attorney (D.A.), not by victims. Exhibit 4–1 on page 76 summarizes some of the key differences between civil law and criminal law. Some wrongful acts provide a basis for both a criminal prosecution and a tort action. Exhibit 4–2 illustrates how this can happen.

1. The term *tort* is French for "wrong."

EXHIBIT 4–1 Civil and Criminal Law Compared

ISSUE	CIVIL LAW	CRIMINAL LAW
Area of concern	Rights and duties between individuals	Offenses against society as a whole
Wrongful act	Harm to a person or to a person's property	Violation of a statute that prohibits some type of activity
Party who brings suit	Person who suffered harm	The state
Standard of proof	Preponderance of the evidence	Beyond a reasonable doubt
Remedy	Damages to compensate for the harm or an equitable remedy	Punishment (fine and/or imprisonment)

In the first part of this chapter, we examine various types of torts, including intentional torts, torts resulting from negligence, and torts for which strict liability (liability without fault) is imposed. We then look at how tort law is being applied to torts committed on the Internet. The second part of the chapter focuses on crime, including crime committed in cyberspace.

EXHIBIT 4–2 Tort Lawsuit and Criminal Prosecution for the Same Act

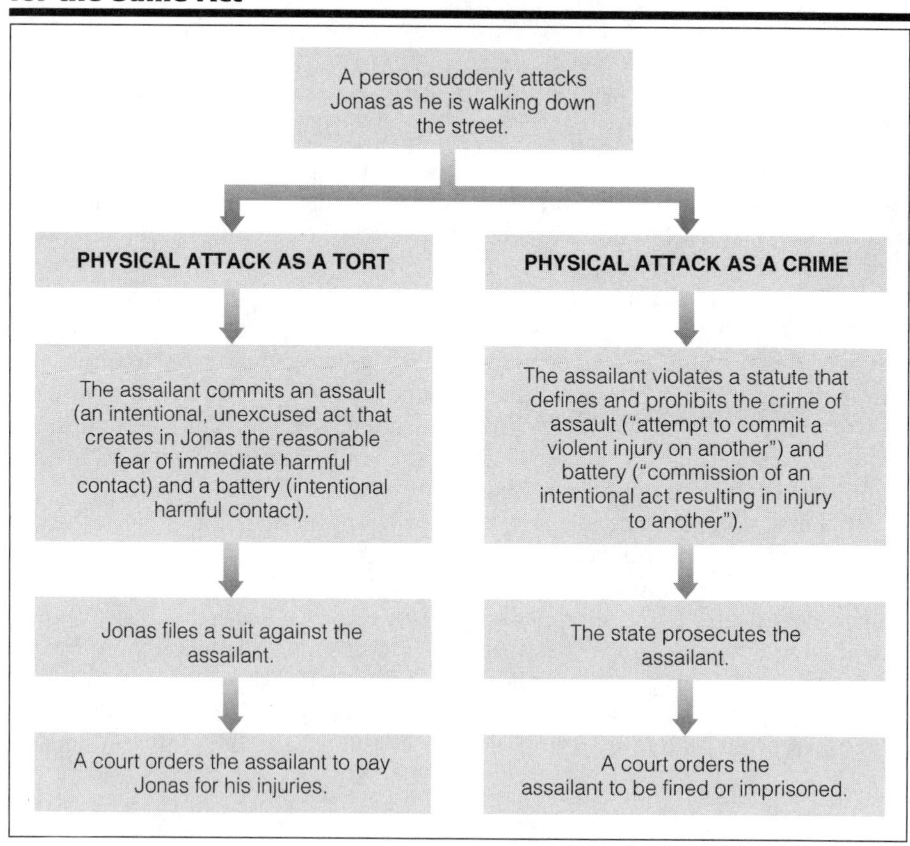

SECTION 1 INTENTIONAL TORTS

An **intentional tort**, as the term implies, requires *intent*. The **tortfeasor** (the one committing the tort) must intend to commit an act, the consequences of which interfere with the personal or business interests of another in a way not permitted by law. An evil or harmful motive is not required–in fact, the actor may even have a beneficial motive for committing what turns out to be a tortious act. In tort law, intent only means that the actor intended the consequences of his or her act or knew with substantial certainty that specific consequences would result from the act. The law generally assumes that individuals intend the *normal* consequences of their actions. Thus, forcefully pushing another–even if done in jest and without any evil motive–is an intentional tort (if injury results), because the object of a strong push can ordinarily be expected to go flying.

Intentional torts fall into two broad classifications: intentional torts against persons and business relationships, and intentional torts against property. We look here at torts that fall within each of these classifications.

On the Web

To find cases and articles on torts in the tort law library at the Internet Law Library's Web site, go to **http://www.lawguru.com/ilawlib**.

INTENTIONAL TORT
A wrongful act knowingly committed.

TORTFEASOR
One who commits a tort.

Intentional Torts against Persons and Business Relationships

Intentional torts against persons and business relationships include assault and battery, false imprisonment, defamation, invasion of the right to privacy, misrepresentation, and wrongful interference.

ASSAULT AND BATTERY Any intentional, unexcused act that creates in another person a reasonable apprehension or fear of immediate harmful or offensive contact is an **assault.** Note that apprehension is not the same as fear. If a contact is such that a reasonable person would want to avoid it, and if there is a reasonable basis for believing that the contact will occur, then the plaintiff suffers apprehension whether or not he or she is afraid.

ASSAULT
Any word or action intended to make another person fearful of immediate physical harm; a reasonably believable threat.

The *completion* of the act that caused the apprehension, if it results in harm to the plaintiff, is a **battery,** which is defined as an unexcused and harmful or offensive physical contact *intentionally* performed. Any unpermitted, offensive contact, whether harmful or not, is a battery. The contact can involve any part of the body or anything attached to it–for example, a hat or other item of clothing, a purse, or a chair or an automobile in which one is sitting. Whether the contact is offensive is determined by the *reasonable person standard.*[2] The contact can be made by the defendant or by some force the defendant sets in motion–for example, a rock thrown.

BATTERY
The unprivileged, intentional touching of another.

A number of legally recognized defenses can be raised by a defendant who is sued for assault, battery, or both:

1. *Consent.* When a person consents to the act that damages him or her, there is generally no liability for the damage done.

2. *Self-defense.* An individual who is defending his or her life or physical well-being can claim self-defense. In a situation of either *real* or *apparent*

2. The reasonable person standard is an objective test of how a reasonable person would have acted under the same circumstances. See the subsection entitled "The Duty of Care and Its Breach" later in this chapter.

danger, a person may normally use whatever force is *reasonably* necessary to prevent harmful contact.

3. *Defense of others.* An individual can act in a reasonable manner to protect others who are in real or apparent danger.

4. *Defense of property.* Reasonable force may be used in attempting to remove intruders from one's home, although force that is likely to cause death or great bodily injury normally cannot be used just to protect property.

FALSE IMPRISONMENT *False imprisonment* is defined as the intentional confinement or restraint of another person's activities without justification. The confinement can be accomplished through the use of physical barriers, physical restraint, or threats of physical force. Moral pressure does not constitute false imprisonment.

Businesspersons are often confronted with suits for false imprisonment after they have attempted to confine a suspected shoplifter for questioning. Under the privilege to detain granted to merchants in some states, a merchant can use the defense of *probable cause* to justify delaying a suspected shoplifter. Probable cause exists when the evidence to support the belief that a person is guilty outweighs the evidence against that belief. The detention, however, must be conducted in a *reasonable* manner and for only a *reasonable* length of time.

DEFAMATION
Any published or publicly spoken false statement that causes injury to another's good name, reputation, or character.

SLANDER
Defamation in oral form.

LIBEL
Defamation in writing or other form (such as in a videotape) having the quality of permanence.

ACTIONABLE
Capable of serving as the basis of a lawsuit.

DEFAMATION The tort of **defamation** of character involves wrongfully hurting a person's good reputation. The law imposes a general duty on all persons to refrain from making false, defamatory statements of fact about others. Breaching this duty orally involves the tort of **slander;** breaching it in writing involves the tort of **libel.** The tort of defamation also arises when a false statement of fact is made about a person's product, business, or title to property. We deal with these torts later in this chapter.

Four types of utterances are considered to be slander *per se,* which means that no proof of injury or harm is required for these utterances to be **actionable:**

1. A statement that another has a loathsome communicable disease.

2. A statement that another has committed improprieties while engaging in a profession or trade.

3. A statement that another has committed or has been imprisoned for a serious crime.

4. A statement that an unmarried woman is unchaste.

The Publication Requirement. The basis of the tort of defamation is the publication of a statement or statements that hold an individual up to contempt, ridicule, or hatred. *Publication* here means that the defamatory statements are communicated to persons other than the defamed party. If Thompson writes Andrews a private letter falsely accusing him of embezzling funds, the action does not constitute libel. If Peters falsely states that Gordon is dishonest and incompetent when no one else is around, the action does not constitute slander. In neither case was the message communicated to a third party.

The courts have generally held that even dictating a letter to a secretary constitutes publication. Moreover, if a third party overhears defamatory statements by chance, the courts usually hold that this also constitutes publication.

Defamatory statements made via the Internet are actionable as well (discussed later in this chapter). Any individual who repeats (republishes) defamatory statements normally is liable even if that person reveals the source of the statements.

Defenses to Defamation. Truth is almost always a defense against a defamation charge. In other words, if a defendant in a defamation case can prove that the allegedly defamatory statement of fact was actually true, normally no tort has been committed.

In some circumstances, a person will not be liable for defamatory statements because he or she enjoys a **privilege,** or immunity. For example, statements made by attorneys and judges in the courtroom during a trial are absolutely privileged. So are statements made by legislators during congressional floor debate, even if the legislators make such statements maliciously—that is, knowing them to be untrue.

In general, defamatory statements that are made about **public figures** (public officials who exercise substantial governmental power and any persons in the public limelight) and published in the press are privileged if they are made without "actual malice." To be made with **actual malice,** a statement must be made *with either knowledge of falsity or a reckless disregard of the truth.*[3] Public figures must prove actual malice because statements made about them are usually related to matters of public interest. Public figures also generally have access to a public medium for answering disparaging falsehoods about themselves; private individuals do not.

PRIVILEGE
In tort law, the ability to act contrary to another person's right without that person's having legal redress for such acts. Privilege may be raised as a defense to defamation.

PUBLIC FIGURES
Individuals who are thrust into the public limelight. Public figures include government officials and politicians, movie stars, well-known businesspersons, and generally anybody who becomes known to the public because of his or her position or activities.

ACTUAL MALICE
Real and demonstrable evil intent. In a defamation suit, a statement made about a public figure normally must be made with actual malice (with either knowledge of its falsity or a reckless disregard of the truth) for liability to be incurred.

INVASION OF PRIVACY A number of sources of law, including constitutional law and statutory law, protect privacy rights. The invasion of another's privacy can also constitute a tort. Under tort law, four acts qualify as invasion of privacy:

1. *The use of a person's name, picture, or other likeness for commercial purposes without permission.* This tort is usually called the tort of appropriation.
2. *Intrusion on an individual's affairs or seclusion.* This tort has been held to extend to eavesdropping by wiretap and unauthorized scanning of a bank account.
3. *Publication of information that places a person in a false light.* This could be a story attributing to someone ideas not held or actions not taken by that person. (This could involve the tort of defamation as well.)
4. *Public disclosure of private facts about an individual that an ordinary person would find objectionable.*

A pressing issue in today's online world has to do with the privacy rights of Internet users. For an exploration of this issue, see this chapter's *E-Guidelines* feature on the next page.

FRAUDULENT MISREPRESENTATION A misrepresentation leads another to believe in a condition that is different from the condition that actually exists.

3. *New York Times Co. v. Sullivan,* 376 U.S. 254, 84 S.Ct. 710, 11 L.Ed.2d 686 (1964).

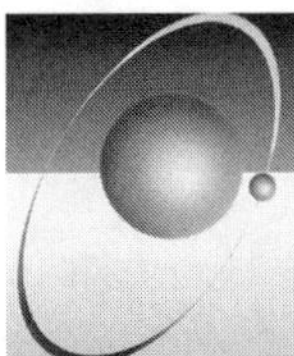

E-Guidelines

The Protection of Privacy Rights in Cyberspace

You may not know it, but when you surf the Web you usually do not do so anonymously. When you visit a Web site, the site's owner or operator often knows where you are located, the kind of computer you have, the name of your Internet service provider, and other details. In fact, a 1998 Federal Trade Commission (FTC) survey of 1,400 Web sites found that although more than 85 percent of the sites collected personal information on visitors, only 14 percent of these sites informed visitors of their information-collecting practices.

Ironically, at a time when the value of personal information is higher than ever, the ability of individuals to control how that information is used is at a low point. A growing concern today is how to protect Internet users' privacy rights without impeding the development of e-commerce and the flow of information online.

The Value of Personal Information

In February 1999, Free-PC, a company based in Pasadena, California, announced that it would distribute 10,000 free Compaq computers immediately (and some 90,000 more computers in the future). Within days, the company received more than 1.2 million applications. What did Free-PC expect to get in return? The answer is—information. Those who received the computers had to disclose their ages, incomes, hobbies, and a variety of other details about their lives. They also had to permit their online surfing to be tracked.

Online companies realize that profits can be made by gathering and using personal customer information, selling it to third parties, or sharing it with partners. A user's name and everything connected to it have become valuable commodities to be purchased, sold, and otherwise exchanged for a profit in today's electronic marketplace.

Web Site Privacy Policies and Guidelines

To ward off possible government action, as well as to avoid liability under existing laws, most online businesses are now taking steps to create and implement Web site privacy policies. Web site privacy guidelines are available from a number of online privacy groups and other organizations, including the Online Privacy Alliance, the Internet Alliance, and the Direct Marketing Association. Some organizations, including the Better Business Bureau, have even developed a "seal of approval" that Web-based businesses can display at their sites if they follow the organization's privacy guidelines.

Online privacy guidelines generally recommend that businesses post a notice on their Web sites about the type of information being collected, how it will be used, and the parties to whom it will be disclosed. Other recommendations include allowing Web site visitors to access and correct or remove personal information and giving visitors an "opt-in" or "opt-out" choice. For example, if a user selects an "opt-out" policy, the personal data collected by the site owner would be kept private.

Ultimately, new technology may make privacy a structural component of the Internet. For example, software is currently being developed by Microsoft and other firms that would enable Web browsers to display a warning if a user visits a Web site that does not have a privacy policy or that collects data the user does not wish to disclose.

Because of these and other efforts, the FTC recently proposed to Congress that pending legislative action be postponed for a time to see if the online industry can regulate itself. For self-regulation to be effective, however, online companies and privacy organizations will need to agree on uniform privacy policy standards and devise appropriate enforcement mechanisms. These obstacles may be difficult—if not impossible—to overcome.

CHECKLIST

- ☑ Any company involved in e-commerce today should consider creating and implementing a Web site privacy policy to avoid liability for violating the privacy rights of Web site visitors.
- ☑ Online businesses should also consider joining an online privacy organization, both to obtain guidelines for privacy policies and to promote further self-regulation of e-commerce.

The tort of **fraudulent misrepresentation**, or *fraud,* involves intentional deceit for personal gain. The tort includes several elements:

FRAUDULENT MISREPRESENTATION (FRAUD)
Any misrepresentation, either by misstatement or omission of a material fact, knowingly made with the intention of deceiving another and on which a reasonable person would and does rely to his or her detriment.

1. A misrepresentation of material facts or conditions with knowledge that they are false or with reckless disregard for the truth.
2. An intent to induce another party to rely on the misrepresentation.
3. A justifiable reliance on the misrepresentation by the deceived party.
4. Damages suffered as a result of that reliance.
5. A causal connection between the misrepresentation and the injury suffered.

For fraud to occur, more than mere **puffery**, or *seller's talk,* must be involved. Fraud exists only when a person represents as a fact something he or she knows is untrue. For example, it is fraud to claim that the roof of a building does not leak when one knows it does. Facts are objectively ascertainable, whereas seller's talk is not. "I am the best architect in town" is seller's talk. The speaker is not trying to represent something as fact, because the term *best* is a subjective, not an objective, term.

PUFFERY
A salesperson's often exaggerated claims concerning the quality of property offered for sale. Such claims involve opinions rather than facts and are not considered to be legally binding promises or warranties.

WRONGFUL INTERFERENCE Torts involving wrongful interference with another's business rights generally fall into two categories—interference with a contractual relationship and interference with a business relationship.

Wrongful Interference with a Contractual Relationship. Three elements are necessary for wrongful interference with a contractual relationship to occur:

1. A valid, enforceable contract must exist between two parties.
2. A third party must know that this contract exists.
3. This third party must *intentionally* cause one of the two parties to the contract to breach the contract, and the interference must be for the purpose of advancing the economic interest of the third party.

The contract may be between a firm and its employees or a firm and its customers, suppliers, competitors, or other parties. Sometimes a competitor of a firm draws away a key employee. If the original employer can show that the competitor induced the breach of the employment contract—that is, that the employee would not normally have broken the contract—damages can be recovered.

The following case illustrates the elements of the tort of wrongful interference with a contractual relationship in the context of an agreement not to compete.

CASE 4.1 Kallok v. Medtronic, Inc.

Supreme Court of Minnesota, 1998.
573 N.W.2d 356.
http://www.lawlibrary.state.mn.us/archive/sctjl.html[a]

a. This page is part of the Web site for the "Minnesota State Court System" maintained by the Minnesota state government. It lists, in alphabetical order, Minnesota Supreme Court opinions and orders that have been issued since May 2, 1996, with first party names beginning with the letter J, K, or L. Scroll down the list to the *Kallok* case and click on the docket number to access the opinion.

COMPANY PROFILE *Medtronic, Inc., (**http://www.medtronic.com**) is the world's leading manufacturer of implantable biomedical devices. The company was started in 1949 by Earl Bakken, who was then a graduate student at the University of Minnesota, and Palmer Hermundslie, who worked in a lumberyard. The company's initial focus was the repair of hospital laboratory equipment. Today, Medtronic's most important products relate to cardiovascular and neurological health.*

CASE 4.1—Continued

Medtronic makes the most often prescribed heart pacemakers, as well as heart valves, implantable neurostimulation and drug-delivery systems, catheters used in angioplasties, and other products. Medtronic sells these products in more than 120 countries.

BACKGROUND AND FACTS Michael Kallok signed a series of noncompete agreements when he worked for Medtronic. The agreements restricted his ability to work for Medtronic's competitors, including Angeion Corporation. When Kallok later approached Angeion for a job, he told it about the agreements. Angeion consulted with its attorneys, who advised that Kallok would not breach the agreements by accepting a job with Angeion. Angeion did not tell the attorneys all of the details of the agreements, however. After Kallok resigned from Medtronic to work for Angeion, he and Angeion filed a suit in a Minnesota state court against Medtronic, asserting that the noncompete agreements were unenforceable. Medtronic counterclaimed, alleging wrongful interference by Angeion. Angeion argued that its hiring of Kallok was justified because it consulted attorneys first. The court held Angeion liable and, among other things, awarded Medtronic damages. Kallok and Angeion appealed. The state intermediate appellate court reversed the award of damages. Medtronic appealed to the Minnesota Supreme Court.

IN THE LANGUAGE OF THE COURT. . .
ANDERSON, Justice.

* * * *

Medtronic easily established the * * * elements [of a cause of action for tortious interference with a contractual relationship]. First, as Kallok signed valid noncompete agreements, it is evident that a contract existed between him and Medtronic. Second, Angeion knew of the existence of Kallok's noncompete agreements before it hired him. * * * Third, * * * Angeion * * * procured the breach of his noncompete agreements by offering him the * * * position that he eventually accepted.

* * * Angeion, however, asserts that * * * its actions were justified because it consulted with its outside legal counsel before hiring Kallok * * * . We conclude that Angeion's argument lacks merit.

* * * Angeion did not fully inform its outside counsel about Kallok's background at Medtronic or the intricacies of his noncompete agreements. Had Angeion candidly provided its attorneys with all relevant information * * * Angeion would have understood that hiring Kallok would cause him to breach his noncompete agreements with Medtronic. * * *

* * * *

* * * As a result, Medtronic was forced into court to protect the legitimate interest embodied in Kallok's noncompete agreements. * * * We hold that the [trial] court * * * correctly allowed Medtronic to recover from Angeion the * * * expenses it incurred in enforcing its noncompete agreements with Kallok.

DECISION AND REMEDY The Minnesota Supreme Court reversed the decision of the lower court. The state supreme court reinstated Medtronic's award of damages for Angeion's interference with the noncompete agreements between Medtronic and Kallok.

FOR CRITICAL ANALYSIS—Social Consideration *What might be the result for our society if there were no cause of action for wrongful interference with a contractual relationship?*

Wrongful Interference with a Business Relationship. Individuals devise countless schemes to attract business, but they are forbidden by the courts to interfere unreasonably with another's business in their attempts to gain a share of the market. There is a difference between *competitive practices* and *predatory behavior.* The distinction usually depends on whether a business is attempting to attract customers in general or to solicit only those customers who have already shown an interest in the similar product or service of a specific competitor.

For example, if a shopping center contains two shoe stores, an employee of Store A cannot be positioned at the entrance of Store B for the purpose of diverting customers to Store A. This type of activity constitutes the tort of wrongful interference with a business relationship, often referred to as interference with a prospective (economic) advantage, and it is commonly considered to be an unfair trade practice.

Defenses to Wrongful Interference. A person will not be liable for the tort of wrongful interference with a contractual or business relationship if it can be shown that the interference was justified, or permissible. Bona fide competitive behavior is a permissible interference even if it results in the breaking of a contract.

For example, if Jerrod's Meats advertises so effectively that it induces Sam's Restaurant to break its contract with Burke's Meat Company, Burke's Meat Company will be unable to recover against Jerrod's Meats on a wrongful interference theory, because advertising is legitimate competitive behavior.

Intentional Torts against Property

Intentional torts against property include trespass to land, trespass to personal property, and conversion. Land is *real property* and things permanently attached to the land. *Personal property* consists of all other items, which are basically movable. Thus, a house and lot are real property, whereas the furniture inside a house is personal property.

TRESPASS TO LAND The tort of **trespass to land** occurs any time a person, without permission, enters onto, above, or below the surface of land that is owned by another; causes anything to enter onto the land; or remains on the land or permits anything to remain on it. Note that actual harm to the land is not an essential element of this tort, because the tort is designed to protect the right of an owner to exclusive possession. Common types of trespass to land include walking or driving on the land; shooting a gun over the land; throwing rocks or spraying water on a building that belongs to someone else; building a dam across a river, thus causing water to back up on someone else's land; and placing part of one's building on an adjoining landowner's property.

TRESPASS TO LAND
The entry onto, above, or below the surface of land owned by another without the owner's permission or legal authorization.

In some jurisdictions, a trespasser is liable for damage caused to the property and generally cannot hold the owner liable for injuries that the trespasser sustains on the premises. Other jurisdictions apply a "reasonable duty" rule. For example, a landowner may have a duty to post a notice if the property is patrolled by guard dogs or to place a fence around a swimming pool to limit access by children. An owner can remove a trespasser from the premises—or detain a trespasser on the premises for a reasonable time—through the use of reasonable force without being liable for assault and battery or false imprisonment.

If it can be shown that the trespass was warranted, as when a trespasser enters to assist someone in danger, a defense exists.

TRESPASS TO PERSONAL PROPERTY
The unlawful taking or harming of another's personal property; interference with another's right to the exclusive possession of his or her personal property.

TRESPASS TO PERSONAL PROPERTY When any individual harms the personal property of another or otherwise interferes with the personal property owner's right to exclusive possession and enjoyment of that property, **trespass to personal property** occurs. If Kelly takes Ryan's business law book as a practical joke and hides it so that Ryan is unable to find it for several days prior to a final examination, Kelly has engaged in a trespass to personal property.

If it can be shown that trespass to personal property was warranted, then a complete defense exists. Most states, for example, allow automobile repair shops to hold a customer's car (under what is called an *artisan's lien*) when the customer refuses to pay for repairs already completed.

CONVERSION
The wrongful taking, using, or retaining possession of personal property that belongs to another.

CONVERSION The tort of **conversion** occurs when a person deprives an owner of personal property without that owner's permission and without just cause. Conversion is the civil side of crimes related to theft. A store clerk who steals merchandise from the store commits a crime and engages in the tort of conversion at the same time. When conversion occurs, the lesser offense of trespass to personal property usually occurs as well. If the initial taking of the property was a trespass, retention of that property is conversion. If the initial taking of the property was permitted by the owner or for some other reason is not a trespass, failure to return it may still be conversion.

A successful defense against the charge of conversion is that the purported owner does not in fact own the property or does not have a right to possess it that is superior to the right of the holder. Necessity is another possible defense against conversion. If Abrams takes Mendoza's cat, Abrams is guilty of conversion. If Mendoza sues Abrams, Abrams must return the cat or pay damages. If, however, the cat had rabies and Abrams took the cat to protect the public, Abrams has a valid defense—necessity.

CONCEPT SUMMARY 4.1 INTENTIONAL TORTS

CATEGORY	NAME OF TORT
Intentional Torts against Persons and Business Relationships	1. *Assault and battery*—Any unexcused and intentional act that causes another person to be apprehensive of immediate harm is an assault. An assault resulting in physical contact is battery. 2. *False imprisonment*—An intentional confinement or restraint of another person's movement without justification. 3. *Defamation (libel or slander)*—A false statement of fact, not made under privilege, that is communicated to a third person and that causes damage to a person's reputation. For public figures, the plaintiff must also prove that the statement was made with actual malice. 4. *Invasion of privacy*—Publishing or otherwise making known or using information relating to a person's private life and affairs, with which the public had no legitimate concern, without that person's permission or approval.

Concept Summary 4.1 Intentional Torts (continued)

Category	Name of Tort
Intentional Torts against Persons and Business Relationships (continued)	5. *Fraudulent misrepresentation (fraud)*—A false representation made by one party, through misstatement of facts or through conduct, with the intention of deceiving another and on which the other reasonably relies to his or her detriment. 6. *Wrongful interference with a contractual or a business relationship*—The knowing, intentional interference by a third party with an enforceable contractual relationship or an established business relationship between other parties for the purpose of advancing the economic interests of the third party.
Intentional Torts against Property	1. *Trespass to land*—The invasion of another's real property without consent or privilege. Specific rights and duties apply once a person is expressly or impliedly established as a trespasser. 2. *Trespass to personal property*—The intentional interference with an owner's right to use, possess, or enjoy his or her personal property without the owner's consent. 3. *Conversion*—The wrongful taking and use of another person's personal property for the benefit of the tortfeasor or another. 4. *Disparagement of property*—Any economically injurious falsehood that is made about another's product or property; an inclusive term for the torts of *slander of quality* and *slander of title.*

DISPARAGEMENT OF PROPERTY When economically injurious falsehoods are made not about another's reputation but about another's product or property, **disparagement of property** occurs. *Disparagement of property* is a general term for torts that can be more specifically referred to as *slander of quality* or *slander of title.*

DISPARAGEMENT OF PROPERTY
An economically injurious falsehood made about another's product or property. A general term for torts that are more specifically referred to as slander of quality or slander of title.

Slander of Quality. Publishing false information about another's product, alleging it is not what its seller claims, constitutes the tort of **slander of quality.** This tort has also been given the name **trade libel.** The plaintiff must prove that actual damages proximately resulted from the slander of quality. That is, it must be shown not only that a third person refrained from dealing with the plaintiff because of the improper publication but also that the plaintiff suffered damages because the third person refrained from dealing with him or her.

SLANDER OF QUALITY (TRADE LIBEL)
The publication of false information about another's product, alleging that it is not what its seller claims.

TRADE LIBEL
The publication of false information about another's product, alleging it is not what its seller claims; also referred to as slander of quality.

Slander of Title. When a publication falsely denies or casts doubt on another's legal ownership of property, and when this results in financial loss to the property's owner, the tort of **slander of title** may exist. Usually, this is an intentional tort in which someone knowingly publishes an untrue statement about another's ownership of certain property with the intent of discouraging a third person from dealing with the person slandered. For example, it would be difficult for a car dealer to attract customers after competitors published a notice that the dealer's stock consisted of stolen autos.

SLANDER OF TITLE
The publication of a statement that denies or casts doubt on another's legal ownership of any property, causing financial loss to that property's owner.

SECTION 2 NEGLIGENCE

NEGLIGENCE
The failure to exercise the standard of care that a reasonable person would exercise in similar circumstances.

In contrast to intentional torts, in torts involving **negligence**, the tortfeasor neither wishes to bring about the consequences of the act nor believes that they will occur. The actor's conduct merely creates a risk of such consequences. If no risk is created, there is no negligence. Moreover, the risk must be foreseeable; that is, it must be such that a reasonable person engaging in the same activity would anticipate the risk and guard against it. In determining what is reasonable conduct, courts consider the nature of the possible harm. A very slight risk of a dangerous explosion might be unreasonable, whereas a distinct possibility of someone's burning his or her fingers on a stove might be reasonable.

To succeed in a negligence action, the plaintiff must prove the following:

1. That the defendant owed a duty of care to the plaintiff.
2. That the defendant breached that duty.
3. That the plaintiff suffered a legally recognizable injury.
4. That the defendant's breach caused the plaintiff's injury.

We discuss here each of these four elements of negligence.

The Duty of Care and Its Breach

DUTY OF CARE
The duty of all persons, as established by tort law, to exercise a reasonable amount of care in their dealings with others. Failure to exercise due care, which is normally determined by the "reasonable person standard," constitutes the tort of negligence.

REASONABLE PERSON STANDARD
The standard of behavior expected of a hypothetical "reasonable person." The standard against which negligence is measured and that must be observed to avoid liability for negligence.

Central to the tort of negligence is the concept of a **duty of care.** This concept arises from the notion that if we are to live in society with other people, some actions can be tolerated and some cannot; some actions are right and some are wrong; and some actions are reasonable and some are not. The basic principle underlying the duty of care is that people are free to act as they please so long as their actions do not infringe on the interests of others.

The law of torts defines and measures the duty of care by the **reasonable person standard.** In determining whether a duty of care has been breached, for example, the courts ask how a reasonable person would have acted in the same circumstances. The reasonable person standard is said to be (though in an absolute sense it cannot be) objective. It is not necessarily how a particular person would act. It is society's judgment on how an ordinarily prudent person *should* act. If the so-called reasonable person existed, he or she would be careful, conscientious, prudent, even tempered, and honest. The degree of care to be exercised varies, depending on the defendant's occupation or profession, his or her relationship with the plaintiff, and other factors.

DUTY OF LANDOWNERS Landowners are expected to exercise reasonable care to protect from harm individuals coming onto their property. As mentioned earlier, in some jurisdictions landowners are held to have a duty to protect even trespassers against certain risks. Landowners who rent or lease premises to tenants are expected to exercise reasonable care to ensure that the tenants and their guests are not harmed in common areas, such as stairways.

BUSINESS INVITEES
Those people, such as customers or clients, who are invited onto business premises by the owner of those premises for business purposes.

Retailers and other firms that explicitly or implicitly invite persons to come onto their premises are usually charged with a duty to exercise reasonable care to protect these **business invitees.** For example, if you entered a supermarket, slipped on a wet floor, and sustained injuries as a result, the owner of the supermarket would be liable for damages if, when you slipped, there was no sign warning that the floor was wet.

Some risks, of course, are so obvious that an owner need not warn of them. For example, a business owner does not need to warn customers to open a door before attempting to walk through it. Other risks, however, even though they may seem obvious to a business owner, may not be so in the eyes of another, such as a child. For example, a hardware store owner may not think it is necessary to warn customers that, if climbed, a stepladder leaning against the back wall of the store could fall down and harm them. It is possible, though, that a child could tip the ladder over while climbing it and be hurt as a result.

DUTY OF PROFESSIONALS If an individual has knowledge, skill, or intelligence superior to that of an ordinary person, the individual's conduct must be consistent with that status. Professionals–including physicians, dentists, psychiatrists, architects, engineers, accountants, and lawyers, among others–are required to have a standard minimum level of special knowledge and ability. Therefore, in determining what constitutes reasonable care in the case of professionals, the court takes their training and expertise into account. In other words, an accountant cannot defend against a lawsuit for negligence by stating, "But I was not familiar with that general principle of accounting."

The Injury Requirement and Damages

To recover damages (receive compensation), the plaintiff in a tort lawsuit must prove that he or she suffered a *legally recognizable* injury. That is, the plaintiff must have suffered some loss, harm, wrong, or invasion of a protected interest. If no harm or injury results from a given negligent action, there is nothing to compensate–and no tort exists. For example, if you carelessly bump into a passerby, who stumbles and falls as a result, you may be liable in tort if the passerby is injured in the fall. If the person is unharmed, however, there normally can be no suit for damages, because no injury was suffered.

Causation

Another element necessary to a tort is *causation*. If a person breaches a duty of care and someone suffers an injury, the wrongful activity must have caused the harm for a tort to have been committed.

CAUSATION IN FACT AND PROXIMATE CAUSE In deciding whether the requirement of causation is met, the court must address two questions:

1. *Is there causation in fact?* Did the injury occur because of the defendant's act, or would it have occurred anyway? If an injury would not have occurred without the defendant's act, then there is causation in fact. **Causation in fact** can usually be determined by use of the *but for* test: "but for" the wrongful act, the injury would not have occurred. Theoretically, causation in fact is limitless. One could claim, for example, that "but for" the creation of the world, a particular injury would not have occurred. Thus, as a practical matter, the law has to establish limits, and it does so through the concept of proximate cause.

CAUSATION IN FACT
An act or omission without ("but for") which an event would not have occurred.

PROXIMATE CAUSE
Legal cause; exists when the connection between an act and an injury is strong enough to justify imposing liability.

2. *Was the act the proximate cause of the injury?* **Proximate cause**, or *legal cause*, exists when the connection between an act and an injury is strong enough to justify imposing liability. Consider an example. Ackerman carelessly leaves a campfire burning. The fire not only burns down the forest but also sets off an explosion in a nearby chemical plant that spills chemicals into a river, killing all the fish for a hundred miles downstream and ruining the economy of a tourist resort. Should Ackerman be liable to the resort owners? To the tourists whose vacations were ruined? These are questions of proximate cause that a court must decide.

FORESEEABILITY Questions of proximate cause are linked to the concept of foreseeability, because it would be unfair to impose liability on a defendant unless the defendant's actions created a *foreseeable* risk of injury. Probably the most cited case on the concept of foreseeability as a requirement for proximate cause—and as a measure of the extent of the duty of care generally—is the *Palsgraf* case. The question before the court was as follows: Does the defendant's duty of care extend only to those who may be injured as a result of a foreseeable risk, or does it extend also to persons whose injuries could not reasonably be foreseen?

CASE 4.2 Palsgraf v. Long Island Railroad Co.

Court of Appeals of New York, 1928.
248 N.Y. 339,
162 N.E. 99.

BACKGROUND AND FACTS The plaintiff, Palsgraf, was waiting for a train on a station platform. A man carrying a package was rushing to catch a train that was moving away from a platform across the tracks from Palsgraf. As the man attempted to jump aboard the moving train, he seemed unsteady and about to fall. A railroad guard on the car reached forward to grab him, and another guard on the platform pushed him from behind to help him board the train. In the process, the man's package, which (unknown to the railroad guards) contained fireworks, fell on the railroad tracks and exploded. There was nothing about the package to indicate its contents. The repercussions of the explosion caused scales at the other end of the train platform to fall on Palsgraf, causing injuries for which she sued the railroad company. At the trial, the jury found that the railroad guards had been negligent in their conduct. The railroad company appealed. The appellate court affirmed the trial court's judgment, and the railroad company appealed to New York's highest state court.

IN THE LANGUAGE OF THE COURT. . .
CARDOZO, C.J. [Chief Justice.]

* * * *

The conduct of the defendant's guard, if a wrong in its relation to the holder of the package, was not a wrong in its relation to the plaintiff, standing far away. Relatively to her it was not negligence at all. * * *

* * * *

* * * What the plaintiff must show is "a wrong" to herself; i.e., a violation of her own right, and not merely a wrong to someone else[.] * * * *The risk reasonably to be perceived defines the duty to be obeyed[.]* * * * Here, by concession, there was nothing in the situation to suggest to the most cautious mind that the parcel wrapped in newspaper would spread wreckage through the station. If the guard had thrown it down knowingly and willfully, he would not

have threatened the plaintiff's safety, so far as appearances could warn him. His conduct would not have involved, even then, an unreasonable probability of invasion of her bodily security. Liability can be no greater where the act is inadvertent. [Emphasis added.]

* * * One who seeks redress at law does not make out a cause of action by showing without more that there has been damage to his person. If the harm was not willful, he must show that the act as to him had possibilities of danger so many and apparent as to entitle him to be protected against the doing of it though the harm was unintended. * * * The victim does not sue * * * to vindicate an interest invaded in the person of another. * * * He sues for breach of a duty owing to himself.

* * * [To rule otherwise] would entail liability for any and all consequences, however novel or extraordinary.

DECISION AND REMEDY Palsgraf's complaint was dismissed. The railroad had not been negligent toward her, because injury to her was not foreseeable. Had the owner of the fireworks been harmed, and had he filed suit, there could well have been a different result.

FOR CRITICAL ANALYSIS–Social Consideration *If the guards had known that the package contained fireworks, would the court have ruled differently? Would it matter that the guards were motivated by a desire to help the man board the train and not by a desire to harm anyone?*

Defenses to Negligence

The basic defenses to liability in negligence cases are (1) assumption of risk and (2) contributory and comparative negligence.

ASSUMPTION OF RISK A plaintiff who voluntarily enters into a risky situation, knowing the risk involved, will not be allowed to recover. This is the defense of **assumption of risk.** For example, a driver entering an automobile race knows there is a risk of being injured or killed in a crash. The driver has assumed the risk of injury. The requirements of this defense are (1) knowledge of the risk and (2) voluntary assumption of the risk.

ASSUMPTION OF RISK
A defense against negligence that can be used when the plaintiff is aware of a danger and voluntarily assumes the risk of injury from that danger.

Of course, the plaintiff does not assume a risk different from or greater than the risk normally carried by the activity. In our example, the race driver assumes the risk of being injured in the race but not the risk that the banking in the curves of the racetrack will give way during the race because of a construction defect.

CONTRIBUTORY AND COMPARATIVE NEGLIGENCE Traditionally, if a plaintiff's own negligence contributed to his or her injury, this *contributory negligence* was a comlete defense to liabillity. Today, in most states, however, a **comparative negligence** standard is applied. Under this doctrine, both the plaintiff's negligence and the defendant's negligence are taken into consideration, and damages are awarded accordingly. Some jurisdictions have adopted a "pure" form of comparative negligence that allows the plaintiff to recover

COMPARATIVE NEGLIGENCE
A theory in tort law under which the liability for injuries resulting from negligent acts is shared by all parties who were negligent (including the injured party), on the basis of each person's proportionate negligence.

damages even if his or her fault is greater than that of the defendant. Many states' comparative negligence statutes, however, contain a "50 percent" rule, under which the plaintiff recovers nothing if he or she was more than 50 percent at fault.

SECTION 3 STRICT LIABILITY IN TORT

STRICT LIABILITY
Liability regardless of fault. In tort law, strict liability may be imposed on defendants in cases involving defective products, abnormally dangerous activities, or dangerous animals.

Another category of torts is **strict liability**, or liability without fault. A significant application of strict liability is in the area of product liability—liability of manufacturers and sellers for harmful or defective products. If a consumer is injured by a defective product, the seller of the product may be held strictly liable—liable without regard to the seller's intentions or exercise of due care—for the injury. (Product liability may also be based on negligence or fraud.) Strict liability may also be imposed in cases involving abnormally dangerous activities or dangerous animals.

SECTION 4 CYBER TORTS

CYBER TORT
A tort committed in cyberspace.

FLAME
An online message in which one party attacks another in harsh, often personal, terms.

In the area of torts, as in other areas of the law affected by the new technology, there are more questions than answers. One of the foremost issues is the question of who should be held liable for a **cyber tort** (a tort committed in cyberspace). For example, who should be held liable when someone in a newsgroup posts a defamatory **flame** (an online message in which one party attacks another in harsh, often personal, terms)? Should an Internet service provider (ISP) be liable for the remark if the ISP was unaware that it was being made? Who should be held liable for an employee's defamatory remark on a company bulletin board?

Other questions involve issues of proof. How, for example, can it be proved that an online defamatory remark was "published" (which requires that a third party see or hear it)? How can the identity of the person who made the remark be discovered? Can an ISP be forced to reveal the source of an anonymous comment? Answers to some of these questions are explored in the following sections.

Defamation Online

Online forums allow anyone—customers, employees, or crackpots—to complain about a business firm. The complaint could concern the firm's personnel, policies, practices, or products, and it might have an impact on the business of the firm. This is possible regardless of whether the complaint is justified and whether it is true.

If a statement is not true, it may constitute defamation. Defamation is any published or publicly spoken false statement that causes injury to another's good name, reputation, or character. Like other torts, defamation is governed by state law, and the elements of the tort can vary from state to state. As discussed earlier in this chapter, generally a plaintiff must show that a statement was false, was not subject to a privilege, was communicated to a third person, and resulted in damage to the plaintiff. A public figure must also show that the statement was made with actual malice.

LIABILITY OF INTERNET SERVICE PROVIDERS Newspapers, magazines, and television and radio stations may be held liable for defamatory remarks that they disseminate, even if those remarks are prepared or created by others. Under the Communications Decency Act of 1996, however, Internet service providers (ISPs), or "interactive computer service providers," are not liable with respect to such material.[4] An ISP typically provides access to the Internet through a local phone number and may provide other services, including access to databases available only to the ISP's subscribers.

A California state court extended the 1996 CDA even further when it ruled that eBay, the online auction house, could not be held liable for the sale of pirated sound recordings on its Web site. The judge concluded that eBay's function was as an interactive service provider, not a seller responsible for items sold on its site.[5]

In the following widely publicized case, the court focused chiefly on the question of whether America Online, Inc., should be held liable for defamatory statements made by one of its subscribers.

---

4. 47 U.S.C. Section 230.

5. *Stoner v. eBay, Inc.* (Cal.Super.Ct. 2000). For further details on this unpublished decision, see "California Judge Finds eBay Immune under CDA," *e-commerce Law & Strategy*, November 2000, p. 9.

CASE 4.3 Blumenthal v. Drudge

United States District Court,
District of Columbia, 1998.
992 F.Supp. 44.
http://www.courttv.com/legaldocs/cyberlaw/drudge2.html[a]

COMPANY PROFILE *Founded in 1985, America Online, Inc. (AOL) (**http://www.aol.com**), operates two global Internet online services: AOL Interactive Services and CompuServe Interactive Services. This makes AOL the world's largest interactive computer service, or Internet service provider (ISP). AOL also operates AOL Studios, which develops original and local content for AOL's online and Web-based brands, including AOL, AOL.com, CompuServe, and Digital City. As many as fifty million subscribers or other users use AOL as a conduit to receive and disseminate huge quantities of information over its computer network. In 1998, AOL merged with Netscape. In 2000, AOL bought Time Warner.*

a. This site is Court TV Online's "Technology and Computers" section within its "Legal Documents" collection.

BACKGROUND AND FACTS Under a licensing agreement with America Online, Inc. (AOL), the *Drudge Report,* an online political publication, was made available free to all AOL subscribers. According to the agreement, AOL could remove content that it determined was in violation of AOL's "standard terms of service." One issue of the *Drudge Report* contained an article charging that Sidney Blumenthal, an assistant to the president of the United States, "has a spousal abuse past that has been effectively covered up." Blumenthal's spouse, Jacqueline Blumenthal, also worked in the White House as the director of a presidential commission. When the *Report's* editor, Matt Drudge, learned that the article was false, he printed a retraction and publicly apologized to the Blumenthals. The Blumenthals filed a suit in a federal district court against Drudge, AOL, and others, alleging in part that the original remarks were defamatory. AOL filed a motion for summary judgment.

CASE 4.3–Continued

IN THE LANGUAGE OF THE COURT. . .
PAUL L. FRIEDMAN, District Judge.

* * * *

* * * AOL was nothing more than a provider of an interactive computer service on which the *Drudge Report* was carried, and Congress has said quite clearly [in the Communications Decency Act (CDA) of 1996] that such a provider shall not be treated as a "publisher or speaker" and therefore may not be held liable in tort.

* * * *

Plaintiffs make the additional argument, however, that * * * Drudge was not just an anonymous person who sent a message over the Internet through AOL. He is a person with whom AOL contracted, whom AOL paid * * * and whom AOL promoted to its subscribers and potential subscribers as a reason to subscribe to AOL. * * *

* * * *

If it were writing on a clean slate, this Court would agree with plaintiffs. * * * But Congress has made a different policy choice by providing immunity even where the interactive service provider has an active, even aggressive role in making available content prepared by others. * * * Congress has conferred immunity from tort liability as an incentive to Internet service providers to self-police the Internet for obscenity and other offensive material, even where the self-policing is unsuccessful or not even attempted.

DECISION AND REMEDY The court granted AOL's motion for summary judgment. The court held that under the CDA, an Internet service provider is not liable for failing to edit, withhold, or restrict access to defamatory remarks that it disseminates but did not create.

FOR CRITICAL ANALYSIS–Economic Consideration *What considerations might have led Congress to exempt ISPs from liability for defamation?*

PIERCING THE VEIL OF ANONYMITY A threshold barrier to anyone who seeks to bring an action for online defamation is discovering the identity of the person who posted a defamatory message online. ISPs can disclose personal information about their customers only when ordered to do so by a court. Because of this, businesses and individuals are increasingly resorting to lawsuits against "John Does." Then, using the authority of the courts, they can obtain from ISPs the identities of the persons responsible for the messages. In one case, for example, several Internet critics published allegedly defamatory statements about a Pennsylvania court judge. The judge sued the "John Does" for libel, and the court ordered America Online to give the names of the defendant "Does."[6]

In another case, Eric Hvide, a former chief executive of a company called Hvide Marine, sued a number of "John Does" who had posted allegedly defam-

6. For a discussion of this case, see "Judge's Online Critics Lose Their Anonymity," *The National Law Journal,* November 27, 2000, p. A7.

atory statements about his company on various online message boards. Hvide, who eventually lost his job, sued the Does for libel in a Florida court, which ruled that Yahoo! and America Online had to reveal the identities of the defendant Does.[7]

How the courts will rule when these and similar cases come to trial, if they do, is not yet clear. In a first-ever decision of its kind, however, a U.S. district court awarded $675,000 to a physician who was, in the jury's opinion, a victim of online libel. When the physician, Dr. Sam D. Graham, Jr., was chair of the Urology Department at Emory University's School of Medicine, a posting on a Yahoo! message board suggested that he had taken kickbacks from a urology company after giving his department's pathology business to the company. Graham resigned from his position and sued the anonymous poster for libel. Because the poster was not actually a Yahoo! customer, discovering the poster's identity was difficult. After extensive investigation, however, and, according to Graham's attorney, a lot of "dumb luck," Graham finally discovered the identity of the person who posted the message. The case went to trial, and the court ruled in Graham's favor.[8]

Tort Liability and Computer Viruses

As everybody knows, viruses sent into cyberspace can cause significant damage to computer systems "infected" by the viruses. At issue today is whether tort theories can be used to obtain compensation for damages caused by viruses. To date, adapting tort law to virus-caused damages has been difficult because it is not all that clear who should be held liable for these damages.

For example, who should be held liable for damages caused by the "ILOVEYOU" virus that spread around the globe in 2000 and caused an estimated $10 billion in damage? Of course, the person who wrote the virus is responsible. But what about the producer of the e-mail software that the virus accessed to spread itself so rapidly? What about the antivirus software companies? Were they negligent in failing to market products that were capable of identifying and disabling the virus before damage occurred? Another question is whether the users themselves should share part of the blame. After all, even after the virus had received widespread publicity, users continued to open e-mail attachments containing the virus.

Determining what tort duties apply in cyberspace and the point at which one of those duties is breached will not be an easy task for the courts. Causation, for example, becomes difficult to establish in a cyber world without territorial boundaries. Furthermore, if the courts attribute liability to software producers, what might happen? For example, suppose that a company's software was found to be 20 percent responsible for the damage caused by the "ILOVEYOU" virus. That would mean the company would be liable for $2 billion in damages. Such extensive liability would bankrupt many software companies.[9]

---

7. *Does v. Hvide,* 770 So.2d 1237 (Fla.App.3d 2000).

8. *Graham v. Oppenheimer* (E.D. Va. 2000). For details on this unpublished decision, see "Net Libel Verdict Is Upheld," *The National Law Journal,* December 25, 2000, p. A19.

9. For a further discussion of this issue, see Christopher J. McGuire, "Old Torts Never Die—They Just Adapt to the Internet," *The National Law Journal,* September 25, 2000, pp. B15–16.

SECTION 5 CRIMES

To find a glossary of terms used in criminal law, view actual forms that are filled out during the course of an arrest, and learn about some controversial issues in criminal law, go to **http://tqd.advanced.org/2760/home.htm**.

FELONY
A crime—such as arson, murder, rape, or robbery—that carries the most severe sanctions, usually ranging from one year in a state or federal prison to the forfeiture of one's life.

Just as torts can be committed in cyberspace, so can crimes. How existing criminal laws and newly enacted laws are being applied to crimes in the cyber world will be examined in the next section. Here, we look at some of the basics of criminal law.

As you learned earlier in this chapter, crimes differ from torts in several significant ways. One of the major differences between the two types of wrongful acts is that normally a crime is defined by statute and subject to penalties set forth in the relevant statute.

Generally, crimes are classified as felonies or misdemeanors, depending on their degree of gravity. **Felonies** are serious crimes punishable by death or by imprisonment in a federal or state penitentiary for one year or longer.[10] Under federal law and in most states, any crime that is not a felony is considered a **misdemeanor.** Misdemeanors are crimes punishable by a fine or by incarceration (imprisonment) for up to one year. If confined, the guilty party goes to a local jail instead of a penitentiary. Disorderly conduct and trespass are common misdemeanors.

Types of Crime

To find your state's criminal code, select "State" under the link to "Laws: Cases and Codes," at **http://www.findlaw.com**.

MISDEMEANOR
A lesser crime than a felony, punishable by a fine or imprisonment for up to one year in other than a state or federal penitentiary.

ROBBERY
The act of forcefully and unlawfully taking personal property of any value from another; force or intimidation is usually necessary for an act of theft to be considered a robbery.

LARCENY
The wrongful taking and carrying away of another person's personal property with the intent to permanently deprive the owner of the property.

The number of actions that are designated as criminal is nearly endless. Federal, state, and local laws provide for the classification and punishment of thousands of different criminal acts. Here, we discuss five categories of criminal acts: violent crime, property crime, public order crime, white-collar crime, and computer crime.

VIOLENT CRIME AGAINST PERSONS Some types of crime are called *violent crimes,* or crimes against persons, because they cause others to suffer harm or death. Murder is a violent crime. So is sexual assault, or rape. Assault and battery are also classified as violent crimes—as mentioned earlier, they also constitute torts. **Robbery**—defined as the taking of money, personal property, or any other article of value from a person by means of force or fear—is also a violent crime.

PROPERTY CRIME The most common type of criminal activity is property crime, or those crimes in which the goal of the offender is some form of economic gain or the damaging of property. Robbery is a form of property crime, as well as a violent crime, because the offender seeks to gain the property of another. Larceny and forgery also fall within the general category of property crime.

Larceny. Any person who wrongfully or fraudulently takes and carries away another person's personal property is guilty of **larceny.** Larceny includes the fraudulent intent to deprive an owner permanently of property. Many business-related larcenies entail fraudulent conduct. Shoplifting and employee theft are

10. Some states, such as North Carolina, consider felonies to be punishable by incarceration for at least two years.

forms of larceny that result in substantial business monetary losses each year in the United States. Larceny does not involve force or fear. Therefore, picking pockets is larceny, not robbery.

Stealing computer programs may constitute larceny even though the "property" consists of magnetic impulses. Stealing computer time may also be considered larceny. Intercepting cellular phone calls to obtain another's phone card number–and then using that number to place long-distance calls, often overseas–is a form of property theft.

Forgery. The fraudulent making or altering of any writing in a way that changes the legal rights and liabilities of another is **forgery**. If, without authorization, Severson signs Bennett's name to the back of a check made out to Bennett, Severson is committing forgery. Forgery also includes changing trademarks, falsifying public records, counterfeiting, and altering legal documents.

FORGERY
The fraudulent making or altering of any writing in a way that changes the legal rights and liabilities of another.

PUBLIC ORDER CRIME Historically, societies have always outlawed activities that are considered contrary to public values and morals. Today, the most common public order crimes include public drunkenness, prostitution, gambling, and illegal drug use. These crimes are sometimes referred to as *victimless crimes* because they harm only the offender. From a broader perspective, however, they are deemed detrimental to society as a whole because they often create an environment that may give rise to property and violent crimes.

WHITE-COLLAR CRIME Crimes occurring in the business context are popularly referred to as white-collar crimes. Although there is no official definition of **white-collar crime**, the term is commonly used to mean an illegal act or series of acts committed by an individual or business entity using some nonviolent means to obtain a personal or business advantage. The crimes discussed next normally occur only in the business environment and thus fall into the category of white-collar crime. Note, though, that certain property crimes, such as larceny and forgery, may also fall into this category if they occur within the business context.

WHITE-COLLAR CRIME
Nonviolent crime committed by individuals or corporations to obtain a personal or business advantage.

Embezzlement. When a person entrusted with another person's property or funds fraudulently appropriates that property or those funds, **embezzlement** occurs. Typically, embezzlement involves an employee who steals funds from his or her employer. Banks face this problem, and so do a number of businesses in which corporate officers or accountants "doctor" the books to cover up the fraudulent conversion of funds for their own benefit. Embezzlement is not larceny, because the wrongdoer does not physically take the property from the possession of another, and it is not robbery, because no force or fear is used.

EMBEZZLEMENT
The fraudulent appropriation of money or other property by a person to whom the money or property has been entrusted.

Mail and Wire Fraud. One of the most potent weapons against white-collar criminals is the Mail Fraud Act of 1990.[11] Under this act, it is a federal crime to use the mails to defraud the public. Illegal use of the mails must involve (1) mailing or causing someone else to mail a writing–something written,

11. 18 U.S.C. Sections 1341–1342.

printed, or photocopied—for the purpose of executing a scheme to defraud, and (2) contemplating or organizing a scheme to defraud by false pretenses. If, for example, Johnson advertises by mail the sale of a cure for cancer that he knows to be fraudulent because it has no medical validity, he can be prosecuted for fraudulent use of the mails.

Federal law also makes it a crime (wire fraud) to use wire, radio, or television transmissions to defraud.[12] Violators may be fined up to $1,000, imprisoned for up to five years, or both. If the violation affects a financial institution, the violator may be fined up to $1 million, imprisoned for up to thirty years, or both.

COMPUTER CRIME
Any wrongful act that is directed against computers and computer parties, or wrongful use or abuse of computers or software.

COMPUTER CRIME The American Bar Association defines **computer crime** as any act that is directed against computers and computer parts, that uses computers as instruments of crime, or that involves computers and constitutes abuse. A variety of different types of crime can be committed with or against computers, including the cyber crimes discussed in the next section. The dependence of businesses on computer operations has left firms vulnerable to sabotage, fraud, embezzlement, and the theft of proprietary data, such as trade secrets or other intellectual property (discussed in Chapters 5 and 6).

Many computer crimes fall into the broad category of financial crimes. Computer networks provide opportunities for employees and others to commit crimes that can involve serious economic losses. For example, employees of accounting and computer departments can transfer monies among accounts with little effort and often with less risk than that involved in transactions evidenced by paperwork. The potential for crime in the area of financial transactions is great; most monetary losses from computer crime are suffered in this area.

The theft of computer equipment and the theft of goods with the aid of computers (such as by manipulating inventory records to disguise the theft of goods) are subject to the same criminal and tort laws as thefts of other physical property. In many jurisdictions, the unauthorized use of computer data or services is considered larceny. Other computer crimes include vandalism and destructive programming. A knowledgeable individual, such as an angry employee whose job has just been terminated, can do a considerable amount of damage to computer data and files. Destructive programming in the form of viruses, as mentioned earlier, presents an ongoing problem for businesspersons and other computer users today.

12. 18 U.S.C. Section 1343.

CONCEPT SUMMARY 4.2 TYPES OF CRIMES

CRIME CATEGORY	DEFINITION AND EXAMPLES
Violent Crime against Persons	1. *Definition*—Crimes that cause others to suffer harm or death. 2. *Examples*—Murder, assault and battery, sexual assault (rape), and robbery.
Property Crime	1. *Definition*—Crimes in which the goal of the offender is some form of economic gain or the damaging of property; the most common form of crime. 2. *Examples*—Larceny and forgery.
Public Order Crime	1. *Definition*—Crimes contrary to public values and morals. 2. *Examples*—Public drunkenness, prostitution, gambling, and illegal drug use.

CONCEPT SUMMARY 4.2 Types of Crimes (continued)

Crime Category	Definition and Examples
White-Collar Crime	1. *Definition*—An illegal act or series of acts committed by an individual or business entity using some nonviolent means to obtain a personal or business advantage; usually committed in the course of a legitimate occupation. 2. *Examples*—Embezzlement, and mail and wire fraud.
Computer Crime	1. *Definition*—Any act that is directed against computers and computer parts, that uses computers as instruments of crime, or that involves computers and constitutes abuse. 2. *Examples*—Virtually all crimes involving computer use or abuse, including financial crimes (such as embezzlement), the theft of computer equipment, the theft of goods or services with the aid of computers, and destructive programming (such as viruses).

The Essentials of Criminal Liability

Two elements must exist for a person to be convicted of a crime: (1) the performance of a prohibited act, and (2) a specified state of mind, or intent, on the part of the actor. To establish criminal liability, there must be a *concurrence* between the act and the intent. In other words, these two elements must occur together.

THE CRIMINAL ACT Every criminal statute prohibits certain behavior. Most crimes require an act of *commission;* that is, a person must *do* something in order to be accused of a crime. In criminal law, an act of omission can be a crime, but only when a person has a legal duty to perform the omitted act. Failure to file a tax return is an example of an omission that is a crime.

STATE OF MIND A wrongful mental state is as necessary as a wrongful act in establishing guilt. The mental state, or requisite intent, required to establish guilt for a crime is indicated in the applicable statute or law. Murder, for example, involves the guilty act of killing another human being, and the guilty mental state is the desire, or intent, to take another's life. For theft, the guilty act is the taking of another person's property, and the mental state involves both the awareness that the property belongs to another and the desire to deprive the owner of it.

Defenses to Criminal Liability

In certain circumstances, the law may allow a person to be excused from criminal liability because he or she lacks the required mental state. Criminal defendants may also be relieved of criminal liability if they can show that their criminal actions were justified (by a need to protect one's life or property, for example), given the circumstances. Among the most important defenses to criminal liability are infancy, insanity, and entrapment. Also, in some cases, defendants are given *immunity* from prosecution and thus relieved, at least in part, of criminal liability for their actions. We look next at each of these defenses.

INFANCY The term *infant,* as used in the law, refers to any person who has not yet reached the age of majority. In all states, certain courts handle cases involving children who are alleged to have violated the law. In some states, a child will be treated as an adult and tried in a regular court if he or she is above a certain age (usually fourteen) and is guilty of a felony, such as rape or murder.

INSANITY Just as a child is often judged incapable of the state of mind required to commit a crime, so also may be someone suffering from a mental illness. The courts have had difficulty deciding what standards should be used to measure sanity for the purposes of a criminal trial. Almost all federal courts and about half of the states do not hold a person responsible for criminal conduct if, as a result of mental disease or defect, the person lacked the capacity to appreciate the wrongfulness of the conduct or to obey the law.

Some states use a test under which a criminal defendant is not responsible if, at the time of the offense, he or she did not know the nature and quality of the act or did not know that the act was wrong. Other states use the irresistible-impulse test. Under this test, a person may be found insane even if he or she was aware that a criminal act was wrong, providing that some "irresistible impulse" resulting from a mental deficiency drove him or her to commit the crime.

ENTRAPMENT
In criminal law, a defense in which the defendant claims that he or she was induced by a public official—usually an undercover agent or police officer—to commit a crime that he or she would otherwise not have committed.

ENTRAPMENT The defense of **entrapment** is designed to prevent police officers or other government agents from encouraging crimes in order to apprehend persons wanted for criminal acts. In the typical entrapment case, an undercover agent *suggests* that a crime be committed and somehow pressures or induces an individual to commit it. The agent then arrests the individual for the crime. The crucial issue is whether a person who committed a crime was predisposed to commit the crime or did so because the agent induced it.

IMMUNITY At times, the state may wish to obtain information from a person accused of a crime. Accused persons are understandably reluctant to give information if it will be used to prosecute them, and they cannot be forced to do so. The privilege against self-incrimination is granted by the Fifth Amendment to the Constitution. To obtain information from a person accused of a crime, the state can grant *immunity* from prosecution or agree to prosecute for a less serious offense in exchange for the information. Once immunity is given, the person can no longer refuse to testify.

Constitutional Safeguards

Criminal law brings the force of the state, with all of its resources, to bear against the individual. The U.S. Constitution provides specific safeguards to protect the rights of individuals and to prevent the arbitrary use of power on the part of those who act for the government. The United States Supreme Court has ruled that most of these safeguards apply not only in federal but also in state courts. These safeguards include the following:

1. The Fourth Amendment protection from unreasonable searches and seizures.

2. The Fourth Amendment requirement that no warrant for a search or an arrest be issued without probable cause.

3. The Fifth Amendment requirement that no one be deprived of "life, liberty, or property without due process of law."

4. The Fifth Amendment prohibition against **double jeopardy** (trying someone twice for the same criminal offense).[13]

DOUBLE JEOPARDY
A situation occurring when a person is tried twice for the same criminal offense; prohibited by the Fifth Amendment to the Constitution.

5. The Fifth Amendment requirement that no person be required to be a witness against (incriminate) himself or herself.

6. The Sixth Amendment guarantees of a speedy trial, a trial by jury, a public trial, the right to confront witnesses, and the right to a lawyer at various stages in some proceedings.

7. The Eighth Amendment prohibitions against excessive bail and fines and cruel and unusual punishment.

Under what is known as the **exclusionary rule,** all evidence obtained in violation of the constitutional rights spelled out in the Fourth, Fifth, and Sixth Amendments normally is not admissible at trial. All evidence derived from the illegally obtained evidence is known as the "fruit of the poisonous tree," and such evidence normally must also be excluded from the trial proceedings. For example, if a confession is obtained after an illegal arrest, the arrest is the "poisonous tree," and the confession, if "tainted" by the arrest, is the "fruit." The purpose of the exclusionary rule is to deter police misconduct.

EXCLUSIONARY RULE
In criminal procedure, a rule under which any evidence that is obtained in violation of the accused's constitutional rights guaranteed by the Fourth, Fifth, and Sixth Amendments, as well as any evidence derived from illegally obtained evidence, will not be admissible in court.

SECTION 6 CYBER CRIMES

A **cyber crime** is a crime that occurs in the virtual community of the Internet. The "location" of cyber crime—cyberspace—raises new issues in the investigation of crimes and the prosecution of perpetrators. It is the unique nature of the Internet that causes one of the toughest problems in enforcing laws against cyber crimes: the issue of jurisdiction. A person who commits an act against a business in California, where the act is a cyber crime, might never have set foot in California but instead might reside in New York, or even in Canada, where the act may not be a crime. If the crime were committed via e-mail, would the e-mail constitute sufficient "minimum contacts" for the victim's state to exercise jurisdiction?

CYBER CRIME
A crime that occurs online, in the virtual community of the Internet, as opposed to the physical world.

Other problematic concerns relate to the difficulty of applying traditional laws, which were designed to protect persons from physical harm or to safeguard their physical property, to crimes committed in cyberspace. For example, a federal statute makes it illegal to threaten physical violence against property. A threat to delete computer files, however, does not involve physical violence against property.

13. The prohibition against double jeopardy means that once a criminal defendant is found not guilty of a particular crime, the government may not reindict the person and retry him or her for the same crime. The prohibition against double jeopardy does not preclude a *civil* suit's being brought against the same person by the crime victim to recover damages. For example, a person found not guilty of assault and battery in a criminal case may be sued by the victim in a civil tort case for damages. Additionally, a state's prosecution of a crime will not prevent a separate federal prosecution of the same crime, and vice versa. For example, a defendant found not guilty of violating a state law can be tried in federal court for the same act, if the act is defined as a crime under federal law.

The online environment also makes it difficult to identify and prosecute those who commit cyber crimes. Cyber criminals do not leave physical traces, such as fingerprints or DNA samples, as evidence of their crimes. Even electronic "footprints" can be hard to find and follow. For example, e-mail may be sent through a remailer, an online service that guarantees that a message cannot be traced to its source. Thus, a perplexing problem facing lawmakers today is the difficulty of detecting and prosecuting cyber crimes.

Types of Cyber Crimes

Cyber crimes can take numerous forms. Here we look at several types of activities that constitute cyber crimes—cyber stalking, cyber theft, online pornography, gambling in cyberspace, hacking activities, and cyber terrorism.

CYBER STALKING California enacted the first stalking law in 1990, in response to the contemporary murders of six women—including Rebecca Schaeffer, a television star—by the men who had harassed them. The law made it a crime to harass or follow a person while making a "credible threat" that puts that person in reasonable fear for his or her safety or the safety of the person's immediate family.[14] Most other states have also enacted stalking laws.

Generally speaking, stalking laws in about half of the states require a physical act (following the victim). **Cyber stalkers**—stalkers who commit their crimes in cyberspace—find their victims through Internet relay chat (or live chat), Usenet newsgroups or other bulletin boards, and e-mail. None of these communications requires that a stalker physically "follow" his or her prey. For this reason, these statutes do not apply in the online community. About three-quarters of the stalking laws in the other states *could* apply in cyberspace, because those statutes deem tools of harassment to include written communications (e-mail) or telephones (Internet connections).

CYBER STALKER
A person who commits the crime of stalking in cyberspace. Generally, stalking consists of harassing a person and putting that person in reasonable fear for his or her safety or the safety of the person's immediate family.

As of this writing, seven states have statutes that specifically address stalking by computer, or cyber stalking. It is also a federal crime to harass someone by means of interstate "telecommunications devices."[15] Some of the state statutes are based on California's law and require a "credible threat." Others require only an intention to harass, annoy, or alarm.[16]

CYBER THEFT In cyberspace, thieves are not subject to the physical limitations of the "real" world. A thief can steal data stored in a networked computer with dial-in access from anywhere on the globe. Only the speed of the connection and the thief's computer equipment limit the quantity of data that can be stolen.

For this reason, laws written to protect physical property are difficult to apply in cyberspace. For example, the federal statute that bans the interstate transportation of stolen property refers to "goods, wares and merchandise."[17] At least

14. Cal. Penal Code Section 646.9.
15. 47 U.S.C. Section 223(1)(A) and (B). See also 18 U.S.C. Section 875. Another possibility was indicated in 1998, when a former University of California student was convicted under federal civil rights law for sending hate e-mail to Asian students.
16. See, for example, Conn. General Statutes Sections 53a-182b and 53a-183.
17. 18 U.S.C. Section 2314.

one court has held that this does not apply to intangible property such as computer data.[18] Another federal statute makes it illegal to threaten physical violence to property.[19] A threat to delete files may not qualify.

To address abuses that stem from the misuse of the new technology, Congress amended the Counterfeit Access Device and Computer Fraud and Abuse Act of 1984 with the National Information Infrastructure Protection Act of 1996.[20] The 1996 act provides, among other things, that a person who accesses a computer online, without authority, to obtain classified, restricted, or protected data, or attempts to do so, is subject to criminal prosecution. These data could include financial and credit records, medical records, legal files, military and national security files, and other confidential information in government or private computers. The crime has two elements: accessing a computer without authority and taking the data.

This theft is a felony if it is committed for a commercial purpose or for private financial gain, or if the value of the stolen data (or computer time) exceeds $5,000. Penalties include fines and imprisonment for up to twenty years. A victim of computer theft can also bring a civil suit against the violator to obtain damages, an injunction, and other relief.

ONLINE PORNOGRAPHY The First Amendment to the U.S. Constitution guarantees the freedom of speech. According to the United States Supreme Court, however, certain forms of speech, including obscene speech, will not be protected under that amendment. Yet what, exactly, is obscene speech? From time to time, the Court has grappled with this question. Frequently, the determination is left to state and local authorities, who customarily base their definitions of obscenity on community standards. Generally, though, in the interests of preventing the abuse of children, the Court has upheld state statutes prohibiting the sale and possession of child pornography. At the federal level, the Child Protection Act of 1984 made it a crime to receive knowingly through the mails sexually explicit depictions of children.

The problem facing the courts and lawmakers today is how to control obscenity and child pornography that is disseminated via the Internet. In 1996, Congress first attempted to protect minors from pornographic materials on the Internet by passing the Communications Decency Act (CDA). The act made it a crime to make available to minors online any "obscene or indecent" message that "depicts or describes, in terms patently offensive as measured by contemporary communication standards, sexual or excretory activities or organs." The act was immediately challenged in court as an unconstitutional infringement on free speech.

When the case eventually came before the Supreme Court, the Court agreed that the act imposed unconstitutional restraints on free speech. In the eyes of the Court, the terms *indecent* and *patently offensive* covered large amounts of nonpornographic material with serious educational or other value. The Court thus invalidated the law.[21] Later attempts by Congress to curb pornography on the Internet have also been held unconstitutional by the courts. (See this chapter's *Controversial Issues* feature for a further discussion of this issue.)

18. *United States v. Brown,* 925 F.2d 1301 (10th Cir. 1991).
19. 18 U.S.C. Section 1951(a).
20. 18 U.S.C. Section 1030.
21. *Reno v. American Civil Liberties Union,* 521 U.S. 844, 117 S.Ct. 2329, 138 L.Ed.2d 874 (1997).

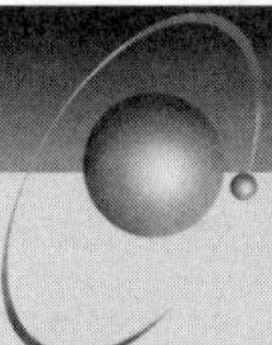

Controversial Issues in the Online World

Is Virtual Pornography a Crime?

The history of legislation involving pornography is long, complicated, and often inconsistent. One area of law in the field of pornography, however, that seems to be well settled involves child pornography. Whether it be photos on paper, moving images on video, or both of these transmitted on the Internet, federal and state laws are quite clear about the illegality of involving minors in lewd and lascivious visual products.

A new controversy has arisen in this area nonetheless. It involves the depiction of "fake" minors engaged in sexual acts in still photos as well as in movies.

Supercomputing Leads the Way to Virtual Pornography

Today's office- and home-based personal computers would have been considered the supercomputers of just a few years ago. The processing speeds, coupled with the size of the permanent memory and the size of the hard disks on today's computers, allow for digital image creation at a relatively low cost. Current software programs allow digital images to be produced that are extremely lifelike. Indeed, digital images are used in most Hollywood movies today, often without the viewer knowing that the images are "fake." When this relatively new and inexpensive technology is applied to pornography, the results are amazingly real. If a computer programmer, using just his or her computer, creates a lifelike set of child actors and has them, through commands on his or her computer, engage in sexual acts, is this a violation of child pornography laws?

This controversy surrounds the main issue underlying child pornography laws. Such laws are meant to protect children, and in particular those who are involved in actual child pornography. If no children are actually involved, is this also a violation of child pornography laws?

Congress and the Courts Take a Stand, but the Controversy Is Far from Over

In 1996, Congress passed the Child Pornography Prevention Act.[a] This act bans the distribution and possession of computer-generated images that appear to depict minors engaging in lewd and lascivious behavior. There is a basic tension between the 1996 act and the First Amendment to the United States Constitution. Those who believe that the 1996 act is unconstitutional say that it creates, for the first time in our history, a "thought crime." In contrast, those who support the act argue that the availability of child pornography on the Web, whether it be virtual or real, encourages the abuse of children. As Professor Eric M. Freedman of Hoftra Law School stated, the 1996 law "proceeds on the premise that the underlying idea is so pathological that it should be banned from public discourse."[b]

To date, cases challenging the law's constitutionality have come before four federal appellate courts, which have reached conflicting conclusions on the issue. To resolve these conflicts, in January 2001 the United States Supreme Court agreed to review a case decided by the U.S. Court of Appeals for the Ninth Circuit in 1999. That court struck down the 1996 law, concluding that it was unconstitutionally vague and overbroad. The court pointed out that the government can place significant restraints on free speech rights only if the restraints are necessary to promote a compelling government interest. In the court's eyes, the government only has a compelling interest in protecting children from actual, not "fake," child pornography.[c]

By the time you read this book, the Supreme Court may have ruled on this controversy. Until then, to be sure, the debate over whether virtual pornography should be a crime will continue in earnest.

FOR CRITICAL ANALYSIS

Do you agree with the Ninth Circuit Court of Appeals that the government does not have a compelling interest in preventing children from virtual child pornography? Explain.

a. 18 U.S.C. Section 2256.

b. As quoted in Adam Liptak, "When Is a Fake Too Real? That's Virtually Uncertain," *The New York Times,* January 28, 2001, p. 3.

c. *Free Speech Coalition v. Reno,* 198 F.3d 1083 (9th Cir. 1999); rehearing denied, 220 F.3d 1113 (2000).

GAMBLING IN CYBERSPACE In general, gambling contracts are illegal. All states have statutes that regulate gambling—defined as any scheme that involves the distribution of property by chance among persons who have paid valuable consideration for the opportunity (chance) to receive the property. In some states, certain forms of gambling, such as casino gambling or horse racing, are legal. Many states also have legalized state-operated lotteries, as well as lotteries (such as bingo) arranged for charitable purposes. A number of states also allow gambling on Native American reservations.

One of the challenges facing both the federal and state governments today is how to enforce gambling laws in an online environment. Now, virtually any person, even a fourteen-year-old with a credit card, can play blackjack or other gambling games on the Internet. Given that annual expenditures on gambling are estimated to be between $100 billion and $500 billion a year, the questions raised by online gambling are certainly not about to go away.

Jurisdictional Challenges. As noted earlier, jurisdictional issues become complicated in crimes committed via the Internet. Certainly, this is true with respect to online gambling. For example, in those states that do not allow casino gambling or off-track betting, what can a state government do if residents of the state place bets online? After all, states have no constitutional authority to regulate activities that occur in other states. Complicating the problem is the fact that many Internet gambling sites are located outside the United States in countries in which Internet gambling is legal, and no state government has jurisdiction over activities that take place in other countries. Of course, under certain conditions a state court can exercise jurisdiction over an out-of-state party that has a threshold level of contacts ("minimum contacts") with the state. A number of courts have shown a willingness to exercise jurisdiction over gambling sites located out of state—or even out of the country—based on the assumption that Internet advertising of gambling sites constitutes minimum contacts.[22]

Where Does the Gambling Occur? Another threshold issue in regulating online gambling has to do with determining where the physical act of placing a bet on the Internet occurs. Is it where the gambler is located or where the gambling site is based? For example, suppose that a resident of New York places bets via the Internet at a gambling site located in Antigua. Is the actual act of "gambling" taking place in New York or in Antigua? According to a New York trial court, the act of entering a bet and transmitting information from New York to Antigua via the Internet was adequate to constitute gambling activity within New York.[23] How the majority of courts will decide this question, however, is not yet clear.

Collecting Credit-Card Gambling Debts. Many states have laws that bar the collection of illegal gambling debts. Given that nearly 90 percent of Internet gambling is accomplished through the use of credit cards, these laws may have significant implications for credit-card companies, banks, and other issuers of

---

22. See, for example, *Minnesota v. Granite Gate Resorts, Inc.*, 568 N.W.2d 715 (Minn.App. 1997), aff'd, 176 N.W.2d 747 (Minn. 1998); and *Thompson v. Handa-Lopez, Inc.*, 998 F.Supp. 734 (W.D.Tex. 1998).
23. *People v. World Interactive Gaming Corp.* (N.Y.Sup.Ct. July 29, 1999); unpublished opinion.

credit cards. Specifically, will credit-card issuers be able to collect debts from cardholders who use their cards to obtain funds for online gambling?

In a series of class-action cases against credit-card companies that are currently before the federal courts, the plaintiffs have alleged that they should not have to pay credit-card debts that they incurred for gambling purposes. Clearly, the courts' decisions in these cases will have important consequences for the online gambling industry. In the meantime, opponents of Internet gambling are pressuring Congress to pass legislation that would prohibit the use of the Internet for gambling purposes. Additionally, four states—Illinois, Louisiana, Nevada, and Texas—already have specifically banned Internet gambling.

HACKER
A person who uses one computer to break into another. Professional computer programmers refer to such persons as "crackers."

CYBER TERRORIST
A hacker whose purpose is to exploit a target computer for a serious impact, such as the corruption of a program to sabotage a business.

HACKING AND CYBER TERRORISM Persons who use one computer to break into another are often referred to as **hackers.** Hackers who break into computers without authorization commit cyber theft. Often, their principal aim is to prove how smart they are by gaining access to others' password-protected computers and causing random data errors or making unpaid-for telephone calls.[24] Such crimes should not be taken lightly, but from a larger perspective, they might be considered the equivalent of new-tech car theft.

Cyber terrorists, however, are hackers who aim not to gain attention but to remain undetected in order to exploit computers for a more serious impact. Just as a "real" terrorist might explode a bomb to shut down an embassy, a cyber terrorist might explode a "logic bomb" to shut down a central computer. Other goals might include a wholesale theft of data, such as a merchant's customer files, or the monitoring of a computer to discover a business firm's plans and transactions. A cyber terrorist might want to insert false codes or data. For example, the processing control system of a food manufacturer could be changed to alter the levels of ingredients so that consumers of the food would become ill.

Crime Control versus Civil Liberties

In spite of the difficulties involved in detecting and prosecuting cyber crimes, law enforcement officials have had some success. They have been able to discover the identities of those who commit cyber wrongs, such as hackers who access others' databases without authorization and programmers who create and transmit online destructive viruses. Governments in some countries, such as Russia, have succeeded in controlling Internet crime to some extent by monitoring the e-mail and other electronic transmissions of users of certain Internet service providers. In the United States, however, any government attempt to monitor Internet use to detect criminal conspiracies or activities would likely be challenged as violating the constitutional rights of Americans.

Consider the Carnivore program launched by the Federal Bureau of Investigation (FBI) in 1999. The program was established to monitor e-mail and other online transmissions to and from particular criminal suspects. Although the FBI states that the program is used only under court order and is closely supervised by officials in the Department of Justice, it has nonetheless elicited

24. The total cost of crime on the Internet is estimated to be several billion dollars annually, but two-thirds of that total is said to consist of unpaid-for toll calls.

a great deal of controversy. Critics claim that this unprecedented form of communications surveillance is a threat to Americans' privacy rights because, in addition to targeting criminal suspects, the government could also monitor the communications of innocent citizens. As a result of public concern over the program, Congress has been holding hearings to see if the program can be justified.

TERMS AND CONCEPTS

QUESTIONS AND CASE PROBLEMS

4–1. Causation. Ruth carelessly parks her car on a steep hill, leaving the car in neutral and failing to engage the parking brake. The car rolls down the hill, knocking down an electric line. The sparks from the broken line ignite a grass fire. The fire spreads until it reaches a barn one mile away. The barn houses dynamite, and the burning barn explodes, causing part of the roof to fall on and injure a passing motorist, Jim. Can Jim recover damages from Ruth? Why or why not?

4–2. Wrongful Interference. Lothar owns a bakery. He has been trying to obtain a long-term contract with the owner of Martha's Tea Salons for some time. Lothar starts a local advertising campaign on radio and television and in the newspaper. This advertising campaign is so persuasive that Martha decides to break the contract she has had with Harley's Bakery so that she can patronize Lothar's bakery. Is Lothar liable to Harley's Bakery for the tort of wrongful interference with a contractual relationship? Is Martha liable for this tort? For anything?

4–3. Tort Theories. On the morning of October 2, 1989, a fire started by an arsonist broke out in the Red Inn in Provincetown, Massachusetts. The inn had smoke detectors, sprinklers, and an alarm system, all of which alerted the guests, but there were no emergency lights or clear exits. Attempting to escape, Deborah Addis and James Reed, guests at the inn, found the first-floor doors and windows locked. Ultimately, they forced open a second-floor window and jumped out. To recover for their injuries, they filed a suit in a Massachusetts state court against Tamerlane Corp., which operated the inn under a lease, and others (including Duane Steele, who worked for the owner of the inn). Under what tort theory discussed in this chapter might Addis and Reed recover damages from Tamerlane and the others? What must they prove to recover damages under this theory? Discuss fully. [*Addis v. Steele,* 38 Mass.App.Ct. 433, 648 N.E.2d 773 (1995)]

4–4. Embezzlement. Faulkner, a truck driver, was hauling a load of refrigerators from San Diego to New York for the trucking company that employed him. He departed from his assigned route and stopped in Las Vegas, where he attempted to display and sell some of the refrigerators to a firm. Although the refrigerators never left the truck, to display them he had to break the truck's seals, enter the cargo department, and open two refrigerator cartons. The store owner refused to purchase the appliances, and when Faulkner left the store, he was arrested. He was later convicted under federal law for the embezzlement of an interstate shipment. Faulkner appealed, claiming that the charge of embezzlement should not apply because the property had not been physically removed from the owner's possession. Will the appellate court agree with Faulkner? Explain. [*United States v. Faulkner,* 638 F.2d 129 (9th Cir. 1981)]

4–5. Criminal Liability. On the grounds of a school, Gavin T., a fifteen-year-old student, was eating lunch. He threw a half-eaten apple toward the outside wall of a classroom some distance away. The apple sailed through a slowly closing door and struck a teacher who was in the room. The teacher was knocked to the floor and lost consciousness for a few minutes. Gavin was charged, in a California state court, with assault by "any means of force likely to produce great bodily injury." The court found that he did not intend to hit the teacher but only intended to see the apple splatter against the outside wall. To send a "message" to his classmates that his actions were wrong, however, the court convicted him of the charge. Should Gavin's conviction be reversed on appeal? Why or why not? [*In re Gavin T.,* 66 Cal.App.4th 238, 77 Cal.Rptr.2d 701 (1998)]

4–6. Fifth Amendment. The federal government was investigating a corporation and its employees. The alleged criminal wrongdoing, which included the falsification of corporate books and records, occurred between 1993 and 1996 in one division of the corporation. In 1999, the corporation pled guilty and agreed to cooperate in an investigation of the individuals who might have been involved in the improper corporate activities. "Doe I," "Doe II," and "Doe III" were officers of the corporation during the period in which the illegal activities occurred and worked in the division where the wrongdoing took place. They were no longer working for the corporation, however, when, as part of the subsequent investigation, the government asked them to provide specific corporate documents in their possession. All three asserted the Fifth Amendment privilege against self-incrimination. The government asked a federal district court to order the three to produce the records. Corporate employees can be compelled to produce corporate records in a criminal proceeding, because they hold the records as representatives of the corporation, to which the Fifth Amendment privilege against self-incrimination does not apply. Should *former* employees also be compelled to produce corporate records in their possession? Why or why not? [*In re Three Grand Jury Subpoenas* Duces Tecum *Dated January 29, 1999,* 191 F.3d 173 (2d Cir. 1999)]

4–7. Defamation. An unidentified person posted messages on America Online, Inc. (AOL), advertising for sale t-shirts and other items with offensive slogans related to the 1995 bombing of the federal building in Oklahoma City. Buyers were instructed to call the business phone number of Ken Zeran, who knew nothing about the ad. Zeran received a high volume of calls, consisting of derogatory messages and death threats. He called AOL and was assured that the messages would be removed. The postings remained up for five days, however, during which time the angry calls to Zeran intensified. Zeran filed a suit in a federal district court against AOL, arguing in part that AOL was liable for unreasonably delaying the removal of the defamatory messages. Why would the court rule in AOL's favor? [*Zeran v. America Online, Inc.,* 129 F.3d 327 (4th Cir. 1997)]

WEB EXERCISES

Go to **http://lec.westbuslaw.com**, the Web site that accompanies this text. Select "Internet Applications," and then click on "Chapter 4." There you will find the following Internet research exercises that you can perform to learn more about privacy rights in an online world and cyber crime:

Activity 4–1: Privacy Rights in Cyberspace

Activity 4–2: Cyber Crime

CHAPTER 5

Intellectual Property—Patents and Copyrights

Concepts Covered

After reading this chapter, you should be able to:

1. Summarize the law protecting patents.
2. Discuss how technology is affecting patents.
3. Describe the law protecting copyrights.
4. State what legal protection exists for copyrights in digital form.
5. Explain how international law covers patents, copyrights, and other intellectual property.

"The Internet, by virtue of its ability to mesh what will be hundreds of millions of people together, . . . is . . . a profoundly different capability that by and large human beings have not had before."

Tony Rutkowski, 1943–
(Executive Director of the Internet Society, 1994–1996)

Most people think of wealth in terms of houses, land, cars, stocks, and bonds. Wealth, however, also includes **intellectual property**, which consists of the products that result from intellectual, creative processes. Although it is an abstract term for an abstract concept, intellectual property is nonetheless wholly familiar to virtually everyone. *Trademarks, service marks, copyrights,* and *patents* are all forms of intellectual property. The book you are reading is copyrighted. Undoubtedly, the personal computer you use at home is trademarked. Exhibit 5–1 on pages 108 and 109 offers a comprehensive summary of these forms of intellectual property, as well as intellectual property that consists of *trade secrets*. In this chapter, we examine patents and copyrights in some detail. Trademarks and trade secrets will be covered in Chapter 6.

INTELLECTUAL PROPERTY
Property resulting from intellectual, creative processes. Patents, trademarks, and copyrights are examples of intellectual property.

The study of intellectual property law is important because intellectual property has taken on increasing significance, not only within the United States but globally as well. Today, ownership rights in intangible intellectual property are more important to the prosperity of many U.S. companies than are their tangible assets. A major challenge to businesspersons today is how to protect these valuable rights in the online world.

The need to protect creative works was voiced by the framers of the U.S. Constitution over two hundred years ago: Article I, Section 8, of the U.S. Constitution authorized Congress "[t]o promote the Progress of Science and useful Arts, by securing for limited Times to Authors and Inventors the exclusive Right to their respective Writings and Discoveries." Laws protecting patents, trademarks, and copyrights are explicitly designed to protect and reward inventive and artistic creativity. Although intellectual property law limits the

EXHIBIT 5–1 Forms of Intellectual Property

	PATENT	COPYRIGHT	TRADEMARKS (SERVICE MARKS AND TRADE DRESS)	TRADE SECRETS
Definition	A grant from the government that gives an inventor exclusive rights to an invention.	An intangible property right granted to authors and originators of a literary work or artistic production that falls within specified categories.	Any distinctive word, name, symbol, or device (image or appearance), or combination thereof, that an entity uses to identify and distinguish its goods or services from those of others.	Any information (including formulas, patterns, programs, devices, techniques, and processes) that a business possesses and that gives the business an advantage over competitors who do not know the information or processes.
Requirements	An invention must be: 1. Novel. 2. Not obvious. 3. Useful.	Literary or artistic works must be: 1. Original. 2. Fixed in a durable medium that can be perceived, reproduced, or communicated. 3. Within a copyrightable category.	Trademarks, service marks, and trade dress must be sufficiently distinctive (or must have acquired a secondary meaning) to enable consumers and others to distinguish the manufacturer's, seller's, or business user's products or services from those of competitors.	Information and processes that have commercial value, that are not known or easily ascertainable by the general public or others, and that are reasonably protected from disclosure.
Types or Categories	1. Utility (general). 2. Design. 3. Plant (flowers, vegetables, and so on).	1. Literary works (including computer programs). 2. Musical works. 3. Dramatic works. 4. Pantomime and choreographic works. 5. Pictorial, graphic, and sculptural works. 6. Films and audiovisual works. 7. Sound recordings.	1. Strong, distinctive marks (such as fanciful, arbitrary, or suggestive marks). 2. Marks that have acquired a secondary meaning by use. 3. Other types of marks, including certification marks and collective marks. 4. Trade dress (such as a distinctive decor, menu, or style or type of service).	1. Customer lists. 2. Research and development. 3. Plans and programs. 4. Pricing information. 5. Production techniques. 6. Marketing techniques. 7. Formulas. 8. Compilations.
How Acquired	By filing a patent application with the U.S. Patent and Trademark Office and receiving that office's approval.	Automatic (once in tangible form); to recover for infringement, the copyright must be registered with	1. At common law, ownership is created by use of mark. 2. Registration (either with the U.S. Patent and Trademark Office or with the	Through the originality and development of information and processes that are unique to a business, that are unknown by others, and that would

EXHIBIT 5–1 Forms of Intellectual Property (Continued)

	PATENT	COPYRIGHT	TRADEMARKS (SERVICE MARKS AND TRADE DRESS)	TRADE SECRETS
How Acquired (continued)		the U.S. Copyright Office.	appropriate state office) gives constructive notice of date of use. 3. Federal registration is permitted if the mark is currently in use or if the applicant intends use within six months (period can be extended to three years). 4. Federal registration can be renewed between the fifth and sixth years and, thereafter, every ten years.	be valuable to competitors if they knew of the information and processes.
Rights	An inventor has the right to make, use, sell, assign, or license the invention during the duration of the patent's term. The first to invent has patent rights.	The author or originator has the exclusive right to reproduce, distribute, display, license, or transfer a copyrighted work.	The owner has the right to use the mark or trade dress and to exclude others from using it. The right of use can be licensed or sold (assigned) to another.	The owner has the right to sole and exclusive use of the trade secrets and the right to use legal means to protect against misappropriation of the trade secrets by others. The owner can license or assign a trade secret.
Duration	Twenty years from the date of application; for design patents, fourteen years.	1. For authors: the life of the author, plus 70 years. 2. For publishers: 95 years after the date of publication or 120 years after creation.	Unlimited, as long as it is in use. To continue notice by registration, the registration must be renewed by filing.	Unlimited, as long as not revealed to others.
Civil Remedies for Infringement	Monetary damages, which include reasonable royalties and lost profits, *plus* attorneys' fees. (Treble damages are available for intentional infringement.)	Actual damages, plus profits received by the infringer; or statutory damages of not less than $500 and not more than $20,000 ($100,000, if infringement is willful); *plus* costs and attorneys' fees.	1. Injunction prohibiting future use of mark. 2. Actual damages, plus profits received by the infringer (can be increased to three times the actual damages under the Lanham Act). 3. Impoundment and destruction of infringing articles. 4. Plus costs and attorneys' fees.	Monetary damages for misappropriation (the Uniform Trade Secrets Act permits punitive damages up to twice the amount of actual damages for willful and malicious misappropriation); plus costs and attorneys' fees.

economic freedom of some individuals, it does so to protect the freedom of others to enjoy the fruits of their labors—in the form of profits.

SECTION 1 PATENTS

PATENT
A government grant that gives an inventor the exclusive right or privilege to make, use, or sell his or her invention for a limited time period. The word *patent* usually refers to some invention and designates either the instrument by which patent rights are evidenced or the patent itself.

A **patent** is a grant from the government that gives an inventor the exclusive right to make, use, and sell an invention for a period of twenty years from the date of filing the application for a patent. Patents for a fourteen-year period are given for designs, as opposed to inventions. For either a regular patent or a design patent, the applicant must demonstrate to the satisfaction of the U.S. Patent and Trademark Office that the invention, discovery, process, or design is genuine, novel, useful, and not obvious in light of current technology. A patent holder gives notice to all that an article or design is patented by placing on it the word *Patent* or *Pat.* plus the patent number. In contrast to patent law in other countries, in the United States patent protection is given to the first person to invent a product or process, even though someone else may have been the first to file for a patent on that product or process.

Patent Infringement

If a firm makes, uses, or sells another's patented design, product, or process without the patent owner's permission, the tort of patent infringement occurs. Patent infringement may arise even though the patent owner has not put the patented product in commerce. Patent infringement may also occur even though not all features or parts of an invention are copied. (With respect to a patented process, however, all steps or their equivalents must be copied in order for infringement to occur.)

Often, litigation for patent infringement is so costly that the patent holder will instead offer to sell to the infringer a license to use the patented design, product, or process (licensing will be discussed in Chapter 6). Indeed, in many cases, the costs of detection, prosecution, and monitoring are so high that patents are valueless to their owners, because the owners cannot afford to protect them.

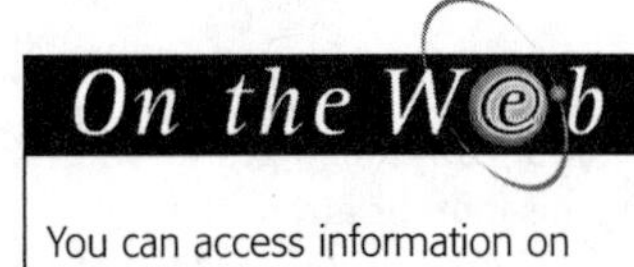

You can access information on patent law at **http://www.patents.com**.

In the past, parties involved in patent litigation also faced another problem: it was often hard to predict the outcome of litigation because jurors found it difficult to understand the issues in dispute. This was particularly true when the claims involved patents on complicated products—such as sophisticated technological or biotechnological products. In a significant case decided in 1996, *Markman v. Westview Instruments, Inc.*,[1] the United States Supreme Court held that it is the responsibility of judges, not juries, to interpret the scope and nature of patent claims. In other words, before a case goes to the jury, the judge must interpret the nature of the claim and give the jury instructions based on that interpretation.

1. 517 U.S. 370, 116 S.Ct. 1384, 134 L.Ed.2d 577 (1996).

Patents for Software

To perform patent searches and to access information on the patenting process, go to **http://www.bustpatents.com**.

At one time, it was difficult for developers and manufacturers of software to obtain patent protection because many software products simply automate procedures that can be performed manually. In other words, these computer programs do not meet the "novel" and "not obvious" requirements previously mentioned. Also, the basis for software is often a mathematical equation or formula, which is not patentable. In 1981, however, the United States Supreme Court held that it is possible to obtain a patent for a process that incorporates a computer program–providing, of course, that the process itself is patentable.[2] Subsequently, many patents have been issued for software-related inventions.

Another obstacle to obtaining patent protection for software is the procedure for obtaining patents. The process can be expensive and slow. The time element is a particularly important consideration for someone wishing to obtain a patent on software. In light of the rapid changes and improvements in computer technology, delay could undercut the product's success in the marketplace.

Despite these difficulties, patent protection is used in the computer industry. If a patent is infringed, the patent holder may sue for an injunction, damages, and the destruction of all infringing copies, as well as attorneys' fees and court costs.

Business Process Patents

A controversial patent issue today involves patents for business processes. These patents have become particularly troublesome with respect to Internet-related activities.

Traditionally, patents have been granted to inventions that are "new and useful processes, machines, manufacturers, or compositions of matter, or any new and useful improvements thereof." The Patent and Trademark Office (PTO) routinely rejected computer systems and software applications because they were deemed not to be useful processes, machines, articles of manufacture, or compositions of matter. They were simply considered mathematical algorithms, abstract ideas, or "methods of doing business."

In a landmark 1998 case, however, *State Street Bank & Trust Co. v. Signature Financial Group, Inc.*,[3] the U.S. Court of Appeals for the Federal Circuit ruled that only three categories of subject matter will always remain unpatentable: (1) the laws of nature; (2) natural phenomena; and (3) abstract ideas. After this decision, the field of business process patents became wide open.

INTERNET COMPANIES AND BUSINESS PROCESS PATENTS Following the *State Street* decision, numerous Internet companies applied for business process patents. Walker Digital, founded by Jay Walker, applied for a business process patent for its idea of allowing consumers on the Internet to make offers for airline tickets. Participating airlines could accept the offers or not. This system is called a "Dutch auction." When Walker Digital received the patent, Priceline.com was

2. *Diamond v. Diehr*, 450 U.S. 175, 101 S.Ct. 1048, 67 L.Ed.2d 155 (1981).
3. 149 F.3d 1368 (Fed. Cir. 1998).

born. The company went public and soon reached a market capitalization of $18 billion. Jay Walker had 50 percent of the stock and became an instant multibillionaire.[4]

Technology companies began to file business process patents in droves after Walker Digital succeeded with its patent application. For example, About.com obtained a patent titled "Elaborative Internet Data Mining System." This business process patent covers a system that creates and pulls together the Web content of a large range of topics onto a single Web site. Amazon.com obtained a business process patent for its "one-click" ordering system (a method of processing credit-card orders securely without asking, more than once, for the customer's card number or other personal information, such as the customer's name and address). Indeed, the U.S. Patent and Trademark Office saw an 800 percent rise in the issuance of Internet-related patents from 1997 to the beginning of 2000.

THE CONTROVERSY OVER BUSINESS PROCESS PATENTS Those in favor of business process patents argue that venture capitalists are more inclined to invest in Internet and high-tech companies if they believe such start-ups can obtain patents for their business processes. Certainly, venture capitalists were inclined to shower Priceline.com with millions of dollars when they sensed that the company would obtain a patent on its online version of a Dutch auction system for selling airline tickets.

In contrast, there are many who believe that business process patents will have a chilling effect on Internet businesses. The more these patents are granted for some of the building blocks of e-commerce, the more those involved in e-commerce will have to pay licensing fees to use such building blocks. Consider an analogy: had a business process patent been applied to the granting of frequent flyer miles, then all airlines would have to pay a license fee for such programs.

Consider further that virtually all business process patents for Internet firms have been granted for processes that have existed for a long time in the real world. Priceline.com's use of the Dutch auction system is simply the electronic version of an auction system that has been around for centuries. The Internet company Cybergold received a business process patent on its use of incentives—paying people to look at its Web ads. Such incentive systems are neither new nor nonobvious. In the real world they have been around for hundreds of years, if not more. Essentially, they are no different from enclosing a dollar bill with a survey and asking people to fill out the survey and send it in.

The U.S. Patent and Trademark Office can be accessed at **http://www.uspto.gov**.

Online Patent Databases

A significant development relating to patents is the availability online of the world's patent databases. The U.S. Patent and Trademark Office provides at its Web site searchable databases covering U.S. patents granted since 1976. This page of the USPTO is illustrated in Exhibit 5–2. The European Patent Office (EPO)

4. Even with the patent, however, Priceline.com was unable to make profits as predicted. Its market capitalization dropped to only a few hundred million dollars in 2001.

Exhibit 5–2 Patent Databases of the U.S. Patent and Trademark Office

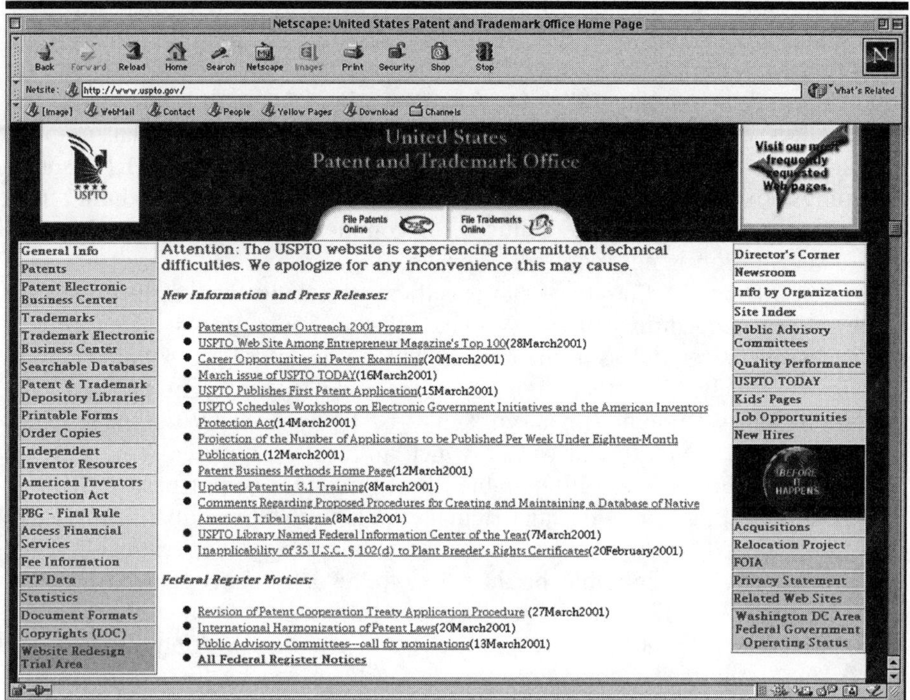

maintains at its Web site databases covering all patent documents in sixty-five nations and the legal status of patents in twenty-two of those countries.

SECTION 2 COPYRIGHTS

A **copyright** is an intangible property right granted by federal statute to the author or originator of a literary or artistic production of a specified type. Currently, copyrights are governed by the Copyright Act of 1976,[5] as amended. Works created after January 1, 1978, are automatically given statutory copyright protection for the life of the author plus 70 years. For copyrights owned by publishing houses, the copyright expires 95 years from the date of publication or 120 years from the date of creation, whichever is first. For works by more than one author, the copyright expires 70 years after the death of the last surviving author.

COPYRIGHT
The exclusive right of authors to publish, print, or sell an intellectual production for a statutory period of time. A copyright has the same monopolistic nature as a patent or trademark, but it differs in that it applies exclusively to works of art, literature, and other works of authorship, including computer programs.

Copyrights can be registered with the U.S. Copyright Office in Washington, D.C. A copyright owner no longer needs to place the symbol © or the term *Copr.* or *Copyright* on the work, however, to have the work protected against infringement. Chances are that if somebody created it, somebody owns it.

5. 17 U.S.C. Sections 101 *et seq.*

For information on copyrights, go to the U.S. Copyright Office at **http://lcweb.loc.gov/copyright**.

What Is Protected Expression?

Works that are copyrightable include books, records, films, artworks, architectural plans, menus, music videos, product packaging, and computer software. To obtain protection under the Copyright Act, a work must be original and fall into one of the following categories: (1) literary works; (2) musical works; (3) dramatic works; (4) pantomimes and choreographic works; (5) pictorial, graphic, and sculptural works; (6) films and other audiovisual works; and (7) sound recordings. To be protected, a work must be "fixed in a durable medium" from which it can be perceived, reproduced, or communicated. Protection is automatic. Registration is not required.

Section 102 of the Copyright Act specifically excludes copyright protection for any "idea, procedure, process, system, method of operation, concept, principle, or discovery, regardless of the form in which it is described, explained, illustrated, or embodied." Note that it is not possible to copyright an *idea*. The underlying ideas embodied in a work may be freely used by others. What is copyrightable is the particular way in which an idea is expressed. Whenever an idea and an expression are inseparable, the expression cannot be copyrighted. Generally, anything that is not an original expression will not qualify for copyright protection. Facts widely known to the public are not copyrightable. Page numbers are not copyrightable, because they follow a sequence known to everyone. Mathematical calculations are not copyrightable.

Compilations of facts, however, are copyrightable. Section 103 of the Copyright Act defines a compilation as "a work formed by the collection and assembling of preexisting materials or data that are selected, coordinated, or arranged in such a way that the resulting work as a whole constitutes an original work of authorship." The key requirement in the copyrightability of a compilation is originality. Therefore, the White Pages of a telephone directory do not qualify for copyright protection when the information that makes up the directory (names, addresses, and telephone numbers) is not selected, coordinated, or arranged in an original way.[6] In one case, even the Yellow Pages of a telephone directory did not qualify for copyright protection.[7]

Copyright Infringement

Whenever the form or expression of an idea is copied, an infringement of copyright has occurred. The reproduction does not have to be exactly the same as the original, nor does it have to reproduce the original in its entirety. If a substantial part of the original is reproduced, there is copyright infringement.

Those who infringe copyrights may be liable for damages or criminal penalties. These range from actual damages or statutory damages, imposed at the court's discretion, to criminal proceedings for willful violations. Actual damages are based on the harm caused to the copyright holder by the infringement, while statutory damages, not to exceed $150,000, are provided for under the Copyright Act. Criminal proceedings may result in fines and/or imprisonment.

---

6. *Feist Publications, Inc. v. Rural Telephone Service Co.*, 499 U.S. 340, 111 S.Ct. 1282, 113 L.Ed.2d 358 (1991).

7. *Bellsouth Advertising & Publishing Corp. v. Donnelley Information Publishing, Inc.*, 999 F.2d 1436 (11th Cir. 1993).

An exception to liability for copyright infringement is made under the "fair use" doctrine. In certain circumstances, a person or organization can reproduce copyrighted material without paying royalties (fees paid to the copyright holder for the privilege of reproducing the copyrighted material). Section 107 of the Copyright Act provides as follows:

> [T]he fair use of a copyrighted work, including such use by reproduction in copies or phonorecords or by any other means specified by [Section 106 of the Copyright Act], for purposes such as criticism, comment, news reporting, teaching (including multiple copies for classroom use), scholarship, or research, is not an infringement of copyright. In determining whether the use made of a work in any particular case is a fair use the factors to be considered shall include–
>
> (1) the purpose and character of the use, including whether such use is of a commercial nature or is for nonprofit educational purposes;
> (2) the nature of the copyrighted work;
> (3) the amount and substantiality of the portion used in relation to the copyrighted work as a whole; and
> (4) the effect of the use upon the potential market for or value of the copyrighted work.

Because these guidelines are very broad, the courts determine whether a particular use is fair on a case-by-case basis. Thus, anyone reproducing copyrighted material may still be subject to a violation. In determining whether a use is fair, courts have often considered the fourth factor to be the most important.

The following case indicates what must be proved to win a case involving charges of copyright infringement of a musical work.

CASE 5.1 Repp v. Webber

United States Court of Appeals,
Second Circuit, 1997.
132 F.3d 882.

http://www.tourolaw.edu/2ndCircuit/December97[a]

HISTORICAL AND CULTURAL SETTING
Musical works fall within the category of works of authorship that can be protected by copyright. A protected musical work can consist of lyrics or music alone, or of both lyrics and music, as in a song. A musical work can exist in a number of different forms, including a tape, a compact disk, and sheet music. To determine whether a copyright of a musical work has been infringed, an expert might dissect the works into musical phrases and compare those phrases to other works by the same, or other, composers. Pitch and rhythm—the elements of a melody—might also be dissected and compared. Harmony—the chordal elements that support the melody—can be an additional important element in comparing pop compositions.

BACKGROUND AND FACTS Over a period of thirty years, Ray Repp wrote and published more than 120 musical compositions, including the song "Till You," which was registered with the U.S. Copyright Office in 1978. Repp included "Till You" on his album "Benedicamus" and in two books of sheet music, and performed the song in over two hundred concerts. Andrew Lloyd Webber, the composer of such musicals as *Cats* and *Evita,* wrote the musical

a. This is the "Decisions for December 1997" page within the collection of opinions of the U.S. Court of Appeals for the Second Circuit. Scroll down the list of cases to the entry for the *Repp* case. Click on the case name to read the court's opinion.

CASE 5.1—Continued

Phantom of the Opera in 1983 and 1984. Claiming that "Phantom Song," one of the songs in *Phantom of the Opera,* infringed on the copyright of "Till You," Repp and others filed a suit in a federal district court against Lloyd Webber and others. Lloyd Webber responded that he never heard of Repp or "Till You" and that "Phantom Song" was an "independent creation." Musical experts offered conflicting testimony about the similarity of the songs' melodies, harmonics, and phrases. Despite this conflict, the court stated that "the two songs do not share a striking similarity" and issued a summary judgment for Lloyd Webber. The court added that Repp failed to show "Phantom Song" was not created independently. Repp appealed to the U.S. Court of Appeals for the Second Circuit.

IN THE LANGUAGE OF THE COURT. . .
MINER, Circuit Judge:

* * * *

While there was little, if any, evidence demonstrating access, there was considerable evidence that "Phantom Song" is so strikingly similar to "Till You" as to preclude the possibility of independent creation and to allow access to be inferred without direct proof. * * * Two highly qualified experts * * * gave unequivocal opinions based on musicological analyses. * * *

* * * The issue of "striking similarity," by virtue of the supported opinions of the experts * * * was shown to be a genuine issue of material fact. Access to the music of Repp being an essential element of his case, it cannot be said that there is an absence of evidence to support proof of that element through the inference generated by the striking similarity of the two pieces.

* * * *

* * * The plaintiffs here have established a *prima facie* case of access through striking similarity * * * . Whether the evidence of independent creation here is sufficient to rebut the *prima facie* case established in this action is a question for the factfinder * * * .

DECISION AND REMEDY The U.S. Court of Appeals reversed the decision of the lower court and remanded the case. Because the issues of "striking similarity" and "independent creation" were disputed, there was a genuine disagreement about the material facts and summary judgment was not appropriate.

FOR CRITICAL ANALYSIS—Cultural Consideration *Considering that there are a limited number of musical notes and a limited number of works into which those notes can be composed, should the fact that infringement might be "subconscious" affect liability in a copyright suit?*

Copyright Protection for Software

In 1980, Congress passed the Computer Software Copyright Act, which amended the Copyright Act of 1976 to include computer programs in the list of creative works protected by federal copyright law. The 1980 statute, which classifies computer programs as "literary works," defines a computer program as a "set of statements or instructions to be used directly or indirectly in a computer in order to bring about a certain result."

Because of the unique nature of computer programs, the courts have had many difficulties in applying and interpreting the 1980 act. In a series of cases decided in the 1980s, the courts held that copyright protection extended not only to those parts of a computer program that can be read by humans, such as the "high-level" language of a source code, but also to the binary-language object code of a computer program, which is readable only by the computer.[8] Additionally, such elements as the overall structure, sequence, and organization of a program were deemed copyrightable.[9]

By the early 1990s, the issue had evolved into whether the "look and feel"—the general appearance, command structure, video images, menus, windows, and other screen displays—of computer programs should also be protected by copyright. Although the courts have disagreed on this issue, the tendency has been *not* to extend copyright protection to look-and-feel aspects of computer programs. For example, in 1995 the Court of Appeals for the First Circuit held that Lotus Development Corporation's menu command hierarchy for its Lotus 1-2-3 spreadsheet was not protectable under the Copyright Act. The court deemed that the menu command hierarchy is a "method of operation," and Section 102 of the Copyright Act specifically excludes methods of operation from copyright protection.[10] The decision was affirmed by the United States Supreme Court in 1996.[11]

A major problem facing today's businesspersons is how to protect copyrighted materials, including software, in cyberspace. See this chapter's *E-Guidelines* feature on the next page for a discussion of this issue.

Copyrights in Digital Information

Copyright law is probably the most important form of intellectual property protection on the Internet. This is because much of the material on the Internet consists of works of authorship (including multimedia presentations, software, and database information). These works are the traditional focus of copyright law. Copyright law is also important because the nature of the Internet requires that data be "copied" to be transferred online. Copies are a significant part of the traditional controversies arising in this area of the law.

THE COPYRIGHT ACT OF 1976 As explained earlier in this chapter, copyright law is concerned chiefly with the creation, distribution, and sale of protected works of authorship. When Congress drafted the principal U.S. law governing copyrights, the Copyright Act of 1976, cyberspace did not exist for most of us. The threat to copyright owners was posed not by computer technology but by unauthorized tangible copies of works and the sale of rights to movies, television, and other media.

---

8. See *Stern Electronics, Inc. v. Kaufman*, 669 F.2d 852 (2d Cir. 1982); and *Apple Computer, Inc. v. Franklin Computer Corp.*, 714 F.2d 1240 (3d Cir. 1983).

9. *Whelan Associates, Inc. v. Jaslow Dental Laboratory, Inc.*, 797 F.2d 1222 (3d Cir. 1986).

10. *Lotus Development Corp. v. Borland International, Inc.*, 49 F.3d 807 (1st Cir. 1995).

11. *Lotus Development Corp. v. Borland International, Inc.*, 517 U.S. 843, 116 S.Ct. 804, 113 L.Ed.2d 610 (1996). This issue may again come before the Supreme Court for a decision, because only eight justices heard the case, and there was a tied vote; the effect of the tie was to affirm the lower court's decision.

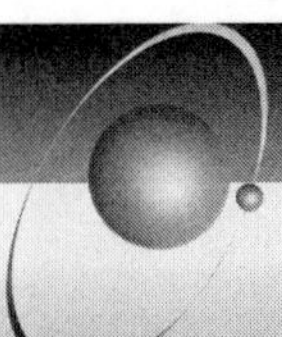

E-Guidelines

Copyright Protection in a Digital Age

Most intellectual property does not sell for the cost of production plus a normal profit. Rather, intellectual property is sold at a price that reflects heavy research costs for ingenious ideas. Any property that involves high development costs and low production costs is vulnerable to "piracy"—the unauthorized copying and use of the property.

In the past, copying intellectual products was time consuming, and the pirated copies were worse than the originals. In today's online world, however, things have changed. Millions of unauthorized copies can now be reproduced simply by clicking a mouse, and pirated duplicates of copyrighted works obtained via the Internet are exactly the same as the originals—after all, they are digitized.

How Big Is the Problem?

The Business Software Alliance estimates that half of the global market for software is supplied today by pirated products. The International Federation of the Phonographic Industry believes that 20 percent of recorded music is pirated. Much of the piracy of intellectual property, especially software and music, is deemed "altruistic." People illegally give intellectual property away not to make any money but because they want to be generous. There is also a problem with respect to copyright law, which makes a distinction between reproduction for public use (which requires the copyright holder's permission) and reproduction for private use (which, within limits, does not require such permission). The difficulty here is distinguishing between private and public use.

Additionally, current copyright law is based on national boundaries. The Internet, however, knows no such limits. Despite attempts to increase protection for intellectual property on a global level (discussed later in this chapter), countries vary widely in their implementation and enforcement of international agreements.

Is There Any Solution to the Problem?

Is there any current solution to the increasing problem of the piracy of intellectual property via the Internet? The simple answer is no. Efforts to find partial solutions are being made, nonetheless. One such attempt is the development of pirate-proof ways of transmitting materials. For example, IBM has developed so-called secure packaging for sending digital information over the Internet.

New technologies are also simplifying the task of searching online databases for pirated copies of copyrighted materials. Providers of online "business intelligence," such as Cyveillance, Ewatch, and Cybercheck, help companies detect and combat infringing uses of their software, text, music, or other copyrighted works. These "digital detectives" use special

Some of the issues that were unimagined when the Copyright Act was drafted have posed thorny questions for the courts. For example, to sell a copy of a work, permission of the copyright holder is necessary. Because of the nature of cyberspace, however, one of the early controversies was determining at what point an intangible, electronic "copy" of a work has been made. The courts have held that loading a file or program into a computer's random access memory, or RAM, constitutes the making of a "copy" for purposes of copyright law.[12] RAM is a portion of a computer's memory into which a file, for example, is loaded so that it can be accessed (read or written over). Thus, a copyright is infringed when

12. *MAI Systems Corp. v. Peak Computer, Inc.*, 991 F.2d 511 (9th Cir. 1993).

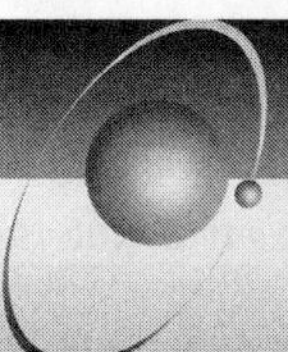

E-Guidelines, Continued

Copyright Protection in a Digital Age

search tools, called "spiders" or "robots," to monitor the Web for sites containing copyrighted works, such as music files.

Once an infringing use is detected, the copyright owner has several options. The owner can send a cease-and-desist (warning) letter to the infringer, take the infringer to court, or issue a license to the infringer. Often, the last option is preferred, simply because the other two may be impractical. For one thing, efforts to shut down infringing Web sites have had limited success. In part, this is because of the ease with which a "mirror" site can be created—at a new location. Initiating a lawsuit against a Web site or user may also be difficult because of jurisdictional problems (see Chapter 2).

Government Efforts to Protect Copyright Holders

The government has also taken action to protect copyright holders. In 1997, Congress passed the No Electronic Theft (NET) Act, which extended criminal liability for the piracy of copyrighted materials to a broader group. Prior to the act, criminal penalties could be imposed only if unauthorized copies were exchanged for financial gain. To combat "altruistic" piracy, the NET imposes criminal penalties on persons who exchange unauthorized copies of copyrighted works, such as software, even though they realize no profit from the exchange. The act also imposes penalties on those who make unauthorized electronic copies of books, magazines, movies, or music for *personal* use, thus altering the traditional "fair use" doctrine. The criminal penalties for violating the act are steep; they include fines as high as $250,000 and incarceration for up to five years.

More recently, in 1998, Congress passed the Digital Millennium Copyright Act (see Appendix A), which allows civil and criminal penalties to be imposed on persons who circumvent encryption software or other technological antipiracy protection. Global efforts are also under way to protect intellectual property, including copyrights. (Some of these efforts are mentioned elsewhere in this chapter.)

CHECKLIST

- ☑ Anybody who has ownership rights in intellectual property should be aware that it is increasingly possible for the property to be pirated via the Internet.
- ☑ Businesspersons must weigh potential benefits against potential costs when deciding how many resources can be devoted to combating the online piracy of their copyrighted works.

a party downloads software into RAM if that party does not own the software or otherwise have a right to download it.[13]

Other rights, including those relating to the revision of "collective works" such as magazines, were acknowledged thirty years ago but were considered to have only limited economic value. Today, technology has made some of those rights vastly more significant. How does the old law apply to these rights? That was one of the questions in the following case.

13. *DSC Communications Corp. v. Pulse Communications, Inc.*, 170 F.3d 1354 (Fed. Cir. 1999).

CASE 5.2 Tasini v. The New York Times Co.

United States Court of Appeals,
Second Circuit, 1999.
192 F.3d 356.
http://www.touro.edu.2ndcircuit/September99[a]

BACKGROUND AND FACTS

Magazines and newspapers, including the *New York Times,* buy and publish articles written by freelance writers. Unless the parties agree otherwise, under Section 201(c) of the Copyright Act the writers retain the copyrights in the separate articles, but the publishers obtain copyrights in the "collective work." Besides circulating hard copies of their periodicals, these publishers sell the contents to e-publishers for inclusion in online and other electronic databases. Jonathan Tasini and five other freelance writers filed a suit in a federal district court against the New York Times Company and other publishers, including the e-publishers, contending that the e-publication of the articles violated the Copyright Act. The publishers responded, among other things, that the Copyright Act gave them a right to produce "revisions" of their publications. The writers argued that articles included in e-databases were not "revisions." The publishers filed a motion for summary judgment, which the court granted. The writers appealed to the U.S. Court of Appeals for the Second Circuit.

a. On this page, scroll down to the case name and click on it to access the opinion.

IN THE LANGUAGE OF THE COURT. . .

WINTER, Chief Judge.

* * * *

* * * [Under Section 201(c) of the Copyright Act] the privilege granted to a collective-work [publisher] to use individually copyrighted contributions is limited to the reproduction and distribution of the individual contribution as part of: (i) "that particular [that is, the original] collective work"; (ii) "any revision of that collective work"; or (iii) "any later collective work in the same series." Because it is undisputed that the electronic databases are neither the original collective work—the particular edition of the periodical—in which the Authors' articles were published nor a later collective work in the same series, appellees [the publishers] rely entirely on the argument that each database constitutes a "revision" of the particular collective work in which each Author's individual contribution first appeared. We reject that argument.

* * * *

The most natural reading of the "revision" of "that collective work" clause is that the Section 201(c) privilege protects only later editions of a particular issue of a periodical, such as the final edition of a newspaper. Because later editions are not identical to earlier editions, use of the individual contributions in the later editions might not be protected under the preceding clause. Given the context provided by the surrounding clauses, this interpretation makes perfect sense. It protects the use of an individual contribution in a collective work that is somewhat altered from the original in which the copyrighted article was first published, but that is not in any ordinary sense of language a "later" work in the "same series."

* * * *

Moreover, * * * if the contents of an electronic database are merely a "revision" of a particular "collective work," e.g., the August 16, 1999 edition of *The New York Times,* then the third clause of the privilege sentence—permitting the reproduction and distribution of an individually copyrighted work as part of "a later collective work in the same series"—would be superfluous. An electronic database can contain hundreds or thousands of editions of hundreds or thousands of periodicals, including newspapers, magazines, anthologies, and encyclopedias. To view the contents of databases as revisions would eliminate any need for a privilege for "a later collective work in the same series."

DECISION AND REMEDY The U.S. Court of Appeals for the Second Circuit held that the publishers, to put the contents of their periodicals into e-databases and onto CD-ROMs, needed the permission of the writers whose articles were included in the periodicals. The court reversed the lower court's summary judgment and remanded the case with instructions to enter a judgment for the writers.

FOR CRITICAL ANALYSIS–Political Consideration *When technology creates a situation in which rights such as those in this case are more valuable than originally anticipated, should the law be changed to redistribute the economic benefit of those rights?*

THE DIGITAL MILLENNIUM COPYRIGHT ACT OF 1998 The Digital Millennium Copyright Act of 1998 (see Appendix A) created civil and criminal penalties for anyone who circumvents encryption software or other technological antipiracy protection. Also prohibited are the manufacture, import, sale, or distribution of devices or services for circumvention.

There are exceptions to fit the needs of libraries, scientists, universities, and others. In general, the new law does not restrict the "fair use" of circumvention for educational and other noncommercial purposes. For example, circumvention is allowed to test computer security, to conduct **encryption** research, to protect personal privacy, or to allow parents to monitor their children's use of the Internet. The exceptions are to be reconsidered every three years.

ENCRYPTION
The process by which a message (plaintext) is transformed into something (ciphertext) that the sender and receiver intend third parties not to understand.

An Internet service provider (ISP) is not liable for any copyright infringement by its customer if the ISP is unaware of the subscriber's violation. An ISP may be held liable only after learning of the violation and failing to take action to shut the subscriber down. A copyright holder has to act promptly, however, by pursuing a claim in court, or the subscriber has the right to be restored to online access.

Recently, a court applied the 1998 act to the DVD code-cracking software called DeCCS. For a discussion of this case, see this chapter's *Controversial Issues* feature on the next page.

MP3 and File-Sharing Technology

At one time, music fans swapped compact disks (CDs) and recorded the songs that they liked from others' CDs onto their own cassettes. This type of "file sharing" was awkward at best. After the Internet became popular, it was not long before a few enterprising programmers decided to create software to compress large data files, particularly those associated with music. The reduced size of such files allows for the feasibility of transmitting music over the Internet. The most widely known compression and decompression system is MP3. This system gives music fans the ability to "rip" songs or entire CDs onto their computer or onto a portable listening device, such as Rio. It was only a matter of time before someone figured out that it would be great for music fans to be able to access other music fans' files via the Internet.

Controversial Issues in the Online World

Code-Cracking Software for DVDs Online—The Courts Speak

Digital versatile disks (DVDs) promise to give a boost to the at-home movie rental and purchase industry. DVDs provide numerous advantages over traditional videocassettes. For one thing, they are more compact. They also offer superior audio and video quality. Additionally, they provide for numerous enhancements, such as directors' commentaries, separate foreign language audio tracks, and various foreign language subtitles. Not surprisingly, the owners of motion picture copyrights have a vested interest in preventing renters and owners of DVDs from making the contents of those DVDs available on the Internet. All DVDs include an encryption system created to protect against the unauthorized copying of the contents of the DVDs.

Cracking the Code

Almost as soon as encryption technology was used to safeguard the contents of DVDs, the code was cracked by a group of hackers, including nineteen-year-old Norwegian Jon Johansen. His decryption program, called DeCCS, was quickly made available on the Internet. One such site was 2600.com, owned by Ed Corly. Almost immediately after DeCCS was posted, a group of movie companies, including Disney and Twentieth Century-Fox, filed suit.

Violation of the Digital Millennium Copyright Act

In what was seen as a victory for the motion picture industry, U.S. District Court Judge Lewis A. Kaplan ruled that DeCCS violated the Digital Millennium Copyright Act of 1998.[a] As discussed elsewhere in this chapter, this act essentially prohibits individuals from breaking encryption programs put in place to protect digital versions of intellectual property such as movies, music, and the like. After all, reasoned the court, since the posting of DeCCS, along with a separate video-compression program known as Divx, the pirating of movies has become increasingly common on the Internet.

The defendants argued that software programs designed to break encryption schemes were simply a form of constitutionally protected speech. The court, however, rejected the free speech argument. "Computer code is not purely expressive any more than the assassination of a political figure is purely a political statement. . . . The Constitution, after all, is a framework for building a just and democratic society. It is not a suicide pact," stated Judge Kaplan.

New Forms of Encryption May Curb DVD Piracy

New forms of encryption and copyright protection are being developed right now. If successful, they may at least slow down the amount of piracy on the Internet. New DVD-Audio discs contain a digital "watermark" that can be tracked. In this way, if pirated copies of the watermarked DVD-Audio disc are found, record labels can better pursue the originator of such pirated copies. Additionally, the sound quality of DVD-Audio discs that are copied is of much lower quality than the originals.

New versions of Microsoft's Media Player software allow digital restrictions dictated by copyright holders. The software then scrambles the digital output so that it cannot be recorded. Finally, IBM is developing an encryption system, which it believes will prevent DVD piracy.

If the past is any predictor of the future, however, no matter how well a copyrighted work is encrypted, the technically skilled will be able to "crack" the encryption code, thereby allowing pirated copies to resurface.

FOR CRITICAL ANALYSIS

Will the decision in the *Universal City Studios* case have any practical effect, given that literally thousands of copies of DeCCS already existed on the Internet before the decision was made?

a. *Universal City Studios, Inc. v. Reimerdes,* 111 F.Supp.2d 294 (S.D.N.Y. 2000).

File sharing via the Internet is accomplished through what is called **peer-to-peer (P2P) networking.** The concept is simple. Rather than going through a central Web server, P2P involves numerous personal computers (PCs) that are connected to the Internet. Files stored on one PC can be accessed by others who are members of the same network. Sometimes this is called a **distributed network.** In other words, parts of the network are distributed all over the country or the world.

PEER-TO-PEER (P2P) NETWORKING
A technology that allows Internet users to access files on other users' computers.

DISTRIBUTED NETWORK
A network that can be used by persons located (distributed) around the country or the globe to share computer files.

In all file-sharing arrangements, copyright issues abound. After all, if you took this textbook to your local copy center and asked for fifty copies to resell to your classmates, you would face copyright problems. The materials in this text are copyrighted in order for the authors and the publisher to be rewarded for their efforts and to cover the expense of publishing the text. While Congress allows for "fair use," copying the entire book for resale would not fall under that exception to copyright law. File sharing, when it involves copyrighted materials, creates a copyright violation problem. Clearly, recording artists and their labels stand to lose large amounts of royalties and revenues if relatively few CDs are purchased and then made available on distributed networks, from which everyone can then get them for free.

In the following widely publicized case, several firms in the recording industry sued Napster, Inc., the owner of the popular Napster Web site. The firms alleged that Napster was contributing to copyright infringement on the part of those who downloaded CDs from other computers in the Napster file-sharing system. At issue was whether Napster could be held vicariously liable for the infringement.[14]

14. Vicarious (substitute) liability exists when one person is subject to liability for another's actions. A common example of this is in the employment context, when an employer is held vicariously liable by third parties for torts committed by employees in the course of their employment.

CASE 5.3 A&M Records, Inc. v. Napster, Inc.

United States Court of Appeals,
Ninth Circuit, 2001.
239 F.3d 1004.

HISTORICAL AND TECHNOLOGICAL SETTING *In 1987, the Moving Picture Experts Group set a standard file format for the storage of audio recordings in a digital format called MPEG-3, abbreviated as "MP3." Digital MP3 files are created through a process called "ripping." Ripping software allows a computer owner to copy an audio compact disk (CD) directly onto a computer's hard drive by compressing the audio information on the CD into the MP3 format. The MP3's compressed format allows for rapid transmission of digital audio files from one computer to another by e-mail or any other file-transfer protocol.*

BACKGROUND AND FACTS Napster, Inc. (**http://www.napster.com**), facilitates the transmission of MP3 files among the users of its Web site through a process called "peer-to-peer" file sharing. Napster allows users to (1) make MP3 music files stored on individual computer hard drives available for copying by other Napster users, (2) search for MP3 music files stored on other users' computers, and (3) transfer exact copies of the contents of other users' MP3 files from one computer to another via the Internet. These functions are made possible by Napster's MusicShare software, available free of charge from Napster's site, and Napster's network servers and server-side software. Napster provides technical support for the indexing and searching of MP3 files. A&M Records, Inc., and others engaged in the commercial recording, distribution, and sale of copyrighted musical compositions and sound recordings filed a suit in a

CASE 5.3–Continued

federal district court against Napster, alleging copyright infringement. The court issued a preliminary injunction ordering Napster to stop "engaging in, or facilitating others in copying, downloading, uploading, transmitting, or distributing plaintiffs' copyrighted musical compositions and sound recordings, * * * without express permission of the rights owner." Napster appealed to the U.S. Court of Appeals for the Ninth Circuit.

IN THE LANGUAGE OF THE COURT. . .
BEEZER, Circuit Judge:

* * * *

* * * In the context of copyright law, vicarious liability extends * * * to cases in which a defendant has the right and ability to supervise the infringing activity and also has a direct financial interest in such activities.

* * * *

The ability to block infringers' access to a particular environment for any reason whatsoever is evidence of the right and ability to supervise. Here, plaintiffs have demonstrated that Napster retains the right to control access to its system. Napster has an express reservation of rights policy, stating on its website that it expressly reserves the "right to refuse service and terminate accounts in [its] discretion, including, but not limited to, if Napster believes that user conduct violates applicable law * * * or for any reason in Napster's sole discretion, with or without cause."

To escape imposition of vicarious liability, the reserved right to police must be exercised to its fullest extent. Turning a blind eye to detectable acts of infringement for the sake of profit gives rise to liability.

The district court correctly determined that Napster had the right and ability to police its system and failed to exercise that right to prevent the exchange of copyrighted material. * * *

Napster, however, has the ability to locate infringing material listed on its search indices, and the right to terminate users' access to the system. The file name indices, therefore, are within the "premises" that Napster has the ability to police. We recognize that the files are user-named and may not match copyrighted material exactly (for example, the artist or song could be spelled wrong). For Napster to function effectively, however, file names must reasonably or roughly correspond to the material contained in the files, otherwise no user could ever locate any desired music. As a practical matter, Napster, its users and the record company plaintiffs have equal access to infringing material by employing Napster's "search function."

Our review of the record requires us to accept the district court's conclusion that plaintiffs have demonstrated a likelihood of success on the merits of the vicarious copyright infringement claim. Napster's failure to police the system's "premises," combined with a showing that Napster financially benefits from the continuing availability of infringing files on its system, leads to the imposition of vicarious liability.

DECISION AND REMEDY The U.S. Court of Appeals for the Ninth Circuit affirmed the lower court's decision that Napster was obligated to police its own system and had likely infringed the plaintiffs' copyrights. Holding that the injunction was "overbroad," however, the appellate court remanded the case for a clarification of

CASE 5.3—Continued

Napster's responsibility to determine whether music on its Web site was copyrighted.

FOR CRITICAL ANALYSIS—Technological Consideration *How might the Napster system be put to commercially significant but noninfringing uses?*

File Sharing—What the Future Holds

In spite of the court's ruling in the *Napster* case, file sharing continues. Indeed, there are now a number of Napster clones. One is Aimster.com, which has about three million users. Another is iMesh.com, which has four million users with about 300,000 users online at any one time. BearShare.com and LimeWare.com have file-sharing networks using the Gnutella technology (a decentralized P2P search system).

Clearly, file sharing via the Internet is here to stay, and file sharing is not just for downloading others' stored music files. Rather, there are an unlimited number of uses for distributed networks. Currently, for example, many researchers allow their home computers' computing power to be accessed through file-sharing software so that very large mathematical problems can be solved quickly. Additionally, those who work on a project but who are located throughout the country or the world use file-sharing programs in order to advance their project rapidly. A new product called *Groove* is supposed to make the management of large projects with many workers increasingly efficient, speedy, and popular.

Intel Corporation, the maker of the chips that go into most of the world's computers, has often stated that file sharing is the wave of the future. Indeed, Intel is currently working with a group of eighteen companies, including IBM and Hewlett-Packard, to develop standards in this area. Intel envisions consumers and companies alike creating self-organizing Web communities. These groups could consist of employees at a single company, family members, or any group with common interests.

SECTION 3 INTERNATIONAL PROTECTION FOR INTELLECTUAL PROPERTY

For many years, the United States has been a party to various international agreements relating to intellectual property rights. For example, the Paris Convention of 1883, to which about ninety countries are signatory, allows parties in one country to file for patent and trademark protection in any of the other member countries. Other international agreements in this area include the Berne Convention and the TRIPS agreement.

On the Web

You can find extensive information on copyright law—including the texts of the Berne Convention and other international treaties on copyright issues—at the Web site of the Legal Information Institute at Cornell University's School of Law at **http://www.law.cornell.edu/topics/copyright.html**.

The Berne Convention

Under the Berne Convention of 1886, an international copyright agreement, if an American writes a book, his or her copyright in the book must be recognized by every country that has signed the convention. Also, if a citizen of a country that has not signed the convention first publishes a book in a country that has signed, all other countries that have signed the convention must recognize that author's copyright. Copyright notice is not needed to gain protection under the Berne Convention for works published after March 1, 1989.

Currently, the laws of many countries as well as international laws are being updated to reflect changes in technology and the expansion of the Internet. Copyright holders and other owners of intellectual property generally agree that changes in the law are needed to stop the increasing international piracy of their property. These developments will be covered in more detail shortly.

The Berne Convention and other international agreements have given some protection to intellectual property on a global level. Another significant worldwide agreement to increase such protection is the Trade-Related Aspects of Intellectual Property Rights agreement—or, more simply, the TRIPS agreement.

The TRIPS Agreement

The TRIPS agreement was signed by representatives from over one hundred nations in 1994. It was one of several documents that were annexed to the agreement that created the World Trade Organization, or WTO, in 1995. The TRIPS agreement established, for the first time, standards for the international protection of intellectual property rights, including patents, trademarks, and copyrights for movies, computer programs, books, and music.

Prior to the TRIPS agreement, one of the difficulties faced by U.S. sellers of intellectual property in the international market was that another country might either lack laws to protect intellectual property rights or fail to enforce what laws it had. To address this problem, the TRIPS agreement provides that each member country must include in its domestic laws broad intellectual property rights and effective remedies (including civil and criminal penalties) for violations of those rights.

Generally, the TRIPS agreement provides that member nations must not discriminate (in terms of the administration, regulation, or adjudication of intellectual property rights) against foreign owners of such rights. In other words, a member nation cannot give its own nationals (citizens) favorable treatment without offering the same treatment to nationals of all member countries. For example, if a U.S. software manufacturer brings a suit for the infringement of intellectual property rights under Japan's national laws, the U.S. manufacturer is entitled to receive the same treatment as a Japanese domestic manufacturer. Each member nation must also ensure that legal procedures are available for parties who wish to bring actions for infringement of intellectual property rights. Additionally, as part of the agreement creating the WTO, a mechanism for settling disputes among member nations was established.

Particular provisions of the TRIPS agreement refer to patent, trademark, and copyright protection for intellectual property. The agreement specifically provides copyright protection for computer programs by stating that compilations of data, databases, and other materials are "intellectual creations" and are to be protected as copyrightable works. Other provisions relate to trade secrets and the rental of computer programs and cinematographic works.

The World Intellectual Property Organization (WIPO) Copyright Treaty of 1996

Technology, particularly the Internet, offers new outlets for creative products. It also makes them easier to steal—copyrighted works can be pirated and distributed around the world quickly and efficiently. To curb this crime, in 1996 the World Intellectual Property Organization (WIPO) enacted the WIPO Copyright Treaty, a special agreement under the Berne Convention. The purpose was to upgrade global standards of copyright protection, particularly for the Internet.

Special provisions of the WIPO treaty relate to rights in digital data. The treaty strengthens some rights for copyright owners, in terms of their application in cyberspace, but leaves other questions unresolved. For example, the treaty does not make clear what, for purposes of international law, constitutes the making of a "copy" in electronic form. The United States signed the WIPO treaty in 1996 and implemented its terms in the Digital Millennium Copyright Act of 1998.

The World Intellectual Property Organization offers information on the background of intellectual property, including copyrights, and its international protection at **http://www.wipo.org/eng/newindex/intellct.htm**.

TERMS AND CONCEPTS

copyright 113
distributed network 123
encryption 121
intellectual property 107
patent 110
peer-to-peer (P2P) networking 123

QUESTIONS AND CASE PROBLEMS

5–1. Patent Infringement. John and Andrew Doney invented a hard-bearing device for balancing rotors. Although they registered their invention with the U.S. Patent and Trademark Office, it was never used as an automobile wheel balancer. Some time later, Exetron Corp. produced an automobile wheel balancer that used a hard-bearing device with a support plate similar to that of the Doneys. Given the fact that the Doneys had not used their device for automobile wheel balancing, does Exetron's use of a similar hard-bearing device infringe on the Doneys' patent?

5–2. Copyright Infringement. Max plots a new Batman adventure and carefully and skillfully imitates the art of DC Comics to create an authentic-looking Batman comic. Max is not affiliated with the owners of the copyright to Batman. Can Max publish the comic without infringing on the owners' copyright?

5–3. Fair Use Doctrine. Professor Wise is teaching a summer seminar in business torts at State University. Several times during the course, he makes copies of relevant sections from business law texts and distributes them to his students. Wise does not realize that the daughter of one of the textbook authors is a member of his seminar. She tells her father about Wise's copying activities, which have taken place without her father's or his publisher's permission. Her father sues Wise for copyright infringement. Wise claims protection under the fair use doctrine. Who will prevail? Explain.

5–4. Copyright Infringement. In which of the following situations would a court likely hold Ursula liable for copyright infringement?

(a) From a scholarly journal at the library, Ursula photocopies ten pages relating to a topic on which she is writing a term paper.

(b) Ursula makes blouses, dresses, and other clothes and sells them in her small shop. She advertises some of the outfits as Guest items, hoping that customers might mistakenly assume that they were made by Guess, the well-known clothing manufacturer.

(c) Ursula teaches Latin American history at a small university. She has a VCR and frequently tapes television programs relating to Latin America. She then takes the videos to her classroom so that her students can watch them.

5–5. Copyright Protection. One day during algebra class, Diedra, an enterprising fourteen-year-old student, began drawing designs on her shoelaces. By the end of the class, Diedra had decorated her shoelaces with the name of the school, Broadson Junior High, written in blue and red (the school colors) and with pictures of bears, the school's mascot. After class, she showed the designs to her teacher, Mrs. Laxton. When Diedra got home that night, she wrote about her idea in her diary, in which she also drew her shoelace design. Mrs. Laxton had been trying to think of how she could build school spirit. She thought about Diedra's shoelaces and decided to go into business for herself. She called her business Spirited Shoelaces and designed shoelaces for each of the local schools, decorating the shoelaces in each case with the school's name, mascot, and colors. The business became tremendously profitable. Even though Diedra never registered her idea with the patent or copyright office, does she nonetheless have intellectual property rights in the shoelace design? Will her diary account be sufficient proof that she created the idea? Discuss.

5–6. Copyright Infringement. James Smith, the owner of Michigan Document Services, Inc. (MDS), a commercial copy shop, concluded that it was unnecessary to obtain the copyright owners' permission to reproduce copyrighted materials in coursepacks. Smith publicized his conclusion, claiming that professors would not have to worry about any delay in production at his shop. MDS then compiled, bound, and sold coursepacks to students at the University of Michigan without obtaining the permission of copyright owners. Princeton University Press and two other publishers filed a suit in a federal district court against MDS, alleging copyright infringement. MDS claimed that its coursepacks were covered under the fair use doctrine. Were they? Explain. [*Princeton University Press v. Michigan Document Services, Inc.*, 99 F.3d 1381 (6th Cir. 1996)]

5–7. Copyrights. Webbworld operates a Web site called Neptics, Inc. The site accepts downloads of certain images from third parties and makes these images available to any user who accesses the site. Before being allowed to view the images, however, the user must pay a subscription fee of $11.95 per month. Over a period of several months, images were available that were originally created by or for Playboy Enterprises, Inc. (PEI). The images were displayed at Neptics's site without PEI's permission. PEI filed a suit in a federal district court against Webbworld, alleging copyright infringement. Webbworld argued in part that it should not be held liable because, like an Internet service provider that furnishes access to the Internet, it did not create or control the content of the information available to its subscribers. Do you agree with Webbworld? Why or why not? [*Playboy Enterprises, Inc. v. Webbworld*, 968 F.Supp. 1171 (N.D.Tex. 1997)]

WEB EXERCISES

Go to **http://lec.westbuslaw.com**, the Web site that accompanies this text. Select "Internet Applications," and then click on "Chapter 5." There you will find the following Internet research exercise that you can perform to learn about a recent development with respect to patent rights:

Activity 5–1: BountyQuest

CHAPTER 6

Intellectual Property—Trademarks, Cyber Marks, and Trade Secrets

Concepts Covered

After reading this chapter, you should be able to:

1. Define the term *virtual property*.
2. Discuss the law protecting trademarks.
3. Indicate what legal protection exists for cyber marks.
4. Describe how the law protects trade secrets.
5. Give examples of how technology is affecting the laws that govern trademarks, cyber marks, and trade secrets.

"The protection of trademarks is the law's recognition of the psychological function of symbols. If it is true that we live by symbols, it is no less true that we purchase goods by them."

Felix Frankfurter, 1882–1965
(Associate justice of the United States Supreme Court, 1939–1962)

The legal issues relating to *virtual property*—property in cyberspace—are essentially legal questions involving intellectual property. As discussed in Chapter 5, intellectual property consists of trademarks, patents, copyrights, and trade secrets. Legal protection for these forms of property makes it possible to market goods and services profitably, which provides an incentive to sell competitive goods and services.

Trademarks and trade secrets are the types of intellectual property that are discussed in this chapter. Much of the law relating to the use of this property outside cyberspace is well settled. In the context of cyberspace, however, a fundamental issue has to do with the degree of legal protection that should be given to virtual property. If the protection is inadequate, the incentive to make new works available online will be reduced. If the protection is too strict, the free flow and fair use of data will be impaired.

SECTION 1 TRADEMARKS AND RELATED PROPERTY

A **trademark** is a distinctive mark, motto, device, or implement that a manufacturer stamps, prints, or otherwise affixes to the goods it produces so that they may be identified on the market and their origin vouched for. At common law, the person who used a symbol or mark to identify a business or product was protected in the use of that trademark. Clearly, if one used the trademark of another, it would lead consumers to believe that one's goods were made by the other. The law seeks to avoid this kind of confusion. We examine in this section various aspects of the law governing trademarks.

TRADEMARK
A distinctive mark, motto, device, or implement that a manufacturer stamps, prints, or otherwise affixes to the goods it produces so that they may be identified on the market and their origins made known. Once a trademark is established (under the common law or through registration), the owner is entitled to its exclusive use.

In the following famous case concerning Coca-Cola, the defendants argued that the Coca-Cola trademark was entitled to no protection under the law, because the term did not accurately represent the product.

CASE 6.1 The Coca-Cola Co. v. The Koke Co. of America

Supreme Court of the United States, 1920.
254 U.S. 143,
41 S.Ct. 113,
65 L.Ed. 189.

http://www.findlaw.com/casecode/supreme.html[a]

COMPANY PROFILE *John Pemberton, an Atlanta pharmacist, invented a caramel-colored, carbonated soft drink in 1886. His bookkeeper, Frank Robinson, named the beverage Coca-Cola after two of the ingredients, coca leaves and kola nuts. Asa Candler bought the Coca-Cola Company (***http://www.cocacolacompany.com***) in 1891, and within seven years, he made the soft drink available in all of the United States, as well as in parts of Canada and Mexico. Candler continued to sell Coke aggressively and to open up new markets, reaching Europe before 1910. In doing so, however, he attracted numerous competitors, some of whom tried to capitalize directly on the Coke name.*

a. In the "Citation Search" section, enter "254" in the left box and "143" in the right box, and click "Get It" to access the opinion.

BACKGROUND AND FACTS The Coca-Cola Company sought to enjoin (prevent) the Koke Company of America and other beverage companies from, among other things, using the word *Koke* for their products. The Koke Company of America and other beverage companies contended that the Coca-Cola trademark was a fraudulent representation and that Coca-Cola was therefore not entitled to any help from the courts. The Koke Company and the other defendants alleged that the Coca-Cola Company, by its use of the Coca-Cola name, represented that the beverage contained cocaine (from coca leaves), which it no longer did. The trial court granted the injunction against the Koke Company, but the appellate court reversed the lower court's ruling. Coca-Cola then appealed to the United States Supreme Court.

IN THE LANGUAGE OF THE COURT. . .
Mr. Justice *HOLMES* delivered the opinion of the Court.

* * * *

* * * Before 1900 the beginning of [Coca-Cola's] good will was more or less helped by the presence of cocaine, a drug that, like alcohol or caffeine or opium, may be described as a deadly poison or as a valuable item of the pharmacopeia according to the rhetorical purposes in view. The amount seems to have been very small,[b] but it may have been enough to begin a bad habit and after the Food and Drug Act of June 30, 1906, if not earlier, long before this suit was brought, it was eliminated from the plaintiff's compound. * * *

* * * Since 1900 the sales have increased at a very great rate corresponding to a like increase in advertising. The name now characterizes a beverage to be had at almost any soda fountain. It means a single thing coming from a single source, and well known to the community. It hardly would be too much to say that the drink characterizes the name as much as the name the drink. In other words Coca-Cola probably means to most persons the plaintiff's familiar product to be had everywhere rather than a compound of particular substances. * * * [B]efore this suit was brought the plaintiff had advertised to the public that it must not expect and would not find cocaine, and had eliminated everything tending to suggest cocaine effects except the name and the picture of [coca] leaves and nuts, which probably conveyed little or nothing to most who saw it. It appears to us that it would be going too far to deny the plaintiff relief against a palpable fraud because possibly here and there an ignorant person might call for the drink with the hope for incipient cocaine intoxication. The plaintiff's position must be judged by the facts as they were when the suit was begun, not by the facts of a different condition and an earlier time.

b. In reality, until 1903 the amount of active cocaine in each bottle of Coke was equivalent to one "line" of cocaine.

DECISION AND REMEDY The district court's injunction was allowed to stand. The competing beverage companies were enjoined from calling their products Koke.

FOR CRITICAL ANALYSIS–Social Consideration *How can a court determine when a particular nickname for a branded product has entered into common use?*

Statutory Protection of Trademarks

Statutory protection of trademarks and related property is provided at the federal level by the Lanham Trade-Mark Act of 1946.[1] The Lanham Act was enacted in part to protect manufacturers from losing business to rival companies that used confusingly similar trademarks. The Lanham Act incorporates the common law of trademarks and provides remedies for owners of trademarks who wish to enforce their claims in federal court. Many states also have trademark statutes.

In 1995, Congress amended the Lanham Act by passing the Federal Trademark Dilution Act,[2] which extended the protection available to trademark owners by creating a federal cause of action for trademark **dilution.** Until the passage of this amendment, federal trademark law only prohibited the unauthorized use of the same mark on competing–or on noncompeting but "related"–goods or services when such use would likely confuse consumers as to the origin of those goods and services. Trademark dilution laws, which have also been enacted by about half of the states, protect "distinctive" or "famous" trademarks (such as Jergens, McDonald's, RCA, and Macintosh) from certain unauthorized uses of the marks *regardless* of a showing of competition or a likelihood of confusion.

DILUTION
With respect to trademarks, a doctrine under which distinctive or famous trademarks are protected from certain unauthorized uses of the marks regardless of a showing of competition or a likelihood of confusion. Congress created a federal cause of action for dilution in 1995 with the passage of the Federal Trademark Dilution Act.

In one of the first cases to be decided under the 1995 act's provisions, a federal court held that a famous mark may be diluted not only by the use of an *identical* mark but also by the use of a *similar* mark. The lawsuit was brought by Ringling Bros.–Barnum & Bailey, Combined Shows, Inc., against the state of Utah. Ringling Bros. claimed that Utah's use of the slogan "The Greatest Snow on Earth"–to attract visitors to the state's recreational and scenic resorts–diluted the distinctiveness of the circus's famous trademark, "The Greatest Show on Earth." Utah moved to dismiss the suit, arguing that the 1995 provisions only protect owners of famous trademarks against the unauthorized use of identical marks. The court disagreed and refused to grant Utah's motion to dismiss the case.[3]

Trademark Registration

Trademarks may be registered with the state or with the federal government. To register for protection under federal trademark law, a person must file an application with the U.S. Patent and Trademark Office in Washington, D.C. Under current law, a mark can be registered (1) if it is currently in commerce or (2) if the applicant intends to put it into commerce within six months.

To access the federal database of registered trademarks directly, go to **http://www.uspto.gov/tmdb/index.html**.

Under extenuating circumstances, the six-month period can be extended by thirty months, giving the applicant a total of three years from the date of notice of trademark approval to make use of the mark and file the required use statement. Registration is postponed until the mark is actually used. Nonetheless, during this waiting period, any applicant can legally protect his or her trademark against a third party who previously has neither used the mark nor filed an application for it. Registration is renewable between the fifth and sixth years after the initial registration and every ten years thereafter (every twenty years for those trademarks registered before 1990).

1. 15 U.S.C. Sections 1051–1127.
2. 15 U.S.C. Section 1125.
3. *Ringling Bros.–Barnum & Bailey, Combined Shows, Inc. v. Utah Division of Travel Development*, 935 F.Supp. 736 (E.D.Va. 1996).

Registration of a trademark with the U.S. Patent and Trademark Office gives notice on a nationwide basis that the trademark belongs exclusively to the registrant. The registrant is also allowed to use the symbol ® to indicate that the mark has been registered. Whenever that trademark is copied to a substantial degree or used in its entirety by another, intentionally or unintentionally, the trademark has been *infringed* (used without authorization). When a trademark has been infringed, the owner of the mark has a cause of action against the infringer. A person need not have registered a trademark in order to sue for trademark infringement, but registration does furnish proof of the date of inception of the trademark's use.

Distinctiveness of Mark

A central objective of the Lanham Act is to reduce the likelihood that consumers will be confused by similar marks. For that reason, only those trademarks that are deemed sufficiently distinctive from all competing trademarks will be protected. A trademark must be sufficiently distinct to enable consumers to identify the manufacturer of the goods easily and to distinguish between those goods and competing products.

STRONG MARKS Fanciful, arbitrary, or suggestive trademarks are generally considered to be the most distinctive (strongest) trademarks. This is because these types of marks are normally taken from outside the context of the particular product and thus provide the best means of distinguishing one product from another.

Fanciful trademarks include invented words, such as Xerox for one manufacturer's copiers and Kodak for another company's photographic products. Arbitrary trademarks include actual words used with products that have no literal connection to the words, such as English Leather used as a name for an after-shave lotion (and not for leather processed in England). Suggestive trademarks are those that suggest something about a product without describing the product directly. For example, the trademark Dairy Queen suggests an association between the products and milk, but it does not directly describe ice cream.

SECONDARY MEANING Descriptive terms, geographical terms, and personal names are not inherently distinctive and do not receive protection under the law until they acquire a secondary meaning. A secondary meaning may arise when customers begin to associate a specific term or phrase (such as London Fog) with specific trademarked items (coats with London Fog labels). Whether a secondary meaning becomes attached to a term or name usually depends on how extensively the product is advertised, the market for the product, the number of sales, and other factors. Once a secondary meaning is attached to a term or name, a trademark is considered distinctive and is protected. Even a shade of color can qualify for trademark protection, once customers associate the color with the product.[4]

GENERIC TERMS Generic terms, such as *bicycle* and *computer,* receive no protection, even if they acquire secondary meanings. A particularly thorny problem arises when a trademark acquires generic use. For example, *aspirin* and *thermos* were originally the names of trademarked products, but today the words are used generically. Other examples are *escalator, trampoline, raisin bran, dry ice, lanolin, linoleum, nylon,* and *corn flakes.* Even so, the courts will not allow another firm to use those marks in such a way as to deceive a potential consumer. In the following case, the issue before the court was whether the phrase "You Have Mail" is a generic term.

4. *Qualitex Co. v. Jacobson Products Co.,* 514 U.S. 159, 115 S.Ct. 1300, 131 L.Ed.2d 248 (1995).

CASE 6.2 America Online, Inc. v. AT&T Corp.

United States District Court,
Eastern District of Virginia, 1999.
64 F.Supp.2d 549.

BACKGROUND AND FACTS In the late 1960s and early 1970s, AT&T Corporation developed started using "YOU HAVE MAIL" in its e-mail notification service for its members. AT&T provides Internet access to subscribers through its WorldNet Service. Since 1998, when a member visits the WorldNet home page, a "You Have Mail!" notification window pops up. AOL filed a suit in a federal district court against AT&T, alleging in part trademark infringement of the phrase "YOU HAVE MAIL," which AOL claimed to own. AT&T filed a motion for summary judgment, asking the court to rule that the term was generic.

IN THE LANGUAGE OF THE COURT. . .
HILTON, J. [Judge.]

* * * *

* * * [A] plaintiff who is seeking to establish a valid trademark must show that the primary significance of the term in the minds of the consuming public is not the product but the producer. * * * [T]he following evidence [may] be used to determine the primary significance of a mark: (1) competitors' use of the mark, (2) plaintiff's use of the mark, (3) dictionary definitions, (4) media usage, (5) testimony of persons in the trade, and (6) consumer surveys.

* * * *

* * * Under the primary significance test, the "mail" component of YOU HAVE MAIL means "e-mail."

First, the Court notes that even AOL uses the words "mail" and "e-mail" interchangeably. For example, in its * * * complaint AOL repeatedly uses the word "mail" as referring to "e-mail." * * *

Next, it is undisputed that numerous competitors of AOL use "mail" as a synonym for "e-mail." * * *

Regarding media usage and testimony of persons involved in the trade, [there are] numerous examples of the books printed to describe the e-mail notification features used by both UNIX and AOL. All of the authors, without fail, use "mail" and "e-mail" interchangeably. * * *

Last, the Court would note that * * * consumer surveys [are used] as a means of determining whether the primary significance of a mark is generic. However, when determining whether a mark is generic, the Court is not to consider whether the mark has acquired any secondary meaning, because generic marks with secondary meaning are still not entitled to protection. * * *

* * * *

The primary significance of the phrase YOU HAVE MAIL indicates to the public-at-large what the service is, not where it came from. * * * Further, this holding does not rest on considering solely the "mail" component of the phrase YOU HAVE MAIL. * * * The "you" and the "have" of YOU HAVE MAIL (either separately or together) do not carry with them any especial significance which would change the primary significance of the mark as previously stated. Since the "you," "have," and "mail" of YOU HAVE MAIL are all used for their everyday, common meaning, the phrase as a whole is generic * * * .

DECISION AND REMEDY The court granted a summary judgment in favor of AT&T. The court ruled that "You have mail" is a generic expression and therefore cannot be owned by AOL.

FOR CRITICAL ANALYSIS–Social Consideration *Particular shapes, sounds, colors, and even scents that have acquired secondary meanings have qualified for trademark protection. As the court noted, however, generic marks will not be protected, even if they have acquired secondary meanings. Why is this a principle of trademark law?*

Trade Dress

TRADE DRESS
The image and overall appearance of a product—for example, the distinctive decor, menu, layout, and style of service of a particular restaurant. Basically, trade dress is subject to the same protection as trademarks.

The term **trade dress** refers to the image and overall appearance of a product—for example, the distinctive décor, menu, layout, and style of service of a particular restaurant. Basically, trade dress is subject to the same protection as trademarks. In cases involving trade dress infringement, as in trademark infringement cases, a major consideration is whether consumers are likely to be confused by the allegedly infringing use.

Service, Certification, and Collective Marks

SERVICE MARK
A mark used in the sale or the advertising of services, such as to distinguish the services of one person from the services of others. Titles, character names, and other distinctive features of radio and television programs may be registered as service marks.

CERTIFICATION MARK
A mark used by one or more persons, other than the owner, to certify the region, materials, mode of manufacture, quality, or accuracy of the owner's goods or services. When used by members of a cooperative, association, or other organization, such a mark is referred to as a collective mark. Examples of certification marks include the "Good Housekeeping Seal of Approval" and "UL Tested."

COLLECTIVE MARK
A mark used by members of a cooperative, association, or other organization to certify the region, materials, mode of manufacture, quality, or accuracy of the specific goods or services. Examples of collective marks include the labor union marks found on tags of certain products and the credits of movies, which indicate the various associations and organizations that participated in the making of the movies.

A **service mark** is similar to a trademark but is used to distinguish the services of one person or company from those of another. For example, each airline has a particular mark or symbol associated with its name. Titles and character names used in radio and television are frequently registered as service marks.

Other marks protected by law include certification marks and collective marks. A **certification mark** is used by one or more persons other than the owner to certify the region, materials, mode of manufacture, quality, or accuracy of the owner's goods or services. When used by members of a cooperative, association, or other organization, it is referred to as a **collective mark.** Examples of certification marks are the phrases "Good Housekeeping Seal of Approval" and "UL Tested." Collective marks appear at the ends of motion picture credits to indicate the various associations and organizations that participated in the making of the films. The union marks found on the tags of certain products are also collective marks.

Trade Names

TRADE NAME
A term that is used to indicate part or all of a business's name and that is directly related to the business's reputation and goodwill. Trade names are protected under the common law (and under trademark law, if the name is the same as the firm's trademarked property).

Trademarks apply to *products.* The term **trade name** is used to indicate part or all of a business's name, whether the business is a sole proprietorship, a partnership, or a corporation. Generally, a trade name is directly related to a business and its goodwill. A trade name may be protected as a trademark if the trade name is the same as the name of the company's trademarked product—for example, Coca-Cola. Unless also used as a trademark or service mark, a trade name cannot be registered with the federal government. Trade names are protected under the common law, however. As with trademarks, words must be unusual or fancifully used if they are to be protected as trade names. The word *Safeway,* for example, was held by the courts to be sufficiently fanciful to obtain protection as a trade name for a foodstore chain.[5]

Section 2 CYBER MARKS

CYBER MARK
A trademark in cyberspace.

In cyberspace, trademarks are sometimes referred to as **cyber marks.** Here, we look at trademark-related issues in cyberspace and how new laws and the courts are addressing these issues. One concern relates to the rights of a mark's owner to use the mark as part of a domain name (Internet address). Other issues have to do with cybersquatting, meta tags, trademark dilution on the Web, and the use of licensing as a way to avoid liability for infringing on another's intellectual property rights.

Domain Names

Remember from Chapter 3 that one of the difficulties businesses face today has to do with securing rights to use their trademarks in domain names (Internet

5. *Safeway Stores v. Suburban Foods,* 130 F.Supp. 249 (E.D.Va. 1955).

addresses). This problem emerged during the 1990s as e-commerce expanded on a worldwide scale. For one thing, of the five top level domains (TLDs) then available, only one—*.com*—could be used by commercial enterprises. The others (*.org, .net, .edu, .int, .mil, .gov*) were initially provided for use by nonprofit organizations, Internet service providers, educational institutions, international organizations, the military, and government agencies, respectively. Additionally, there were about two hundred nation-specific TLDs, such as *.us* for the United States or *.fr* for France.

On the Web

An online magazine that deals, in part, with intellectual property issues is *Law Technology Product News* at **http://www.ljextra.com/ltpn**.

As e-commerce expanded, the *.com* TLD became widely used by businesses on the Web. In fact, by 1998 nearly 85 percent of registered domain names used the *.com* TLD.[6] Competition among firms with identical or similar names and products for the second level domains preceding the *.com* TLD led, understandably, to disputes over domain name rights. As discussed in Chapter 3, the Internet Corporation for Assigned Names and Numbers (ICANN) has played a leading role in facilitating the settlement of domain name disputes worldwide. As the overseer of domain name distribution on the Internet, ICANN also recently approved several new TLDs for use in domain names. (These new TLDs, and the procedures used by ICANN in selecting new registrars, have given rise to considerable controversy—see this chapter's *Controversial Issues* feature for a discussion of this issue.)

Anticybersquatting Legislation

One of the early questions concerning cyber marks had to do with cybersquatting. **Cybersquatting** occurs when a person registers for a domain name that is the same as, or confusingly similar to, the trademark of another and then offers to sell the domain name back to the trademark owner. During the 1990s, cybersquatting became a contentious issue and led to much litigation. Often in controversy in these cases was whether cybersquatting constituted a commercial use of the mark so as to violate federal trademark law. Additionally, it was not always easy to separate cybersquatting from legitimate business activity. Although no clear rules emerged from this litigation, many courts held that cybersquatting violated trademark law.[7]

CYBERSQUATTING
An act that occurs when a person registers for a domain name that is the same as, or confusingly similar to, the trademark of another and offers to sell the domain name back to the trademark owner.

In 1999, Congress addressed this issue by passing the Anticybersquatting Consumer Reform Act (ACRA), which amended the Lanham Act—the federal law protecting trademarks discussed earlier in this chapter. The ACRA makes it illegal for a person to "register, traffic in, or use" a domain name if (a) the name is identical or confusingly similar to the trademark of another and (b) if the one registering, trafficking in, or using the domain name has a "bad faith intent" to profit from that trademark. The act does not define what constitutes bad faith. Instead, it lists several factors that courts can consider in deciding whether bad faith exists. Some of these factors are the trademark rights of the other person, the intent to divert consumers in a way that could harm the goodwill represented by the trademark, whether there is an offer to transfer or sell the domain name to the trademark owner, and whether there is an intent to use the domain name to offer goods and services.

The ACRA applies to all domain name registrations, even domain names registered before the passage of the act. Successful plaintiffs in suits brought under the act can collect actual damages and profits, or elect to receive statutory damages of from $1,000 to $100,000. In fact, immediately after the act's passage, a number of trademark owners filed suits against cybersquatters to recover damages. The following case included a request for statutory damages under the act.

6. Lee B. Burgunder, *Legal Aspects of Managing Technology*, 2d ed. (Cincinnati: South-Western College Publishing, 2001), p. 434.
7. See, for example, *Panavision International, L.P. v. Toeppen*, 141 F.3d 1316 (9th Cir. 1998).

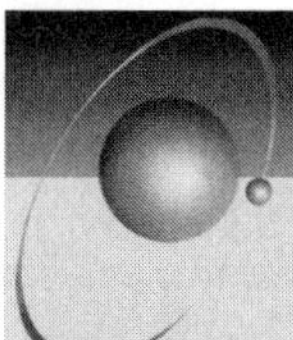

Controversial Issues in the Online World

ICANN's Process for Choosing New TLDs Comes under Fire

In 1997, the U.S. Government directed the secretary of the Department of Commerce to privatize the domain name system in a manner that increased competition and facilitated international participation in its management. The end result of the Commerce Department's efforts was the creation, in October 1998, of the Internet Corporation for Assigned Names and Numbers (ICANN), a private, nonprofit organization, to act as a technical coordination body for the Internet.

Part of the impetus behind ICANN's creation was to remove domain name registration oversight from the U.S. government to a private organization that could work to serve the broader interests of the international community. Previously, because the Internet developed from a U.S. military and research network, domain name registration had been under the direction of U.S. government organizations. From 1993 to 1998, Network Solutions, Inc. (NSI), under a contract with the U.S. government, exclusively controlled the allocation of domain names. Recently, though, ICANN has been accused of being too subjective in its selection of new top level domain (TLD) names for use in Internet addresses and too secretive in its procedures.

ICANN Approves More TLDs

For some time, Internet businesses had clamored for more choices with respect to TLDs. In response to this desire, ICANN let it be known that it would be selecting some new TLDs for use in Internet addresses. The Internet community responded with nearly two hundred proposed new TLDs for ICANN to consider. In November 2000, ICANN approved the following seven new TLDs:

.biz (for businesses)
.info (for general use)
.name (for individuals)
.pro (for professionals)
.museums (for museums)
.coop (for business cooperatives)
.aero (for the aviation industry)

Criticism of ICANN's Approval Process

Many were disappointed at ICANN's choices for the new TLDs. In fact, due to mounting criticism of ICANN's approval process, Congress decided to hold hearings on this issue. In February 2000, the new chair of the House Subcommittee on Telecommunications and the Internet, Republican Fred Upton of Michigan, called hearings because he said he had questions about whether the ICANN TLD decision-making process was too subjective. Upton also questioned whether the process thwarted competition. In particular, he and others were concerned about ICANN's refusal to approve TLDs that would segregate Web content for children and adults. Creating two new TLDs that would have included *.kids* and *.XXX* would have done this.

At the hearings, Democratic representative Edward Markey of Massachusetts raised issues about the procedure itself. He said that it was more shrouded in mystery than events at the Vatican.

In front of the same committee, Dr. Vinton G. Cerf, chair of ICANN, offered a defense to the selection process. He pointed out that ICANN's effort was not to find "the best applications," but simply to ask the Internet community to offer a set of options from which ICANN could select a limited number. He pointed out that from the very beginning, ICANN had made it known that only a small number of new TLDs would be selected. He further pointed out that more than four thousand public comments were received after the nearly two hundred proposed new TLDs were posted on ICANN's Web site. Thus, he believed that the process was fair and open.

New TLDs—A Blessing or A Curse?

Apart from the controversy associated with the selection process for the new TLDs, there is also the question of how valuable these new TLDs will be for Internet users and businesses. Some argue that the increased number of TLDs will make Internet navigation more confusing.

Additionally, some contend that although the additional TLDs will allow businesses and individuals to obtain desirable domain names, they will also complicate the process of protecting corporate trademarks. This is because, in order to protect their trademarks, businesses often buy up all available domain names associated with a particular word or set of words. With additional TLDs, this becomes more difficult. For example, if you market a product called XYZ, you would want to own the domain name XYZ.com, as well as XYZ.biz and possibly, depending on the nature of your product, XYZ.coop or XYZ.aero or XYZ.info.

There also is a cost factor, because registering for domain names is not free. In fact, the Gartner Group, Inc., in Stamford, Connecticut, estimates that companies now have to spend an average of about $70,000 a year to maintain a domain name strategy to protect their trademarks.

FOR CRITICAL ANALYSIS

Do you think that it is wise to entrust control over domain name distribution to a private organization, such as ICANN? Would it be any fairer to have a U.S. government agency control this process? Can you think of any other alternative that would be acceptable to the worldwide community of Internet users?

CASE 6.3 E. & J. Gallo Winery v. Spider Webs Ltd.

United States District Court,
Southern District of Texas, 2001.
129 F.Supp.2d 1033.

BACKGROUND AND FACTS In 1999, Steve and Pierce Thumann and their father, Fred, created Spider Webs Ltd., a partnership, to, according to Steve, "develop Internet address names." Spider Webs registered nearly two thousand Internet domain names for an average of $70 each, including the names of cities, the names of buildings, names related to a business or trade (such as air conditioning or plumbing), and the names of famous companies. It offered many of the names for sale on its Web site and through eBay.com. Through Network Solutions, Inc., Spider Webs registered the domain name "ERNESTANDJULIOGALLO.COM" in Spider Webs's name. E. & J. Gallo Winery (Gallo), the well-known California winery founded by Ernest and Julio Gallo, filed a suit against Spider Webs, alleging, in part, violations of the Anticybersquatting Consumer Protection Act (ACPA). Gallo asked the court for, among other things, statutory damages. During the suit, Spider Webs published anticorporate articles and opinions, and discussions of the suit and of the risks associated with alcohol use, at the URL "ERNESTANDJULIOGALLO.COM." Gallo filed a motion for summary judgment.

IN THE LANGUAGE OF THE COURT. . .
CRONE, Magistrate J. [Judge.]

* * * *

* * * [Gallo] has a distinctive and famous trademark and * * * the domain name "ERNESTANDJULIOGALLO.COM" is nearly indistinguishable from Gallo's "ERNEST & JULIO GALLO" trademark. * * * Other federal courts have agreed that domain names that are substantially the same as a trademark are confusingly similar and create a presumption of confusion. In this instance, Spider Webs' domain name "ERNESTANDJULIOGALLO.COM" is confusingly similar to Gallo's registered trademark "ERNEST & JULIO GALLO."

The ACPA lists nine factors a court may consider when determining whether a domain name was registered in bad faith * * * . The statute further provides, however, that "[b]ad faith intent * * * shall not be found in any case in which the court determines that the person believed and had reasonable grounds to believe that the use of the domain name was a fair use or otherwise lawful." * * *

* * * *

In the case at bar [now before the court], a review of the nine factors provides ample evidence that Spiders Webs used, registered, or trafficked in the domain name ERNESTANDJULIOGALLO.COM with a bad faith intent to profit from the sale of the domain name. Gallo has a registered trademark in the name "ERNEST & JULIO GALLO," while Spider Webs has no intellectual property interest in the name "ERNESTANDJULIOGALLO" aside from its registered domain name. Furthermore, the domain name "ERNESTANDJULIOGALLO.COM" does not include the legal name of Spider Webs Ltd., the company that registered the domain name, or of its partners * * * . Spider Webs has never used the domain name in connection with the bona fide offering of any goods or services. It has, however, used the name to develop a web site on which it has made derogatory comments about the instant [present] litigation and about alcohol. * * * Moreover, Spider Webs' use of the web site to criticize E. & J. Gallo Winery and to comment on the present litigation served only to disparage Gallo and diminish its goodwill. * * *

* * * *

* * * Prior to the enactment of the ACPA, a number of courts had found cybersquatting to be unlawful under both federal and state antidilution laws.

CASE 6.3—Continued

* * * Steve Thumann admitted that Spider Webs did not seek advice from counsel prior to acquiring the domain name at issue as to whether it might be engaging in infringing conduct. Courts addressing the issue have found that such a failure supports a finding of bad faith.

DECISION AND REMEDY The court granted Gallo's motion for summary judgment and awarded Gallo $25,000 in statutory damages. The court permanently enjoined the Thumanns from using the Internet domain name "ERNESTANDJULIOGALLO.COM" and from registering any domain name that contains the word "Gallo" or the words "Ernest" and "Julio" in combination. Finally, the court ordered the Thumanns to transfer to Gallo the registered domain name "ERNESTANDJULIOGALLO.COM."

FOR CRITICAL ANALYSIS—Social Consideration *Why is cybersquatting considered a violation of trademark law?*

Meta Tags

META TAGS
Words inserted into a Web site's key words field to increase the site's appearance in search engine results.

Search engines compile their results by looking through a Web site's key words field. Meta tags, or key words, may be inserted in this field to increase a site's appearance in search engine results, even though the site has nothing to do with the inserted words. Using this same technique, one site may appropriate the key words of other sites with more frequent hits, so that the appropriating site appears in the same search engine results as the more popular site. One use of meta tags was at issue in the following case.

CASE 6.4 Playboy Enterprises, Inc. v. Welles

United States District Court,
Southern District of California, 1998.
7 F.Supp.2d 1098.
http://www.Loundy.com/CASES/Playboy_v_Wells.html[a]

BACKGROUND AND FACTS Playboy Enterprises, Inc. (PEI), maintains Web sites to promote *Playboy* magazine and PEI models. PEI's trademarks include the terms *Playboy, Playmate,* and *Playmate of the Year.* Terri Welles is a self-employed model and spokesperson, who was featured as the "Playmate of the Year" in June 1981. Welles maintains a Web site titled "Terri Welles—Playmate of the Year 1981." As meta tags, Welles's site uses the terms *Playboy* and *Playmate,* among others. PEI asked Welles to stop using these terms, but she refused. PEI filed a suit in a federal district court against Welles, asking the court to order her to, among other things, stop using those terms as meta tags. PEI argued, in part, that this constituted trademark infringement under the Lanham Act. Welles responded in part that her use of the terms is a "fair use," because she was and is the "Playmate of the Year 1981."

a. This is a page within the E-LAW site of David J. Loundy, an attorney and author. Note that to access this site you must use the misspelled version of Welles's name given in this URL.

IN THE LANGUAGE OF THE COURT. . .
GRAHAM, District Judge.

* * * *

In a case where the mark is used only to describe the goods or services of [a] party, or their geographic origin, trademark law recognizes a "fair use" defense. * * *

* * * *

It is clear that defendant is selling Terri Welles and only Terri Welles on the website. There is no overt attempt to confuse the websurfer into believing that her site is a Playboy-related website. In this case, then, defendant's use of the term Playmate of the Year 1981 is descriptive of and used fairly and in good faith only to describe [herself]. * * *

With respect to the meta tags, the court finds there to be no trademark infringement where defendant has used plaintiff's trademarks in good faith to index the content of her website. * * * *Much like the subject index of a card catalog, the meta tags give the websurfer using a search engine a clearer indication of the content of a website.* The use of the term *Playboy* is not an infringement because it references not only her identity as a "Playboy Playmate of the Year 1981," but it may also reference the legitimate editorial uses of the term *Playboy* contained in the text of defendant's website. [Emphasis added.]

DECISION AND REMEDY The court held that a party can use another's trademarks as meta tags when those marks describe the party who uses them. The court ruled that Welles was entitled to the "fair use" of the "Playboy" and "Playmate" marks as meta tags.

FOR CRITICAL ANALYSIS–Technological Consideration *Why would PEI encourage its models to use its marks outside cyberspace but attempt to block such uses within cyberspace?*

Dilution in the Online World

As discussed earlier in this chapter, trademark *dilution* occurs when a trademark is used, without authorization, in a way that diminishes the distinctive quality of the mark. Unlike trademark infringement, a dilution cause of action does not require proof that consumers are likely to be confused by a connection between the unauthorized use and the mark. For this reason, the products involved do not have to be similar. In the first case alleging dilution on the Web, a court precluded the use of "candyland.com" as the URL for an adult site. The suit was brought by the maker of the "Candyland" children's game and owner of the "Candyland" mark.[8]

In one interesting case, a court issued an injunction on the ground that spamming under another's logo is trademark dilution.[9] In that case, Hotmail, Inc., provided e-mail services and worked to dissociate itself from spam. Van$ Money Pie, Inc., and others spammed thousands of e-mail customers, using the free e-mail Hotmail as a return address. The court ordered the defendants to stop.

Licensing

One of the ways to make use of another's mark (or another's copyright, patent, or trade secret), while avoiding litigation, is to obtain a license to do so. A license in this context is essentially an agreement to permit the use of a mark for certain purposes. A licensee (the party obtaining the license) might be allowed to use the mark of the licensor (the party issuing the license) as part of the name of its company, or as part of its domain name, without otherwise using the mark on any products or services.

In 1999, the National Conference of Commissioners on Uniform State Laws approved the Uniform Computer Information Transactions Act (UCITA) and submitted it to the states for adoption. The act was drafted to address problems unique to electronic contracting and to the purchase and sale (licensing) of

8. *Hasbro, Inc. v. Internet Entertainment Group, Ltd.*, 1996 WL 84853 (W.D.Wash. 1996).
9. *Hotmail Corp. v. Van$ Money Pie, Inc.*, 47 U.S.P.Q.2d 1020 (N.D.Cal. 1998).

computer information, such as software. Appendix H at the end of this text sets forth some of the important provisions of the UCITA.

SECTION 3 TRADE SECRETS

TRADE SECRET
Information or a process that gives a business an advantage over competitors who do not know the information or process.

Some business processes and information that are not, or cannot be, patented, copyrighted, or trademarked are nevertheless protected against appropriation by competitors as trade secrets. **Trade secrets** consist of customer lists, plans, research and development, pricing information, marketing techniques, production techniques, and generally anything that makes an individual company unique and that would have value to a competitor.

State and Federal Law on Trade Secrets

Under Section 757 of the *Restatement of Torts,* "One who discloses or uses another's trade secret, without a privilege to do so, is liable to the other if (1) he discovered the secret by improper means, or (2) his disclosure or use constitutes a breach of confidence reposed in him by the other in disclosing the secret to him." The theft of confidential business data by industrial espionage, as when a business taps into a competitor's computer, is a theft of trade secrets without any contractual violation and is actionable in itself.

Until recently, virtually all law with respect to trade secrets was common law. In an effort to reduce the unpredictability of the common law in this area, a model act, the Uniform Trade Secrets Act, was presented to the states in 1979 for adoption. Parts of the act have been adopted in more than twenty states. Typically, a state that has adopted parts of the act has adopted only those parts that encompass its own existing common law. (In 1996, Congress passed the Economic Espionage Act, which made the theft of trade secrets a federal crime.)

Does a trade secret lose its protection under the Uniform Trade Secrets Act when an employee commits it to memory rather than takes it in written form? That was the question in the following case.

CASE 6.5 Ed Nowogroski Insurance, Inc. v. Rucker

Supreme Court of Washington, 1999.
137 Wash.2d 427,
971 P.2d 936.

BACKGROUND AND FACTS Jerry Kiser, Darwin Rieck, and Michael Rucker worked as sales representatives for Ed Nowogroski Insurance, Inc., an insurance agency. When friction developed among the agency and Kiser, Rieck, and Rucker, the three quit to go to work for Potter, Leonard and Cahan, Inc., a competing insurance firm. During their employment with Potter, the former Nowogroski employees used Nowogroski customer lists to attract business. Kiser and Rucker used written client information that they had copied from their former employer's files. Rieck worked chiefly from memory. The Nowogroski agency filed a suit in a Washington state court against its former employees and their new employer, alleging misappropriation of trade secrets. The court concluded that the client information fit the definition of a trade secret under the Uniform Trade Secrets Act and issued a judgment in Nowogroski's favor. The court decided, however, that only the written information was protected and did not award damages for the use of the memorized data. Nowogroski appealed to an intermediate state appellate court, which held that there is no distinction between written and memorized information and ordered a recalculation of the damages. The defendants appealed to the Washington Supreme Court.

IN THE LANGUAGE OF THE COURT. . .
HILTON, J. [Judge.]

* * * *

The Uniform Trade Secrets Act does not distinguish between written and memorized information. The Act does not require a plaintiff to prove actual theft or conversion of physical documents embodying the trade secret information to prove misappropriation. The Washington Uniform Trade Secrets Act defines a "trade secret" to include compilations of information which have certain characteristics without regard to the form that such information might take. The definition of "misappropriation" includes unauthorized "disclosure or use." * * * [T]wo types of information mentioned in the Uniform Trade Secrets Act as examples of trade secrets include "method" and "technique"; these do not imply the requirement of written documents.

* * * *

The form of information, whether written or memorized, is immaterial under the trade secrets statute; the Uniform Trade Secrets Act makes no distinction about the form of trade secrets. Whether the information is on a CD, a blueprint, a film, a recording, a hard paper copy or memorized by the employee, the inquiry is whether it meets the definition of a trade secret under the Act and whether it was misappropriated. Absent a contract to the contrary, an employee is free to compete against his or her former employer, and a former employee may use general knowledge, skills and experience acquired during the prior employment in competing with a former employer. However, an employee may not use or disclose trade secrets belonging to the former employer to actively solicit customers from a confidential customer list. In this case, the former employees actively solicited customers from the employer's customer lists, which the trial court found to be of independent value because unknown and subject to reasonable efforts to keep secret. * * * [W]e conclude the Court of Appeals was correct in holding that there is no legal distinction between written and memorized information under the Uniform Trade Secrets Act and in remanding for a recalculation of damages.

DECISION AND REMEDY The Washington Supreme Court affirmed the judgment of the state intermediate appellate court. Under the Uniform Trade Secrets Act, there is no legal distinction between written and memorized information.

FOR CRITICAL ANALYSIS–Economic Consideration *For many businesses, trade secrets are their most valuable assets. What incentives might employers offer to their employees to keep them from revealing the company's trade secrets to competing firms?*

Trade Secrets in Cyberspace

The nature of the new technology undercuts a business firm's ability to protect its confidential information, including trade secrets.[10] For example, a dishonest employee could e-mail trade secrets in a company's computer to a competitor or a future employer. If e-mail is not an option, the employee might walk out with the information on a computer disk.

The Cyberspace Law Institute offers articles and information on such topics as trade secrets at **http://www.cli.org**.

10. Note that in a recent case, the court indicated that customers' e-mail addresses may constitute trade secrets. See *T-N-T Motorsports, Inc. v. Hennessey Motorsports, Inc.*, 965 S.W.2d 18 (Tex.App.–Hous. [1 Dist.] 1998), rehearing overruled (1998), petition dismissed (1998).

One of the problems posed by cyberspace is that traditional strategies designed to prevent employees from revealing trade secrets do not adapt well to the cyber environment. For example, traditionally employers who are concerned about protecting their trade secrets have included confidentiality clauses or even **covenants not to compete** in their employment contracts. In a covenant not to compete, an employee (typically, a middle-level or upper-level management employee) agrees not to work for a competitor or not to start competing businesses for a specified period of time after termination of employment. Such agreements are legal so long as the specified period of time is not excessive in duration and the geographic restriction is reasonable. The problem is, no geographic restriction is possible in cyberspace, as the court noted in the following case.

COVENANT NOT TO COMPETE
A contractual promise to refrain from competing with another party for a certain period of time (not excessive in duration) and within a reasonable geographic area.

CASE 6.6 Earthweb, Inc. v. Schlack

United States District Court, Southern District of New York, 1999. 71 F.Supp.2d 299.

BACKGROUND AND FACTS Mark Schlack worked in the publishing industry for fifteen years, holding such positions as senior editor and editor in chief for print magazines, including *BYTE* and *Web Builder.* In October 1998, Schlack began working for EarthWeb, Inc., as the company officer responsible for the content of the firm's Web sites. The parties signed an employment agreement under which Schlack agreed that "for a period of twelve (12) months after the termination of [his] employment with EarthWeb, [he] shall not, directly or indirectly, work * * * for any person or entity that directly competes with EarthWeb." In September 1999, Schlack resigned to accept a position with ITworld.com, a subsidiary of International Data Group.[a] Unlike EarthWeb, ITworld.com planned to post original content. EarthWeb filed a suit in a federal district court against Schlack. EarthWeb asked the court to issue a preliminary injunction, on the basis of the employment agreement, to prevent Schlack from working for ITworld.com. EarthWeb argued in part that Schlack's services to EarthWeb were "unique" and "extraordinary." The court applied New York state law.

a. International Data Group (IDG) (**http://www.idg.com**) is the world's leading provider of IT print-based information, generating over $3 billion in annual revenues through 290 publications and 240 Web sites in more than 75 countries.

IN THE LANGUAGE OF THE COURT. . .
PAULEY, District Judge.

* * * *

* * * In New York, non-compete covenants will be enforced only if reasonably limited in scope and duration, and only to the extent necessary (1) to prevent an employee's solicitation or disclosure of trade secrets, (2) to prevent an employee's release of confidential information regarding the employer's customers, or (3) in those cases where the employee's services to the employer are deemed special or unique.

The policy underlying this strict approach rests on notions of employee mobility and free enterprise. Once the term of an employment agreement has expired, the general public policy favoring robust and uninhibited competition should not give way merely because a particular employer wishes to insulate himself from competition. Important, too, are the powerful considerations of public policy which militate [work] against sanctioning the loss of a man's livelihood. On the other hand, the employer is entitled to protection from unfair or illegal conduct that causes economic injury.

Applying these principles here, EarthWeb's restrictive covenant * * * [fails] to pass muster * * * .

* * * *

As a threshold matter, this Court finds that the one-year duration of EarthWeb's restrictive covenant is too long given the dynamic nature of this industry, its lack of geographical borders, and Schlack's former cutting-edge position with EarthWeb where his success depended on keeping abreast of daily changes in content on the Internet. * * *

* * * *

Contrary to EarthWeb's contention, Schlack's services are not "unique and extraordinary." Such characteristics have traditionally been associated with various categories of employment where the services are dependent on an employee's special talents; such categories include musicians, professional athletes, actors and the like. However, in order to justify enforcement of a restrictive covenant, more must * * * be shown to establish such a quality than that the employee excels at his work or that his performance is of high value to his employer. It must also appear that his services are of such character as to make his replacement impossible or that the loss of such services would cause the employer irreparable injury. EarthWeb has not shown that the nature of Schlack's services are unique or that he cultivated the type of special client relationships that [are] worthy of protection * * * .

DECISION AND REMEDY The court denied EarthWeb's request for a preliminary injunction. The court concluded that EarthWeb did not prove the covenant not to compete in the employment agreement with Schlack was reasonable and necessary to protect EarthWeb's interests.[b]

FOR CRITICAL ANALYSIS–Technological Consideration *Should the constant and rapid changes in the IT industry influence courts' decisions in such cases as this one?*

b. The case was appealed to the U.S. Court of Appeals for the Second Circuit, which remanded and later affirmed the lower court's decision. *EarthWeb, Inc. v. Schlack,* remanded, 205 F.3d 1322 (2d Cir. 2000), aff'd __ F.3d __ (2d Cir. 2000).

TERMS AND CONCEPTS

certification mark 134
collective mark 134
covenant not to compete 142
cyber mark 134
cybersquatting 135
dilution 131
meta tags 138
service mark 134
trade dress 134
trade name 134
trade secret 140
trademark 129

QUESTIONS AND CASE PROBLEMS

6–1. Trademark Infringement. Alpha Software, Inc., announced a new computer operating system to be marketed under the name McSoftware. McDonald's Corp. wrote Alpha a letter stating that the use of this name infringed on the McDonald's family of trademarks characterized by the prefix "Mc" attached to a generic term. Alpha claimed that "Mc" had come into generic use as a prefix and therefore McDonald's had no trademark rights to the prefix itself. Alpha filed an action seeking a declaratory judgment from the court that the mark McSoftware did not infringe on McDonald's federally registered trademarks or common law rights to its marks and would not constitute an unfair trade practice. What factors must the court consider in deciding this issue? What will be the probable outcome of the case? Explain.

6–2. Trademark Infringement. CBS, Inc., owns and operates Television City, a television production facility in Los Angeles that is home to many television series. The name Television City is broadcast each week in connection with each show. CBS sells T-shirts, pins, watches, and so on emblazoned with "CBS Television City." CBS registered the name Television City with the U.S. Patent and Trademark Office as a service mark "for television production services."

David and William Liederman wished to open a restaurant in New York City using the name Television City. Besides food, the restaurant would sell television memorabilia such as T-shirts, sweatshirts, and posters. When CBS learned of the Liedermans' plans, it asked a federal district court to order them not to use the name Television City in connection with their restaurant. Does CBS's registration of the Television City mark ensure its exclusive use in all markets and for all products? If not, what factors might the court consider to determine whether the Liedermans can use the name Television City in connection with their restaurant? [*CBS, Inc. v. Liederman,* 866 F.Supp. 763 (S.D.N.Y. 1994)]

6–3. Trade Secrets. William Redmond, as the general manager for PepsiCo, Inc., in California, had access to the company's inside information and trade secrets. In 1994, Redmond resigned to become chief operating officer for the Gatorade and Snapple Co., which makes and markets Gatorade and Snapple and is a subsidiary of the Quaker Oats Co. PepsiCo brought an action in a federal district court against Redmond and Quaker Oats, seeking to prevent Redmond from disclosing PepsiCo's secrets. The court ordered Redmond not to assume new duties that were likely to trigger disclosure of those secrets. The central issue on appeal was whether a plaintiff can obtain relief for trade secret misappropriation on showing that a former employee's new employment will inevitably lead him or her to rely on the plaintiff's trade secrets. How should the court rule on this issue? Discuss fully. [*PepsiCo v. Redmond,* 54 F.3d 1262 (7th Cir. 1995)]

6–4. Trademarks. Sara Lee Corp. manufactures pantyhose under the L'eggs trademark. Originally, L'eggs were sold in egg-shaped packaging, a design that Sara Lee continues to use with its product. Sara Lee's only nationwide competitor in the same pantyhose markets is Kayser-Roth Corp. When Kayser-Roth learned of Sara Lee's plan to introduce L'eggs Everyday, a new line of hosiery, Kayser-Roth responded by simultaneously introducing a new product, Leg Looks. Sara Lee filed a complaint in a federal district court against Kayser-Roth, asserting that the name Leg Looks infringed on the L'eggs mark. Does Kayser-Roth's Leg Looks infringe on Sara Lee's L'eggs? Why or why not? [*Sara Lee Corp. v. Kayser-Roth Corp.,* 81 F.3d 455 (4th Cir. 1996)]

6–5. Trademark Infringement. Elvis Presley Enterprises, Inc. (EPE), owns all of the trademarks of the Elvis Presley estate. None of these marks is registered for use in the restaurant business. Barry Capece registered "The Velvet Elvis" as a service mark for a restaurant and tavern with the U.S. Patent and Trademark Office. Capece opened a nightclub called "The Velvet Elvis" with a menu, décor, advertising, and promotional events that evoked Elvis Presley and his music. EPE filed a suit in a federal district court against Capece and others, claiming, among other things, that "The Velvet Elvis" service mark infringed on EPE's trademarks. During the trial, witnesses testified that they thought the club was associated with Elvis Presley. Should Capece be ordered to stop using "The Velvet Elvis" mark? Why or why not? [*Elvis Presley Enterprises, Inc. v. Capece,* 141 F.3d 188 (5th Cir. 1998)]

6–6. Trademark Infringment. A&H Sportswear Co., a swimsuit maker, obtained a trademark for its MIRACLESUIT in 1992. The MIRACLESUIT design makes the wearer appear slimmer. The MIRACLESUIT was widely advertised and discussed in the media. The MIRACLESUIT was also sold for a brief time in the Victoria's Secret (VS) catalogue, which is published by Victoria's Secret Catalogue, Inc. In 1993, Victoria's Secret Stores, Inc., began selling a cleavage-enhancing bra, which was named THE MIRACLE BRA and for which a trademark was obtained. The next year, THE MIRACLE BRA swimwear debuted in the VS catalogue and stores. A&H filed a suit in a federal district court against VS Stores and VS Catalogue, alleging in part that THE MIRACLE BRA mark, when applied to swimwear, infringed on the MIRACLESUIT mark. A&H argued that there was a "possibility of confusion" between the marks. The VS entities contended that the appropriate standard was "likelihood of confusion" and that in this case, there was no likelihood of confusion. In whose favor will the court rule, and why? [*A&H Sportswear, Inc. v. Victoria's Secret Stores, Inc.,* 166 F.3d 197 (3d Cir. 1999)]

6–7. Cyber Marks. Playboy Enterprises, Inc. (PEI), owns the rights to the cyber marks "Playboy," "Playboy magazine," and "Playmate." Without authorization, Calvin Designer Label used the terms as meta tags for its Web sites on the Internet. As tags, the terms were invisible to viewers (in black type on a black background), but they caused the Web sites to be returned at the top of the list of a search engine query for "Playboy" or "Playmate." PEI filed a suit in a federal district court against Calvin Designer Label, alleging, among other things, trademark infringement. Should the court order the defendant to stop using the terms as tags? Why or why not? [*Playboy Enterprises, Inc. v. Calvin Designer Label,* 985 F.Supp. 1220 (N.D.Cal. 1997)]

WEB EXERCISES

Go to **http://lec.westbuslaw.com**, the Web site that accompanies this text. Select "Internet Applications," and then click on "Chapter 6." There you will find the following Internet research exercise that you can perform to learn more about intellectual property rights:

Activity 6–1: Gray-Market Goods

Unit 2

Management and E-Commerce

Contents

CHAPTER 7
E-Contracting

Concepts Covered

After reading this chapter, you should be able to:

1. Discuss the requirements for a valid contract and the kinds of circumstances in which contracts will not be enforceable.
2. Describe the remedies available to the innocent party when a contract is breached, or broken.
3. Define what constitutes an e-signature and the legal validity of such signatures.
4. Summarize the background and general coverage of the Uniform Computer Information Transactions Act (UCITA).
5. State some of the major provisions of the Uniform Electronic Transactions Act (UETA).

"The law of toasters, televisions, and chain saws is not appropriate for contracts involving online databases, artificial intelligence systems, software, multimedia, and Internet trade in information."

Prefatory Note
Uniform Computer Information Transactions Act

E-CONTRACT
A contract that is entered into in cyberspace and is evidenced only by electronic impulses (such as those that make up a computer's memory), rather than, for example, a typewritten form.

Contract law forms the basis for most commercial activity. This is as true for business in the computer industry, and in cyberspace in particular, as it is for business in general. E-commerce is a growing part of this commercial activity, with business-to-business (B2B) transactions estimated to soon exceed a trillion dollars annually.

The question is whether doing business in cyberspace creates any special contract problems or calls for any other changes in the law as it has traditionally been applied to contracts. Of course, the overriding goal should be to facilitate e-commerce.

Many observers argue that the development of cyberspace is revolutionary and new legal theories, and new law, are needed to govern **e-contracts**, or contracts entered into in e-commerce. To date, most courts have applied traditional common law principles to cases arising in the e-environment. In the first part of this chapter, we examine these principles of contract law. Then we turn to a discussion of some new laws that have been created to apply in situations in which traditional laws governing contracts have sometimes been thought inadequate.[1]

1. In the session of Congress in 2000, for example, more than four hundred bills were introduced that contained the word "Internet." Only a few of these were enacted, however, and most of those did not have much legal effect.

SECTION 1 THE LAW GOVERNING CONTRACTS

Although aspects of contract law vary from state to state, much of it is based on the common law. In 1932, the American Law Institute compiled the *Restatement of the Law of Contracts*. This work is a nonstatutory, authoritative exposition of the present law on the subject of contracts and is currently in its second edition (although a third edition is in the process of being drafted). Often, the second edition of the *Restatement of the Law of Contracts* is referred to simply as the *Restatement (Second) of Contracts*.

Article 2 of the Uniform Commercial Code (UCC), which governs **sales contracts** (contracts for the sale of goods), occasionally departs from common law contract rules. Generally, the different treatment of contracts falling under the UCC stems from the general policy of encouraging commerce. To the extent that the common law has not been modified by the UCC, however, the common law of contracts also applies to sales contracts. For example, the common law requirements for a valid contract, which will be discussed shortly, are also applicable to sales contracts. In general, the rule is that whenever there is a conflict between a common law contract rule and the UCC, the UCC controls. In other words, when a UCC provision addresses a certain issue, the UCC governs; when the UCC is silent, the common law governs. In the discussion of the common law of contracts that follows, we indicate some of the ways in which the UCC significantly changes the common law with respect to sales contracts.

With respect to Article 2, keep in mind that this article deals with the sale of *goods;* it does not deal with real property (real estate), services, or intangible property such as stocks and bonds. Thus, if the subject matter of a dispute is goods, the UCC governs. If it is real estate or services, the common law applies. The relationship between general contract law and the law governing sales of goods is illustrated in Exhibit 7–1 on the next page.

On the Web

For information on the *Restatements of the Law,* including the *Restatement (Second) of Contracts,* go to the American Law Institute's Web site at **http://www.ali.org**.

SALES CONTRACT
A contract for the sale of goods under which the ownership of goods is transferred from a seller to a buyer for a price.

On the Web

You can access the Uniform Commercial Code (UCC), including Article 2, at the Web site of the University of Pennsylvania Law School. Go to **http://www.law.upenn.edu/bll/ulc/ulc.htm**.

SECTION 2 CONTRACT FORMATION

According to the *Restatement (Second) of Contracts,* a **contract** is "a promise or a set of promises for the breach of which the law gives a remedy, or the performance of which the law in some way recognizes as a duty."[2] A **promise** is an assurance that one will or will not do something in the future. Simply put, a contract is any agreement (based on a promise or an exchange of promises) that can be enforced in court.

To form a valid contract, several requirements must be met. The parties must agree to form a contract, consideration (something of value) must be received or promised, the parties must have contractual capacity, and the contract must be formed for a legal purpose. We look next at each of these requirements.

CONTRACT
An agreement that can be enforced in court; formed by two or more parties, each of whom agrees to perform or to refrain from performing some act now or in the future.

PROMISE
A declaration that something either will or will not happen in the future.

Agreement

An essential element for contract formation is **agreement**—the parties must agree on the terms of the contract and manifest to each other their mutual assent to the same bargain. Ordinarily, agreement is evidenced by two events: an *offer*

AGREEMENT
A meeting of two or more minds in regard to the terms of a contract; usually broken down into two events—an offer by one party to form a contract, and an acceptance of the offer by the person to whom the offer is made.

2. *Restatement (Second) of Contracts.*

EXHIBIT 7–1 The Law Governing Contracts

This exhibit graphically illustrates the relationship between general contract law and the law governing contracts for the sale of goods. Sales contracts are not governed exclusively by Article 2 of the Uniform Commercial Code but are also governed by general contract law whenever it is relevant and has not been modified by the UCC.

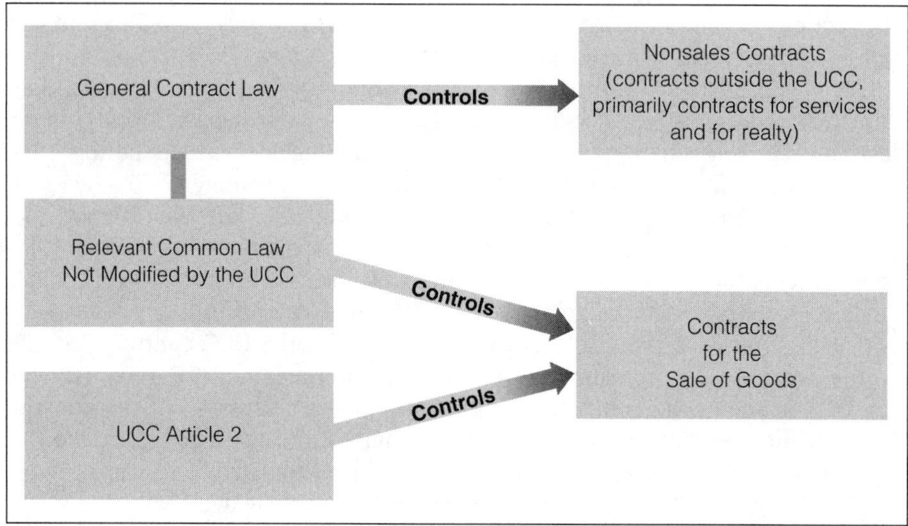

and an *acceptance*. One party offers a certain bargain to another party, who then accepts that bargain.

OFFER
A promise or commitment to perform or refrain from performing some specified act in the future.

OFFEROR
A person who makes an offer.

OFFEREE
A person to whom an offer is made.

OFFER An **offer** is a promise or commitment to do or refrain from doing some specified thing in the future. Three elements are necessary for an offer to be effective:

- The **offeror** (the party making the offer) must have a serious intention to become bound by the offer.
- The terms of the offer must be reasonably certain, or definite, so that the parties and the court can ascertain the terms of the contract. (Note that in contracts for the sale of goods, the UCC relaxes the requirement of definiteness somewhat by stating that a contract can still arise even if certain terms, such as price and delivery terms, are left "open," or unspecified.[3])
- The offer must be communicated by the offeror to the **offeree** (the party to whom the offer is made), resulting in the offeree's knowledge of the offer.

The communication of an effective offer to an offeree gives the offeree the power to transform the offer into a legally binding contract by an acceptance—provided, of course, that the other requirements for a valid contract are met. The offeree, naturally, also has the option of rejecting the offer or rejecting the offer and simultaneously making another offer, called a counteroffer. In a counter-

3. See Section 204 of UCC Article 2—or, as citations to the UCC are usually given, UCC 2–204. You can access the UCC and its provisions by going to the Web site given earlier in this chapter in an *On the Web* section.

offer, the offeree becomes the offeror—offering to form a contract with different terms. For example, suppose that Duffy offers to work for Wong for $50,000. Wong responds, "Your price is too high. I'll offer to hire you for $40,000." Wong's response is a counteroffer, because it terminates Duffy's offer and creates a new offer by Wong.

Both a rejection of the offer by the offeree or the making of a counteroffer by the offeree terminate the original offer. The original offer can also be terminated by the offeror by *revoking* (withdrawing) the offer (unless the offer is irrevocable)—but *only* if the revocation is accomplished before the offeree accepts the offer.[4] If the offeree has already accepted the offer, then both parties are bound in contract—the offeror cannot revoke the offer at this point. Additionally, an offer will terminate automatically by law in some circumstances, such as when the specific subject matter of the offer is destroyed, the offeror or offeree dies or becomes incompetent, or a new law is passed that makes the contract illegal. An offer will also terminate automatically by law when the period of time specified in the offer has passed, or, if no time for acceptance is specified in the offer, when a *reasonable* period of time has passed. What constitutes a reasonable period of time depends on the subject matter of the contract, business and market conditions, and other relevant circumstances.

The 'Lectric Law Library provides information on contract law, including a definition of a contract, the elements required for a contract, and so on, at the Laypeople's Law Lounge, through the link "Contracts," at **http://www.lectlaw.com**.

ACCEPTANCE As mentioned, an offeree's **acceptance** of an offer results in a legally binding contract (if all of the other elements of a valid contract are present). One requirement of an acceptance is that it be *unequivocal.* In other words, the terms of the offer must be accepted exactly as stated by the offeror. This principle of contract law is known as the **mirror image rule**—the terms of the acceptance must be the same as ("mirror") the terms of the offer. If the acceptance is subject to new conditions or if the terms of the acceptance materially change the original offer, the acceptance may be deemed a counteroffer that implicitly rejects the original offer. One of the ways in which the UCC has significantly modified the common law of contracts is by providing that an offeree's inclusion of additional terms in an acceptance will not necessarily prevent a contract from being formed.[5]

Another requirement, for most types of contracts, is that the acceptance be communicated to the offeror. A significant problem with respect to contract formation has to do with the timeliness of acceptances. The general rule is that acceptance of an offer is timely if it is made before the offer is terminated. Problems arise, however, when the parties involved are not dealing face to face. In such cases, acceptance takes effect at the time the acceptance is communicated via the mode expressly or impliedly authorized by the offeror. This is the **mailbox rule.** Under this rule, if the communication is sent by an authorized medium, an acceptance becomes valid when it is sent (even if it is never received by the offeror).

ACCEPTANCE
(1) In contract law, the offeree's notification to the offeror that the offeree agrees to be bound by the terms of the offeror's proposal. Although historically the terms of acceptance had to be the mirror image of the terms of the offer, the Uniform Commercial Code provides that even modified terms of the offer in a definite expression of acceptance constitute a contract. (2) In negotiable instruments law, the drawee's signed agreement to pay a draft when presented.

MIRROR IMAGE RULE
A common law rule that requires, for a valid contractual agreement, that the terms of the offeree's acceptance adhere exactly to the terms of the offeror's offer.

MAILBOX RULE
A rule providing that an acceptance of an offer becomes effective on dispatch (on being placed in a mailbox), if mail is, expressly or impliedly, an authorized means of communication of acceptance to the offeror.

4. "Irrevocable" offers cannot be revoked by the offeror. Irrevocable offers include the option cotnract, in which the offeror promises to hold the offer open for a specified period of time in return for a payment, and the "merchant's firm offer," which arises when a merchant-offeror gives assurances in a signed writing that the offer will remain open during a time period stated in the offer or, if no time period is stated, for a reasonable period of time (limited to three months).

5. See UCC 2–207, which provides that a contract for the sale of goods is formed if the offeree makes a definite expression of acceptance (such as signing the form in the appropriate location), even though the terms of the acceptance modify or add to the terms of the original offer.

Most offerors do not indicate expressly their preferred method of acceptance. In those cases, acceptance of an offer may be made by any medium that is *reasonable under the circumstances.* Several factors determine whether the acceptance was reasonable: the nature of the circumstances at the time the offer was made, the means used by the offeror to transmit the offer, and the reliability of the offer's delivery. If, for example, an offer was sent by FedEx overnight delivery because an acceptance was urgently required, the offeree's attempt to accept by fax would be deemed reasonable. In the e-contracting environment, the issues of the timeliness and method of acceptance may not arise. This is because persons often accept online offers simply by clicking on a box stating "I agree" or "I accept." Such **click-on agreements** are becoming widely used with the expansion of e-commerce and the formation of contracts online.

CLICK-ON AGREEMENT
This occurs when a buyer, completing a transaction on a computer, is required to indicate his or her assent to be bound by the terms of an offer by clicking on a button that says, for example, "I agree." Sometimes referred to as a *click-on license* or a *click-wrap agreement.*

Consideration

Another requirement for a valid contract is consideration. **Consideration** is usually defined as the value (such as money) given in return for a promise (such as the promise to sell a stamp collection on receipt of payment). No promise is enforceable without consideration.

CONSIDERATION
Generally, the value given in return for a promise. The consideration, which must be present to make the contract legally binding, must be something of legally sufficient value and bargained for and must result in a detriment to the promisee or a benefit to the promisor.

Often, consideration is broken down into two parts: (1) something of *legal value* must be given in exchange for the promise, and (2) there must be a *bargained-for* exchange. The "something of legal value" may consist of a return promise that is bargained for. It may also consist of performance, which may be an act, a forbearance (refraining from action), or the creation, modification, or destruction of a legal relation.

Once a contract has been formed, the general common law rule is that the terms of the contract cannot be modified without further consideration. The UCC, however, states that an agreement modifying a contract for the sale of goods "needs no consideration to be binding."[6]

On the Web

To learn more about how the courts decide such issues as whether consideration was lacking for a particular contract, look at relevant case law, which can be accessed through Cornell University's School of Law site at **http://www.law.cornell.edu/topics/contracts.htm**.

LEGAL SUFFICIENCY OF CONSIDERATION For a binding contract to be created, consideration must be *legally sufficient.* To be legally sufficient, consideration for a promise must be either *legally detrimental to the promisee* or *legally beneficial to the promisor.* A party can incur legal detriment by either promising to give legal value (such as the payment of money) or by a forbearance or a promise of forbearance—that is, by refraining from or promising to refrain from doing something that the party had a legal right to do.

ADEQUACY OF CONSIDERATION Adequacy of consideration refers to the fairness of the bargain. In general, a court will not question the adequacy of consideration if the consideration is legally sufficient. Parties are normally free to bargain as they wish. If people could sue merely because they had entered into an unwise contract, the courts would be overloaded with frivolous suits.

In extreme cases, a court may consider the adequacy of consideration in terms of its amount or worth because inadequate consideration may indicate fraud, duress, undue influence, or a lack of bargained-for exchange. It may also

6. See UCC 2-209.

reflect a party's incompetence (for example, an individual might have been too intoxicated or simply too young to make a contract).

PROMISSORY ESTOPPEL In some circumstances, contracts will be enforced even though consideration is lacking. Under the doctrine of **promissory estoppel**, a person who has reasonably and substantially relied on the promise of another may be able to obtain some measure of recovery. The following elements are required:

PROMISSORY ESTOPPEL
A doctrine that applies when a promisor makes a clear and definite promise on which the promisee justifiably relies; such a promise is binding if justice will be better served by the enforcement of the promise. *See also* Estoppel

1. There must be a clear and definite promise.
2. The promisee must justifiably rely on the promise.
3. The reliance normally must be of a substantial and definite character.
4. Justice will be better served by enforcement of the promise.

If these requirements are met, a promise may be enforced even though it is not supported by consideration. In essence, the promisor will be *estopped* (prevented) from asserting the lack of consideration as a defense. For example, suppose that your uncle tells you, "I'll pay you $150 a week so you won't have to work anymore." In reliance on your uncle's promise, you quit your job, but your uncle refuses to pay you. Under the doctrine of promissory estoppel, you may be able to enforce such a promise.[7]

Capacity

For a contract to be deemed valid, the parties to the contract must have **contractual capacity**—the legal ability to enter into a contractual relationship. Courts generally presume the existence of contractual capacity, but there are some situations in which capacity is lacking or may be questionable. In many situations, a party may have the capacity to enter into a valid contract but also have the right to avoid liability under it.

CONTRACTUAL CAPACITY
The threshold mental capacity required by the law for a party who enters into a contract to be bound by that contract.

Minors usually are not legally bound by contracts. Subject to certain exceptions, the contracts entered into by a minor are *voidable* (capable of being canceled, or avoided) at the option of that minor. The minor has the option of *disaffirming* (renouncing) the contract and setting aside the contract and all legal obligations arising from it. An adult who enters into a contract with a minor, however, cannot avoid his or her contractual duties on the ground that the minor can do so. Unless the minor exercises the option to disaffirm the contract, the adult party is bound by it.

Intoxication is a condition in which a person's normal capacity to act or think is inhibited by alcohol or some other drug. If the person was sufficiently intoxicated to lack mental capacity, the transaction is voidable at the option of the intoxicated person even if the intoxication was purely voluntary.

If a person has been adjudged mentally incompetent by a court of law and a guardian has been appointed, any contract made by the mentally incompetent person is *void*—no contract exists. Only the guardian can enter into binding legal duties on the incompetent person's behalf.

7. *Ricketts v. Scothorn*, 57 Neb. 51, 77 N.W. 365 (1898).

Legality

A contract to do something that is prohibited by federal or state statutory law is illegal and, as such, void from the outset and thus unenforceable. For example, all states require that members of certain professions or occupations—including physicians, lawyers, real estate brokers, architects, electricians, and stockbrokers—obtain licenses allowing them to practice.

When a person enters into a contract with an unlicensed individual, the contract may still be enforceable, depending on the nature of the licensing statute. Some states expressly provide that the lack of a license in certain occupations bars the enforcement of work-related contracts. If the statute does not expressly declare this, one must look to the underlying purpose of the licensing requirements for a particular occupation. If the purpose is to protect the public from unauthorized practitioners, a contract involving an unlicensed individual normally is illegal and unenforceable. If the underlying purpose of the statute is to raise government revenues, however, a contract entered into with an unlicensed practitioner generally is enforceable—although the unlicensed person is usually fined.

Additionally, a contract that calls for a tortious act (the commission of a tort) is illegal and unenforceable. Some contracts, such as contracts that restrain trade (anticompetitive contracts) or contracts that are so oppressive to innocent parties that they "shock the conscience" of the court, are not enforceable; they are said to be contrary to public policy. In other words, these contracts will not be enforced because of the negative impact they would have on society.

SECTION 3 DEFENSES TO CONTRACT ENFORCEABILITY

A contract has been entered into by two parties with full legal capacity and for a legal purpose. The contract is supported by consideration. The contract thus meets the four requirements for a valid contract. Nonetheless, the contract may be unenforceable if the parties have not genuinely assented to its terms or if the contract is not in the proper form—such as in writing, if the law requires it to be in writing.

Genuineness of Assent

GENUINENESS OF ASSENT
Knowing and voluntary assent to the terms of a contract. If a contract is formed as a result of a mistake, misrepresentation, undue influence, or duress, genuineness of assent is lacking, and the contract will be voidable.

Lack of **genuineness of assent** can be used as a defense to the contract's enforceability. Genuineness of assent may be lacking because of a mistake, misrepresentation, undue influence, or duress.

MISTAKE It is important to distinguish between *mistakes of fact* and *mistakes of value or quality.* If a mistake concerns the future market value or quality of the object of the contract, the mistake is one of *value,* and the contract normally can be enforced by either party. Each party is considered to have assumed the risk that the value will change or prove to be different from what he or she thought. Without this rule, almost any party who did not receive what he or she considered a fair bargain could argue mistake.

Only a mistake of fact allows a contract to be avoided. Mistakes of fact occur in two forms—*unilateral* and *mutual (bilateral).* A unilateral mistake occurs when only one party to the contract makes a mistake as to some *material fact*—a fact important to the subject matter of the contract. The general rule is that a unilateral mistake does not afford the mistaken party any right to relief from the contract, although there are some exceptions to this rule. For example, if a contractor's bid was low because he or she made a mistake in addition when totaling the estimated costs, any contract resulting from the bid may be rescinded. (**Rescission** is the act of canceling, or nullifying, a contract.)

RESCISSION
A remedy whereby a contract is canceled and the parties are returned to the positions they occupied before the contract was made; may be effected through the mutual consent of the parties, by their conduct, or by court decree.

When *both* of the parties are mistaken about the same material fact, either party can rescind the contract. For example, if the parties to a contract attach materially different meanings to a contract term that is subject to more than one reasonable interpretation, their mutual misunderstanding may allow the contract to be rescinded.

FRAUDULENT MISREPRESENTATION When an innocent party is fraudulently induced to enter into a contract, the contract usually can be avoided because that party has not *voluntarily* consented to its terms. Normally, the innocent party can either rescind the contract and be restored to his or her original position or enforce the contract and seek damages for any injuries resulting from the fraud.

Fraudulent misrepresentation occurs when one party to a contract misrepresents a material fact to the other party, with the intention of deceiving the other party, and the other party justifiably relies on the misrepresentation. To collect damages, a party must also have been injured. To obtain rescission of a contract, or to defend against the enforcement of a contract on the basis of fraudulent misrepresentation, in most states a party need not have suffered an injury.

FRAUDULENT MISREPRESENTATION (FRAUD)
Any misrepresentation, either by misstatement or omission of a material fact, knowingly made with the intention of deceiving another and on which a reasonable person would and does rely to his or her detriment.

Justifiable reliance on misrepresented facts is at issue in the following case, which involved the following questions: Is a job applicant justified in relying on a prospective employer's glowing statements about the future of the employer's business? Would it make any difference if an offered position were "at will"—that is, if the job could be terminated by either employee or employer at any time for any reason?

CASE 7.1 Meade v. Cedarapids, Inc.

United States Court of Appeals, Ninth Circuit, 1999.
164 F.3d 1218.
http://www.ca9.uscourts.gov [a]

BACKGROUND AND FACTS William Meade, Leland Stewart, Doug Vierkant, and David Girard applied for, and were offered, jobs at the El-Jay Division of Cedarapids, Inc., in Eugene, Oregon. During the interviews, each applicant asked about El-Jay's future. They were told, among other things, that El-Jay was a stable company with few downsizings and layoffs, sales were up and were expected to increase, and production was expanding. Cedarapids management had already planned to close El-Jay, however. Each applicant signed an at-will employment agreement. To take the job at El-Jay, each new employee either quit his present job or passed up other employment opportunities. Each employee and his family then moved to Eugene. When El-Jay closed soon after they started their new jobs, Meade and the others filed a suit in a federal district court against Cedarapids, alleging, in part, fraudulent misrepresentation, based on the statements made to them during their job interviews. The court granted a summary judgment in favor of Cedarapids. The plaintiffs appealed to the U.S. Court of Appeals for the Ninth Circuit.

a. Click on the "OPINIONS" oval. From that page, click on "1999," and when the menu opens, click on "January." Scroll down to the case name and click on it to access the case.

CASE 7.1–Continued

IN THE LANGUAGE OF THE COURT. . .
EZRA, * * * Judge:

* * * *

The district court held that Plaintiffs were not justified in relying on representations and omissions made during their pre-employment negotiations, as a matter of law, because Plaintiffs each signed an at-will employment agreement. That Plaintiffs' employment with Defendants was at-will does not defeat their justified reliance on Defendants' representations about El-Jay. Even in the presence of language stating "no promises about employment have been made," an action for fraud in the inducement of a contract is possible. The representation Plaintiffs relied upon in this case is that El-Jay was growing and expanding. Plaintiffs were not relying on representations as to the duration of their employment. Plaintiffs accepted at-will employment, but they accepted at-will employment with a company that represented its Eugene facility as growing while failing to disclose and/or concealing that it was closing.

Furthermore, Plaintiffs contend that their injuries were suffered as a result of the fraudulent inducement to enter employment, not the premature termination of that employment. The district court apparently treated the claims as breach of contract claims rather than claims of fraudulent inducement to form a contract.

Finally, Plaintiffs maintain that allowing at-will employment to defeat Plaintiffs' reliance would effectively allow employers to make any representations to prospective employees and then not fulfill those representations once employment began. We agree. Although Plaintiffs had no reasonable expectations for employment of any particular duration, they reasonably relied on statements as to the company's future growth, particularly when given in response to Plaintiffs' concerns. If Plaintiffs can prove Defendants' representations were knowingly or recklessly false, then a reasonable trier of fact could find the requisite elements of the tort of fraudulent misrepresentation.

DECISION AND REMEDY The U.S. Court of Appeals for the Ninth Circuit reversed the lower court's grant of summary judgment in favor of the defendants on the claim of fraudulent misrepresentation and remanded the case for further proceedings. An employer may be held liable for misrepresenting its future business plans to prospective employees.

FOR CRITICAL ANALYSIS–Social Consideration *Suppose that one of the plaintiffs had learned from a reliable source (outside of El-Jay) that Cedarapids management planned to close the El-Jay division. Would that plaintiff still have a cause of action for fraudulent misrepresentation? Why or why not?*

UNDUE INFLUENCE Undue influence arises from special kinds of relationships in which one party can greatly influence another party, thus overcoming that party's free will. Undue influence can arise from a number of confidential or fiduciary relationships:[8] attorney-client, physician-patient, guardian-ward, parent-child, husband-wife, or trustee-beneficiary. The essential feature of undue influence is that the party being taken advantage of does not, in reality,

8. A *fiduciary relationship* is one involving a high degree of trust and confidence.

exercise free will in entering into a contract. A contract entered into under excessive or undue influence lacks genuine assent and is therefore voidable.

DURESS Assent to the terms of a contract is not genuine if one of the parties is *forced* into the agreement. Forcing a party to do something, including entering into a contract, through fear created by threats is legally defined as *duress*. In addition, blackmail or extortion to induce consent to a contract constitutes duress. Duress is both a defense to the enforcement of a contract and a ground for the rescission of a contract.

Professor Eric Talley of the University of Southern California provides an interesting discussion of the history and current applicability of the Statute of Frauds, both internationally and in the United States, at **http://www-bcf. usc.edu/~etalley/frauds.html**.

The Statute of Frauds

An otherwise valid contract may be unenforceable if it is not in the proper form. For example, certain types of contracts are required to be in writing. If a contract is required by law to be in writing and there is no written evidence of the contract, it may not be enforceable.

Almost every state has a statute that stipulates what types of contracts must be in writing or be evidenced by a written memorandum signed by the party against whom enforcement is sought, unless certain exceptions apply. This statute is commonly referred to as the **Statute of Frauds.**[9]

STATUTE OF FRAUDS
A state statute under which certain types of contracts must be in writing to be enforceable.

The following types of contracts are said to fall "within" or "under" the Statute of Frauds and therefore require a writing:

1. Contracts involving interests in land.
2. Contracts that cannot by their terms be performed within one year from the date of formation.
3. Collateral, or secondary, contracts, such as promises to answer for the debt or duty of another and promises by the administrator or executor of an estate to pay a debt of the estate personally—that is, out of his or her own pocket.
4. Promises made in consideration of marriage.
5. Under the Uniform Commercial Code (UCC), contracts for the sale of goods priced at $500 or more.[10]

In some states, an oral contract that would otherwise be unenforceable under the Statute of Frauds may be enforced under the doctrine of promissory estoppel, based on detrimental reliance. Recall that if a promisor makes a promise on which the promisee justifiably relies to his or her detriment, a court may *estop* (prevent) the promisor from denying that a contract exists. In these circumstances, an oral promise can be enforceable notwithstanding the Statute of Frauds if the reliance was foreseeable to the person making the promise and if injustice can be avoided only by enforcing the promise.

A number of cases involving the Statute of Frauds have to do with the second item listed above—contracts that cannot by their terms be performed within

9. The name is misleading because the statute neither applies to fraud nor invalidates any type of contract. Rather, it denies *enforceability* to certain contracts that do not comply with its requirements.

10. The UCC provides for some exceptions to this rule. For example, if a contract requires goods to be specially manufactured for the buyer, the contract may be enforceable in some circumstances. Additionally, the UCC's "partial performance" exception provides that an oral contract for the sale of goods is enforceable to the extent that performance actually took place—that is, to the extent payment has been made and accepted or that goods have been received and accepted. See UCC 2-201(3).

one year from the date of formation. The test for determining whether an oral contract is enforceable under this "one-year rule" is not whether an agreement is *likely* to be performed within a year but whether performance is *possible* within one year. In the following case, the question before the court was whether an oral contract for lifetime employment was enforceable.

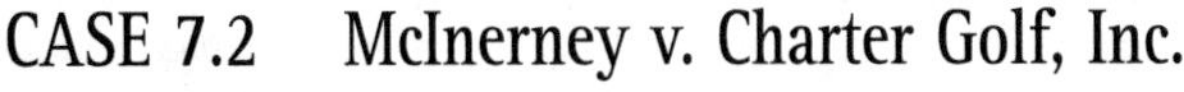

CASE 7.2 McInerney v. Charter Golf, Inc.

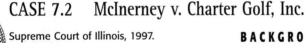

Supreme Court of Illinois, 1997.
176 Ill.2d 482,
680 N.E.2d 1347,
223 Ill.Dec. 911.
http://www.state.il.us/court/Opinions/SupremeCourt/1997/May/Opinions/HTML/80248.txt[a]

HISTORICAL AND SOCIAL SETTING *The purpose of the English Statute of Frauds was to prohibit "many fraudulent practices, which are commonly endeavored to be upheld by perjury and subordination of perjury." The statutes of frauds in the United States seek to do the same by barring lawsuits based on nothing more than verbal statements. The one-year provision recognizes that with the passage of time evidence becomes stale and memories fade. This provision protects not just the parties to a contract but also the courts from charlatans, liars, and the problems of proof accompanying oral contracts.*

a. This is a page within a Web site maintained by the state of Illinois that includes some of the recent "Opinions of the Illinois Supreme and Appellate Courts."

BACKGROUND AND FACTS Charter Golf, Inc., manufactures and sells golf apparel and supplies. Dennis McInerney had worked as a Charter sales representative for about a year when he was offered a position with Hickey-Freeman, Inc., one of Charter's competitors. Jerry Montiel, Charter's president, urged McInerney to turn down the offer and promised to guarantee him a 10 percent commission "for the remainder of his life." Montiel also promised McInerney that he would be subject to discharge only for dishonesty or disability. McInerney accepted Montiel's offer. Three years later, Charter fired McInerney. He filed a suit in an Illinois state court against Charter, alleging breach of contract. Charter argued in part that Montiel's oral promises were not enforceable because they were not capable of being performed within one year. The trial court ruled in favor of Charter, and the state intermediate appellate court affirmed. McInerney appealed to the Supreme Court of Illinois.

IN THE LANGUAGE OF THE COURT. . .
Justice *HEIPLE* delivered the opinion of the court:

* * * *

* * * A "lifetime" employment contract is, in essence, a permanent employment contract. Inherently, it anticipates a relationship of long duration—certainly longer than one year. In the context of an employment-for-life contract, we believe that the better view is to treat the contract as one not to be performed within the space of one year from the making thereof. To hold otherwise would eviscerate [remove the essence from] the policy underlying the statute of frauds and would invite confusion, uncertainty, and outright fraud. Accordingly, we hold that a writing is required for the fair enforcement of lifetime employment contracts.

* * * *

In sum, though an employee's promise to forgo another job opportunity in exchange for a guarantee of lifetime employment is consideration to support the formation of a contract, the statute of frauds requires that contracts for lifetime employment be in writing.

DECISION AND REMEDY The Supreme Court of Illinois affirmed the lower court's decision. The state supreme court held that an employer's promise of lifetime employment in exchange for an employee's promise to forgo a job opportunity needs to be in writing to satisfy the Statute of Frauds.

FOR CRITICAL ANALYSIS–Social Consideration *If the Statute of Frauds were repealed—as it has been in some countries—what might be the effects on the outcomes of cases such as McInerney's?*

SECTION 4 CONTRACT PERFORMANCE AND REMEDIES

There are several ways that one's contractual duties can be terminated. The most common way to terminate one's contractual duties, however, is by the **performance** of those duties. Failure to perform one's contractual duties as promised results in a **breach** of the contract. When one party breaches a contract, the other party (the nonbreaching party) can seek remedies.

PERFORMANCE
In contract law, the fulfillment of one's duties arising under a contract with another; the normal way of discharging one's contractual obligations.

BREACH
To violate a law, by an act or an omission, or to break a legal obligation that one owes to another person or to society.

Contract Performance

Conditions expressly stated in a contract must be fully satisfied for complete performance to take place. A party who in good faith performs substantially all of the terms of a contract, however, can usually enforce the contract against the other party under the doctrine of *substantial performance*. Generally, performance that provides a party with the important and essential benefits of a contract, in spite of any omission or deviation from the terms, is substantial performance.

Because substantial performance is not perfect, the other party is entitled to damages to compensate for the failure to comply with the contract. The measure of the damages is the cost to bring the object of the contract into compliance with its terms, if that cost is reasonable under the circumstances. If the cost is unreasonable, the measure of damages is the difference in value between the performance that was rendered and the performance that would have been rendered if the contract had been performed completely.

Law Guru can lead you to other sources of law relating to contract performance. Go to **http:lawguru.com/lawlinks.html**.

After a contract has been made, performance may become impossible in an objective sense. For example, the subject matter of the contract may be destroyed, one of the parties to a personal contract may die or become incapacitated prior to performance, or performance may become illegal due to a change in the law. In these situations, the law excuses parties from their contractual performance duties under what is known as the doctrine of *impossibility of performance*.

Under the doctrine of *commercial impracticability,* courts may excuse parties from their performance obligations when the performance becomes much more difficult or expensive than originally contemplated at the time the contract was formed. For someone to successfully invoke this doctrine, however, the anticipated performance must become *extremely* difficult or costly.

Contract Remedies

A *remedy* is the relief provided for an innocent party when the other party has breached the contract. It is the means employed to enforce a right or to redress an injury. The most common remedies available to a nonbreaching party include damages, rescission and restitution, and specific performance.[11]

DAMAGES
Money sought as a remedy for a breach of contract or for a tortious act.

DAMAGES A breach of contract entitles the nonbreaching party to sue for money (damages). **Damages** are designed to compensate a party for the loss of the bargain.[12] Generally, innocent parties are to be placed in the position they would have occupied had the contract been fully performed.[13] Damages compensating the nonbreaching party for the loss of the bargain are known as *compensatory damages.* These damages compensate the injured party only for damages actually sustained and proved to have arisen directly from the loss of the bargain caused by the breach of contract. They simply replace what was lost because of the wrong.

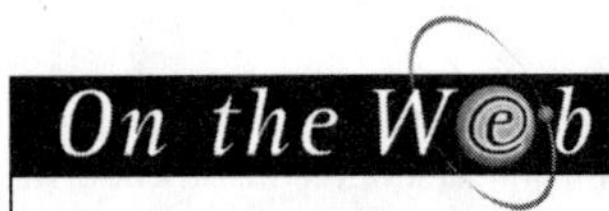

Information on contract law, including breach of contract and remedies, is available at **http://www.nolo.com/Chunkcm/CM9.html**.

The amount of compensatory damages is the difference between the value of the breaching party's promised performance and the value of his or her actual performance. This amount is reduced by any loss that the injured party has avoided, however. Expenses that are caused directly by a breach of contract—such as those incurred to obtain performance from another source—are known as *incidental damages.* For example, if you are hired to perform certain services during August for $3,000, but the employer breaches the contract and you find another job that pays only $500, you can recover $2,500 as compensatory damages, plus the expenses to find the other job as incidental damages.

Foreseeable damages that result from a party's breach of contract are called *consequential damages,* or *special damages.* They differ from compensatory damages in that they are caused by special circumstances beyond the contract itself. They flow from the consequences, or results, of a breach. To recover consequential damages, the breaching party must know (or have reason to know) that special circumstances will cause the nonbreaching party to suffer an additional loss.

RESCISSION AND RESTITUTION As already discussed, *rescission* is essentially an action to undo, or terminate, a contract—to return the contracting parties to the positions they occupied prior to the transaction. When fraud, a mistake, duress, undue influence, misrepresentation, or lack of capacity to contract is present, unilateral rescission is available as a remedy. The failure of one party to perform entitles the other party to rescind the contract. Generally, to rescind a contract, both parties must make *restitution* to each other by returning goods, property, or money previously conveyed.

SPECIFIC PERFORMANCE
An equitable remedy requiring exactly the performance that was specified in a contract; usually granted only when money damages would be an inadequate remedy and the subject matter of the contract is unique (for example, real property).

SPECIFIC PERFORMANCE The equitable remedy of **specific performance** calls for the performance of the act promised in the contract. Normally, however, spe-

11. UCC Article 2 contains several provisions applying to remedies available when a sales contract is breached. See the sections included in Parts 6 and 7 of Article 2.

12. Bear in mind that although a nonbreaching party may succeed in obtaining damages from a court from the breaching party, the court's judgment may be difficult to enforce. The breaching party may not have sufficient funds or assets to pay the damages awarded.

13. *Hawkins v. McGee,* 84 N.H. 114, 146 A. 641 (1929).

cific performance will not be granted unless the party's legal remedy (money damages) is inadequate. For this reason, contracts for the sale of goods rarely qualify for specific performance—substantially identical goods can be bought or sold in the market. If the goods are unique, however, such as in a case involving a painting or a rare book, a court of equity will decree specific performance.

Generally, courts refuse to grant specific performance of personal-service contracts—contracts that require one party to work personally for another party. Public policy strongly discourages involuntary servitude.[14] Moreover, the courts do not want to have to monitor a continuing service contract if supervision would be difficult—as it would be if the contract required the exercise of personal judgment or talent. A court cannot assure meaningful performance in such a situation.[15]

SECTION 5 E-SIGNATURES

In many cases a contract, to be enforced, requires the signature of the party against whom enforcement is sought. A significant issue in the context of e-commerce has to do with how electronic signatures, or **e-signatures**, can be created and verified on e-contracts.

E-SIGNATURE
An electronic sound, symbol, or process attached to or logically associated with a record and executed or adopted by a person with the intent to sign the record, according to the Uniform Electronic Transactions Act.

Before the days when most people could write, they signed documents with an "X." Then came the handwritten signature, followed by typed signatures, printed signatures, and, most recently, digital signatures that are transmitted electronically. Throughout the evolution of signature technology, debates over what constitutes a valid signature have occurred, and with good reason—without some consensus on what constitutes a valid signature, little business or legal work could be accomplished.

E-Signature Technologies

Today, there are numerous technologies that allow electronic documents to be signed. These include digital signatures and alternative technologies.

The most prevalent e-signature technology is the *asymmetric cryptosystem,* which creates a digital signature using two different (asymmetric) cryptographic "keys." In such a system, a person attaches a digital signature to a document using a private key, or code. The key has a publicly available counterpart. Anyone can use it with the appropriate software to verify that the digital signature was made using the private key. A **cybernotary**, or legally recognized certification authority, issues the key pair, identifies the owner of the keys, and certifies the validity of the public key. The cybernotary also serves as a repository for public keys. Cybernotaries already are available, but they do not operate within any existing legal framework because they are so new.

CYBERNOTARY
A legally recognized certification authority that issues the keys for digital signatures, identifies their owners, certifies their validity, and serves as a repository for public keys.

Another type of signature technology, known as *signature dynamics,* involves capturing a sender's signature using a stylus and an electronic digitizer pad. A

14. The Thirteenth Amendment to the U.S. Constitution prohibits involuntary servitude, and thus a court will not order a person to perform under a personal-service contract. A court may grant an order (injunction) prohibiting that person from engaging in similar contracts in the future for a period of time, however.

15. Similarly, courts often refuse to order specific performance of construction contracts because courts are not set up to operate as construction supervisors or engineers.

computer program takes the signature's measurements, the sender's identity, the time and date of the signature, and the identity of the hardware. This information is then placed in an encrypted *biometric token* attached to the document being transmitted. To verify the authenticity of the signature, the recipient of the document compares the measurements of the signature with the measurements in the token. When this type of e-signature is used, it is not necessary to have a third party verify the signatory's identity.

Other forms of e-signature have been—or are now being—developed as well. For example, some e-signatures use "smart cards." A smart card is a credit-card–size device that is embedded with code and other data. As with credit and debit cards, this smart card can be inserted into computers to transfer information. Unlike those other cards, however, a smart card could be used to establish a person's identity as validly as a signature on a piece of paper. In addition, technological innovations now under way will allow an e-signature to be evidenced by an image of one's retina, fingerprint, or face that is scanned by a computer and then matched to a numeric code. The scanned image and the numeric code are registered with security companies that maintain files on an accessible server that can be used to authenticate a transaction.

State Laws Governing E-Signatures

Most states have laws governing e-signatures. The problem is that the state e-signature laws are not uniform. Some states—California is a notable example—provide that many types of documents cannot be signed with e-signatures, while other states are more permissive in this respect. Additionally, some states recognize the validity of only digital signatures, while others permit other types of e-signatures.

In an attempt to create more uniformity among the states, the National Conference of Commissioners on Uniform State Laws promulgated the Uniform Electronic Transactions Act (UETA) in 1999. The UETA defines an *e-signature* as "an electronic sound, symbol, or process attached to or logically associated with a record and executed or adopted by a person with the intent to sign the record."[16] A **record** is "information that is inscribed on a tangible medium or that is stored in electronic or other medium and is retrievable in perceivable form."[17]

RECORD
Information that is either inscribed in a tangible medium or stored in an electronic or other medium and that is retrievable, according to the Uniform Electronic Transactions Act. The Uniform Computer Information Transactions Act uses *record* instead of *writing*.

This definition of *e-signature* includes encrypted digital signatures, names (intended as signatures) at the ends of e-mail, and a click on a Web page if the click includes the identification of the person. The UETA also states, among other things, that a signature may not be denied legal effect or enforceability solely because it is in electronic form. (Other aspects of the UETA are discussed later in this chapter.)

Federal Law on E-Signatures and E-Documents

In 2000, Congress enacted the Electronic Signatures in Global and National Commerce Act (E-SIGN Act) to provide that no contract, record, or signature

16. UETA 102(8).
17. UETA 102(15).

may be "denied legal effect" solely because it is in an electronic form. In other words, under this law, an electronic signature is as valid as a signature on paper, and an electronic document can be as enforceable as a paper one.

For an electronic signature to be enforceable, the contracting parties must have agreed to use electronic signatures. For an electronic document to be valid, it must be in a form that can be retained and accurately reproduced.

Contracts and documents that are exempt include court papers, divorce decrees, evictions, foreclosures, health-insurance terminations, prenuptial agreements, and wills. Also, the only agreements governed by the Uniform Commercial Code (UCC) that fall under this law are those covered by Articles 2 and 2A, and UCC 1–107 and 1–206.

Despite the limitations, the E-SIGN Act expands enormously the possibilities for contracting online. From a remote location, a businessperson might open an account with a financial institution, obtain a mortgage or other loan, buy insurance, and purchase real estate over the Internet. Payments and transfers of funds could be done entirely online. This can avoid the time and costs associated with producing, delivering, signing, and returning paper documents. (See this chapter's *E-Guidelines* on the next page for a further discussion of the E-SIGN Act and its implications for e-commerce.)

SECTION 6 THE UNIFORM COMPUTER INFORMATION TRANSACTIONS ACT

Among the proposed new laws that go beyond the existing law is the Uniform Computer Information Transactions Act (UCITA). The UCITA is a draft of legislation suggested to the states by the National Conference of Commissioners on Uniform State Laws (NCCUSL) and the American Law Institute (ALI). These organizations have initiated many of the most significant laws that apply to traditional commerce, including the Uniform Commercial Code (UCC).

The UCITA's History

In the early 1990s, with the continued development of the software industry, it became apparent that Article 2 of the Uniform Commercial Code (UCC), which deals with the sale of goods (tangible property), could not be applied to most transactions involving software.

There are two basic reasons for this. First, software is not a "good" (tangible property)—it is electronic information (intangible property). Second, the "sale" of software generally involves a license (right to use) rather than a sale (passage of title from the seller to the purchaser). The producer of the software either directly contracted with the licensee (user) or used a distribution system—for example, authorizing retailers to distribute (sell) copies of the producer's software to customers (end users). Because neither involved the sale of goods, new rules needed to be established.

During the next eight years, the development of these new rules by a drafting committee of the NCCUSL were widely discussed and debated in a variety of forums. Controversy surrounded the proposed drafts, which probably engendered more comment from more groups than has any other proposed uniform act.

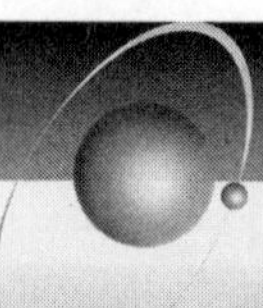

E-Guidelines

E-Signatures: What Lies Ahead?

Many have heralded the Electronic Signatures in Global and National Commerce Act (E-SIGN Act), which became effective October 1, 2000, as the single most important piece of technology legislation ever enacted. According to one observer, "Not since notarized written signatures replaced wax and signet rings has history seen such a fundamental change in contract law."[a] Perhaps to underscore the act's historic significance, President Clinton signed the act into law in Philadelphia, the city in which the U.S. Constitution was drafted over 224 years ago and signed with quill pens (in contrast to the digital signature used by President Clinton).

As discussed elsewhere in this chapter, the act provided that electronic signatures, or e-signatures, are legally valid and enforceable. Although a contract signed electronically may be invalid or unenforceable for other reasons, it cannot be deemed unenforceable merely because an electronic signature or electronic record was used in its formation.

a. Mark Ballard, "E-SIGN a Nudge, Not Revolution," *The National Law Journal*, September 25, 2000, p. B1.

Who Will Benefit from E-SIGN?

Today, business-to-consumer (B2C) transactions make up the bulk of Internet e-commerce traffic. Some predict that as a result of the E-SIGN Act, consumers will readily turn to the Internet to purchase even more items than they currently do, including homes, groceries, online novels, and the like. Yet until the online industry comes up with a system of obtaining and protecting digital signatures, and convincing consumers that they are safe and secure, consumers will be wary of using them.

Others believe that the real beneficiaries will be parties engaged in business-to-business (B2B) transactions, which can easily involve substantial sums and complicated agreements to be performed over time. By giving legal effect to e-signatures, the E-SIGN Act increased the acceptability of e-contracts and, because of the time and cost savings e-contracts generate, they will likely become much more widely used in the B2B marketplace.

What the Act Did Not Do

What the act did *not* do is provide any standard for authenticating e-signatures or include solutions to other problems associated with e-contracting. How will the technology be managed? What kind of signature verification process will be required? If encryption "keys" are

PROPOSED UCC ARTICLE 2B Initially, the drafters tried to modify Article 2 of the UCC to incorporate the licensing of goods with the sale of goods. In 1995, the NCCUSL decided that a separate article to be titled "Article 2B—Licenses" was needed. The drafting committee consisted of representatives of the NCCUSL and the ALI, members of the American Bar Association, and Professor Raymond T. Nimmer (University of Houston Law Center), who served as committee reporter. The first drafts issued by this committee covered the licensing of *all* information. A number of powerful industry groups, including broadcast groups, music associations, and print publishers, objected to this broad inclusion. As a result, the drafting committee narrowed the scope of Article 2B to the licensing of computer information only and retained coverage of electronic contracting.

A final proposed draft of Article 2B was published early in 1999. The ALI, which has approved and supported passage of all of the other articles of the UCC, rejected Article 2B. In April 1999, the NCCUSL and the ALI issued a press release stating that the draft would no longer be a proposed addition (Article 2B) to the UCC, but would be submitted as a separate uniform act entitled the Uniform Computer Information Transactions Act (UCITA).

E-Guidelines, Continued

used, how will they be generated? Where can you get one? Will there be digital notaries? What if a hacker or other technologically sophisticated person "steals" one's signature and "forges" electronic documents with it? Basically, the act left these and other questions to be decided by the parties to e-commerce contracts, the technology industry, and the states.

There is another problem. An element common to all valid signatures is that they evidence an *intent to be bound* by the document that is being signed. Section 1–201(39) of the Uniform Commercial Code, for example, provides that a signature may include "any symbol executed or adopted by a party with present intention to authenticate a writing." Thus, any symbol, including an X, a person's initials, or even a thumbprint, can suffice as a signature—but *only* if the symbol is used with the intention of authenticating the writing. Section 106(5) of the E-SIGN Act emphasizes the intent factor by defining an electronic signature as any "electronic sound, symbol, or process, attached to or logically associated with a contract or other record and executed or adopted by a person with the intent to sign the record." Yet how can intent be measured in the electronic-contracting environment? How do you know if an online party even has contractual capacity? Again, this question is left up to the parties and the states to decide.

A major goal of the E-SIGN Act was to encourage e-commerce through the use of electronic signatures. Yet the act itself does not accomplish this goal. More sigificant will be how quickly the states and the marketplace adopt uniform standards for authenticating e-signatures—as this technology is the key to the expansion of e-commerce.

CHECKLIST

- ☑ At the time the E-SIGN Act was passed, twenty-two states already had enacted some form of electronic-transactions laws, and another twenty-four states had addressed e-commerce contracts in some way. Before forming e-contracts, businesspersons should become aware of what the law is in their states with respect to electronic transactions.
- ☑ Businesspersons generally should also keep in mind what the E-SIGN Act did *not* do. As indicated above, certain contract elements, including the intent to be bound by a signature and the contractual capacity of the parties, may be difficult to determine when forming e-contracts. Thus, businesspersons should take steps to avoid problems in these areas when contracting in the online environment.

RECOMMENDATION TO THE STATES The NCCUSL, by removing the draft as a part of the UCC, could proceed on its own to recommend to the states that they enact the UCITA—ALI approval was not required. In July 1999, the delegates of the NCCUSL approved the draft, by a vote of forty-three to six, for submission to the states for adoption.

For more information about the current status of the UCITA, and to learn more about other uniform laws proposed by the NCCUSL, see the appendix at the end of this chapter about the NCCUSL's Web site.

OPPOSITION AND AMENDMENTS The UCITA, as it was proposed in 1999, met opposition from a number of industry associations, state insurance commissions, and consumer groups. In fact, the industry associations indicated that they would strongly oppose state adoptions. These industry associations included the Motion Picture Association of America, Magazine Publishers of America, the Newspaper Association of America, the National Cable Television Association, the National Association of Broadcasters, the Recording Industry Association of America, and the telecommunications industry. Perhaps this opposition contributed substantially to the fact that there were only two state adoptions in 1999.

Because of the resistance and the concerns of these groups, plus the need for clarity concerning whether transactions involving the relationships between an insured and the insurer were excluded, the NCCUSL worked out a package of amendments for passage in August 2000. These amendments basically excluded from the UCITA the business activities of the members of these industry organizations. On passage of the amendments, the associations agreed formally in writing to withdraw their opposition to the individual states' enactment of the UCITA.

Some consumer groups still oppose the passage of the UCITA. See this chapter's *Controversial Issues in the Online World* for a discussion of this issue.

The UCITA's Coverage and Content

COMPUTER INFORMATION
Information in electronic form obtained from or through use of a computer, or that is in digital or an equivalent form capable of being processed by a computer.

The UCITA establishes a comprehensive set of rules covering contracts involving computer information. **Computer information** is "information in electronic form obtained from or through use of a computer, or that is in digital or equivalent form capable of being processed by a computer."[18]

Under this definition, the act covers contracts to license or purchase software, contracts to create a computer program, contracts for computer games, contracts for online access to databases, contracts to distribute information on the Internet, "diskettes" that contain computer programs, online books, and other similar contracts.

THE UCITA MAY APPLY TO ONLY PART OF A TRANSACTION The UCITA does not apply generally to the sale of goods even if software is embedded in or used in the production of the goods (except a computer). Examples are television sets, stereos, books, and automobiles. It also does not apply to traditional movies, records, or cable. These industries are specifically excluded for the most part.

When a transaction includes computer information as defined in the act and subject matter other than computer information, the UCITA generally provides that if the primary subject matter deals with computer information rights, the act applies to the entire transaction. If this is not the primary subject matter, the act applies only to the part "of the transaction involving computer information, informational rights in it and creation or modification of it."

DEFAULT RULES
Rules that apply under the Uniform Computer Information Transactions Act only in the absence of an agreement between contracting parties to the contrary.

PARTIES CAN "OPT OUT" As with most other uniform acts that apply to business, the UCITA allows the parties to waive or vary the provisions of the act by a contract. The parties may even agree to "opt out" of the act and, for contracts not covered by the act, to "opt in." In other words, the UCITA expressly recognizes the freedom to contract and supports the idea that this is a basic principle of contract law.

The UCITA stresses the parties' agreement, but the act's provisions apply in the absence of an agreement.[19] These provisions are called **default rules.** As with

18. UCITA 102(10).
19. UCITA 113.

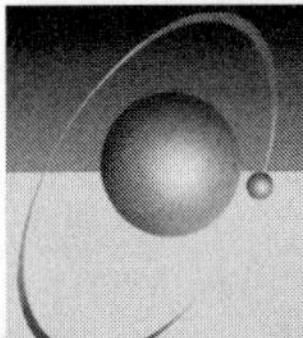

Controversial Issues in the Online World

Does the UCITA Favor the Software Industry over Consumers?

Some consumer groups argue that the UCITA favors the software industry and will have harsh effects for consumers. One of the initial concerns of these groups was the licensor's right of electronic self-help under the act. As you will read later in this chapter (see the discussion of electronic self-help on page 174), this concern was addressed by the August 2000 amendments. The Amendments prohibited the use of electronic self-help with respect to mass-market transactions—transactions involving consumer contracts or in which computer information is directed to the general public (mass-market transactions will be discussed shortly.

Notwithstanding these amendments, a number of consumer advocates continue to oppose the UCITA. Among other things, they object to the automatic enforceability of licensing agreements, including shrink-wrap and click-on agreements, which can easily go unread by consumers. Even in printed documents, consumers often do not take the time to read the "fine print." Consumer groups that object to the enforceability of licensing agreements claim that this problem is even more prevalent with shrink-wrap and click-on agreements. Also viewed as objectionable are the limits on the rights of a licensee when a licensor knows that licensed software contains serious defects.

FOR CRITICAL ANALYSIS

Some persons argue that the communications revolution brought about by the Internet and the rapid expansion of e-commerce empowers corporations, but not individuals—whose privacy and human connection with others will only be diminished. In what ways is this argument supported or undercut by the UCITA?

other uniform statutes, rules relating to good faith, diligence, public policy, unconscionability, and related principles cannot be varied or deleted by agreement.

RIGHTS AND RESTRICTIONS The licensing of information is the primary method used for transferring computer information in business today. A license contract involves a transfer of computer information, such as software, from a seller (the licensor) to a buyer (the licensee). The licensee is given certain rights to use and control the computer information during the license period. Title does not pass, and quite often the license places restrictions on the licensee's use of, and rights to copy and control, the computer information. Many of the sections of the UCITA deal with the rights and restrictions that can be imposed on the parties in the license.

FROM CONTRACT FORMATION TO CONTRACT REMEDIES The UCITA, which consists of nine "parts," covers everything from the formation of a contract to construction rules, warranties available, transfer of interests and financing arrangements, performance rules, breach of contract, and remedies. This arrangement resembles that of UCC Article 2. The UCITA's table of contents is shown in Exhibit 7–2 on the next page.

Highlights of the UCITA

The UCITA resembles UCC Article 2. Both acts have similar general provisions, including definitions (approximately sixty-six) and formal requirements (such as a Statute of Frauds, which, in the case of the UCITA, requires a written

EXHIBIT 7–2 UCITA's Table of Contents

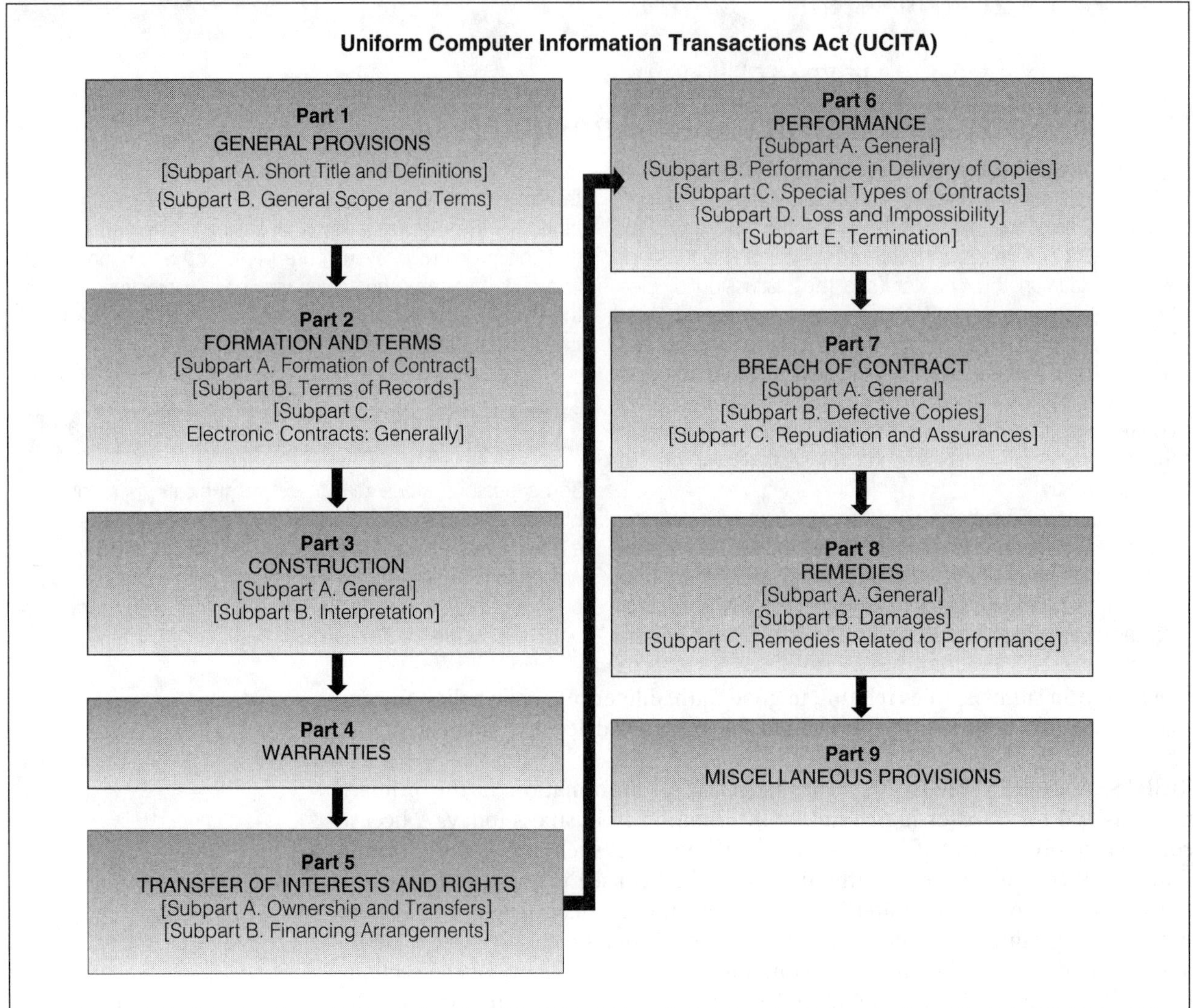

memorandum when a contract requires a payment of $5,000 or more). The UCITA also includes rules for offer and acceptance, as well as other provisions comparable to those found in Article 2.[20]

The UCITA goes further, however, with provisions covering the contracting parties' choice of law and choice of forum, the UCITA's relationship to federal law and other state laws, and many others.[21] These provisions make the UCITA more comprehensive in scope than UCC Article 2.

20. See, for example, UCITA 111.

21. See, for example, UCITA 109 and 110.

The next sections describe some of the UCITA's highlights. Note that most of them address situations that arise due to the unique nature of licensing computer information.

For a comprehensive review of the Uniform Computer Information Transactions Act, go to **http://www.ucitaonline.com**.

MASS-MARKET LICENSES Basically, a *mass-market* transaction is either (1) a consumer contract or (2) a transaction in which the computer information is directed to the general public and the end-user licensee acquires the information in a retail transaction.

A **mass-market license** is an electronic form contract that is usually presented along with a package of purchased computer information. These licenses are commonly received by having the license contract shrink-wrapped or, in the case of an online transaction, click-wrapped with the computer information (when the purchaser clicks on a certain link).

MASS-MARKET LICENSE
An e-contract that is presented with a package of computer information in the form of a click-on license or a shrink-wrap license.

These licenses are different from negotiated licenses in that mass-market licenses are automatically enforceable, as long as the terms are readily available and the licensee has had an opportunity to review the license terms.

If the licensee does not want the computer information for any reason, the UCITA allows the licensee to return the computer information for a refund and recover any reasonable expenses incurred in removing and returning the computer information. The UCITA provides that these rights of returning and entitlement to reasonable expenses cannot be waived or disclaimed by the licensor.

WARRANTIES Article 2 of the UCC provides for both express warranties and implied warranties. *Express warranties* are affirmations of fact that are made by a seller about a product being sold and that go to the basis of the bargain. Implied warranties arise in any sale of goods falling under UCC Article 2. The *implied warranty of merchantability* is a warranty that the goods being sold are reasonably fit for the general purpose for which they are sold. The *implied warranty of fitness for a particular purpose* is a warranty that the goods sold are fit for a particular purpose, if the buyer is relying on the seller's skill or judgment in selecting goods that are fit for the buyer's purpose. UCC Article 2 allows sellers to disclaim warranties, provided the disclaimers meet certain requirements set out in the UCC so that the buyer is fully aware of the disclaimers.[22]

The UCITA provides for basically the same warranties as Article 2. Thus, a licensor's affirmations of fact or promises concerning computer information (as a basis for the bargain) constitute express warranties.[23] Implied warranties are also provided for by the act (and can be disclaimed, as under UCC Article 2).[24] The UCITA's implied warranties of merchantability and fitness are closely tailored to the information's content and the "compatibility of the computer systems."[25]

AUTHENTICATION AND ATTRIBUTION Before the emergence of electronic contracting, parties generally knew each other, and many contracts contained

22. UCC Article 2's provisions on warranties made in sales contracts are set forth in UCC 2–313, 2–314, 2–315, and 2–316.
23. UCITA 402.
24. UCITA 401.
25. UCITA 403 and 405.

the signatures of the parties. Today, we deal with electronic signatures, or e-signatures. We want to be sure that the "person" sending the electronic message is in fact the person whose electronic message is being transmitted. For this reason, like the revisions of other statutes, the UCITA's rules were revised to provide for the authentication of e-signatures.

AUTHENTICATE
To sign a record, or with the intent to sign a record, to execute or to adopt an electronic sound, symbol, or the like to link with the record.

To **authenticate** means to sign a record, or with the intent to sign a record, to execute or to adopt an electronic sound, symbol, or the like to link with the record. As noted earlier in this chapter, a *record* is information that is inscribed in either a tangible medium or stored in an electronic or other medium and that is retrievable. The UCITA uses the word *record* instead of *writing.*

To ensure that the person sending the electronic computer information is the same person whose e-signature accompanies the information, the UCITA has a procedure, referred to as the *attribution procedure,* that sets forth steps for identifying a person who sends an electronic communication. These steps, which can be specified by the contracting parties, can be simple or complex as long as they are commercially reasonable.

Attribution procedures can also have an effect on liability for errors in the message content. If the attribution procedure is in place to detect errors, the party who conforms to the procedure is not bound by the error. Consumers who make unintended errors are not bound as long as the consumer notifies the other party promptly, returns the computer information received, and has not benefited from its use.

Under the UCITA, as under previous law, there is no requirement that all of the terms in a contract actually must have been read by all of the parties to be effective. For example, clicking on a link that states to do so is to agree to certain terms can be enough. The following case illustrates a court's evaluation of the validity of a clause in a click-on agreement.

CASE 7.3 Caspi v. Microsoft Network, L.L.C.[a]

New Jersey Superior Court,
Appellate Division, 1999.
323 N.J.Super. 118,
732 A.2d 528.
http://lawlibrary.rutgers.edu/search.shtml[b]

BACKGROUND AND FACTS Microsoft Network, LLC (MSN), is an online computer service. Before becoming an MSN member, a prospective subscriber is prompted by MSN software to view multiple computer screens of information, including a membership agreement that contains a forum-selection clause.[c] This clause calls for any claims against MSN to be litigated in the state of Washington. MSN's membership agreement appears on the computer screen in a scrollable window next to blocks providing the choices "I Agree" and "I Don't Agree." Prospective members have the option to click "I Agree" or "I Don't Agree" at any point while scrolling through the agreement. Registration proceeds only after the potential subscriber has the opportunity to view, and assents to, the membership agreement. No charges are incurred until a subscriber clicks on "I Agree." Steven Caspi was a subscriber. Alleging that MSN rolled over his membership into a more expensive plan without notice,[d] Caspi filed a suit in a New Jersey

a. *L.L.C.,* or *LLC,* is an abbreviation for limited liability company, a hybrid form of business enterprise that limits the liability of its members and offers special tax advantages.

b. This Web site is maintained by Rutgers University School of Law—Camden. This page contains links to recent opinions of the New Jersey state courts. In the "Additional Information:" row, click on "Search by party name." When that page opens, in the first column, click the "Appellate Division" box. In the second column, in the "First Name" box, enter "Caspi" and click on "Submit Form." When the results appear, click on the appropriate link to access the opinion.

c. A *forum-selection clause* in a contract designates the court, the jurisdiction, or the dispute-resolution entity to decide any disputes arising under the contract.

d. This is known as *unilateral negative option billing,* a practice at one time condemned by the attorneys general of twenty-one states, including New Jersey's, with regard to an MSN competitor, America Online, Inc.

state court against MSN. Other subscribers, claiming to represent 1.5 million members, joined the suit. MSN filed a motion to dismiss on the ground that the forum-selection clause called for the suit to be heard in the state of Washington. The court granted the motion. The plaintiffs appealed to a state intermediate appellate court, arguing that they did not have adequate notice of the clause and therefore it was not part of their contracts.

IN THE LANGUAGE OF THE COURT. . .
KESTIN, J.A.D. [Judge, Appellate Division.]

* * * *

The scenario presented here is different [from a case in which a forum selection clause appeared in the fine print on the back of a cruise ticket] because of the medium used, electronic versus printed; but, in any sense that matters, there is no significant distinction. The plaintiffs in [the other case] could have perused all the fine-print provisions of their travel contract if they wished before accepting the terms by purchasing their cruise ticket. The plaintiffs in this case were free to scroll through the various computer screens that presented the terms of their contracts before clicking their agreement.

Also, it seems clear that there was nothing extraordinary about the size or placement of the forum selection clause text. By every indication we have, the clause was presented in exactly the same format as most other provisions of the contract. It was the first item in the last paragraph of the electronic document. We note that a few paragraphs in the contract were presented in upper case typeface, presumably for emphasis, but most provisions, including the forum selection clause, were presented in lower case typeface. We discern nothing about the style or mode of presentation, or the placement of the provision, that can be taken as a basis for concluding that the forum selection clause was proffered unfairly, or with a design to conceal or deemphasize its provisions. To conclude that plaintiffs are not bound by that clause would be equivalent to holding that they were bound by no other clause either, since all provisions were identically presented. Plaintiffs must be taken to have known that they were entering into a contract; and no good purpose, consonant [in agreement or accord] with the dictates of reasonable reliability in commerce, would be served by permitting them to disavow particular provisions or the contracts as a whole.

The issue of reasonable notice regarding a forum selection clause is a question of law for the court to determine. We agree with the trial court that, in the absence of a better showing than has been made, plaintiffs must be seen to have had adequate notice of the forum selection clause.

DECISION AND REMEDY The state intermediate appellate court affirmed the decision of the lower court. The forum-selection clause contained in the click-on subscriber agreement was valid and enforceable, because it was presented in the same format as most of the rest of the agreement and potential subscribers had sufficient opportunity to view it.

FOR CRITICAL ANALYSIS–Economic Consideration *Many attorneys advise their business clients that it is especially important, when forming e-contracts, to include forum-selection clauses. Would including such a clause be more important when forming an e-contract than when forming a traditional, printed contract?*

ACCESS CONTRACT
Under the Uniform Computer Information Transactions Act (UCITA), "a contract to obtain by electronic means access to, or information from an information processing system of another person, or the equivalent of such access."

ACCESS CONTRACTS The UCITA defines an **access contract** as "a contract to obtain by electronic means access to, or information from an information processing system of another person, or the equivalent of such access." This is important for most of us, if for no other reason than our ability to use the Internet. Section 611 of the UCITA, however, has special rules governing available times and manner of access.

SUPPORT AND SERVICE CONTRACTS TO CORRECT PERFORMANCE PROBLEMS The UCITA covers licensor support and service contracts, but no licensor is required to provide such support and service.[26] Computer software support contracts are common, and once made, the licensor is obligated to comply with the express terms of the support contract or, if the contract is silent on an issue, to do what is reasonable in light of ordinary business standards.

ELECTRONIC SELF-HELP The UCITA allows the licensor to cancel, repossess, prevent continued use, and take similar actions on a licensee's breach of a license. The act permits the licensor to undertake "electronic self-help" to enforce the licensor's rights through electronic means.

Outside the UCITA, "self-help" refers to the right of a lessor, for example, under Article 2A of the UCC, to repossess a leased computer if the lessee fails to make payments according to the terms of the lease. A lender may have this same right under UCC Article 9 if a borrower fails to make payments on a loan secured by a computer.

In a transaction governed by the UCITA, electronic self-help includes the right of a software licensor to install a "turn-off" function in the software so that if the licensee violates the terms of the license, the software can be disabled from a distance. This right is most important to a small firm that licenses its software to a much larger company. Electronic self-help may be the licensor's only practical remedy if the license is breached.

There are some limitations on this right.[27] For example, the amendments to the UCITA passed in August 2000 prohibit electronic self-help in mass-market transactions. In addition, the remedy is not available unless the parties agree to permit electronic self-help. The licensor must give notice of the intent to use the self-help remedy at least fifteen days before doing so, along with full disclosure of the nature of the breach and information to enable the licensee to cure the breach or to communicate with the licensor concerning the situation.

A licensor is entitled on a licensee's breach to incidental and consequential damages. Of course, a licensor must attempt to mitigate those damages, but electronic self-help cannot be used if the licensor "has reason to know that its use will result in substantial injury or harm to the public health or safety or grave harm to the public interest affecting third persons involved in the dispute."

These limitations on the use of electronic self-help cannot be waived or varied by contract.

26. See UCITA 612.
27. See UCITA 816.

SECTION 7 THE UNIFORM ELECTRONIC TRANSACTIONS ACT

As mentioned earlier in this chapter, another uniform law proposed by the National Conference of Commissioners on Uniform State Laws (NCCUSL) concerning e-commerce is the Uniform Electronic Transactions Act (UETA). The goal of the UETA is not to create rules for electronic transactions—for example, the act does not require digital signatures—but to support the enforcement of e-contracts.

The Validity of E-Contracts

Under the UETA, contracts entered into online, as well as other electronic documents, are presumed valid. In other words, a contract is not unenforceable simply because it is in electronic form. The UETA does not apply to transactions governed by the UCC or the UCITA, or to wills or testamentary trusts.

The UETA and the UCITA Compared

The UETA and the UCITA have many similarities. The drafters of the laws attempted to make them consistent. Both proposals provide for such items as the following:

1. The equivalency of records and writings.
2. The validity of e-signatures.
3. The formation of contracts by e-agents.
4. The formation of contracts between an e-agent and a natural person.
5. The attribution of an electronic act to a person if it can be proved that the act was done by the person or his or her agent.
6. A provision that parties do not need to participate in e-commerce to make binding contracts.

These two uniform laws also have differences. Those differences include the following:

1. The UETA supports all electronic transactions, but it does not create rules for them. The UCITA concerns only contracts that involve computer information, but for those contracts, the UCITA imposes rules.
2. The UETA does not apply unless contracting parties agree to use e-commerce in their transactions. The UCITA applies to any agreement that falls within its scope.

In sum, the chief difference between the UETA and the UCITA is that the UCITA addresses e-commerce issues that the UETA does not. Those issues, and how the UCITA deals with them, were discussed in the previous sections.

TERMS AND CONCEPTS

acceptance 149
access contract 170
agreement 148
authenticate 168
breach 157
click-on agreement 150
computer information 164
consideration 150
contract 147
contractual capacity 151
cybernotary 159
damages 158
default rules 164
e-contract 146
e-signature 159
fraudulent misrepresentation 153
genuineness of assent 152
mailbox rule 149
mass-market license 167
mirror image rule 149
offer 148
offeree 148
offeror 148
performance 157
promise 147
promissory estoppel 151
record 160
rescission 153
sales contract 147
specific performance 158
Statute of Frauds 155

QUESTIONS AND CASE PROBLEMS

7–1. The One-Year Rule. On January 1, Damon, for consideration, orally promised to pay Gary $300 a month for as long as Gary lived, with the payments to be made on the first day of every month. Damon made the payments regularly for nine months and then made no further payments. Gary claimed that Damon had breached the oral contract and sued Damon for damages. Damon contended that the contract was unenforceable because, under the Statute of Frauds, contracts that cannot be performed within one year must be in writing. Discuss whether Damon will succeed in this defense.

7–2. Assent. Juan is an elderly man who lives with his nephew, Samuel. Juan is totally dependent on Samuel's support. Samuel tells Juan that unless he transfers a tract of land he owns to Samuel for a price 15 percent below market value, Samuel will no longer support and take care of him. Juan enters into the contract. Discuss fully whether Juan can set aside this contract.

7–3. Attribution. Frank, an employee for Lloyd & Wright Architects, orders drafting supplies costing $4,500 from Precision Equipment, Inc., through Precision's Web site at precisionequip.com. On the order page at the site, Frank is asked to type in his name, company name, e-mail address, phone number, a credit-card or Precision account number, and the personal identification number (PIN) issued by the seller. The precisionequip.com site asks Frank to check this information before clicking "SUBMIT," at which time the order will be accepted and the supplies will be shipped. For purposes of the UCITA, what part of this transaction could be considered an attribution procedure? Is there an enforceable contract between Lloyd & Wright and Precision under the UCITA, even though there is nothing in writing? Explain.

7–4. Click-On Agreements. Anne is a reporter for *Daily Business Journal,* a print publication consulted by investors and other businesspersons. Anne often uses the Internet to perform research for the articles that she writes for the publication. While visiting the Web site of Cyberspace Investments Corporation, Anne reads a pop-up window that states, "Our business newsletter, *E-Commerce Weekly,* is available at a one-year subscription rate of $5 per issue. To subscribe, enter your e-mail address below and click 'SUBSCRIBE.' By subscribing, you agree to the terms of the subscriber's agreement. To read this agreement, click 'AGREEMENT.'" Anne enters her e-mail address, but does not click on "AGREEMENT" to read the terms. Has Anne entered into an enforceable contract to pay for *E-Commerce Weekly?* Explain.

7–5. Remedies. Mary enters into a licensing agreement with Scientific Research Corporation to obtain certain data for Chemical Engineering, Inc. The agreement requires an initial registration fee and a monthly subscription fee for the data, which is owned by, and available only from, Scientific Research. Chemical Engineering pays the initial fee and the first month's subscription charge, but Scientific Research refuses to provide Chemical Engineering with access to the data. Chemical Engineering files a suit against Scientific Research. How might the court rule, and why? If the court rules in Chemical Engineering's favor, what remedies are available?

7–6. Oral Contracts. Samuel DaGrossa and others were planning to open a restaurant. At some point prior to August 1985, DaGrossa orally agreed with Philippe LaJaunie that LaJaunie, in exchange for his contribution in designing, renovating, and managing the restaurant, could purchase a one-third interest in the restaurant's stock if the restaurant was profitable in its first year of operations. The restaurant opened in March 1986, and a few weeks later, LaJaunie's employment was terminated. LaJaunie brought an action to enforce the stock-purchase agreement. Is the agreement enforceable? Why, or why not? [*LaJaunie v. DaGrossa,* 159 A.D.2d 349, 552 N.Y.S.2d 628 (1990)]

7–7. Fraudulent Misrepresentation. In 1987, United Parcel Service Co. and United Parcel Service of America, Inc. (together known as "UPS"), decided to change its parcel delivery business from relying on contract carriers to establishing its own airline. During the transition, which took sixteen months, UPS hired 811 pilots. At the time, UPS expressed a desire to hire pilots who remained throughout that period with its contract carriers, which included Orion Air. A UPS representative met with more than fifty Orion pilots and made promises of future employment. John Rickert, a captain with Orion, was one of the pilots. Orion ceased operation after the UPS transition, and UPS did not hire Rickert, who obtained employment about six months later as a second officer with American Airlines, but at a lower salary. Rickert filed a suit in a Kentucky state court against UPS, claiming, in part, fraud based on the promises made by the UPS representative. UPS filed a motion for a directed verdict. What are the elements for a cause of action based on fraudulent misrepresentation? In whose favor should the court rule in this case, and why? [*United Parcel Service, Inc. v. Rickert,* 996 S.W.2d 464 (Ky. 1999)]

WEB EXERCISES

Go to **http://lec.westbuslaw.com**, the Web site that accompanies this text. Select "Internet Applications," and then click on "Chapter 7." There you will find the following Internet research exercise that you can perform to learn more about e-contracting:

Activity 7–1: E-Contracts

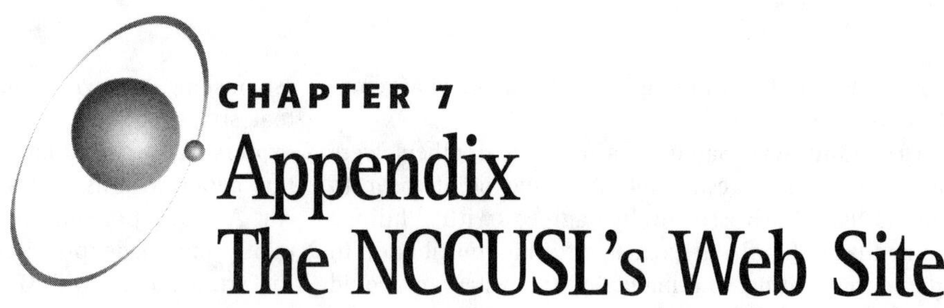

CHAPTER 7 Appendix The NCCUSL's Web Site

The text of the law has always been available to the public in published form. The law has never been as accessible, however, as it is now on the Internet. This means that businesspersons can be better informed about their legal rights and responsibilities today than they could even ten years ago.

One important cyberspace connection to the text of the law is the Web site of the National Conference of Commissioners on Uniform State Laws (NCCUSL).

To connect to the Web site of the National Conference of Commissioners on Uniform State Laws (NCCUSL), log on at **http://www.nccusl.org**.

Site Map

The site is divided into ten sections. On one page, the NCCUSL provides information about itself ("About Us"), including its history, rules, and bylaws. On another page, the NCCUSL details the projects on which it is currently working ("Drafting Projects Underway"). "Topics under Discussion" lists subjects that the organization has assigned to its committees to review as subjects for draft legislation. The site also contains links to the NCCUSL's press releases ("Newsroom") and "What's New."

Most informative are the updates on the jurisdictions that have introduced and adopted the NCCUSL's proposed laws ("Legislative Status and Information on Uniform Acts"). This page includes, for each proposed act, a "Legislative Fact Sheet," a "Summary," and a selection of "Questions and Answers." The other sections at this site are "Meetings," "Links," "Contact Us," and "Site Map."

The UCITA and UETA Links

As of this writing, only two states—Maryland and Virginia—had adopted the UCITA. It had been introduced, however, in at least six other jurisdictions—Delaware, Hawaii, Illinois, New Jersey, Alabama, and the District of Columbia—although no action was expected for the remainder of these states' legislative sessions. Twenty-nine states had enacted, or considered enacting, the UETA.

On the Web

To read one of the drafts of the UCITA or the UETA, go to a site that contains the drafts of many of the uniform laws the NCCUSL has issued. This site, maintained by the University of Pennsylvania Law School, is at **http://www.law.upenn.edu/bll/ulc/ulc**.

The NCCUSL's Web site includes an update of this short list of the states that have adopted the UCITA and the UETA or considered them for adoption. The site also contains summaries of the acts and "Question and Answer" sections concerning these proposed laws.

To access the NCCUSL's most recent information about the UCITA, select "Legislative Status and Information on Uniform Acts," and then click on the box entitled "By Subject Matter." Then select "Business Laws," scroll down to "Computer Information Transactions," and click on the type of information you desire. To find similar information about the UETA, follow the same steps, but in "Business Laws," scroll down to "Electronic Transactions," and click on the appropriate link.

CHAPTER 8

Risk Management and Information Security

Concepts Covered

After reading this chapter, you should be able to:

1. Indicate when an insurable interest arises in regard to life and property insurance.
2. Distinguish between an insurance broker and an insurance agent.
3. Summarize some of the clauses that are typically included in insurance contracts.
4. Indicate what is meant by the term *information security* and why this form of security is important.
5. Describe some of the measures that businesses can implement to accomplish and maintain information security.

"Insurance is part charity and part business, but all common sense."

Calvin Coolidge, 1872–1933
(Thirtieth president of the United States, 1923–1929)

Many precautions can be taken to protect against the hazards of life. For example, an individual can wear a seat belt to protect against automobile injuries or install smoke detectors to guard against the risk of injury from fire. Of course, no one can predict whether an accident or a fire will ever occur, but individuals and businesses must establish plans to protect their personal and financial interests should some event threaten to undermine their security.

Traditionally, businesses have purchased insurance to help protect their interests. **Insurance** is a contract by which the insurance company (the insurer) promises to pay a sum of money or give something of value to another (either the insured or the beneficiary) to compensate the other for a particular, stated loss. Basically, insurance is an arrangement for transferring and allocating risk, which can be described as a prediction concerning potential loss based on known and unknown factors. **Risk management** normally involves the transfer of certain risks from the individual to an insurance company by a contractual agreement. In the first part of this chapter, we look at the types of risks that insurance can protect against and at the nature of insurance contracts.

In today's online world, businesses face special risks that may not be covered by traditional types of insurance. For example, suppose that the Celeste

INSURANCE
A contract in which, for a stipulated consideration, one party agrees to compensate the other for loss on a specific subject by a specified peril.

RISK
A prediction concerning potential loss based on known and unknown factors.

RISK MANAGEMENT
Planning that is undertaken to protect one's interest should some event threaten to undermine its security. In the context of insurance, risk management involves transferring certain risks from the insured to the insurance company.

Company sells its products via its Web site. The buyers purchase the products using their credit cards. A hacker accesses the business's server containing the customers' credit-card numbers and then uses those numbers to purchase goods. The Celeste Company may be liable to the credit-card companies for negligence if it failed to maintain appropriate security measures to protect the data from unauthorized access. Guarding against liability due to the theft or loss of computer information and systems is an important part of conducting business in cyberspace. Consider that one recent survey of major corporations revealed that, during the 1990s, over 98 percent of the companies had been targets of computer-related crimes. In the second part of this chapter, we examine some of the steps being taken by online businesses today to maximize **information security.**

INFORMATION SECURITY
The ability to control access to computer information.

SECTION 1 INSURANCE TERMINOLOGY AND CONCEPTS

Like other areas of law, insurance has its own special concepts and terminology, a knowledge of which is essential to an understanding of insurance law.

Insurance Terminology

POLICY
In insurance law, a contract between the insurer and the insured in which, for a stipulated consideration, the insurer agrees to compensate the insured for loss on a specific subject by a specified peril.

PREMIUM
In insurance law, the price paid by the insured for insurance protection for a specified period of time.

UNDERWRITER
In insurance law, the insurer, or the one assuming a risk in return for the payment of a premium.

An insurance contract is called a **policy**; the consideration paid to the insurer is called a **premium**; and the insurance company is sometimes called an **underwriter.** The parties to an insurance policy are the *insurer* (the insurance company) and the *insured* (the person covered by its provisions).

Insurance contracts are usually obtained through an *agent,* who usually works for the insurance company, or through a *broker,* who is ordinarily an independent contractor. When a broker deals with an applicant for insurance, the broker is, in effect, the applicant's agent. In contrast, an insurance agent is an agent of the insurance company, not an agent of the applicant. As a general rule, the insurance company is bound by the acts of its agents when they act within the scope of the agency relationship. In most situations, state law determines the status of all parties writing or obtaining insurance.

The Concept of Risk Pooling

All types of insurance companies use the principle of *risk pooling;* that is, they spread the risk among a large number of people—the pool—to make the premiums small compared with the coverage offered. Life insurance companies, for example, know that only a small proportion of the individuals in any particular age group will die in any one year. If a large percentage of people in this age group pay premiums to the company in exchange for a benefit payment in the event of death, there will be a sufficient amount of money to pay the beneficiaries of the policyholders who die. Through the extensive correlation of data over a period of time, insurers can estimate fairly accurately the total amount they will have to pay if they insure a particular group, as well as the rates that they will have to charge each member of the group so they can make the necessary payments and still show a profit.

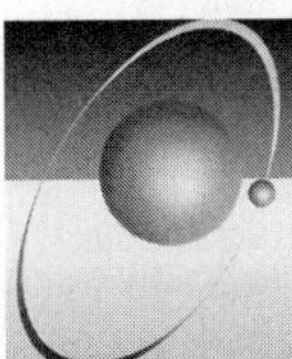

E-Guidelines

Risk Management in Cyberspace

As mentioned elsewhere, companies doing business online face many risks that are not covered by traditional types of insurance (see Exhibit 8–1 on page 182). Not surprisingly, a growing number of companies are now offering policies designed to cover Web-related risks.

Insurance Coverage for Web-Related Risks

For example, consider the types of coverage offered by Net Secure, a venture undertaken by IBM, several insurance companies, and a New York broker. Net Secure provides insurance protection against losses resulting from programming errors; network and Web site disruptions; the theft of electronic data and assets, including intellectual property; Web-related defamation, copyright infringement, and false advertising; and the violation of users' privacy rights.

InsureTrust.com, an insurer affiliated with three leading insurance companies—American International Group, Lloyd's of London, and Reliance National—offers similar coverage. Insurance for Web-related perils is also being added to the offerings of existing insurers, such as Lloyd's of London, Hartford Insurance, and the Chubb Group of Insurance Companies. Clearly, the market for these new types of insurance coverage is rapidly evolving, and new policies will continue to appear.

Customized Policies

Unlike traditional insurance policies, which are generally drafted by insurance companies and presented to insurance applicants on a "take-it-or-leave-it" basis, Internet-particular policies are usually customized to provide protection against specific risks faced by diverse types of businesses. For example, an Internet service provider will face different risks than an online merchant, and a banking institution will face dissimilar risks than a law firm. The specific business-related risks are taken into consideration when determining the policy premium.

CHECKLIST

- ☑ Before selecting a technology policy, businesspersons need to do some homework. Specifically, they need to determine to what types of risks their Web businesses expose them and try to obtain an insurance policy that specifically protects them against those risks.
- ☑ As when procuring any type of insurance coverage, businesspersons should read the policy carefully before committing to it. Often, buried within the fine print of a policy are various exclusions—risks that are not covered by the policy.
- ☑ Businesspersons should not be "penny wise and pound foolish" when it comes to insurance protection. While insurance coverage may seem expensive, it may be much less costly than defending against a lawsuit. Often, the cost of coverage can be reduced by purchasing a policy with a high deductible.

Classifications of Insurance

Insurance is classified according to the nature of the risk involved. For example, fire insurance, casualty insurance, life insurance, and title insurance apply to different types of risk. Furthermore, policies of these types differ in the persons and interests that they protect. This is reasonable because the types of losses that are expected and the types that are foreseeable or unforeseeable vary with the nature of the activity. See Exhibit 8–1 beginning on the next page for a list of various insurance classifications. (For a relatively new type of insurance coverage, see this chapter's *E-Guidelines* feature.)

EXHIBIT 8–1 Insurance Classifications

TYPE OF INSURANCE	COVERAGE
Accident	Covers expenses, losses, and suffering incurred by the insured because of accidents causing physical injury and any consequent disability; sometimes includes a specified payment to heirs of the insured if death results from an accident.
All-risk	Covers all losses that the insured may incur except those resulting from fraud on the part of the insured.
Automobile	May cover damage to automobiles resulting from specified hazards or occurrences (such as fire, vandalism, theft, or collision); normally provides protection against liability for personal injuries and property damage resulting from the operation of the vehicle.
Casualty	Protects against losses that may be incurred by the insured as a result of being held liable for personal injuries or property damage sustained by others.
Credit	Pays to a creditor the balance of a debt on the disability, death, insolvency, or bankruptcy of the debtor; often offered by lending institutions.
Decreasing-term life	Provides life insurance; requires uniform payments over the life (term) of the policy, but with a decreasing face value (amount of coverage).
Employer's liability	Insures employers against liability for injuries or losses sustained by employees during the course of their employment; covers claims not covered under workers' compensation insurance.
Fidelity or guaranty	Provides indemnity against losses in trade or losses caused by the dishonesty of employees, the insolvency of debtors, or breaches of contract.
Fire	Covers losses to the insured caused by fire.
Floater	Covers movable property, as long as the property is within the territorial boundaries specified in the contract.
Group	Provides individual life, medical, or disability insurance coverage but is obtainable through a group of persons, usually employees; the policy premium is paid either entirely by the employer or partially by the employer and partially by the employee.
Health	Covers expenses incurred by the insured resulting from physical injury or illness and other expenses relating to health and life maintenance.
Homeowners'	Protects homeowners against some or all risks of loss to their residences and the residences' contents or liability arising from the use of the property.
Key-person	Protects a business in the event of the death or disability of a key employee.
Liability	Protects against liability imposed on the insured resulting from injuries to the person or property of another.
Life	Covers the death of the policyholder. On the death of the insured, an amount specified in the policy is paid by the insurer to the insured's beneficiary.
Major medical	Protects the insured against major hospital, medical, or surgical expenses.
Malpractice	Protects professionals (doctors, lawyers, and others) against malpractice claims brought against them by their patients or clients; a form of liability insurance.
Marine	Covers movable property (including ships, freight, and cargo) against certain perils or navigation risks during a specific voyage or time period.
Mortgage	Covers a mortgage loan; the insurer pays the balance of the mortgage to the creditor on the death or disability of the debtor.

EXHIBIT 8–1 Insurance Classifications (Continued)

TYPE OF INSURANCE	COVERAGE
No-fault auto	Covers personal injury and (sometimes) property damage resulting from automobile accidents. The insured submits his or her claims to his or her own insurance company, regardless of who was at fault. A person may sue the party at fault or that party's insurer only in cases involving serious medical injury and consequent high medical costs. Governed by state "no-fault" statutes.
Term life	Provides life insurance for a specified period of time (term) with no cash surrender value; usually renewable.
Title	Protects against any defects in title to real property and any losses incurred as a result of existing claims against or liens on the property at the time of purchase.

Insurable Interest

A person can insure anything in which he or she has an **insurable interest.** Without this insurable interest, there is no enforceable contract, and a transaction to purchase insurance coverage would have to be treated as a wager. The existence of an insurable interest is a primary concern in determining liability under an insurance policy.

INSURABLE INTEREST
An interest either in a person's life or well-being or in property that is sufficiently substantial that insuring against injury to (or the death of) the person or against damage to the property does not amount to a mere wagering (betting) contract.

LIFE INSURANCE In regard to life insurance, one must have a reasonable expectation of benefit from the continued life of another to have an insurable interest in that person's life. The insurable interest must exist *at the time the policy is obtained.* The benefit may be pecuniary (related to money), or it may be founded on the relationship between the parties (by blood or affinity). Close family relationships give a person an insurable interest in the life of another. Generally, blood or marital relationships fit this category. A husband can take out an insurance policy on his wife and vice versa; parents can take out life insurance policies on their children; brothers and sisters, on each other; and grandparents, on grandchildren—as all these are close family relationships. A policy that a person takes out on his or her spouse remains valid even if they divorce, unless a specific provision in the policy calls for its termination on divorce.

Key-person insurance is insurance obtained by an organization on the life of a person who is important to that organization. Because the organization expects to receive some pecuniary gain from the continuation of the key person's life or some financial loss from the key person's death, the organization has an insurable interest. Typically, a partnership will insure the life of each partner, because the death of any one partner will cause some degree of loss to the partnership. Similarly, a corporation has an insurable interest in the life expectancy of a key executive whose death would result in financial loss to the company. If a firm insures a key person's life and then that person leaves the firm and dies, the firm can collect on the insurance policy, provided it continued to pay premiums.

PROPERTY INSURANCE With respect to real and personal property, an insurable interest exists when the insured derives a pecuniary benefit from the preservation and continued existence of the property—that is, one has an insurable interest in property when one would sustain a pecuniary loss from its destruction. The insurable interest in property must exist when the loss occurs. Both a mortgagor (such as homeowner who has financed the purchase of his or her home through a mortgage loan) and a mortgagee (such as the bank that holds the mortgage) have an insurable interest in the mortgaged property. So do a landlord and a tenant in leased property. John or Jane Doe, however, cannot obtain fire insurance on the White House.

SECTION 2 THE INSURANCE CONTRACT

For a summary of the law governing insurance contracts in the United States, including rules of interpretation, go to **http://www.consumerlawpage.com/article/insureds.shtml**.

An insurance contract is governed by the general principles of contract law, although the insurance industry is heavily regulated by the states.[1] Customarily, a party offers to purchase insurance by submitting an insurance application to the insurance company. The company can either accept or reject the offer. Sometimes, the insurance company's acceptance is conditional—on the results of a life insurance applicant's medical examination, for example. For the insurance contract to be binding, consideration (in the form of a premium) must be given, and the parties forming the contract must have the required contractual capacity to do so.

Application for Insurance

The filled-in application form for insurance is usually attached to the policy and made a part of the insurance contract. Thus, an insurance applicant is bound by any false statements that appear in the application (subject to certain exceptions). Because the insurance company evaluates the risk factors based on the information included in the insurance application, misstatements or misrepresentations can void a policy, especially if the insurance company can show that it would not have extended insurance if it had known the facts.[2]

Effective Date

The effective date of an insurance contract—that is, the date on which the insurance coverage begins—is important. In some instances, the insurance applicant is not protected until a formal written policy is issued. In other situations, the applicant is protected between the time the application is received and the time the insurance company either accepts or rejects it. Four facts should be kept in mind:

1. A broker is the agent of an applicant. Therefore, if the broker fails to procure a policy, the applicant normally is not insured. According to general principles of agency law, if the broker fails to obtain policy coverage and the

1. The states were given authority to regulate the insurance industry by the McCarran-Ferguson Act of 1945, 15 U.S.C. Sections 1011–1015.

2. See, for example, *Berthiaume v. Minnesota Mutual Life Insurance Co.*, 388 N.W.2d 15 (Minn. App. 1986).

applicant is damaged as a result, the broker is liable to the damaged applicant-principal for the loss.

2. A person who seeks insurance from an insurance company's agent is usually protected from the moment the application is made, provided—in the case of life insurance—that some form of premium has been paid. Between the time the application is received and the time it is either rejected or accepted, the applicant is covered (possibly subject to certain conditions, such as passing a physical examination). Usually, the agent will write a memorandum, or **binder,** indicating that a policy is pending and stating its essential terms.

BINDER
A written, temporary insurance policy.

3. If the parties agree that the policy will be issued and delivered at a later time, the contract is not effective until the policy is issued and delivered or sent to the applicant, depending on the agreement. Thus, any loss sustained between the time of application and the delivery of the policy is not covered.

4. Parties may agree that a life insurance policy will be binding at the time the insured pays the first premium, or the policy may be expressly contingent on the applicant's passing a physical examination. If the applicant pays the premium and passes the examination, the policy coverage is continuously in effect. If the applicant pays the premium but dies before having the physical examination, then in order to collect, the applicant's estate normally must show that the applicant would have passed the examination had he or she not died. An insurance contract may also include a clause stating that the applicant must be "still insurable" on the effective date of the policy.[3]

In sum, coverage on an insurance policy can begin when a binder is written; when the policy is issued; or, depending on the terms of the contract, after a certain period of time has elapsed.

Provisions and Clauses

Some of the important provisions and clauses contained in insurance contracts are defined and discussed in the following subsections.

PROVISIONS MANDATED BY STATUTE If a statute mandates that a certain provision be included in insurance contracts, a court will deem that an insurance policy contains the provision regardless of whether the parties actually included it in the language of their contract. If a statute requires that any limitations regarding coverage be stated in the contract, a court will not allow an insurer to avoid liability for a claim through reliance on an unexpressed limitation.

INCONTESTABILITY CLAUSES Statutes commonly require that a life or health-insurance policy provide that after the policy has been in force for a specified length of time—often two or three years—the insurer cannot contest statements made in the application. This is known as an *incontestability clause.* Once a policy becomes incontestable, the insurer cannot later avoid a claim on the basis of, for example, fraud on the part of the insured, unless the clause provides an exception for that circumstance. The clause does not prohibit an insurer's refusal

3. See, for example, *Life Insurance Co. of North America v. Cichowlas,* 659 So.2d 1333 (Fla.App. 4th 1995).

or reduction of payment for a claim due to nonpayment of premiums, failure to file proof of death within a certain period, or lack of an insurable interest.

COINSURANCE CLAUSES Often, when taking out fire insurance policies, property owners insure their property for less than full value. Part of the reason for this is that most fires do not result in a total loss. To encourage owners to insure their property for an amount as close to full value as possible, a standard provision of fire insurance policies is a coinsurance clause. Typically, a *coinsurance clause* provides that if the owner insures the property up to a specified percentage—usually 80 percent—of its value, he or she will recover any loss up to the face amount of the policy. If the insurance is for less than the fixed percentage, the owner is responsible for a proportionate share of the loss.

Coinsurance applies only in instances of partial loss. For example, if the owner of property valued at $100,000 took out a policy in the amount of $40,000 and suffered a loss of $30,000, the recovery would be $15,000. The formula for calculating the recovery amount is as follows:

$$\frac{\text{amount of insurance } (\$40{,}000)}{\text{coinsurance percentage } (80\%) \times \text{property value } (\$100{,}000)} = \text{recovery percentage } (50\%)$$

$$\text{recovery percentage } (50\%) \times \text{amount of loss } (\$30{,}000) = \text{recovery amount } (\$15{,}000)$$

If the owner had taken out a policy in the amount of $80,000, then according to the same formula, the full loss would have been recovered.

APPRAISAL AND ARBITRATION CLAUSES Most fire insurance policies provide that if the parties cannot agree on the amount of a loss covered under the policy or on the value of the property lost, an *appraisal* can be demanded. An appraisal is an estimate of the property's value determined by suitably qualified individuals who have no interest in the property. Typically, two appraisers are used, one being appointed by each party. A third party, or umpire, may be called on to resolve differences. Other types of insurance policies also contain provisions for appraisal and arbitration when the insured and insurer disagree as to the value of a loss.

MULTIPLE INSURANCE COVERAGE If an insured has *multiple insurance coverage*—that is, policies with several companies covering the same insurance interest—and the amount of coverage exceeds the loss, the insured can collect from each insurer only the company's *proportionate* share of the liability, relative to the total amount of insurance. Many fire insurance policies include a pro rata clause, which requires that any loss be shared proportionately by all carriers. For example, if Grumbling insured $50,000 worth of property with two companies, and each policy had a liability limit of $40,000, on the property's total destruction Grumbling could collect only $25,000 from each insurer.

ANTILAPSE CLAUSES A life insurance policy may provide, or a statute may require a policy to provide, that it will not automatically lapse if no payment is made on the date due. Ordinarily, under an *antilapse provision,* the insured has a *grace period* of thirty or thirty-one days within which to pay an overdue premium. If the insured fails to pay a premium altogether, there are alternatives to cancellation:

- The insurer may be required to extend the insurance for a period of time.
- The insurer may issue a policy with less coverage to reflect the amount of the payments made.
- The insurer may pay to the insured the policy's **cash surrender value**–the amount the insurer has agreed to pay on the policy's cancellation before the insured's death. (In determining this value, the following factors are considered: the period that the policy has already run, the amount of the premium, the insured's age and life expectancy, and amounts to be repaid on any outstanding loans taken out against the policy.)

CASH SURRENDER VALUE
The amount that the insurer has agreed to pay to the insured if a life insurance policy is canceled before the insured's death.

When the insurance contract states that the insurer cannot cancel the policy, these alternatives are important.

Interpreting Provisions of an Insurance Contract

The courts are increasingly cognizant of the fact that most people do not have the special training necessary to understand the intricate terminology used in insurance policies. The words used in an insurance contract have their ordinary meanings and are interpreted by courts in light of the nature of the coverage involved. When there is an ambiguity in the policy, the provision is interpreted against the insurance company. When it is unclear whether an insurance contract actually exists because the written policy has not been delivered, the uncertainty is resolved against the insurance company. The court presumes that the policy is in effect unless the company can show otherwise. Similarly, an insurer must take care to make sure that the insured is adequately notified of any change in coverage under an existing policy.

In the following case, a business and its insurance company disputed whether the language of the contract meant that the insurer should cover losses caused by business interruptions that occurred when a power outage caused computer systems to be inoperable for a time.

CASE 8.1 American Guarantee & Liability Insurance Co. v. Ingram Micro, Inc.

United States District Court,
District of Arizona, 2000.
__ F.Supp.2d __.

BACKGROUND AND FACTS Ingram Micro, Inc. (**http://www.ingrammicro.com**), is a wholesale distributor of microcomputer products. The company uses a computer network (the Impulse System) to track its transactions. Ingram's entire operation depends on the proper functioning of Impulse. Ingram obtained an insurance policy from American Guarantee & Liability Insurance Company to insure Ingram's "property, business income and operations." The policy insured against "[a]ll [r]isks of direct physical loss or damage from any cause." Ingram's computers, including Impulse, were insured under the policy. In December 1998, Ingram experienced a half-hour power outage. The mainframe computers lost all of their programming information, which Ingram employees had to reload. Due to a malfunctioning matrix switch, Impulse was not restored to full operation for nearly eight hours. Ingram filed a claim under its policy with American. American denied the claim, and each party filed a suit in a federal district court against the other. Both parties filed motions for summary judgment.

CASE 8.1–Continued

IN THE LANGUAGE OF THE COURT. . .
MARQUEZ, Senior District J. [Judge.]

* * * *

American and its expert witnesses admit that Ingram's mainframe computers and the matrix switch did not function as before the power outage and that certain data entry and reconfiguration processes were necessary to make Impulse operate as it had before the power outage. American argues, however, that the computer system and the matrix switch were not "physically damaged" because their capability to perform their intended functions remained intact. The power outage did not adversely affect the equipment's inherent ability to accept and process data and configuration settings when they were subsequently reentered into the computer system.

Ingram argues that the fact that the mainframe computers and the matrix switch retained the ability to accept the restored information and eventually operate as before does not mean that they did not undergo "physical damage." Ingram offers a broader definition of this term and contends that "physical damage" includes loss of use and functionality.

At a time when computer technology dominates our professional as well as personal lives, the Court must side with Ingram's broader definition of "physical damage." The Court finds that *"physical damage" is not restricted to the physical destruction or harm of computer circuitry but includes loss of access, loss of use, and loss of functionality.* [Emphasis added.]

The Court is not alone in this interpretation. * * *

* * * Lawmakers around the country have determined that when a computer's data [are] unavailable, there is damage; when a computer's services are interrupted, there is damage; and when a computer's software or network is altered, there is damage. Restricting the Policy's language to that proposed by American would be archaic.

* * * *

In this case, Ingram does allege property damage—that as a result of the power outage, Ingram's computer system and world-wide computer network physically lost the programming information and custom configurations necessary for them to function. * * * It wasn't until Ingram employees manually reloaded the lost programming information that the mainframes were "repaired." Impulse was "physically damaged" for eight hours. Ingram employees "repaired" Impulse by physically bypassing a malfunctioning matrix switch. Until this restorative work was conducted, Ingram's mainframes and Impulse were inoperable.

DECISION AND REMEDY The court granted Ingram's motion for summary judgment and denied American's motion. The court concluded that "physical damage" to a computer, under a policy insuring against that risk, is not restricted to the physical destruction of, or harm to, the circuitry but includes loss of access, loss of use, and loss of functionality.

FOR CRITICAL ANALYSIS–Economic Consideration *Why would an insurer attempt to avoid paying a property damage claim for the loss of access, use, or functionality of a computer?*

Cancellation

The insured can cancel a policy at any time, and the insurer can cancel under certain circumstances. When an insurance company can cancel its insurance contract, the policy or a state statute usually requires that the insurer give advance written notice of the cancellation. Any premium paid in advance and not yet earned may be refundable. The insured may also be entitled to a life insurance policy's cash surrender value.

The insurer may cancel an insurance policy for various reasons, depending on the type of insurance. For example, automobile insurance can be canceled for nonpayment of premiums or suspension of the insured's driver's license. Property insurance can be canceled for nonpayment of premiums or for other reasons, including the insured's fraud or misrepresentation, gross negligence, or conviction for a crime that increases the hazard against which the policy insures. Life and health policies can be canceled because of false statements made by the insured in the application, but cancellation can only take place before the effective date of an incontestability clause. An insurer cannot cancel—or refuse to renew—a policy because of the national origin or race of an applicant or because the insured has appeared as a witness in a case brought against the company.

State laws normally impose a requirement that an insured must be notified in writing of an insurance policy cancellation.[4] The same requirement applies when only part of a policy is canceled. The exact form that this notice should take is not always specified, however, and the issue in the following case was what and how much notice are sufficient to effect a cancellation.

4. At issue in one case was whether a notification of cancellation included on a diskette sent to the insured constituted "written notice" of cancellation. The court held that the computerized document, which could be printed out as "hard copy," constituted written notice. See *Clyburn v. Allstate Insurance Co.*, 826 F.Supp. 955 (D.S.C. 1993).

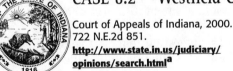

CASE 8.2 Westfield Cos. v. Rovan, Inc.

Court of Appeals of Indiana, 2000.
722 N.E.2d 851.
http://www.state.in.us/judiciary/opinions/search.html[a]

BACKGROUND AND FACTS Rovan, Inc., repairs and renovates automobiles and recreational vehicles in Indiana. Cheryl Robinson is the president of Rovan. In 1997, Westfield Companies issued an insurance policy to Rovan. The policy was more than one hundred pages long and contained forty-two "forms," which were listed by description, not by number. In January 1998, Rovan leased from Cheryl's son Brandon a 1995 Chevy pickup truck. As part of the lease, Rovan agreed to provide insurance for Brandon when he drove the truck. A copy of the lease was forwarded to Westfield, which added the Chevy to Rovan's policy. Westfield also added a clause (the "Lessor Endorsement") to cover Brandon when he drove a vehicle that he leased to Rovan. In March, Rovan replaced the lease of the Chevy with a lease of a 1998 Ford Mustang GT from Brandon under the same terms and conditions as the previous lease. Westfield was notified of the change and, in the policy, deleted the Chevy and added the Mustang. Westfield sent to Rovan an "Amended Common Policy Declaration" that noted the change in vehicles and stated, at the bottom, "DELETED FORM CA2001 07/97. This endorsement changes your policy. Please attach it to

a. In the "Select one or more opinion groups to search" section, click on the box next to "Appeals Court." In the "Please enter the case number, party name(s), key word or phrases, separated by commas" box, type "Rovan," and click on "SEARCH." When the results return, click on "converted file msm" to access the opinion.

CASE 8.2—Continued

your original policy." FORM CA2001 07/97 was the Lessor Endorsement. In June, Cheryl agreed to replace the Mustang with Brandon's 1997 Dodge pickup truck. Within a few days, Brandon, while driving the Dodge, was involved in an accident that left three minors dead and two others seriously injured. Westfield filed a request with an Indiana state court for a declaratory judgment that its policy had not covered Brandon at the time of the accident. The court granted a summary judgment in favor of Rovan. Westfield appealed to a state intermediate appellate court.

IN THE LANGUAGE OF THE COURT. . .

MATTINGLY, Judge.

* * * *

The question of what and how much notice of cancellation by the insurer is sufficient to effectively cancel an insurance policy is one of first impression for [never before decided by] this court. While generally in the absence of a specific statutory or policy provision, any form of notice of cancellation is sufficient, we hold *such notice must positively and unequivocally inform the insured of the insurer's intention that the policy cease to be binding.* * * * [Emphasis added.]

In this case, no form of notice of cancellation is required by either Policy provision or statute. Therefore, Westfield was required to send Rovan only such notice as would positively and unequivocally inform Rovan that Westfield was canceling the Lessor Endorsement. Westfield argues the Amended Common Policy Declaration was sufficient. * * * Westfield argues the statement at the bottom deleting Form CA2001 07/97 (the Lessor Endorsement) in conjunction with the sentences recognizing the Amended Common Policy Declaration as a change in the policy is sufficient to provide notice of cancellation. We disagree and find the phrase "DELETED FORM CA2001 07/97" decidedly cryptic and completely uninformative. All it expresses is that one out of some forty-two forms contained in the Policy had been deleted. It does not suggest the importance or practical consequences of this deletion by positively and unequivocally informing Rovan that the Lessor Endorsement would cease to be binding. In other words, it is not a clear expression of intent to cancel so as to be apparent to the ordinary person.

We are not persuaded by Westfield's suggesting that "[a]nyone who looked at the Policy could easily correlate the form number with the title of the form." The Policy is well over one hundred pages long and contains roughly forty-two separately numbered "forms" of various page lengths. The several tables of contents list the parts of the Policy by description, not by form number. The only way for one to determine which form had been deleted would be to examine each and every page of the Policy. In this case, the search would have uncovered the Lessor Endorsement approximately three-quarters of the way through the Policy located immediately after the "Nuclear Energy Liability Exclusion Endorsement."

Westfield, by failing to provide notice of cancellation, did not effectively cancel coverage under the Lessor Endorsement. Accordingly, the Lessor Endorsement remained in effect on * * * the date of the accident.

DECISION AND REMEDY The state intermediate appellate court affirmed the summary judgment in Rovan's favor. Westfield had not provided sufficient notice of its cancellation of coverage because the notice did not "positively and unequivocally inform the insured of the insurer's intention."

FOR CRITICAL ANALYSIS–Ethical Consideration *What if the policy in this case had only been, say, three pages long instead of over one hundred pages long? What if it had been five, ten, fifteen, or fifty pages? At what point should it be assumed that the insurer's intent to cancel the policy, in the method used in this case, will be "apparent to the ordinary person"?*

Basic Duties and Rights

Essentially, the parties to an insurance contract are responsible for the obligations the contract imposes.

In applying for insurance, for example, the obligation to act in good faith means that a party must reveal everything necessary for the insurer to evaluate the risk. In other words, the applicant must disclose all material facts. These include all facts that would influence an insurer in determining whether to charge a higher premium or to refuse to issue a policy altogether.

Once the insurer has accepted the risk, and on the occurrence of an event giving rise to a claim, the insurer has a duty to investigate to determine the facts. When a policy provides insurance against third party claims, the insurer is obligated to make reasonable efforts to settle such a claim. If a settlement cannot be reached, then regardless of the claim's merit, the insurer must defend any suit against the insured. Usually, a policy provides that in this situation the insured must cooperate. A policy provision may expressly require the insured to attend hearings and trials, to help in obtaining evidence and witnesses, and to assist in reaching a settlement.

Defenses against Payment

An insurance company can raise any of the defenses that would be valid in any ordinary action on a contract, as well as some defenses that do not apply in ordinary contract actions. If the insurance company can show that the policy was procured through fraud or misrepresentation, for example, it may have a valid defense for not paying on a claim. (The insurance company may also have the right to disaffirm or rescind an insurance contract.) An absolute defense exists if the insurer can show that the insured lacked an insurable interest–thus rendering the policy void from the beginning. Improper actions, such as those that are against public policy or that are otherwise illegal, can also give the insurance company a defense against the payment of a claim or allow it to rescind the contract.

The insurance company can be prevented, or estopped, from asserting some defenses that are normally available. For example, if a company tells an insured that information requested on a form is optional and the insured provides it anyway, the company cannot use the information to avoid its contractual obligation under the insurance contract. Similarly, incorrect statements as to the age of the insured normally do not provide the insurance company with a way to escape payment on the death of the insured. Also, incontestability clauses prevent the insurer from asserting certain defenses. Some states follow the *concurrent causation doctrine,* which requires that the insurer pay on a claim when the accident was due to more than one cause, at least one of which was covered under the policy.[5]

In the following case, an insurance company attempted to avoid payment under a policy for life and disability insurance by claiming that the policy owner did not have an insurable interest, thus rendering the policy void from the outset.

5. This doctrine was enunciated by the California Supreme Court in *State Farm Mutual Automobile Insurance Co. v. Partridge,* 10 Cal.3d 94, 514 P.2d 123, 109 Cal.Rptr. 811 (1973). Subsequently, a number of other states, particularly in the Midwest, adopted the doctrine. But see *Vanguard Insurance Co. v. Clarke,* 438 Mich. 463, 475 N.W.2d 48 (1991), in which the Michigan Supreme Court rejected the doctrine.

CASE 8.3 Paul Revere Life Insurance Co. v. Fima

United States Court of Appeals, Ninth Circuit, 1997.
105 F.3d 490.
http://www.cae9.uscourts.gov[a]

BACKGROUND AND FACTS Raoul Fima applied to Paul Revere Life Insurance Company for a disability policy. On the application, Fima stated his income as $105,000 for the previous year and $85,000 for the current year. Fima's actual income for those years was $21,603 and $6,320, respectively. The policy included the following incontestability clause: "After your policy has been in force for two years, . . . we cannot contest the statements in the application." Three years later, when Fima filed a claim under the policy, Revere discovered the truth regarding Fima's income. Revere filed a suit in a federal district court against Fima, seeking to have the policy declared void *ab initio* (from the beginning) on the ground that he lacked an insurable interest. The court denied the request. Revere appealed.

a. In the left column, click on the "Opinions" icon. On that page, click on "1997" to open the menu. Click on "January," then scroll down the list to the name of the case, and click on it to access the opinion.

IN THE LANGUAGE OF THE COURT. . .
BRUNETTI, Circuit Judge:

* * * *

Fima had an insurable interest under California Insurance Code [S]ection 10110 as a matter of law. Section 10110 states that "[e]very person has an insurable interest in the life and health of * * * [h]imself." Because Fima had an insurable interest under [S]ection 10110, his disability insurance policy was not void *ab initio.*

* * * *

* * * Because that policy is not void *ab initio* and because the period for contesting the policy has passed under the incontestability clause, Revere may not now challenge the terms of the policy or the extent of Fima's insurable interest.

DECISION AND REMEDY The U.S. Court of Appeals for the Ninth Circuit affirmed the judgment of the lower court. Every person has an insurable interest in his or her own life and health.

FOR CRITICAL ANALYSIS–Ethical Consideration *What is the underlying rationale for including incontestability clauses in insurance contracts?*

SECTION 3 TYPES OF INSURANCE

There are four general types of insurance coverage: life insurance, fire and homeowners' insurance, automobile insurance, and business liability insurance. We now examine briefly the coverage available under each of these types of insurance. In the course of our discussion, we point out certain features and provisions as they relate to the law, with special emphasis on life and fire insurance policies.

On the Web

The law firm of Anderson Kill & Olick usually includes a number of articles relating to insurance on its Web site—click on "What's New" at **http://www.andersonkill.com/home2.cgi**.

Life Insurance

There are five basic types of life insurance:

1. Whole life is sometimes referred to as straight life, ordinary life, or cash-value insurance. This type of insurance provides protection with a cumulated cash surrender value that can be used as collateral for a loan. Premiums are paid by the insured during the insured's entire lifetime, with a fixed payment to the beneficiary on death.

2. Limited-payment life might be a twenty-payment life policy. Premiums are paid for a stated number of years, after which the policy is paid up and fully effective during the insured's life. Naturally, premiums are higher than for whole life. This insurance has a cash surrender value.

3. Term insurance is a type of policy for which premiums are paid for a specified term. Payment on the policy is due only if death occurs within the term period. Premiums are less expensive than for whole life or limited-payment life, and there is usually no cash surrender value. Frequently, this type of insurance can be converted to another type of life insurance.

4. Endowment insurance involves fixed premium payments that are made for a definite term. At the end of the term, a fixed amount is to be paid to the insured or, on the death of the insured during the specified period, to a beneficiary. Thus, this type of insurance represents both term insurance and a form of *annuity* (the right to receive fixed, periodic payments for life or—as in this case—for a term of years). Endowment insurance has a rapidly increasing cash surrender value, but premiums are high, as payment is required at the end of the term even if the insured is still living.

5. Universal life is a type of insurance that combines some aspects of term insurance and some of whole life insurance. Every payment, usually called a "contribution," involves two deductions made by the issuing life insurance company. The first one is a charge for term insurance protection; the second is for company expenses and profit. The money that remains after these deductions earns interest for the policyholder at a rate determined by the company. The interest-earning money in the policy is called the policy's cash value, but that

WHOLE LIFE
A life insurance policy in which the insured pays a level premium for his or her entire life and in which there is a constantly accumulating cash value that can be withdrawn or borrowed against by the borrower. Sometimes referred to as straight life insurance.

LIMITED-PAYMENT LIFE
A type of life insurance for which premiums are payable for a definite period, after which the policy is fully paid.

TERM INSURANCE
A type of life insurance policy for which premiums are paid for a specified term. Payment on the policy is due only if death occurs within the term period. Premiums are less expensive than for whole life or limited-payment life, and there is usually no cash surrender value.

ENDOWMENT INSURANCE
A type of insurance that combines life insurance with an investment so that if the insured outlives the policy, the face value is paid to him or her; if the insured does not outlive the policy, the face value is paid to his or her beneficiary.

UNIVERSAL LIFE
A type of insurance that combines some aspects of term insurance with some aspects of whole life insurance.

term does not mean the same thing as it does for a traditional whole life insurance policy. With a universal life policy, the cash value grows at a variable interest rate rather than at a predetermined rate.

The rights and liabilities of the parties in life insurance contracts are basically dependent on the insurance agreement. A few features deserve special attention.

LIABILITY The life insurance contract determines not only the extent of the insurer's liability but, generally, whether the insurer is liable on the death of the insured. Most life insurance contracts exclude liability for death caused by suicide, military action during war, execution by a state or federal government, and even a mishap that occurs while the insured is a passenger in a commercial vehicle. In the absence of exclusion, most courts today construe any cause of death to be one of the insurer's risks.

ADJUSTMENT DUE TO MISSTATEMENT OF AGE The insurance policy constitutes the agreement between the parties. The application for insurance is part of the policy and is usually attached to the policy. When the insured misstates his or her age in the application, an error is introduced, particularly as to the amount of premiums paid. Misstatement of age is not a material error sufficient to allow the insurer to void the policy. Instead, on discovery of the error, the insurer will adjust the premium payments and/or benefits accordingly.

ASSIGNMENT Most life insurance policies permit the insured to change beneficiaries. When this is the case, in the absence of any prohibition or notice requirement, the insured can assign the rights to the policy (for example, as security for a loan) without the consent of the insurer or the beneficiary. If the beneficiary's right is *vested*—that is, has become absolute, entitling the beneficiary to payment of the proceeds—the policy cannot be assigned without the consent of the beneficiary. For the most part, life insurance contracts permit assignment and require notice only to the insurer to be effective.

CREDITORS' RIGHTS Unless insurance proceeds are exempt under state law, the insured's interest in life insurance is an asset that is subject to the rights of judgment creditors. These creditors generally can reach insurance proceeds payable to the insured's estate, proceeds payable to anyone if the payment of premiums constituted a fraud on creditors, and proceeds payable to a named beneficiary unless the beneficiary's rights have vested. Creditors, however, cannot compel the insured to make available the cash surrender value of the policy or to change the named beneficiary to that of the creditor. Almost all states exempt at least a part of the proceeds of life insurance from creditors' claims.

TERMINATION Although the insured can cancel and terminate the policy, the insurer generally cannot do so. Therefore, termination usually takes place only on the occurrence of the following:

1. Default in premium payments that causes the policy to lapse.
2. Death and payment of benefits.
3. Expiration of the term of the policy.
4. Cancellation by the insured.

Fire and Homeowners' Insurance

There are basically two types of insurance policies for a home—standard fire insurance policies and homeowners' policies.

STANDARD FIRE INSURANCE POLICIES The standard fire insurance policy protects the homeowner against fire and lightning, as well as damage from smoke and water caused by the fire or the fire department. Most fire insurance policies are classified according to the type of property covered and the extent (amount) of the issuer's liability. Exhibit 8–2 lists typical fire insurance policies.

As with life insurance, certain features and provisions of fire insurance deserve special mention. In reading the following, it is important to note some basic differences in the treatment of life and fire policies.

Liability. The insurer's liability is determined from the terms of the policy. Most policies, however, limit recovery to losses resulting from *hostile* fires—basically, those that break out or begin in places where no fire was intended to burn. A *friendly* fire—one burning in a place where it was intended to burn—is not covered. Therefore, smoke from a fireplace is not covered, but smoke from a fire caused by a defective electrical outlet is covered. Sometimes, owners add "extended coverage" to the fire policy to cover losses from "friendly" fires.

If the policy is a *valued* policy (see Exhibit 8-2) and the subject matter is completely destroyed, the insurer is liable for the amount specified in the policy. If it is an *open* policy, the extent of actual loss must be determined, and the insurer is liable only for the amount of the loss or for the maximum amount specified in the policy, whichever is less. For partial losses, actual loss must always be determined, and the insurer's liability is limited to that amount. Most insurance policies permit the insurer either to restore or replace the property destroyed or to pay for the loss.

EXHIBIT 8–2 Typical Fire Insurance Policies

TYPE OF POLICY	COVERAGE
Blanket	Covers a class of property rather than specific property, because the property is expected to shift or vary in nature. A policy covering the inventory of a business is an example.
Floater	Usually supplements a specific policy. It is intended to cover property that may change in either location or quantity. To illustrate, if the painting mentioned below under "specific policy" were to be exhibited during the year at numerous locations throughout the state, a floater policy would be desirable.
Open	A policy in which the value of the property insured is not agreed on. The policy usually provides for a maximum liability of the insurer, but payment for loss is restricted to the fair market value of the property at the time of loss or to the insurer's limit, whichever is less.
Specific	Covers a specific item of property at a specific location. An example is a particular painting located in a residence or a piece of machinery located in a factory or business.
Valued	A policy in which, by agreement, a specific value is placed on the subject to be insured to cover the eventuality of its total loss.

Proof of Loss. Fire insurance policies require the insured to file with the insurer, within a specified period or immediately (within a reasonable time), proof of loss as a condition for recovery. Failure to comply *could* allow the insurance carrier to avoid liability. Courts vary somewhat on the enforcement of such clauses.

Occupancy Clause. Most standard policies require that the premises be occupied at the time of loss. The relevant clause states that if the premises become vacant or unoccupied for a given period, unless consent by the insurer is given, the coverage is suspended until the premises are reoccupied. Persons going on extended vacations should check their policies regarding this point.

Assignment. Before a loss has occurred, a fire insurance policy is not assignable without the consent of the insurer. The theory is that the fire insurance policy is a personal contract between the insured and the insurer. The nonassignability of the policy is extremely important in the purchase of a house. The purchaser must procure his or her own insurance. If the purchaser wishes to assume the remaining insurance coverage period of the seller, consent of the insurer is essential.

To illustrate: Ann is selling her home and lot to Jeff. Ann has a one-year fire policy with Ajax Insurance Company, with six months of coverage remaining at the date on which the sale is to close. Ann agrees to assign the balance of her policy, but Ajax has not given its consent. One day after passage of the deed, a fire totally destroys the house. Can Jeff recover from Ajax?

The answer is no, as the policy is actually voided on the closing of the transaction and the deeding of the property. The reason the policy is voided is that Ann no longer has an insurable interest at the time of loss, and Jeff has no rights in a nonassignable policy.

HOMEOWNERS' POLICIES A homeowners' policy provides protection against a number of risks under a single policy, allowing the policyholder to avoid the cost of buying each protection separately. There are two basic types of homeowners' coverage:

1. *Property coverage* includes the garage, house, and other private buildings on the policyholder's lot. It also includes the personal possessions and property of the policyholder at home, in travel, or at work. It pays additional expenses for living away from home because of a fire or some other covered peril.
2. *Liability coverage* is for personal liability in case someone is injured on the insured's property, the insured damages someone else's property, or the insured injures someone else who is not in an automobile.

Perils insured under property coverage often include fire, lightning, wind, hail, vandalism, and theft (of personal property). Personal property that is typically not included under property coverage, in the absence of a specific provision, includes such items as motor vehicles, farm equipment, airplanes, and boats. Coverage for other property, such as jewelry and securities, is usually limited to a specified dollar amount.

Liability coverage under a homeowners' policy applies when others are injured or property is damaged because of the unsafe condition of the policyholder's premises. It also applies when the policyholder is negligent. It does not normally apply, however, if the liability arises from business or professional activities or from the operation of a motor vehicle. These are subjects for separate policies. Also excluded is liability arising from intentional misconduct. Similar to liability coverage is coverage for the medical payments of others who are injured on the policyholder's property and coverage for property of others that is damaged by a member of the policyholder's family.

Renters, too, take out insurance policies to protect against losses to personal property. Renters' insurance covers personal possessions against various perils and includes coverage for additional living expenses and liability.

Automobile Insurance

There are two basic kinds of automobile insurance: liability insurance and collision and comprehensive insurance.

LIABILITY INSURANCE Automobile liability insurance covers bodily injury and property damage liability. Liability limits are usually described by a series of three numbers, such as 100/300/50. This means that the policy, for one accident, will pay a maximum of $100,000 for bodily injury to one person, a maximum of $300,000 for bodily injury to more than one person, and a maximum of $50,000 for property damage. Many insurance companies offer liability up to $500,000 and sometimes higher.

Individuals who are dissatisfied with the maximum liability limits offered by regular automobile insurance coverage can purchase separate coverage under an *umbrella policy.* Umbrella limits sometimes go as high as $5 million. Umbrella policies also cover personal liability in excess of the liability limits of a homeowners' policy.

COLLISION AND COMPREHENSIVE INSURANCE Collision insurance covers damage to the insured's car in any type of collision. Usually, it is not advisable to purchase full collision coverage (otherwise known as zero deductible). The price per year is relatively high, because it is likely that some small repair jobs will be required each year. Most people prefer to take out coverage with a deductible of $100, $250, or $500, which costs substantially less than zero-deductible coverage.

Comprehensive insurance covers loss, damage, and destruction due to fire, hurricane, hail, vandalism, and theft. It can be obtained separately from collision insurance.

OTHER AUTOMOBILE INSURANCE Other types of automobile insurance coverage include the following:

1. *Uninsured motorist coverage.* Uninsured motorist coverage insures the driver and passengers against injury caused by any driver without insurance or by a hit-and-run driver. Certain states require that it be included in all auto insurance policies sold.

2. *Accidental death benefits.* Sometimes referred to as *double indemnity,* accidental death benefits provide a lump sum to named beneficiaries if the policyholder dies in an automobile accident. This coverage generally costs very little, but it may not be necessary if the insured has a sufficient amount of life insurance.

3. *Medical payment coverage.* Medical payment coverage provided by an auto insurance policy pays hospital and other medical bills and sometimes funeral expenses. This type of insurance protects all the passengers in the insured's car when the insured is driving.

OMNIBUS CLAUSE
A provision in an automobile insurance policy that protects the vehicle owner who has taken out the insurance policy and anyone who drives the vehicle with the owner's permission.

4. *Other-driver coverage.* An **omnibus clause**, or an *other-driver clause,* protects the vehicle owner who has taken out the insurance and anyone who drives the vehicle with the owner's permission. This coverage may be held to extend to a third party who drives the vehicle with the permission of the person to whom the owner gave permission.

5. *No-fault insurance.* Under no-fault statutes, claims arising from an accident are made against the claimant's own insurer, regardless of who was at fault. In some cases—for example, when injuries involve expensive medical treatment—an injured party may seek recovery from another party or insurer. In those instances, the injured party may collect the maximum amount of no-fault insurance and still sue for total damages from the party at fault, although usually, on winning an award, the injured party must reimburse the insurer for its no-fault payments.

Business Liability Insurance

A business may be vulnerable to all sorts of risks. A key employee may die or become disabled; a customer may be injured when using a manufacturer's product; the patron of an establishment selling liquor may leave the premises and injure a third party in an automobile accident; or a professional may overlook some important detail, causing liability for malpractice. Should the first situation arise (for instance, if the company president dies), the firm may have some protection under a key-person insurance policy, discussed previously. In the other circumstances, other types of insurance may apply.

GENERAL LIABILITY Comprehensive general liability insurance can protect against virtually as many risks as the insurer agrees to cover. For example, among the types of coverage that a business might wish to acquire is protection from liability for injuries arising from on-premises events not otherwise covered, such as company social functions. Some specialized establishments, for example, taverns, may be subject to liability in individualized circumstances, and policies can be drafted to meet their needs. To illustrate, in many jurisdictions statutes impose liability on a seller of liquor when a buyer of the liquor, intoxicated as a result of the sale, injures a third party. Legal protection may extend not only to immediately consequent injuries, such as quadriplegia resulting from an automobile accident, but also to the loss of financial support suffered by a family because of the injuries. Insurance can provide coverage for these injuries and financial losses.

PRODUCT LIABILITY Manufacturers may be subject to liability for injuries that their products cause, and product liability insurance can be written to match specific products' risks. Coverage can be procured under a comprehensive general liability policy or under a separate policy. The coverage may include payment for expenses involved in recalling and replacing a product that has proved to be defective.

PROFESSIONAL MALPRACTICE In recent years, professionals—attorneys, physicians, architects, and engineers, for example—have increasingly become the targets of negligence suits. Professionals may purchase malpractice insurance to protect themselves against such claims. The large judgments in some malpractice suits have received considerable publicity and are sometimes cited in what has been called "the insurance crisis," because they have contributed to a significant increase in malpractice insurance premiums.

WORKERS' COMPENSATION Workers' compensation insurance covers payments to employees who are injured in accidents arising out of and in the course of employment (that is, on the job). Workers' compensation is governed by state statutes.

SECTION 4 INFORMATION SECURITY

Understandably, a major concern regarding computer information is its security. As mentioned in Chapter 4, the most common types of computer crime are thefts of confidential information and trade secrets. Individuals and businesses, as well as other organizations and institutions, want to be assured that others do not overhear, record, or otherwise gain access to their computer information.

A breach of information security erodes public confidence and can lead to a loss of business. It can also result in the imposition of civil or criminal liability on the employer or business. Civil liability may be based on a claim that privacy interests were violated or that there was a breach of a duty of care (see the discussion of torts in Chapter 4). Criminal liability may be founded on a federal or state statute. In the remaining pages of this chapter, we look at some of the steps that can be taken to protect computer information.

Steps to Secure Information

Special care must be taken with electronic data to accomplish and maintain information security. Steps that businesspersons can take to protect their computer information include the following:

- Decide what information needs to be protected, and why.
- Make sure that all of those who are authorized to use the information understand why security is necessary.
- Decide on a system of security. (Some possibilities are covered in the pages that follow.)
- Explain to those with access to the information what they need to do to protect it.
- Forbid access to the computer system to outsiders.
- Test the security system periodically, once it is in place. If necessary, an outside firm can be hired for this purpose.
- Enforce the use of the security system.

Employment Policies

Although outside hackers and spies are a threat, the acts of employees, former employees, and other "insiders" are responsible for most computer abuse, including breaches of information security. When an insider's security breach injures a third party, the employer may be held liable. For these reasons, employees and others should be told that any form of computer abuse is against company policy, is illegal, and will be the basis for employment termination.

To ensure that confidential information is protected, employees and others may be required to sign confidentiality agreements. Such agreements typically provide that the employees will not disclose confidential information during or after employment without the employer's consent.

Monitoring certain computer-related employee activities may be appropriate, but if monitoring is to take place, employees should be informed. Usually, it is legal to monitor employees' e-mail communications and Web travels as long as the employee is told about the monitoring. Another safeguard is to distribute information only to those who need to know it. Still other security measures include facility lockups, visitor screenings, and announced briefcase checks.

Computer System Safeguards

Computers that are connected to an internal network or to the Internet can be subject to a breach of security. E-mail, for example, is vulnerable to interception along the path of its transmission over the Internet and on receipt. In this respect, e-mail is more like a postcard than a sealed letter. Without security protection, a networked computer should not be considered safe.

Many sources of software offer security programs that can be easily used. For example, most word processing programs include a "password" function. To gain access to information within the program, a user must know the password. A document that can be unlocked only with the password can be e-mailed as an attachment, providing some security. This security is minimal, however. Most password systems are easily breached. This helps persons who have forgotten their passwords, but hackers can also unlock confidential communications with little effort.

Another popular method to assure an increased degree of security for e-mail is to use some form of cryptography. Encryption hardware is useful to those who often encrypt their documents or data, or who want to encrypt all of the information on their computers. This hardware is available in the form of computer chips and is commonly used in automatic teller machines (ATMs). These chips quickly encrypt, or decrypt, information. Additionally, effective **firewalls** can be installed at the interface between computers and the Internet to protect against unwanted intruders. Firewalls can also be used to keep internal network segments secure.

FIREWALL
A barrier between networked computers and the network to which they are connected.

State and Federal Statutes

When there is a breach of information security, there are laws that can be used to prosecute the offenders. Almost all of the states have enacted statutes directed at computer abuse, including breaches of information security. The two primary federal statutes targeted at breaches of information security are the Computer Fraud and Abuse Act of 1984[6] and the federal wire fraud statute.[7]

6. 18 U.S.C. Section 1030.
7. 18 U.S.C. Section 1343.

COMPUTER FRAUD AND ABUSE ACT The Computer Fraud and Abuse Act (CFAA) prohibits seven types of activities related to "protected computers," which include computers used by the federal government, by a financial institution, or in interstate or foreign commerce or communication. The proscribed activities include the following:

- Intentional unauthorized access to obtain information relating to the national defense of the United States.
- Intentional unauthorized access to obtain financial information.
- Intentional unauthorized access to a nonpublic federal computer.
- Unauthorized access with the intent to defraud and obtaining through that access a thing of value worth more than $5,000.
- An intentional transmission that damages a protected computer, or intentional unauthorized access that causes other harm.
- Intentional trafficking in passwords with the intent to defraud.
- An intentional transmission of a threat to damage a protected computer, with the intent to extort.

The CFAA defines *damage* as a "loss aggregating at least $5,000 in value during any one-year period to one or more individuals." In the following case, the question was whether the term *individual* includes a corporation.

CASE 8.4 United States v. Middleton

United States Court of Appeals,
Ninth Circuit, 2000.
231 F.3d 490.

BACKGROUND AND FACTS Nicholas Middleton worked as the personal computer administrator for Slip.net, an Internet service provider. His responsibilities included installing software and hardware on the company's computers and providing technical support to its employees. He had extensive knowledge of Slip.net's internal systems, including employee and computer program passwords. Dissatisfied with his job, Middleton quit. Through various subterfuges, Middleton obtained access to a computer that the company had named "Lemming." Slip.net used Lemming to perform internal administrative functions and to host customers' Web sites. Lemming also contained the software for a new billing system. Middleton changed all the administrative passwords, altered the computer's registry, and deleted the entire billing system and two internal databases. To correct the damage cost Slip.net more than 150 man-hours, in addition to the expense of an outside consultant and new software. Middleton was convicted of intentionally causing damage to a "protected computer" without authorization, in violation of the CFAA. He appealed to the U.S. Court of Appeals for the Ninth Circuit, arguing that the term *individual*, as used in the statute, did not include a corporation.

IN THE LANGUAGE OF THE COURT. . .
GRABER, Circuit Judge:

* * * *

In 1996, Congress amended [the CFAA] to its current form, using the term "protected computer" and concomitantly expanding the number of computers that the statute "protected." The 1996 amendments also altered the definition of damage to read, "loss aggregating at least $5,000 in value during any one-year period to one or more individuals." We have found no explanation for this

CASE 8.4–Continued

change. We do not believe, however, that this change evidences an intent to limit the statute's reach.

To the contrary, Congress has consciously broadened the statute consistently since its original enactment. The Senate Report on the 1996 amendments notes:

> As intended when the law was originally enacted, the Computer Fraud and Abuse statute facilitates addressing in a single statute the problem of computer crime. * * * *As computers continue to proliferate in businesses and homes, and new forms of computer crimes emerge, Congress must remain vigilant to ensure that the Computer Fraud and Abuse statute is up-to-date and provides law enforcement with the necessary legal framework to fight computer crime.* [Emphasis added.]

The report instructs that "the definition of 'damage' is amended to be sufficiently broad to encompass the types of harm against which people should be protected." The report notes that the interaction between the provision that prohibits conduct causing damage and the provision that defines damage will prohibit a hacker from stealing passwords from an existing log-on program, when this conduct requires "all system users to change their passwords, *and requires the system administrator to devote resources to resecuring the system.* * * * If the loss to the victim meets the required monetary threshold, the conduct should be criminal, and the victim should be entitled to relief." The reference to a "system administrator" suggests that a corporate victim is involved. That is, if Congress intended to limit the definition of the crime to conduct causing financial damage to a natural person only, its report would not use the example of a "system administrator" devoting resources to fix a computer problem as illustrative of the "damage" to be prevented and criminalized. The Senate Report's reference to the proliferation of computers in businesses as well as homes provides additional evidence of the Senate's intent to extend the statute's protections to corporate entities. [Emphasis added.]

DECISION AND REMEDY The U.S. Court of Appeals for the Ninth Circuit concluded that the CFAA's term *individual* included a corporation. The court affirmed Middleton's conviction. He was sentenced to three years' probation, subject to a condition of 180 days in community confinement, and ordered to pay $9,147 in restitution.

FOR CRITICAL ANALYSIS–Ethical Consideration *Review the tort law principles discussed in Chapter 4, and then answer the following question: Could Slip.net have sued Lemming in tort to obtain damages to compensate Slip.net for the harms caused by Lemming's actions? Explain.*

OTHER FEDERAL STATUTES The federal wire fraud statute (discussed in Chapter 4) applies to fraud committed over the Internet, in interstate commerce. This can cover a crime that results from a transmission between two computers in, for example, New York, because it cannot be predicted which path the transmission will take–it may even travel via Europe or Asia. Other federal statutes that may apply include the Economic Espionage Act of 1996, which prohibits trade secret theft;[8] the Anticounterfeiting Consumer Protection Act of 1996,

8. 18 U.S.C. Sections 1831–1839.

which increased penalties for stealing copyrighted or trademarked property;[9] the National Stolen Property Act of 1988, which concerns the interstate transport of stolen property;[10] and the Racketeer Influenced and Corrupt Organizations Act (RICO), which prohibits racketeering activity.[11]

Information Security Group

In January 2001, the U.S. Commerce Department and nineteen information technology companies formed the Information Technology Information Sharing and Analysis Center (IT-ISAC). The members of the IT-ISAC currently include such firms as Microsoft Corporation, International Business Machines Corporation (IBM), and Intel Corporation.

The IT-ISAC members intend to share information about security issues to improve protection against breaches of information security. The members plan to exchange information about cyber threats and attacks, as well as countermeasures and security practices. The objective is to safeguard e-commerce.

9. See 18 U.S.C. Section 2311 note.
10. 18 U.S.C. Sections 2311, 2314, and 2315.
11. RICO incorporates twenty-six separate types of federal crimes and nine types of state felonies, and declares that if a person commits two of these offenses, he or she is guilty of "racketeering activity." See 18 U.S.C. Section 1961(1)(A).

TERMS AND CONCEPTS

binder 181
cash surrender value 183
endowment insurance 189
firewall 196
information security 176
insurable interest 179
insurance 175
limited-payment life 189
omnibus clause 195
policy 176
premium 176
risk 175
risk management 175
term insurance 189
underwriter 176
universal life 189
whole life 189

QUESTIONS AND CASE PROBLEMS

8–1. Insurable Interest. Adia owns a house and has an elderly third cousin living with her. Adia decides she needs fire insurance on the house and a life insurance policy on her third cousin to cover funeral and other expenses that will result from her cousin's death. Adia takes out a fire insurance policy from Ajax Insurance Co. and a $10,000 life insurance policy from Beta Insurance Co. on her third cousin. Six months later, Adia sells the house to John and transfers title to him. Adia and her cousin move into an apartment. With two months remaining on the Ajax policy, a fire totally destroys the house; at the same time, Adia's third cousin dies. Both insurance companies tender back premiums but claim they have no liability under the insurance contracts, as Adia did not have an insurable interest. Discuss their claims.

8–2. Assignment of Insurance. Sapata has an ordinary life insurance policy on her life and a fire insurance policy on her house. Both policies have been in force for a number of years. Sapata's life insurance names her son, Rory, as beneficiary. Sapata has specifically removed her right to change beneficiaries, and the life policy is silent on right of assignment. Sapata is going on a one-year European vacation and borrows money from Leonard to finance the trip. Leonard takes an assignment of the life insurance policy as security for the loan, as the policy has accumulated a substantial cash surrender value. Sapata also rents out her house to Leonard and assigns to him her fire insurance policy. Discuss fully whether Sapata's assignment of these policies is valid.

8–3. Coinsurance Clauses. Fritz has an open fire insurance policy on his home for a maximum liability of $60,000. The policy has a number of standard clauses, including the right of the insurer to restore or rebuild the property in lieu of a monetary payment, and it has a standard coinsurance clause. A fire in Fritz's house virtually destroys a utility room and part of the kitchen. The fire was caused by the overheating of an electric water heater. The total damage to the property is $10,000. The property at the time of loss is valued at $100,000. Fritz files a proof-of-loss claim for $10,000. Discuss the insurer's liability in this situation.

8–4. Multiple Insurance Coverage. Lori has a large house. She secures two open fire insurance policies on the house. Her policy with the Ajax Insurance Co. is for a maximum of $100,000, and her policy with the Beta Insurance Co. is for a maximum of $50,000. Lori's house burns to the ground. The value of the house at the time of the loss is $120,000. Discuss the liability of Ajax and Beta to Lori.

8–5. Insurer's Defenses. Kirk Johnson applied for life insurance with New York Life Insurance Co. on October 7, 1986. In answer to a question about smoking habits, Johnson stated that he had not smoked in the past twelve months and that he had never smoked cigarettes. In fact, Johnson had smoked for thirteen years, and during the month prior to the insurance application, he was smoking approximately ten cigarettes per day. Johnson died on July 17, 1988, for reasons unrelated to smoking. Johnson's father, Lawrence Johnson, who was the beneficiary of the policy, filed a claim for the insurance proceeds. While investigating the claim, New York Life discovered Kirk Johnson's misrepresentation and denied the claim. The company canceled the policy and sent Lawrence Johnson a check for the premiums that had been paid. Lawrence Johnson refused to accept the check, and New York Life brought an action for a declaratory judgment (a court determination of a plaintiff's rights). What should the court decide? Discuss fully. [*New York Life Insurance Co. v. Johnson,* 923 F.2d 279 (3d Cir. 1991)]

8–6. Insurer's Defenses. Jeffrey Duke purchased a life insurance policy on his own life from New England Mutual Life Insurance Co. Duke listed as his beneficiary his lover and business adviser, William Remmelink. On his insurance application, however, Duke described his beneficiary as merely his business partner. After Duke died of acquired immune deficiency syndrome (AIDS), New England Mutual brought an action against William Johnson, the executor of Duke's estate, to rescind (cancel) the insurance contract on the ground that Duke had "materially misrepresented his relationship with his beneficiary." Johnson claimed that New England Mutual's attempt to rescind the contract was in bad faith and asked for both punitive damages and attorneys' fees. During the trial, an underwriter with twenty-four years of experience testified that New England Mutual had never before rescinded a policy because of a misrepresentation regarding the relationship between the beneficiary and the insured. Did Duke mischaracterize his relationship with his beneficiary? If so, was such a misrepresentation material? How should the court decide? [*New England Mutual Life Insurance Co. v. Johnson,* 155 Misc.2d 680, 589 N.Y.S.2d 736 (1992)]

8–7. Insurer's Defenses. The City of Worcester, Massachusetts, adopted an ordinance in 1990 that required rooming houses to be equipped with automatic sprinkler systems no later than September 25, 1995. In Worcester, James and Mark Duffy owned a forty-eight-room lodging house with two retail stores on the first floor. In 1994, the Duffys applied with General Star Indemnity Co. for an insurance policy to cover the premises. The application indicated that the premises had sprinkler systems. General issued a policy that required, among other safety features, a sprinkler system. Within a month, the premises were inspected on behalf of General. On the inspection form forwarded to the insurer, in the list of safety systems, next to the word "sprinkler" the inspector had inserted only a hyphen. In July 1995, when the premises sustained over $100,000 in fire damage, General learned that there was no sprinkler system. The insurer filed a suit in a federal district court against the Duffys to rescind the policy, alleging misrepresentation in their insurance application about the presence of sprinklers. How should the court rule, and why? [*General Star Indemnity Co. v. Duffy,* 191 F.3d 55 (1st Cir. 1999)]

WEB EXERCISES

Go to **http://lec.westbuslaw.com**, the Web site that accompanies this text. Select "Internet Applications," and then click on "Chapter 8." There you will find the following Internet research exercises that you can perform to learn more about new types of insurance coverage and some of the consequences of settlements in insurance cases:

Activity 8–1: Technoinsurance

Activity 8–2: Disappearing Decisions

Unit 3

Marketing and E-Commerce

Contents

CHAPTER 9
Online Marketing

Concepts Covered

After reading this chapter, you should be able to:

❶ State how jurisdictional issues can arise when engaging in online marketing.

❷ Discuss some of the laws that apply to online marketing methods.

❸ Indicate what provisions should be included in online offers and why those provisions are important.

❹ Explain what shrink-wrap and click-on agreements are.

❺ Summarize the developments to date with respect to e-signatures.

"Trade and commerce, if they were not made of India rubber, would never manage to bounce over the obstacles which legislators are continually putting in their way."

Henry David Thoreau, 1817–1862 (American author)

Marketing has had a long and somewhat slow-moving history. The first marketing campaigns were obviously oral. Businesspeople made their services and products known by telling others and hoping that word of mouth would bring them additional business. With the advent of inexpensive paper, movable type, and printing presses, paper-based marketing campaigns gradually became the accepted form of "getting one's message out." The increasing popularity of newspapers and then magazines allowed businesses to advertise to large numbers of potential customers at relatively low cost.

The use of the electromagnetic spectrum—first radio and then television—added yet another dimension to marketing possibilities. Businesses found that they could reach even larger audiences by using radio and television, but sometimes at a much higher cost. In the meantime, telemarketing became increasingly important for marketing certain goods and services. Indeed, today telemarketing is one of the most cost-effective methods of reaching remote audiences for the sale of some goods and services. For example, textbook publishers often use telemarketing crews to reach professors in small schools, since it is not cost effective to send a salesperson to such schools on a regular basis.

Enter the Internet and the World Wide Web. Online marketing was born not too many years ago, became very popular in the late 1990s, and then settled down to a normal growth rate in the 2000s. In this chapter, you will learn about online marketing and the laws surrounding it. Make no mistake: online marketing is here to stay and can only grow in the future. It will become better, more cost effective, and more exciting as additional individuals and businesses gain access to high-speed Internet networks.

SECTION 1 JURISDICTIONAL ISSUES

Any business selling goods online must keep in mind that the Internet is international in scope. As explained in Chapter 2, this ability of the Internet to bypass national boundaries undercuts the traditional geographical basis for a court to assert jurisdiction.

Considering this fact, some observers speculated that setting up a Web site could subject the owner to a lawsuit anywhere in the world. Others contended that without more, a presence on the Web would not be enough to support jurisdiction over a nonresident defendant. Some even argued that a physical presence in a jurisdiction should be required.

What is emerging in the world's courts is a standard that echoes the requirement of "minimum contacts" applied by the U.S. courts. To compel a defendant to appear, most courts are indicating that a physical presence is not necessary but that minimum contacts–doing business within the jurisdiction, for example–are enough.[1] The effect of this standard is that a business firm has to comply with the laws in any jurisdiction in which it targets customers for its products.

The question then arises whether, in light of current technology, it is possible to do business over the Internet in one jurisdiction but not in another. If a company provides a link on its Web site through which a person in one country can do business with the firm, is it technically possible for that company to block access to persons in other countries? This question was one of the issues in the following case.

1. Currently under negotiation is the Hague Convention on Jurisdiction, which is an international treaty the intention of which is to make civil judgments enforceable across national borders. One issue in the negotiation is whether to require that all disputes be settled in the country of the seller or the country of the buyer. It has also been suggested that mandatory jurisdiction provisions be left out of the treaty.

CASE 9.1 International League Against Racism and Antisemitism v. Yahoo!, Inc.

Tribunal de Grande Instance de Paris, 2000.

HISTORICAL AND TECHNOLOGICAL SETTING *The Internet is a combination of several hundred million computer networks and associated sites that are interconnected throughout the world. Between 1973 and 1980, the U.S. Department of Defense defined a set of procedures by which the networks connected to the Internet could communicate. These procedures are known as Transmission Control Protocol/Internet Protocol, or TCP/IP. Each unit connected to the Internet must have what is known as an IP address, which is a series of numbers. For convenience, the numbers are associated with names, which are referred to as domain names (see Chapters 3 and 6).*

BACKGROUND AND FACTS Yahoo!, Inc., operates a "Yahoo Auctions" Web site (**http://pages.auctions.yahoo.com**) that is directed principally at customers in the United States. Items offered for sale have included objects representing symbols of Nazi ideology. In France, the act of displaying such objects is a crime and is also subject to civil liability. The International League Against Racism and Antisemitism and others filed a suit in the *Tribunal de Grande Instance de Paris* (a French court) against Yahoo and others, seeking an injunction and damages. The court ordered Yahoo to, among other things, "take all necessary measures to dissuade and make impossible any access [by persons in France or French territory] via yahoo.com to the auction service for Nazi merchandise as well as to any other site or service that may be construed as an apology

CASE 9.1–Continued

for Nazism or contesting the reality of Nazi crimes." Two months later, Yahoo returned to the court, arguing in part that the court did not have jurisdiction and that even if it did, Yahoo could not technically do what the court ordered.

IN THE LANGUAGE OF THE COURT. . .
[*JEAN-JACQUES GOMEZ*] the Presiding Justice.

* * * *

* * * YAHOO is aware that it is addressing French parties because upon making a connection to its auctions site from a terminal located in France it responds by transmitting advertising banners written in the French language[.]

* * * [A] sufficient basis is thus established in this case for a connecting link with France, which renders our jurisdiction perfectly competent to rule in this matter[.]

* * * *

* * * [I]t emerges from the [findings of the panel of consultants whom the court appointed to consider technical solutions] that it is possible to determine the physical location of a surfer from the IP address[.]

* * * *

* * * [I]t should be borne in mind that YAHOO Inc. already carries out geographical identification of French surfers or surfers operating out of French territory and visiting its auctions site, insofar as it routinely displays advertising banners in the French language targeted at these surfers, in respect of whom it therefore has means of identification * * * .

* * * [A] request [can] be made to surfers whose IP address is ambiguous * * * to provide a declaration of nationality, which in effect amounts to a declaration of the surfer's geographical origin, which YAHOO could ask for when the home page is reached, or when a search is initiated for Nazi objects * * * immediately before the request is processed by the search engine[.]

* * * [A] combination of [the] two procedures, namely geographical identification and declaration of nationality, would enable a filtering success rate approaching 90% to be achieved[.]

* * * *

* * * [E]ven if YAHOO [is] unable to identify with certainty the surfer's geographical origin, in this case France, it would know the place of delivery, and would be in a position to prevent the delivery from taking place if the delivery address was located in France[.]

DECISION AND REMEDY The court affirmed the injunction, reasoning that the "combination of [the] technical measures at [Yahoo's] disposal" rendered compliance possible. The court gave Yahoo three months to comply, after which it would be fined 100,000 francs (approximately $14,000) for each day that it failed to do so. The court also ordered Yahoo to pay each plaintiff 10,000 francs.[a]

FOR CRITICAL ANALYSIS–Technological Consideration *With this case in mind, how is the technology that underlies the Internet likely to change?*

a. Two months later, in January 2001, Yahoo banned all items of hate, including Nazi memorabilia, from its auction site. In February, however, Yahoo announced that it would not install a filter to block French users' access and filed a suit in a U.S. court, again challenging the French court's judgment on jurisdictional and technological grounds.

SECTION 2 ONLINE MARKETING AND THE LAW

All merchants can advertise their wares, online or offline. Yet in doing so, they cannot go beyond what the law permits. For example, businesses are prohibited from making statements about their products or services that would deceive or mislead consumers. You will read about the laws prohibiting deceptive advertising in the next chapter, in the context of consumer protection. There are also limits on how personal information about consumers who visit an online merchant's Web site can be used—as you will also learn in the next chapter.

Generally, online marketers must be careful to operate within the parameters established by laws covered earlier in this text. The unauthorized use of another's trademark in marketing, for example, could result in extensive liability under trademark law (see Chapter 6). Here we examine how the law applies to two practices commonly used in online marketing—linking to or framing another's Web page and direct e-mail marketing. We also look at how online businesses have been dealing with "cybergripers"—those who complain online about a business's products or practices.

Linking and Framing

When a user clicks on an icon, or highlighted or underlined text, that is programmed to be a hypertext link, the user is immediately taken to a new online location. The link may lead to another point within the same site or to a different, unrelated site somewhere else in cyberspace.

Sometimes, a site owner may ask the permission of other owners to link to their sites, but this is not normally done. Linking by underlining the name of a linked site is legal and does not require permission. Linking is considered one of the primary factors in the success of Internet commerce, and is part of the revolution of the new technology. Site owners are less agreeable to *framing,* however.

An online magazine that deals, in part, with intellectual property issues is *Law Technology Product News* at **http://www.ljextra.com/ltpn**.

FRAMING OTHERS' WEB PAGES If a linking site is a framing site, the pages of the linked site will appear in a window of the original site. With frames, a single site can let users view several sites simultaneously. Using linking and framing technology, any site owner can divert traffic from another site. This may be desired because search engines base their results on the number of hits (visits to a site). More hits can mean more advertising revenue and more sales. An owner may even appropriate a competitor's content and hide it, so that an unsuspecting user is transported to the appropriator's site even though he or she cannot see the appropriated material. This is a violation of trademark law (and copyright law).

AVOIDING LIABILITY FOR TRADEMARK INFRINGEMENT Although the law is not settled on this issue, framing has given rise to lawsuits alleging trademark violation. For example, in one case, Ticketmaster Corporation sued Microsoft Corporation in a federal district court, alleging that Microsoft Network's unauthorized links to interior pages of Ticketmaster's site constituted trademark infringement and unfair competition. Ticketmaster argued that its Web site is the same as a trademark and that it should be allowed to control the way in which others use it. Because the case was settled by the parties in 1999, we do not know how the court might have ruled.

The issue will likely come up again, however, and to be on the safe side, owners of linking sites should take several precautions. Consent should be obtained if a link falsely implies an affiliation between the sites, if a link uses the linked site's logo or trademark, if an imaged link is used, if the link is "deep" (to internal pages), or if a frame modifies or distorts the linked site. Also, consent should be obtained if the linked site requests or requires it, or if the link diverts advertising revenue from the linked site. Finally, a linking site should include a disclaimer.

Direct E-Mail Marketing

DIRECT E-MAIL
Volume e-mailing via the Internet to customers and others advertise goods or services; the online equivalent of direct mail.

On the Web

For an online article from the *New York Times* on the use of direct e-mail in marketing, go to **http://www.nytimes.com/library/tech/00/12/biztech/technology/13schw.html**.

SPAM
Bulk, unsolicited ("junk") e-mail.

The online equivalent of direct mail is **direct e-mail.** Increasingly, online businesses are finding that direct e-mail is less expensive and results in more responses than "click-through" banner ads on Web sites. E-mail can be sent to customers only, as most of it is, or to a wider group of Internet users to advertise new or upgraded products. Generally, though, direct e-mailers should be careful not to cross the line between permissible and impermissible e-mailings.

Bulk, unsolicited e-mail ("junk" e-mail) sent to all of the users on a particular e-mailing list is often called **spam.** Because spam can waste user time and network bandwidth (the amount of data that can be transmitted within a certain time), some individuals and organizations have attempted to curb its use. The Internet is a public forum, however. Under the First Amendment, this limits what can be done to restrict the use of spam.

In California, an unsolicited e-mail ad must state in its subject line that it is an ad ("ADV:"). The ad must also include a toll-free phone number or return e-mail address through which the recipient can contact the sender to request that no more ads be e-mailed.[2] An Internet service provider (ISP) can bring a successful suit in a California state court against a spammer who violates the ISP's policy that prohibits or restricts unsolicited e-mail ads. The court can award damages of up to $25,000 per day.[3]

In the following antispam case, an ISP argued in a federal district court that spamming is trespassing. Would the court accept this argument and block the sending of unsolicited ads to the ISP's subscribers?

2. Ca. Bus. & Prof. Code Section 17538.4.
3. Ca. Bus. & Prof. Code Section 17538.45.

CASE 9.2 Compuserve, Inc. v. Cyber Promotions, Inc.

United States District Court,
Southern District of Ohio, 1997.
962 F.Supp. 1015.
http://www.Loundy.com/CASES/CompuServe_v_Cyber_Promo.html[a]

BACKGROUND AND FACTS Through a nationwide computer network, CompuServe, Inc., operates a communication service that includes e-mail for CompuServe subscribers. E-mail sent to the subscribers is processed and stored on CompuServe's equipment. Cyber Promotions, Inc., is in the business of sending unsolicited e-mail ads, or spam, to Internet users. CompuServe subscribers complained to the service about Cyber Promotions's ads, and many canceled their subscriptions. Handling the ads also placed a tremendous burden on CompuServe's equipment. CompuServe told Cyber Promotions to stop using CompuServe's equipment to process and store the ads—in

a. This page is at the E-LAW Web site, "the home page of David J. Loundy, an attorney and author."

effect, to stop sending the ads to CompuServe subscribers. Ignoring the demand, Cyber Promotions stepped up the volume of its ads. After CompuServe attempted unsuccessfully to block the flow with screening software, it filed a suit against Cyber Promotions in a federal district court, seeking an injunction on the ground that the ads constituted trespass to personal property.

IN THE LANGUAGE OF THE COURT. . .
GRAHAM, District Judge.

* * * *

* * * [An] actor may commit a trespass by an act which brings him [or her] into an intended physical contact with a chattel [property] in the possession of another[.]

* * * It is undisputed that plaintiff has a possessory interest in [a right to possess] its computer systems. Further, defendants' contact with plaintiff's computers is clearly intentional. Although electronic messages may travel through the Internet over various routes, the messages are affirmatively directed to their destination.

* * * *

* * * Harm to the personal property or diminution of its quality, condition, or value as a result of defendants' use can also be the predicate for liability. * * * To the extent that defendants' multitudinous electronic mailings demand the disk space and drain the processing power of plaintiff's computer equipment, those resources are not available to serve CompuServe subscribers. Therefore, the value of that equipment to CompuServe is diminished even though it is not physically damaged by defendants' conduct.

* * * *

Many subscribers have terminated their accounts specifically because of the unwanted receipt of bulk e-mail messages. Defendants' intrusions into CompuServe's computer systems, insofar as they harm plaintiff's business reputation and goodwill with its customers, are actionable.

DECISION AND REMEDY The court held that spamming is trespassing. The court issued an injunction, ordering Cyber Promotions to stop distributing its ads to e-mail addresses maintained by CompuServe.

FOR CRITICAL ANALYSIS–Technological Consideration *If Web site links on a system caused the linked site to be overloaded with requests for information, could that constitute a trespass to personal property?*

A COUNTER TO SPAM—OPT-IN E-MAIL ADVERTISING In order to avoid spamming issues, online marketers create alliances with online communities, such as iVillage.com and dollars4mail.com. These communities consist of subscribers who have agreed to the terms and conditions of the communities. One of the terms normally is that the subscriber or member opts in to receive a limited number of direct e-mail advertisements. This is called "opt-in advertising." Thus, those who are members of, say, iVillage.com or dollars4mail.com have explicitly agreed to receive targeted e-mail ads.

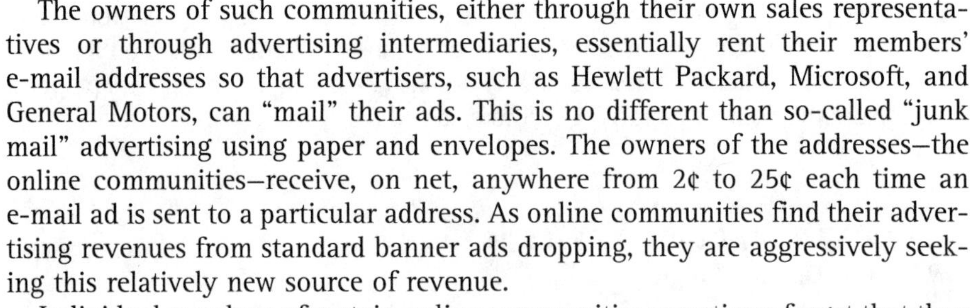

The owners of such communities, either through their own sales representatives or through advertising intermediaries, essentially rent their members' e-mail addresses so that advertisers, such as Hewlett Packard, Microsoft, and General Motors, can "mail" their ads. This is no different than so-called "junk mail" advertising using paper and envelopes. The owners of the addresses—the online communities—receive, on net, anywhere from 2¢ to 25¢ each time an e-mail ad is sent to a particular address. As online communities find their advertising revenues from standard banner ads dropping, they are aggressively seeking this relatively new source of revenue.

For links to Web sites devoted to eliminating spam and other related activities, go to **http://www.spamcop.com**.

Individual members of certain online communities sometimes forget that they ever signed up. When they receive an e-mail ad sponsored by a particular online community to which they subscribe, they believe that they have been "spammed." They then report the supposed spam to their Internet service provider (ISP) or to one of several Web groups, such as SpamCop, that are dedicated to eliminating spam from the Internet. On numerous occasions, such complaints of alleged spam have been completely inaccurate. Nonetheless, the supposedly offending "spammer" may get temporarily or permanently "kicked off" the Internet backbone. So far there have been no lawsuits in such cases, but they are bound to occur. These spam-fighting Internet entities often give total credence to the complaint, without accepting the explanation of the targeted "spammer."

It is interesting to make the comparison between paper junk mail and so-called electronic junk mail. While annoyed recipients of paper junk mail can request that their names be taken off certain mailing lists, very little publicity surrounds such actions. Moreover, throwing out a piece of junk mail without opening it is simple and relatively costless. But the same is true for spam. Deleting it without opening it is virtually costless. Moreover, on the front of virtually all e-mail advertisements, there is a place to unsubscribe. Indeed, it is simpler to "unsubscribe" to a particular mailing list on the Web than it is to get your name eliminated from a mailing list used for paper advertisements. Nonetheless, Internet users seem to be much more irritated about online junk advertising than they are about offline junk advertising.

DOUBLE OPT IN—REDUCING THE RISK EVEN MORE Online community owners sometimes go one step further to assure that they are not accused of spamming. Not only do they require their subscribers to sign a terms and conditions agreement, which gives permission to the community owners to allow direct e-mail ads, but such communities also send out a separate explicit agreement to each member of the community. This agreement restates that the members who click on an acceptance to the agreement are consenting to receive targeted e-mail ads; hence, the appellation *double opt in*. Some online advertisers will only rent e-mail addresses from communities that have double opt-in agreements for each member.

Dealing with Cybergripers

A recurring challenge for owners of trademarks has to do with Web sites—often referred to "cybergriping" or "sucks" sites—that are established solely for the purpose of criticizing the products or services sold by owners of the marks. For example, walmartsucks.com is a site devoted to critical comments on Wal-Mart's policies and services. Is there anything online businesses can do to ward off these cyber attacks on their reputations and goodwill?

TRADEMARK PROTECTION VERSUS FREE SPEECH RIGHTS There is little that trademark owners can do to protect themselves against these sites, because, in the United States at least, the courts have been reluctant to hold that such domain names infringe on the trademark owners' rights. After all, one of the primary reasons trademarks are protected under U.S. law is to prevent customers from becoming confused over the origins of the goods for sale—and a cybergriping site would certainly not create such confusion. Furthermore, American courts give extensive protection to free speech rights, including the right to express opinions about companies and their products. Of course, when such opinions are defamatory—consisting of false statements that are harmful to the reputation of another—a trademark owner may have recourse under the tort theories of fraud or disparagement of property (see Chapter 4).

PREVENTIVE TACTICS Many businesses have concluded that while they cannot control what people say about them, they can make it more difficult for it to be said—by buying up insulting domain names before the cybergripers can register for them. For example, United Parcel Service (UPS) recently bought UPSstinks.com, IHateUPS.com, UPSBites.com, and a number of similar names. According to Ram Mohan, the founder of the Internet research site Company Sleuth, "Tech-savvy companies used to do this occasionally, but now it's more mainstream, almost standard." Indeed, a study by Company Sleuth of recent domain name registrations revealed that in August 2000 nearly 250 companies had registered domain names containing "stinks," "bites," "sucks," or similarly disparaging words. Wal-Mart alone registered for more than two hundred anti-Wal-Mart names.[4]

SECTION 3 FORMING CONTRACTS ONLINE

One of the basic requirements of contract law is that the parties to a contract agree to the contract's terms. Usually, agreement is separated into two distinct events, offer and acceptance. One party (the **offeror**) makes an offer to form a contract containing certain terms, and the other party (the **offeree**) agrees to accept that offer.

OFFEROR
A person who makes an offer.

OFFEREE
A person to whom an offer is made.

When an offer is effectively accepted by the offeree, a legally binding contract comes into existence, providing other requirements for a valid contract are met. These other requirements are consideration (something of value must be given), contractual capacity (legal competence), and legality (the contract must be for a legal purpose). Additionally, to be enforceable, the parties must have genuinely assented to its terms. If the contract was formed due to fraud, for example, or due to a mistake, then genuineness of assent is lacking. To be enforceable, the contract must also be in the proper form—in writing, for example, if the law so requires.

4. David Stretfield, "Making Bad Names for Themselves: Firms Preempt Critics with Nasty Domains," *The Washington Post*, September 8, 2000, p. A1.

Today, numerous contracts are being formed online. Many of these contracts involve business-to-consumer (B2C) sales. Consumers purchase books, CDs, software, airline tickets, clothing, computers, and a host of other goods via the Internet. An increasing number of transactions involve business-to-business (B2B) sales. (For a discussion of the growth in the B2B marketplace, see this chapter's *Controversial Issues* feature.) Although the medium through which these sales contracts are generated has changed, the age-old problems attending contract formation have not. Disputes concerning contracts formed online continue to center around contract terms and whether the parties voluntarily assented to those terms.

Online Offers

Sellers doing business via the Internet can protect themselves against contract disputes and legal liability by creating offers that clearly spell out the terms that will govern their transactions if the offers are accepted.

DRAFTING THE OFFER Online offers should not be casually drafted. Rather, they must be carefully constructed and address all key terms and conditions so that, on their acceptance, the resulting contract clearly delineates the obligations of the parties. All important terms should be conspicuous and easily viewed by potential buyers. The seller's Web site should include a hypertext link to a page containing the full contract so that potential buyers are made aware of the terms to which they are assenting. At a minimum, the offer (contract) should include the following provisions:

- A provision specifying the remedies available to the buyer if the goods turn out to be defective or if the contract is otherwise breached, or broken. Any limitation of remedies should be clearly spelled out.
- A forum-selection clause (indicating the forum, or location, for the resolution of any dispute that may arise under the contract). This clause will help to avert future jurisdictional problems, which often arise in online transactions, and also help ensure that the seller will not be required to appear in court in a distant state.
- The statute of limitations governing the transaction (that is, the time period within which a legal action can be brought over a dispute concerning the contract).
- A clause that clearly indicates what constitutes the buyer's agreement to the terms of the offer.
- A provision specifying how payment for the goods and of any applicable taxes must be made.
- A statement of the seller's refund and return policies.
- Disclaimers of liability for certain uses of the goods. For example, an online seller of business forms may add a disclaimer that the seller does not accept responsibility for the buyer's reliance on the forms rather than on an attorney's advice.
- How the information gathered about the buyer will be used by the seller. (See the discussion of privacy rights in Chapter 4 and in the next chapter for more information on this topic.)

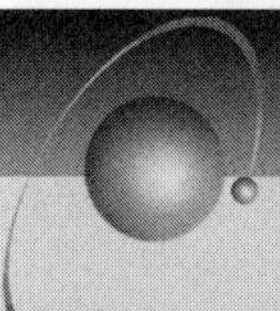

Controversial Issues in the Online World

The Burgeoning Business-to-Business Online Marketplace

The concept of an auction has been around for thousands of years. The most famous auction site on the Internet—eBay—has been around for only several years. Initially, eBay online auctions consisted of individuals selling items to other individuals, called consumer-to-consumer, or C2C, transactions. Eventually, merchants began selling overstocks and other items directly to consumers through the eBay auction site and on many other similar sites that were created, such as Yahoo Auction. These types of online auction sales have been labeled business-to-consumer, or B2C, transactions.

Enter the B2B Market

It wasn't long before the power of the Internet to reduce the cost of doing business became apparent. The result has been the advent of numerous business-to-business (B2B) online sites. These have taken on many forms. Some are simply a collection of supplier sites linked together with powerful software. They enable a business that wishes to purchase, for example, paper supplies to search a B2B sales site to find the lowest price among a variety of competing businesses that sell paper supplies.

More generally, though, online B2B sites have created a giant marketplace for the exchange of goods and services, the likes of which has never before been seen. One of the largest is Covisint. This Internet marketplace is jointly owned by five large automakers: General Motors, Ford, DaimlerChrysler, Renault, and Nissan Motors. Covisint's online joint venturers also include two information technology companies, Commerce One and Oracle. The five automakers plan to eventually funnel their combined annual spending of over $300 billion through this single Internet portal. Automobile manufacturer suppliers might add another $500 billion. The goal, of course, is to achieve significant cost savings. This Internet site features procurement, online quoting, and collaborative product design. It is estimated that the automobile makers using Covisint will reduce costs by up to 5 percent—which translates into millions of dollars per year for each company. This site offers auctions, catalogues, and expansion of supply-change management.

Similar sites exist in virtually every industry now. Boeing Company has created a B2B exchange for the aerospace industry. Its participants include Lockheed Martin Corporation, Raytheon Company, and BAE Systems, all three of which are Boeing's largest competitors. In the wood-products industry, Weyerhaeuser has created an exchange that includes its competitors, International Paper and Georgia-Pacific Corporation.

Potential Government Concerns

When competitors get together, governments get worried. Consequently, regulatory agencies in the United States, Germany, and elsewhere have been examining carefully the functions of large electronic B2B exchanges that are funded and supported by competitors in a single industry. It took months before the Federal Trade Commission (FTC) decided, in late 2000, to give regulatory approval to the automakers that established Covisint. The FTC indicated that it wanted to make sure that automakers were not simply collaborating to form an illegal cartel, the sole aim of which was to fix prices and harm competing suppliers. Undoubtedly, the FTC will examine B2B Web sites in the areas of health care, steel manufacturing, agriculture, and aerospace, to name only a few.

FOR CRITICAL ANALYSIS

Traditional methods used to procure goods have been via mail, fax, and phone. Does procurement online via B2B create any new legal issues?

An important rule to keep in mind is that the offeror controls the offer, and thus the resulting contract. This means that you should anticipate what terms you want to include in a contract and provide for them in the offer. Of course, it may be that a standardized contract form may serve your purposes. As indicated in this chapter's *E-Guidelines* feature on the next page, however, care should be taken when using such forms.

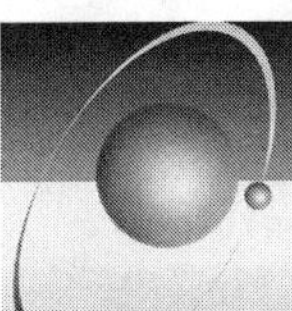

E-Guidelines

Online Contract Forms

Before the printing press, every contract form had to be handwritten. Since the advent of printing, however, most standard contract forms have been readily available at low cost. The introduction of computers into legal practice obviated the need to use preprinted forms and further allowed attorneys to customize contract forms for each given situation. This procedure has been both simplified and expanded by the inclusion of contract forms on simple-to-use CD-ROMs, such as Quicken's *Business Lawyer.* Now the Internet has made available an even larger variety of contract forms, as well as other legal and business forms.

Where to Obtain Online Contract Forms

The 'Lectric Law Library has a collection of forms at **http://www.lectlaw.com/form.html**. In addition to actual forms, there are comments on how the forms should be used and filled out. The site includes forms for the assignment of a contract, a contract for sale of a motor vehicle, and many others. Another excellent online resource for various types of forms is FindForms, at **http://www.findforms.com**.

Other online forms collections can be found at LegalWiz.com (go to **http://www.legalwiz.com/forms.htm**), a Web site that provides free legal forms, including a form that can be used to sell personal property. At **http://www.legaldocs.com**, you will find an electronic forms book that offers hundreds of standardized legal forms, some of which are free. Washburn University School of Law has a Web page containing links to an extensive number of forms archives at **http://www.washlaw.edu/legalforms/legalforms.html**. Finally, many law firms post legal forms, including contract forms, on their Web sites as well. For example, see the Web site of Bornstein & Naylor (at **http://www.netset.com/~mb/free.htm**).

More Sources for Online Forms and Advice

Recently, some online legal sites have been offering not only contract forms, but also online chats with lawyers, all for a small fee. For example, **http://www.uslaw.com** offers online chats with lawyers for $9.95 for a single session of up to thirty minutes. For $24.95, you can obtain an annual subscription. A special site for small-business owners is **http://www.lawvantage.com**. Some documents are free; others require a fee or an annual subscription. Another Web site, **http://www.mylawyer.com**, offers many consumer documents at prices starting at $9.95.

CHECKLIST

- ☑ Businesspersons should be aware that online contract forms for specific types of contracts are *standardized*—meaning that they contain the terms and conditions that typically appear in such contracts. In other words, such forms should be carefully scrutinized to ensure that they contain terms and conditions specific to the needs of particular contracting parties.
- ☑ The expanding number of forms collections on the Web means that businesspersons can "shop around" for the forms that most closely meet their purposes. Often, businesses download generic contract forms and alter them to suit their special needs. Then they go to their business law firms and ask for a review. This saves them a considerable amount of legal fees.
- ☑ Businesspersons who engage in online commerce can post their own customized contract forms on their Web sites for prospective customers or others to review or use. For example, an online merchant may include an offer to purchase or sell certain goods or services and provide a means by which the offer can be accepted—such as by clicking on a box stating, "I agree."

DISPLAYING THE OFFER The seller's Web site should include a hypertext link to a page containing the full contract so that potential buyers are made aware of the terms to which they are assenting. The contract generally must be displayed online in a readable format, such as 12-point typeface. All provisions should be reasonably clear. For example, if a seller is offering certain goods priced according to a complex price schedule, that schedule must be fully provided and explained.

INDICATING HOW THE OFFER CAN BE ACCEPTED An online offer should also include some mechanism by which the customer may accept the offer. Typically, online sellers include boxes containing the words "I agree" or "I accept the terms of the offer" that offerees can click on to indicate acceptance.

Online Acceptances

In many ways, **click-on agreements** are the Internet equivalents of **shrink-wrap agreements** (or *shrink-wrap licenses,* as they are sometimes called). A *shrink-wrap agreement* is an agreement the terms of which are expressed inside a box in which the goods are packaged. (The term *shrink-wrap* refers to the plastic that covers the box.) Usually, the party who opens the box is told that he or she agrees to the terms by keeping whatever is in the box. When the purchaser opens the software package, he or she agrees to abide by the terms of the limited license agreement.

In most cases, a shrink-wrap agreement is not between a retailer and a buyer, but between the manufacturer of the hardware or software and the ultimate buyer-user of the product. The terms generally concern warranties, remedies, and other issues associated with the use of the product.

Section 2–204 of the Uniform Commercial Code (UCC), the law governing sales contracts, provides that any contract for the sale of goods "may be made in any manner sufficient to show agreement, including conduct by both parties which recognizes the existence of a contract." Thus, a buyer's failure to object to terms contained within a shrink-wrapped software package (or an online offer) may constitute an acceptance of the terms by conduct.[5] We look next at how the law has been applied to both shrink-wrap and click-on agreements.

CLICK-ON AGREEMENT This occurs when a buyer, completing a transaction on a computer, is required to indicate his or her assent to be bound by the terms of an offer by clicking on a button that says, for example, "I agree." Sometimes referred to as a *click-on license* or a *click-wrap agreement.*

SHRINK-WRAP AGREEMENT An agreement whose terms are expressed inside a box in which goods are packaged. Sometimes called a *shrink-wrap license.*

On the Web

You can access the Uniform Commercial Code (UCC), including Article 2, at the Web site of the University of Pennsylvania Law School. Go to **http://www.law.upenn.edu/bll/ulc/ulc.htm**.

SHRINK-WRAP AGREEMENTS—ENFORCEABLE CONTRACT TERMS In many cases, the courts have enforced the terms of shrink-wrap agreements the same as the terms of other contracts. Sometimes the courts have reasoned that by including the terms with the product, the seller proposed a contract that the buyer could accept by using the product after having an opportunity to read the terms.

Also, it seems practical from a business's point of view to enclose a full statement of the legal terms of a sale with the product rather than to read the statement over the phone, for example, when a buyer calls in an order for the product.

The issue in the following case was whether the court should enforce a clause in a shrink-wrap license under Article 2 of the Uniform Commercial Code (UCC), the law governing sales contracts. The specific issue in the case was whether the limitation on liability in the clause was enforceable against a buyer of the software.

5. See, for example, *ProCD, Inc. v. Zeidenberg,* 86 F.3d 1447 (7th Cir. 1996).

CASE 9.3 M. A. Mortenson Co. v. Timberline Software Corp.

Washington Supreme Court, 2000.
140 Wash.2d 568,
998 P.2d 305.
http://www.findlaw.com/11stategov/wa/waca.html[a]

BACKGROUND AND FACTS Beginning in 1990, M. A. Mortenson Company, a nationwide construction contractor, bought software from Timberline Software Corporation. The software analyzed construction project requirements and bid information from subcontractors, and found the lowest-cost combination of subcontractors to do the work. The software was distributed subject to a license set forth on the outside of each disk's pouch and the inside cover of the instruction manuals. The first screen that appeared each time the program was used also referred to the license, which included a limitation on Timberline's liability arising from the use of the software. When Mortenson upgraded its computer system in 1993, it bought Timberline's upgraded software, *Precision Bid Analysis.* This software required the use of special "protection device " hardware. After Mortenson used *Precision* to prepare a bid, it was discovered that the bid was $1.95 million less than it should have been. The software had a bug. Timberline was already aware of the problem and had provided a newer version of *Precision* to some of its other customers. Mortenson filed a suit in a Washington state court against Timberline, alleging that the software was defective. Mortenson asserted that the shrink-wrap limitation on Timberline's liability was not part of the parties' contract. Timberline filed a motion for summary judgment, which the court granted. A state intermediate appellate court affirmed the order. Mortenson appealed to the Washington Supreme Court.

a. This page is part of a Web site maintained by FindLaw. The page contains links to recent opinions of the Washington state courts. In the "Supreme Court" section, click on "2000." When the page opens, scroll to "May. 04, 2000" and the name of the case. Click on "67796-4" to access the opinion.

IN THE LANGUAGE OF THE COURT. . .
JOHNSON, J. [Justice.]

* * * *

[UCC 2–204] states:

(1) A contract for sale of goods may be made in any manner sufficient to show agreement, including conduct by both parties which recognizes the existence of such a contract.

* * * *

* * * We * * * hold under [UCC 2–204] the terms of the license were part of the contract between Mortenson and Timberline, and Mortenson's use of the software constituted its assent to the agreement, including the license terms.

The terms of Timberline's license were either set forth explicitly or referenced in numerous locations. The terms were included within the shrinkwrap packaging of each copy of *Precision Bid Analysis;* they were present in the manuals accompanying the software; they were included with the protection devices for the software, without which the software could not be used. The fact the software was licensed was also noted on the introductory screen each time the software was used. Even accepting Mortenson's contention it never saw the terms of the license, as we must do on summary judgment, *it was not necessary for Mortenson to actually read the agreement in order to be bound by it.* [Emphasis added.]

Furthermore, [UCC 1–201(3)] defines an "agreement" as "the bargain of the parties in fact as found in their language or by implication from other circumstances including course of dealing or usage of trade or course of performance * * * ." Mortenson and Timberline had a course of dealing; Mortenson had purchased licensed software from Timberline for years prior to its upgrade to *Precision Bid Analysis*. All Timberline software, including the prior version of *Bid Analysis* used by Mortenson since at least 1990, is distributed under license. Moreover, extensive testimony and exhibits before the trial court demonstrate an unquestioned use of such license agreements throughout the software industry. Although Mortenson questioned the relevance of this evidence, there is no evidence in the record to contradict it. * * *

As the license was part of the contract between Mortenson and Timberline, its terms are enforceable unless objectionable on grounds applicable to contracts in general.

DECISION AND REMEDY The Washington Supreme Court affirmed the decision of the lower court. The shrink-wrap license that accompanied Timberline's software was enforceable, and its limitation on Timberline's liability caused by use of the software was valid. The parties had dealt with each other for years, and the terms of the license, which was similar to those used throughout the software industry, were set forth in several locations.

FOR CRITICAL ANALYSIS–Ethical Consideration *Is it fair to hold that a person can be bound by an agreement that he or she has not read? Why, or why not?*

SHRINK-WRAP AGREEMENTS–PROPOSALS FOR ADDITIONAL TERMS Not all of the terms presented in shrink-wrap agreements have been enforced. One important consideration is whether the parties form their contract before or after the seller communicates the terms of the shrink-wrap agreement to the buyer. If a court finds that the buyer learned of the shrink-wrap terms *after* the parties entered into a contract, the court might conclude that those terms were proposals for additional terms, which were not part of the contract unless the buyer expressly agreed to them.

In the following case, the court was asked to decide, among other things, whether to enforce an arbitration clause that was part of a set of "Standard Terms and Conditions" included in every box of every computer the defendant sold.

CASE 9.4 Klocek v. Gateway, Inc.

United States District Court, District of Kansas, 2000. 104 F.Supp.2d 1332.

BACKGROUND AND FACTS Whenever it sells a computer, Gateway, Inc., includes a copy of its "Standard Terms and Conditions Agreement" in the box that contains the power cables and instruction manuals. At the top of the first page, in a printed box and in emphasized type, is the following: "NOTE TO THE CUSTOMER: * * * By keeping your Gateway 2000 computer system beyond five (5) days after the date of delivery, you accept these Terms and Conditions." This document is four pages long and contains sixteen numbered paragraphs. Paragraph 10 states, "DISPUTE RESOLUTION. Any dispute or controversy arising out of or relating to this Agreement or its interpretation shall be settled exclusively and finally by arbitration." William Klocek bought a Gateway computer. Dissatisfied when it proved to be incompatible with his other computer equipment, he filed a suit in a federal district court against Gateway and others, alleging in part breach of contract. Gateway filed a motion to dismiss, asserting that Klocek was required to submit his claims to arbitration under Gateway's "Standard Terms." Klocek argued that these terms were not part of the contract for the purchase of the computer.

CASE 9.4—Continued

IN THE LANGUAGE OF THE COURT. . .

VRATIL, District Judge.

* * * *

* * * [UCC 2–207] provides:

Additional terms in acceptance or confirmation. (1) A definite and seasonable [timely] expression of acceptance or a written confirmation which is sent within a reasonable time operates as an acceptance even though it states terms additional to or different from those offered or agreed upon, unless acceptance is expressly made conditional on assent to the additional or different terms.

(2) The additional terms are to be construed as proposals for addition to the contract [if the contract is not between merchants].

* * * *

Under [UCC] 2–207, [Gateway's] Standard Terms constitute either an expression of acceptance or written confirmation. As an expression of acceptance, the Standard Terms would constitute a counter-offer [a return offer that simultaneously rejects the original offer] only if Gateway expressly made its acceptance conditional on plaintiff's [Klocek's] assent to the additional or different terms. The conditional nature of the acceptance must be clearly expressed in a manner sufficient to notify the offeror [Klocek] that the offeree [Gateway] is unwilling to proceed with the transaction unless the additional or different terms are included in the contract. Gateway provides no evidence that at the time of the sales transaction, it informed plaintiff that the transaction was conditioned on plaintiff's acceptance of the Standard Terms. Moreover, the mere fact that Gateway shipped the goods with the terms attached did not communicate to plaintiff any unwillingness to proceed without plaintiff's agreement to the Standard Terms.

Because plaintiff is not a merchant, additional or different terms contained in the Standard Terms did not become part of the parties' agreement unless plaintiff expressly agreed to them. Gateway argues that plaintiff demonstrated acceptance of the arbitration provision by keeping the computer more than five days after the date of delivery. Although the Standard Terms purport to work that result, Gateway has not presented evidence that plaintiff expressly agreed to those Standard Terms. Gateway states only that it enclosed the Standard Terms inside the computer box for plaintiff to read afterwards. It provides no evidence that it informed plaintiff of the five-day review-and-return period as a condition of the sales transaction, or that the parties contemplated additional terms to the agreement. * * * Thus, * * * the Court overrules Gateway's motion to dismiss.

DECISION AND REMEDY The court denied Gateway's motion to dismiss. The court reasoned that it would enforce the arbitration provision in Gateway's "Standard Terms" if they were part of the contract for the sale of the computer. The court concluded that those terms were not part of the contract, because Gateway did not show, as required under UCC 2–207, that it told Klocek its acceptance of the deal was conditioned on his agreeing to those terms or that he agreed to them.[a]

FOR CRITICAL ANALYSIS—Technological Consideration *The court in this case applied UCC provisions to an electronic contract. Can you think of some unique aspects of electronic contracting that would not be covered by traditional laws, such as the UCC?*

a. Klocek's complaint was later dismissed on the ground that his claim did not satisfy the court's amount-in-controversy requirement for diversity jurisdiction. See *Klocek v. Gateway, Inc.,* 104 F.Supp.2d 1332 (D.Kan. 2000).

EXHIBIT 9–1 A Click-On Disclaimer

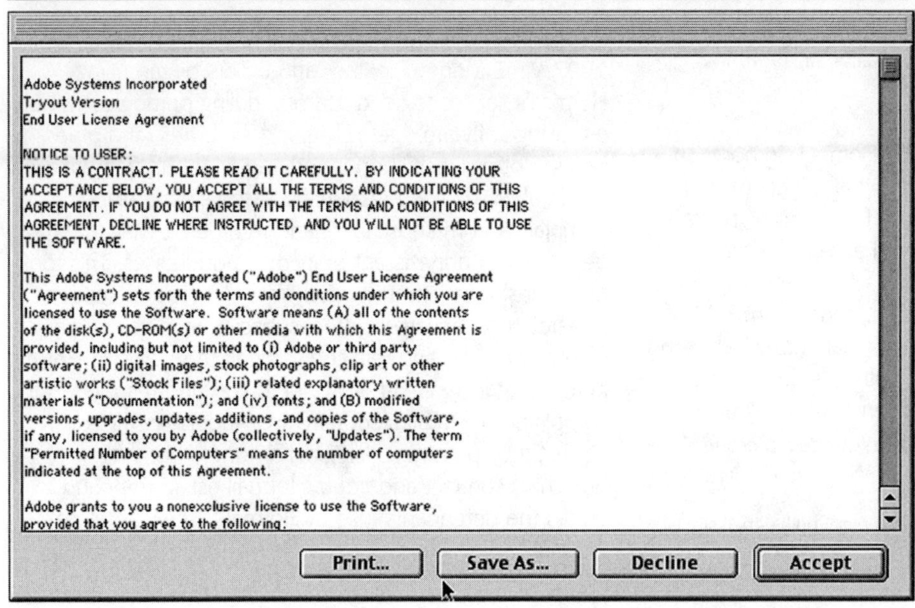

Adobe Systems Incorporated
Tryout Version
End User License Agreement

NOTICE TO USER:
THIS IS A CONTRACT. PLEASE READ IT CAREFULLY. BY INDICATING YOUR ACCEPTANCE BELOW, YOU ACCEPT ALL THE TERMS AND CONDITIONS OF THIS AGREEMENT. IF YOU DO NOT AGREE WITH THE TERMS AND CONDITIONS OF THIS AGREEMENT, DECLINE WHERE INSTRUCTED, AND YOU WILL NOT BE ABLE TO USE THE SOFTWARE.

This Adobe Systems Incorporated ("Adobe") End User License Agreement ("Agreement") sets forth the terms and conditions under which you are licensed to use the Software. Software means (A) all of the contents of the disk(s), CD-ROM(s) or other media with which this Agreement is provided, including but not limited to (i) Adobe or third party software; (ii) digital images, stock photographs, clip art or other artistic works ("Stock Files"); (iii) related explanatory written materials ("Documentation"); and (iv) fonts; and (B) modified versions, upgrades, updates, additions, and copies of the Software, if any, licensed to you by Adobe (collectively, "Updates"). The term "Permitted Number of Computers" means the number of computers indicated at the top of this Agreement.

Adobe grants to you a nonexclusive license to use the Software, provided that you agree to the following:

CLICK-ON AGREEMENTS As described earlier, a click-on agreement (also sometimes called a *click-on license* or *click-wrap agreement*) occurs when a buyer, completing a transaction on a computer, is required to indicate his or her assent to be bound by the terms of an offer by clicking on a button that says, for example, "I agree." The terms may be contained on a Web site through which the buyer is obtaining goods or services, or they may appear on a computer screen when software is loaded. Exhibit 9–1 contains the language of a click-on disclaimer that accompanies a package of software made and marketed by Adobe Systems, Inc.

As mentioned, Article 2 of the UCC provides that acceptance can be made by conduct. The *Restatement (Second) of Contracts,* a compilation of common law contract principles, has a similar provision. It states that parties may agree to a contract "by written or spoken words or by other action or by failure to act."[6] With these provisions in mind, it seems that a binding contract can be created over the Internet by clicking on an "I agree" button.

The following case was the first to involve the enforceability of a click-on agreement. The court was asked to decide, among other things, whether the defendants had breached certain "Terms of Service" that were posted on a Web site and accompanied by an "I agree" button, which the defendants had clicked.

6. *Restatement (Second) of Contracts,* Section 19.

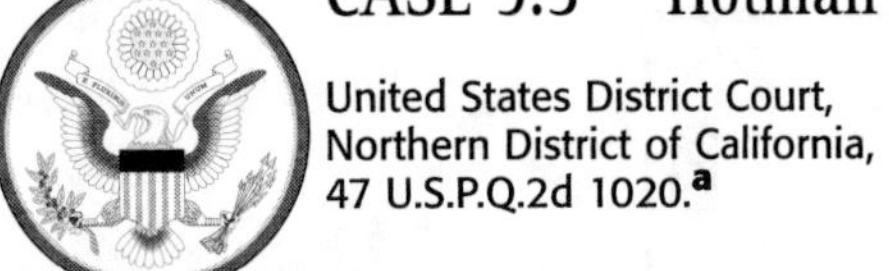

CASE 9.5 Hotmail Corp. v. Van$ Money Pie, Inc.

United States District Court,
Northern District of California, 1998.
47 U.S.P.Q.2d 1020.[a]

BACKGROUND AND FACTS Hotmail Corporation provides free e-mail service to more than eighty million subscribers. To obtain the service, at Hotmail's Web site a prospective subscriber clicks on an "I accept" button to agree to Hotmail's "Terms of Service." These terms prohibit a subscriber from using the service to send *spam*.[b] All of the millions of daily e-mail messages that subscribers send and receive automatically display Hotmail's domain name "hotmail.com" and its signature statement "Get Your Private, Free Email at **http://www.hotmail.com**." In 1997, Van$ Money Pie, Inc., and others began using Hotmail's service to send spam peddling pornography, bulk e-mailing software, "get-rich-quick" schemes, and other items. Hotmail was soon inundated with hundreds of thousands of misdirected responses to the spam, including complaints from subscribers and returned e-mail that had been sent to nonexistent or incorrect addresses. This took up a substantial amount of Hotmail's computer capacity, threatened to adversely affect subscribers in sending and receiving e-mail, and resulted in significant costs to Hotmail in terms of increased personnel to sort and respond to the complaints. Hotmail filed a suit in a federal district court against the spammers, alleging, among other things, breach of contract and fraud. Hotmail asked the court to enjoin the defendants' use of Hotmail's service before the trial.

a. This reporter is the *United States Patent Quarterly, Second Series*, which is published by the Bureau of National Affairs, Inc., in Washington, D.C.

b. As mentioned, *spam* is unsolicited commercial bulk e-mail similar to junk mail sent through the U.S. Postal Service.

IN THE LANGUAGE OF THE COURT. . .

WARE, J. [Judge.]

* * * *

Breach of Contract

* * * The evidence supports a finding that plaintiff will likely prevail on its breach of contract claim and that there are at least serious questions going to the merits of this claim in that plaintiff has presented evidence of the following: that defendants obtained a number of Hotmail mailboxes and access to Hotmail's services; that in so doing defendants agreed to abide by Hotmail's Terms of Service which prohibit using a Hotmail account for purposes of sending spam and/or pornography; that defendants breached their contract with Hotmail by using Hotmail's services to facilitate sending spam and/or pornography; that Hotmail complied with the conditions of the contract except those from which its performance was excused; and that if defendants are not enjoined they will continue to create such accounts in violation of the Terms of Service.

Fraud and Misrepresentation

* * * The cause of action for fraud includes willfully deceiving another with intent to induce him to alter his position to his injury or risk by asserting, as a fact, that which is not true, by one who has no reasonable ground for believing it to be true; or by suppressing a fact, by one who is bound to disclose it, or who gives information of other facts which are likely to mislead for want of communication of that fact; or by making a promise without any intention of performing it.

* * * The evidence supports a finding that plaintiff will likely prevail on its fraud and misrepresentation claim and that there are at least serious questions going to the merits of this claim in that plaintiff has presented evidence of the

following: that defendants fraudulently obtained a number of Hotmail accounts, promising to abide by the Terms of Service without any intention of doing so and suppressing the fact that such accounts were created for the purpose of facilitating a spamming operation, and that defendants' fraud and misrepresentation caused Hotmail to allow defendants to create and use Hotmail's accounts to Hotmail's injury. In addition, the evidence supports a finding that defendants' falsification of e-mails to make it appear that such messages and the responses thereto were authorized to be transmitted via Hotmail's computers and stored on Hotmail's computer system—when defendants knew that sending such spam was unauthorized by Hotmail—constitutes fraud and misrepresentation, and that Hotmail relied on such misrepresentations to allow the e-mails to be transmitted over Hotmail's services and to take up storage space on Hotmail's computers, to Hotmail's injury.

DECISION AND REMEDY The court concluded that Hotmail was entitled to a preliminary injunction on several grounds, including the likelihood that Hotmail would prevail on its breach of contract and fraud claims. In reaching this conclusion, the court recognized Hotmail's online service agreement, with its click-on acceptance button, to be an enforceable contract.

FOR CRITICAL ANALYSIS–Social Consideration *In your opinion, are most consumers fully aware of the legal consequences of clicking an "I agree" box on a Web site?*

Electronic Signatures[7]

Forming online contracts, or e-contracts, has numerous advantages, but there are also some drawbacks—unless precautions are taken. One issue has to do with signatures. Many laws and regulations require a "signature" for regulatory compliance or to validate a transaction and make it enforceable. For example, under the UCC's Statute of Frauds provision any contract for the sale of goods priced at $500 or more must be in writing to be enforceable, and it must be signed by the party against whom enforcement is sought. Thus, when a contract requires a signature, those forming online contracts need to make some provision for what kind of electronic signature (e-signature) will be used to both (1) establish the identity of the person signing and (2) validate or authenticate the document as an intentional legal act of the signer.

E-SIGNATURE TECHNOLOGIES Today, there are numerous technologies that allow electronic documents to be signed. These include digital signatures and alternative technologies.

The most prevalent e-signature technology is the *asymmetric cryptosystem*, which creates a digital signature using two different (asymmetric) cryptographic "keys." In such a system, a person attaches a digital signature to a document using a private key, or code. The key has a publicly available counterpart.

7. You may have been assigned this material in a previous chapter. If so, you may skip this section on e-signatures.

CYBERNOTARY
A legally recognized certification authority that issues the keys for digital signatures, identifies their owners, certifies their validity, and serves as a repository for public keys.

Anyone can use it with the appropriate software to verify that the digital signature was made using the private key. A **cybernotary**, or legally recognized certification authority, issues the key pair, identifies the owner of the keys, and certifies the validity of the public key. The cybernotary also serves as a repository for public keys. Cybernotaries already are available, but they do not operate within any existing legal framework because they are so new.

Another type of signature technology, known as *signature dynamics,* involves capturing a sender's signature using a stylus and an electronic digitizer pad. A computer program takes the signature's measurements, the sender's identity, the time and date of the signature, and the identity of the hardware. This information is then placed in an encrypted *biometric token* attached to the document being transmitted. To verify the authenticity of the signature, the recipient of the document compares the measurements of the signature with the measurements in the token. When this type of e-signature is used, it is not necessary to have a third party verify the signatory's identity.

Other forms of e-signature have been—or are now being—developed as well. For example, technological innovations now under way will allow an e-signature to be evidenced by an image of one's retina, fingerprint, or face that is scanned by a computer and then matched to a numeric code. The scanned image and the numeric code are filed with security companies that maintain files on an accessible server that can be used to authenticate a transaction.

STATE LAWS GOVERNING E-SIGNATURES Most states have laws governing e-signatures. The problem is that the state e-signature laws are not uniform. In an attempt to create more uniformity among the states, the National Conference of Commissioners on Uniform State Laws promulgated the Uniform Electronic Transactions Act (UETA) in 1999. The UETA defines an *e-signature* as "an electronic sound, symbol, or process attached to or logically associated with a record and executed or adopted by a person with the intent to sign the record."[8]

This definition of *e-signature* includes encrypted digital signatures, names (intended as signatures) at the ends of e-mail, and a click on a Web page if the click includes the identification of the person. The UETA also states, among other things, that a signature may not be denied legal effect or enforceability solely because it is in electronic form.

The law firm of Baker & McKenzie offers a summary of the scope and applicability of the E-SIGN Act of 2000 on its Web site. Go to **http://www.bmck.com/ecommerce/E-SIGN_Act.htm**.

FEDERAL LAW ON E-SIGNATURES AND E-DOCUMENTS In 2000, Congress enacted the Electronic Signatures in Global and National Commerce Act (E-SIGN Act) to provide that no contract, record, or signature may be "denied legal effect" solely because it is in an electronic form. In other words, under this law, an electronic signature is as valid as a signature on paper, and an electronic document can be as enforceable as a paper one. For an electronic signature to be enforceable, the contracting parties must have agreed to use electronic signatures. For an electronic document to be valid, it must be in a form that can be retained and accurately reproduced.

What the act did *not* do is provide any standard for authenticating e-signatures or include solutions to other problems associated with e-contracting. How will the technology be managed? What kind of signature verification process will be

8. UETA 102(8).

required? If encryption "keys" are used, how will they be generated? Where can you get one? Will there be digital notaries? What if a hacker or other technologically sophisticated person steals one's signature and forges electronic documents with it? Basically, the act left these and other questions to be decided by the parties to e-commerce contracts, the technology industry, and the states.

There is another problem. An element common to all valid signatures is that they evidence an *intent to be bound* by the document that is being signed. Section 1–201(39) of the Uniform Commercial Code, for example, provides that a signature may include "any symbol executed or adopted by a party with present intention to authenticate a writing." Thus, any symbol, including an X, a person's initials, or even a thumbprint, can suffice as a signature—but *only* if the symbol is used with the intention of authenticating the writing. Section 106(5) of the E-SIGN Act emphasizes the intent factor by defining an electronic signature as any "electronic sound, symbol, or process, attached to or logically associated with a contract or other record and executed or adopted by a person with the intent to sign the record." Yet how can intent be measured in the electronic-contracting environment? How do you know if an online party even has contractual capacity? Again, this question is left up to the parties and the states to decide.

SECTION 4 PARTNERING AGREEMENTS

One way that online sellers and buyers can overcome signature problems, as well as disputes over terms and conditions in their e-contracts, is to form partnering agreements. In a **partnering agreement**, a seller and a buyer who frequently do business with each other agree in advance on the terms and conditions that will apply to all transactions subsequently conducted electronically. The partnering agreement can also establish special access and identification codes to be used by the buyer and seller when transacting business electronically.

PARTNERING AGREEMENT
An agreement between a seller and a buyer who frequently do business with each other on the terms and conditions that will apply to all subsequently formed electronic contracts.

A partnering agreement reduces the likelihood that disputes under the contract will arise, because the buyer and the seller have agreed, in their partnering agreement, to the terms and conditions that will accompany each sale. Furthermore, if a dispute does arise, a court or arbitration forum will be able to refer to the partnering agreement when determining the parties' intent with respect to subsequent contracts. Of course, even with a partnering agreement there remains the possibility of fraud. If an unauthorized person uses a purchaser's designated access number and identification code, it may be some time before the problem is discovered.

TERMS AND CONCEPTS

click-on agreement 213
cybernotary 220
direct e-mail 206
offeree 209
offeror 209
partnering agreement 221
shrink-wrap agreement 213
spam 206

QUESTIONS AND CASE PROBLEMS

9–1. Click-On Agreements. Paul is a financial analyst for King Investments, Inc., a brokerage firm. Paul uses the Internet to investigate the background and activities of companies that might be good investments for King's customers. While visiting the Web site of Business Research, Inc., Paul sees on his screen a message that reads, "Welcome to business-research.com. By visiting our site, you have been entered as a subscriber to our e-publication, *Companies Unlimited*. This publication will be sent to you daily at a cost of $7.50 per week. An invoice will be included with *Companies Unlimited* every four weeks. You may cancel your subscription at any time." Has Paul entered into an enforceable contract to pay for *Companies Unlimited?* Why, or why not?

9–2. Linking. Ticket Sales, Inc. (TS), operates a ticket brokerage on the Internet, selling tickets for athletic events through its Web site. For each event, there is a separate interior page with its own URL. Each page contains information about the event and directions on how to buy tickets. On the site's home page is a "Statement of Terms," which includes a clause prohibiting linking, but TS does not require its customers to agree to the terms before buying tickets. Tkts.com Corp. operates a clearinghouse on the Internet, informing customers where they can buy tickets to events. For each event, Tkts.com maintains a Web page that includes basic information and a link to a ticket broker's page, which is usually a TS event page. Tkts.com explains on its site that it does not sell tickets and that the links connect to services that do. Is Tkts.com violating the law?

9–3. Shrink-Wrap Terms. Over the phone, Rich and Enza Hill ordered a computer from Gateway 2000, Inc. Inside the box were the computer and a list of contract terms, which provided that the terms governed the transaction unless the customers returned the computer within thirty days. Among those terms was a clause that required any claims to be submitted to arbitration. The Hills kept the computer for more than thirty days before complaining to Gateway about the computer's components and its performance. When the matter was not resolved to their satisfaction, the Hills filed a suit in a federal district court against Gateway, arguing, among other things, that the computer was defective. Gateway asked the court to enforce the arbitration clause. The Hills claimed that this term was not part of a contract to buy the computer because the list on which it appeared had been in the box and they did not see the list until after the computer was delivered. Is the term a part of the contract? Why or why not? [*Hill v. Gateway 2000, Inc.*, 105 F.3d 1147 (7th Cir. 1997)]

9–4. License Agreements. Management Computer Controls, Inc. (known as "MC 2"), is a Tennessee corporation in the business of selling software. Charles Perry Construction, Inc., is a Florida corporation. Perry entered into two contracts with MC 2 to buy software designed to perform estimating and accounting functions for construction firms. Each contract was printed on a standard order form containing a paragraph that referred to a license agreement. The license agreement included a choice-of-forum and choice-of-law provision: "Agreement is to be interpreted and construed according to the laws of the State of Tennessee. Any action, either by you or MC 2, arising out of this Agreement shall be initiated and prosecuted in the Court of Shelby County, Tennessee, and nowhere else." Each of the software packages arrived with the license agreement affixed to the outside of the box. Additionally, the boxes were sealed with an orange sticker bearing the following warning: "By opening this packet, you indicate your acceptance of the MC 2 license agreement." Alleging that the software was not suitable for use with Windows NT, Perry filed a suit against MC 2 in a Florida state court. MC 2 filed a motion to dismiss the complaint on the ground that the suit should be heard in Tennessee. How should the court rule? Why? [*Management Computer Controls, Inc. v. Charles Perry Construction, Inc.*, 743 So.2d 627 (Fla.App. 1 Dist. 1999)]

9–5. Click-On Agreements. America Online, Inc. (AOL), is, among other things, an Internet service provider (ISP). AOL promotes its service through the mass distribution of its software. Mark Williams, a Massachusetts resident, installed on his computer the edition of the software known as "AOL Version 5.0." After it was loaded, a request appeared on Williams's computer screen, asking him to agree to "Terms of Service." To read the terms, Williams had to click "Read Now" boxes twice. The terms included a clause that stated all disputes were to be submitted to a Virginia state court. Williams later claimed that the installation of the software caused unauthorized changes to the configuration of his computer so he could no longer access non-AOL ISPs, was unable to run non-AOL e-mail programs, and was unable to access personal information and files. Williams and others filed a suit in a Massachusetts state court against AOL, alleging in part unfair or deceptive acts or practices in violation of state law. On the basis of the forum-selection clause in the "Terms of Service," AOL filed a motion to dismiss. Should the court grant the motion? Why or why not? [*Williams v. America Online, Inc.*, 2001 WL 135825 (Mass.Super. 2001)]

9–6. Cybergriping. Lockheed Corp. has used the name "Lockheed" since the 1930s. In 1995, Lockheed merged with Martin Marietta Corp., both of which were large companies with international reputations. The product of that merger, Lockheed Martin Corp., one of the world's largest and best-known aerospace, electronics, and advanced materials manufacturers, continued to use the Lockheed name. In 1998, Dan Parisi registered the domain names "lockheedsucks.com" and "lockheedmartinsucks.com." Parisi used the names to point to a Web site that offered visitors an opportunity to vent their views on Lockheed and other companies. Lockheed demanded that Parisi transfer the names to it. Parisi refused. Lockheed filed a complaint with the World Intellectual Property Organization Arbitration and Mediation Center (WIPO Center), asking it to transfer the names. Lockheed contended in part that the names were "confusingly similar" to Lockheed's trademarks. Parisi responded that "no one would reasonably believe [Lockheed] operates a website that appends the word 'sucks' to its name and then uses it to criticize corporate America." In whose favor should the WIPO Center rule, and why? [*Lockheed Martin Corp. v. Parisi*, WIPO Case No. D2000-1015 (2000)]

9–7. Spam. America Online, Inc. (AOL), provides services to its customers (members), including the transmission of e-mail to and from other members and across the Internet. To become a member, a person must agree not to use AOL's computers to send bulk, unsolicited, commercial e-mail (spam). AOL uses filters to block spam, but bulk e-mailers sometimes use other software to thwart the filters. National Health Care Discount, Inc. (NHCD), sells discount optical and dental service plans. To generate leads for NHCD's products, sales representatives, who included AOL members, sent more than 300 million pieces of spam through AOL's computer system. Each item cost AOL an estimated $.00078 in equipment expenses. Some of the spam used false headers and other methods to hide the source. After receiving more than 150,000 complaints, AOL asked NHCD to stop. When the spam continued, AOL filed a suit in a federal district court against NHCD, alleging in part trespass to chattels—an unlawful interference with another's rights to possess personal property. AOL asked the court for a summary judgment on this claim. Did the spamming constitute trespass to chattels? Explain. [*America Online, Inc. v. National Health Care Discount, Inc.*, 121 F.Supp.2d 1255 (N.D.Iowa, 2000)]

WEB EXERCISES

Go to **http://lec.westbuslaw.com**, the Web site that accompanies this text. Select "Internet Applications," and then click on "Chapter 9." There you will find the following Internet research exercise that you can perform to learn more about online business-to-business transactions:

Activity 9–1: The B2B Marketplace

CHAPTER 10

Consumer Protection and Privacy Issues

Concepts Covered

After reading this chapter, you should be able to:

1. Summarize the major consumer protection laws.
2. Indicate some specific ways in which consumers are protected against deceptive advertising and sales practices.
3. List and describe the major laws protecting privacy rights.
4. Explain how personal information is collected and used by online marketers.
5. Discuss what the government has and has not done with respect to the privacy of online personal information.

"Subject to specific constitutional limitations, when the legislature has spoken, the public interest has been declared in terms well nigh conclusive."

William O. Douglas
(Associate justice of the United States Supreme Court, 1939–1975)

The marketing strategies you read about in the previous chapter are closely tied to the topics covered in this chapter—consumer protection and privacy issues. After all, the goal of many marketing efforts is to sell goods or services to **consumers**, defined as persons who make purchases primarily for personal, family, or household use. Those who market and sell goods, whether online or offline, are subject to laws designed to protect consumers from certain marketing practices, such as deceptive advertising.

In this chapter, we first examine some consumer protection laws that are relevant to e-commerce transactions. We then look at an issue of increasing concern not only to consumers but to all groups in society: how to protect privacy rights in the online environment.

CONSUMER
One whose purchases are made primarily for person, family, or household use.

CONSUMER LAW
The body of statutes, agency rules, and judicial decisions protecting consumers of goods and services from dangerous or mislabeled products, unfair credit practices, deceptive advertising, and so on.

SECTION 1 FEDERAL LAWS PROTECTING CONSUMERS

Generally, all statutes, administrative agency rules, and common law judicial decisions that serve to protect the interests of consumers are classified as **consumer law**. Traditionally, in disputes involving consumers, it was assumed that the freedom to contract carried with it the obligation to live by the deal made. Over time, this attitude has changed considerably. Today, myriad federal and state laws protect consumers from unfair trade practices, unsafe products, discriminatory or unreasonable credit requirements, and other problems related to consumer transactions. Nearly every agency and department of the federal government has an office of consumer affairs, and most states have one or more such offices to help consumers. Also, typically the attorney general's office assists consumers at the state level.

One of the earliest federal consumer protection laws—and still one of the most important—was the Federal Trade Commission Act of 1914.[1] The act created the Federal Trade Commission (FTC) to carry out the broadly stated goal of preventing unfair and deceptive trade practices, including deceptive advertising.[2]

Deceptive Advertising

Advertising will be deemed deceptive if a consumer would be misled by the advertising claim. Vague generalities and obvious exaggerations are permissible. These claims are known as *puffing*. When a claim takes on the appearance of literal authenticity, however, it may create problems. Advertising that *appears* to be based on factual evidence but that in fact is not will be deemed deceptive. A classic example is provided by a 1944 case in which the claim that a skin cream would restore youthful qualities to aged skin was deemed deceptive.[3]

On the Web

To learn what the Federal Trade Commission (FTC) is currently doing to protect consumers, go to the FTC's Web site at **http://www.ftc.gov**.

Some advertisements contain "half-truths," meaning that the presented information is true but incomplete, and it leads consumers to a false conclusion. For example, the makers of Campbell's soups advertised that "most" Campbell's soups were low in fat and cholesterol and thus were helpful in fighting heart disease. What the ad did not say was that Campbell's soups are high in sodium, and high-sodium diets may increase the risk of heart disease. The FTC ruled that Campbell's claims were thus deceptive. Advertising that contains an endorsement by a celebrity may be deemed deceptive if the celebrity actually makes no use of the product.

A major challenge in today's legal environment has to do with deceptive advertising practices on the Internet. See this chapter's *E-Guidelines* on the next page for a discussion of this issue.

BAIT-AND-SWITCH ADVERTISING The FTC has promulgated specific rules to govern advertising techniques. One of the most important rules is contained in the FTC's "Guides Against Bait Advertising,"[4] issued in 1968. The rule seeks to prevent **bait-and-switch advertising**—that is, advertising a very low price for a particular item that will likely be unavailable to the consumer, who will then be encouraged to purchase a more expensive item. The low price is the "bait" to lure the consumer into the store. The salesperson is instructed to "switch" the consumer to a different, more expensive item. Under the FTC guidelines, bait-and-switch advertising occurs if the seller refuses to show the advertised item, fails to have in stock a reasonable quantity of the item, fails to promise to deliver the advertised item within a reasonable time, or discourages employees from selling the item.

BAIT-AND-SWITCH ADVERTISING Advertising a product at a very attractive price (the "bait") and then informing the consumer, once he or she is in the store, that the advertised product is either not available or is of poor quality; the customer is then urged to purchase ("switched" to) a more expensive item.

1. 15 U.S.C. Sections 41–58.
2. 15 U.S.C. Section 45.
3. *Charles of the Ritz Distributing Corp. v. Federal Trade Commission*, 143 F.2d 676 (2d Cir. 1944).
4. 16 C.F.R. Part 238.

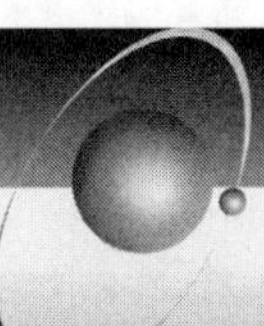

E-Guidelines

Government Agencies Tackle Internet Fraud

The expanding world of e-commerce has created many benefits for consumers. It has also led to some challenging problems, including fraud conducted via the Internet.

What the FTC Has Done

For many years, the Federal Trade Commission (FTC) has fought deceptive advertising in printed materials and in radio and television broadcasts. Since the 1990s, it has spent a considerable portion of its resources on fighting deceptive advertising on the Internet. The FTC has moved particularly quickly on commercial Internet fraud schemes. It has even provided "hot links" on Web sites that it has targeted. A hot link takes the user to the FTC's own Web site, on which the complaint, restraining order, and other documents in the case can be read and downloaded.

Actions by Other Agencies

Other agencies are also fighting online fraud and false advertising. For example, the Securities and Exchange Commission (SEC) has initiated actions against dozens of entities that have perpetrated online investment scams. One fraudulent scheme involved twenty thousand investors, who lost in all more than $3 million. Some cases have involved false claims about the earnings potential of home-business programs, such as the claim that one could "earn $4,000 or more each month." Others have concerned claims for "guaranteed credit repair."

The Department of Transportation (DOT) has also brought actions against purported online violators of advertising and disclosure laws. In one case, the DOT fined Virgin Airlines for failing to disclose the true price of a flight that it advertised on the Web. Also, the Consumer Product Safety Commission (CPSC) has created what it calls a one-stop Web site at which it provides information that allows consumers to avoid the most obvious fraud problems on the Web and elsewhere.

CHECKLIST

- ☑ All business entities must be aware that the laws and government regulations controlling standard "paper" commerce and advertising apply equally to the Internet.
- ☑ Businesspersons should realize that even though Internet sites are seemingly infinite in number, the vastness of this number will not prevent federal and state agency "watchdogs" from discovering fraud and false advertising. An increasing number of government regulatory dollars are going into policing the Internet.

CEASE-AND-DESIST ORDER
An administrative or judicial order prohibiting a person or business firm from conducting activities that an agency or court has deemed illegal.

COUNTERADVERTISING
New advertising that is undertaken pursuant to a Federal Trade Commission order for the purpose of correcting earlier false claims that were made about a product.

FTC ACTIONS AGAINST DECEPTIVE ADVERTISING The FTC receives complaints from many sources, including competitors of alleged violators, consumers, consumer organizations, trade associations, Better Business Bureaus, government organizations, and state and local officials. If enough consumers complain and the complaints are widespread, the FTC will investigate the problem. If the FTC concludes that a given advertisement is unfair or deceptive, it drafts a formal complaint, which is sent to the alleged offender. The company may agree to settle the complaint without further proceedings, or the FTC can conduct a hearing in which the company can present its defense.

If the FTC succeeds in proving that an advertisement is unfair or deceptive, it usually issues a **cease-and-desist order** requiring that the challenged advertising be stopped. It might also impose a sanction known as **counteradvertising** by requiring the company to advertise anew—in print, on radio, and on television—to inform the public about the earlier misinformation. The FTC may institute **multiple product orders,** which require a firm to cease and desist from false advertising not only in regard to the product that was the subject of the action but also in regard to all of the firm's other products.

MULTIPLE PRODUCT ORDER
An order issued by the Federal Trade Commission to a firm that has engaged in deceptive advertising by which the firm is required to cease and desist from false advertising not only in regard to the product that was the subject of the action but also in regard to all the firm's other products.

Is it false or misleading to advertise a product as effective when its effectiveness results only from users' belief that it works? The court addressed this issue in the following case.

CASE 10.1 Federal Trade Commission v. Pantron I Corp.

United States Court of Appeals,
Ninth Circuit, 1994.
33 F.3d 1088.

BACKGROUND AND FACTS Pantron I Corporation sold the Helsinki Formula as a "cure" for baldness. Pantron claimed that the product reduced hair loss and promoted hair growth. The Federal Trade Commission filed a suit in a federal district court against Pantron and its owner, Hal Lederman, alleging that these claims constituted an unfair or deceptive trade practice. The court concluded in part that the product had a "placebo effect"—that is, that it worked when its users believed it would. The court issued an order that, among other things, allowed Pantron to continue claiming its product "works some of the time for a lot of people." The FTC appealed this order.

IN THE LANGUAGE OF THE COURT. . .
REINHARDT, Circuit Judge:

* * * *

* * * Where, as here, a product's effectiveness arises solely as a result of the placebo effect, a representation that the product is effective constitutes a false advertisement even though some consumers may experience positive results. In such circumstances, the efficacy claim is misleading because the [product] is not inherently effective, its results being attributable to the psychosomatic [psychologically induced] effect produced by * * * advertising * * * .

* * * Under the evidence in the record before us, it appears that massaging vegetable oil on one's head would likely produce the same positive results as using the Helsinki Formula. * * * [A] court should not allow a seller to rely on such a placebo effect in supporting a claim of effectiveness * * * . [W]ere we to hold otherwise, advertisers would be encouraged to foist unsubstantiated claims on an unsuspecting public in the hope that consumers would believe the ads and the claims would be self-fulfilling.

DECISION AND REMEDY The U.S. Court of Appeals for the Ninth Circuit reversed this part of the lower court's order and remanded the case. Pantron could not continue to claim that its product "works some of the time for a lot of people."

FOR CRITICAL ANALYSIS—Political Consideration *What other government actions might have been taken against Pantron and the Helsinki Formula, which was sold through the mail?*

Telemarketing and Electronic Advertising

The law firm of Arent Fox offers extensive information relating to advertising law at **http://www.advertisinglaw.com**.

The pervasive use of the telephone to market goods and services to homes and businesses led to the passage in 1991 of the Telephone Consumer Protection Act (TCPA).[5] The act prohibits telephone solicitation using an automatic telephone dialing system or a prerecorded voice. Most states also have laws regulating telephone solicitation. The TCPA also makes it illegal to transmit ads via fax without first obtaining the recipient's permission. (Similar issues have arisen with respect to junk e-mail, called "spam"—see the previous chapter for a discussion of this topic.)

The act is enforced by the Federal Communications Commission and also provides for a private right of action. Consumers can recover any actual monetary loss resulting from a violation of the act or receive $500 in damages for each violation, whichever is greater. If a court finds that a defendant willfully or knowingly violated the act, the court has the discretion to treble the damages awarded.

The Telemarketing and Consumer Fraud and Abuse Prevention Act[6] of 1994 directed the FTC to establish rules governing telemarketing and to bring actions against fraudulent telemarketers. The FTC's Telemarketing Sales Rule[7] of 1995 requires a telemarketer, before making a sales pitch, to inform the recipient that the call is a sales call and to identify the seller's name and the product being sold. The rule makes it illegal for telemarketers to misrepresent information (including facts about their goods or services, earnings potential, profitability, the risk attending an investment, or the nature of a prize). Additionally, telemarketers must inform the people they call of the total cost of the goods being sold, any restrictions on obtaining or using the goods, and whether a sale will be considered to be final and nonrefundable. A telemarketer must also remove a consumer's name from its list of potential contacts if the customer so requests.

The following case involved telemarketers engaged in allegedly deceptive advertising.

5. 47 U.S.C. Sections 227 *et seq.*
6. 15 U.S.C. Sections 6101–6108.
7. 16 C.F.R. Sections 310.1–310.8.

CASE 10.2 Federal Trade Commission v. Growth Plus International Marketing, Inc.

United States District Court,
Northern District of Illinois, 2001.
____F.Supp.3d ____.

BACKGROUND AND FACTS A group of Canadian corporations and individuals engaged in a telemarketing enterprise to sell Canadian lottery packages to consumers in the United States. What the telemarketers did not tell the consumers is that the sales were illegal. In fact, the sellers affirmatively misrepresented that they were authorized to make the sales. They also misrepresented the buyers' chances of winning and used high-pressure sales tactics. The corporations included Growth Plus International Marketing, Inc., also doing business as Growth Potential International, GPIM, and GPI; Gains International Marketing, Inc., also doing business as Gains Wealth International; and Ploto Computer Services, Inc. The individuals included Victor Thiruchelvam, Jessie Nadarajah, Kandan Nadarajah, Arudchelvam Nagamuthu, and Julie Turgeon. The Federal Trade Commission (FTC) filed a suit in a federal district court against Growth and the others, alleging deceptive advertising. The FTC asked the court for, among other things, a preliminary injunction.

IN THE LANGUAGE OF THE COURT. . .

ASPEN, Acting Chief District J. [Judge.]

* * * *

* * * When the [Federal Trade] Commission seeks an injunction, the "public interest" test applies, which involves two factors: (a) the likelihood that the Commission will ultimately succeed on the merits, and (b) the balance of the equities. * * *

* * * *

* * * The evidentiary materials at this point establish a strong case that the defendants were guilty of numerous misrepresentations or omissions. For example, (a) the defendants told customers that it was legal for them to sell the lottery tickets in the United States, when it was not; (b) the defendants told customers that they were authorized by the Canadian government to sell lottery tickets, when in fact they were not; (c) the defendants represented to consumers that they had a good chance of winning the lottery because they would be playing with a large pool of people, without disclosing that the odds of winning were roughly 1 in 14 million. This information that was misrepresented or concealed plainly was material to the consumers' decisions to purchase the tickets: The knowledge that the sale of the tickets was illegal under federal law and that the "good chance" of winning was in fact a 1 in 14 million shot certainly are the types of information that would likely affect the decision of whether to participate in the lottery. And, in fact, the Commission has provided sworn statements from several consumers indicating that they would not have purchased the lottery tickets had they known that the sales of tickets were illegal.

* * * For these same reasons, the Commission has made a strong case that it will likely prevail on the merits of its claim that defendants have violated the Telemarketing Sales Rule, which prohibits sellers and telemarketers from making false or misleading statements to induce persons to acquire goods or services.

* * * Turning to the balance of the equities, the Court notes that although private equities may be considered, public equities receive far greater weight. In this case, the balance of equities weighs heavily in favor of the issuance of preliminary injunctive relief. There is a strong public interest in an immediate halt to illegal sale of lottery tickets accomplished through the use of misleading devices. By contrast, the Court perceives very little private interest in the continuance of such sales pending further proceedings in the case * * * .

DECISION AND REMEDY The court granted the FTC's request for a preliminary injunction. The court concluded that the FTC made a strong case against the defendants, whose misrepresentations misled consumers.

FOR CRITICAL ANALYSIS–Technological Consideration *Is it likely that the result in this case would have been different if the defendants had offered the Canadian lottery tickets for sale only on the Internet?*

For current articles concerning consumer issues, go to the Alexander Law Firm's "Consumer Law Page," which is online at **http://consumerlawpage.com/intro.html**.

Telephone and Mail-Order Sales

Sales made by either telephone or mail order are the greatest source of complaints to the nation's Better Business Bureaus. Many mail-order firms are far removed from most of their buyers, thus making it burdensome for buyers to bring complaints against them. To a certain extent, consumers are protected under federal laws prohibiting mail fraud, which were discussed in Chapter 4, and under state consumer protection laws that parallel and supplement the federal laws.

The FTC Mail or Telephone Order Merchandise Rule of 1993, which amended the FTC Mail-Order Rule of 1975,[8] provides specific protections for consumers who purchase goods via phone lines or through the mails. The 1993 rule extended the 1975 rule to include sales in which orders are transmitted by computer, fax machine, or some similar means involving telephone lines. Among other things, the rule requires mail-order merchants to ship orders within the time promised in their catalogues or advertisements, to notify consumers when orders cannot be shipped on time, and to issue a refund within a specified period of time when a consumer cancels an order.

In addition, the Postal Reorganization Act of 1970[9] provides that *unsolicited* merchandise sent by U.S. mail may be retained, used, discarded, or disposed of in any manner deemed appropriate. The recipient has no obligation to the sender in this situation.

Online Deceptive Advertising

In 2000, to help businesses comply with existing laws prohibiting deceptive advertising, the FTC issued new guidelines.[10] The guidelines do not set forth new rules but rather describe how existing laws apply to online advertising. Generally, the rules emphasize that any ads—online or offline—must be truthful and not misleading, and that any claims made in any ads must be substantiated. Additionally, ads cannot be unfair, defined in the guidelines as "caus[ing] or . . . likely to cause substantial consumer injury that consumers could not reasonably avoid and that is not outweighed by the benefit to consumers or competition."

The guidelines also call for "clear and conspicuous" disclosure of any qualifying or limiting information. The FTC suggests that advertisers should assume that consumers will not read an entire Web page. Therefore, to satisfy the "clear and conspicuous" requirement, advertisers should place the disclosure as close as possible to the claim being qualified, or include the disclosure within the claim itself. If such placement is not feasible, the next-best placement would be a section of the page to which a consumer could easily scroll. Generally, hyperlinks to a disclosure are recommended only for lengthy disclosures or for disclosures that must be repeated in a variety of locations on the Web page.

---

8. 6 C.F.R. Sections 435.1–435.2.
9. 39 U.S.C. Section 3009.
10. *Advertising and Marketing on the Internet: Rules of the Road,* September 2000.

SECTION 2 STATE CONSUMER PROTECTION LAWS

Thus far, our primary focus has been on federal legislation. State laws, however, often provide more sweeping and significant protections for the consumer than do federal laws. Recall from Chapter 1 that the Uniform Commercial Code (UCC), which has been adopted in virtually all states, governs contracts for the sale and lease of goods. Some of the UCC's provisions, including those governing warranties, offer important protections for consumers against unfair practices on the part of sellers and lessors. The federal Magnuson-Moss Warranty Act supplements the UCC provisions in cases involving both a consumer transaction of at least $10 and an express written warranty.

Virtually all states also have specific consumer protection acts, often titled "deceptive trade practices acts." Although state consumer protection statutes vary widely in their provisions, a common thread runs through most of them. Typically, state consumer protection laws are directed at deceptive trade practices, such as a seller's providing false or misleading information to consumers. As mentioned, state laws often provide broad protection for consumers. A prime example is the Texas Deceptive Trade Practices Act of 1973, which forbids a seller from selling to a buyer anything that the buyer does not need or cannot afford.

Increasingly, consumers are purchasing goods and services via the Internet from online merchants using electronic contracts, or e-contracts. As you read in the previous chapter, the National Conference of Commissioners on Uniform State Laws has recently promulgated a uniform act (the Uniform Computer Information Transactions Act) that, if widely adopted by the states, will provide uniform principles for e-contracts throughout the nation. As also noted in the previous chapter, the 1999 federal legislation validating e-signatures means that contracts that are formed and signed electronically now have the force of law.

SECTION 3 E-CONTRACTS AND CONSUMER WELFARE

The laws just mentioned are clearly a boon for e-commerce, which, to be sure, creates actual and potential savings for most consumers. These savings may be monetary or simply a savings in time—the time not wasted by leaving one's house to purchase an item. While there are many advantages to e-commerce, consumers continue to be plagued by problems stemming from contracts formed online. Recall from this chapter's *E-Guidelines* feature that online fraud is a growing problem. Additional difficulties, while they may not constitute fraud, also exist.

A government-sponsored Web site that contains reports on consumer issues and provides information for consumers is **http://www.consumer.gov**.

Late Deliveries

Most e-retailing sites do 40 to 60 percent of their business in the ten weeks before Christmas. The closer it is to Christmas, the greater the number of orders. Consequently, the pressure to deliver in time for Christmas is great. After the first truly significant e-commerce Christmas selling season in 1999, irate consumers throughout the country raised their collective voice against several dozen online selling sites for failing to deliver orders on time.

In July 2000, the FTC reached a settlement with seven online retailers. The FTC complaint alleged that the following companies had violated their agreements with consumers: Toysrus.com, Inc.; Macys.com, Inc.; KBkids.com, LLC; CDNow, Inc.; Patriot Computer Corp.; Original Honey Baked Ham Company; and MinidisNow.com. The FTC found that these online merchants failed to ship Christmas gifts on time and simultaneously failed to notify their customers of these delays. As a result, the companies were ordered to pay fines ranging from $20,000 to $350,000. The FTC stated that the steep fines would serve as a warning to other online retailers that they would be held liable for violating delivery rules if they repeated this type of behavior the following Christmas. Toysrus.com decided to reduce the probability of such an event reoccurring by forming an alliance with Amazon.com to launch a joint site. This alliance allows Amazon to help Toysrus.com handle traffic and avoid Christmas delivery delays.

The Problem of Hidden Costs

The FTC has also taken action against certain sites because they failed to fully disclose the terms of attractive offers that turned out to have hidden costs. For example, several online retailers, including Buy.com and Value America, Inc., advertised "free" and "low-cost" computers to online shoppers. What these companies failed to disclose, however, was that there were numerous hidden costs associated with such purported bargains. Individuals would obtain the free or low-cost computers only after they agreed to a three-year Internet service subscription. Moreover, the Internet subscription services offered were often ones that charged an hourly rate or required long-distance telephone charges because the affiliated Internet service provider had no local access numbers.

The Issue of Fine Print

When someone talks about "reading the fine print," he or she is usually referring to contractual terms printed on an agreement. In cyberspace, e-contracts often contain the same amount of fine print, but there is a difference–while it may be difficult to read the fine print on a printed page, it is often even more difficult to read it on a computer screen, particularly if that screen is not very large. Not surprisingly, most people do not read the fine print in e-contracts. Clicking on "I agree" while engaging in online e-commerce may not be done with full knowledge of to what type of e-contract one is actually agreeing. So far, there has been little regulatory work in this area.

Short-Term versus Long-Term Contracts

Most e-contracts currently involve short-term agreements, such as for the sale and delivery of goods. But what if electronic contracts become routinely used for long-term agreements, such as mortgages or insurance agreements? A long-term contract signed and stored on a computer may not be accessible in the long run without upgrading one's software and perhaps hardware. Typically, during the life of a long-term loan contract, such as an automobile loan or a mortgage, the loan will be purchased by two or more banks. How does the borrower continue to communicate with the ultimate owner of that loan contract?

In addition, what if a borrower's hard disk crashes, leaving the borrower without the original contract? At a minimum, all significant contracts, whether they are short term or long term, should be copied onto a removable storage source, such as a Zip disk or similar storage device.

SECTION 4 PRIVACY ISSUES IN THE ONLINE WORLD

While some of the concerns over e-contracting remain speculative, the concern over privacy issues in the online world is not. Until relatively recently, most privacy issues concerned the public's belief that personal information collected by government agencies posed a threat to individual privacy. In other words, typical privacy issues in the past related to personal information that government agencies, including the Federal Bureau of Investigation (FBI), might obtain and keep about an individual. Later, concerns about what banks and insurance companies might know and transmit to others about individuals became an issue. One of the major concerns of consumers in recent years has been the increasing value of personal information for online marketers—who are willing to pay a high price to those who collect and sell them such information.

Indeed, in today's online world, some people believe that privacy rights are quickly becoming a thing of the past. "Cookies" on their hard drives allow Internet users' Web movements to be tracked. Technology is now available that makes it possible to connect previously anonymous Internet users to actual geographic locations. Furthermore, any person who wants to purchase goods from online merchants or auctions inevitably must reveal some personal information, which may include the purchaser's name, address, Social Security number, and credit-card number.

In the remaining pages of this chapter, we look at issues relating to privacy rights in the online world, beginning with a discussion of current laws protecting privacy rights. As you will see, there is a growing tension between the goal of promoting e-commerce and the need to protect individual privacy rights online.

SECTION 5 LAWS PROTECTING PRIVACY RIGHTS

Privacy rights are protected by both state and federal laws. The earliest protection for privacy interests was under tort law, a topic you read about in Chapter 4. In this section, after discussing the invasion of privacy as a tort, we look at the protection of privacy rights under the U.S. Constitution and various federal statutes. Note that state constitutions and statutes also protect individuals' privacy rights, often to a significant degree. Because of their diversity, we focus here on the federal Constitution and federal laws.

Tort Law

Remember from Chapter 4 that a tort is defined as wrongful conduct and is part of civil, as opposed to criminal, law. The idea that privacy should be regarded as a distinct tort for which a remedy should be made available was first proposed in an article by Samuel Warren and Louis Brandeis titled "The Right to Privacy," which was published in the *Harvard Law Review* in 1890.[11] The article

11. Samuel D. Warren and Louis D. Brandeis, "The Right to Privacy," 4 *Harvard Law Review* 193 (1890).

proposed that, given the growing excesses of the press, the invasion of privacy should be recognized as a separate interest protected by law.

Some scholars refer to this article as the most famous law review article of all time. Certainly, its influence on the courts was immediate and extensive. Beginning in the 1890s, a number of courts advanced the privacy doctrine proposed by Warren and Brandeis. Today, tort law safeguards individual privacy rights through the tort of *invasion of privacy.* As you learned in Chapter 4, under tort law four acts are considered to qualify as invasion of privacy:

- The use of a person's name, picture, or other likeness for commercial purposes without permission (the tort of appropriation).
- Intrusion on an individual's affairs or seclusion.
- Publication of information that places a person in a false light.
- Public disclosure of private facts about an individual that an ordinary person would find objectionable.

In the marketplace, celebrity endorsements are often considered a valuable selling tool. What originated as a concern for the right to be left alone has evolved into a tool to control the commercial use–and thus protect the economic value–of one's name, voice, signature, photograph, and likeness.

In 1971, California enacted a commercial appropriation statute that complements the common law tort of appropriation.[12] Does this statute apply when copyrighted photos are displayed on a commercial Web site without the copyright holder's permission? That was the issue in the following case.

12. California Civil Code Section 3344.

CASE 10.3 KNB Enterprises v. Matthews

California Court of Appeals,
Second District, 2000.
78 Cal.App.4th 362,
92 Cal.Rptr.2d 713.

HISTORICAL AND TECHNOLOGICAL SETTING *Usenet is a public forum on the Internet where individuals can participate in the open exchange of information. Usenet provides information through more than 30,000 user groups. These groups generally provide information regarding topics of public interest. This information includes, among other things, messages, recipes, software, and pictures. Access to Usenet is not possible through an ordinary Web browser but requires a computer program known as a newsreader.*

BACKGROUND AND FACTS KNB Enterprises operates a Web site known as webvirgins, which provides erotic photos for a fee. KNB owns the copyrights to all of the photos that it displays. To promote the site, KNB uploads sample images to certain Usenet newsgroups. Anyone with access to Usenet can view the sample images at no charge, and can download the images. Greg Matthews used a software program on Usenet to identify and copy photos, including more than 400 of KNB's images, which featured more than 450 models. Without KNB's permission, Matthews displayed the images on his own commercial Web site, Justpics. Justpics charged its customers a monthly membership fee to view the photos, which were displayed in their original state, but without KNB's accompanying text, captions, and headers. KNB filed a suit in a California state court against Matthews, claiming that the models' likenesses were misappropriated under the California appropriation statute. Matthews argued that the federal Copyright Act (see Chapter 5) preempted KNB's claim.[a] The court granted a summary judgment in Matthews's favor, and KNB appealed to a state intermediate appellate court.

a. Under the U.S. Constitution, a claim based on a state statute is preempted when there is a valid federal statute on the same subject. In such a case, the federal statute takes precedence.

IN THE LANGUAGE OF THE COURT. . .

ORTEGA, Acting P.J. [Presiding Judge.]

* * * *

The issue we face is whether the * * * models' claims, which plaintiff [KNB] asserts by right of assignment,[b] are preempted by federal copyright law. * * * [F]or preemption to occur under the [Copyright] Act, two conditions must be met: first, the subject of the claim must be a work fixed in a tangible medium of expression and come within the subject matter or scope of copyright protection, and second, the right asserted under state law must be equivalent to the exclusive rights contained in [the Copyright Act].

There can be no dispute that photographs are copyrightable. Photographs clearly fall within the [Copyright Act's] classification of "pictorial, graphic and sculptural works." * * *

It is also undisputed that the unauthorized commercial display of the copyrighted photographs on defendant's website constituted an infringement of plaintiff's exclusive rights [under the Copyright Act]. * * *

* * * *

* * * [R]ight of publicity claims generally are not preempted by the Copyright Act. Invasion of privacy may sometimes occur by acts of reproduction, distribution, performance, or display, but inasmuch as the essence of the tort does not lie in such acts, preemption should not apply. The same may be said of the right of publicity. * * * [A] likeness [does] not become a work of authorship simply because [it is] embodied in a copyrightable work such as a photograph.

* * * In our view, a [right of publicity] claim is preempted * * * where an actor or model with no copyright interest in the work seeks to prevent the exclusive copyright holder from displaying the copyrighted work. We do not believe a [right of publicity] claim is preempted * * * where, as here, the defendant [Matthews] has no legal right to publish the copyrighted work.

Returning to the two-part test for determining preemption * * *, we conclude neither condition has been met in this case. First, the subjects of the claims are the models' likenesses, which are not copyrightable even though embodied in a copyrightable work * * * . Second, the right asserted under the state statute, the right of publicity, does not fall within the subject matter of copyright. Accordingly, we conclude the [state law] claims are not preempted by federal copyright law.

b. An *assignment* occurs when an original party to a contract transfers his or her rights under the contract to a third party—someone who was not a party to the original contract.

DECISION AND REMEDY The state intermediate appellate court concluded that because a likeness is not copyrightable, even if it is captured in a copyrighted photo, the claim against Matthews was not the equivalent of a copyright infringement claim and was not preempted by copyright law. The court reversed the lower court's judgment and remanded the case for further proceedings.

FOR CRITICAL ANALYSIS–Political Consideration *What advantage might a party realize in obtaining a court's judgment that a suit is subject to federal, and not state, law?*

Constitutional Protection of Privacy Rights

The U.S. Constitution does not explicitly mention a general right to privacy, and only relatively recently have the courts regarded the right to privacy as a constitutional right. Louis Brandeis, when he became a Supreme Court justice, continued to advocate privacy rights. In a 1928 Supreme Court case, *Olmstead v. United States,*[13] he stated in his dissent that the right to privacy is "the most comprehensive of rights and the right most valued by civilized men." The majority of the justices at that time did not agree, and it was not until the 1960s that a majority on the Supreme Court endorsed the view that the Constitution protected individual privacy rights.

In a landmark 1965 case, *Griswold v. Connecticut,*[14] the Supreme Court invalidated a Connecticut law that effectively prohibited the use of contraceptives. The Court held that the law violated the right to privacy. Justice William O. Douglas formulated a unique way of reading this right into the Bill of Rights (the first ten amendments to the Constitution). He claimed that "emanations" from the rights guaranteed by the First, Third, Fourth, Fifth, and Ninth Amendments formed and gave "life and substance" to "penumbras" (partial shadows) around these guaranteed rights. These penumbras included an implied constitutional right to privacy.

When we read these amendments, we can see the foundation for Justice Douglas's reasoning. Consider the Fourth Amendment. By prohibiting unreasonable searches and seizures, the amendment effectively protects individuals' privacy. Consider also the words of the Ninth Amendment: "The enumeration in the Constitution of certain rights, shall not be construed to deny or disparage others retained by the people." In other words, just because the Constitution, including its amendments, does not specifically mention the right to privacy does not mean that this right is denied to the people. Indeed, in a recent survey of America Online subscribers, respondents ranked privacy second behind freedom of speech and ahead of freedom of religion. A recent Harris poll showed that almost 80 percent of those questioned believed that if the framers were writing the Constitution today, they would add privacy as an important right.[15]

Federal Statutes Protecting Privacy Rights

In the last several decades, Congress has enacted a number of statutes that protect the privacy of individuals in various areas of concern (see Exhibit 10–1). In the 1960s, Americans were sufficiently alarmed by the accumulation of personal information in government files that they pressured Congress to pass laws permitting individuals to access their files. Congress responded in 1966 with the Freedom of Information Act, which allows any person to request copies of any information on him or her contained in federal government files. In 1974, Congress passed the Privacy Act, which also gives persons the right to access such information.

---

13. 277 U.S. 438, 48 S.Ct. 564, 72 L.Ed. 2d 944 (1928).
14. 381 U.S. 479, 85 S.Ct. 1678, 14 L.Ed. 2d 510 (1965).
15. *Public Perspective,* November/December 2000, p. 9.

EXHIBIT 10–1 Federal Legislation Relating to Privacy

TITLE	PROVISIONS CONCERNING PRIVACY
Freedom of Information Act (1966)	Provides that individuals have a right to obtain access to information about them collected in government files.
Fair Credit Reporting Act (1970)	Provides that consumers have the right to be informed of the nature and scope of a credit investigation, the kind of information that is being compiled, and the names of the firms or individuals who will be receiving the report.
Crime Control Act (1973)	Safeguards the confidentiality of information amassed for certain state criminal systems.
Family and Educational Rights and Privacy Act (1974)	Limits access to computer-stored records of education-related evaluations and grades in private and public colleges and universities.
Privacy Act (1974)	Protects the privacy of individuals about whom the federal government has information. Specifically, the act provides as follows: 1. Agencies originating, using, disclosing, or otherwise manipulating personal information must ensure the reliability of the information and provide safeguards against its misuse. 2. Information compiled for one purpose cannot be used for another without the concerned individual's permission. 3. Individuals must be able to find out what data concerning them are being compiled and how the data will be used. 4. Individuals must be given a means by which to correct inaccurate data.
Tax Reform Act (1976)	Preserves the privacy of personal financial information.
Right to Financial Privacy Act (1978)	Prohibits financial institutions from providing the federal government with access to customers' records unless a customer authorizes the disclosure.
Electronic Fund Transfer Act (1978)	Prohibits the use of a computer without authorization to retrieve data in a financial institution's or consumer reporting agency's files.
Cable Communications Policy Act (1984)	Regulates access to information collected by cable service operators on subscribers to cable services.
Electronic Communications Privacy Act (1986)	Prohibits the interception of information communicated by electronic means.
Driver's Privacy Protection Act (1994)	Prevents states from disclosing or selling a driver's personal information without the driver's consent.
Health Insurance Portability and Accountability Act (1996)	Prohibits the use of a consumer's medical information for any purpose other than that for which such information was provided, unless the consumer expressly consents to the use. Final rules under the act, issued by the Department of Health and Human Services, became effective on April 14, 2001.
Children's Online Privacy Protection Act (1998)	Requires operators of Web sites aimed at children under the age of thirteen to clearly provide notice about the information being collected and how it will be used; requires verifiable parental consent for certain types of information about children.
Financial Services Modernization Act (Gramm-Leach-Bliley Act) (1999)	Requires all financial institutions to provide customers with information on their privacy policies and practices; prohibits the disclosure of nonpublic personal information about a consumer to an unaffiliated third party unless strict disclosure and opt-out requirements are met. Final rules under the act, issued by the Federal Trade Commission, became mandatory on July 1, 2001.

Other acts passed in the 1970s and 1980s gave further protection to privacy rights with respect to financial records, electronic fund transfers, and other areas. More recently, Congress has passed a number of laws, including those discussed next, in response to privacy concerns raised by the widespread use of the Internet.

THE DRIVER'S PRIVACY PROTECTION ACT In 1994, Congress passed the Driver's Privacy Protection Act (DPPA) when it learned that states were selling information obtained by state motor vehicle departments to commercial database suppliers. As a result, personal information given by those who applied for driver's licenses or vehicle registrations was finding its way to Web sites that anyone could access. This information included people's names, addresses, telephone numbers, vehicle descriptions, Social Security numbers, medical information, and photographs.

Congress was pressured to take action after an actress, Rebecca Schaeffer, was killed by a stalker who obtained her address—which was not published in any phone book—from state driver's license records. Subsequent congressional investigation unearthed many similar incidents in which motor vehicle files were used to locate, threaten, and harm women trying to escape domestic abuse, as well as other victims. The 1994 act prevents states from disclosing or selling a driver's personal information without the driver's consent.

The state of South Carolina challenged the constitutionality of the DPPA in the following case.

CASE 10.4 Reno v. Condon

Supreme Court of the United States, 2000.
528 U.S. 141,
120 S.Ct. 666,
145 L.Ed.2d 587.
http://supct.law.cornell.edu/supct/supct.January.2000.html[a]

BACKGROUND AND FACTS Each state's Department of Motor Vehicles (DMV) requires drivers and automobile owners to provide personal information, including a name, address, telephone number, and Social Security number, as a condition of obtaining a driver's license or registering an automobile. Many states sell this information to individuals and businesses. Wisconsin's DMV, for example, receives approximately $8 million each year from the sale of this information. Before a state can sell this data, under the DPPA a driver must consent to its release. In other words, a person must choose to "opt in." There are exceptions for government use, motor vehicle recalls, and certain other circumstances. In contrast to the federal DPPA, under South Carolina state law, information in DMV records is available to anyone who promises not to use it for telemarketing. The information is not released only if a South Carolina driver affirmatively "opts out." Charles Condon, the attorney general of South Carolina, filed a suit in a federal district court against Janet Reno, then the attorney general of the United States, alleging that the DPPA violated the U.S. Constitution. The court granted an injunction to prevent the DPPA's enforcement, and the U.S. Court of Appeals for the Fourth Circuit upheld the order. Reno appealed to the United States Supreme Court.

a. This page includes a list of the January 2000 decisions of the United States Supreme Court. Scroll down the list of cases to the *Reno v. Condon* case, and click on the name to access the opinion.

IN THE LANGUAGE OF THE COURT. . .
Chief Justice *REHNQUIST* delivered the opinion of the Court.

* * * *

The United States asserts that the DPPA is a proper exercise of Congress's authority to regulate interstate commerce under the Commerce Clause. The

United States bases its Commerce Clause argument on the fact that the personal, identifying information that the DPPA regulates is a "thin[g] in interstate commerce," and that the sale or release of that information in interstate commerce is therefore a proper subject of congressional regulation. We agree with the United States' contention. The motor vehicle information which the States have historically sold is used by insurers, manufacturers, direct marketers, and others engaged in interstate commerce to contact drivers with customized solicitations. The information is also used in the stream of interstate commerce by various public and private entities for matters related to interstate motoring. Because drivers' information is, in this context, an article of commerce, its sale or release into the interstate stream of business is sufficient to support congressional regulation. * * *

But the fact that drivers' personal information is, in the context of this case, an article in interstate commerce does not conclusively resolve the constitutionality of the DPPA. In [other cases] we held federal statutes invalid * * * because those statutes violated the principles of federalism contained in the Tenth Amendment.[b] * * * While Congress has substantial powers to govern the Nation directly, including in areas of intimate concern to the States, the Constitution has never been understood to confer upon Congress the ability to require the States to govern according to Congress' instructions.

* * * Congress cannot compel the States to enact or enforce a federal regulatory program. * * * Congress cannot circumvent that prohibition by conscripting the States' officers directly. The Federal Government may neither issue directives requiring the States to address particular problems, nor command the States' officers, or those of their political subdivisions, to administer or enforce a federal regulatory program.

* * * *

* * * [However, the] DPPA does not require the States in their sovereign capacity to regulate their own citizens. The DPPA regulates the States as the owners of databases. It does not require the South Carolina Legislature to enact any laws or regulations, and it does not require state officials to assist in the enforcement of federal statutes regulating private individuals. We accordingly conclude that the DPPA is consistent with the constitutional principles * * * .

DECISION AND REMEDY The United States Supreme Court reversed the judgment of the U.S. Court of Appeals for the Fourth Circuit. The Supreme Court held that the DPPA was a proper exercise of Congress's power under the commerce clause and did not violate other constitutional provisions.

FOR CRITICAL ANALYSIS–Ethical Consideration *Are there any ethical reasons why a state should keep private its drivers' personal information?*

b. Under the Tenth Amendment to the U.S. Constitution, "[t]he powers not delegated to the United States by the Constitution, nor prohibited by it to the States, are reserved to the States respectively, or to the people."

THE REGULATION OF MEDICAL INFORMATION In 1996, Congress passed the Health Insurance Portability and Accountability Act[16] to regulate the privacy of individuals' medical and health-care information. In part, the act was prompted by concerns over the ease with which such information could be transmitted via the Internet. The Department of Health and Human Services (HHS) has issued rules under the act,[17] which became final on April 14, 2001. The regulations prohibit the use of a consumer's medical information for any purpose other than that for which such information was provided, unless the consumer expressly consents to the use. The HHS rules concerning medical-records privacy, which cover both electronic and paper records, apply to all health-care providers, as well as to insurance companies.

Anyone intentionally disclosing prohibited information faces criminal fines of up to $50,000 and imprisonment for up to a year. Any willful intent to sell such information is punishable by a fine of up to $250,000 and imprisonment for up to ten years.

PROTECTION OF ONLINE FINANCIAL INFORMATION In 1999, Congress passed the Financial Services Modernization Act,[18] also known as the Gramm-Leach-Bliley Act, in an attempt to delineate how financial institutions can treat customer data. The Federal Trade Commission (FTC) determined the final rules[19] pursuant to the act. The final rules became mandatory on July 1, 2001. In general, the act and its implementing rules place restrictions and affirmative obligations on financial institutions to protect consumers' customer data and privacy. All financial institutions must provide customers with information on their privacy policies and practices. No financial institution can now disclose nonpublic personal information about a consumer to an unaffiliated third party unless restrictive disclosure and opt-out requirements are met.

The FTC's implementing rules (which are found in a 159-page booklet) not only cover standard financial institutions, such as banks, but also online mortgage brokers, real estate brokers, and tax preparers. Interestingly, the rules cover data obtained through any "cookies" used to track consumers' actions on the Web. One business group that is bound to be hurt by the legislation is credit bureaus. They routinely sell information that contains names, addresses, Social Security numbers, and so on to help debt collectors and private investigators locate people. In the future, such information cannot be sold without the prior approval of each individual covered.

PROTECTING CHILDREN'S ONLINE PRIVACY Privacy advocates believe that children are especially vulnerable to invasion of their privacy. Congress was sufficiently convinced of this problem to pass the Children's Online Privacy

16. 18 U.S.C. Sections 24, 669, 1035, 1347, 1518, 3486; 26 U.S.C. Sections 220, 4980C–4980E, 6039F, 6050Q, 7702B, 9801–9806; 29 U.S.C. Sections 1181–1187; 42 U.S.C. Sections 300qq-1, 300qq-11, 300qq-12, 300qq-13, 300qq-21, 300qq-22, 300qq-23, 300qq-41–300qq-47, 300qq-91, 300qq-92, 1320a-7c, 1320a-7d, 1320a-7e, 1320–1320d-8, 1395b-5, 1395ddd; and others.

17. 45 C.F.R. Parts 142, 160, and 164.

18. 12 U.S.C. Sections 24a, 248b, 1820a, 1828b, 1831v–1831y, 1848a, 2908, 4809; 15 U.S.C. Sections 80b-10a, 6701, 6711–6717, 6731–6735, 6751–6766, 6781, 6801–6809, 6821–6827, 6901–6910; and others.

19. 12 C.F.R. Part 40.

Protection Act (COPPA) of 1998.[20] COPPA requires operators of Web sites aimed at children under the age of thirteen to clearly provide notice about the information being collected and how it will be used. Operators must also allow parents to review and change such information and to approve what will be done with it.

Certain types of personal information about children can only be obtained after the Web site operator has obtained **verifiable parental consent.** Such parental consent can be in the form of (a) a digital signature, (b) a credit-card number, (c) a signed or "clicked on" consent form, (d) a verifiable call to a toll-free number, or (e) an e-mail response using a password. Such a verifiable parental consent must be obtained before any information about children under age thirteen can access the chat rooms and message boards of child-oriented Web sites.

VERIFIABLE PARENTAL CONSENT
Under the Children's Online Privacy and Protection Act (COPPA) of 2000, a requirement that parental consent must be obtained by Web site operators before any information about children under the age of thirteen can access chat rooms and message boards of child-oriented Web sites.

Subsequent to the final implementation of COPPA, a number of child-oriented Web sites closed down. Their owners claimed they could not possibly afford to abide by the final regulations mandated by COPPA.

SECTION 6 ONLINE MARKETING AND PRIVACY CONCERNS

One of the reasons that personal information is so valuable to online companies is that it allows them to market their products and services more effectively than before. Advertisers prefer to target their online ads to those who might be most receptive to such ads. For example, a firm selling lockable gun racks knows that it will get a higher response rate when it advertises in a gun-enthusiasts' magazine than in, say, *Time* magazine. This is called **targeted marketing.** On the Web, a firm selling financial services will have a greater response rate if its banner ads are viewed by a Web surfer already on a financial information Web site.

TARGETED MARKETING
Advertising directed to ("targeted" at) a specific group of consumers who, judging from their interests and past purchasing habits, would be the most likely purchasers of the product being marketed.

Advertisers who wish to send out e-mail ads will obtain better response rates if they target such ads to e-mail addresses of people who have shown an interest in their particular product or service field. For example, the same seller of lockable gun racks will get a higher response rate by sending e-mail messages to users of a gun information Web site than by sending e-mails to all subscribers of an Internet service provider (ISP).

The Doubleclick, Inc., Problem Brings Online Privacy Issues to the Forefront

One of the largest online advertising intermediary companies is Doubleclick, Inc. Doubleclick sells banner ads, button ads, flash ads, and other types of ads used online. A person who opens such ads typically has a "cookie" set on his or her hard drive that allows Doubleclick and its advertisers to track the user's online movements. In particular, it can be learned whether a Web surfer comes back to a particular Web site on which he or she has clicked on ads before.

Doubleclick decided that it wanted to use such information in a more profitable way. It merged with Abacus Direct Corporation in a deal valued at $1.7 billion. Abacus had developed software that would link data it collected online,

20. 15 U.S.C. Sections 6501–6506.

through the use of cookies, to consumers' real names and addresses collected offline. Once the public got wind of what Doubleclick was planning to do, government spokespersons as well as privacy advocacy groups raised such a media storm that Doubleclick, Inc., had to abandon its plans to use the consumer information database that it had acquired through its purchase of Abacus.

Developing Digital Silhouettes of Internet Users

As Doubleclick, Inc., began to back away from developing profiles of individual Internet users, other companies attempted to fill the void. Predictive Networks, Inc., developed software that builds profiles of Internet users after tracking their clicks across the Web. The agreements that Predictive Networks have in place involve ISPs, which can track where their subscribers go on the Web. Predictive's software can follow the users and gain insights into the ages, incomes, hobbies, and, more important, shopping preferences of Web surfers. Consider an example. A Web surfer visits an airline site, and then goes to the Web site of the New York Museum of Modern Art. Using Predictive's profile model, that Web surfer might immediately be sent a banner ad for a New York City travel guide from Amazon.com.

In its defense against irate privacy advocates, Predictive Networks says that it only keeps *scores* that reveal implied preferences and demographic data. No ISP or advertiser can ever view an individual profile. It is Predictive that sends the ads directly to users, thereby protecting users' privacy. Privacy advocates are worried that Predictive's software will eventually be used by others, including cable companies.

The value of Predictive's software to advertisers is the targeted nature of the advertising sent out. Rather than sending banner ads to a general group of Web surfers, banner ads can be sent to those people who are most likely to be interested in the product or service advertised.

Monitoring Response Rates to Targeted E-Mail Ads—An Invasion of Privacy?

Most Internet users receive e-mail advertisements. In some cases, a user might become a member of a Web community and explicitly agree to accept e-mail advertisements in exchange for being able to access that particular Web page. For example, suppose that you are a subscriber to a gardening Web site. In order to receive the gardening information on a regular basis online, you would probably have to accept the terms and conditions of that Web site. Very likely, one of the terms would be that you agree to receive e-mail advertisements.

An advertiser that is promoting a new indoor plant fertilizer may wish to advertise the product using targeted e-mail ads. An obvious target is the subscriber list of the gardening Web site. When the advertiser sends out the targeted e-mails (targeted e-mails are not considered spam—see the discussion of this issue in the previous chapter), that advertiser wishes to know how many subscribers to the gardening Web page actually opened the e-mail ads. Technically this is relatively easy to determine by use of what is called a **JavaScript.** Lists of e-mail addresses that generate high response rates are therefore valuable to potential advertisers who want to send out targeted e-mails.

JAVASCRIPT
A programming language that enhances the capabilities of Web pages.

Federal and state regulators, however, complain that the use of JavaScripts to determine what percentage of people receiving an e-mail ad actually opened that ad is a violation of individual privacy rights. Proposed regulations and legislation would make it illegal to use JavaScripts to obtain this information.

Consumer Concerns over Online Privacy

For some time, when the issue of online privacy was discussed, a common response to the issue was, "Why should I be concerned about privacy if I have nothing to hide?" As Yale Law School professor Jeffrey Rosen points out, however, this response misses the point. Regardless of whether we have anything to hide, the uncertainty about whether our actions are observed or tracked by others causes us to lead more restrictive lives. According to Rosen, "We are just beginning to recognize the scope of surveillance," and Americans need to educate themselves on the way personal information is being obtained and used, both by corporate entities and the government.[21]

Certainly, a majority of Americans today are understandably concerned about what is happening in the online world. According to a report recently published by the University of California at Los Angeles, Americans are quite aware of–and concerned about–their lack of privacy on the Internet. The study showed that almost two-thirds of Internet users and more than three-quarters of nonusers either agreed or strongly agreed with the statement that "people who go online put their privacy at risk."[22] A survey conducted by the FTC in 2000 showed that an even larger majority of Americans are concerned about the effects of e-commerce on privacy: 92 percent of the respondents stated that they do not trust online companies to keep personal information confidential. Significantly, 80 percent of the respondents recommended that legislation be enacted to protect privacy rights in the online environment.[23]

SECTION 7 WEB SITE PRIVACY POLICIES

In response to consumers' privacy concerns, many Web site owners now post privacy policies on their sites. These policies generally state what kind of information about the sites' visitors will be collected and how it will be used. Some policies allow users to decide whether the information being gathered by the Web site can be disclosed to others and for what purposes. Other policies simply state that Web users, by visiting the site, indicate their acceptance of the terms and conditions of the privacy policy. If a site visitor does not agree to the terms and conditions, he or she is advised not to use the site. Excerpts from a typical privacy policy are presented in Exhibit 10–2 on the next page.

In the last several years, a number of independent, nonprofit organizations have developed model Web site privacy policies and guidelines for online

---

21. Jeffrey Rosen, *The Unwanted Gaze: The Destruction of Privacy in America* (Westminster, Md.: Random House, 2000).

22. This report, titled "Surveying the Digital Future" and based on an extensive study of attitudes concerning Internet use, was published in 2000 by the UCLA Center for Communication Policy. It is available online at http://www.college.ucla.edu/InternetReport.

23. The results of this survey are reported online at http://www.ftc.gov/reports/privacy2000.pdf.

EXHIBIT 10–2 Excerpts from a Typical Privacy Policy

dollars4mail.com is committed to maintaining your online privacy. We developed this Privacy Statement to demonstrate that we are committed to protecting all individuals who utilize our Web-based e-mail services, and all other services that we do and will provide. . . . When you use our free Web-based e-mail service, you implicitly consent to our collection, use, and disclosure of information about you, as described below. We reserve the right to change the following policies from time to time. Therefore, we recommend that you consult this Privacy Policy Statement periodically.

* * * *

When you sign up for our free e-mail service and income opportunity "get paid to read e-mail ads," we collect specific information on your age, gender, etc. We do this in order to send you the appropriate advertisements for you to get paid to read. Obviously, the more closely we can match your tastes with what our advertisers are selling, the more effective will be their advertising campaigns. This will ultimately lead to their desiring to continue advertising with us. The end result is that you will continue to be able to earn money by reading their ads. . . . Thus, for every subscriber of our growing community we collect the standard information about who you are and where you live and so on, as well as demographic information about your age, household size, income level, education, and so on. We also find out about your use of the Internet, what kind of car you drive, etc. This information is used only in conjunction with better targeting the ads that will be sent to you. Our goal is for you not only to make a lot of money by reading these ads, but for you to receive information that is actually useful in making your consumer choices.

To learn more about TRUSTe, including its origins and sample privacy policy, go to **http://www.truste.org**.

businesses to use. One of the best known of these organizations is TRUSTe. Web site owners that agree to TRUSTe's privacy standards are allowed to post the TRUSTe "seal of approval" on their Web sites. The idea behind the seal, which many describe as the online equivalent of the "Good Housekeeping Seal of Approval," is to allay users' fears about privacy problems.

The FTC's Role

In view of these developments, as well as new software that permits users to crush or filter out cookies, the Federal Trade Commission (FTC) has largely decided to allow the online industry to regulate itself with respect to the acquisition and sale of personal information. As in other areas of consumer protection, however, the FTC does maintain some oversight. If people complain to the FTC about a particular Web site's unfair or deceptive practices, the FTC may investigate and bring an action against the site's owner. Somewhat ironically, several FTC actions against online companies have been based on the companies' violations of their own Web site privacy policies. According to the FTC, such violations constitute deceptive practices.

The Case against GeoCities

In 1998, in the first case involving Internet privacy, the FTC brought an action against GeoCities, a provider of free home pages and e-mail addresses. On its

Web site, GeoCities (later bought by Yahoo!) told new members that it would not share the information that it collected with any third party without the permission of the persons from whom it was collected; rather, it would "use it to gain a better understanding of who is visiting GeoCities."

GeoCities, however, treated the failure of a member or visitor to click on a box that would let the user opt out of marketing offers as "permission" to share the information. The FTC charged that GeoCities had "misrepresent[ed] the purposes for which it collect[ed] personal identifying information from children and adults." The FTC also claimed that GeoCities sold the data to third parties who then targeted advertising at specific GeoCities's users, depending on their profiles.

Without admitting any wrongdoing, GeoCities agreed to change its policies on disclosing user information and abide by privacy standards established by the FTC. These standards, which the FTC developed during the GeoCities proceedings, included the following fixed elements:

- Notice of the Web site's privacy policy.
- Consumer choice with respect to any information collected.
- An outline of safeguards that render secure all consumer information data.
- The ability of the consumer to correct and update information.
- Parental control if a child is involved.
- An enforcement mechanism.

After the GeoCities action, the FTC's Internet Task Force (ITF) began to periodically surf the Internet to review advertising and privacy claims made on Web sites. If the ITF concludes that a claim does not meet the FTC's requirements, the FTC will notify the Web site's administrator of the violation and give the site thirty days to comply with requested changes.

Web Site Policies and the Sale of Business Assets

The problem for many online businesses is that personal information about their customers is often their most valuable asset. What if the company goes bankrupt and the major assets that can be sold to pay debts owed to creditors consist of personal information about the site's customers? In this situation, can such data be sold? For a discussion of this issue, see this chapter's *Controversial Issues* feature on the next page.

Government Sites Often Fail Privacy Tests

The General Accounting Office did a privacy audit of numerous government sites in September 2000. Almost all of them failed to meet the standards that the FTC seeks to impose on private sites. Few of them informed users of a Web site's data-collection procedures. Even fewer gave users options about whether and how the sites could use and collect the users' personal information. Few kept users' personal information secure from unauthorized use. In all, of the sixty-five government Web sites audited, 97 percent of the sites (including the FTC's site) did not meet the full criteria established by the FTC. Additionally, over 20 percent of the sixty-five government Web sites allowed third party online marketing companies to deposit cookies.

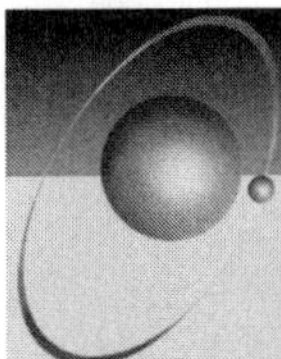

Controversial Issues in the Online World

E-Bankruptcies

Anyone who starts a new business knows the chilling fact: out of one hundred businesses that are founded, ten will prosper in the long run. Internet companies are certainly no different. In the late 1990s, they could do no wrong and their stock market valuation soared. By 2000, though, the bloodbath started as investors realized that many of these companies would never turn a profit. Internet companies were increasingly unable to obtain additional financing from venture capitalists. As a result, the number of "dot.com" bankruptcies increased—during the year 2000, nearly one hundred e-tailers declared bankruptcy.

What Happens When a Company's "Assets" Consist of Personal Data?

Typically, during bankruptcy proceedings, the company or an official appointed by the bankruptcy court sells off a company's assets and distributes the proceedings to the company's creditors. Yet e-companies present a unique problem: What happens if the company's "assets" consist largely of personal information about the company's customers? Can these assets be sold without violating the privacy rights of the customers?

Consider what happened when high-flying and quickly falling Internet company Toysmart.com went bankrupt and attempted to auction its customer names and profiles to the highest bidder. The hue and cry about violation of privacy rights was heard around the country. After all, Toysmart's Web site promised that such information would never be revealed or shared with a third party. Moreover, Toysmart was a licensee of TRUSTe. The Federal Trade Commission (FTC) and at least forty state attorneys general filed suit against the company, claiming that Toysmart had engaged in deceptive trade practices. A settlement was reached in which Toysmart agreed to sell the customer data only as part of a package that would include the entire Web site and only if the buyer was in the same business and agreed to abide by the same privacy policy developed by Toysmart.

Subsequently, the Texas attorney general sued Living.com, a failed furniture retailer, to prevent that company from selling customer data. Under a settlement reached by the parties, Living.com can go ahead with the sale but only if customers are allowed to opt out of the sale of their data to a third party.

Relaxing Web Site Policies

In the wake of the Toysmart case, a number of Web sites revised their privacy policies to reflect the possibility of a future sale of personal information to third parties. Yet consumers of such sites complained that revising a Web site privacy policy in such a way is essentially a breach of the promise made to customers in the previous policy. For example, Amazon.com came under fire when it revised its privacy policy in 2000. Amazon.com had previously collected personal customer information at a time when its privacy policy stated that it would not sell, trade, or rent customers' personal information to others. Amazon.com later changed its privacy policy to permit disclosure of this personal information to third parties. To inform its 23 million customers of this change in its privacy policy, Amazon.com simply stated on its Web site, "As we continue to develop our business, we might sell or buy stores or assets . . . . [C]ustomer information generally is one of the transferred business assets."

Two U.S. privacy groups, EPIC and Junkbusters, immediately complained to the FTC that Amazon had engaged in deceptive trade practices.[a] The FTC has yet to release the results of its investigation.

FOR CRITICAL ANALYSIS

Is allowing customers to opt out of a sale a sufficient safeguard of personal privacy rights? Would Web site customers read such a notice? Would it be better to require Web companies to get customer permission before any sale of customer information?

a. You can read Junkbusters's letter to the FTC by accessing its Web site at **http://www.junkbusters.com/amazon.html**.

SECTION 8 SHOULD MORE BE DONE TO PROTECT PRIVACY RIGHTS?

One of the questions facing both consumers and online marketers today is whether the government should step in and pass legislation to protect consumers' online privacy rights. A number of privacy advocates and consumer groups, including the Consumer Federation of America and the Electronic Privacy Information Center, are urging Congress to pass legislation to protect online privacy rights.

Notably, even some groups within the online industry believe that the federal government should take action. For example, the Hewlett-Packard Company recently called for federal legislation of consumer privacy rights. Subsequently, the American Electronics Association (AEA), the country's largest and oldest high-tech trade association, recently reversed its antiregulatory policy and issued "principles" for Congress to consider when writing new Internet privacy rules. The AEA principles call for new rules requiring e-commerce Web sites to notify consumers about the kind of information being collected and to give them the opportunity to choose not to surrender such information.

Most online industry groups, however, including the Information Technology Association of America and the Information Technology Industry Council, continue to support the self-regulation model. Nonetheless, the change in the AEA's stance on regulation reflects a growing concern about the pressure being put on state governments to regulate online companies. The belief is that if the federal government does not act to protect online privacy, online marketers could be subject to varying state laws, which would hamper e-commerce.

Currently, Congress is considering a number of bills that address online privacy issues. Given the mounting pressure on Congress brought by civil rights groups, consumers, and now even some groups within the online industry, it is likely that Congress will take some kind of action in the near future.

TERMS AND CONCEPTS

bait-and-switch advertising 225
cease-and-desist order 226
consumer 224
consumer law 224
counteradvertising 226
JavaScript 242
multiple product orders 227
targeted marketing 241
verifiable parental consent 241

QUESTIONS AND CASE PROBLEMS

10–1. Unsolicited Merchandise. Andrew, a resident of California, received a flyer in the U.S. mail announcing a new line of regional cookbooks distributed by the Every-Kind Cookbook Co. Andrew was not interested and threw the flyer away. Two days later, Andrew received in the mail an introductory cookbook entitled *Lower Mongolian Regional Cookbook*, as announced in the flyer, on a "trial basis" from Every-Kind. Andrew was not interested but did not go to the trouble of returning the cookbook. Every-Kind demanded payment of $20.95 for the *Lower Mongolian Regional Cookbook*. Discuss whether Andrew can be required to pay for the cookbook.

10–2. Privacy. Alpha Communications Corp. is an online marketing company. Alpha tracks consumer browsing habits on the Web by planting cookies on consumers' hard drives. The cookies are planted from sites with posted privacy policies. Alpha does this tracking for commercial purposes—the company sells the information about the browsing habits to online retailers—and without the permission of the consumers. Beth, a consumer, complains that Alpha's practices violate the law. Is Beth correct? Why or why not?

10–3. Consumer Protection. Fireside Rocking Chair Co. advertised in the newspaper a special sale price of $159 on machine-caned rocking chairs. In the advertisement was a drawing of a natural-wood rocking chair with a caned back and seat. The average person would not be able to tell from the drawing whether the rocking chair was machine caned or hand caned. Hand-caned rocking chairs sold for $259. Lowell and Celia Gudmundson went to Fireside because they had seen the ad for the machine-caned rocking chair and were interested in purchasing one. The Gudmundsons arrived on the morning the sale began. Fireside's agent said the only machine-caned rocking chairs he had were painted lime green and were priced at $159. He immediately turned the Gudmundsons' attention to the hand-caned rocking chairs, praising their quality and pointing out that for the extra $100, the hand-caned chairs were surely a good value. The Gudmundsons, preferring the natural-wood machine-caned rocking chair for $159 as pictured in the advertisement, said they would like to order one. The Fireside agent said he could not order a natural-wood, machine-caned rocking chair. Discuss fully whether Fireside has violated any consumer protection laws.

10–4. Deceptive Advertising. Dennis and Janice Geiger saw an advertisement in a newspaper for a Kimball Whitney spinet piano on sale for $699 at McCormick Piano & Organ Co. Because the style of the piano drawn in the advertisement matched their furniture, the Geigers were particularly interested in the Kimball. When they went to McCormick Piano & Organ, however, they learned that the drawing closely resembled another, more expensive Crest piano and that the Kimball spinet looked quite different from the piano sketched in the drawing. The salesperson told the Geigers that she was unable to order the spinet piano in the style requested by the Geigers. When the Geigers asked for the names of other customers who had purchased the advertised pianos, the salesperson became hysterical and said she would not, under any circumstances, sell the Geigers a piano. The Geigers then brought suit against the piano store, alleging that the store had engaged in deceptive advertising in violation of Indiana law. Had McCormick Piano & Organ Co. engaged in deceptive advertising? Explain. [*McCormick Piano & Organ Co. v. Geiger,* 412 N.E.2d 842 (Ind.App. 1980)]

10–5. Deceptive Advertising. Thompson Medical Co. marketed a new cream called Aspercreme that was supposed to help arthritis victims and others suffering from minor aches. Aspercreme contained no aspirin. Thompson's television advertisements stated that the product provided "the strong relief of aspirin right where you hurt" and showed the announcer holding up aspirin tablets as well as a tube of Aspercreme. The Federal Trade Commission held that the advertisements were misleading, because they led consumers to believe that Aspercreme contained aspirin. Thompson Medical Co. appealed this decision and argued that the advertisements never actually stated that the product contained aspirin. How should the court rule? Discuss. [*Thompson Medical Co. v. Federal Trade Commission,* 791 F.2d 189 (D.C.Cir. 1986)]

10–6. Privacy. In February 1999, Carl Adler mailed a driver's license renewal application form and a check for $28 to the New York Department of Motor Vehicles (DMV). The form required Adler's Social Security number, which he intentionally omitted. The DMV returned the application and check, and told him to supply his Social Security number or send proof that the Social Security Administration could not give him a number. Claiming a right to privacy, Adler refused to comply. The DMV responded that federal law authorizes the states to obtain Social Security numbers from individuals in the context of administering certain state programs, including driver's license programs, and that Adler's application would not be processed until he supplied the number. Adler filed a suit in a New York state court against the DMV, asserting in part that it was in violation of the federal Privacy Act of 1974. Adler asked the court to, among other things, order the DMV to renew his license. Should the court grant Adler's request? Why, or why not? [*Adler v. Jackson,* 712 N.Y.S.2d 240 (Sup. 2000)]

10–7. Privacy. "Anonymous Publicly Traded Company" (APTC) is a corporation with its principal place of business in Indiana. APTC filed a suit in an Indiana state court against "John Does 1 through 5," asserting that the defendants, whose identities were unknown, made defamatory statements about APTC in Internet chat rooms. APTC also claimed that the defendants were current or former employees who breached their fiduciary duties to the company by publishing confidential information about APTC on the Internet. As part of the discovery process, APTC asked a Virginia state court to subpoena America Online, Inc. (AOL), for the names of and other information pertaining to four AOL subscribers. AOL filed a motion in the Virginia court to block the subpoena, arguing that APTC should identify itself. APTC contended that it had a valid privacy interest that would be advanced by permitting it to remain anonymous and that revealing its identity would "harm the shareholders," but the company did not offer evidence of any potential "damage to the value of the corporation." The court denied the motion. AOL appealed to a state intermediate appellate court. Should APTC be allowed to proceed anonymously? Explain. [*America Online, Inc. v. Anonymous Publicly Traded Co.*, 542 S.E.2d 377 (Va. 2001)]

WEB EXERCISES

Go to **http://lec.westbuslaw.com** the Web site that accompanies this text. Select "Internet Applications," and then click on "Chapter 10." There you will find the following Internet research exercise that you can perform to learn more about consumer law:

Activity 10–1: Consumer Law

Unit 4

Human Resources and E-Commerce

Contents

CHAPTER 11
Employment Relationships and Web Technology

Concepts Covered

After reading this chapter, you should be able to:

1. Differentiate between an employee and an independent contractor.
2. Discuss how Web technology has affected job-recruitment practices.
3. Summarize the major statutes prohibiting employment discrimination.
4. List some of the problems that may arise in the formation and enforcement of employment contracts.
5. Explain why employment policies should include provisions relating to information security.

"Liberty of contract is not an absolute concept. It is relative to many conditions of time and place and circumstance."

Benjamin Cardozo, 1870–1938
(Associate justice of the United States Supreme Court, 1932–1938)

Any company doing business online must be aware of its rights and obligations with respect to its employees. For one thing, online employers need to know what kind of liability they may incur for actions undertaken by their employees in the course and scope of their employment. Additionally, employers often hire persons to help develop technological tools, such as software. A significant question may then arise: Who has ownership rights in the technology—the employee who developed it or the company that hired the employee? Generally, the answers to these and similar questions are found in the common law governing agency relationships.

Other common law principles apply to employment relationships as well. For example, when an employment contract is formed, the common law governing contracts comes into play. Additionally, the common law doctrine of **employment at will**, which traditionally was the basic law governing employment, continues to apply to employment relationships. Under this doctrine, normally either party can terminate the employment relationship at any time and for any reason, *unless* the termination would violate the terms of an employment contract or a federal or state statute. Recall from Chapter 1 that common law doctrines only apply to areas *not* covered by statutory law. The common law employment-at-

EMPLOYMENT AT WILL
A common law doctrine under which either party may terminate an employment relationship at any time for any reason, unless a contract specifies otherwise.

will doctrine has thus been displaced to a significant extent by statutory law governing employment relationships.

In this chapter, we first examine agency law and its applicability to e-commerce. We then look at some of the laws governing employment relationships. All firms, including online businesses, that engage in interstate commerce and employ a specified number of workers are subject to federal statutes regulating employment relationships. Exhibit 11–1 summarizes the major federal statutes governing the workplace today, several of which we discuss in the text of this chapter.

EXHIBIT 11–1 Major Federal Statutes Regulating Employment Relationships

AREA COVERED	MAJOR APPLICABLE FEDERAL STATUTE
Hours and Wages	*Fair Labor Standards Act of 1938*–Establishes requirements for overtime pay, minimum wages, and the employment of minors (persons under the age of eighteen).
Labor Laws	*National Labor Relations Act of 1935*–Regulates labor-management relationships; established the rights of employees to engage in collective bargaining and to strike; created the National Labor Relations Board to oversee union elections and to prevent employers from engaging in unfair and illegal union-related activities and unfair labor practices.
Worker Health and Safety	1. *Occupational Safety and Health Act of 1970*–Requires employers to meet specific standards to promote safety in the workplace and establishes penalties for violations. 2. *State workers' compensation laws*–Establish administrative procedures for compensating workers injured on the job.
Income Security	1. *Social Security Act of 1935*–Provides for old-age (retirement), survivors, and disability insurance; funded by contributions by both employers and employees. 2. *Medicare*–Administered by the Social Security Administration for people sixty-five years of age and older and for some under the age of sixty-five who are disabled; funded by contributions by both employers and employees. 3. *Employee Retirement Income Security Act of 1974*–Establishes standards for private pension plans offered by employers. 4. *Federal Unemployment Tax Act of 1935*–Requires employers that fall under the provisions of the act to pay unemployment taxes at regular intervals; administered by state governments.
Health and Life Insurance	*Consolidated Omnibus Budget Reconciliation Act of 1985*-Prohibits the elimination of a worker's medical, optical, or dental insurance coverage on the voluntary or involuntary termination of the worker's employment. Workers have up to sixty days to decide whether or not to continue with the employer's group insurance plan.
Family and Medical Leave	*Family and Medical Leave Act of 1993*–Requires employers who have fifty or more employees to provide employees with up to twelve weeks of family or medical leave during any twelve-month period. During an employee's leave, the employer must continue the worker's health-care coverage and guarantee employment in the same or a comparable position when the employee returns to work (exceptions are made for key employees).
Employment Discrimination	1. *Title VII of the Civil Rights Act of 1964*–Prohibits employment discrimination on the basis of race, color, national origin, religion, or gender. 2. *Age Discrimination in Employment Act of 1967*–Prohibits discrimination against job applicants or employees who are forty years old or older. 3. *Americans with Disabilities Act of 1990*–Requires that the needs of persons with disabilities be accommodated by employers unless to do so would create an "undue hardship."

SECTION 1 AGENCY RELATIONSHIPS

AGENCY
A relationship between two parties in which one party (the agent) agrees to represent or act for the other (the principal).

AGENT
A person who agrees to represent or act for another, called the principal.

PRINCIPAL
In agency law, a person who agrees to have another, called the agent, act on his or her behalf.

One of the most common, important, and pervasive legal relationships is that of **agency**. In an agency relationship between two parties, one of the parties, called the **agent**, agrees to represent or act for the other, called the **principal**. The principal has the right to control the agent's conduct in matters entrusted to the agent. By using agents, a principal can conduct multiple business operations simultaneously in various locations. Thus, for example, contracts that bind the principal can be made at different places with different persons at the same time.

A familiar example of an agent is a corporate officer who serves in a representative capacity for the owners of the corporation. In this capacity, the officer has the authority to bind the principal (the corporation) to a contract. Indeed, agency law is essential to the existence and operation of a corporate entity, because only through its agents can a corporation function and enter into contracts.

Types of Agency Relationships

Agency relationships commonly exist between employers and employees. Agency relationships may sometimes also exist between employers and independent contractors who are hired to perform special tasks or services.

EMPLOYER-EMPLOYEE RELATIONSHIPS Normally, all employees who deal with third parties are deemed to be agents. All employment laws (state and federal) apply only to the employer-employee relationship. Statutes governing Social Security, withholding taxes, workers' compensation, unemployment compensation, workplace safety laws, employment discrimination, and the like are applicable only when an employer-employee relationship exists. *These laws do not apply to the independent contractor.*

Because employees may be deemed agents of their employers, agency law and employment law overlap considerably. Agency relationships, though, as will become apparent, can exist outside an employer-employee relationship and thus have a broader reach than do employment laws.

EMPLOYER–INDEPENDENT CONTRACTOR RELATIONSHIPS Independent contractors are not employees, because by definition, those who hire them have no control over the details of their work performance. Section 2 of the *Restatement (Second) of Agency* defines an **independent contractor** as follows:

INDEPENDENT CONTRACTOR
One who works for, and receives payment from, an employer but whose working conditions and methods are not controlled by the employer. An independent contractor is not an employee but may be an agent.

> [An independent contractor is] a person who contracts with another to do something for him but who is not controlled by the other nor subject to the other's right to control with respect to his physical conduct in the performance of the undertaking. He may or may not be an agent.

Building contractors and subcontractors are independent contractors, and a property owner does not control the acts of either of these professionals. Truck drivers who own their equipment and hire out on a per-job basis are independent contractors, but truck drivers who drive company trucks on a regular basis are usually employees.

The relationship between a principal and an independent contractor may or may not involve an agency relationship. To illustrate: An owner of real estate who hires a real estate broker to negotiate a sale of his or her property not only has contracted with an independent contractor (the real estate broker) but also has established an agency relationship for the specific purpose of assisting in the sale of the property. Another example is an insurance agent, who is both an independent contractor and an agent of the insurance company for which he or she sells policies.

Criteria for Establishing Employee Status

A question that frequently comes before the courts is whether a worker should be deemed an employee or an independent contractor. How a court decides this issue can have a significant effect on the rights and liabilities of the parties.

For example, employers normally are held liable as principals for the actions of their employee-agents if those actions are carried out within the scope of employment. Additionally, federal and state statutory laws governing employment discrimination, workplace safety, and compensation for on-the-job injuries normally apply only to employees—not to independent contractors. The tax liability of employers is also affected by the determination of worker status. Whereas employers are responsible for certain taxes, such as Social Security and unemployment taxes, with respect to employees, they are not responsible for these taxes if their workers are classified as independent contractors.

FACTORS CONSIDERED BY THE COURTS In deciding whether a worker is categorized as an employee or an independent contractor, courts often consider the following questions:

1. How much control can the employer exercise over the details of the work? (If an employer can exercise considerable control over the details of the work and the day-to-day activities of the worker, this indicates employee status. This is perhaps the most important factor weighed by the courts in determining employee status.)

2. Is the worker engaged in an occupation or business distinct from that of the employer? (If so, this points to independent-contractor status, not employee status.)

3. Is the work usually done under the employer's direction or by a specialist without supervision? (If the work is usually done under the employer's direction, this indicates employee status.)

4. Does the employer supply the tools at the place of work? (If so, this indicates employee status.)

5. For how long is the person employed? (If the person is employed for a long period of time, this indicates employee status.)

6. What is the method of payment—by time period or at the completion of the job? (Payment by time period, such as once every two weeks or once a month, indicates employee status.)

7. What degree of skill is required of the worker? (If a great degree of skill is required, this may indicate that the person is an independent contractor hired for a specialized job and not an employee.)

FACTORS CONSIDERED BY THE INTERNAL REVENUE SERVICE Often, the criteria for determining employee status are established by a statute or administrative agency regulation. The Internal Revenue Service (IRS), for example, has guidelines for its auditors to follow in determining whether a worker is an independent contractor or an employee. In the past, auditors were to consider twenty factors in making such a decision. New guidelines effective in 1997, however, encourage IRS examiners to look closely at just one of those factors—the degree of control the business exercises over the worker.

The IRS tends to scrutinize closely a firm's classification of a worker as an independent contractor rather than an employee, because employers can avoid certain tax liabilities by hiring independent contractors instead of employees. Regardless of the firm's classification of a worker's status as an independent contractor, if the IRS decides that the worker should be classified as an employee, the employer will be responsible for paying any applicable Social Security, withholding, and unemployment taxes.

Sometimes, it is advantageous to have employee status—to take advantage of laws protecting employees, for example. At other times, it may be advantageous to have independent-contractor status—for instance, for tax purposes. (For other examples of the implications of independent-contractor versus employee status, see this chapter's *E-Guidelines* feature.)

The following case involved a dispute over ownership rights in a computer program. Under the Copyright Act of 1976, any copyrighted work created by an employee within the scope of his or her employment at the request of the employer is a "work for hire," and the employer owns the copyright to the work. When an employer hires an independent contractor, however, normally the contractor owns the copyright unless the parties agree in writing that the work is a "work for hire." The outcome of the case hinged on whether the creator of the program, at the time it was created, was an employee or an independent contractor.

CASE 11.1 Graham v. James

United States Court of Appeals,
Second Circuit, 1998.
144 F.3d 229.
http://www.findlaw.com/casecode/courts/2nd.html[a]

BACKGROUND AND FACTS Richard Graham marketed CD-ROM disks containing compilations of shareware, freeware, and public-domain software.[b] With five to ten thousand programs per disk, Graham needed a file-retrieval program to allow users to access the software on the disks. Larry James agreed to create the program in exchange for, among other things, credit on the final product. James built into the final version of the program a notice attributing authorship and copyright to himself. Graham removed the notice, claiming that the program was a work for hire and the copyright was his. Graham used the program on several subsequent releases. James sold the program to another CD-ROM publisher. Graham filed a suit in a federal district court against James, alleging, among other things, copyright infringement. The court ruled that James was an independent contractor and that he owned the copyright. Graham appealed the ruling.

a. This is a page, part of the Findlaw Web site, with links to some of the opinions of the U.S. Court of Appeals for the Second Circuit. In the "Select Year" and "Select Month" pull-down menus, select "1998" and "May," respectively. When that page opens, scroll down the list of cases to the *Graham* case and click on the link to access it.

b. *Shareware* is software released to the public to sample, with the understanding that anyone using it will register with the author and pay a fee. *Freeware* is software available for use at no charge. *Public-domain software* is software unprotected by copyright.

IN THE LANGUAGE OF THE COURT. . .
JACOBS, Circuit Judge.

* * * *

The Copyright Act provides, *inter alia* [among other things], that "a work prepared by an employee within the scope of his or her employment" is a work for hire. "[T]he employer or other person for whom the work [for hire] was prepared is considered the author" and the employer owns the copyright * * * .

* * * *

* * * [In determining whether a hired party is an employee, the important factors are:] (i) the hiring party's right to control the manner and means of creation; (ii) the skill required; (iii) the provision of employee benefits; (iv) the tax treatment of the hired party; and (v) whether the hiring party had the right to assign additional projects to the hired party. * * *

We are persuaded by the district court's conclusion that James was an independent contractor. Almost all of the * * * factors line up in favor of that conclusion: James is a skilled computer programmer, he was paid no benefits, no payroll taxes were withheld, and his engagement by Graham was project-by-project. The only * * * factor arguably favoring Graham is his general control over the work; but the district court has found, plausibly, that Graham's participation in the development of the [file-retrieval program] was minimal and that his instructions to James were very general.

DECISION AND REMEDY The U.S. Court of Appeals for the Second Circuit affirmed the lower court's judgment on this issue. The court agreed that James owned the copyright because he was an independent contractor when he developed the program.

FOR CRITICAL ANALYSIS–Economic Consideration *What are some other advantages of being an independent contractor? What might be some disadvantages?*

Liability for Contracts Formed by Agents

Liability for contracts formed by an agent depends in part on whether the agent was authorized to form the contract. Generally, unless a principal has authorized the agent, expressly or impliedly, to form a particular type of contract, the principal will not be liable for any such contract formed by the agent. The principal's liability for agents' contracts also depends on how the principal is classified. A **disclosed principal** is a principal whose identity is known by the third party at the time the contract is made by the agent. A **partially disclosed principal** is a principal whose identity is not known by the third party, but the third party knows that the agent is or may be acting for a principal at the time that the contract is made. An **undisclosed principal** is a principal whose identity is totally unknown by the third party, and the third party has no knowledge that the agent is acting in an agency capacity at the time the contract is made.[1]

Generally, assuming that an agent acts within the scope of his or her authority, a disclosed, partially disclosed, or undisclosed principal is liable to a third

DISCLOSED PRINCIPAL
A principal whose identity is known to a third party at the time the agent makes a contract with the third party.

PARTIALLY DISCLOSED PRINCIPAL
A principal whose identity is unknown by a third person, but the third person knows that the agent is or may be acting for a principal at the time the agent and the third person form a contract.

UNDISCLOSED PRINCIPAL
A principal whose identity is unknown by a third person, and the third person has no knowledge that the agent is acting for a principal at the time the agent and the third person form a contract.

1. *Restatement (Second) of Agency,* Section 4.

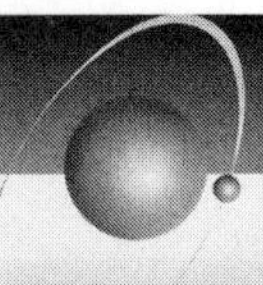

E-Guidelines

Employee Rights for Contingent Workers

Not surprisingly, many employers prefer to designate certain workers as independent contractors rather than as employees. After all, if a worker is an independent contractor, the employer is not required to pay the employer's share of Social Security taxes (as is required for employees) or bear the administrative expense of withholding taxes from the worker's paycheck. Furthermore, the employer need not provide employee benefits—such as pension plans, stock option plans, group insurance coverage, and so on—to independent contractors. Finally, the employer is free from many of the obligations imposed on employers under laws protecting employees, such as laws regulating safety in the workplace and laws protecting employees from discrimination. As illustrated in the *Graham v. James* case presented earlier, workers also benefit at times from having independent-contractor status.

Another option for employers who wish to save on costs, including the cost of benefits provided to employees, is to hire "temporary" workers through an employment agency. In this situation, the worker is an employee of the agency, rather than an employee of the hiring company, and the agency is responsible for withholding taxes and so on. A number of employers have resorted to hiring "temps" on a long-term basis to avoid having to provide employee benefits to those workers.

Increasingly, though, employers who use independent contractors and temps are finding that their contractual designations of these workers may not hold up under scrutiny. The Internal Revenue Service (IRS) or a court may hold that, despite the agreement between the worker and the employer, the worker is in fact an employee, either under the common law of agency or under a statutory definition of an employee. Under agency law, as stated elsewhere in this chapter, the most important factor in deciding this question is the degree of control that the employer exercises over the worker—although other factors also bear on the outcome.

Employee Benefits for Temps

In 1999, the Court of Appeals for the Ninth Circuit handed down a decision in *Vizcaino v. Microsoft*[a] that has serious implications for employers. The events that led to the lawsuit were set in motion in 1990, when the IRS determined that a number of Microsoft Corporation's independent contractors were actually employees of the company for tax purposes. The IRS arrived at this conclusion based on the significant control that Microsoft exercised over the independent contractors' work performance. As a result of the IRS's findings, Microsoft was ordered to pay back payroll taxes for hundreds of independent contractors who should have been classified as employees. Rather than contest the ruling, Microsoft required most of the workers in question, as well as a number of its other independent contractors, to become associated with employment agencies and work for Microsoft as "temps"—or lose the opportunity to work for Microsoft.

Workers who refused to register with employment agencies, as well as some who did register, sued Microsoft. The workers alleged that they were actually employees of the

a. 173 F.3d 713 (9th Cir. 1999).

party for a contract made by the agent. If the principal is disclosed, an agent has no contractual liability for the nonperformance of the principal or the third party. If the principal is partially disclosed, in most states the agent is also treated as a party to the contract, and the third party can hold the agent liable for contractual nonperformance.[2] When neither the fact of agency nor the identity of the principal is disclosed, the undisclosed principal is normally bound to perform, but the agent is personally liable for the undisclosed principal's nonperformance.

2. *Restatement (Second) of Agency,* Section 321.

E-Guidelines, Continued

company and, as such, entitled to participate in Microsoft's stock option plan for employees. Microsoft countered that it need not provide such benefits because each of the workers had signed an independent-contractor agreement specifically stating that the worker was responsible for his or her own benefits. When the case ultimately reached the Court of Appeals for the Ninth Circuit, the court held that the independent contractors were in fact "common law employees" under agency law. Notably, the court held that being an employee of a temporary employment agency did not preclude the employee from having the status of a common law employee of Microsoft at the same time.

Employment Discrimination and Independent Contractors

It is often assumed that laws prohibiting employment discrimination apply only to direct (employer-employee) employment relationships. Employers, though, should be wary of making this assumption. For one thing, independent contractors may have a cause of action against their employers under 42 U.S.C. Section 1981, which was enacted as part of the Civil Rights Act of 1866. That section prohibits discrimination on the basis of race in the formation or enforcement of contracts, including contracts between employers and independent contractors.

For another, a number of courts have held that independent contractors have standing to sue their employers under the major federal law prohibiting employment discrimination—Title VII of the Civil Rights Act of 1964. (This law prohibits discrimination in the workplace on the basis of race, color, ethnic origin, religion, or gender.)

Moreover, at least one court has held that Title VII's definition of the term *employee* is sufficiently broad that it embraces even an employee of an independent contractor. In *NME Hospitals, Inc. v. Rennels*,[b] an employee who worked for a pathology laboratory that provided services to a hospital sued the hospital for gender discrimination. The hospital argued that the plaintiff did not have standing to sue because she was an employee of an independent contractor and not of the hospital. The court, however, pointed out that Title VII affords relief to any "person claiming to be aggrieved." All the plaintiff need show is that some sort of employment relationship existed between the plaintiff and a third party and that the third party (in this case, the hospital) "controlled access to the plaintiff's employment opportunities and denied or interfered with the access based on unlawful criteria."

b. 994 S.W.2d 142 (Tex. 1999).

CHECKLIST

- ☑ Employers should be wary of trying to cut costs by using independent contractors or temps, because such workers may be deemed employees by a court or under IRS guidelines.
- ☑ Employers should also take steps to avoid discrimination against *any* worker, regardless of whether the worker is an employee, an independent contractor, or even an employee of an independent contractor.

When an undisclosed principal is in breach and the agent is forced to pay the third party, the agent is entitled to indemnification by the principal. It was the principal's duty to perform, even though his or her identity was undisclosed,[3] and failure to do so will make the principal ultimately liable. Once the undisclosed principal's identity is revealed, the third party generally can elect to hold either the principal or the agent liable on the contract.

3. If the agent is a gratuitous agent, and the principal accepts the benefits of the agent's contract with a third party, the principal will be liable to the agent on the theory of quasi contract.

Liability for Torts Committed by Agents

Obviously, an agent is liable for his or her own torts. A principal may also be liable for an agent's torts if they result from one of the following:

- The principal's own tortious conduct (conduct involving a tort, or civil wrong—see Chapter 4).
- The principal's authorization of a tortious act.
- The agent's unauthorized but tortious misrepresentation made within the scope of the agency.

TORTS COMMITTED BY EMPLOYEES If the agent is an employee, whose conduct the principal-employer controls, the employer may also be liable for torts committed by the employee in the course of employment under the doctrine of ***respondeat superior.***[4] Under this doctrine, the principal-employer is liable for any harm caused to a third party by an agent-employee acting within the scope of employment. For example, when an employee's security breach causes customers to suffer harm, the employer may be held liable. The doctrine of *respondeat superior* imposes **vicarious liability** on the employer—that is, liability without regard to the personal fault of the employer for torts committed by an employee in the course or scope of employment.[5] Therefore, third persons injured through the negligence of an employee can sue either the employee who was negligent or the employer, if the employee's negligent conduct occurred while the employee was acting within the scope of employment.

RESPONDEAT SUPERIOR
In Latin, "Let the master respond." A doctrine under which a principal or an employer is held liable for the wrongful acts committed by agents or employees while acting within the course and scope of their agency or employment.

VICARIOUS LIABILITY
Legal responsibility placed on one person for the acts of another.

At early common law, a servant (employee) was viewed as the master's (employer's) property. The master was deemed to have absolute control over the servant's acts and was held strictly liable for them no matter how carefully the master supervised the servant. The rationale for the doctrine of *respondeat superior* is based on the principle of social duty that requires every person to manage his or her affairs, whether accomplished by the person or through agents, so as not to injure another. Liability is imposed on employers because they are deemed to be in a better financial position to bear the loss. The superior financial position carries with it the duty to be responsible for damages.

Most *intentional* torts that employees commit have no relation to their employment; thus, their employers will not be held liable. Under the doctrine of *respondeat superior,* however, the employer may be liable for intentional torts of the employee that are committed within the course and scope of employment, just as the employer is liable for negligence. For example, an employer is liable when an employee (such as a "bouncer" at a nightclub or a security guard at a department store) commits assault and battery or false imprisonment while acting within the scope of employment.

TORTS COMMITTED BY INDEPENDENT CONTRACTORS The general rule concerning liability for the acts of independent contractors is that the employer is not liable for physical harm caused to a third person by the negligent act of an

---

4. Pronounced ree-*spahn*-dee-uht soo-*peer*-ee-your. The doctrine of *respondeat superior* applies not only to employer-employee relationships but also to other principal-agent relationships in which the principal has the right of control over the agent.

5. In this respect, the theory of *respondeat superior* is similar to the theory of strict liability—see Chapter 4.

independent contractor in the performance of the contract. An employer who has no legal power to control the details of the physical performance of a contract cannot be held liable. Here again, the test is the *right to control*. Because an employer bargains with an independent contractor only for results and retains no control over the manner in which those results are achieved, the employer is generally not expected to bear the responsibility for torts committed by an independent contractor.

E-AGENT
A computer program, or electronic or other automated means used to independently initiate an action or to respond to electronic messages or performances without review by an individual, according to the Uniform Computer Information Transactions Act.

SECTION 2 E-AGENTS

An electronic agent, or **e-agent**, is not a person but a semiautonomous computer program that is capable of executing specific tasks.[6] Examples of e-agents in e-commerce include software that can search through many databases and retrieve only relevant information for the user.

Some e-agents are used to make purchases on the Internet. An Internet user might employ one of the following e-agents to search the Web for a particular book: PriceScan, MX Bookfinder, and Bestbookbuys. Any one of these e-agents will scour the Web for the lowest price for that particular book title. Once found, the e-agent usually offers links to the appropriate Web sites. Other shopping e-agents locate other specific products in online catalogues and actually negotiate product acquisition, as well as delivery.

For information on PriceScan, go to **http://www.pricescan.com**.

What Agency Law Applies?

Under traditional agency law, contracts formed by an agent normally are legally binding on the principal *if* the principal authorized the agent, either expressly or impliedly, to form the contracts. One of the controversies involving e-agents concerns the extent of an e-agent's authority to act on behalf of its principal. Consider a not-too-uncommon example.

Software that an e-agent might find for its principal will undoubtedly involve a click-on agreement. E-agents searching the Internet may run into a variety of such click-on agreements, which contain different terms and conditions. If the e-agent ignores the terms and conditions of a licensing agreement outlined in the click-on setting, is the principal bound by the agreement? Conversely, a click-on agreement may exempt a third party from liability resulting from an underlying product or service. Is the principal bound by this term? With respect to human agents, the courts occasionally have found that an agent could not agree to such a term without explicit authority.

To avoid problems created by the use of e-agents, some online stores have blocked e-agents from accessing pricing information. Other online merchants are developing click-on agreements that can be understood by a computer and that are therefore more conspicuous for e-agents.

In the following case, the court addressed the issue of a principal's liability for the actions of its e-agent.

6. The Uniform Computer Information Transactions Act (UCITA), discussed later in this chapter, defines an *e-agent* as "a computer program, electronic or other automated means used to independently initiate an action or to respond to electronic messages or performances without review by an individual" [UCITA 102(a)(28)].

CASE 11.2 eBay, Inc. v. Bidder's Edge, Inc.

United States District Court,
Northern District of California, 2000.
100 F.Supp.2d 1058.

HISTORICAL AND TECHNOLOGICAL SETTING *A spider (also known as a Web crawler or a software robot, sometimes shortened to "bot") is a computer program that operates, or crawls, across the Internet to perform searching, copying, and retrieving functions. A spider is capable of executing thousands of instructions per minute, far in excess of what a human can accomplish. Spiders consume the processing and storage resources of a system, making that portion of the system's capacity unavailable to the system owner or other users. Consumption of sufficient system resources slows the processing of the system and can overload it, causing a malfunction or crash. A severe malfunction can result in a loss of data and an interruption in services.*

BACKGROUND AND FACTS eBay, Inc. (online at **http://www.ebay.com**), is an Internet-based, person-to-person trading site that offers sellers the ability to list items for sale and prospective buyers the ability to search those listings and bid on items.[a] Bidder's Edge, Inc. (BE), is the owner and operator of an auction aggregation site designed to offer online auction buyers the ability to search for items across numerous online auctions without having to search each host site individually. In 1998, eBay gave BE permission to include information regarding some eBay-hosted auctions. In 1999, BE wanted to increase its coverage, and eBay verbally approved BE crawling the eBay Web site for ninety days. To reduce the load on eBay's system in the future, eBay wanted BE to run a search only in response to a user query. BE wanted to recursively crawl the eBay system to compile its own auction database. Other aggregation sites agreed to eBay's terms, but BE refused. When BE's spider continued to crawl the eBay system, eBay filed a suit in a federal district court against BE, alleging, among other things, trespass to chattels, or personal property (see Chapter 4). eBay filed a motion for a preliminary injunction.

a. eBay currently has over 8 million registered users. Over 400,000 new items are added to the site every day. Every minute, 600 bids are placed on almost 3 million items. Users currently perform, on average, 10 million searches per day on eBay's database.

IN THE LANGUAGE OF THE COURT. . .
WHYTE, District Judge:

* * * *

If BE's activity is allowed to continue unchecked, it would encourage other auction aggregators to engage in similar recursive searching of the eBay system such that eBay would suffer irreparable harm from reduced system performance, system unavailability, or data losses. * * *

* * * *

* * * If eBay were a brick and mortar auction house with limited seating capacity, eBay would appear to be entitled to reserve those seats for potential bidders, to refuse entrance to individuals (or robots) with no intention of bidding on any of the items, and to seek preliminary injunctive relief against non-customer trespassers eBay was physically unable to exclude. * * * The court concludes that under the circumstances present here, BE's ongoing violation of eBay's fundamental property right to exclude others from its computer system potentially causes sufficient irreparable harm to support a preliminary injunction.

* * * *

If eBay's irreparable harm claim were premised solely on the potential harm caused by BE's current crawling activities, evidence that eBay had licensed others to crawl the eBay site would suggest that BE's activity would not result in irreparable harm to eBay. However, * * * eBay has carefully chosen to permit crawling by a limited number of aggregation sites that agree to abide by [eBay's] terms * * * . Such [permission] does not support the inference that carte blanche crawling of the eBay site would pose no threat of irreparable harm.

* * * *

BE argues that even if eBay will be irreparably harmed if a preliminary injunction is not granted, BE will suffer greater irreparable harm if an injunction is granted. According to BE, lack of access to eBay's database will result in a two-thirds decrease in the items listed on BE, and a one-eighth reduction in the value of BE, from $80 million to $70 million. * * * Barring BE from automatically querying eBay's site does not prevent BE from maintaining an aggregation site including information from eBay's site.

Moreover, * * * a defendant who builds a business model based upon a clear violation of the property rights of the plaintiff cannot defeat a preliminary injunction by claiming the business will be harmed if the defendant is forced to respect those property rights.

DECISION AND REMEDY The court concluded that eBay showed at least a possibility of suffering irreparable harm and that BE did not show a balance of hardships in its favor. The court granted eBay's motion for a preliminary injunction, ordering BE to stop accessing eBay's computers with a spider without eBay's written authorization.

FOR CRITICAL ANALYSIS—Economic Consideration *Why would BE object to complying with eBay's request to perform the same function as other aggregation sites and search engines in general?*

E-Agents and the UCITA

As mentioned in Chapter 6, in 1999 the National Conference of Commissioners on Uniform State Laws promulgated the Uniform Computer Information Transactions Act (UCITA).[7] The act was drafted to address problems unique to electronic contracting and to the purchase and sale (licensing) of computer information, such as software. Among other things, the act specifically addresses the issue of e-agents. Section 107(d) of the UCITA provides that any individual or company that uses an e-agent "is bound by the operations of the electronic agent, even if no individual was aware of or reviewed the agent's operations or the results of the operations." The liability of individuals and companies for the acts of e-agents, however, is qualified by Section 206(a) of the UCITA, which states that "a court may grant appropriate relief if the operations resulted from fraud, electronic mistake, or the like."

SECTION 3 RECRUITING EMPLOYEES

Because employees normally are deemed agents of their employers, the common law of agency necessarily permeates the employment environment. In addition, other laws govern employment relationships. Here, after a discussion of how Web technology has changed job-recruitment procedures, we look at the major federal statutes prohibiting discrimination in the workplace. These laws come

You can find an "Employee Hiring Form Package" that includes everything from employment contract forms to guidelines on how to comply with laws prohibiting discrimination in hiring at **http://www.lycos.com/business/hr.html**.

7. Excerpts from the UCITA are included in Appendix F at the end of this text.

into play even before an employment relationship is established—that is, during the hiring process.

Web Technology and Employee Recruitment

Searching for the perfect job candidate has never been easy. Typically, employers would advertise positions in local, regional, and/or national newspapers, as well as in trade or professional journals. Given how the Internet has affected all aspects of business and professional life, it is not surprising that it has also changed the way people search for jobs or for job candidates.

ELECTRONIC POSTING Although many employers continue to advertise openings in relevant printed media, today they can also advertise online. They can take advantage of Web technology to make searching for job candidates much easier than it was in the past. An obvious vehicle for advertising job opportunities is the company's own Web site. Most large firms today devote a section of their Web sites to employment issues, including job listings. Employers can also post jobs in online areas—such as bulletin boards and newsgroups—that they know will be accessed by those in the relevant trade or profession.

In addition, employers can access an increasing number of online sources that will advertise a job position available on numerous Web sites—for a fee, of course. For example, workindex.com offers what it calls "one-stop job posting." By using this service employers can reach qualified candidates who access as many as seven hundred Web sites and newsgroups. Jobbankusa.com offers a similar service. You can find myriad other Web sites offering job-placement services in specialized areas simply by accessing a search engine, such as Yahoo!, and keying in the word "employment."

Note that the online job marketplace is particularly suited to employers who are seeking to fill positions relating to the computer industry. This is because those who work in this industry are the most likely persons to be searching for jobs online.

DRAFTING EMPLOYMENT ADS AND RÉSUMÉS—THE IMPORTANCE OF KEY WORDS When drafting ads that will be posted online, employers should keep in mind that those searching for jobs on the Web will be using key words in their searches. This means that important job requirements should be phrased in such a way that online job searchers can find the ad when searching the Web.

Those who draft résumés to be posted online also need to forget résumé formats of the past, when the appearance of a résumé was a major concern. They also need to ignore writing styles of the past—for example, using active verbs (such as "Published newsletter!" or "Researched articles!") to sound dynamic. While correct spelling and brevity are still important qualities in a résumé, just as important in the online world are relevant key words, such as the name of a spread-sheet program or programming language with which the job seeker is familiar.

Laws Prohibiting Discriminatory Hiring Procedures

In the past several decades, judicial decisions, administrative agency actions, and legislation have restricted the ability of employers, as well as unions, to discriminate against workers on the basis of race, color, religion, national origin, gender, age, or disability. A class of persons defined by one or more of these criteria is known as a **protected class.** Several federal statutes prohibit **employment discrimination** against members of protected classes. These laws apply to the hiring process, as well as to employment relationships once a worker has accepted a job with a company.

PROTECTED CLASS
A class of persons with identifiable characteristics who historically have been victimized by discriminatory treatment for certain purposes. Depending on the context, these characteristics include age, color, gender, national origin, race, and religion.

EMPLOYMENT DISCRIMINATION
Treating employees or job applicants unequally on the basis of race, color, national origin, religion, gender, age, or disability; prohibited by federal statutes.

TITLE VII OF THE CIVIL RIGHTS ACT OF 1964 The most important federal statute prohibiting discrimination in the workplace is Title VII of the Civil Rights Act of 1964.[8] Title VII and its amendments prohibit employment discrimination on the basis of race, color, religion, national origin, and gender at any stage of employment. Title VII applies to employers affecting interstate commerce with fifteen or more employees, labor unions with fifteen or more members, labor unions that operate hiring halls (to which members go regularly to be rationed jobs as they become available), employment agencies, and state and local governing units or agencies. A special section of the act prohibits discrimination in most federal government employment.

Title VII prohibits both intentional discrimination and unintentional discrimination. The latter occurs when an employer's job requirements, such as those involving educational achievement, have an unintended discriminatory impact on a protected class. Unless the employer can prove that a specific requirement having a discriminatory effect is a *business necessity,* the employer may be liable for violating Title VII—and liability under Title VII can be extensive. If a plaintiff successfully proves that unlawful discrimination occurred, a number of remedies are available, including compensatory damages and (if an employer acted with malice or reckless indifference to an individual's rights) punitive damages. The amount of damages is limited by the statute to specific sums against specific employers—ranging from $50,000 against employers with one hundred or fewer employees to $300,000 against employers with more than five hundred employees.

An excellent source for information on various forms of employment discrimination is the Equal Employment Opportunity Commission's Web site at **http://www.eeoc.gov**.

Compliance with Title VII is monitored by the Equal Employment Opportunity Commission (EEOC), which, on receiving a complaint of discrimination, may investigate the matter and sue the employer. Alternatively, the EEOC may decline to investigate the claim and allow the employee to bring a lawsuit against the employer.

DISCRIMINATION BASED ON AGE The Age Discrimination in Employment Act (ADEA) of 1967, as amended, prohibits employment discrimination on the basis of age against individuals forty years of age or older. The act also prohibits mandatory retirement for nonmanagerial workers. For the act to apply, an employer must have twenty or more employees, and the employer's business activities must affect interstate commerce. The EEOC administers the ADEA, but the act also permits private causes of action against employers for age discrimination.

Numerous cases of alleged age discrimination have been brought against employers who, to cut costs, hired younger, lower-salaried workers to replace older, higher-salaried employees. Whether a firing is discriminatory or simply

8. 42 U.S.C. Sections 2000e–2000e-17.

part of a rational business decision to prune the company's ranks is not always clear. Companies generally defend a decision to discharge a worker by asserting that the worker could no longer perform his or her duties or that the worker's skills were no longer needed. The employee must prove that the discharge was motivated, at least in part, by age bias. Proof that qualified older employees are generally discharged before employees who are younger or that co-workers continually made unflattering age-related comments about the discharged worker may be enough.

DISCRIMINATION BASED ON DISABILITY The most significant statute prohibiting employment (and other types of) discrimination against persons who have disabilities is the Americans with Disabilities Act (ADA) of 1990. Basically, the ADA requires that employers "reasonably accommodate" the needs of persons with disabilities unless to do so would cause the employer to suffer an "undue hardship." This act is also administered by the EEOC, and the same remedies that are available under Title VII are available to victims of disability-based discrimination. In addition, employers who repeatedly violate the act may be ordered to pay fines of up to $100,000.

The ADA is broadly drafted to define persons with disabilities as persons with physical or mental impairments that "substantially limit" their everyday activities. More specifically, the ADA defines *disability* as "(1) a physical or mental impairment that substantially limits one or more of the major life activities of such individuals; (2) a record of such impairment; or (3) being regarded as having such an impairment." Health conditions that have been considered disabilities under federal law include blindness, alcoholism, heart disease, cancer, muscular dystrophy, cerebral palsy, paraplegia, diabetes, acquired immune deficiency syndrome (AIDS), being infected by the human immunodeficiency virus (HIV), and morbid obesity (defined as existing when an individual's weight is two times that of a normal person).[9]

One issue that frequently arises in ADA cases is whether a person whose impairment is mitigated by medication or a corrective device qualifies for protection under the ADA. In 1999, the United States Supreme Court addressed this issue in a case involving two pilots whose severe myopia could be corrected with glasses or contact lenses. The Court held that a person is not disabled (substantially limited in any major life activity) under the ADA if he or she has a condition that can be corrected with medication, or one, such as poor vision, that can be rectified with corrective devices, such as glasses.[10]

Reasonable Accommodation. If a job applicant or an employee with a disability can perform essential job functions with reasonable accommodation, the employer must make the accommodation. Required modifications may include installing ramps for a wheelchair, establishing flexible working hours, creating or modifying job assignments, and creating or improving training materials and procedures. Employers, however, are not required to hire or retain workers who, because of their disabilities, pose a "direct threat to the health or safety" of themselves or their co-workers.

---

9. *Cook v. Rhode Island Department of Mental Health,* 10 F.3d 17 (1st Cir. 1993).
10. *Sutton v. United Airlines, Inc.,* 527 U.S. 471, 119 S.Ct. 2139, 144 L.Ed.2d 450 (1999).

Generally, employers should give primary consideration to employees' preferences in deciding what accommodations should be made. If an applicant or employee fails to let the employer know how his or her disability can be accommodated, the employer may avoid liability for failing to hire or retain the individual on the ground that the individual has failed to meet the "otherwise qualified" requirement.[11] Employers should be cautious in making this assumption in cases involving mental illness, though. For example, in one case, an employee was held to have a cause of action against his employer under the ADA even though the employee never explicitly told the employer how his disability could be accommodated.[12]

Employers who do not accommodate the needs of persons with disabilities must demonstrate that the accommodations would cause *undue hardship.* Generally, the law offers no uniform standards for identifying what is an undue hardship other than the imposition of a "significant difficulty or expense" on the employer. Usually, the courts decide whether an accommodation constitutes an undue hardship on a case-by-case basis. In one case, the court decided that paying for a parking space near the office for an employee with a disability was not an undue hardship.[13] In another case, the court held that accommodating the request of an employee with diabetes for indefinite leave until his disease was under control would create an undue hardship for the employer, because the employer would not know when the employee was returning to work.[14]

Job Applications and Preemployment Physical Exams. Employers must modify their job-application process so that those with disabilities can compete for jobs with those who do not have disabilities. A job announcement that has only a phone number, for example, would discriminate against potential job applicants with hearing impairments. Thus, the job announcement must also provide an address.

Employers are restricted in the kinds of questions they may ask on job-application forms and during preemployment interviews. Furthermore, employers cannot require persons with disabilities to submit to preemployment physicals unless such exams are required of all other applicants. Employers can condition an offer of employment on the employee's successfully passing a medical examination, but disqualifications must result from the discovery of problems that render the applicant unable to perform the job for which he or she is to be hired.

SECTION 4 THE EMPLOYMENT CONTRACT

One of the questions that arises when an employer hires new employees is whether a written contract should be formed. A **contract** can be defined as an agreement between two or more parties, based on an exchange of promises, that can be enforced in court. A contract may be oral, or it may be in writing. In the employment context, whenever an employer hires a worker, the employer has

CONTRACT
An agreement that can be enforced in court; formed by two or more parties, each of whom agrees to perform or to refrain from performing some act now or in the future.

11. See, for example, *Beck v. University of Wisconsin Board of Regents,* 75 F.3d 1130 (7th Cir. 1996); and *White v. York International Corp.,* 45 F.3d 357 (10th Cir. 1995).
12. *Bultemeyer v. Fort Wayne Community Schools,* 100 F.3d 1281 (7th Cir. 1996).
13. See *Lyons v. Legal Aid Society,* 68 F.3d 1512 (2d Cir. 1995).
14. *Myers v. Hase,* 50 F.3d 278 (4th Cir. 1995).

essentially formed a contract with that worker. If the contract is oral, however, it may be difficult for either party to enforce the contract.

At times, oral employment contracts may be advantageous to employers. As mentioned earlier in this chapter, under the common law doctrine of employment at will, employers are free to terminate a worker's employment for any or no reason. (Exceptions are sometimes made to the at-will doctrine, as you will read shortly.) If a written employment contract states that employees can only be fired for certain reasons, such as for "good cause," however, the employer must abide by this contract provision or face liability for **breaching,** or breaking, the contract. At other times, written employment contracts are advantageous to the employer, particularly when hiring key personnel whose services may be essential to the company's growth or prosperity.

BREACH
To violate a law, by an act or an omission, or to break a legal obligation that one owes to another person or to society.

AGREEMENT
A meeting of two or more minds in regard to the terms of a contract; usually broken down into two events—an offer by one party to form a contract, and an acceptance of the offer by the person to whom the offer is made.

CONSIDERATION
Generally, the value given in return for a promise. The consideration, which must be present to make the contract legally binding, must be something of legally sufficient value and bargained for and must result in a detriment to the promisee or a benefit to the promisor.

PROMISSORY ESTOPPEL
A doctrine that applies when a promisor makes a clear and definite promise on which the promisee justifiably relies; such a promise is binding if justice will be better served by the enforcement of the promise.

Elements of a Contract

For a valid contract to be formed, four requirements must be met. First, the parties must agree to form a contract. Usually, a contractual **agreement** is manifested by an *offer* and an *acceptance*—one person makes an offer to form a contract, and the other party accepts that offer. Under contract law, the offer and acceptance must meet certain criteria. For example, the one making the offer must have a serious intention to become bound by the offer, and the terms of the offer must be sufficiently definite to allow the parties and a court to ascertain what the contract terms are in the event the contract is breached. The person accepting the offer must accept the terms exactly as stated in the offer, or contractual agreement will not exist.

Second, each party must give **consideration** (something of value, such as wages in return for work) for the contract. Exceptions to this rule are made in certain circumstances, however. For example, under the doctrine of **promissory estoppel,** a person who has reasonably and substantially relied on the promise of another may be able to obtain some measure of recovery. Under this doctrine, a court may enforce an otherwise unenforceable promise based on the party's *detrimental reliance* on a contractual promise—to avoid the injustice that would otherwise result. The one making the contractual promise will be *estopped* (prevented) from asserting the lack of consideration as a defense to contract formation. Third, to form a valid contract, the parties must have the required legal competence to form a contract. Finally, the contract cannot be for an illegal purpose.

If these four elements are present, a valid contract exists. If one party fails to perform the promises made in the contract, the other party will be entitled to remedies. Usually, the remedy for a breach of contract is money damages. At times, however, a court may grant one of the equitable remedies mentioned in Chapter 1. If any of the four elements required for a valid contract is lacking, a valid contract has not come into existence.

In the following case, an individual sought to recover damages under the doctrine of promissory estoppel from a prospective employer that reneged on its promise of employment.

On the Web

To learn more aboout how the courts decide such issues as whether consideration was lacking for a particular contract, look at relevant case law, which can be accessed through Cornell University's School of Law site at **http://www.law.cornell.edu/topics/contracts.html**.

CASE 11.3 Goff-Hamel v. Obstetricians & Gynecologists, P.C.

Supreme Court of Nebraska, 1999.
256 Neb. 19,
588 N.W.2d 798.
http://www.findlaw.com/11stategov/ne/neca.html[a]

BACKGROUND AND FACTS Julie Goff-Hamel worked for Hastings Family Planning. After eleven years, Goff-Hamel was earning $24,000, plus benefits: six weeks' paid maternity leave, six weeks' vacation, twelve paid holidays, twelve sick days, educational reimbursement, and medical and dental insurance. In July 1993, representatives of Obstetricians & Gynecologists, P.C.,[b] (Obstetricians)—including part owner Dr. George Adam and personnel consultant Larry Draper—asked Goff-Hamel to work for Obstetricians. Adam told Goff-Hamel that the position was full-time, at a salary of $10 per hour, and included two weeks' paid vacation, three or four paid holidays, uniforms, and an educational stipend. A retirement plan would start after the end of the second year, retroactive to the end of the first year. The job did not include health insurance. Goff-Hamel agreed to start in October and gave notice to Hastings in August. She was given uniforms for her new job and a copy of her work schedule. The day before she was supposed to start, Draper told her that she need not report to work and that Janel Foote, the wife of Dr. Terry Foote, a part owner, opposed her hiring. Goff-Hamel filed a suit in a Nebraska state court against Obstetricians, seeking damages in part on the basis of detrimental reliance. The court concluded that because she was to be employed at will, her employment could be terminated at any time—which included before she began working—and issued a summary judgment in favor of Obstetricians. Goff-Hamel appealed to the Nebraska Supreme Court.

a. On this page, click on "January" under "1999." On the page that opens, scroll down to the case name, and click on "19990129" to access the opinion.
b. *P.C.* is an abbreviation for "professional corporation," which is a special form for a business entity.

IN THE LANGUAGE OF THE COURT. . .
WRIGHT, J. [Justice.]

* * * *

Other jurisdictions which have addressed the question of whether a cause of action for promissory estoppel can be stated in the context of a prospective at-will employee are split on the issue. Some have held that an employee can recover damages incurred as a result of resigning from the former at-will employment in reliance on a promise of other at-will employment. They have determined that when a prospective employer knows or should know that a promise of employment will induce an employee to leave his or her current job, such employer shall be liable for the reliant's damages. * * * [T]hey have concluded that the employee would have continued to work in his or her prior employment if it were not for the offer by the prospective employer. Although damages have not been allowed for wages lost from the prospective at-will employment, damages have been allowed based upon wages from the prior employment and other damages incurred in reliance on the job offer.

In contrast, other jurisdictions have held as a matter of law that a prospective employee cannot recover damages incurred in reliance on an unfulfilled promise of at-will employment, concluding that reliance on a promise consisting solely of at-will employment is unreasonable as a matter of law because the employee should know that the promised employment could be terminated by the employer at any time for any reason without liability. These courts have stated that an anomalous [abnormal] result occurs when recovery is allowed

CASE 11.3–Continued

for an employee who has not begun work, when the same employee's job could be terminated without liability 1 day after beginning work.

* * * *

* * * [W]e conclude under the facts of this case that promissory estoppel can be asserted in connection with the offer of at-will employment and that the trial court erred in granting Obstetricians summary judgment. *A cause of action for promissory estoppel is based upon a promise which the promisor [the one making the promise] should reasonably expect to induce action or forbearance on the part of the promisee [the one to whom the promise is made] [and] which does in fact induce such action or forbearance.* * * * [Emphasis added.]

* * * *

The facts are not disputed that Obstetricians offered Goff-Hamel employment. Apparently, at the direction of the spouse of one of the owners, Obstetricians refused to honor its promise of employment. It is also undisputed that Goff-Hamel relied upon Obstetricians' promise of employment to her detriment in that she terminated her employment of 11 years. Therefore, under the facts of this case, the trial court should have granted summary judgment in favor of Goff-Hamel on the issue of liability.

DECISION AND REMEDY The Nebraska Supreme Court reversed the judgment of the trial court. The state supreme court held that promissory estoppel can be asserted in connection with an offer of at-will employment. The court remanded the case for a determination of the amount of damages to which Goff-Hamel was entitled.

FOR CRITICAL ANALYSIS–Economic Consideration *If you were a judge in the trial court to which this case was remanded, what factors would you consider in determining the amount of damages that should be awarded to Goff-Hamel?*

Defenses to Contract Enforceability

Even if a valid contract is formed, certain defenses can be raised against the contract's enforceability. For example, one party may claim that he or she did not genuinely assent to the contract's terms or that the contract was not in the proper form—such as in writing, if the law requires it to be in writing.

GENUINENESS OF ASSENT
Knowing and voluntary assent to the terms of a contract. If a contract is formed as a result of a mistake, misrepresentation, undue influence, or duress, genuineness of assent is lacking, and the contract will be voidable.

GENUINENESS OF ASSENT A court will not enforce a contract if **genuineness of assent** is lacking. Generally, genuineness of assent will be lacking if the contract was formed due to a mistake, a fraudulent misrepresentation, undue influence, or duress. In these situations, normally a contract can be avoided—that is, the party successfully claiming that genuineness of assent is lacking will not be required to perform any obligations under the contract. In cases involving fraudulent misrepresentation, damages may be awarded if it can be shown that the misrepresentation was intentional and that the innocent party justifiably relied to his or her detriment on the misrepresentation.

During job interviews, in order to lure qualified employees, prospective employers sometimes "promise the moon" and paint their companies' prospects as bright. Employers must be careful, though, to avoid any conduct that could be interpreted by a court as fraudulent misrepresentation. For example, in one case, during a job interview the company told a job candidate that it would be able to fund long-term projects and showed the candidate a financial statement that showed profitable operations. In fact, the financial statement was not the most recent one, which showed losses. The candidate was hired, but he was laid off a year later because of the firm's financial difficulties. A court held that the company's actions amounted to fraudulent misrepresentation.[15]

THE STATUTE OF FRAUDS Another defense to contract enforceability is that the contract was not in the proper form. For example, almost every state has a statute that stipulates what types of contracts must be in writing. This statute is commonly referred to as the **Statute of Frauds.**[16] If a contract is required by law to be in writing and there is no written evidence of the contract, it may not be enforceable.

STATUTE OF FRAUDS
A state statute under which certain types of contracts must be in writing to be enforceable.

Among the types of contracts that fall under the Statute of Frauds are contracts that cannot, by their terms, be performed within one year from the date of their formation. In other words, any contract, including an employment contract, that cannot be performed within one year's time must be in writing to be enforceable. The test for determining whether an oral contract is enforceable under this "one-year rule" is not whether an agreement is *likely* to be performed within a year but whether performance is *possible* within one year. Under this rule, an oral contract for a long-term project that would necessarily require more than a year's time to complete would not be enforceable. One court has even held that an oral contract for lifetime employment was not enforceable.[17]

Covenants Not to Compete

As discussed in Chapter 6, one of the concerns of employers in today's cyber age is protecting their trade secrets—customer lists, marketing techniques, or any business process or information that makes an individual company unique and that would have value to a competitor. To protect against the disclosure of trade secrets to competitors, employers often include *covenants not to compete* in their employment contracts with managerial employees.

In a covenant not to compete, the employee agrees not to work for a competitor or to start a competing business for a specified period of time after terminating employment. Such agreements are generally legal so long as the specified period of time is not excessive in duration and the geographical restriction is reasonable. Basically, the restriction on competition must be reasonable—that is, not any greater than necessary to protect a legitimate business interest.

The 'Lectric Law Library provides information on contract law, including a definition of a contract, the elements required for a contract, and so on, at the Laypeople's Law Lounge, through the link "Contracts," at **http://www.lectlaw.com**.

One of the problems for Internet companies with respect to covenants not to compete is determining what are "reasonable" time and geographic restrictions with respect to Web-related work. As one court noted, a time restriction of one year, which courts traditionally have found to be reasonable, may be too long, given the rapid pace of development in communications technology.

15. *Hord v. Environmental Research Institute of Michigan*, 228 Mich.App. 638, 579 N.W.2d 133 (1998).
16. The name is misleading because the statute neither applies to fraud nor invalidates any type of contract. Rather, it denies *enforceability* to certain contracts that do not comply with its requirements.
17. See, for example, *McInerney v. Charter Golf, Inc.*, 176 Ill.2d 482, 680 N.E.2d 1347, 223 Ill.Dec. 911 (1997).

Additionally, considering the lack of geographic borders on the Internet, what could possibly be a reasonable geographic restriction in cyberspace?[18]

Implied Contracts—An Exception to the At-Will Doctrine

Employers should be aware that even if no written employment contract is formed, a court may find that an *implied* contract was formed. If the employee is fired outside the terms of the implied contract, he or she may succeed in an action for breach of contract even though no written employment contract exists.

For example, an employer's manual or personnel bulletin may state that, as a matter of policy, workers will be dismissed only for good cause. If the employee is aware of this policy and continues to work for the employer, a court may find that there is an implied contract based on the terms stated in the manual or bulletin. Promises that an employer makes to employees regarding discharge policy may also be considered part of an implied contract. If the employer fires a worker in a manner contrary to the procedure promised, a court may hold that the employer has violated the implied contract and is liable for damages. Most state courts will consider this claim and judge it by traditional contract standards.

A few states have gone further and held that all employment contracts contain an implied covenant of good faith. This means that both sides promise to abide by the contract in good faith. If an employer fires an employee for an arbitrary or unjustified reason, the employee can claim that the covenant of good faith was breached and the contract violated.

SECTION 5 EMPLOYMENT TERMINATION

While it may be relatively easy to hire an employee, it may be extremely difficult to fire him or her without risking liability for violating some legal duty. Another potential risk is that a departing employee may do extensive damage to the firm's computerized databases.

Wrongful Discharge—Liability under Statutory Law

WRONGFUL DISCHARGE
An employer's termination of an employee's employment in violation of an employment contract or laws that protect employees.

Whenever an employer discharges an employee in violation of a statute protecting employees, the employee may bring an action for **wrongful discharge.** If an employee's discharge violates one of the federal statutes prohibiting employment discrimination discussed earlier in this chapter, the employer may face extensive liability.

Moreover, most states also have statutes that prohibit employment discrimination. Generally, the kinds of discrimination prohibited under federal legislation are also prohibited by state laws. In addition, state statutes often provide protection for certain individuals who are not protected under federal laws. For example, a New Jersey appellate court has held that anyone over the age of eighteen was entitled to sue for age discrimination under the state law, which

18. At least one court has commented on these problems. See *EarthWeb v. Schlack*, 71 F.Supp.2d 299 (S.D.N.Y. 1999). This case was presented in Chapter 6 as Case 6.6.

specified no threshold age limit.[19] Furthermore, state laws prohibiting discrimination may apply to firms with fewer employees than the threshold number required under federal statutes, thus offering protection to a greater number of workers. Finally, state laws may provide for additional damages that are not provided for under federal statutes.

Wrongful Discharge—Exceptions to the At-Will Doctrine

As stated above, whenever an employer discharges an employee in violation of an employment contract or a statutory law protecting employees, the employee may bring an action for wrongful discharge. If an employer's actions do not violate any express employment contract or statute, the question is whether the employer has violated a common law doctrine. Because of the harsh effects of the employment-at-will doctrine for employees, courts have carved out various exceptions to the doctrine. As mentioned earlier, even when no written employment contract exists, a court may find that an employee's termination constitutes the breach of an implied contract. Other exceptions to the at-will doctrine may be based on tort theory and public policy.

EXCEPTIONS BASED ON TORT THEORY In a few cases, the discharge of an employee may give rise to an action for wrongful discharge under tort theories. Abusive discharge procedures may result in the tort of defamation (discussed in Chapter 4) or the tort known as *intentional infliction of emotional distress.* In one case, a restaurant had suffered some thefts of supplies, and the manager announced that he would start firing waitresses alphabetically until the thief was identified. The first waitress fired said that she suffered great emotional distress as a result. The state's highest court upheld her claim as stating a valid cause of action.[20]

Some courts have permitted workers to sue their employers under the tort theory of fraud. Under this theory, an employer may be held liable for making false promises to a prospective employee if the employee detrimentally relies on the employer's representations by taking the job. For example, suppose that an employer induces a prospective employee to leave a lucrative job and move to another state by offering "a long-term job with a thriving business." In fact, the employer is having significant financial problems. Furthermore, the employer is planning a merger that will involve the elimination of the position offered to the prospective employee. If the employee takes the job in reliance on the employer's representations and is fired shortly thereafter, the employee may be able to bring an action against the employer for fraud.[21]

EXCEPTIONS BASED ON PUBLIC POLICY The most widespread common law exception to the employment-at-will doctrine is an exception made on the basis of **public policy.** Courts may apply this exception when an employer fires a worker for reasons that violate a fundamental public policy of the jurisdiction.

PUBLIC POLICY
A government policy based on widely held societal values and (usually) expressed or implied in laws or regulations.

19. *Bergen Commercial Bank v. Sisler,* 307 N.J.Super. 333, 704 A.2d 1017 (1998).
20. *Agis v. Howard Johnson Co.,* 371 Mass. 140, 355 N.E.2d 315 (1976).
21. See, for example, *Lazar v. Superior Court of Los Angeles Co.,* 12 Cal.4th 631, 909 P.2d 981, 49 Cal.Rptr.2d 377 (1996).

Generally, the courts require that the public policy involved must be expressed clearly in the statutory law governing the jurisdiction. The public policy against employment discrimination, for example, is expressed clearly in federal and state statutes. Thus, if a worker is fired for discriminatory reasons but has no cause of action under statutory law (for example, if the workplace has too few employees to be covered by the statute), that worker may succeed in a suit against the employer for wrongful discharge in violation of public policy.[22]

Sometimes, an employer will direct an employee to perform an illegal act. If the employee refuses to perform the act, the employer may decide to fire the worker. Similarly, employees who "blow the whistle" on the wrongdoing of their employers often find themselves disciplined or even out of a job. **Whistleblowing** occurs when an employee tells a government official, upper-management authorities, or the press that his or her employer is engaged in some unsafe or illegal activity. Whistleblowers on occasion have been protected from wrongful discharge for reasons of public policy. For example, a bank was held to have wrongfully discharged an employee who pressured the employer to comply with state and federal consumer credit laws.[23]

WHISTLEBLOWING
An employee's disclosure to government, the press, or upper-management authorities that the employer is engaged in unsafe or illegal activities.

Damaging Actions by Departing Employees

Some disgruntled employees who have quit or been fired from their jobs have caused substantial damage to their employers' interests. For example, a departing employee might unleash a virus into the company's computer system or otherwise destroy or alter electronic databases. He or she may download valuable customer lists to use in a competing business or e-mail confidential trade secrets to the company's competitors.

In one case, a former employee of Intel Corporation, Ken Hamidi, became a thorn in Intel's side when he criticized the company's policies in e-mail sent to current employees. Hamidi, an engineer who had operated an Intel employee Web site, e-mailed from 25,000 to 35,000 messages at a time to Intel employees. Intel eventually took Hamidi to court, and the court ordered Hamidi to cease sending e-mails to Intel employees.[24]

Another illustration of what a departing employee might do is provided by a criminal case that involved two competing software developers, Borland International, Inc., and Symantec. Eugene Wang, a Borland vice president, expressed dissatisfaction with his job and quit. Other Borland officers reviewed Wang's e-mail files and found messages to Gordon Eubanks, Symantec's president and chief executive officer. Believing that the messages contained trade secrets and other confidential information, Borland filed a civil suit to recover damages and also notified the police. After an investigation, criminal charges, including the theft of trade secrets, were filed against both Wang and Eubanks.[25]

22. See, for example, *Molesworth v. Brandon,* 341 Md. 621, 672 A.2d 608 (1996).
23. *Harless v. First National Bank in Fairmont,* 162 W.Va. 116, 246 S.E.2d 270 (1978).
24. *Intel Corp. v. Hamidi,* 1999 WL 450944 (Cal.Super. 1999).
25. *People v. Eubanks,* 14 Cal.4th 580, 14 Cal.4th 1282D, 927 P.2d 310, 59 Cal.Rptr.2d 200 (1996), as modified on denial of rehearing (1997). The charges were dismissed after Borland paid a substantial part of the cost of the criminal investigation. The California Supreme Court felt that Borland's payment made it unlikely that the defendants would receive fair treatment.

In the following case, a business firm's competitor engaged in a systematic scheme to hire away key employees from the firm to obtain its trade secrets. Some of these employees, while still working for the firm, used its computers to send trade secrets to the competitor via e-mail.

CASE 11.4 Shurgard Storage Centers, Inc. v. Safeguard Self Storage, Inc.

United States District Court, Western District of Washington, 2000. 119 F.Supp.2d 1121.

COMPANY PROFILE *Shurgard Storage Centers, Inc. (**http://www.shurgard.com**), is the industry leader in full and self-service storage facilities in the United States and Europe. Shurgard's outstanding growth over the most recent twenty-five-year period was due to its development and construction of top-quality storage centers. Shurgard devised a sophisticated system of creating market plans, identifying appropriate development sites, and evaluating whether a site would provide a high return on an investment. Shurgard created a marketing team to carry out these tasks for each potential market. The teams became familiar with the market, identified potential acquisition sites, and developed relationships with market participants to obtain preferred sites.*

BACKGROUND AND FACTS Shurgard and Safeguard Self Storage, Inc., are competitors in the self-storage business. In late 1999, Safeguard offered a job to Eric Leland, a regional development manager for Shurgard. Because of his position with Shurgard, Leland had full access to the firm's confidential business plans, expansion plans, and other trade secrets. Leland began e-mailing this information to Safeguard, without Shurgard's knowledge or approval. After quitting Shurgard and beginning work for Safeguard, Leland continued to disclose Shurgard's secrets. Meanwhile, Safeguard recruited and hired other Shurgard employees with intimate knowledge of Shurgard's business practices. Shurgard filed a suit in a federal district court against Safeguard, claiming in part violations of the Computer Fraud and Abuse Act (CFAA) of 1986. Safeguard filed a motion to dismiss this claim.

IN THE LANGUAGE OF THE COURT. . .

ZILLY, District Judge.

* * * *

Under [CFAA Section] 1030(a)(2)(C), "[w]hoever * * * intentionally accesses a computer without authorization or exceeds authorized access, and thereby obtains * * * information from any protected computer if the conduct involved an interstate or foreign communication * * * shall be punished" as provided in section (c) of the statute. Additionally, [Section] 1030(g) provides that "[a]ny person who suffers damage or loss by reason of a violation of this section may maintain a civil action against the violator to obtain compensatory damages and injunctive relief or other equitable relief." [Under Section 1030(e)(2)(B)] a "protected computer" means a computer "which is used in interstate or foreign commerce or communication." [Under Section 1030(e)(6)] "[t]he term 'exceeds authorized access' means to access a computer with authorization and to use such access to obtain or alter information in the computer that the accesser is not entitled so to obtain or alter."

* * * *

The defendant's [Safeguard's] * * * ground for challenging the plaintiff's [Shurgard's] claim is that the plaintiff has not alleged that its former employees did not have authorized access to the information in question. The defendant notes that the plaintiff alleged that Mr. Leland had full access to all the

CASE 11.4–Continued

information allegedly transferred to the defendant. Accordingly, the defendant argues that the plaintiff cannot maintain an action under [the CFAA] because it has not alleged that anyone accessed its computers without authorization or exceeded authorized access to those computers.

The plaintiff responds by arguing that the authorization for its former employees ended when the employees began acting as agents for the defendant. The plaintiff * * * argues that when Mr. Leland or other former employees used the plaintiff's computers and information on those computers in an improper way they were "without authorization."

* * * *

Under the *Restatement (Second) of Agency* [Section 112] * * * : Unless otherwise agreed, the authority of an agent terminates if, without knowledge of the principal, he acquires adverse interests or if he is otherwise guilty of a serious breach of loyalty to the principal. Under this rule, the authority of the plaintiff's former employees ended when they allegedly became agents of the defendant. Therefore, * * * they lost their authorization and were "without authorization" when they allegedly obtained and sent the proprietary information to the defendant via e-mail.

DECISION AND REMEDY The court denied Safeguard's request to dismiss Shurguard's claim. The court held that a computer user who has authorized access to a computer and its programs loses that authorization when he or she uses those programs in an unauthorized way.

FOR CRITICAL ANALYSIS–Economic Consideration *What exactly do employees steal when they transmit confidential information without authorization via e-mail, considering that the original material is still on the owner's computers?*

SECTION 6 EMPLOYMENT POLICIES AND INFORMATION SECURITY[26]

Damage caused by the actions of departing employees is just one of the challenges faced by today's employers with respect to information security. Generally, individuals and businesses, as well as other organizations and institutions, want to be assured that others do not overhear, record, or otherwise gain access to their computer information. As mentioned in Chapter 4, the most common types of computer crime are thefts of confidential information and trade secrets.

A breach of information security erodes public confidence and can lead to a loss of business. It can also result in the imposition of civil or criminal liability on the employer or business. Civil liability may be based on a claim that privacy interests were violated or that there was a breach of a duty of care (see the discussion of torts in Chapter 4). Criminal liability may be founded on a federal or state statute. We look next at some of the steps that can be taken to protect computer information.

26. You may have been assigned this material in a previous chapter. If so, you may skip this section on information security.

Steps to Secure Information

Special care must be taken with electronic data to accomplish and maintain information security. Steps that businesspersons can take to protect their computer information include the following:

- Decide what information needs to be protected, and why.
- Make sure that all of those who are authorized to use the information understand why security is necessary.
- Decide on a system of security. (Some of the possibilities are covered in the pages that follow.)
- Explain to those with access to the information what they need to do to protect it.
- Forbid access to the computer system to outsiders.
- Test the security system periodically, once it is in place. If necessary, an outside firm can be hired for this purpose.
- Enforce the use of the security system.

Employment Policies

Although the acts of outside hackers and spies are a threat, the acts of employees, former employees, and other "insiders" are responsible for most computer abuse, including breaches of information security. When an insider's security breach injures a third party, the employer may be held liable. For these reasons, employees and others should be told that any form of computer abuse is against company policy, is illegal, and will be the basis for employment termination.

To ensure that confidential information is protected, employees and others may be required to sign confidentiality agreements. Such agreements typically provide that the employees will not disclose confidential information during or after employment without the employer's consent. Another safeguard is to distribute information only to those who need to know it. Still other security measures include facility lockups, visitor screenings, and announced briefcase checks.

Monitoring some computer-related employee activities may be appropriate, but if monitoring is to be done, employees should be told. Usually, it is legal to monitor employees' e-mail communications and Web surfing as long as the employee is told about the monitoring. Monitoring employees' online activities will be discussed at length in the next chapter.

Computer System Safeguards

Computers that are connected to an internal network or to the Internet can be vulnerable to a breach of security. E-mail, for example, is subject to interception along the path of its transmission over the Internet and on receipt. In this respect, e-mail is more like a postcard than a sealed letter. Without security protection, a networked computer should not be considered safe.

Many sources of software offer security programs that can be easily used. For example, most word processing programs include a "password" function. To gain access to information within the program, a user must know the password. A document that can be unlocked only with the password can be e-mailed as an attachment, providing some security. This security is minimal, however. Most password systems are easily breached. This helps persons who have forgotten their passwords, but hackers can also unlock confidential communications with little effort.

Another popular method of assuring improved security for e-mail is to use some form of cryptography. Encryption hardware is useful to those who often encrypt their documents or data, or who want to encrypt all of the information on their computers. This hardware is available in the form of computer chips and is commonly used in automatic teller machines (ATMs). These chips quickly encrypt, or decrypt, information. Additionally, effective **firewalls** can be installed at the interface between computers and the Internet to protect against unwanted intruders. Firewalls can also be used to keep internal network segments secure.

FIREWALL
A system composed of hardware and software to prevent unauthorized access to a network by an outsider.

TERMS AND CONCEPTS

QUESTIONS AND CASE PROBLEMS

11–1. Computer Abuse. Ann is an employee of Beta Communications Corporation. In a company restructuring, Ann's position is eliminated and she is given five days' notice. On May 5, Ann's last day of work, she e-mails some of Beta's confidential files to one of Beta's competitors. On the same day, Ann creates a computer virus, which she calls "Tornado," and releases it into Beta's computer system. Tornado wipes out the data on Beta's drives and makes it impossible for the computers to boot up for five hours. Ann programmed Tornado to reactivate on the fifth day of each month. Does Beta have any recourse against Ann? Discuss.

11–2. Discrimination Based on Disability. Ananda is a hearing-impaired repairperson currently employed with the Southwestern Telephone Co. Her job requires her to drive the company truck to remote rural areas in all kinds of weather, to climb telephone poles, to make general repairs to telephone lines, and so on. She has held this position for five years, a full year longer than any other employee, and she is quite competent. Ananda recently applied for a promotion to the position of repair crew coordinator, a position that would require her to be in constant communication with all repairpersons in the field. Southwestern rejected Ananda's application, stating that the company "needs someone in this critical position who can speak and hear clearly, someone who does not suffer from any hearing disability." Ananda says she could easily perform the essentials of the job if Southwestern would provide her with a sign interpreter. Although Southwestern agrees that Ananda is otherwise qualified for the coordinator position, the company has concluded that the cost of hiring an interpreter would be prohibitive, and therefore it should not be required to accommodate her disability under the Americans with Disabilities Act. Who is correct? Discuss.

11–3. E-Agents. Alpha Business Products, Inc., sells software on its Web site through an online ordering system, an e-agent. Through this system, Beth, a purchasing agent for Medical Insurance Company, orders an upgrade for Medical's word processing software. Before completing the order, Beth enters, in a "Comments" box, the following statement: "We will accept this upgrade if we are satisfied with the software after ten days' trial use." Do Alpha and Medical have a contract under the UCITA? Do they have a contract under the UETA? Discuss.

11–4. Employment at Will. Robert Adams worked as a delivery truck driver for George W. Cochran & Co. Adams persistently refused to drive a truck that lacked a required inspection sticker and was subsequently fired as a result of his refusal. Adams was an at-will employee, and Cochran contended that because there was no written employment contract stating otherwise, Cochran was entitled to discharge Adams at will—that is, for cause or no cause. Adams sought to recover $7,094 in lost wages and $200,000 in damages for the "humiliation, mental anguish and emotional distress" that he had suffered as a result of being fired from his job. Under what legal doctrines discussed in this chapter—or exceptions to those doctrines—might Adams be able to recover damages from Cochran? Discuss fully. [*Adams v. George W. Cochran & Co.,* 597 A.2d 28 (D.C.App. 1991)]

11–5. Employee versus Independent Contractor. Stephen Hemmerling was a driver for the Happy Cab Co. Hemmerling paid certain fixed expenses and abided by a variety of rules relating to the use of the cab, the hours that could be worked, the solicitation of fares, and so on. Rates were set by the state. Happy Cab did not withhold taxes from Hemmerling's pay. While driving a cab, Hemmerling was injured in an accident and filed a claim against Happy Cab in a Nebraska state court for workers' compensation benefits. Such benefits are not available to independent contractors. On what basis might the court hold that Hemmerling is an employee? Explain. [*Hemmerling v. Happy Cab Co.,* 247 Neb. 919, 530 N.W.2d 916 (1995)]

11–6. Wrongful Discharge. Stephen Fredrick, a pilot for Simmons Airlines, Inc., criticized the safety of the aircraft that Simmons used on many of its flights and warned the airline about possible safety problems. Simmons took no action. After one of the planes crashed, Fredrick appeared on the television program *Good Morning America* to discuss his safety concerns. The same day, Fredrick refused to allow employees of Simmons to search his personal bags before a flight that he was scheduled to work. Claiming insubordination, the airline terminated Fredrick. Fredrick filed a suit in a federal district court against Simmons, claiming, among other things, retaliatory discharge for his public criticism of the safety of Simmons's aircraft and that this discharge violated the public policy of providing for safe air travel. Simmons responded that an employee who "goes public" with his or her concerns should not be protected by the law. Will the court agree with Simmons? Explain. [*Fredrick v. Simmons Airlines Corp.,* 144 F.3d 500 (7th Cir. 1998)]

11–7. Spiders. Register.com is, among other things, a registrar of Internet domain names. Like all registrars, Register.com is required to provide free to the public an online, interactive database, called the WHOIS database, containing the names and contact information of its registrants. Verio, Inc., although not a registrar of domain names, is a direct competitor of Register.com in providing other services. Verio used automated software—a spider, or robot (or bot)—to collect the WHOIS data and use it for mass e-mail solicitations (spam) in a marketing initiative called Project Henhouse. Register.com complained to Verio, which stopped the spam but continued to collect the data with its spider. Register.com filed a suit in a federal district court against Verio, alleging, in part, trespass to chattels (personal property) and asking for an injunction. Verio responded in part that its use of a spider to collect the WHOIS data did not harm Register.com's computers. How should the court rule, and why? [*Register.com v. Verio, Inc.,* 126 F.Supp.2d 238 (S.D.N.Y. 2000)]

WEB EXERCISES

Go to **http://lec.westbuslaw.com**, the Web site that accompanies this text. Select "Internet Applications," and then click on "Chapter 11." There you will find the following Internet research exercises that you can perform to learn more about agency and employment relationships:

Activity 11–1: Employees or Independent Contractors?

Activity 11–2: Americans with Disabilities

CHAPTER 12

Monitoring Employees' Activities

Concepts Covered

After reading this chapter, you should be able to:

1. Explain what sexual harassment is and how it can occur in the online workplace.
2. Discuss how e-mailed documents may be used in litigation and why retention policies for e-documents are important.
3. Indicate how, and how extensively, employees' activities are monitored.
4. Identify the major laws protecting employee privacy rights.
5. Describe how an Internet-use policy may shield an employer from liability for violating employee privacy rights.

"We are rapidly entering the age of no privacy, where everyone is open to surveillance at all times; where there are no secrets."

William O. Douglas, 1898–1980 (Associate justice of the United States Supreme Court, 1939–1975)

One of the most notable developments in the employment arena in recent years is the expansion of the working area into cyberspace. Increasingly, the courts are holding that employer-provided e-mail systems, electronic bulletin boards, and the like are part of the workplace. As such, employment laws that govern the workplace also apply to the cyber workplace.

Employees' use of the Internet may expose employers to losses or liability on many fronts. Employees may unwittingly infect the employer's computer files with a virus by downloading software. As you read in Chapter 4, computer viruses can cause a firm to incur substantial losses. Another risk is that employees could reproduce, without authorization, copyright-protected materials on the Internet (see Chapter 5). Still another risk is that confidential information, such as trade secrets, contained in e-mail or voice mail messages could fall into the hands of an outside party—see the discussion of this issue in Chapter 6 and in the previous chapter. Finally, personal use of the Internet by employees cuts into their work time, which is a major concern for many employers today.

In this chapter, we first discuss how employers can also incur losses or liability from other online activities, such as using e-mail to harass co-workers or to exchange candid remarks that can be used as evidence in a lawsuit. We then look at some of the ways in which employers, in an attempt to shield themselves from liability, monitor their employees' online communications. Understandably, employers' monitoring activities have raised important legal issues.

Specifically, how far can employers go in their surveillance of employee activities without infringing on employee rights? As you will see, developing a comprehensive Internet-use policy is an important proactive measure that employers can take to avoid liability for employees' use of the Internet.

SECTION 1 LIABILITY FOR ONLINE HARASSMENT

As noted in the previous chapter, Title VII of the Civil Rights Act of 1964 prohibits discrimination against employees on the basis of race, color, national origin, religion, and gender. Title VII also protects employees against **sexual harassment**, which is regarded as a form of gender-based discrimination. Over the last decade, most of the cases involving employment discrimination alleged sexual harassment or some other form of gender discrimination. Note, however, that Title VII protects employees from harassment based on race, color, national origin, or religion as well.

SEXUAL HARASSMENT
In the employment context, the granting of job promotions or other benefits in return for sexual favors or language or conduct that is so sexually offensive that it creates a hostile working environment.

What Constitutes Harassment?

Sexual harassment can take two forms: *quid pro quo* harassment and hostile-environment harassment. *Quid pro quo* is a Latin phrase that is often translated to mean "something in exchange for something else." ***Quid pro quo* harassment** occurs when job opportunities, promotions, salary increases, and so on are given in return for sexual favors. According to the United States Supreme Court, **hostile-environment harassment** occurs when "the workplace is permeated with discriminatory intimidation, ridicule, and insult, that is sufficiently severe or pervasive to alter the conditions of the victim's employment and create an abusive working environment."[1]

***QUID PRO QUO* HARASSMENT**
A form of sexual harassment that occurs when job opportunities, promotions, salary increases, and other benefits are given in return for sexual favors.

HOSTILE-ENVIRONMENT HARASSMENT
According to the United States Supreme Court, a form of harassment that occurs when the workplace is "permeated with discriminatory intimidation, ridicule, and insult, that is sufficiently severe or pervasive to alter the conditions of the victim's employment and create an abusive working environment."

Generally, the courts apply this Supreme Court guideline on a case-by-case basis. Some courts have held that just one incident of sexually offensive conduct–such as a sexist remark by a co-worker or a photo on an employer's desk of his bikini-clad wife–can create a hostile environment.[2] At least one court has held that a worker may recover damages under Title VII because *other* persons were harassed sexually in the workplace.[3] According to some employment specialists, employers should assume that hostile-environment harassment has occurred if an employee claims that it has.

Employees' online activities can create a hostile working environment in many ways. Racial jokes, ethnic slurs, or other comments contained in e-mail may become the basis for a claim of hostile-environment harassment or other form of discrimination. A worker who sees sexually explicit images on a co-worker's computer screen may find the images offensive and claim that they create a hostile working environment.

On the Web

The law firm of Arent Fox posts articles on current issues in the area of employment law, including sexual harassment, on its Web site at **http://www.arentfox.com**.

Harassment by Supervisors

What if an employee is harassed by a manager or supervisor of a large firm, and the firm itself (the "employer") is not aware of the harassment? Should the

1. *Harris v. Forklift Systems*, 510 U.S. 17, 114 S.Ct. 367, 126 L.Ed.2d 295 (1993).
2. For other examples, see *Radtke v. Everett*, 442 Mich. 368, 501 N.W.2d 155 (1993); and *Nadeau v. Rainbow Rugs, Inc.*, 675 A.2d 973 (Me. 1996).
3. *Leibovitz v. New York City Transit Authority*, 4 F.Supp.2d 144 (E.D.N.Y. 1998).

employer be held liable for the harassment nonetheless? For some time, the courts were in disagreement on this issue. Typically, employers were held liable for Title VII violations by the firm's managerial or supervisory personnel in *quid pro quo* harassment cases regardless of whether the employer knew about the harassment. In hostile-environment cases, in contrast, the majority of courts tended to hold employers liable only if the employer knew or should have known of the harassment and failed to take prompt remedial action.

In 1998, in two separate cases, the United States Supreme Court issued some significant guidelines relating to the liability of employers for their supervisors' harassment of employees in the workplace. In *Faragher v. City of Boca Raton*,[4] the Court held that an employer (a city) could be held liable for a supervisor's harassment of employees even though the employer was unaware of the behavior. The Court reached this conclusion primarily because, although the city had a written policy against sexual harassment, the policy had not been distributed to city employees. Additionally, the city had not established any procedures that could be followed by employees who felt that they were victims of sexual harassment. In *Burlington Industries, Inc. v. Ellerth*,[5] the Court ruled that a company could be held liable for the harassment of an employee by one of its vice presidents even though the employee suffered no adverse job consequences.

In these two cases, the Court set forth some common-sense guidelines on liability for harassment in the workplace that will be helpful to employers and employees alike. On the one hand, employees benefit by the ruling that employers may be held liable for their supervisors' harassment even though the employers were unaware of the actions and even though the employees suffered no adverse job consequences. On the other hand, the Court made it clear in both decisions that employers have an affirmative defense against liability for their supervisors' harassment of employees if the employers can show that (1) they have taken "reasonable care to prevent and correct promptly any sexually harassing behavior" (by establishing effective harassment policies and complaint procedures, for example), and (2) the employee suing for harassment failed to follow these policies and procedures.

Harassment by Co-Workers

For a list of facts about sexual harassment published by the Equal Employment Opportunity Commission, go to **http://www.eeoc.gov/facts/fs-sex.html**.

Often, and particularly in the online environment, employees alleging harassment complain that the actions of co-workers, not supervisors, are responsible for creating a hostile working environment. In such cases, the employee still has a cause of action against the employer. Generally, though, the employer will be held liable only if it knew or should have known about the harassment and failed to take immediate remedial action.

For example, in *Daniels v. WorldCom, Inc.*,[6] Angela Daniels, an employee of Robert Half International under contract to WorldCom.Inc., received racially harassing e-mailed jokes from another employee. After receiving the jokes, Daniels complained to WorldCom managers. Shortly afterward, the company issued a warning to the offending employee about the proper use of the e-mail

4. 524 U.S. 725, 118 S.Ct. 2275, 141 L.Ed.2d 662 (1998).
5. 524 U.S. 742, 118 S.Ct. 2257, 141 L.Ed.2d 633 (1998).
6. 1998 WL 91261 (N.D.Tex. 1998).

system and held two meetings to discuss company policy on the use of the system. In Daniels's suit against WorldCom for racial discrimination, a federal district court concluded that the employer was not liable for its employee's racially harassing e-mails because the employer took prompt remedial action.

In another case, Deborah Schwenn, an employee of Anheuser-Busch, Inc., complained to her supervisor that she had received sexually harassing e-mail on the computer terminal attached to the forklifts she used in the warehouse. A week later, Schwenn met with a company official, who promised to investigate her complaint. Within two days, the official had printed and reviewed all e-mail on warehouse computers, interviewed witnesses, and issued a memo to all employees restating the company's sexual-harassment policy and warning against the abuse of e-mail. After several more incidents of alleged harassment, Schwenn left her job at Anheuser-Busch and filed a suit in a federal district court against the employer, alleging, among other things, discrimination in retaliation for complaining about the e-mail. Because the employer had not disciplined Schwenn in any way for her complaint and had instead investigated the allegations, the court held that the employer had not discriminated against her.[7]

The following case involved charges of gender-based, hostile-environment harassment arising from comments posted by the plaintiff's co-employees on an online bulletin board. A threshold issue in the case was whether the bulletin board constituted "an integral part of the workplace." If it was not, the employer could not be held liable for the harassment.

7. *Schwenn v. Anheuser-Busch, Inc.*, 1998 WL 166845 (N.D.N.Y. 1998).

CASE 12.1 Blakey v. Continental Airlines, Inc.

New Jersey Supreme Court, 2000.
164 N.J. 38,
751 A.2d 538.
http://lawlibrary.rutgers.edu/search.shtml[a]

HISTORICAL AND TECHNOLOGICAL SETTING *CompuServe, Inc., a subsidiary of America Online, Inc., is the Internet service provider for Continental Airlines, Inc. CompuServe provides Continental's pilots and other crew members with online access to their flight schedules. As part of the service, CompuServe makes a "Crew Members Forum" available for the exchange of ideas and information via messages and threads.*[b] *Through customized software, any individual with a Continental pilot or crew member identification number can access the Forum. This includes chief pilots and assistant chief pilots, who are considered management within Continental. Technical assistance is provided by system operators (SYSOPS), who are volunteer crew members.*

a. This page, which is part of a Web site maintained by Rutgers School of Law in Camden, New Jersey, includes a search box for a database of the recent opinions of the New Jersey state courts. In the box, type "Blakey" and click on the "Search" link. When the results appear, scroll down the list and click on the *Blakey* case name to access the opinion.
b. A *thread* is a sequence of responses to an initial message posting. This enables a user to follow or join an individual discussion.

BACKGROUND AND FACTS Tammy Blakey, a pilot for Continental Airlines since 1984, was that airline's first female captain, and one of only five Continental pilots to fly an Airbus, or A300, aircraft. Shortly after qualifying to be a captain on the A300, Blakey complained of sexual harassment and a hostile working environment based on conduct and comments directed at her by male co-employees. Specifically, Blakey complained to Continental's management about pornographic photos and vulgar gender-based comments directed at her in her plane's cockpit and other work areas. Blakey pursued claims against Continental with the Equal Employment Opportunity Commission and in a federal district court. Meanwhile, Continental pilots published a series of harassing, gender-based, defamatory messages about Blakey on the Forum. When the federal court refused to consider

CASE 12.1–Continued

these threads, Blakey filed a complaint based on the messages in a New Jersey state court against Continental and others. She alleged, in part, gender-based harassment arising from a hostile work environment. Continental filed a motion for summary judgment on this claim, which the court granted. A state intermediate appellate court upheld the summary judgment, and Blakey appealed to the New Jersey Supreme Court.

IN THE LANGUAGE OF THE COURT. . .
O'HERN, J. [Justice.]

* * * *

* * * When an employer knows or should know of the harassment and fails to take effective measures to stop it, the employer has joined with the harasser in making the working environment hostile. The employer, by failing to take action, sends the harassed employee the message that the harassment is acceptable and that the management supports the harasser. "Effective" remedial measures are those reasonably calculated to end the harassment. * * *

* * * *

* * * Continental's liability [depends] on whether the Crew Members Forum was such an integral part of the workplace that harassment on the Crew Members Forum should be regarded as a continuation or extension of the pattern of harassment that existed in the Continental workplace.

Our common experience tells us how important are the extensions of the workplace where the relations among employees are cemented or sometimes sundered. If an "old boys' network" continued, in an after-hours setting, the belittling conduct that edges over into harassment, what exactly is the outsider (whether black, Latino, or woman) to do? Keep swallowing the abuse or give up the chance to make the team? We believe that severe or pervasive harassment in a work-related setting that continues a pattern of harassment on the job is sufficiently related to the workplace that an informed employer who takes no effective measures to stop it, sends the harassed employee the message that the harassment is acceptable and that the management supports the harasser. * * *

* * * *

CompuServe's role may * * * be analogized to that of a company that builds an old-fashioned bulletin board. If the maker of an old-fashioned bulletin board provided a better bulletin board by setting aside space on it for employees to post messages, we would have little doubt that messages on the company bulletin board would be part of the workplace setting. Here, the Crew Members Forum is an added feature to the company bulletin board.

DECISION AND REMEDY The New Jersey Supreme Court reversed the judgment of the lower court and remanded the case for further proceedings. The state supreme court indicated that the trial court was to determine, among other things, which messages were harassing, whether Continental had notice of those messages, and the severity or pervasiveness of the harassing conduct.

FOR CRITICAL ANALYSIS–Social Consideration *Does the holding in the* Blakey *case mean that employers have a duty to monitor their employees' e-mail and other online communications?*

Same-Gender Harassment

The courts have also had to address the issue of whether men who are harassed by other men, or women who are harassed by other women, are also protected by laws that prohibit gender-based discrimination in the workplace. For example, what if the male president of a firm demands sexual favors from a male employee? Does this action qualify as sexual harassment? For some time, the courts were widely split on this question. In 1998, in *Oncale v. Sundowner Offshore Services, Inc.*,[8] the Supreme Court resolved the issue by holding that Title VII protection extends to situations in which individuals are harassed by members of the same gender.

On the Web

The University of North Carolina offers links to an extensive number of sexual-harassment resources at **http://library.uncg.edu/depts/docs/us/harass.html**.

Harassment versus Free Speech Rights

Some employers have defended against claims of sexual harassment by stating that employees, like everyone else, enjoy the right to free speech, which is guaranteed by the First Amendment to the Constitution. Yet where should the line be drawn between free speech rights and speech that is sufficiently offensive as to violate Title VII's prohibition against harassing behavior?

The answer to this question is not all that clear. As one federal appellate court noted, "Where pure expression is involved, Title VII steers into the territory of the First Amendment. . . . [W]hen Title VII is applied to sexual-harassment claims based solely on verbal insults or pictorial or literary matter, the statute imposes content-based . . . restrictions on speech."[9] In another case, an Oregon court held that religious speech that unintentionally creates a hostile environment is constitutionally protected.[10]

SECTION 2 E-MAIL AND THE LITIGATION PROCESS

E-mail offers numerous benefits. Because of its speed, relative inexpensiveness, and ease of use, it has largely replaced hard copy as a means of communication within and between business firms. Yet, as e-mail and Internet use continue to grow in the workplace, so too do the difficulties that go along with them. A significant problem has to do with the use of e-mail as evidence in lawsuits. In part, this dilemma arises because of common misperceptions about the nature of e-mail.

Common Misperceptions about E-Mail

A common misperception about e-mail is that such messages are private. Those sending e-mail thus tend to be more casual–and often more candid–in these communications than they would be if they were writing similar thoughts in interoffice memos or business correspondence using company letterhead. Unlike regular mail, however, which is sent in a sealed envelope, e-mail involves a

8. 523 U.S. 75, 118 S.Ct. 998, 140 L.Ed.2d 207 (1998).
9. *De Angelis v. El Paso Municipal Police Officers Association*, 51 F.3d 591 (5th Cir. 1995).
10. *Meltebeke v. B.O.L.I.*, 903 P.2d 351 (Ore. 1995).

intermediary entity—the employer's computer network. Indeed, in one case an attorney argued that sending an e-mail message via an employer's computer system is like posting a note on someone's desk in plain view.[11]

Another common misperception is that e-mail lacks permanence because it can be so easily deleted. In fact, the e-mail is not really deleted from the computer's hard drive just by a click of the mouse; rather, the delete command clears space on the hard drive that can be overwritten when the computer needs that space. Until the message is overwritten, it can be retrieved. Furthermore, copies of the e-mail message exist not only in the sender's hard drive but also in the hard drives of any recipients of the message, as well as in any servers through which the e-mail might have been routed, if those servers have not erased the e-mail. Finally, many businesses routinely back up computer information, and back-up tapes may contain e-mail that has been sent to the electronic trash bin.

E-Mail as "Smoking Guns"

Recall from Chapter 2 that if a corporation becomes the target of a civil lawsuit or criminal investigation, the company may be required to turn over any documents in its files relating to the matter being litigated. These documents may consist of legal documents, contracts, e-mails, faxes, letters, interoffice memorandums, notebooks, diaries, and other materials, even if they are kept in personal hard-copy or computerized files in the homes of directors or officers. If a company refuses to comply with a request for documents—or destroys the documents—it may be subject to severe court sanctions[12] or even a criminal charge of obstruction of justice.

For an article by an attorney with the law firm of Oldham and Oldham discussing how *not* to create a smoking gun, go to the following Web site: **http://www.twinoaks.com/newsletters.asp?show=69**.

In the litigation context, informal comments made via e-mail can come back to haunt the senders years later, as many firms are learning. For example, e-mail messages exchanged years ago by Microsoft Corporation executives became, for the Department of Justice (DOJ), "smoking guns" (evidence supporting the DOJ's position) in the department's suit against Microsoft for anticompetitive business practices. The DOJ claimed that the e-mail tended to show that Microsoft deliberately tried to monopolize access to the Internet.[13] Note that even if the e-mail has been deleted and no back-up copies are available, the e-mail may have been printed out. At least one court has ruled that a printed-out e-mail message was admissible in court as evidence in these circumstances.[14]

To curb potential litigation problems stemming from the use of e-mail, as well as for other reasons, many firms today have developed e-mail management policies as part of their overall document-retention policies. For a discussion of this issue, see this chapter's *E-Guidelines* feature.

On the Web

For a list of the types of corporate documents that should be retained, go to **http://www.hefcpa.com/docret.html**.

11. *Restuccia v. Burk,* 1996 WL 1329386 (Mass.Super. 1996).

12. See, for example, *Procter & Gamble Co. v. Haugen,* 179 F.R.D. [Federal Rules Decisions] 622 (D.Utah 1998).

13. *United States v. Microsoft Corp.*, 87 F.Supp.2d 30 (D.D.C. 2000). This case is currently on appeal.

14. *Schwenn v. Anheuser-Busch, Inc.*, 1998 WL 166845 (N.D.N.Y. 1998).

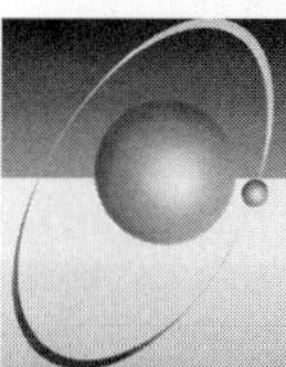

E-Guidelines

Retention Policies for E-Documents

As noted elsewhere, it is not uncommon today for e-mailed documents to be requested during the discovery stage of a lawsuit brought by or against the company. For this reason and others, today's firms are learning that policies on e-document management—particularly with respect to e-mail—are becoming imperative.

Document-retention policies are not new. In the past, however, they involved only a firm's paper documents. Today, a document-retention policy must also take into consideration electronic documents and data, including e-mail.

E-Mail Management Policies

Creating an effective e-mail management policy has now become a priority for most firms. In part, this is to avoid having to produce evidence harmful to a company's interests during litigation, as discussed elsewhere in this chapter. Additionally, e-mail management is necessary because of the sheer volume of employees' e-mail exchanges in today's workplace. In many companies, employees exchange over a million e-mail messages per week. If the company were to keep all e-mail on back-up storage devices, in the event of a lawsuit it could face a time-consuming and costly problem—sorting through millions of messages to locate relevant documents. In one case, for example, the court ordered a defendant to review and produce about 30 million pages of e-mail stored on back-up tapes (at a cost of between $50,000 and $70,000).[a]

To avoid such litigation nightmares, some firms simply delete e-mail after a specified period, such as two weeks or thirty days, and do not include e-mail on their routine back-ups. (Indeed, software by Disappearing, Inc., in San Francisco, and QV Tech, Inc., of Colorado Springs, Colorado, automatically deletes e-mail at a specified time, such as within one day or one week.) Other businesses keep back-up copies of their e-mail forever, in the event that they may need access to those messages at some future time (to defend against a lawsuit, for example). Still other companies print out or make back-up copies of important e-mail and trash the rest, just as they do with paper documents.

Which E-Documents Should Be Retained?

How does a company decide which electronic documents should be retained and which should be destroyed? Generally, e-documents are subject to the same requirements as any of the other records of an organization. By law, corporations are required to keep certain types of documents, such as those specified in the *Code of Federal Regulations* and in regulations issued by government agencies, such as the Occupational Safety and Health Administration.

As a rule, any records that the company is not legally required to keep or that the company is sure it will have no legal need for should be removed from the files and destroyed. A partnership agreement, for example, should be kept. An e-mail message about last year's company picnic, however, should be removed from the electronic files and destroyed; obviously, it is just taking up storage space.

If a company becomes the target of an investigation, it usually must modify its document-retention policy until the investigation has been completed. Company officers, after receiving a subpoena to produce specific types of documents, should instruct the appropriate employees not to destroy relevant e-documents that would otherwise be disposed of as part of the company's normal document-retention program. Generally, company officials must always exercise good faith in deciding what documents should or should not be destroyed when attempting to comply with a subpoena.

CHECKLIST

- ☑ Business owners or managers should consider developing an e-document retention policy to ward off potential litigation problems.
- ☑ Employers should let employees know not only which e-documents should be retained and deleted but also which types of documents should not be created in the first place.

a. *In re Brand Name Prescription Drugs Antitrust Litigation,* 1995 WL 360526 (N.D.Ill. 1995).

SECTION 3 ELECTRONIC MONITORING IN THE WORKPLACE

You can find an excellent summary of electronic monitoring in the workplace and the laws governing this activity at a page on the Web site of the law firm of Morgan Lewis. Go to **http://www.morganlewis.com/art61499.htm**.

In an attempt to avoid liability under various laws, as well as to increase worker productivity, many employers now monitor their employees' use of electronic communications, including those transmitted via the Internet. According to a recent survey of the American Management Association, more than two-thirds of employers engage in some form of surveillance of their employees.[15] The types of surveillance used by these employers are listed in Exhibit 12–1.

Monitoring Software

Tracking employees' Internet use is made easier by a variety of specially designed software products. For example, software such as SurfControl's SuperScout for Business allows employers to track virtually every move made by a worker using the Internet, including the specific Web sites visited by the worker and the time spent surfing the Web. Pearl Software's Cyber Snoop can monitor and log any Web, FTP, e-mail, chat, and newsgroup activity being accessed by employees. The employer can click on any Web site address (URL) in the activity log to access particular sites. Additionally, Cyber Snoop keeps a cache of incoming and outgoing e-mail, which can be read from the URL list window.

Other software, such as Baltimore Technologies' MIMEsweeper, can be used by employers to literally "sweep" through all online communications in the workplace, including e-mail attachments, to detect offensive language or sites. SpectorSoft Corporation recently released monitoring software that takes periodic "screen shots" of employees' computers; employers can then review the screen shots later. MicroData's software can scan 50,000 messages per hour.

EXHIBIT 12–1 Electronic Monitoring in the Workplace

TYPE OF MONITORING	PERCENTAGE OF EMPLOYERS USING EACH TYPE
Storage and review of e-mail	27%
Storage and review of computer files	21%
Video recording of employee job performance	16%
Recording and review of telephone conversations	11%
Storage and review of voice mail messages	6%
SOURCE: American Management Association, 2000.	

15. For a discussion of this survey and its results, see Allison R. Michael and Scott M. Lidman, "Monitoring of Employees Still Growing," *The National Law Journal*, January 29, 2001, p. B9.

Filtering Software

FILTERING SOFTWARE
A computer program that includes a pattern through which data are passed. When designed to block access to certain Web sites, the pattern blocks the retrieval of a site whose URL or key words are on a list within the program.

Often, employer security measures involve the use of **filtering software** as well. Such software prevents access to specified Web sites, such as sites containing pornographic or sexually explicit images. Blocking access to such sites reduces the possibility that employees will transmit images via e-mail that may result in a hostile-environment claim. It also helps to prevent employees from violating any criminal laws governing pornography.

Other filtering software may be used to screen incoming e-mail and block mail that consists of spam or that may contain a virus. For example, Elron Software's Command View Message Inspector flags unsolicited ads and newsletters by searching for suspect words in subject lines and messages.

The use of filtering software by public employers (government agencies) has led to charges that blocking access to Web sites violates employees' rights to free speech, which are guaranteed by the First Amendment to the Constitution. For example, some professors at colleges and universities in Virginia challenged the constitutionality of a Virginia law restricting the ability of state employees to access sexually explicit matter on state-owned or leased computers. The professors complained that their universities blocked access to sites containing sexually explicit materials that were educational, and that the statute interfered with their teaching. In their suit against the state, however, a federal district court held that the statute did not violate the professors' First Amendment rights. The court's ruling was upheld on appeal.[16]

Although the use of filtering software by government institutions has been controversial, this is not an issue in the context of private businesses. This is because the First Amendment's protection of free speech applies to *government* restraints on speech, not restraints imposed in the private sector.

SECTION 4 ELECTRONIC MONITORING VERSUS EMPLOYEE RIGHTS

Clearly, employers need to protect themselves from liability for their employees' online activities. They also have a legitimate concern with monitoring the productivity of their workers. At the same time, employees expect to have a certain zone of privacy in the workplace. Indeed, many lawsuits have involved allegations that employers' intrusive monitoring practices violate employees' privacy rights.

The American Civil Liberties Union (ACLU) has a page on its Web site devoted to employee privacy rights with respect to electronic monitoring. Go to **http://www.aclu.org/library/pbr2.html**.

Statutory Regulation of Monitoring Activities

Generally, there is little specific statutory regulation of monitoring activities. The major statute with which employers must comply is the Electronic Communications Privacy Act (ECPA) of 1986.[17] This act amended existing federal wiretapping law to cover electronic forms of communications, such as communications via cellular telephones or e-mail. The ECPA prohibits the intentional interception of any wire or electronic communication or the intentional disclosure or use of the information obtained by the interception. The act

16. *Urofsky v. Gilmore,* 216 F.3d 401 (4th Cir. 2000).

17. 18 U.S.C. Sections 2510–2521.

excludes from coverage, however, any electronic communications through devices that are "furnished to the subscriber or user by a provider of wire or electronic communication service" and that are being used by the subscriber or user, or by the provider of the service, "in the ordinary course of its business."

This "business-extension exception" to the ECPA permits employers to monitor employee electronic communications in the ordinary course of their businesses. It does not, however, permit employers to monitor employees' personal communications. Under another exception to the ECPA, however, employers may avoid liability under the act if the employees consent to having their electronic communications intercepted by the employer. Thus, an employer may be able to avoid liability under the ECPA by simply requiring employees to sign forms indicating that they consent to such monitoring.

Privacy Rights under Constitutional and Tort Law

The privacy rights of employees are protected by both state and federal laws. The earliest protection for privacy interests was under tort law. Privacy rights are also now protected under the U.S. Constitution as well as by many state constitutions.

THE TORT OF INVASION OF PRIVACY Recall from Chapter 4 that the invasion of another's privacy is a civil wrong, or tort. Under tort law, four acts are considered to qualify as invasion of privacy:

- The use of a person's name, picture, or other likeness for commercial purposes without permission.
- Intrusion on an individual's affairs or seclusion.
- Publication of information that places a person in a false light.
- Public disclosure of private facts about an individual that an ordinary person would find objectionable.

The following case involves a public employee and her employer's threatened disclosure to the media of the personal e-mail messages that she sent or received over the Internet from her work computer. The same rules concerning public disclosure do not apply in the context of private employment. This case illustrates, however, the problems associated with sending and receiving personal e-mail in any workplace in which it is prohibited.

CASE 12.2 Tiberino v. Spokane County

THE SEAL OF THE STATE OF WASHINGTON 1889

Court of Appeals of Washington, Division 3, 2000. 13 P.3d 1104.

BACKGROUND AND FACTS In August 1998, Gina Tiberino was hired as a secretary in the Prosecuting Attorney's Office in Spokane County, Washington. The county provided her with a personal computer with an e-mail application. According to county policy, Tiberino was told that her employer could monitor all e-mail, that she was not to put anything into an e-mail message that she would not want on the front page of a newspaper, and county equipment was not for personal use. In October, Tiberino's co-workers complained that she was using her computer to send personal e-mail over the Internet. Her supervisor reminded her that county computers were not to be used for personal business. In November, she was discharged for unsatisfactory work performance related to her use of e-mail for personal matters. When she threatened to sue the county, her ex-employer printed out all of her e-mail. Of 551 items, 467 were personal messages. When the media asked the prosecutor's office to release copies of the e-mail (more than 3,700 pages), Tiberino filed a suit in a Washington state court against the county to stop the release. The court concluded that the messages were "public records" and refused to grant her request. On Tiberino's appeal, the state intermediate appellate court agreed that the messages were public records and then considered whether, under a state statutory exception, their disclosure would violate her right to privacy.

IN THE LANGUAGE OF THE COURT. . .

KURTZ, C.J. [Chief Judge.]

* * * *

A person's right to privacy is violated only if disclosure of information about the person: (1) [w]ould be highly offensive to a reasonable person, and (2) is not of legitimate concern to the public. * * *

* * * *

Ms. Tiberino argues that the purely personal nature of her e-mails to her mother, sister and friends makes it clear that public disclosure would be highly offensive to any reasonable person. Ms. Tiberino's e-mails contain intimate details about her personal and private life and do not discuss specific instances of misconduct. An individual has a privacy interest whenever information which reveals unique facts about those named is linked to an identifiable individual. * * * Any reasonable person would find disclosure of Ms. Tiberino's e-mails to be highly offensive.

* * * *

For the e-mails to be exempt from disclosure, Ms. Tiberino must also show that the public has no legitimate concern requiring release of the e-mails. Ms. Tiberino contends that the disclosure of private e-mails could decrease the efficiency and morale of government employees. The County argues that the County employees were on notice that the computers should not be used for personal business, so the disclosure of their e-mail would not affect the efficient administration of government.

* * * *

Generally, records of governmental agency expenditures for employee salaries, including vacation and sick leave, and taxpayer-funded benefits are of legitimate public interest and therefore not exempt from disclosure. Certainly, there exists a reasonable concern by the public that government conduct itself fairly and use public funds responsibly.

* * * *

However, * * * [t]he content of Ms. Tiberino's e-mails is personal and is unrelated to governmental operations. Certainly, the public has an interest in seeing that public employees are not spending their time on the public payroll pursuing personal interests. But it is the amount of time spent on personal matters, not the content of personal e-mails or phone calls or conversations, that is of public interest. The fact that Ms. Tiberino sent 467 e-mails over a 40 working-day time frame is of significance in her termination action and the public has a legitimate interest in having that information. But what she said in those e-mails is of no public significance. The public has no legitimate

CASE 12.2–Continued

concern requiring release of the e-mails and they should be exempt from disclosure.

DECISION AND REMEDY The state intermediate appellate court reversed the judgment of the lower court. The appellate court concluded that Tiberino's e-mail messages were "public records," but that they were exempt from public disclosure as personal information.

FOR CRITICAL ANALYSIS–Social Consideration *Instead of serving as a flash point for a lawsuit, as in the* Tiberino *case, how might an employer's monitoring of employees' e-mail prevent litigation?*

CONSTITUTIONAL PROTECTION OF PRIVACY RIGHTS The privacy rights of employees are also protected, to a certain extent, by the U.S. Constitution and state constitutions. Although the federal Constitution does not explicitly mention a right to privacy, the Supreme Court has held that this right can be inferred from constitutional provisions set forth in the Bill of Rights (the first ten amendments to the Constitution).[18] Several state constitutions, including that of California, also provide for privacy rights.

Factors Considered by the Courts in Employee Privacy Cases

When determining whether an employer should be held liable for violating an employee's privacy rights, the courts generally weigh the employer's interests against the employee's reasonable expectation of privacy. Generally, if employees are informed that their communications are being monitored, they cannot reasonably expect those communications to be private. If employees are not informed that certain communications are being monitored, however, the employer may be held liable for invading their privacy.

For example, in one case an employer secretly recorded conversations among his four employees by placing a tape recorder in their common office. The conversations were of a highly personal nature and included harsh criticisms of the employer. The employer immediately fired two of the employees, informing them that their termination was due to their comments on the tape. In the suit that followed, one of the issues was whether the employees, in these circumstances, had a reasonable expectation of privacy. The court held that they did and granted summary judgment in their favor. The employees clearly would not criticize their boss if they did not assume their conversations were private. Furthermore, the office was small, and the employees were careful that no third parties ever overheard their comments.[19]

Privacy Expectations and E-Mail Systems

With respect to e-mail monitoring, the courts have tended to hold for employers in cases brought by employees alleging that their privacy has been invaded.

18. See, for example, *Griswold v. Connecticut,* 381 U.S. 479, 85 S.Ct. 1678, 14 L.Ed.2d 510 (1965).
19. *Dorris v. Abscher,* 179 F.3d 420 (6th Cir. 1999).

This is true even when employees were not informed that their e-mail would be monitored.

In a leading case on this issue, the Pillsbury Company promised its employees that it would not read their e-mail, or terminate or discipline them based on the content of their e-mail. Despite this promise, Pillsbury intercepted employee Michael Smyth's e-mail, decided that it was unprofessional and inappropriate, and fired him. In Pennsylvania, where the discharge occurred, it is against public policy for an employer to fire an employee based on a violation of the employee's right to privacy. In Smyth's suit against the company, he claimed that his termination was a violation of this policy. The court, however, found no "reasonable expectation of privacy in e-mail communications voluntarily made by an employee to his supervisor over the company e-mail system."[20]

Sometimes, employees have argued that they have a reasonable expectation of privacy when their files or e-mail is password protected. Even in this situation, however, courts are reluctant to hold that the employees' privacy interests have been violated if employers access these materials. In one case, a Texas state court refused to recognize an invasion of privacy based on Microsoft Corporation's review and release of e-mail stored in an employee's office computer. Microsoft suspended employee Bill McLaren, Jr., pending an investigation into accusations of sexual harassment and other misconduct. During the suspension, Microsoft read his e-mail. After McLaren was fired, he filed a suit against the employer, claiming that the e-mail, which was in "personal folders" and "protected" by a password, was his personal property. The court reasoned that the computer was given to McLaren to do his job and therefore the e-mail on it was "merely an inherent part of the office environment." All e-mail is transmitted over a network, which makes it accessible to third parties. In this case, the employer also provided the network and the e-mail application.[21]

SECTION 5 OFFSITE EMPLOYEE COMMUNICATIONS

Not too many years ago, employees would often gather around the office water cooler to exchange news and small talk. Comments made during these sessions could include anything from criticisms of management policies to the latest sports statistics to gossip about office employees. Generally, employers were rarely concerned about these personal exchanges among employees. Today, employees are increasingly gathering around what one writer has termed "virtual water coolers"[22]—chat forums or bulletin boards on private Web sites devoted to e-gossip—and the rules of the game are changing.

Industry-Specific Web Sites

Private Web forums include Web sites specifically devoted to news and e-office gossip related to specific trades or industries. For example, a popular site for young lawyers is greedyassociates.com. Here, attorneys exchange information about working conditions and salaries from around the country—information

20. *Smyth v. Pillsbury,* 914 F.Supp. 97 (E.D.Pa.1996).
21. *McLaren v. Microsoft Corp.,* 1999 WL 339015 (Tex.App–Dallas 1999).
22. Adam Cohen, "Click Here for a Hot Rumor about Your Boss," *Time,* September 11, 2000, p. 48.

that in the past was hard to obtain. Truckers can compare experiences and rigs with other truckers at truckinlife.com. Vault.com is a site devoted to the latest news and gossip in the investment banking industry.

A growing concern for many companies is how to deal with cybergriping conducted in offsite forums that damages the companies' reputations. Unlike complaints about a company discussed around the water cooler in the past, complaints registered in cyber forums reach a nationwide audience. If an employer's reputation is damaged by comments on offsite forums, is there anything the employer can do? Not really. Of course, any employer that is defamed by online comments can resort to a suit for libel—a tort that occurs when someone makes a false statement that damages another entity's good name or reputation (see Chapter 4). Such litigation is expensive, however, and there is no guarantee that a court will hold that a particular comment or series of comments were libelous.

Employers can, however, access these sites to learn about the concerns of their employees. For example, when employees at Agency.com, an Internet business strategies firm, complained about management policies, the co-founder of the company paid attention. He made it clear that he took the employees' criticism of the company policies very seriously and that he was committed to employee satisfaction.

Employee Web Sites

One of the attractive aspects of the Internet is its anonymity. On the Web, a person can pose as someone else through the use of a pseudonym or the creation of a new identity. Entering a chat room or a Web site under a false name may seem harmless, especially when the site is open to the public. When someone uses a false identity to access a *private* Web site, however, could that person be held liable to the owner of the site?

This question was at issue in the case presented next. The case involved an employer who, concerned about what employees were saying about management on a private Web site operated by one of the company's employees, used another employee's password to gain access to the site. At issue in the case is whether the employer's actions constituted a violation of the Wiretap Act[23] and Stored Communications Act,[24] both of which had been amended by the ECPA to prohibit unauthorized interception of electronic communications.

23. 18 U.S.C. Sections 2510–2520.
24. 18 U.S.C. Sections 2701–2710.

CASE 12.3 Konop v. Hawaiian Airlines, Inc.

United States Court of Appeals, Ninth Circuit, 2001.
236 F.3d 1035.

BACKGROUND AND FACTS Robert Konop, a pilot for Hawaiian Airlines, Inc., maintained a Web site where he posted bulletins critical of his employer and others. Konop controlled access to the site by requiring visitors to log in with a user name and password. Konop provided user names to certain Hawaiian employees, but not to managers or union representatives. To obtain a password, an eligible employee had to register and consent to an agreement not to disclose the site's contents. Hawaiian vice president James Davis obtained a password by using the name of Hawaiian pilot Gene Wong, with Wong's permission. Wong had never logged into the site and had never agreed to Konop's term of nondisclosure. Konop soon learned that Hawaiian officers were aware of the site's contents and later discovered what Davis had done. Konop filed a suit in a federal district court against Hawaiian, claiming, among other things, that Davis's unauthorized viewing violated the Wiretap Act and the Stored Communications Act. On those claims, the court entered a summary judgment against Konop, who appealed to the U.S. Court of Appeals for the Ninth Circuit.

IN THE LANGUAGE OF THE COURT. . .

BOOCHEVER, Circuit Judge:

* * * *

* * * [In a previous case, a court reasoned] that the logic and policy of the Wiretap Act "require participation by the one charged with an 'interception' in the contemporaneous acquisition of the communication."

A requirement that transmission and acquisition be contemporaneous would be fatal to Konop's claim that Hawaiian violated the Wiretap Act by gaining unauthorized access to his website. There is ordinarily a period of latency between the initial transmission of information for storage on a web server, and the acquisition of that information by its recipients. If interception requires that acquisition and transmission occur contemporaneously, then unauthorized downloading of information stored on a web server cannot be interception.

* * * *

The law by which such acts of downloading are judged has changed significantly, however * * * . The variety of acts constituting interception was expanded by * * * the ECPA * * * .

* * * *

We first note that the Wiretap Act provides but a single definition of "intercept," and that definition does not expressly contain or suggest the contemporaneity requirement. * * *

* * * *

* * * An electronic communication in storage is no more or less private than an electronic communication in transmission. Distinguishing between the two for purposes of protection from interception is irrational and an insupportable result given Congress' emphasis of individual privacy rights during passage of the ECPA.

A 1996 amendment to the Wiretap Act also suggests Congress understood electronic communications to include stored communications unless specified otherwise. The amendment appended a proviso to the Wiretap Act's definition by specifying: "'electronic communication' * * * does not include * * * electronic funds transfer information stored by a financial institution * * * ." The exclusion of certain kinds of stored information from the definition of electronic communication implies that Congress understood the term in ordinary circumstances to include stored information. * * *

We believe that Congress intended the ECPA to eliminate distinctions between protection of private communications based on arbitrary features of the technology used for transmission.

CASE 12.3–Continued

DECISION AND REMEDY The U.S. Court of Appeals for the Ninth Circuit reversed the lower court's judgment with respect to Konop's claims under the Wiretap Act and the Stored Communications Act, and remanded those claims for trial. The appellate court concluded that the contents of private Web sites are "electronic communications" in intermediate storage and, as such, are protected from unauthorized interception under the Wiretap Act and unauthorized access under the Stored Communications Act.

FOR CRITICAL ANALYSIS–Technological Consideration *Does the court's decision in the* Konop *case mean that an unlawful interception occurs every time someone views a Web page?*

Web E-Mail

Some employees are finding ways to skirt their employers' e-mail policies and electronic surveillance. They do this by using any number of free e-mail providers, such as Hotmail and services provided by AltaVista, Excite, and Yahoo! To be free from prying eyes, some employees use encrypted e-mail services, such as those provided free of charge by ZipLip.com or HushMail.com. Other services, including Anonymizer.com and Zero-Knowledge Systems, charge a small fee for encrypted e-mail services.

Even so, employees who use these services may still violate their employers' policies that require any employee use of e-mail to be work related. This is because they need to use company-provided computer systems to access the services.

SECTION 6 DEVELOPING AN INTERNET-USE POLICY

Clearly, the law allows employers to engage in electronic monitoring in the workplace. In fact, cases in which courts have held that an employer's monitoring of electronic communications in the workplace violated employees' privacy rights are few and far between.

Nonetheless, today's business owners and managers would be wise to implement an Internet-use policy. For one thing, in some cases in which plaintiffs claimed that employer monitoring practices violated privacy rights, the juries were reluctant to decide the issue in favor of employers. For another, a clear policy setting forth the company's policy with respect to acceptable Internet use and the monitoring of employees' Internet activities will help to avoid litigation for wrongful discharge when an employee is fired for failure to comply with the policy. As any firm knows, lawsuits are expensive. Just one successful suit for wrongful termination against a small company can bankrupt that firm. Even if a worker does not succeed in the suit, the legal fees incurred by defending against the claim could be devastating for the firm's profits.

One Approach–Obtaining Employees' Consent to Electronic Monitoring

A business that monitors its employees' electronic communications should, first of all, notify its employees of the monitoring. Second, employees should be asked to consent, in writing, to such actions. Generally, as you learned earlier in this chapter, if employees consent to employer monitoring they cannot claim that their privacy rights have been invaded by such practices.

Any Internet-use policy should also spell out the permissible and impermissible uses of the company's communications systems. Additionally, employees should understand why the company monitors workplace communications. Generally, when employees are told the reasons for monitoring and clearly understand what their rights and duties are with respect to company communications systems, they are less offended by the surveillance. To make sure that employees are so informed, the American Management Association recommends that electronic monitoring policies be:

- Clearly defined and disseminated to all employees through all communication channels, from paper to electronic media.
- Addressed in recruitment, orientation, and training programs.
- Discussed in face-to-face meetings between managers and employees, which allow for questions to be answered and concerns aired.
- Illustrated through specific examples of misuse, accompanied by a consistent explanation regarding the application of standards.

It is also important to let employees know what will happen if they violate the policy. The policy might state, for example, that any employee who violates the policy will be subject to disciplinary actions, including termination.

An area of growing concern for employers is whether employees, if they are allowed to use a company e-mail system for nonbusiness uses, may utilize the system to discuss union activities. For an examination of this topic, see this chapter's *Controversial Issues* feature on the next two pages.

An Alternative Approach—No Monitoring

Some companies are finding that the benefits of electronic monitoring may not be worth the costs. E-mail monitoring can be expensive and time consuming, and can lead to employee resentment. Furthermore, employers that monitor employees' e-mail may be liable for harassment charges if they failed to uncover harassing e-mail messages while monitoring. In this situation, a court may hold that the employer "should have known" of the harassment. Some companies are also finding that monitoring does not offer them complete protection against the one damaging message that might be overlooked.

An alternative being pursued by a growing number of companies, particularly in the high-tech industry, is to allow their employees to use their own discretion with respect to Internet use. Hewlett-Packard, for example, does not monitor employees' Internet use or block access to any Web sites. Some observers claim that this "hands-off" approach with respect to employee use of the Internet is a sensible one. For one thing, some highly qualified job candidates may not want to work for a company that monitors their Internet use. For another, there is no evidence that Internet monitoring has increased worker productivity. Finally, how can an employer monitor Internet use while its employees are traveling or working at home—as more and more employees are doing?

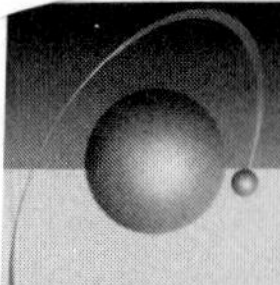

Controversial Issues in the Online World

Internet Policies and Union Activities

Employers with unionized work forces must be especially cautious when drafting Internet policies to avoid violating labor laws. One of the foremost statutes regulating labor is the National Labor Relations Act (NLRA) of 1935.[a] The purpose of the NLRA was to secure for employees the rights to organize; to bargain collectively through representatives of their own choosing; and to engage in concerted activities for organizing, collective bargaining, and other purposes. The act also specifically defined a number of employer practices as unfair to labor:

- Interference with the efforts of employees to form, join, or assist labor organizations or to engage in concerted activities for their mutual aid or protection.
- An employer's domination of a labor organization or contribution of financial or other support to it.
- Discrimination in the hiring of or the awarding of tenure to employees for reason of union affiliation.
- Discrimination against employees for filing charges under the act or giving testimony under the act.
- Refusal to bargain collectively with the duly designated representative of the employees.

a. 20 U.S.C. Sections 151–169.

The act created the National Labor Relations Board (NLRB) to oversee union elections and to prevent employers from engaging in unfair and illegal union-related activities and unfair labor practices. The NLRB has the authority to investigate employees' charges of unfair labor practices and to serve complaints against employers in response to these charges.

Union Election Campaigns

Many disputes between labor and management arise during union election campaigns. Generally, the employer has control over unionizing activities that take place on company property and during working hours. Employers may thus limit the campaign activities of union supporters. For example, an employer may prohibit all solicitations and pamphlets on company property as long as the employer has a legitimate business reason for doing so.

Suppose that a union sought to organize clerks at a department store. Courts have found that an employer can prohibit all solicitation in areas of the store open to the public. Union campaign activities in these circumstances could seriously interfere with the store's business. The employer

SECTION 7 OTHER TYPES OF MONITORING

In addition to monitoring their employees' online activities, employers also engage in other types of employee screening and monitoring practices. These practices, which have included lie-detector tests, drug tests, AIDS tests, and employment screening, have often been subject to challenge as violations of employee privacy rights.

Lie-Detector Tests

At one time, many employers required employees or job applicants to take polygraph examinations (lie-detector tests) in connection with their employment. To protect the privacy interests of employees and job applicants, in 1988 Congress passed the Employee Polygraph Protection Act.[25] The statute prohibits employers from (1) requiring or causing employees or job applicants to take lie-detector

25. 29 U.S.C. Sections 2001 *et seq.*

Controversial Issues in the Online World, Continued

may not, however, discriminate in its prohibition against solicitation in the workplace. For example, the employer could not prohibit union solicitation but allow solicitation for charitable causes. Additionally, companies may not prevent union-related solicitation in work areas as long as the activity is conducted outside working hours—during lunch hours or coffee breaks, for example.

An employer may also campaign among its workers against the union, but the NLRB carefully monitors and regulates the campaign tactics of management. Otherwise, management might use its economic power to coerce the workers to vote not to unionize. For example, an employer might tell its workers, "If the union wins, you'll all be fired." The NLRB prohibits employers from making such threats. If the employer issues threats or engages in other unfair labor practices, the NLRB may certify the union even though it lost the election. Alternatively, the NLRB may ask a court to order a new election.

Is an Employer's E-Mail System a "Work Area"?

An emerging issue has to do with whether employers, if they allow employees to use company-owned e-mail systems for nonbusiness purposes, also must permit employees to use e-mail to exchange messages related to unionization or union activities. In the few cases involving this issue, the NLRB has ruled that, in these circumstances, employees may use e-mail for communicating union-related messages.

Suppose, however, that a company's policy prohibited employees from using e-mail for nonbusiness purposes. Given that employees are permitted to engage in union-related solicitation in work areas as long as they are on a break from work, should they also be able to use their employer's e-mail system while on a break? Is an e-mail system a "work area"? To date, the NLRB has not issued an official ruling on this issue, although Barry Kearney of the NLRB's Division of Advice recently stated that he is looking forward to testing the theory that e-mail systems constitute work areas.[b]

FOR CRITICAL ANALYSIS

What if an employee sends a union-related e-mail message while on a break but the employee receiving it, without knowing its contents, opens it during working hours? Is there anything that can be done to prevent this kind of situation from occurring?

b. As cited in "E-Mail's Sacred Unions," *The Economist*, October 14, 2000. See also Daniel F. Murphy, Jr., "How to Avoid Liability for Monitoring Employee Use of E-Mail and the Internet," *Start-Up & Emerging Companies*, Vol. 1, No. 4 (December 2000), pp. 3–4.

tests or suggesting or requesting that they do so; (2) using, accepting, referring to, or asking about the results of lie-detector tests taken by employees or applicants; and (3) taking or threatening negative employment-related action against employees or applicants based on results of lie-detector tests or on their refusal to take the tests.

Employers excepted from these prohibitions include federal, state, and local government employers; certain security service firms; and companies manufacturing and distributing controlled substances. Other employers may use polygraph tests when investigating losses attributable to theft, including embezzlement and the theft of trade secrets.

Drug Testing

In the interests of public safety and to reduce unnecessary costs, many of today's employers, including the government, require their employees to submit to drug testing. Laws relating to the privacy rights of private-sector employees vary from state to state. Some state constitutions prohibit private employers from testing for drugs, and state statutes may restrict drug testing by private employers in any number of ways. A collective bargaining agreement may also provide protection against drug testing. In some instances, employees have brought actions against their employers for the tort of invasion of privacy.

Constitutional limitations apply to the testing of government employees. The Fourth Amendment provides that individuals have the right to be "secure in their persons" against "unreasonable searches and seizures" conducted by government agents. Drug tests have been held to be constitutional, however, when there was a reasonable basis for suspecting government employees of using drugs. Additionally, when drug use in a particular government job could threaten public safety, testing has been upheld. For example, a U.S. Department of Transportation rule that requires employees engaged in oil and gas pipeline operations to submit to random drug testing was upheld, even though the rule did not require that before being tested the individual must have been suspected of drug use.[26] The court held that the government's interest in promoting public safety in the pipeline industry outweighed the employees' privacy interests.

An ongoing problem with respect to drug testing is that such tests are not foolproof. Suppose that a job applicant is not hired because of a positive drug test. If the results of the test are false, does the applicant have any legal recourse? In one case, for example, after a drug-testing laboratory mistakenly reported to an employer that a job applicant had failed a drug test, the applicant filed a suit against the laboratory. The court granted the employer's request for summary judgment, holding—as have a number of other courts—that while a laboratory may owe a duty of care to the employer for whom it conducts the drug tests, it owes no such duty to the employee being tested.[27]

AIDS Testing

An increasing number of employers are testing their workers for acquired immune deficiency syndrome (AIDS). Few public issues involve more controversy than this practice. Some state laws restrict AIDS testing, and federal statutes offer some protection to employees and job applicants who have AIDS or have tested positive for the AIDS virus. The federal Americans with Disabilities Act of 1990[28] (discussed in the previous chapter), for example, prohibits discrimination against individuals with disabilities, and the term *disability* has been broadly defined to include those individuals with diseases such as AIDS. The law also requires employers to reasonably accommodate the needs of persons with disabilities. Generally, although the law may not prohibit AIDS testing, it may prohibit the discharge of employees based on the results of those tests.

Screening Procedures

An area of concern to potential employees has to do with preemployment screening procedures. What kinds of questions on an employment application or

26. *Electrical Workers Local 1245 v. Skinner,* 913 F.2d 1454 (9th Cir. 1990).
27. *Ney v. Axelrod,* 723 A.2d 719 (Pa.Super. 1999).
28. 42 U.S.C. Sections 12102–12118.

a preemployment test are permissible? What kinds of questions go too far in terms of invading the potential employee's privacy? Is it an invasion of the potential employee's privacy, for example, to ask questions about his or her sexual orientation or religious convictions? Although an employer may believe that such information is relevant to the job for which the individual has applied, the applicant may feel differently about the matter. Generally, questions on an employment application must have a reasonable nexus, or connection, with the job for which an applicant is applying.

TERMS AND CONCEPTS

filtering software 289
hostile-environment harassment 281
quid pro quo harassment 281
sexual harassment 281

QUESTIONS AND CASE PROBLEMS

12–1. Electronic Monitoring. Mark is a salesperson for Regional Cellular Phone Corp. (RCPC). RCPC asks Mark to allow some of his phone conversations with customers to be recorded. RCPC tells Mark that the customers will not be told their calls are being monitored. Mark refuses to consent. RCPC fires Mark for his "negative attitude." Mark files a suit in a state court against RCPC under a state statute that makes eavesdropping a crime. Mark alleges in part that RCPC wrongfully terminated his employment in violation of public policy. Is it a violation of public policy to terminate an employee for refusing to be an "accomplice" or a "victim" of an employer's crime of eavesdropping? Explain.

12–2. Performance Monitoring. A firm fired two of its employees after it had discovered, from reading e-mail on back-up tapes accessed using a "supervisory password," that the employees had exchanged personal e-mails covering forty full pages in a four-month period. The workers sued the employer, claiming that the employer, by reading their personal e-mail, had violated their privacy rights. The employees claimed that their personal e-mail was private, in part because the e-mail system could only be accessed by a password. Additionally, they stated that their employer had never warned them that their e-mail might be monitored. The employer asserted that the employees, who were both computer literate, should have realized that e-mail is never private. Furthermore, several other employees testified that they were aware that management had supervisory passwords and, furthermore, that company representatives had discussed the company's monitoring activities with employees. In deciding whether the employees' privacy rights were violated, what factors will the court consider? What will the court likely decide?

12–3. Privacy Rights. Target Stores hire store security officers (SSOs) to observe, apprehend, and arrest suspected shoplifters. Target views good judgment and emotional stability as important SSO job skills. All SSO job applicants must take a test, called the Psychscreen. Some of the test questions relate to religious beliefs; other questions concern sexual orientation. Sibi Soroka and two other applicants (the plaintiffs) found the test objectionable and brought a class-action suit in a California state court against Dayton Hudson, which operates Target Stores. The plaintiffs claimed that the test violated their privacy rights. Target asserted that a person's religious beliefs or sexual orientation had a bearing on the emotional stability of SSOs and their ability to perform their job responsibilities. Target offered little specific evidence to justify this generalization, however. What factor or factors will the court consider in deciding this issue? Should the court decide that the Psychscreen test violated the job applicants' privacy rights? Explain. [*Soroka v. Dayton Hudson Corp.*, 7 Cal.App.4th 203, 1 Cal.Rptr.2D 77 (1991)]

12–4. Privacy Rights. The Department of Labor (DOL) designated certain DOL employment positions as "sensitive" in regard to public health and safety or national security. Employees holding these positions, called "testing-designated positions" (TDPs) could be subjected to drug testing based on a reasonable suspicion of on-duty or off-duty drug use. The American Federation of Government Employees (AFGE) and others asked a federal district court to, among other things, order the DOL to stop testing based on a reasonable suspicion of off-duty drug use. Should the court decide that the employees' privacy rights outweigh the government's legitimate interests in preventing on-duty or off-duty drug use from impairing TDP employees in the performance of their duties? Why or why not? [*American Federation of Government Employees, AFL–CIO, Local 2391 v. Martin,* 969 F.2d 788 (9th Cir. 1992)]

12–5. Privacy Rights. The city of Los Angeles requires a polygraph examination for police officers who ask to be promoted or transferred into a few specialized divisions where the work is unusually sensitive and requires a high level of integrity. Generally, those who fail the test are not promoted or transferred, but neither are they demoted or otherwise penalized. The Los Angeles Protective League filed a suit against the city in a California state court, asking the court, among other things, to order the city to stop the testing. On what basis might the court grant the league's request? On what basis might it refuse to do so? [*Los Angeles Protective League v. City of Los Angeles,* 35 Cal.App.4th 1535, 42 Cal.Rptr.2d 23 (1995)]

12–6. Performance Monitoring. The Communications Operations Division (COD) of the Milwaukee Police Department (MPD) received incoming emergency calls and coordinated the dispatch of officers. All incoming emergency calls were taped. The taping system was in a glass case in the middle of the COD work area. Also, the employees knew that their supervisors might monitor their calls for evaluation and training purposes. Cynthia Griffin, a COD telecommunicator, filed a suit in a federal district court against the MPD and her supervisors, alleging that they had illegally monitored her personal calls. For what reasons might the court rule in favor of the defendants? [*Griffin v. City of Milwaukee,* 74 F.3d 824 (7th Cir. 1996)]

12–7. Privacy Rights. Patience Oyoyo was a claims analyst in the claims management department of Baylor Healthcare Network, Inc. When questions arose about Oyoyo's performance on several occasions, department manager Debbie Outlaw met with Oyoyo to discuss, among other things, Oyoyo's personal use of a business phone. Outlaw reminded Oyoyo that company policy prohibited excessive personal calls and these would result in the termination of her employment. Outlaw began to monitor Oyoyo's phone usage, noting lengthy outgoing calls on several occasions, including some long-distance calls. Eventually, Outlaw terminated Oyoyo's employment, and Oyoyo filed a suit in a federal district court against Baylor. Oyoyo asserted in part that in monitoring her phone calls, the employer had invaded her privacy. Baylor asked the court to dismiss this claim. In whose favor should the court rule, and why? [*Oyoyo v. Baylor Healthcare Network, Inc.,* __ F.Supp.2d __ (N.D.Tex. 2000)]

WEB EXERCISES

Go to **http://lec.westbuslaw.com**, the Web site that accompanies this text. Select "Internet Applications," and then click on "Chapter 12." There you will find the following Internet research exercise that you can perform to learn more about employment laws and issues:

Activity 12–1: Workplace Monitoring and Surveillance

Unit 5

Finance and E-Commerce

Contents

CHAPTER 13
Business Forms and E-Commerce

Concepts Covered

After reading this chapter, you should be able to:

1. Identify and describe the major traditional forms of business organization.
2. Explain how limited liability companies and limited liability partnerships meet needs not met by traditional forms of business organization.
3. Describe the major characteristics of other business organizational forms.
4. Discuss the law governing franchising relationships and the effect of the Internet on this way of doing business.
5. State some of the methods used for raising financial capital.

"[E]veryone thirsteth after gaine."

Sir Edward Coke, 1552–1634
(English jurist and politician)

ENTREPRENEUR
One who initiates and assumes the financial risks of a new enterprise and who undertakes to provide or control its management.

A basic question facing anyone who wishes to start up a business is which of the several forms of business organization will be most appropriate for the business endeavor. In deciding this question, the **entrepreneur** (one who initiates and assumes the financial risk of a new enterprise) needs to consider a number of factors. Four important factors are (1) ease of creation, (2) the liability of the owners, (3) tax considerations, and (4) the need for capital. Keep these factors in mind as you read about the various business organizational forms available to entrepreneurs.

The three major forms of business organization are the sole proprietorship, the partnership, and the corporation. Two relatively new forms of business enterprise—limited liability companies (LLCs) and limited liability partnerships (LLPs)—offer special advantages to businesspersons, particularly with respect to taxation and liability. There are also a number of other business forms, including joint ventures, syndicates, joint stock companies, business trusts, and cooperatives.

In this chapter, we look at all of these options for business organization. Additionally, we examine private franchises. Although a private franchise is not really a business organizational form, it is a popular way of doing business today.

SECTION 1 MAJOR TRADITIONAL BUSINESS FORMS

Historically, entrepreneurs used the three major forms just mentioned—the sole proprietorship, the partnership, and the corporation—to structure their business enterprises.

Sole Proprietorships

The **sole proprietorship** is the simplest form of businesss. In this form, the owner is the business; thus, anyone who does business without creating a separate business organization has a sole proprietorship. Sole proprietorships constitute over two-thirds of all American businesses. They are also usually small enterprises—about 99 percent of the sole proprietorships existing in the United States have revenues of less than $1 million per year. Sole proprietors can own and manage any type of business from an informal, home-office undertaking to a large restaurant or construction firm.

SOLE PROPRIETORSHIP
The simplest form of business, in which the owner is the business; the owner reports business income on his or her personal income tax return and is legally responsible for all debts and obligations incurred by the business.

The Internet has expanded the ability of sole proprietorships to market their products nationwide without greatly increasing their costs. Does this mean that sole proprietorships should now, for some purposes, be considered the equivalent of corporations and other associational business forms? That was the question presented to the court in the following case.

CASE 13.1 Hsin Ten Enterprise USA, Inc. v. Clark Enterprises

United States District Court,
Southern District of New York, 2000.
__ F.Supp.2d __.

COMPANY PROFILE *Clark Enterprises is a Kansas company with its only established offices in Salina, Kansas. Clark is a sole proprietorship owned and operated by Clifford Clark, who lives in Salina. Through representatives and trade shows, Clark sells "The Exercise Machine," an aerobic exercise device. The Exercise Machine can also be purchased through Clark's Web sites by completing a form online, or by printing a form to submit via mail or fax. Between July 1999, when the product was introduced, and October 2000, Clark sold 1,855 Exercise Machines, for total revenues of more than $500,000.*

BACKGROUND AND FACTS Clark markets the Exercise Machine in direct competition with "The Chi Machine," another aerobic exercise product. The Chi Machine is manufactured and sold by Hsin Ten Enterprise USA, Inc., a corporation with its principal place of business in Farmingdale, New York. Hsin Ten also makes and sells other products under the "Chi" trademark, which it owns. One of Clark's Web sites uses the name "Chi Exerciser 2000" to promote Clark's Exercise Machine, and the term *Chi* is frequently used on the Web sites to refer to the product. Hsin Ten filed a complaint in a federal district court in New York against Clark, asserting trademark infringement and other claims. Clark filed a motion to dismiss the trademark claim in part on the ground that the court did not have venue under 28 U.S.C. Section 1391(c), the applicable statute.[a] That section provides, "For purposes of venue * * * , a defendant that is a corporation shall be deemed to reside in any judicial district in which it is subject to personal jurisdiction." Hsin Ten argued that although Clark is an unincorporated sole proprietorship with its principal offices in Kansas, it should be deemed a "corporation" for venue purposes.

a. As explained in Chapter 2, venue concerns the most appropriate location for a trial.

CASE 13.1–Continued

IN THE LANGUAGE OF THE COURT. . .

SCHEINDLIN, D.J. [District Judge.]

* * * *

On its face, Section 1391(c) applies only to corporations. However, the [United States] Supreme Court has held that it also applies to unincorporated associations. Since then, other courts have held that Section 1391(c) is applicable to partnerships and foreign trusts.

* * * [C]ourts have been unwilling to expand the definition of "corporation" beyond [these] general categories * * * . In fact, at least two other federal courts have declined to extend Section 1391(c) to include sole proprietorships such as Clark.

Hsin Ten argues that Clark is unlike other sole proprietorships because it does business in forty-seven states. Plaintiff contends that Clark "resembles a national corporation in all respects except its choice of legal structure * * * . An entity such as Clark * * * , which obviously enjoys the benefits of doing business on a national scale, should not be granted preferential treatment in venue determinations simply because it chose not to incorporate." Plaintiff's argument is unconvincing.

First, broad geographic distribution does not convert a small sole proprietorship into a corporation. With the advent of the Internet and e-commerce, a sole proprietorship can distribute its products throughout the United States with only a relatively minor investment of resources. Moreover, although Clark does business in forty-seven states, it still is not the type of unincorporated business entity that has been included in the definition of corporation. For instance, * * * [t]he defendant partnership in [one case] was one of only four snowmobile manufacturers in the world [and] had annual sales of over $240 million * * * . By contrast, between July 8, 1999 and October 17, 2000, Clark sold 1,855 Exercise Machines. Although this is impressive for a sole proprietorship, it is hardly remarkable. Nor does it convert Clark to the functional equivalent of a corporation.

Second, expanding the definition of "corporation" would greatly burden sole proprietors. Unlike corporations, partnerships and unincorporated associations—all of which are associations of two or more persons—a sole proprietorship is owned and controlled by a single person. Venue is primarily a question of convenience for litigants and witnesses and venue provisions should be treated in practical terms. In practical terms, expanding the definition of "corporation" to include sole proprietorships would be overly burdensome and inconvenient to sole proprietors, most of whom would be unable to afford the expense of litigating in distant states.

DECISION AND REMEDY The court agreed with Clark that it should not be deemed a "corporation" for venue purposes. The court denied Clark's motion to dismiss other parts of Hsin Ten's complaint, however, and ordered the case to proceed to trial.

FOR CRITICAL ANALYSIS–Technological Consideration *If courts "heard" disputes online, as may occur in the future, what effect might that have had on the court's reasoning in this case?*

ADVANTAGES OF THE SOLE PROPRIETORSHIP A major advantage of the sole proprietorship is that the proprietor receives all of the profits (because he or she assumes all of the risk). In addition, it is often easier and less costly to start a sole proprietorship than to start any other kind of business, as few legal forms are involved. This type of business organization also provides more flexibility than does a partnership or a corporation. The sole proprietor is free to make any decision he or she wishes to concerning the business—whom to hire, when to take a vacation, what kind of business to pursue, and so on. A sole proprietor pays only personal income taxes on the business's profits, which are reported as personal income on the proprietor's personal income tax return. Sole proprietors are also allowed to establish tax-exempt retirement accounts in the form of Keogh plans.[1]

DISADVANTAGES OF THE SOLE PROPRIETORSHIP The major disadvantage of the sole proprietorship is that, as sole owner, the proprietor alone bears the burden of any losses or liabilities incurred by the business enterprise. In other words, the sole proprietor has unlimited liability, or legal responsibility, for all obligations that arise in doing business. This unlimited liability is a major factor to be considered in choosing a business form. The sole proprietorship also has the disadvantage of lacking continuity on the death of the proprietor. When the owner dies, so does the business—it is automatically dissolved. If the business is transferred to family members or other heirs, a new proprietorship is created.

Another disadvantage is that the proprietor's opportunity to raise capital is limited to personal funds and the funds of those who are willing to make loans to him or her. If the owner wishes to expand the business significantly, one way to raise more capital to finance the expansion is to join forces with another entrepreneur and establish a partnership or form a corporation.

Partnerships

A **partnership** arises from an agreement, express or implied, between two or more persons to carry on a business for a profit. Partners are co-owners of a business and have joint control over its operation and the right to share in its profits. Generally, unless the partnership agreement provides otherwise, profits are to be shared equally and losses are to be shared in the same ratio as profits. No particular form of partnership agreement is necessary for the creation of a partnership, but for practical reasons, the agreement should be in writing. Basically, the partners may agree to almost any terms when establishing the partnership so long as they are not illegal or contrary to public policy.

PARTNERSHIP
An agreement by two or more persons to carry on, as co-owners, a business for profit.

For information on the taxation of partnerships, see the article on this topic by Dennis D'Annunzio at **http://www.sunbeltnetwork.com/Journal/Current/D970804dsd.html**.

ADVANTAGES OF THE PARTNERSHIP As with a sole proprietorship, one of the advantages of a partnership is that it can be organized fairly easily and inexpensively. Additionally, the partnership form of business offers important tax advantages. The partnership itself files only an informational tax return with the Internal Revenue Service. In other words, the firm itself pays no taxes. A partner's

1. A *Keogh plan* is a retirement program designed for self-employed persons by which a certain percentage of their income can be contributed to the plan, and interest earnings will not be taxed until funds are withdrawn from the plan, usually after the age of fifty-nine and a half.

profit from the partnership (whether distributed or not) is taxed as individual income to the individual partner.

A partnership may also allow for greater capital contributions to the business than is possible in a sole proprietorship. Two or more persons can invest in the business, and lenders may be more willing to make loans to a partnership than they would be to a sole proprietorship.

For some of the advantages and disadvantages of doing business as a partnership, go to the Small Business Administration's Web site at **http://www.sba.gov/starting/indexfaqs.html**.

DISADVANTAGES OF THE PARTNERSHIP The main disadvantage of the partnership form of business is that the partners are subject to personal liability for partnership obligations. If the partnership cannot pay its debts, the personal assets of the partners are subject to creditors' claims. This disadvantage of the partnership is one of the major reasons that many entrepreneurs choose to form corporations. As will be discussed later in this chapter, in the corporate form of business the owners' liability is limited to the amount of their investments in the business. The limited liability companies and limited liability partnerships also discussed later in this chapter are additional business forms that allow business owners to limit their personal liability for business debts and obligations.

Limited Partnerships

A special form of partnership is the limited partnership. Limited partnerships consist of at least one **general partner** and one or more **limited partners.** A general partner assumes management responsibility for the partnership and so has full responsibility for the partnership and for all debts of the partnership. A limited partner contributes cash or other property and owns an interest in the firm but does not undertake any management duties and is not personally liable for partnership debts beyond the amount of his or her investment.

GENERAL PARTNER
In a limited partnership, a partner who assumes responsibility for the management of the partnership and liability for all partnership debts.

LIMITED PARTNER
In a limited partnership, a partner who contributes capital to the partnership but has no right to participate in the management and operation of the business. The limited partner assumes no liability for partnership debts beyond the capital contributed.

One of the major benefits of becoming a limited partner is this limitation on liability, both with respect to lawsuits brought against the partnership and the amount of money placed at risk. A limited partner can forfeit limited liability by taking part in the management of the business.

Compared with the informal, private, and voluntary agreement that usually suffices for a general partnership, the formation of a limited partnership is a public and formal proceeding that must follow statutory requirements. The partners must sign a **certificate of limited partnership.** The certificate must be filed with the designated state official, usually the secretary of state. The certificate is open to public inspection.

CERTIFICATE OF LIMITED PARTNERSHIP
The basic document filed with a designated state official by which a limited partnership is formed.

Limited Liability Limited Partnerships

A **limited liability limited partnership (LLLP)** is a type of limited partnership. The difference between a limited partnership and an LLLP is that the liability of a general partner in an LLLP is the same as the liability of a limited partner. That is, the liability of all partners is limited to the amount of their investments in the firm.

LIMITED LIABILITY LIMITED PARTNERSHIP (LLLP)
A type of limited partnership. The difference between a limited partnership and an LLLP is that the liability of the general partner in an LLLP is the same as the liability of the limited partner. That is, the liability of all partners is limited to the amount of their investments in the firm.

A few states provide expressly for LLLPs.[2] In states that do not provide for LLLPs but do allow for limited partnerships and limited liability partnerships, a limited partnership should probably still be able to register with the state as an LLLP.

2. See, for example, Colorado Revised Statutes Annotated Section 7-62-109. Other states that provide expressly for limited liability limited partnerships include Delaware, Florida, Missouri, Pennsylvania, Texas, and Virginia.

Corporations

A third and widely used business organizational form is the **corporation.** The corporation, like the limited partnership, is a creature of statute. The corporation's existence as a legal entity generally depends on state law.

CORPORATION
A legal entity formed in compliance with statutory requirements. The entity is distinct from its shareholders-owners.

Responsibility for the overall management of the corporation is entrusted to a board of directors, which is elected by the shareholders (those who have purchased ownership shares in the business). The board of directors hires corporate officers and other employees to run the daily business operations of the corporation.

Today, it is possible to incorporate—and receive a **certificate of incorporation**—via online incorporation services. For further information on this topic, see this chapter's *E-Guidelines* feature on the next page.

CERTIFICATE OF INCORPORATION
The primary document that evidences corporate existence (referred to as articles of incorporation in some states).

ADVANTAGES AND DISADVANTAGES OF THE CORPORATION One of the key advantages of the corporation is that the liability of its owners (shareholders) is limited to their investments. The shareholders usually are not personally liable for the obligations of the corporation. Another advantage is that a corporation can raise capital by selling shares of corporate stock to investors. A key disadvantage of the corporate form is that any distributed corporate income is taxed twice. The corporate entity pays taxes on the firm's income, and when income is distributed to shareholders, the shareholders again pay taxes on that income.

S Corporations

A corporation that meets the qualifying requirements specified in Subchapter S of the Internal Revenue Code can operate as an **S corporation.** If a corporation has S corporation status, it can avoid the imposition of income taxes at the corporate level while retaining many of the advantages of a corporation, particularly limited liability.

S CORPORATION
A close business corporation that has met certain requirements as set out by the Internal Revenue Code and thus qualifies for special income tax treatment. Essentially, an S corporation is taxed the same as a partnership, but its owners enjoy the privilege of limited liability.

QUALIFICATION REQUIREMENTS FOR S CORPORATIONS Among the numerous requirements for S corporation status, the following are the most important:

1. The corporation must be a domestic corporation.
2. The corporation must not be a member of an affiliated group of corporations.
3. The shareholders of the corporation must be individuals, estates, or certain trusts. Nonqualifying trusts and partnerships cannot be shareholders. Corporations can be shareholders under certain circumstances.
4. The corporation must have seventy-five or fewer shareholders.
5. The corporation must have only one class of stock, although not all shareholders need have the same voting rights.
6. No shareholder of the corporation may be a nonresident alien.

On the Web

Cornell University's Legal Information Institute has links to state corporation statutes at **http://fatty.law.cornell.edu/topics/state_statutes.html**.

BENEFITS OF S CORPORATIONS At times, it is beneficial for a regular corporation to elect S corporation status. Benefits include the following:

1. When the corporation has losses, the S election allows the shareholders to use the losses to offset other income.
2. When the stockholder's tax bracket is lower than the tax bracket for regular corporations, the S election causes the corporation's entire income to be taxed in the shareholder's bracket (because it is taxed as personal income),

On the Web

The Center for Corporate Law at the University of Cincinnati College of Law is a good source of information on corporate law at **http://www.law.uc.edu/CCL**.

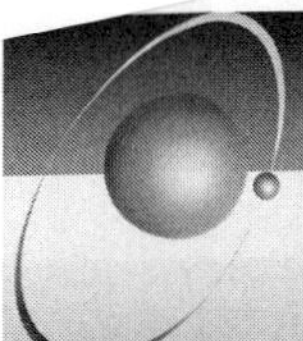

E-Guidelines

Online Incorporation

Today, just about anybody can form a corporation for any lawful purpose in any state. The requirements differ from state to state. You do not have to form your corporation in the state in which you live or the state in which you are doing business, however. In fact, many individuals obtain their corporate charters from the state of Delaware, because it has the fewest legal restrictions on corporate formation and operation. Traditionally, Delaware has also been the state most often chosen for "mail-order incorporation." Today, instead of incorporating by mail, entrepreneurs have the option of incorporating in the states of their choice via online companies that offer incorporation services.

Finding Information on Incorporation Requirements

Most of the more than one hundred companies that offer incorporation services are now online, and you can obtain information about incorporation at their Web sites. For example, at the Web site of The Company Corporation (TCC) of Delaware (at **http://www.incorporate.com**), you can read about the advantages and disadvantages of incorporating your business, the cost of incorporating in your state (or in any other state), and the pros and cons of the various types of corporate entities that are available.

You can find similar information at other sites, including the Web site of Harvard Business Services, Inc. (at **http://www.delawareinc.com**). Here you can find guidelines that will help you choose the type of corporation that best suits your needs, a list of frequently asked questions about incorporation, telephone numbers for each state's corporations division, the annual legal costs of maintaining a corporation, and so on.

Incorporating Online

If you wish to incorporate via an online incorporation service, all you need to do is fill out a form. For example, if you fill out the incorporation forms at the TCC Web site, TCC will then file the forms with the appropriate state office and obtain a certificate of incorporation (corporate charter) for you. Optional TCC services include making arrangements for a registered agent for your corporation, mail-forwarding services, obtaining a tax ID number, and obtaining a domain name registration for your business.

CHECKLIST

- ☑ "Do it yourself" incorporation via online incorporation services may be sufficient for those who are interested in starting small businesses but who have no serious aspirations that their companies will grow much larger.
- ☑ If you believe that the business in which you are going to engage has growth potential and may require significant financing in the future, you are best advised to contact a local lawyer to take you through the necessary steps in incorporating your business.

whether or not it is distributed. This is particularly attractive when the corporation wants to accumulate earnings for some future business purpose.

Because of these tax benefits, many close corporations (corporations in which stockholders are limited to a small group of persons, usually family members) opted for S corporation status in the past. Today, however, the S corporation is losing some of its significance—because the limited liability company and the limited liability partnership (discussed in the next sections) offer similar advantages plus additional benefits, including increased flexibility in forming and operating the business.

SECTION 2 LIMITED LIABILITY COMPANIES

The two most common forms of business organization selected by two or more persons entering into business together are the partnership and the corporation. As explained previously, each form has distinct advantages and disadvantages. For partnerships, the advantage is that partnership income is taxed only once (all income is "passed through" the partnership entity to the partners themselves, who are taxed only as individuals); the disadvantage is the personal liability of the partners. For corporations, the advantage is the limited liability of shareholders; the disadvantage is the double taxation of corporate income. For many entrepreneurs and investors, the ideal business form would combine the tax advantages of the partnership form of business with the limited liability of the corporate enterprise.

A relatively new form of business organization called the **limited liability company (LLC)** is a hybrid form of business enterprise that meets these needs by offering the limited liability of the corporation and the tax advantages of a partnership. LLCs are becoming an increasingly popular organizational form among businesspersons.

LIMITED LIABILITY COMPANY (LLC) A hybrid form of business enterprise that offers the limited liability of the corporation but the tax advantages of a partnership.

IRS rules provide that any unincorporated business will automatically be taxed as a partnership unless it indicates otherwise on the tax form. The exceptions involve publicly traded companies, companies formed under a state incorporation statute, and certain foreign-owned companies. If a business chooses to be taxed as a corporation, it can indicate this choice by checking a box on the IRS form.

Part of the impetus behind creating LLCs in this country is that foreign investors are allowed to become LLC members. Generally, in an era increasingly characterized by global business efforts and investments, the LLC offers U.S. firms and potential investors from other countries flexibility and opportunities greater than those available through partnerships or corporations.

LLC Formation

Like the corporation, an LLC must be formed and operated in compliance with state law. About one-fourth of the states specifically require LLCs to have at least two owners, called **members.** In the rest of the states, although some LLC statutes are silent on this issue, one-member LLCs are usually permitted.

MEMBER The term used to designate a person who has an ownership interest in a limited liability company.

To form an LLC, **articles of organization** must be filed with a central state agency—usually the secretary of state's office. Typically, the articles are required to set forth such information as the name of the business, its principal address, the name and address of a registered agent, the names of the owners, and information on how the LLC will be managed. The business's name must include the words "Limited Liability Company" or the initials "LLC." In addition to filing the articles of organization, a few states require that a notice of the intention to form an LLC be published in a local newspaper.

ARTICLES OF ORGANIZATION The document filed with a designated state official by which a limited liability company is formed.

Note that although the LLC, like the corporation, is a legal entity apart from its owners, for federal jurisdictional purposes an LLC is treated differently than a corporation. The federal jurisdiction statute provides that a corporation is deemed to be a citizen of the state in which it is incorporated and in which it maintains its principal place of business. The statute does not mention the citizenship of partnerships and other unincorporated associations, but courts have tended to regard these entities as citizens of every state in which their members are citizens.

The following case illustrates some of the problems that can arise during the first years of a newly formed enterprise, including an LLC.

CASE 13.2 Skywizard.com, LLC v. Computer Personalities Systems, Inc.

United States District Court,
District of Maine, 2000.
__ F.Supp.2d __.

HISTORICAL AND TECHNOLOGICAL SETTING *The highly competitive Internet service provider (ISP) business comprises approximately 5,000 ISPs nationwide, including America Online, Inc. (AOL), EarthLink, Inc., and Prodigy Communications Corporation. Many variables factor into a consumer's choice of ISP, including name-brand recognition, availability of technical support (AOL offers support twenty-four hours a day, for example), ease of connection to the service, price, availability of a local access phone number, and availability of high-speed connections.*

BACKGROUND AND FACTS Gary Cubeta and Gail Ejdys founded Skywizard.com, LLC, as an ISP. In May 1999, they entered into an agreement with Computer Personalities Systems, Inc. (CPSI), a retailer of computer hardware and software the principal of which, George Cappell, markets products through infomercials on cable television channels. CPSI agreed, among other things, that beginning September 1, it would run, one weekend per month, a "special promotion," according to which a customer who bought a specified computer would receive a year's Internet service through Skywizard.com to start whenever the customer wanted. For each computer sold under this promotion, CPSI agreed to pay Skywizard.com $79. Despite this fee, the ISP incurred a loss of about $44 per year for each "special promotion" subscriber. By March 2000, most of the ISP's subscribers were people who had bought computers through CPSI, including about a third of those who bought the "special promotion" computers. CPSI had failed to run the promotion on September 1, however, and for this reason, among others, Skywizard.com filed a suit in a federal district court against CPSI, alleging breach of contract. Skywizard.com estimated that 1,500 units would have been shipped if the September promotion had run and one-third of the buyers would have subscribed to Skywizard.com, representing lost profits of $67,500.

IN THE LANGUAGE OF THE COURT. . .
COHEN, Magistrate J. [Judge.]

* * * *

Regardless of the number of computers that CPSI may have shipped to customers had a September 1999 Special Promotion aired, the evidence is insufficient to substantiate the amount of Skywizard's damages based on loss of the $79 fee with reasonable probability. As counsel for the defendant pointed out at trial, were all of CPSI's Special Promotion customers to take advantage of the offer of one year's free Internet service (as they theoretically could), the $79 per customer fee would be more than offset by the cost to Skywizard to service all of the new subscribers. Skywizard adduced evidence that as of March 2000 only one-third of CPSI's Special Promotion customers were Skywizard subscribers. If I could conclude with confidence that, had the September 1999 Special Promotion aired, only one-third of the resultant customers would have become Skywizard subscribers, Skywizard would have demonstrated that, by avoiding the cost of servicing the remaining two-thirds of the Special Promotion customers, it lost monies that would have been generated by the $79 fee. However, in view of the newness of the Skywizard enterprise, the fact that Skywizard imposed no deadline within which customers were obliged to accept the offer of one year's free Internet service and the fact that Skywizard's evidence at most amounted to a snapshot of its customer base as of one point in time, I am constrained to conclude that the record is barren of sufficient historic company data from which a reliable projection of the composition of the customer base can be made. In view of the clear breach of contract, an award of nominal damages nonetheless is appropriate.

* * * In light of the foregoing, judgment shall enter in favor of Skywizard and against CPSI in the amount of $100.00.

DECISION AND REMEDY The court held that CPSI breached the contract to run the September promotion, but that damages could not be determined because the life of Skywizard.com had been too short. For these reasons, the court entered a judgment in favor of Skywizard.com for $100 in nominal damages.

FOR CRITICAL ANALYSIS–Economic Consideration *How long should a company's "track record" be to enable it to recover lost profits for a breach of contract?*

Advantages and Disadvantages of LLCs

A key advantage of the LLC is that the liability of members is limited to the amount of their investments. Another significant advantage is that an LLC with two or more members can choose whether to be taxed as a partnership or a corporation. LLCs that want to distribute profits to the members may prefer to be taxed as a partnership, to avoid the "double taxation" characteristic of the corporate entity. Remember that in the corporate form of business, the corporation as an entity pays income taxes on its profits, and the shareholders pay personal income taxes on profits distributed as dividends. Unless the LLC indicates that it wishes to be taxed as a corporation, it is automatically taxed as a partnership by the IRS. This means that the LLC as an entity pays no taxes; rather, as in a partnership, profits are "passed through" the LLC and paid personally by the members.

You can find information on how to form an LLC, including the fees charged in each state for filing LLC articles of organization, at the Web site of BIZCORP International, Inc., at **http://www.bizcorp.com**.

If LLC members want to reinvest profits in the business, however, rather than distribute the profits to members, they may prefer to be taxed as a corporation if corporate income tax rates are lower than personal tax rates. Part of the attractiveness of the LLC for businesspersons is this flexibility with respect to taxation options. For federal income tax purposes, one-member LLCs are automatically taxed as sole proprietorships unless they indicate that they wish to be taxed as corporations. With respect to state taxes, most states follow the IRS rules. Still another advantage of the LLC for businesspersons is the flexibility it offers in terms of business operations and management, as will be discussed shortly.

The disadvantages of the LLC are relatively few. Some of the initial disadvantages with respect to uncertainties over how LLCs would be taxed no longer exist. The only remaining disadvantage of the LLC is that state statutes covering LLCs are not uniform. In an attempt to promote some uniformity among the states in respect to LLC statutes, the National Conference of Commissioners on

Uniform State Laws drafted a Uniform Limited Liability Company Act for submission to the states to consider for adoption. Until all of the states have adopted the uniform law, however, an LLC in one state will have to check the rules in the other states in which the firm does business to ensure that it retains its limited liability.

The LLC Operating Agreement

OPERATING AGREEMENT
In a limited liability company, an agreement in which the members set forth the details of how the business will be managed and operated.

In an LLC, the members themselves can decide how to operate the various aspects of the business by forming an **operating agreement.** Operating agreements typically contain provisions relating to management, how profits will be divided, the transfer of membership interests, whether the LLC will be dissolved on the death or departure of a member, and other important issues.

Operating agreements need not be in writing, and indeed they need not even be formed for an LLC to exist. Generally, though, LLC members should protect their interests by forming a written operating agreement.[3] As with any business arrangement, disputes may arise over any number of issues. If there is no agreement covering the topic being disputed, such as how profits will be divided, the state LLC statute will govern the outcome. For example, most LLC statutes provide that if the members have not specified how profits will be divided among the members, they will be divided equally.

Nolo Press provides information on LLCs and how they are operated at **http://www.nolo.com/encyclopedia/sb_ency.html#Subtopic 164**.

Generally, with respect to issues not covered by an operating agreement or an LLC statute, the principles of partnership law are applied. At issue in the following case was whether partnership law should apply to a dispute between LLC members as to how business receipts were to be divided on the firm's dissolution.

3. Some experts suggest that even a one-member LLC should have an operating agreement. An operating agreement provides evidence that the LLC is a separate entity and thus strengthens the member-owner's protection against being held personally liable for a business obligation.

CASE 13.3 Hurwitz v. Padden

Court of Appeals of Minnesota, 1998.
581 N.W.2d 359.
http://www.courts.state.mn.us/archive/capgi.html[a]

BACKGROUND AND FACTS Thomas Hurwitz and Michael Padden formed a two-person law firm as a partnership without a written agreement. They shared all proceeds on a fifty-fifty basis and reported all income as partnership income. Less than eighteen months later, Hurwitz filed articles of organization with the state of Minnesota to establish the firm as an LLC. More than three years later, Padden told Hurwitz that he wanted to dissolve their professional relationship. They resolved all business issues between them except for a division of fees from several of the firm's cases. Hurwitz filed a suit in a Minnesota state court against Padden, seeking, among other things, a distribution of the fees on a fifty-fifty basis. The court applied the principles of partnership law, ruled that the fees should be divided equally, and entered a judgment in favor of Hurwitz for $101,750. Padden appealed, arguing in part that these principles of partnership law should not apply to an LLC.

a. This page includes a partial list of Minnesota Court of Appeals opinions available in the Minnesota State Law Library online database. The last name of the parties in these cases begins with the letter G, H, or I. Scroll down the list to the *Hurwitz* name and click on the link to read the case.

IN THE LANGUAGE OF THE COURT. . .
SHORT, Judge.

* * * *

* * * [T]he Minnesota Limited Liability Company Act specifically incorporates the definition and use of the term "dissolution" from the Uniform Partnership Act [UPA]. Under both statutes, the entity is not terminated upon dissolution, but continues until all business issues are resolved. Thus, the UPA provides guidance when examining the end stages of either entity's life. * * *

It is undisputed: (1) the firm had no written or oral agreement regarding the division of * * * fees upon dissolution; (2) the firm existed for approximately five-and-a-half years before Padden requested dissolution; (3) a little over five months elapsed between the date of dissolution and the date the parties [filed a suit] to settle the firm's remaining issues; (4) the firm's [disputed] fee cases were acquired before the firm's dissolution; (5) prior to its dissolution, the firm divided fees equally between the parties; and (6) at the time the parties filed suit, the firm was in a winding-up phase. Under these circumstances, partnership principles * * * govern the division of fees obtained from pre-dissolution * * * files. Thus, the * * * fees obtained from pre-dissolution case files must be divided equally between the parties, which is consistent with the pre-dissolution method of allocation.

DECISION AND REMEDY The state intermediate appellate court affirmed the decision of the lower court. The state intermediate appellate court concluded that the disputed fees should be divided equally, as the receipts were divided before the dissolution.

FOR CRITICAL ANALYSIS–Social Consideration *Should the principles of partnership law apply to other forms of business entities?*

LLC Management

Basically, there are two options with respect to the management of an LLC. The members may decide in their operating agreement to be either a "member-managed" or a "manager-managed" LLC.

In a *member-managed* LLC, all of the members participate in management. In a *manager-managed* LLC, the members designate a group of persons to manage the firm. The management group may consist of only members, both members and nonmembers, or only nonmembers. Most LLC statutes provide that unless the members agree otherwise, all members of the LLC will participate in management.

The members of an LLC can also set forth in their operating agreement provisions governing decision-making procedures. For example, the agreement can indicate what procedures are to be followed for choosing or removing managers, an issue on which most LLC statutes are silent. The members are also free to include in the agreement provisions designating when and for what purposes formal members' meetings will be held. In contrast to state laws governing corporations, LLC statutes in most states have no provisions regarding members' meetings. Members may also specify in their agreement how voting rights will be apportioned. If they do not, LLC statutes in most states provide that voting rights are apportioned according to the capital contributions made by each member. Some states provide that, in the absence of an agreement to the contrary, each member has one vote.

SECTION 3 LIMITED LIABILITY PARTNERSHIPS

LIMITED LIABILITY PARTNERSHIP (LLP)
A form of partnership that allows professionals to enjoy the tax benefits of a partnership while limiting their personal liability for the malpractice of other partners.

The **limited liability partnership (LLP)** is similar to the LLC. The difference between an LLP and an LLC is that the LLP is designed more for professionals who normally do business as partners in a partnership. The major advantage of the LLP is that it allows a partnership to continue as a pass-through entity for tax purposes but limits the personal liability of the partners.

The first state to enact an LLP statute was Texas, in 1991. Other states quickly followed suit, and by 1997, virtually all of the states had enacted LLP statutes. Like LLCs, LLPs must be formed and operated in compliance with state statutes. The appropriate form must be filed with a central state agency, usually the secretary of state's office, and the business's name must include either "Limited Liability Partnership" or "LLP."

In most states, it is relatively easy to convert a traditional partnership into an LLP because the firm's basic organizational structure remains the same. Additionally, all of the statutory and common law rules governing partnerships still apply (apart from those modified by the LLP statute). Normally, LLP statutes are simply amendments to a state's already existing partnership law.

For an example of a state law (that of Florida) governing LLPs, go to the Internet Legal Resource Guide's Web page at **http://ilrg.com/whatsnews/statute.html**.

The LLP is especially attractive for two categories of businesses: professional services and family businesses. Professional service companies include law firms and accounting firms. Family limited liability partnerships are basically business organizations in which all of the partners are related (see the discussion later in this chapter). Generally, the LLP allows professionals to avoid personal liability for the malpractice of other partners. Although LLP statutes vary from state to state, generally each state statute limits in some way the liability of partners. For example, Delaware law protects each innocent partner from the "debts and obligations of the partnership arising from negligence, wrongful acts, or misconduct." In North Carolina, Texas, and Washington, D.C., the statutes protect innocent partners from obligations arising from "errors, omissions, negligence, incompetence, or malfeasance." A partner who commits a wrongful act, such as negligence, however, is liable for the results of the act. Also liable is the partner who supervises the party who commits a wrongful act.

On the Web

The law firm of Wordes, Wilshin, Goren & Conner offers a comparison of the advantages and disadvantages of major business forms with respect to various factors, including ease of formation, management, and ability to raise capital, at **http://www.wwgc.com/wwgc-be1.htm**.

SECTION 4 MAJOR BUSINESS FORMS COMPARED

When deciding which form of business organization would be most appropriate, businesspersons normally take several factors into consideration. These factors include ease of creation, the liability of the owners, tax ramifications, and the need for capital. Each major form of business organization offers distinct advantages and disadvantages with respect to these and other factors.

Exhibit 13–1 summarizes the essential advantages and disadvantages of each of the forms of business organization discussed earlier in this chapter.

EXHIBIT 13–1 Major Forms of Business Compared

CHARACTERISTIC	SOLE PROPRIETORSHIP	PARTNERSHIP	CORPORATION
Method of Creation	Created at will by owner.	Created by agreement of the parties.	Charter issued by state–created by statutory authorization.
Legal Position	Not a separate entity; owner is the business.	Not a separate legal entity in many states.	Always a legal entity separate and distinct from its owners–a legal fiction for the purposes of owning property and being a party to litigation.
Liability	Unlimited liability.	Unlimited liability.	Limited liability of shareholders–shareholders are not liable for the debts of the corporation.
Duration	Determined by owner; automatically dissolved on owner's death.	Terminated by agreement of the partners, by the death of one or more of the partners, by withdrawal of a partner, by bankruptcy, and so on.	Can have perpetual existence.
Transferability of Interest	Interest can be transferred, but individual's proprietorship then ends.	Although partnership interest can be assigned, assignee does not have full rights of a partner.	Shares of stock can be transferred.
Management	Completely at owner's discretion.	Each general partner has a direct and equal voice in management unless expressly agreed otherwise in the partnership agreement.	Shareholders elect directors, who set policy and appoint officers.
Taxation	Owner pays personal taxes on business income.	Each partner pays pro rata share of income taxes on net profits, whether or not they are distributed.	Double taxation–corporation pays income tax on net profits, with no deduction for dividends, and shareholders pay income tax on disbursed dividends they receive.
Organizational Fees, Annual License Fees, and Annual Reports	None.	None.	All required.
Transaction of Business in Other States	Generally no limitation.	Generally no limitation.[a]	Normally must qualify to do business and obtain certificate of authority.

a. A few states have enacted statutes requiring that foreign partnerships qualify to do business there.

SECTION 5 SPECIAL BUSINESS FORMS

Besides the business forms already discussed, several other forms can be used to organize a business. For the most part, these other business forms are hybrid organizations–that is, they have characteristics similar to those of partnerships or corporations, or combine features of both.

EXHIBIT 13–1 Major Forms of Business Compared (Continued)

CHARACTERISTIC	LIMITED PARTNERSHIP	LIMITED LIABILITY COMPANY	LIMITED LIABILITY PARTNERSHIP
Method of Creation	Created by agreement to carry on a business for a profit. At least one party must be a general partner and the other(s) limited partner(s). Certificate of limited partnership is filed. Charter must be issued by the state.	Created by an agreement of the owner-members of the company. Articles of organization are filed. Charter must be issued by the state.	Created by agreement of the partners. Certificate of limited liability partnership is filed. Charter must be issued by the state.
Legal Position	Treated as a legal entity.	Treated as a legal entity.	Generally, treated same as a general partnership.
Liability	Unlimited liability of all general partners; limited partners are liable only to the extent of capital contributions.	Member-owners' liability is limited to the amount of capital contributions or investments.	Varies from state to state but usually limits liability of a partner for certain acts committed by other partners.
Duration	By agreement in certificate, or by termination of the last general partner (withdrawal, death, and so on) or last limited partner.	Unless a single-member LLC, can have perpetual existence (same as a corporation).	Terminated by agreement of partners, by death or withdrawal of a partner, or by law (such as bankruptcy).
Transferability of Interest	Interest can be assigned (same as general partnership), but if assignee becomes a member with consent of other partners, certificate must be amended.	Member interests are freely transferable.	Interest can be assigned same as in a general partnership.
Management	General partners have equal voice or by agreement. Limited partners may not retain limited liability if they actively participate in management.	Member-owners can fully participate in management, or member-owners can select managers to manage the firm on behalf of the members.	Same as a general partnership.
Taxation	Generally taxed as a partnership.	LLC is not taxed, and members are taxed personally on profits "passed through" the LLC.	Same as a general partnership.
Organizational Fees, Annual License Fees, and Annual Reports	Organizational fee required; usually not others.	Organizational fee required; others vary with states.	Organizational fee required (such as a set amount per partner); usually not others.
Transaction of Business in Other States	Generally, no limitation.	Generally, no limitation but may vary depending on state.	Generally, no limitation, but state laws vary as to formation and limitation of liability.

Joint Venture

A **joint venture,** which is sometimes referred to as a joint adventure, is a relationship in which two or more persons or business entities combine their efforts or their property for a single transaction or project or a related series of transactions or projects. Joint ventures are taxed like partnerships, and unless otherwise agreed, joint venturers share profits and losses equally. For example, when several contractors combine their resources to build and sell houses in a single development, their relationship is a joint venture.

Joint ventures range in size from very small activities to huge, multimillion-dollar joint actions undertaken by some of the world's largest corporations. Large organizations often investigate new markets or new ideas by forming joint ventures with other enterprises. For instance, General Motors Corporation and Volvo Truck Corporation were involved in a joint venture—Volvo GM—to manufacture heavy-duty trucks and market them in the United States.

A joint venture resembles a partnership. The essential difference is that a joint venture typically involves the pursuit of a single project or series of transactions, and a partnership usually concerns an ongoing business. Of course, a partnership may be created to conduct a single transaction. For this reason, most courts apply the same principles to joint ventures as they apply to partnerships.

JOINT VENTURE
A joint undertaking of a specific commercial enterprise by an association of persons. A joint venture is normally not a legal entity and is treated like a partnership for federal income tax purposes.

SYNDICATE
An investment group of persons or firms brought together for the purpose of financing a project that they would not or could not undertake independently.

Syndicate

A group of individuals getting together to finance a particular project, such as the building of a shopping center or the purchase of a professional basketball franchise, is called a **syndicate,** or an *investment group*. The form of such groups varies considerably. A syndicate may exist as a corporation or as a general or limited partnership. In some cases, the members merely own property jointly and have no legally recognized business arrangement.

JOINT STOCK COMPANY
A hybrid form of business organization that combines characteristics of a corporation (shareholder-owners, management by directors and officers of the company, and perpetual existence) and a partnership (it is formed by agreement, not statute; property is usually held in the names of the members; and the shareholders have personal liability for business debts). Usually, the joint stock company is regarded as a partnership for tax and other legally related purposes.

Joint Stock Company

A **joint stock company** is a true hybrid of a partnership and a corporation. It has many characteristics of a corporation in that (1) its ownership is represented by transferable shares of stock, (2) it is usually managed by directors and officers of the company or association, and (3) it can have a perpetual existence. Most of its other features, however, are more characteristic of a partnership, and it is usually treated like a partnership. As with a partnership, it is formed by agreement (not statute), property is usually held in the names of the members, shareholders have personal liability, and generally the company is not treated as a legal entity for purposes of a lawsuit. In a joint stock company, however, shareholders are not considered to be agents of each other, as would be the case if the company were a true partnership.

BUSINESS TRUST
A voluntary form of business organization in which investors (trust beneficiaries) transfer cash or property to trustees in exchange for trust certificates that represent their investment shares. Management of the business and trust property is handled by the trustees for the use and benefit of the investors. The certificate holders have limited liability (are not responsible for the debts and obligations incurred by the trust) and share in the trust's profits.

Business Trust

A **business trust** is created by a written trust agreement that sets forth the interests of the beneficiaries and the obligations and powers of the trustees. With a business trust, legal ownership and management of the property of the business stay with one or more of the trustees, and the profits are distributed to the beneficiaries.

The business trust was started in Massachusetts in an attempt to obtain the limited liability advantage of corporate status while avoiding certain restrictions on a corporation's ownership and development of real property. The business trust resembles a corporation in many respects. Beneficiaries of the trust, for example, are not personally responsible for the trust's debts or obligations. In fact, in a number of states, business trusts must pay corporate taxes.

Cooperative

COOPERATIVE
An association that is organized to provide an economic service to its members (or shareholders). An incorporated cooperative is a nonprofit corporation. It will make distributions of dividends, or profits, to its owners on the basis of their transactions with the cooperative rather than on the basis of the amount of capital they contributed. Examples of cooperatives are consumer purchasing cooperatives, credit cooperatives, and farmers' cooperatives.

A **cooperative** is an association, either incorporated or not, that is organized to provide an economic service, without profit, to its members (or shareholders). An incorporated cooperative is subject to state laws governing nonprofit corporations. It makes distributions of dividends, or profits, to its owners on the basis of their transactions with the cooperative rather than on the basis of the amount of capital they contribute. Cooperatives that are unincorporated are often treated like partnerships. The members have joint liability for the cooperative's acts.

The cooperative form of business is generally adopted by groups of individuals who wish to pool their resources to gain some advantage in the marketplace. Consumer purchasing co-ops are formed to obtain lower prices through quantity discounts. Seller marketing co-ops are formed to control the market and thereby obtain higher sales prices from consumers. Often, because of their special status, cooperatives are exempt from certain federal laws, such as antitrust laws (laws prohibiting anticompetitive practices).

SECTION 6 PRIVATE FRANCHISES

FRANCHISE
Any arrangement in which the owner of a trademark, trade name, or copyright licenses another to use that trademark, trade name, or copyright, under specified conditions or limitations, in the selling of goods and services.

FRANCHISEE
One receiving a license to use another's (the franchisor's) trademark, trade name, or copyright in the sale of goods and services.

FRANCHISOR
One licensing another (the franchisee) to use his or her trademark, trade name, or copyright in the sale of goods or services.

A **franchise** is defined as any arrangement in which the owner of a trademark, a trade name, or a copyright licenses others to use the trademark, trade name, or copyright in the selling of goods or services. A **franchisee** (a purchaser of a franchise) is generally legally independent of the **franchisor** (the seller of the franchise). At the same time, the franchise is economically dependent on the franchisor's integrated business system. In other words, a franchisee can operate as an independent businessperson but still obtain the advantages of a regional or national organization.

Although the franchise is not really a business organizational form, the franchising arrangement has become widely used by those seeking to make profits. Well-known franchises include McDonald's, KFC, and Burger King.

Types of Franchises

Because the franchising industry is so extensive and so many different kinds of businesses sell franchises, it is difficult to summarize the many types of franchises that now exist. Generally, though, franchises fall into one of the following three classifications: distributorships, chain-style business operations, and manufacturing or processing-plant arrangements.

DISTRIBUTORSHIP A *distributorship* arises when a manufacturing concern (franchisor) licenses a dealer (franchisee) to sell its product. Often, a distributorship covers an exclusive territory. An example is an automobile dealership.

CHAIN-STYLE BUSINESS OPERATION A *chain-style business operation* exists when a franchise operates under a franchisor's trade name and is identified as a member of a select group of dealers that engage in the franchisor's business. The franchisee is generally required to follow standardized or prescribed methods of operation. Often, the franchisor demands that the franchisee maintain certain standards of operation. In addition, sometimes the franchisee is obligated to deal exclusively with the franchisor to obtain materials and supplies. Examples of this type of franchise are McDonald's and most other fast-food chains.

MANUFACTURING OR PROCESSING-PLANT ARRANGEMENT A *manufacturing* or *processing-plant arrangement* exists when the franchisor transmits to the franchisee the essential ingredients or formula to make a particular product. The franchisee then markets it either at wholesale or at retail in accordance with the franchisor's standards. Examples of this type of franchise are Coca-Cola and other soft-drink bottling companies.

Laws Governing Franchising

Because a franchise relationship is primarily a contractual relationship, it is governed by contract law. If the franchise exists primarily for the sale of products manufactured by the franchisor, the law governing sales contracts as expressed in Article 2 of the Uniform Commercial Code applies. Additionally, the federal government and most states have enacted laws governing certain aspects of franchising. Generally, these laws are designed to protect prospective franchisees from dishonest franchisors and to prohibit franchisors from terminating franchises without good cause.

FEDERAL PROTECTION FOR FRANCHISEES Automobile dealership franchisees are protected from automobile manufacturers' bad faith termination of their franchises by the Automobile Dealers' Franchise Act[4]—also known as the Automobile Dealers' Day in Court Act—of 1965. If a manufacturer-franchisor terminates a franchise because of a dealer-franchisee's failure to comply with unreasonable demands (for example, failure to attain an unrealistically high sales quota), the manufacturer may be liable for damages.

Another federal statute is the Petroleum Marketing Practices Act (PMPA)[5] of 1979, which prescribes the grounds and conditions under which a franchisor may terminate or decline to renew a gasoline station franchise. Federal antitrust laws, which prohibit certain types of anticompetitive agreements, may also apply in certain circumstances.

Additionally, the Franchise Rule[6] of the Federal Trade Commission (FTC) requires franchisors to disclose certain material facts relating to the franchise so that a prospective franchisee can make an informed decision about whether to purchase the franchise. The rule was adopted largely to prevent deceptive and unfair practices in the sale of franchises. One difficulty today is how to apply the rule, which was issued decades ago, to the online world. For a further discussion of this topic, see the *Controversial Issues* feature on the next page.

4. 15 U.S.C. Sections 1221 *et seq.*
5. 15 U.S.C. Sections 2801 *et seq.*
6. 16 C.F.R. Part 436.

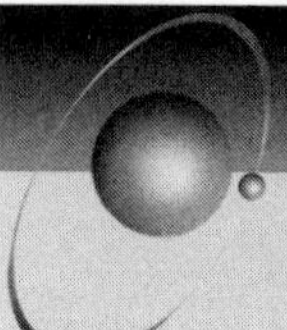

Controversial Issues in the Online World

Should Normal Franchising Rules Apply to the Internet?

Today there are at least 15,000 franchising entities worldwide in seventy-five different kinds of businesses. About 1.2 million franchisees (most of which are in the United States) generate sales approaching $1.5 trillion. The sale of Internet-based franchises may increase these numbers even more. But sales of Internet-based franchises have created a problem, at least in the United States. The Federal Trade Commission (FTC) enacted its Franchise Rule in 1978, when the Internet really did not even exist for most people. That rule, as we pointed out in this chapter, was designed to enable potential franchisees to weigh the risks and benefits of an investment. All aspects of that rule require written disclosures, plus a personal meeting between the franchisor and the prospective franchisee. Such a meeting must take place at least ten business days before the franchise agreement is signed or any payment is made in connection with the purchase of the franchise.

Online Franchising without Any Personal Meeting

The basis of the efficiency of online transactions is that they do not require physical contact between interested parties. A franchisor can communicate to anyone in the world with an Internet connection. When the franchisor has a Web site with downloadable information for prospective franchisees, is this the equivalent of an offer that requires compliance with the FTC's Franchise Rule? Further, does the franchisor have to comply with every different state's franchise regulations?

The Question of Monitoring Is Involved, Too

Given the ease with which franchises can be set up on the Internet, how can the FTC or any other regulatory agency effectively monitor transactions between franchisors and franchisees? Consider Mycity.com (**http://info.mycity.com/franchise.html**). This is a site that creates online Yellow Pages for different cities. Franchisees of Mycity.com sign up clients to be in the Yellow Pages. In essence, all that is involved is intellectual property, for there is no physical presence anywhere.

Regulatory Changes in Sight

For more than a year, the FTC has been proposing changes to its Franchise Rule. One proposed change would require a prospective franchisee to have a proper disclosure document at least fourteen days before the signing of any franchise agreement or any payment to the franchisor. In addition, the franchisee would have to have a franchise form ready for execution five calendar days before signing any contractual agreement. Further, the FTC proposes that there would be an exemption for sophisticated investor transactions, defined as those involving investments in excess of $1.5 million. Finally, the proposed rules would require online franchisors to state very clearly that franchisees would not be entitled to exclusive territorial rights.

FOR CRITICAL ANALYSIS

Given the speed with which online franchises can be created, is it possible for any government agency to effectively regulate these relationships?

STATE PROTECTION FOR FRANCHISEES State legislation tends to be similar to federal statutes and the FTC regulations. For example, to protect franchisees, a state law might require the disclosure of facts that are material to making an informed decision regarding the purchase of a franchise. This could include such information as the actual costs of operation, recurring expenses, and profits earned, along with details substantiating these figures. State deceptive trade practices acts may also prohibit certain types of actions on the part of franchisors.

The Franchise Contract

The franchise relationship is defined by a contract between the franchisor and the franchisee. The franchise contract specifies the terms and conditions of the franchise and spells out the rights and duties of the franchisor and the franchisee. If either party fails to perform its contractual duties, that party may be subject to a lawsuit for breach of contract. Furthermore, if a franchisee is induced to enter into a franchise contract by the franchisor's fraudulent misrepresentation, the franchisor may be liable for damages. Generally, the statutory and case law governing franchising tend to emphasize the importance of good faith and fair dealing in franchise relationships.

Because each type of franchise relationship has its own characteristics, it is difficult to describe the broad range of details a franchising contract may include. In the remaining pages of this chapter, we look at some of the major issues that typically are addressed in a franchise contract.

PAYMENT FOR THE FRANCHISE The franchisee ordinarily pays an initial fee or lump-sum price for the franchise license (the privilege of being granted a franchise). This fee is separate from the various products that the franchisee purchases from or through the franchisor. In some industries, the franchisor relies heavily on the initial sale of the franchise for realizing a profit. In other industries, the continued dealing between the parties brings profit to both. In most situations, the franchisor will receive a stated percentage of the annual sales or annual volume of business done by the franchisee. The franchise agreement may also require the franchisee to pay a percentage of the franchisor's advertising costs and certain administrative expenses.

BUSINESS PREMISES The franchise agreement may specify whether the premises for the business must be leased or purchased outright. In some cases, construction of a building is necessary to meet the terms of the agreement. Certainly, the agreement will specify whether the franchisor supplies equipment and furnishings for the premises or whether this is the responsibility of the franchisee.

LOCATION OF THE FRANCHISE Typically, the franchisor will determine the territory to be served. Some franchise contracts will give the franchisee exclusive rights, or "territorial rights," to a certain geographic area. Other franchise contracts, while they define the territory allotted to a particular franchise, either specifically state that the franchise is nonexclusive or are silent on the issue of territorial rights.

Many franchise lawsuits involve disputes over territorial rights, and this is one area of franchising in which the implied covenant of good faith and fair dealing often comes into play. For example, suppose that a franchisee is not given exclusive territorial rights in the franchise contract, or the contract is silent on the issue. If the franchisor allows a competing franchise to be established nearby, the franchisee may suffer a significant loss in profits. In this situation, a court may hold that the franchisor's actions breached an implied covenant of good faith and fair dealing. At issue in the following case was whether a franchisor had breached this implied covenant.

CASE 13.4 Camp Creek Hospitality Inns, Inc. v. Sheraton Franchise Corp.

United States Court of Appeals, Eleventh Circuit, 1998.
139 F.3d 1396.
http://www.findlaw.com/casecode/courts/11th.html[a]

BACKGROUND AND FACTS In 1990, Camp Creek Hospitality Inns, Inc., entered into a contract with Sheraton Franchise Corporation (a subsidiary of ITT Sheraton Corporation) to operate a Sheraton Inn franchise west of the Atlanta airport. Because another franchisee, the Sheraton Hotel Atlanta Airport, already served that market, Sheraton named Camp Creek's facility "Sheraton Inn Hartsfield-West, Atlanta Airport." Three years later, ITT Sheraton bought a Hyatt hotel in the vicinity of the Atlanta airport and gave it the name "Sheraton Gateway Hotel, Atlanta Airport." The presence of three Sheraton properties in the same market caused some customer confusion. Also, the Inn and the Gateway competed for the same customers, which caused the Inn to suffer a decrease in the growth of its business. Camp Creek filed a suit in a federal district court against Sheraton and others, alleging in part that by establishing the Gateway, ITT Sheraton denied Camp Creek the fruits of its contract in breach of the implied covenant of good faith and fair dealing. The court issued a summary judgment in favor of the defendants. Camp Creek appealed to the U.S. Court of Appeals for the Eleventh Circuit.

a. This Web site is maintained by FindLaw. This page contains links to opinions of the U.S. Court of Appeals for the Eleventh Circuit. In the "select year" and "select month" pull-down menus, select "1998" and "April," respectively. When the results appear, click on the *Camp Creek* case name to access the opinion.

IN THE LANGUAGE OF THE COURT. . .
BIRCH, Circuit Judge:

* * * *

* * * [T]he contract, as executed, says nothing about whether or where Sheraton could establish a competing hotel. * * * Camp Creek had no contractual right to expect the Sheraton Franchise to refrain from licensing the Sheraton name to additional franchises beyond the site of the Inn. By the express terms of the contract, therefore, Sheraton could have authorized a competing franchise directly across the street from the Inn, and Camp Creek would have little recourse.

Sheraton, however, did not establish such a franchise in this case; instead, it purchased and operated the Gateway on its own behalf. * * *

As a result, we must determine whether the implied covenant of good faith and fair dealing permits the Sheraton to establish its own hotel in the same vicinity as the Inn. * * *

* * * Sheraton emphasizes that the Inn has been more profitable every year since the Gateway opened. Camp Creek, however, * * * describe[d] a number of trends present in the market for hotel rooms in the Atlanta area, both before and after Sheraton began operating the Gateway, and present[ed] credible theories and measures of damages attributable to the additional intra-brand competition associated with the Gateway's entry to the market. We hold that Camp Creek's evidence is sufficient to withstand Sheraton's motion for summary judgment on this claim.

DECISION AND REMEDY The U.S. Court of Appeals for the Eleventh Circuit held that unless a franchise contract expressly provides otherwise, a franchisor who competes against a franchisee in the same market could violate the implied covenant of good faith and fair dealing. The court reversed the judgment of the lower court and remanded the case for trial.

FOR CRITICAL ANALYSIS–Economic Consideration *Why would a franchisor compete directly with its franchisee?*

BUSINESS ORGANIZATION AND QUALITY CONTROL The business organization of the franchisee is of great concern to the franchisor. Depending on the terms of the franchise agreement, the franchisor may specify particular requirements for the form and capital structure of the business. The franchise agreement may also provide that standards of operation—relating to such aspects of the business as sales quotas, quality, and record keeping—be met by the franchisee. Furthermore, a franchisor may wish to retain stringent control over the training of personnel involved in the operation and over administrative aspects of the business.

When the franchise is a service operation, such as a motel, the contract often provides that the franchisor will establish certain standards for the facility in order to protect the franchise's name and reputation. Typically, the contract will state that the franchisor is permitted to make periodic inspections to ensure that the standards are being maintained.

PRICING ARRANGEMENTS Franchises provide the franchisor with an outlet for the firm's goods and services. Depending on the nature of the business, the franchisor may require the franchisee to purchase certain supplies from the franchisor at an established price.[7] A franchisor cannot, however, set the prices at which the franchisee will resell the goods, because this may be a violation of state or federal antitrust laws, or both. A franchisor can suggest retail prices but cannot mandate them.

TERMINATION OF THE FRANCHISE The duration of the franchise is a matter to be determined between the parties. Generally, a franchise relationship starts with a short trial period, such as a year, so that the franchisee and the franchisor can determine whether they want to stay in business with one another. Usually, the franchise agreement specifies that termination must be "for cause," such as death or disability of the franchisee, insolvency of the franchisee, breach of the franchise agreement, or failure to meet specified sales quotas. Most franchise contracts provide that notice of termination must be given. If no set time for termination is specified, then a reasonable time, with notice, is implied. A franchisee must be given reasonable time to wind up the business—that is, to do the

7. Although a franchisor can require franchisees to purchase supplies from it, requiring a franchisee to purchase exclusively from the franchisor may violate federal antitrust laws (laws prohibiting certain anticompetitive practices). For two landmark cases on this topic, see *United States v. Arnold, Schwinn & Co.*, 388 U.S. 365, 87 S.Ct. 1956, 18 L.Ed.2d 1249 (1967), and *Fortner Enterprises, Inc. v. U.S. Steel Corp.*, 394 U.S. 495, 89 S.Ct. 1252, 22 L.Ed.2d 495 (1969).

accounting and return the copyright or trademark or any other property of the franchisor.

Franchising Relationships in the Online World

With the growth and development of inexpensive and easy online marketing, it was inevitable that cyberturf conflicts would eventually arise between franchisors and franchisees. Suppose, for example, that a franchise contract grants to the franchisee exclusive rights to sell the franchised product within a certain territory. What happens, then, if the franchisor sells the product from its Web site to anyone anywhere in the world, including in the franchisee's territory? Does this constitute a breach of the franchise contract?

This issue recently came before a panel of arbitrators in an American Arbitration Association (AAA) proceeding. As you learned in Chapter 2, the AAA is a leading provider of arbitration services. The proceeding involved franchise contracts between the Drug Emporium, Inc., and several of its franchisees. The contracts provided that each franchisee had the exclusive right to conduct business in specific geographical areas. The franchisees claimed that the Drug Emporium breached its contractual obligation to honor their territories by using its Web site to sell directly to customers within the franchisees' territories. The arbitrating panel decided in favor of the franchisees and ordered the Drug Emporium not to sell to any potential customers who were physically located within the franchisees' territories.[8]

Because such conflicts can occur not only between the franchisor and its various franchisees but also among competing franchisees, some companies have instituted a specific "no compete" pledge. Coffee Beanery, Ltd., of Flushing, Michigan, has over two hundred physical locations. It set up a single national Web site. The Web site was put up in conjunction with the company's franchisees. Specifically, the home Web page allows interested parties to locate the closest physical franchisee.

SECTION 7 RAISING FINANCIAL CAPITAL

Raising financial capital is critical to entrepreneurial success. In the very early days of a business, sole proprietors or partners may be able to contribute only very limited amounts of capital. If the business becomes successful, the owner or owners may want to raise capital from external sources to expand the business. There are several ways to do this. One way is to borrow funds. Another is to exchange equity (ownership rights) in the company in return for financial capital, either through private arrangements or through public stock offerings.

Loans

A business can raise capital through a bank loan, but this option may not be available for many entrepreneurs. Banks are usually reluctant to lend significant sums to unestablished businesses. Even if a bank is willing to make such a loan, it may require that an entrepreneur personally guarantee repayment.

8. *Emporium Drug Mart, Inc. of Shreveport v. Drug Emporium, Inc.*, No. 71-114-0012600 (American Arbitration Association, September 2, 2000).

If a bank loan is available, the entrepreneur may find it beneficial to obtain one, because raising capital in this way leaves the entrepreneur in full ownership and control of the business (though the loan itself may place some restrictions on future business decisions). Loans with desirable terms may be available from the federal Small Business Administration (SBA). One special SBA program provides loans of up to $25,000 for women, low-income, and minority businesspersons. Some entrepreneurs have even used their credit cards to obtain initial capital.

The following case illustrates some of the problems that can occur in funding a new company.

CASE 13.5 Malihi v. Gholizadeh

Massachusetts Superior Court, 2000.
11 Mass.L.Rptr. 659.

BACKGROUND AND FACTS In January 1996, Ali Malihi, Dariush Gholizadeh, and Ali Kazeroonian founded Worldwide Broadcasting Network (WBN), a corporation, to provide video content over the Internet. WBN was to take material typically shown on television and make it available over the Internet through hundreds of thousands of customized video channels. Gholizadeh and Kazeroonian had technological expertise. Malihi had a financial background, having worked for fourteen years for an investment firm, with over $100 million in assets under his management. Malihi agreed to obtain $5 million in financing for WBN by June. In March, however, Malihi lowered the amount to $2 million and extended the date to October. Meanwhile, he used his own money to fund WBN, including $40,910 for which Malihi asked Gholizadeh to sign promissory notes.[a] At Gholizadeh's insistence, each note provided that repayment depended on his WBN salary, which in turn depended on Malihi's obtaining financing. If Malihi did not obtain financing as agreed, the notes' payment schedule was to be renegotiated. By March 1997, Malihi had not met the $2 million goal and WBN faced a financial crisis. Gholizadeh found an investor willing to help in exchange for WBN stock. When WBN fired Malihi as an employee and discharged him as a director, he filed a suit in a Massachusetts state court against Gholizadeh, seeking payment on the notes.

a. A *promissory note* is a written promise by one person to pay a fixed sum of money to another on demand or on a specified date.

IN THE LANGUAGE OF THE COURT. . .
HINKLE, [Justice.]

* * * *

Defendant [Gholizadeh] argues that, under the language of the promissory notes, he is not obligated to repay the monies loaned him by plaintiff [Malihi] because 1) plaintiff failed to secure the required funding and 2) the parties were unable to renegotiate a mutually acceptable repayment schedule. Defendant contends that unless he agrees to renegotiate the repayment schedule, he has no obligation to repay the money loaned him by plaintiff. That interpretation is not consistent with the express language of the promissory notes.

If the wording of a contract is unambiguous, the contract must be enforced according to its terms. Both promissory notes executed by defendant were subject to the condition that if WBN failed to obtain financing of at least $2,000,000 by October 30, 1996, the schedule of payments, *but not the underlying debt itself,* would be modified and adjusted by the mutual written agreement of the parties.

CASE 13.5–Continued

This provision clearly reflected the parties' understanding that the timing of defendant's repayment, but not the fact of repayment, depended on his receiving a salary from WBN. The promissory notes suggest, although not with any degree of precision, that the repayment period and terms are to be renegotiated if WBN failed to raise $2 million by October 30, 1996. Thus, the express language of the notes enabled defendant to restructure the repayment schedule, but specifically did not excuse him from his obligation to pay the underlying debt.

It is undisputed that WBN failed to obtain $2 million in financing by October 30, 1996, but had secured that amount by early 1997. It is also undisputed that defendant never agreed to a revised payment schedule. Consequently, I find and rule that defendant is liable to plaintiff for payment of the full $40,910 * * * , as well as the interest provided in the notes.

As noted, under the terms of the notes, the parties are required to negotiate a new payment schedule. Because that has not occurred, although defendant is liable for payment of the notes * * * , he is not technically in default, because the parties failed to work out the new payment schedule.

Therefore, judgment will enter for plaintiff on the complaint in the amount of $40,910 plus interest. Defendant and plaintiff shall, within 30 days from the date of judgment, mutually agree in writing on a repayment schedule.

DECISION AND REMEDY The court held that Gholizadeh was obligated to repay the notes, but that technically he was not yet in default. Because Malihi had not obtained the financing for WBN as he had agreed, the parties had to negotiate a new payment schedule.

FOR CRITICAL ANALYSIS–Economic Consideration *In cases involving emerging and start-up ventures, should the courts take into special consideration the firms' need for money?*

Venture Capital

VENTURE CAPITAL
Funds that are invested in, or that are available for investment in, a new corporate enterprise.

VENTURE CAPITALIST
A person or entity that seeks out promising entrepreneurial ventures and funds them in exchange for equity stakes.

Many new businesses raise needed capital by exchanging certain ownership rights (equity) in the firm for **venture capital.** In other words, an outsider contributes money in exchange for an ownership interest in the company. **Venture capitalists** are those who seek out promising entrepreneurial ventures and fund them in exchange for equity stakes. Akin to venture capitalists are individuals, known as "angels," who typically invest somewhat smaller sums in new businesses.

In 1998, venture capitalists invested $14.3 billion in over 2,500 new companies. The average investment was around $5 million.[9] Venture capitalists, in addition to making needed financing available, offer other advantages for entrepreneurs. Venture capitalists are often experienced managers who can provide invaluable assistance to entrepreneurs with respect to strategic business decisions, marketing, and making important business contacts. Obtaining this assistance may be crucial to a new company's success. The disadvantage is that the venture capitalist with a substantial equity stake will demand a corresponding degree of operational control over a company and proportion of future profits.

9. *Time*, September 27, 1999, p. 70.

To attract outside venture capital, you will need a business plan. The plan should be relatively concise (less than fifty pages). It should describe the company, its products, and its anticipated future performance. You may present your plan to a venture capitalist who may then carefully investigate your venture. This may require you to disclose trade secrets, and you should insist that the potential investor sign a confidentiality agreement. If all goes well, you will then negotiate the terms of financing. A key point to be negotiated is how much ownership and control the venture capitalist will receive in exchange for the capital contribution. Exhibit 13–2 summarizes some key issues involved in venture capital negotiations.

Locating Potential Investors

The American Venture Capital Exchange, or AVCE, lists hundreds of companies that seek financing at **http://www.avce.com**.

Technology via the Internet has allowed promoters and others to access, easily and inexpensively, a large number of potential investors. Today, there are several online "matching services." These services specialize in matching potential investors with companies or future companies that are seeking investors. A corporate promoter or a small company seeking capital investment could pay a fee to one of these service companies, which would then include a description of the company in a list that it makes available to investors, also for a fee. Matching services are not new. For decades, several enterprises have provided such services by using computerized databases to match business firms' investment needs with potential investors. What is new is that a number of these service providers are now online, and many of them have significantly expanded the geographic scope of their operations.

A number of companies specialize in matching entrepreneurs in specific industries with potential investors. Also, some companies include listings of companies or start-ups not only in the United States but in other countries as well. Other enterprises restrict their services to firms within a certain region, such as the Pacific Northwest in the United States.

EXHIBIT 13–2 Venture Capital Issues

Type and Quantity of Stock	The venture capitalists will negotiate the amount of stock (which will determine their ownership share of the enterprise) and the type of stock (which will usually be preferred stock).
Stock Preferences	If the venture capitalists receive preferred shares, the shares will generally (1) provide for an annual per-share dividend to be paid before common stockholders receive any dividends and (2) give the venture capitalists priority among shareholders in the event of the firm's liquidation.
Conversion and Antidilution Rights	The preferred shares will be convertible into common stock at the option of the venture capitalists, and the company will be restrained from issuing new stock in an amount that would materially dilute the venture capitalists' ownership interests.
Board of Directors	The venture capitalists will define their proportionate representation on the board of directors.
Registration Rights	Should the company conduct a public offering or register its shares at a later date, the venture capitalists will have the right to have their shares registered also ("piggy-backed"), making those shares more marketable.
Representations and Warranties	The entrepreneur will be required to make representations about the firm's capital structure, its possession of necessary government authorizations, its financial statements, and other material facts.

Garage.com provides a list of start-up companies and summaries of their business plans in the "Garage" area of its site, and a list of potential investors in the "Heaven" area, at **http://www.garage.com**.

Online matching services allow entrepreneurs to reach a wide group of potential investors quickly and with relatively little effort. They also make it possible for a new or existing company to locate investors who are interested in the company's specific type of business venture. Several of these online matching services also offer other kinds of assistance, such as help with creating an effective business plan or tips on how to manage financial issues. Businesspersons, and especially entrepreneurs just starting up their businesses, can also benefit from this type of guidance.

Securities Regulation

Securities regulation is an area of significant concern to those raising capital. Many entrepreneurs do not use venture capitalists but raise money from friends or business acquaintances. Whatever method is used, the investor exchanges capital for an interest in the enterprise. If this interest consists of shares of stock (or otherwise qualifies as a security under federal or state law), the entrepreneur may become subject to extraordinarily detailed regulatory requirements. It may be necessary to register the securities with the Securities and Exchange Commission (SEC) or with the state in which the offering is made, unless the offering falls within an exemption to securities laws. These and other aspects of securities law are discussed in the next chapter.

TERMS AND CONCEPTS

articles of organization 311
business trust 319
certificate of incorporation 309
certificate of limited partnership 308
cooperative 320
corporation 309
entrepreneur 304
franchise 320
franchisee 320
franchisor 320
general partner 308
joint stock company 319
joint venture 319
limited liability company (LLC) 311
limited liability limited partnership (LLLP) 308
limited liability partnership (LLP) 316
limited partner 308
member 311
operating agreement 314
partnership 307
S corporation 309
sole proprietorship 305
syndicate 319
venture capital 328
venture capitalist 328

QUESTIONS AND CASE PROBLEMS

13–1. **Forms of Business Organization.** In each of the following situations, determine whether Georgio's Fashions is a sole proprietorship, a partnership, a limited partnership, or a corporation.

(a) Georgio's defaults on a payment to supplier Dee Creations. Dee sues Georgio's and each of the owners of Georgio's personally for payment of the debt.

(b) Georgio's raises $200,000 through the sale of shares of its stock.

(c) At tax time, Georgio's files a tax return with the IRS and pays taxes on the firm's net profits.

(d) Georgio's is owned by three persons, two of whom are not allowed to participate in the firm's management.

13–2. Choice of Business Form. Jorge, Marta, and Jocelyn are college graduates, and Jorge has come up with an idea for a new product that he believes could make the three of them very rich. His idea is to manufacture soft-drink dispensers for home use and market them to consumers throughout the Midwest. Jorge's personal experience qualifies him to be both first-line supervisor and general manager of the new firm. Marta is a born salesperson. Jocelyn has little interest in sales or management but would like to invest a large sum of money that she has inherited from her aunt. What factors should Jorge, Marta, and Jocelyn consider in deciding which form of business organization to adopt?

13–3. Limited Liability Companies. John, Lesa, and Trevor form an LLC. John contributes 60 percent of the capital, and Lesa and Trevor each contribute 20 percent. Nothing is decided about how profits will be divided. John assumes that he will be entitled to 60 percent of the profits, in accordance with his contribution. Lesa and Trevor, however, assume that the profits will be divided equally. A dispute over the issue arises, and ultimately a court has to decide the issue. What law will the court apply? In most states, what will result? How could this dispute have been avoided in the first place? Discuss fully.

13–4. Franchises. Omega Computers, Inc., is a franchisor that grants exclusive physical territories to its franchisees with retail locations, including Pete's Digital Products. Omega sells over two hundred of the franchises before establishing an interactive Web site. On the site, a customer can order Omega's products directly from the franchisor. When Pete's sets up a Web site through which a customer can also order Omega's products, Omega and Pete file suits against each other, alleging that each is in violation of the franchise relationship. To decide this issue, what factors should the court consider? How might these parties have avoided this conflict? Discuss.

13–5. Indications of Partnership. Sandra Lerner was one of the original founders of Cisco Systems. When she sold her interest in Cisco, she received a substantial amount of money, which she invested, and she became extremely wealthy. Patricia Holmes met Lerner at Holmes's horse training facility, and they became friends. One evening in Lerner's mansion, while applying nail polish, Holmes layered a raspberry color over black to produce a new color, which Lerner liked. Later, the two created other colors with names like "Bruise," "Smog," and "Oil Slick," and titled their concept "Urban Decay." Lerner and Holmes started a firm to produce and market the polishes but never discussed the sharing of profits and losses. They agreed to build the business and then sell it. Together, they did market research, experimented with colors, worked on a logo and advertising, obtained capital from an investment firm, and hired employees. Then Lerner began working to edge Holmes out of the firm. Several months later, when Holmes was told not to attend meetings of the firm's officers, she filed a suit in a California state court against Lerner, claiming, among other things, a breach of their partnership agreement. Lerner responded in part that there was no partnership agreement because there was no agreement to divide profits. Was Lerner right? Why or why not? How should the court rule? [*Holmes v. Lerner,* 74 Cal.App.4th 442, 88 Cal.Rptr.2d 130 (1 Dist. 1999)]

13–6. Limited Liability Companies. Gloria Duchin, a Rhode Island resident, was the sole shareholder and chief executive officer of Gloria Duchin, Inc. (Duchin, Inc.), which manufactured metallic Christmas ornaments and other novelty items. The firm was incorporated in Rhode Island. Duchin Realty, Inc., also incorporated in Rhode Island, leased real estate to Duchin, Inc. The Duchin entities hired Gottesman Co. to sell Duchin, Inc., and to sign with the buyer a consulting agreement for Gloria Duchin and a lease for Duchin Realty's property. Gottesman negotiated a sale, a consulting agreement, and a lease with Somerset Capital Corp. James Mitchell, a resident of Massachusetts, was the chairman and president of Somerset, and Mary Mitchell, also a resident of Massachusetts, was the senior vice president. The parties agreed that to buy Duchin, Inc., Somerset would create a new limited liability company, JMTR Enterprises, L.L.C., in Rhode Island, with the Mitchells as its members. When the deal fell apart, JMTR filed a suit in a Massachusetts state court against the Duchin entities, alleging, among other things, breach of contract. When the defendants tried to remove the case to a federal district court, JMTR argued that the court did not have jurisdiction because there was no diversity of citizenship among the parties; all of the plaintiffs and defendants were citizens of Rhode Island. Is JMTR correct? Why or why not? [*JMTR Enterprises, L.L.C. v. Duchin,* 42 F.Supp.2d 87 (D.Mass. 1999)]

13–7. Partnership. In August 1998, Jea Yu contacted Cameron Eppler, president of Design88, Ltd., to discuss developing a Web site to cater to investors, providing services to its members for a fee. Yu and Patrick Connelly invited Eppler and Ha Tran, another member of Design88, to a meeting to discuss the site. The parties agreed that Design88 would perform certain Web design, implementation, and maintenance functions for 10 percent of the profits from the site, which would be called "The Underground Trader." They signed a "Master Partnership Agreement," which was later amended to include Power Uptik Productions, LLC (PUP). The parties often referred to themselves as partners. From Design88's offices in Virginia, Design88 designed and hosted the site, solicited members through Internet and national print campaigns, processed member applications, provided technical support, monitored access to the site, and negotiated and formed business alliances on the site's behalf. When relations among the parties soured, PUP withdrew. Design88 filed a suit against the others in a Virginia state court. Did a partnership exist among these parties? Explain. [*Design88 Ltd. v. Power Uptik Productions, LLC,* 133 F.Supp.2d 873 (W.D.Va. 2001)]

WEB EXERCISES

Go to **http://lec.westbuslaw.com**, the Web site that accompanies this text. Select "Internet Applications," and then click on "Chapter 13." There you will find the following Internet research exercises that you can perform to learn more about partnerships and limited liability companies:

Activity 13–1: Partnerships
Activity 13–2: Limited Liability Companies

CHAPTER 14

Online Securities Offerings and Regulation

Concepts Covered

After reading this chapter, you should be able to:

❶ Define what is meant by the term *securities*.

❷ Describe the purpose and provisions of the Securities Act of 1933.

❸ Explain the purpose and provisions of the Securities Exchange Act of 1934.

❹ Point out some of the features of state securities laws.

❺ Discuss how securities laws are being applied in the online environment.

"It shall be unlawful for any person in the offer or sale of any security . . . to engage in any transaction, practice, or course of business which operates or would operate as a fraud or deceit upon the purchaser."

Securities Act of 1933, Section 17

As a result of the stock market crash of 1929 and the ensuing economic depression, Congress was pressured to regulate securities trading. The Securities Act of 1933[1] and the Securities Exchange Act of 1934[2] require the disclosure of information to help investors make buying and selling decisions about *securities*—generally defined as any documents evidencing corporate ownership (stock) or debts (bonds). These acts also prohibit deceptive, unfair, and manipulative practices in the purchase and sale of securities. Both acts are administered by the Securities and Exchange Commission (SEC), which was created by the 1934 act.

The online world has brought about some dramatic changes to securities offerings and regulation. Certain businesses can now raise funds via the Internet. Others can allow their shares to be traded via chat rooms. Offering materials can be transmitted on the Web and by using CD-ROMs. The use of the Internet to purchase and sell securities has raised numerous questions. One issue has to do with whether the rules about disclosure should be applied to company-created Web sites. Another thorny issue concerns offshore offerings via the Web. Can the SEC regulate these offerings? Finally, can the SEC effectively "patrol"

1. 15 U.S.C. Sections 77a–77aa.
2. 15 U.S.C. Sections 78a–78mm.

cyberspace to curb securities fraud? The SEC enforcement mechanism for online fraudulent activities has just begun to develop, and so, too, has the law with respect to it.

In this chapter, after a brief discussion of the functions and powers of the SEC, we examine the major laws governing securities offerings and trading. We then look at how these laws are being adapted to the online environment.

SECTION 1 THE SECURITIES AND EXCHANGE COMMISSION

The Center for Corporate Law at the University of Cincinnati College of Law examines all of the acts discussed in this chapter at **http://www.law.uc.edu/CCL**.

As mentioned, the Securities Exchange Act of 1934 created the SEC to administer the 1933 and 1934 acts. The SEC plays a key role in interpreting these acts and in creating regulations governing securities.

The Basic Functions of the SEC

The SEC regulates the securities industry through the following activities:

1. Requiring disclosure of facts concerning offerings of securities listed on national securities exchanges and offerings of certain securities traded over the counter (OTC).

2. Regulating the trade in securities on the national and regional securities exchanges and in the OTC markets.

3. Investigating securities fraud.

4. Requiring the registration of securities brokers, dealers, and investment advisers and regulating their activities.

5. Supervising activities conducted by mutual funds companies.

6. Recommending administrative sanctions, injunctive remedies, and criminal prosecution in cases involving violations of securities laws. (The Fraud Section of the Criminal Division of the U.S. Department of Justice prosecutes violations of federal securities laws.)

The Regulatory Powers of the SEC

Congress has significantly expanded the SEC's powers. To further curb securities fraud, for example, the Securities Enforcement Remedies and Penny Stock Reform Act of 1990[3] increased the types of cases that SEC administrative law judges can hear and the SEC's enforcement options.

The Securities Acts Amendments of 1990 authorized the SEC to seek sanctions against those who violate foreign securities laws.[4] Under the Market Reform Act of 1990, the SEC can suspend trading in securities if prices rise and fall excessively in a short period of time.[5]

The National Securities Markets Improvement Act of 1996 expanded the power of the SEC to exempt persons, securities, and transactions from the requirements of the securities laws.[6] The act also limited the authority of the states

3. 15 U.S.C. Section 77g.
4. 15 U.S.C. Section 78a.
5. 15 U.S.C. Section 78i(h).
6. 15 U.S.C. Sections 77z–3, 78mm.

to regulate certain securities transactions, as well as particular investment advisory firms.[7]

SECTION 2 THE SECURITIES ACT OF 1933

The Securities Act of 1933 governs initial sales of stock by businesses. The act requires that all essential information concerning the issuance of securities be made available to the investing public.

Basically, the courts have interpreted the act's definition of what constitutes a security[8] to mean that a **security** exists in any transaction in which a person (1) invests (2) in a common enterprise (3) reasonably expecting profits (4) derived *primarily* or *substantially* from others' managerial or entrepreneurial efforts.[9]

SECURITIES
Generally, corporate stocks and bonds. A security may also be a note, debenture, stock warrant, or any document given as evidence of an ownership interest in a corporation or as a promise of repayment by a corporation.

The most common forms of securities are stocks and bonds issued by corporations. Securities also include investment contracts in condominiums, franchises, limited partnerships, and oil or gas or other mineral rights.

Registration Statement

If a security does not qualify for an exemption, it must be *registered* before it is offered to the public through the mails or any facility of interstate commerce, including securities exchanges. Issuing corporations must file a *registration statement* with the SEC.

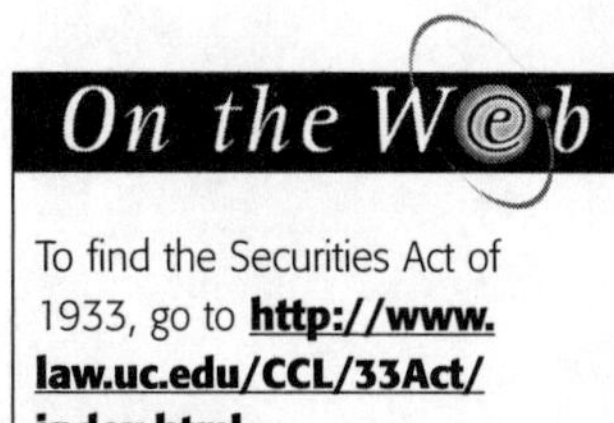

To find the Securities Act of 1933, go to **http://www.law.uc.edu/CCL/33Act/index.html**.

CONTENTS OF THE REGISTRATION STATEMENT The registration statement must include the following:

1. A description of the significant provisions of the security offered for sale and how the registrant intends to use the proceeds of the sale.
2. A description of the registrant's properties and business.
3. A description of the registrant's management; its security holdings; and its remuneration and other benefits, including pensions and stock options. Interests of directors or officers in any material transactions with the corporation must be disclosed.
4. A financial statement certified by an independent public accounting firm.
5. A description of pending lawsuits.

PROSPECTUS A **prospectus** must also be submitted to the SEC as part of the registration statement. The prospectus is created for the purpose of informing potential investors about the security being offered. It contains a description of the security, the issuing corporation, and the risk attached to the security.

PROSPECTUS
A document required by federal or state securities laws that describes the financial operations of the corporation, thus allowing investors to make informed decisions.

OTHER REQUIREMENTS There is a twenty-day waiting period (which can be accelerated by the SEC) after registration before a sale can take place. During this period, oral offers by interested investors to the issuing corporation concerning the proposed securities may occur, and very limited written advertising is allowed.

---

7. 15 U.S.C. Section 80b-3a.
8. See 15 U.S.C. Section 77b(a)(1).
9. *SEC v. W. J. Howey Co.*, 328 U.S. 293, 66 S.Ct. 1100, 90 L.Ed. 1244 (1946).

TOMBSTONE AD
An advertisement, historically in a format resembling a tombstone, of a securities offering. The ad informs potential investors of where and how they may obtain a prospectus.

After the waiting period, the registered securities can be legally bought and sold. Written advertising is allowed only in the form of a **tombstone ad,** so named because historically the format resembled a tombstone. Such ads simply tell the investor where and how to obtain a prospectus.

Exempt Securities

Securities that can be sold without being registered include the following:[10]

1. All bank securities sold prior to July 27, 1933.
2. Commercial paper, if the maturity date does not exceed nine months.
3. Securities of charitable organizations.
4. Securities resulting from a corporate reorganization issued for exchange with the issuer's existing security holders and certificates issued by trustees, receivers, or debtors in possession under the bankruptcy laws.
5. Securities issued exclusively for exchange with the issuer's existing security holders, provided no commission is paid (for example, stock splits).
6. Securities issued to finance the acquisition of railroad equipment.
7. Any insurance, endowment, or annuity contract issued by a state-regulated insurance company.
8. Government-issued securities.
9. Securities issued by banks, savings and loan associations, farmers' cooperatives, and similar institutions subject to supervision by governmental authorities.
10. In consideration of the "small amount involved,"[11] an issuer's offer of up to $5 million in securities in any twelve-month period.

For the last exemption, under Regulation A,[12] the issuer must file with the SEC a notice of the issue and an offering circular, which must also be provided to investors before the sale. Small-business issuers (companies with less than $25 million in annual revenues and less than $25 million in outstanding voting stock) can also utilize an integrated registration and reporting system that uses simpler forms than the full registration system.

Exhibit 14–1 summarizes the securities and transactions (discussed next) that are exempt from the registration requirements.

Exempt Transactions

An issuer of securities that are not exempt under any of the categories listed above can take advantage of certain *exempt transactions*. Because there is some overlap in the exemptions, an offering may qualify for more than one.

SMALL OFFERINGS UNDER REGULATION D During any twelve-month period, offers that involve a small amount of money or are made in a limited manner are, under Regulation D, exempt from the registration requirements.

10. 15 U.S.C. Section 77c.
11. 15 U.S.C. Section 77c(b).
12. 17 C.F.R. Sections 230.251–230.263.

EXHIBIT 14–1 Exemptions under the 1933 Act for Securities Offerings by Businesses

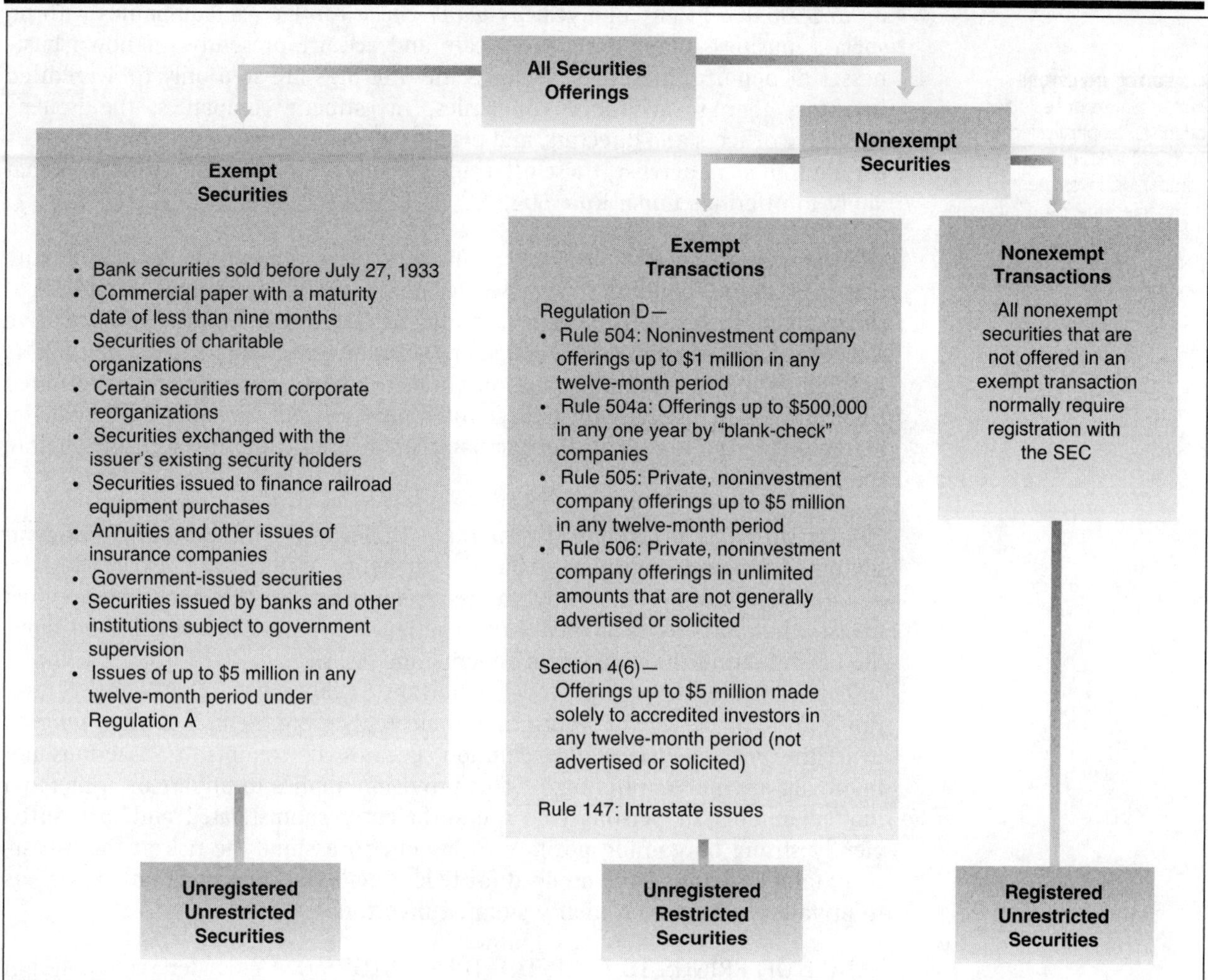

Offerings Up to $1 Million. Noninvestment company offerings up to $1 million in any twelve-month period are exempt, under Rule 504, if no general solicitation or advertising is used; the SEC is notified of the sales; and precaution is taken against nonexempt, unregistered resales.[13] The limits on advertising and unregistered resales do not apply if the offering is made solely in states that provide for registration and disclosure and the securities are sold in compliance with those provisions.[14] *Noninvestment companies* are firms that are not engaged primarily in the business of investing or trading in securities.

13. Precautions to be taken against nonexempt, unregistered resales include asking the investor whether he or she is buying the securities for others; before the sale, disclosing to each purchaser in writing that the securities are unregistered and thus cannot be resold, except in an exempt transaction, without first being registered; and indicating on the certificates that the securities are unregistered and restricted.
14. 17 C.F.R. Section 230.504.

ACCREDITED INVESTORS
In the context of securities offerings, "sophisticated" investors, such as banks, insurance companies, investment companies, the issuer's executive officers and directors, and persons whose income or net worth exceeds certain limits.

Blank-Check Company Offerings Up to $500,000. Under Rule 504a, offerings up to $500,000 in any one year by *blank-check companies* (companies with no specific business plans except to locate and acquire presently unknown businesses or opportunities) are exempt if the offerings are sold only to **accredited investors** (banks, insurance companies, investment companies, the issuer's executive officers and directors, and persons whose income or net worth exceeds certain limits). Otherwise, these offerings are subject to the same conditions that apply to offerings under Rule 504.[15]

Offerings Up to $5 Million. Under Rule 505, private, noninvestment company offerings up to $5 million in any twelve-month period are exempt, regardless of the number of accredited investors, so long as there are no more than thirty-five unaccredited investors; no general solicitation or advertising is used; the SEC is notified of the sales; and precaution is taken against nonexempt, unregistered resales. If a sale involves *any* unaccredited investors, *all* investors must be given material information about the company, its business, and the securities before the sale.[16]

Private Offerings in Unlimited Amounts. Under Rule 506, private offerings in unlimited amounts must meet the requirements of Rule 505, except for the amount limitation. Additionally, the issuer must believe that each unaccredited investor has sufficient knowledge or experience in financial matters to be capable of evaluating the investment's merits and risks.[17]

This exception is perhaps most important to those firms that want to raise funds through the sale of securities without registering them. It is often referred to as the *private placement* exemption, because it exempts "transactions not involving any public offering."[18] This provision applies to private offerings to a limited number of persons who are sufficiently sophisticated and in a sufficiently strong bargaining position to be able to assume the risk of the investment (and who thus have no need for federal registration protection), as well as to private offerings to similarly situated investors.

SMALL OFFERINGS TO ACCREDITED INVESTORS ONLY Under Section 4(6) of the 1933 act, an offer made *solely* to accredited investors is exempt if its amount is not more than $5 million. Any number of accredited investors may participate, but no unaccredited investors may do so. No general solicitation or advertising may be used; the SEC must be notified of all sales; and precaution must be taken against nonexempt, unregistered resales. These are *restricted* securities and may be resold only by registration or in an exempt transaction.[19] (Most securities are, in contrast, *unrestricted* securities.)

INTRASTATE ISSUES Offerings that are restricted to residents of the state in which the issuing company is organized and doing business are exempt if, for nine months after the last sale, no resales are made to nonresidents.[20]

15. 17 C.F.R. Section 230.504a.
16. 17 C.F.R. Section 230.505.
17. 17 C.F.R. Section 230.506.
18. 15 U.S.C. Section 77e(2).
19. 15 U.S.C. Section 77d(6).
20. 15 U.S.C. Section 77c(a)(11); 17 C.F.R. Section 230.147.

RESALES Most securities can be resold without registration. Resales of restricted securities acquired under Rule 504a, Rule 505, Rule 506, or Section 4(6), however, trigger the registration requirements, unless the party selling them complies with Rule 144 or Rule 144A. These rules are sometimes referred to as "safe harbors."

Securities Owned for More Than One Year. Rule 144 exempts restricted securities from registration on resale if the person selling the securities has owned them for at least one year, they are sold in certain limited amounts in unsolicited brokers' transactions, the SEC is given notice of the resale, and there is adequate current public information about the issuer.[21]

A person who has owned the securities for at least two years is not subject to these requirements, unless the person is an *affiliate* (one who controls, is controlled by, or is in common control with the issuer).

Securities Sold Only to Institutional Investors. Securities that at the time of issue are not of the same class as securities listed on a national securities exchange or quoted in a U.S. automated interdealer quotation system may be resold without registration under Rule 144A.[22] They may be sold only to a qualified institutional buyer (an institution, such as an insurance company, an investment company, or a bank, that owns and invests at least $100 million in securities). The seller must take steps to ensure that the buyer knows the seller is relying on this exemption. A sample restricted stock certificate is shown in Exhibit 14–2 on the next page.

Violations of the 1933 Act

It is a violation of the 1933 act to misrepresent or omit facts in a registration statement or prospectus. Liability is also imposed on those who are negligent for not discovering the fraud. Selling securities before the effective date of the registration statement or under an exemption for which the securities do not qualify results in liability.

DEFENSES A defendant can avoid liability if he or she can prove that, even if a statement was not true or a fact was left out, the statement or omission was not material. A defendant can also avoid liability by proving that the plaintiff knew about the misrepresentation and bought the stock anyway.

Any defendant, except the issuer of the stock, can also assert what is called the *due diligence* defense. To use this defense, a person must prove that he or she reasonably believed, at the time the registration statement became effective, that the statements in it were true and there were no omissions of material facts.

CRIMINAL PENALTIES The U.S. Department of Justice brings criminal actions against those who willfully violate the 1933 act. Violators may be penalized by fines up to $10,000, imprisonment up to five years, or both.

---

21. 17 C.F.R. Section 230.144. "Adequate current public information" consists of the reports that certain companies are required to file under the Securities Exchange Act of 1934.
22. 17 C.F.R. Section 230.144A.

EXHIBIT 14–2 A Sample Restricted Stock Certificate

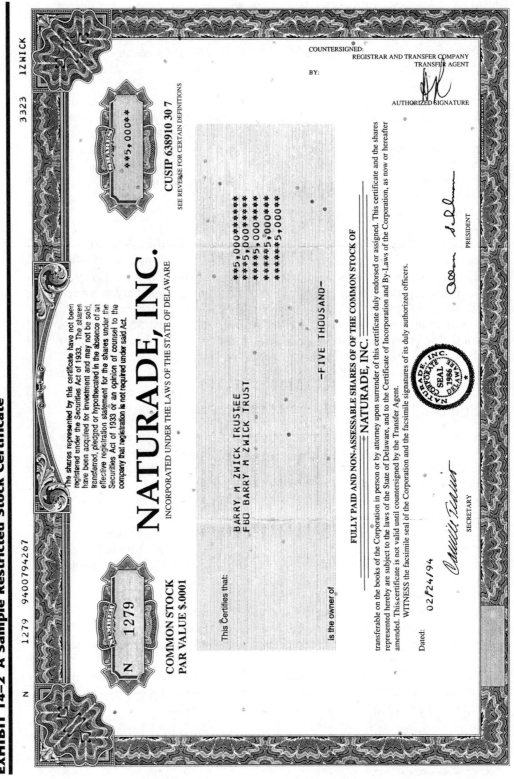

N 1279 9400794267 3323 1ZWICK

The shares represented by this certificate have not been registered under the Securities Act of 1933. The shares have been acquired for investment and may not be sold, transferred, pledged or hypothecated in the absence of an effective registration statement for the shares under the Securities Act of 1933 or an opinion of counsel to the company that registration is not required under said Act.

NUMBER N 1279

SHARES **5,000**

NATURADE, INC.

INCORPORATED UNDER THE LAWS OF THE STATE OF DELAWARE

COMMON STOCK
PAR VALUE $.0001

CUSIP 638910 30 7
SEE REVERSE FOR CERTAIN DEFINITIONS

This Certifies that:

BARRY M ZWICK TRUSTEE
FBO BARRY M ZWICK TRUST

5,000****
5,000**
****5,000****
*****5,000***
******5,000**

is the owner of -FIVE THOUSAND-

FULLY PAID AND NON-ASSESSABLE SHARES OF OF THE COMMON STOCK OF

NATURADE, INC.

transferable on the books of the Corporation in person or by attorney upon surrender of this certificate duly endorsed or assigned. This certificate and the shares represented hereby are subject to the laws of the State of Delaware, and to the Certificate of Incorporation and By-Laws of the Corporation, as now or hereafter amended. This certificate is not valid until countersigned by the Transfer Agent.

WITNESS the facsimile seal of the Corporation and the facsimile signatures of its duly authorized officers.

Dated: 02/24/94

NATURADE, INC. CORPORATE SEAL 1986 DELAWARE

SECRETARY

PRESIDENT

COUNTERSIGNED:
REGISTRAR AND TRANSFER COMPANY
TRANSFER AGENT
BY:
AUTHORIZED SIGNATURE

BANKNOTE CORPORATION OF AMERICA

CIVIL SANCTIONS The SEC is authorized to seek, against those who willfully violate the 1933 act, an injunction against further sales of the securities involved. The SEC can ask the court to grant other relief, such as an order to refund profits. Those who purchase securities and suffer harm as a result of false or omitted statements or other violations may also bring a suit in a federal court to recover their losses and other damages.

SEC RULE 10b-5
A rule of the Securities and Exchange Commission that makes it unlawful, in connection with the purchase or sale of any security, to make any untrue statement of a material fact or to omit a material fact if such omission causes the statement to be misleading.

SECTION 3 THE SECURITIES EXCHANGE ACT OF 1934

The Securities Exchange Act of 1934 provides for the regulation and registration of securities exchanges, brokers, dealers, and national securities associations, such as the National Association of Securities Dealers (NASD). Under Section 12 of the act, the SEC regulates the markets in which securities are traded by maintaining a continuous disclosure system for all corporations with securities on the exchanges and for firms with assets in excess of $10 million and five hundred or more shareholders.

Insider Trading

Section 10(b) of the 1934 act prohibits the use of any manipulative or deceptive device in violation of SEC rules and regulations. Among these rules is **SEC Rule 10b-5**, which prohibits the commission of fraud in connection with the purchase or sale of any security.

Section 10(b) and SEC Rule 10b-5 relate to what is called **insider trading.** Because of their positions, corporate directors and officers often obtain advance inside information that can affect the future market value of the corporate stock. Officers and directors are liable if they take advantage of such information in a personal transaction when they know it is unavailable to the person with whom they are dealing. Section 10(b) and SEC Rule 10b-5 cover not only corporate officers, directors, and majority shareholders but also any persons having access to or receiving information of a nonpublic nature on which trading is based.

INSIDER TRADING
The purchase or sale of securities on the basis of "inside information" (information that has not been made available to the public) in violation of a duty owed to the company whose stock is being traded.

FIDUCIARY DUTY
The duty, imposed on a fiduciary by virtue of his or her position, to act primarily for another's benefit.

In the following classic case, a shareholder alleged that a corporate officer and a corporate director had breached their **fiduciary duties** (duties founded on trust and confidence, the breach of which may expose the breaching party to legal liability) by trading corporate shares on the basis of nonpublic information.

CASE 14.1 Diamond v. Oreamuno

Court of Appeals of New York, 1969.
24 N.Y.2d 494,
248 N.E.2d 910,
301 N.Y.S.2d 78.

BACKGROUND AND FACTS The defendants in this case were the chairman of the board (Oreamuno) and president (Gonzalez) of Management Assistance, Inc. (MAI), a corporation that bought and leased computers, with maintenance services being provided by IBM. The defendants learned that IBM was going to increase its maintenance prices dramatically, to such an extent that MAI's profits would be cut by 75 percent per month. Just before the IBM maintenance price increase was announced, the defendants sold their MAI stock for $28 per share. After IBM publicly announced its price increase, MAI stock fell to $11 per share. The plaintiff (Diamond) brought a shareholder's derivative lawsuit—a suit brought by a shareholder to enforce a corporate cause of action against a third person—on behalf of MAI to recover the profits the defendants had made by selling their shares at the higher price. The trial court granted the defendants' motion to dismiss, and the plaintiff appealed.

CASE 14.1–Continued

IN THE LANGUAGE OF THE COURT. . .
FULD, Chief Judge.

* * * *

Accepting the truth of the complaint's allegations, there is no question but that the defendants were guilty of withholding material information from the purchasers of the shares and, indeed, the defendants acknowledge that the facts asserted constitute a violation of rule 10b-5. * * * Of course, any individual purchaser who could prove an injury as a result of a rule 10b-5 violation can bring his own action for rescission but we have not been referred to a single case in which such an action has been successfully prosecuted where the public sale of securities is involved. The reason for this is that sales of securities, whether through a stock exchange or over-the-counter, are characteristically anonymous transactions, usually handled through brokers, and the matching of the ultimate buyer with the ultimate seller presents virtually insurmountable obstacles. * * *

* * * There is ample room in a situation such as is here presented for a "private Attorney General" to come forward and enforce proper behavior on the part of corporate officials through the medium of the derivative action brought in the name of the corporation. Only by sanctioning such a cause of action will there be any effective method to prevent the type of abuse of corporate office complained of in this case.

DECISION AND REMEDY The court of appeals held that when corporate fiduciaries have breached their duty to the corporation by the use of nonpublic information, a shareholder may bring a derivative action for any profit resulting from the breach of duty.

FOR CRITICAL ANALYSIS–Economic Consideration *Normally, the courts hold that any damages awarded in a shareholder's derivative action should go to the corporation, not to the individual shareholders who bring the suit. Is this fair? Why or why not?*

DISCLOSURE REQUIREMENTS UNDER SEC RULE 10b-5 Any material omission or misrepresentation of material facts in connection with the purchase or sale of a security may violate Section 10(b) and SEC Rule 10b-5. The key to liability is whether the information is *material.* Examples of material facts calling for disclosure include a new discovery, a new product, a change in the financial condition of the firm, and potential litigation against the company.

For information on investor protection and securities fraud, including answers to frequently asked questions on the topic of securities fraud, go to **http://www.securitieslaw.com**.

A company that makes a forward-looking statement, such as a financial forecast, which turns out to be incorrect is not liable for misrepresentation so long as the statement is accompanied by "meaningful cautionary statements identifying important factors that could cause actual results to differ materially from those in the forward-looking statement."[23]

APPLICABILITY OF SEC RULE 10b-5 SEC Rule 10b-5 applies in all cases that concern the trading of securities, registered or unregistered, and that meet the requisites of federal jurisdiction (such as the use of the mails, of stock exchange

23. Private Securities Litigation Reform Act of 1995, 15 U.S.C. Sections 77z-2, 78u-5.

facilities, or of any instrumentality of interstate commerce). Virtually no transaction can be completed without such contact. Also, the states have securities laws, many of which include provisions similar to SEC Rule 10b-5.

OUTSIDERS AND SEC RULE 10b-5 Liability under Section 10(b) of the 1934 act and SEC Rule 10b-5 has been extended to include certain "outsiders"—those who trade on inside information acquired indirectly. Two theories have been developed under which outsiders may be held liable for insider trading: the *tipper/tippee theory* and the *misappropriation theory.*

Tipper/Tippee Theory. Anyone who acquires inside information as a result of a corporate insider's breach of his or her fiduciary duty can be liable under SEC Rule 10b-5. This liability extends to **tippees** (those who receive "tips" from insiders) and even remote tippees (tippees of tippees).

TIPPEE
A person who receives inside information.

To establish liability, there must be a breach of a duty not to disclose inside information, the disclosure must be made in exchange for personal benefit, and the tippee must know of this breach (or should have known of it) and benefit from it.[24] Is the offering of a tip as a gift of profits to someone with whom the insider has a close relationship enough to infer that the insider realized a personal benefit? That was at issue in the following case.

24. See, for example, *Chiarella v. United States,* 445 U.S. 222, 100 S.Ct. 1108, 63 L.Ed.2d 348 (1980); and *Dirks v. SEC,* 463 U.S. 646, 103 S.Ct. 3255, 77 L.Ed.2d 911 (1983).

CASE 14.2 SEC v. Warde

United States Court of Appeals,
Second Circuit, 1998.
151 F.3d 42.
http://www.tourolaw.edu/2ndcircuit/July98[a]

BACKGROUND AND FACTS Edward Downe was a close friend of Fred Sullivan, chairman of Kidde, Inc. At Sullivan's request, Downe became a director of Kidde. Thomas Warde was a good friend of Downe. In June 1987, Sullivan learned that Kidde was the target of a takeover attempt by Hanson Trust PLC, a British firm. After negotiations, the Kidde board announced in August that it would merge with Hanson. The price of Kidde stock increased, and warrants for the shares, which had been priced at $1 in June, went to $26.50.[b] Between learning about the takeover attempt in June and the merger in August, Downe and Warde bought and sold warrants several times, earning very large profits. The SEC filed a suit in a federal district court against Warde and others, alleging insider trading in violation, in part, of Section 10(b). Warde contended that his purchases were based on market savvy, rumor, and public information. The jury found him liable. The court ordered him to pay more than $3 million in penalties and interest. Warde appealed to the U.S. Court of Appeals for the Second Circuit.

a. This page provides access to opinions of the U.S. Court of Appeals for the Second Circuit decided in July 1998. Scroll down the list of cases to the *Warde* case and click on the link to access the opinion.

b. A *warrant* is an agreement to buy stock at a certain price before a certain date. If, before the warrant is exercised, the price goes up, the buyer profits. If the price never exceeds the level in the warrant, the warrant is worthless.

IN THE LANGUAGE OF THE COURT. . .
LEVAL, Circuit Judge:

* * * *

To affirm Warde's liability as a tippee * * * , we must find sufficient evidence to permit a reasonable finding that * * * Downe benefitted by the disclosure to Warde. * * *

CASE 14.2—Continued

* * * *

* * * [In *Dirks v. SEC,* 463 U.S. 646, 103 S.Ct. 3255, 77 L.Ed.2d 911 (1983), the United States] Supreme Court * * * made plain that to prove a Section 10(b) violation, the SEC need not show that the tipper expected or received a specific or tangible benefit in exchange for the tip. Rather, the "benefit" element of Section 10(b) is satisfied when the tipper "intend[s] to benefit the * * * recipient" or "makes a gift of confidential information to a trading relative or friend."

Under this standard, Downe clearly benefitted from Warde's inside trades. Warde's trades "resemble[d] trading by the insider himself followed by a gift of the profits to the recipient." The close friendship between Downe and Warde suggests that Downe's tip was "inten[ded] to benefit" Warde, and therefore allows a jury finding that Downe's tip breached a duty under Section 10(b).

DECISION AND REMEDY The U.S. Court of Appeals for the Second Circuit affirmed the lower court's decision, concluding that the SEC presented sufficient evidence to support every element necessary to hold Warde liable. Warde was ordered to pay the fines, with interest.

FOR CRITICAL ANALYSIS—Social Consideration *How does the decision in this case make it easier for the SEC to win in other insider-trading cases?*

Misappropriation Theory. Liability for insider trading may also be established under the misappropriation theory. If an individual misappropriates (wrongfully obtains) inside information and trades on it for his or her personal gain, then the individual is held liable on the theory that the individual stole information rightfully belonging to another.

Insider Reporting

Officers, directors, and certain large stockholders[25] of Section 12 corporations are required to file reports with the SEC concerning their ownership and trading of the corporation's securities.[26] To discourage such insiders from using nonpublic information about their companies to their personal benefit in the stock market, Section 16(b) of the 1934 act provides for the recapture by the corporation of *all profits* realized by the insider on any purchase and sale or sale and purchase of the corporation's stock within any six-month period.

Although Section 16(b) applies to stock, warrants, options, and securities convertible into stock, the SEC exempts a number of transactions under SEC Rule 16b-3.[27] Exhibit 14–3 compares the effects of SEC Rule 10b-5 and Section 16(b).

25. Those stockholders owning 10 percent of the class of equity securities registered under Section 12 of the 1934 act.

26. 15 U.S.C. Section 78*l*.

27. 17 C.F.R. Section 240.16b-3.

EXHIBIT 14–3 Comparison of Coverage, Application, and Liability under SEC Rule 10b-5 and Section 16(b)

	RULE 10b-5	SECTION 16(b)
Subject matter of transaction	Any security (does not have to be registered).	Any security (does not have to be registered).
Transactions covered	Purchase or sale.	Short-swing purchase and sale or short-swing sale and purchase.
Who is subject to liability?	Virtually anyone with inside information under a duty to disclose–including officers, directors, controlling stockholders, and tippees.	Officers, directors, and certain holders of large amounts of stock.
Is omission or misrepresentation necessary for liability?	Yes.	No.
Any exempt transactions?	No.	Yes, a variety of exemptions.
Is direct dealing with the party necessary?	No.	No.
Who may bring an action?	A person transacting with an insider, the SEC, or a purchaser or seller damaged by a wrongful act.	Corporation and shareholder by derivative action.

Violations of the 1934 Act

Violations of Section 10(b) and SEC Rule 10b-5 of the 1934 act include insider trading. This is a criminal offense, with criminal penalties, and violators may also be subject to civil liability. For sanctions to be imposed, however, there must be *scienter*[28]–an intent to defraud or knowledge of misconduct. *Scienter* can be proved by showing a defendant made false statements or wrongfully failed to disclose material facts.

SCIENTER
Knowledge by the misrepresenting party that material facts have been falsely represented or omitted with an intent to deceive.

Violations of Section 16(b) include the sale by insiders of stock acquired less than six months before the sale. These violations are subject to civil sanctions. *Scienter* is not required.

In the following case, investors charged a corporation with violations of Section 10(b) and SEC Rule 10b-5. The question before the court was whether the investors alleged sufficient facts to indicate *scienter.*

28. Pronounced sy-*en*-ter.

CASE 14.3 In re MCI Worldcom, Inc., Securities Litigation

United States District Court,
Eastern District of New York, 2000.
93 F.Supp.2d 276.

BACKGROUND AND FACTS In early 1999, MCI Worldcom, Inc., began negotiating to buy SkyTel Communications, Inc., then a leading provider of wireless messaging services. When investors heard rumors of the deal, the price of SkyTel stock rose 12 percent. On the morning of May 25, an Internet news service, the Company Sleuth, reported that MCI had registered "skytelworldcom.com" as an Internet domain name.[a] SkyTel's stock price rose 16 percent before noon. At noon, Barbara Gibson, an MCI spokesperson and Senior Manager of Corporate Communication, told the media that the name registration was done by an employee acting alone and "is not an indication of official company intention." Immediately following Gibson's statement, SkyTel's stock price fell to less than the previous day's price. On May 28, MCI announced that it would buy all of SkyTel's stock for $1.3 billion. Paul Curnin and other investors who sold the stock between May 25 and 28 filed a suit in a federal district court against MCI, alleging violations of Section 10(b) and SEC Rule 10b-5. Claiming a failure to properly plead *scienter,* MCI filed a motion to dismiss.

a. It is common for business firms to register domain names before their actual use to protect them from cybersquatters (see Chapter 6).

IN THE LANGUAGE OF THE COURT. . .
GLASSER, District Judge.

* * * *

* * * [A] plaintiff can plead [*scienter*] in one of two ways: (1) by identifying circumstances indicating conscious or reckless behavior by the defendant, or (2) by alleging facts showing a motive to commit fraud and a clear opportunity to do so. * * *

* * * *

To show motive, plaintiffs must show concrete benefits to a defendant that could be realized by one or more of the false statements and wrongful nondisclosures alleged. * * * Plaintiffs assert that MCI was motivated to artificially deflate the price of SkyTel stock in order to help ensure that the acquisition price would not have to be increased. It also did so to make the intended takeover [of SkyTel] more attractive and at a higher premium than if SkyTel's stock price had remained higher because of the merger rumors reignited by the news stories reporting on the registration of the skytelworldcom.com domain name.

* * * *

In response, defendant asserts that plaintiffs fail to allege that Gibson had any knowledge of the confidential merger negotiations, and that such knowledge cannot be assumed or conclusorily asserted. MCI argues that if Gibson is not alleged to have had any knowledge of the confidential merger negotiations, opportunity has not been sufficiently alleged. * * * [I]t is reasonable to assume [,however, that] the official MCI spokesperson, the Senior Manager of Corporation Communications at MCI, did know of an impending merger which was announced three days later.

* * * *

* * * Defendant argues that its alleged motive is insufficient as a matter of law because the alleged fraud did not entail any "concrete" economic benefit to MCI and, therefore, it was not in MCI's economic interests to deflate the price of SkyTel shares.

* * * [B]eing able to acquire a company for a significantly reduced price is a sufficient economic benefit to satisfy the motive requirement for *scienter.* * * *

* * * *

Plaintiffs have also alleged facts that constitute strong circumstantial evidence of conscious misbehavior or recklessness by MCI. * * * [T]hree days prior to the announcement of the merger, MCI's official corporate spokesperson falsely denied any "official company intention" regarding the registration of a domain name that was an obvious combination of MCI's and SkyTel's names. The [investors] understood the denial to mean there would be no takeover, as evidenced by the drop in SkyTel's price. * * * [I]t was MCI itself that registered the domain name, and not, as Ms. Gibson suggested, an MCI employee acting alone.

DECISION AND REMEDY The court denied the motion to dismiss. The investors successfully alleged *scienter* through motive and opportunity, as well as facts from which an inference of conscious misbehavior or recklessness could be drawn.

FOR CRITICAL ANALYSIS–Technological Consideration *What effect has the Internet had on the opportunity to commit violations of the securities laws, as well as to avoid such violations?*

CRIMINAL PENALTIES For violations of Section 10(b) and SEC Rule 10b-5, an individual may be fined up to $1 million, imprisoned up to ten years, or both. A partnership or a corporation may be fined up to $2.5 million.

To examine the Securities Exchange Act of 1934, go to **http://www. law.uc.edu/CCL/34Act/index.html**.

CIVIL SANCTIONS The SEC can bring suit in a federal district court against anyone violating or aiding in a violation of the 1934 act or SEC rules.[29] The court may assess as a penalty as much as triple the profits gained or the loss avoided by the guilty party. Profit or loss is "the difference between the purchase or sale price of the security and the value of that security as measured by the trading price of the security at a reasonable period of time after public dissemination of the nonpublic information."[30]

The Insider Trading and Securities Fraud Enforcement Act of 1988 enlarged the class of persons who may be subject to civil liability for insider-trading violations. This act also gave the SEC authority to award **bounty payments** (rewards given by government officials for acts beneficial to the state) to persons providing information leading to the prosecution of insider-trading violations.[31]

BOUNTY PAYMENT
A reward (payment) given to a person or persons who perform a certain service—such as informing legal authorities of illegal actions.

Private parties may sue violators of Section 10(b) and Rule 10b-5. A private party may obtain rescission of a contract to buy securities or damages to the extent of the violator's illegal profits. Those found liable have a right to seek contribution from those who share responsibility for the violations, including

29. 15 U.S.C. Section 78u(d)(2)(A).
30. 15 U.S.C. Section 78u(d)(2)(C).
31. 15 U.S.C. Section 78u-1.

accountants, attorneys, and corporations.[32] For violations of Section 16(b), a corporation can bring an action to recover the short-swing profits.

SECTION 4 REGULATION OF INVESTMENT COMPANIES

INVESTMENT COMPANY
A company that acts on behalf of many smaller shareholder-owners by buying a large portfolio of securities and professionally managing that portfolio.

MUTUAL FUND
A specific type of investment company that continually buys or sells to investors shares of ownership in a portfolio.

Investment companies act on behalf of their shareholders/owners by buying a portfolio of securities and managing that portfolio professionally. A **mutual fund** is an investment company that continually buys or sells to investors shares of ownership in a portfolio. Investment companies are regulated by the Investment Company Act of 1940,[33] as expanded by the Investment Company Act Amendments of 1970 and the Securities Acts Amendments of 1975. The National Securities Markets Improvement Act of 1996 increased the SEC's authority to regulate these companies by limiting the states' authority.

Under the 1940 act, an investment company is any entity that (1) "is . . . engaged primarily . . . in the business of investing, reinvesting, or trading in securities" or (2) is engaged in such business and more than 40 percent of the company's assets consist of investment securities. Excluded are banks, insurance companies, savings and loan associations, finance companies, oil and gas drilling firms, charitable foundations, tax-exempt pension funds, and other special types of institutions.

All investment companies must register with the SEC by filing a notification of registration. Each year, registered investment companies must file reports with the SEC. To safeguard company assets, all securities must be held in the custody of a bank or stock exchange member.

Dividends may be paid only from accumulated, undistributed net income. Also, there are restrictions on investment activities. For example, investment companies cannot buy securities on the margin (pay only part of the total price, borrowing the rest) or sell short (sell shares not yet owned).

SECTION 5 STATE SECURITIES LAWS

BLUE SKY LAWS
State laws that regulate the offer and sale of securities.

All states have their own corporate securities laws, or **blue sky laws**, that regulate the offer and sale of securities within individual state borders. (The phrase *blue sky laws* dates to a 1917 United States Supreme Court decision in which the Court declared that the purpose of such laws was to prevent "speculative schemes which have no more basis than so many feet of 'blue sky.'"[34]) State securities laws apply only to intrastate transactions, and exemptions from federal law are not exemptions from state laws, but under the National Securities Markets Improvement Act of 1996, the SEC exclusively regulates most of the national securities activities.

---

32. A private cause of action under Section 10(b) and SEC Rule 10b-5 cannot be brought against accountants and others who "aid and abet" violations of the act. Only the SEC can bring actions against so-called aiders and abettors. See *SEC v. Fehn,* 97 F.3d 1276 (9th Cir. 1996).

33. 15 U.S.C. Sections 80a-1 to 80a-64.

34. *Hall v. Geiger-Jones Co.,* 242 U.S. 539, 37 S.Ct. 217, 61 L.Ed. 480 (1917).

SECTION 6 ONLINE SECURITIES OFFERINGS AND DISCLOSURES

The Spring Street Brewing Company, headquartered in New York, made history when it became the first company to attempt to sell securities via the Internet. Through its online initial public offering (IPO), which ended in early 1996, Spring Street raised about $1.6 million. No commissions were paid to any brokers or any underwriters. The offering was made pursuant to Regulation A, which, as mentioned earlier in this chapter, allows small-business issuers to use a simplified registration procedure.

Any company wishing to make an IPO of securities over the Internet has to comply with filing requirements dictated by federal and state law. Because such filings are costly and time consuming, online IPOs are particularly attractive to small companies and start-up ventures that may find it difficult to raise capital from institutional investors or through underwriters.

Rules for the Online Delivery of Offering Materials

One of the early questions posed by online offerings was whether the delivery of securities information via the Internet met the requirements of the Securities Act, which traditionally were applied to the delivery of paper documents. The SEC addressed this issue in its October 1995 interpretive release titled *Use of Electronic Media for Delivery Purposes.*[35] In this release, the SEC stated that "[t]he use of electronic media should be at least an equal alternative to the use of paper-based media" and that anything that can be delivered in paper under the current securities laws might also be delivered in electronic form.

A law firm specializing in securities regulation then asked the SEC to comment on whether a prospectus in downloadable form would meet SEC requirements. In essence, the SEC concluded that it did. There was no change in the substantive law of disclosure; only the delivery vehicle has changed.

Basically, then, when the Internet is used for delivery of a prospectus, the same rules apply as for the delivery of a paper prospectus. They are:

- *Timely and adequate notice of the delivery of information.* Hosting a prospectus on a Web site does not constitute adequate notice, but separate e-mails or even postcards will satisfy the SEC's notice requirements.
- *The online communication system must be easily accessible.* This is very simple to do today because virtually anyone interested in purchasing securities has access to the Web.
- *Some evidence of delivery must be created.* This is a complicated issue with respect to the delivery of prospectuses via the Web. Today, though, this requirement is relatively easy to satisfy. Those making online offerings can require an e-mail return receipt verification of any materials sent electronically.

Once the three requirements above have been satisfied, successful delivery of the prospectus has occurred.

35. Securities Act Release No. 33-7233 (October 6, 1995). The rules governing the use of electronic transmissions for delivery purposes were subsequently confirmed in Securities Act Release No. 33-7289 (May 9, 1996) and expanded in Securities Act Release No. 33-7856 (April 28, 2000).

Potential Liability Created by Online Offering Materials

All printed prospectuses indicate that only the information given in the prospectuses can be used in conjunction with making an investment decision in the securities offered. The same wording, of course, appears on Web-based offerings. Those who create such Web-based offerings may be tempted, however, to go one step further. They may include hyperlinks to other sites that might have analyzed the future prospects of the company, the products and services sold by the company, or the offering itself.

If, for example, a hyperlink goes to an analyst's Web page in which the company is heavily touted, potential investor lawsuits may ensue. These might occur if, after the IPO, the stock price falls. By placing the hyperlink on the Web site of the offering company, that company is impliedly supporting the information presented on the linked page. In such a situation, the company may be liable under federal securities laws.[36] (For other ways in which Web site materials may lead to liability under federal securities laws, see this chapter's *E-Guidelines* feature.)

Remember also that for Regulation D offerings, only accredited investors may participate in such private placements. If the offeror (the entity making the offering) places the offering circular on its Web site for general consumption by anybody on the Internet, potential problems may occur. General solicitation is restricted, obviously, because Regulation D offerings are private placements. If anyone can have access to the offering circular on the Web, the Regulation D exemption may be disqualified.

Putting It All Together—Sight, Sound, Moving Pictures, and Internet Road Shows

With the increased availability of high-speed Internet access, full multimedia presentation of prospectuses, background material, and the ubiquitous "road show" can now be delivered via the Internet. Road shows, as they are commonly called, are part of the sales presentation for any IPO. Road shows are expensive for the offering company, however. They require planning, travel, accommodations, the renting of hotel space where presentations can be made, and so on. Electronic road shows, in contrast, require significant up-front expenditures for their creation, but after that, the cost per location for the presentation is very low.

The first electronic road show was conducted by Primary Care Centers of America in 1996, pursuant to a Regulation D offering. Since then, the SEC has approved other electronic road shows, including those created by Net RoadShow and Thompson Financial Services, Inc.

Electronic road shows must follow the SEC guidelines mentioned earlier on the use of electronic media for delivery purposes. In general, electronic road shows must adhere to the guidelines that apply to live road shows, which are as follows:

- A qualified investor has to contact an institutional salesperson at one of the underwriting investment banks in order to view the road show.

36. See, for example, *In re Syntec Corp.*, 95 F.3d. 92 (9th Cir. 1996).

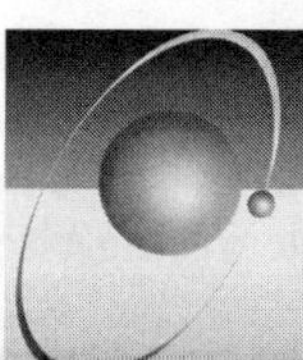

E-Guidelines

Liability for Information Posted on Company Web Sites

Any small or large company can easily have a subcontractor create, develop, and implement a company Web site. Virtually every major corporation and most small corporations have company Web sites today. Web designers, though, cannot create the content for a company Web site. They must ask for content from the company itself. Not surprisingly, most Web designers wish to "fill up" a newly created company Web site with more and more content. A Webmaster usually takes over once the Web site is created. This Webmaster frequently will continue to ask the company for additional content.

Investor Relations on the Web

A typical publicly held corporation has on its Web site a series of Web pages under the heading "Investor Relations." Rather than simply referring the curious Web surfer to the printed materials and those officially filed with the SEC, most companies provide Web-based stories about past, present, and expected future events. Companies need to be cautious in what they include on their Web sites, however, to avoid violating SEC rules. In particular, if a company is engaging in any type of securities offering, rosy statements about the future prospects of the company posted on the company's Web site may come back to haunt management.

Even in the normal course of business, it is possible that optimistic statements posted on the company's Web site may prove unwise. For example, suppose that a company posts a press release on its Web site stating that its earnings for 2002 were $300 million and that the company expects to double those earnings in 2003. In early 2003, the company learns that its 2002 earnings were, in fact, only $200 million and that the earnings could not possibly climb to $600 million in 2003. Next suppose that the firm does not remove the former statement, which is now misleading, from its Web site. In this situation, the company would face potential liability for violating the disclosure requirements of the Securities Exchange Act of 1934.

Hyperlinked Materials

A company also may face potential liability for misleading reports by securities analysts and magazine articles that are hyperlinked to the company's Web site. Even though the information may have been accurate when it was published, a viewer might reasonably rely on the information after it becomes outdated—and the company, by hyperlinking the materials to its Web page, could be held liable for violating SEC disclosure requirements.

Whenever a company's stock price falls dramatically, class-action attorneys may attempt to show that there was a class of investors who purchased the securities based on misleading information posted on the Web site. Thus, nothing can be taken for granted when providing information to investors.

CHECKLIST

- ☑ Each company that has an official company Web site should first develop and enforce a set of guidelines for Web postings, keeping in mind the remaining points in this list.
- ☑ No superfluous information should be posted on the Web site. For the most part, the Web is not new to anyone. Therefore, Web-savvy investors only wish to see the most important information.
- ☑ A securities lawyer who understands disclosure requirements should assist in developing a policy for Web postings.
- ☑ There should always be a time limit for any posted materials; after the time period has expired, the materials should be removed from the site.
- ☑ If a lawsuit is pending, a corporate Web site should be reexamined in light of the lawsuit. Inappropriate materials should be removed from the Web site.

- The qualified investor must be of the same type who would ordinarily be invited to attend a live road show.
- All qualified investors must utilize an access code in order to view the road show on the Internet—no outsiders may have free access to the Web road show.

- Logs must be maintained for those who receive the access code, which must be changed every day to ensure that a qualified investor can only view the road show once.
- The Web version of a road show will present graphs and everything else at a similar speed as a live road show.
- All qualified investors viewing the electronic road show must indicate that they will not download it for further viewing by other people.
- Qualified investors must freely indicate that they understand that the electronic road show is not a prospectus and that they must view the actual prospectus before making a decision to purchase the offered securities.

Online Securities Offerings by Foreign Companies

One of the questions raised by Internet transactions has to do with securities offerings by foreign companies. Traditionally, foreign companies have not been able to offer new shares to the U.S. public without first registering them with the SEC. Today, however, anybody in the world can offer shares of stock worldwide via the Web.

The SEC asks that foreign issuers on the Internet implement measures to warn U.S. investors. For example, a foreign company offering shares of stock on the Internet must add a disclaimer on its Web site stating that it has not gone through the registration procedure in the United States. If the SEC believes that a Web site's offering of foreign securities has been targeted at U.S. residents, it will pursue that company in an attempt to require it to register in the United States.[37]

SECTION 7 ONLINE SECURITIES FRAUD

A major problem facing the SEC today is how to enforce the antifraud provisions of the securities laws in the online environment. An ongoing problem, as you may have read elsewhere in this book, is how to curb online investment scams. One fraudulent investment scheme involved twenty thousand investors, who lost, in all, more than $3 million. Some cases have involved false claims about the earnings potential of home business programs, such as the claim that one could "earn $4,000 or more each month." Others have concerned claims for "guaranteed credit repair."

Here we look at some other significant Internet-related issues concerning securities fraud, including the use and abuse of Internet chat rooms to praise or criticize certain securities. Today, there are tens of thousands of online chat rooms devoted to the buying and selling of securities. None of these are official sites of any companies, securities dealers, or other professionals. The increasing abuse of these online chat forums for private gain in securities trading has become almost rampant, yet what can the SEC do to curb such speech? Clearly, the chat rooms cannot be shut down. After all, the First Amendment to the U.S. Constitution guarantees freedom of speech. Yet where does one draw the line between free speech and statements made to manipulate stock prices? Other issues relate to fictitious press releases and illegal offerings of securities.

---

37. International Series Release No. 1125, March 23, 1998.

Using Chat Rooms to Manipulate Stock Prices

"Pumping and dumping" occurs when a person who has purchased a particular stock heavily promotes ("pumps up") that stock—thereby creating a great demand for it and driving up its price—and then sells ("dumps") it. The concept of pumping up a stock and then dumping it is quite old. In the online world, however, the process can occur much more quickly and efficiently. In 1995, this type of cyber fraud resulted in six SEC cases. By 2001, the SEC had brought an estimated one hundred actions against online perpetrators of such fraud.

The most famous case in this area involved Jonathan Lebed, a fifteen-year-old savvy stock trader and Internet user from New Jersey. While Lebed was the first minor that the SEC charged with securities fraud, he certainly will not be the last. The SEC charged that Lebed bought thinly traded stocks. After the purchases, he flooded stock-related chat rooms, particularly at Yahoo!'s finance boards, with messages touting those stocks' virtues. He used numerous false names so that no one would know that a single person was posting the messages. He said that the stock was the most "undervalued stock in history" and that its price would jump by 1,000 percent "very soon." When other investors attempted to buy the stock, the price would go up quickly, and Lebed would sell out. The resourceful teenager even posted a "limit order" with his broker so that if the price went up while he was attending school, he would not miss out on selling his stocks. The SEC forced the teenager to repay almost $300,000 in gains plus interest. He was allowed, however, to keep about $500,000 of profits he made trading small-company stocks that he also touted on the Internet.

In the following case, the court refers to pumping and dumping stock as "scalping." At issue in the case was whether a stock owner's use of the Internet to tout stock that he had purchased had a duty to disclose his interest in the stock.

CASE 14.4 SEC v. Park

United States District Court,
Northern District of Illinois, 2000.
99 F.Supp.2d 889.

COMPANY PROFILE *In 1997, Yun Soo Oh Park began posting messages on Internet bulletin boards regarding stocks, investing, and other financial subjects. In the first three months of 1998, Park posted thousands of messages under the names "Tokyo Joe" or "TokyoMex." Soon deluged with requests for more stock picks and trading advice, Park formed Societe Anonyme Corporation and set up a Web site called "Tokyo Joe's" (***http://www.tokyojoe.com***) to sell his advice to fee-paying "members." By May 2000, Park, who is the firm's sole officer and shareholder and operates the corporation (renamed Tokyo Joe's Societe Anonyme) from his home, had collected more than $1.1 million in fees.*

BACKGROUND AND FACTS Through the Tokyo Joe's Web site, Park e-mails, posts, and discusses stock picks, reactions to the day's markets, and trading tips. He updates the information on the site at irregular intervals throughout the day. Generally, he first composes and sends e-mail alerts about his stock picks and posts them on the site. Then he discusses the picks in a members-only chat room, and later may post some of his picks on a portion of the site accessible to the public. Finally, he often posts his picks on public Internet bulletin boards. The SEC filed a suit in a federal district court against Park, alleging that through his advice to the members of Tokyo Joe's, Park manipulated and affected the price of stocks that he would buy and sell, in violation of Section 10(b) of the Securities Exchange Act of 1934 and Rule 10b-5. The SEC alleged, among other things, that Park failed to disclose

CASE 14.4–Continued

material facts because he never revealed his own interests in the stocks that he advised others to buy or sell. Park asked the court to dismiss the complaint, arguing in part that he did not have a duty to disclose that information.

IN THE LANGUAGE OF THE COURT. . .

KOCORAS, District Judge.

* * * *

In order to state a claim under [Rule] 10b-5, a claimant must either allege material misstatements or material omissions by a person having a duty to disclose. Although Defendants [Park and his corporation] do not claim that the SEC has not alleged material misstatements, they argue that with respect to the SEC claims which allege violations based on omissions of material fact, the SEC has failed to allege a duty to disclose.

Fraud liability does not attach [arise] for failure to disclose material information unless a party is under the duty to so disclose. A duty to disclose exists when one party possesses information that the other party is entitled to know because of a fiduciary or other similar relation of trust and confidence between them. The SEC contends that Defendants had a duty to disclose because they were "investment advisers" and because they were involved in scalping. Although [the Investment Advisers Act, a different statute] may impose a duty on an "investment adviser" to disclose his scalping, it is unclear whether this duty extends to disclosures under the [Securities] Exchange Act. It seems that the duty to disclose under [Section] 10(b) and Rule 10b-5 must arise from a relationship outside securities law. Thus, Defendants' status as "investment advisers" would not create a duty to disclose.

However, it is possible that Defendants may have a relationship of trust and confidence with [their] subscribers so as to impose on them a duty to disclose their scalping activity. * * * Defendants allegedly had an ongoing relationship with their subscribers and communicated with them electronically on a daily basis. That Defendants' advice and stock picks were sometimes directed at a group and not at the individual does not necessarily mean that the subscribers did not place trust and confidence in Defendants. Moreover, Defendants did communicate through e-mails to individual accounts and addressed individual questions in the chat room. Also, subscribers were apparently placing some degree of trust and confidence in Defendants' particular advice since they were willing to pay a not-insubstantial fee for information and services that they could have acquired practically for free through other web sites, cable t.v. programs, and newspapers.

* * * [A] person who intends to engage in scalping assumes a duty to disclose his interest in the targeted stock.

Thus, because the alleged facts may show that Defendants enjoyed a relationship of trust and confidence with their subscribers or may have assumed a duty to disclose their scalping, the SEC has properly alleged its claims based on Defendants' omission.

DECISION AND REMEDY The court denied the motion to dismiss. A party who is in a relationship of trust and confidence with another has a duty to reveal his or her interest in any stock that the party advises the other to buy or sell.[a]

a. Without admitting or denying the charges, in 2001 Park and his corporation agreed to pay more than $750,000, including $325,000 in what the SEC called illegal profits and $430,000 in penalties.

FOR CRITICAL ANALYSIS–Ethical Consideration *Even if there were no legal duty to disclose an interest in stock that a person touts to others with whom he or she enjoys a relationship of trust and confidence, would there be an ethical duty to reveal the interest?*

Fact versus Opinion

The SEC typically claims that fraud occurs when a false statement of fact is made. Many of Jonathan Lebed's statements (discussed earlier), however, were simply opinions, such as "this stock is headed for $20." Opinions can never be labeled true or false at the time they are made; otherwise they would not be opinions. As long as a person has a "genuine belief" that such an opinion is true, then no fraud is presumably involved.

In the following case, which involved allegations of libel (see Chapter 4), the court had to decide whether negative statements made in an Internet chat room about a company constituted "statements of opinion" or "statements of fact."

CASE 14.5 Global Telemedia International, Inc. v. Does

United States District Court,
Central District of California, 2001.
__ F.Supp.2d __.

COMPANY PROFILE *Global Telemedia International, Inc. (GTMI) (**http://www.gtmi.com**), is a telecommunications company. GTMI owns manufacturing, telecommunications, Internet service provider (ISP) facilities, software development plants, and other offices in Australia, Malaysia, the Philippines, the United States, and other nations. Incorporated in 1984 and operated by various management teams, GTMI was taken over by Jonathon Bentley-Stevens in 1999. GTMI's stock is traded publicly on the National Association of Securities Dealers Over-the-Counter Bulletin Board (OTCBB).*[a]

a. The OTCBB is a service that provides real-time quotes, last-sale prices, and volume information for the stocks of over-the-counter (OTC) companies. An OTC company typically is not listed or traded on a national securities exchange.

BACKGROUND AND FACTS In June 1999, GTMI's stock was trading at about $0.80 per share. By March 2000, the price had increased to $4.70 per share. That month, persons using the aliases ELECTRICK_MAN and BDAMAN609 began posting messages in the GTMI chat room on the Raging Bull Web site.[b] Most of the messages were critical of GTMI and its officers. In April, GTMI's stock price dropped to below $1.00 per share. Over the next six months, ELECTRICK_MAN, BDAMAN609, and more than thirty others posted negative comments about GTMI in the Raging Bull chat room. By October, GTMI's stock was closing at $0.25 a share. GTMI and its officers filed a suit in a

b. Raging Bull is a financial service Web site that organizes chat rooms dedicated to publicly traded companies. Raging Bull does not control the postings in its chat rooms. No special expertise or status is required to post a message. Messages include straightforward commentary, as well as personal invectives. Posters typically are identified by aliases.

CASE 14.5–Continued

California state court against the posters. (ELECTRICK_MAN was identified as "Reader" and BDAMAN609 as "Barry King." The others were listed as "BUSTEDAGAIN40" and "Does 4 through 35.") The plaintiffs asserted claims based on, among other things, trade libel and defamation (see Chapter 4). The suit was moved to a federal district court. Reader and King filed motions to strike the libel and defamation claims from the complaint.

IN THE LANGUAGE OF THE COURT. . .
DAVID O. CARTER, District Judge.

* * * *

Trade libel requires that Reader and King published a false statement which induced others not to deal with Plaintiffs, knowing it was false or acting with reckless disregard of its falsity, and caused Plaintiff monetary damages. Defamation requires a false statement of fact made with malice that caused damage.

Both Reader and King argue that their statements were opinion and that opinions are not actionable * * * .

* * * *

To determine whether a statement is an opinion or fact, the Court must look at the totality of the circumstances. This entails examining the statement in its broad context, which includes the general tenor of the entire work, the subject of the statement, the setting, and the format of the work. Then, the specific context and content of the statement is examined, analyzing the extent of figurative or hyperbolic language used and the reasonable expectations of the audience in that particular situation. Finally, the Court must determine whether the statement is sufficiently factual to be susceptible of being proved true or false.

* * * *

Here, the general tenor, the setting and the format of both Reader's and King's statements strongly suggest that the postings are opinion. The statements were posted anonymously in the general cacophony of an Internet chatroom in which about 1,000 messages a week are posted about GTMI. The postings at issue were anonymous as are all the other postings in the chatroom. They were part of an ongoing, freewheeling and highly animated exchange about GTMI and its turbulent history. At least several participants in addition to Defendants were repeat posters, indicating that the posters were just random individual investors interested in exchanging their views with other investors.

Importantly, the postings are full of hyperbole, invective, shorthand phrases and language not generally found in fact-based documents, such as corporate press releases or SEC filings. * * *

* * * *

In sum, neither Reader's nor King's postings are statements of fact. Given the general context of the postings, the colorful and figurative language of the individual postings, [and] the inability to prove the statements true or false, * * * the postings are opinions.

DECISION AND REMEDY The court granted the motions to strike. The court concluded that Reader and King's postings were not statements of fact but opinions, which are not libelous or defamatory.

FOR CRITICAL ANALYSIS–Social Consideration *Should Web site operators such as Raging Bull, which was not a defendant in this case, be held liable for the statements posted on their sites?*

Chat-Room Fakes Get Caught

Chat rooms are a fertile breeding ground for fakers as well. In 2001, one such set of fakers was sued by E*Trade Group, Inc., an online stockbrokerage firm. Similar to other Internet companies, E*Trade's share price had fallen rather dramatically in 2000 and during the early part of 2001. At that time, a group of imposters used the name of the chief executive of E*Trade, Christos Cotsakos. In one such message, the imposters stated that "I made a killing on my stock options!" They added a nice touch by having Mr. Cotsakos also say that he was "sorry" that other investors lost money in his company's stock. Additionally, numerous postings were made by the imposters in which customers and investors in the company were crudely disparaged.

E*Trade sought an injunction to prohibit individuals from posing as E*Trade executives. It is not clear as yet how the courts will respond to the E*Trade suit. Although in the *Global Telemedia* case just presented the court held that opinions could not be a basis for a libel suit, the courts may view the false statements made by an imposter in a totally different light.

Some have asked a more philosophical question about supposed fraud committed in online chat forums. If some investor is willing to believe essentially anonymous information posted on the Web, where anybody can say anything he or she wants to say, should the SEC intervene? Or should the person acting on such unreliable advice be solely responsible for any losses incurred?

Posting Fictitious Press Releases

Establishing one's "opinion" in an online chat room is one thing. Creating a totally fraudulent press release and sending it out on the Web clearly involves fraud. Twenty-three-year-old college student Mark Jakob posted a fictitious press release through Internet Wire, a company for which he had worked previously. The release alluded to an SEC investigation of a certain firm for improper accounting practices.

Several news services picked up the negative press release. The company's stock plummeted until stock market authorities stopped its trading. The negative press release caused the total market valuation of the company to fall by $2.4 billion. The Federal Bureau of Investigation quickly traced the e-mail containing the press release that Jakob sent to Internet Wire. He sent it from an account at the Library Media Technology Center at El Camino Community College in Redondo Beach, California, where he was a part-time student. Since then, Jakob has been arrested and indicted on eleven counts of securities fraud.

Jakob benefited by the negative publicity because he had "shorted" the stock; that is, he sold the stock without actually owning it, thereby implicitly borrowing the shares. He awaited the price drop; then he "covered" his short position by buying the stock cheaply, thereby making a profit. In this case, the profit was $338,000.

Illegal Securities Offerings

In the first case of its kind, the SEC filed suit against three individuals for illegally offering securities on an Internet auction site.[38] In essence, all three indicated that their companies would go public soon. They attempted to sell unregistered securities via the Web auction sites. All of these actions were in violation of Section 5, 17(a)(1) and 17(a)(3) of the 1933 securities act.

In 2001, the SEC brought a variety of Internet-related fraud cases, many of them related to the initial three cases filed above. For example, in March 2001, the SEC filed twelve separate actions in cases involving solicitations to invest in private companies that purportedly were going to go public (through an IPO).

One such case involved Jerry Chidester, who was the sole shareholder and chief executive of Chidwhite Enterprises, Inc., of Austin, Texas. Chidester used e-mails and a Web page to collect almost $100,000 by offering stock credits to investors who paid "an administrative fee" of $10. The credits were to be redeemed for common stock when the company completed its IPO. In the e-mails and on the Web page, Chidester maintained that the SEC had already approved the IPO (although the SEC had never approved such a registration) and that investors' shares would be valued at $20 to $50 a share. Six thousand investors were defrauded by the twenty-six-year-old entrepreneur.

Increasing SEC Surveillance and Prosecution

As the number and types of online securities frauds increase, the SEC is attempting to keep pace by expanding its online fraud division. It has created an automated surveillance system for online stock frauds. This system, which is constantly being updated, scans the Internet for words and phrases commonly used by fraud perpetrators, such as "get rich quick!" The SEC has been criticized for privacy violations, but it continues to pursue its efforts through its Office of Internet Enforcement, the so-called "Cyberforce." Several hundred employees work in this division.

38. *In re Davis,* SEC Administrative File No. 3-10080, 10/20/99; *In re Haas,* SEC Administrative File No. 3-10081, 10/20/99; *In re Sitaras,* SEC Administrative File No. 3-10082, 10/20/99.

TERMS AND CONCEPTS

accredited investor 338
blue sky law 348
bounty payment 347
fiduciary duties 341
insider trading 341
investment company 348
mutual fund 348
prospectus 335
scienter 345
SEC Rule 10b-5 341
security 335
tippee 343
tombstone ad 336

QUESTIONS AND CASE PROBLEMS

14–1. Registration Requirements. A corporation incorporated and doing business in Florida, Estrada Hermanos, Inc., decides to sell $1 million worth of its no-par-value common stock to the public. The stock will be sold only within the state of Florida. Jose Estrada, the chairman of the board, says the offering need not be registered with the Securities and Exchange Commission. His brother, Gustavo, disagrees. Who is right? Explain.

14–2. Registration Requirements. Huron Corp. has 300,000 common shares outstanding. The owners of these outstanding shares live in several different states. Huron has decided to split the 300,000 shares two for one. Will Huron Corp. have to file a registration statement and prospectus on the 300,000 new shares to be issued as a result of the split? Explain.

14–3. SEC Rule 10b-5. Danny Cherif was employed by the First National Bank of Chicago in its International Financial Institutions Department from 1979 until 1987, when Cherif's position was eliminated because of an internal reorganization. Cherif, using a forged memo to the bank's security department, caused his magnetic identification (ID) card—which he had received as an employee to allow him to enter the bank building—to remain activated after his employment was terminated. Cherif used his ID card to enter the building at night to obtain confidential financial information from the bank's Specialized Finance Department regarding extraordinary business transactions, such as tender offers. During 1988 and 1989, Cherif made substantial profits through securities trading based on this information. Eventually, Cherif's activities were investigated by the Securities and Exchange Commission (SEC), and Cherif was charged with violating Section 10(b) and SEC Rule 10b-5 by misappropriating and trading on inside information in violation of his fiduciary duties to his former employer. Cherif argued that the SEC had wrongfully applied the misappropriation theory to his activities, because as a former employee, he no longer had a fiduciary duty to the bank. Explain whether Cherif is liable under SEC Rule 10b-5. [*SEC v. Cherif,* 933 F.2d 403 (7th Cir. 1991)]

14–4. SEC Rule 10b-5. Louis Ferraro was the chairman and president of Anacomp, Inc. In June 1988, Ferraro told his good friend Michael Maio that Anacomp was negotiating a tender offer for stock in Xidex Corp. Maio passed on the information to Patricia Ladavac, a friend of both Ferraro and Maio. Maio and Ladavac immediately purchased shares in Xidex stock. On the day that the tender offer was announced—an announcement that caused the price of Xidex shares to increase—Maio and Ladavac sold their Xidex stock and made substantial profits (Maio made $211,000 from the transactions, and Ladavac gained $78,750). The SEC brought an action against the three individuals, alleging that they had violated, among other laws, SEC Rule 10b-5. Maio and Ladavac claimed that they had done nothing illegal. They argued that they had no fiduciary duty either to Anacomp or to Xidex, and therefore they had no duty to disclose or abstain from trading in the stock of those corporations. Had Maio and Ladavac violated SEC Rule 10b-5? Discuss fully. [*SEC v. Maio,* 51 F.3d 623 (7th Cir. 1995)]

14–5. Section 10(b). Joseph Jett worked for Kidder, Peabody & Co., a financial services firm owned by General Electric Co. (GE). Over a three-year period, Jett allegedly engaged in a scheme to generate false profits at Kidder, Peabody to increase his performance-based bonuses. When the scheme was discovered, Daniel Chill and other GE shareholders who had bought stock in the previous year filed a suit in a federal district court against GE. The shareholders alleged that GE had engaged in securities fraud in violation of Section 10(b). They claimed that GE's interest in justifying its investment in Kidder, Peabody gave GE "a motive to willfully blind itself to facts casting doubt on Kidder's purported profitability." On what basis might the court dismiss the shareholders' complaint? Discuss fully. [*Chill v. General Electric Co.,* 101 F.3d 263 (2d Cir. 1996)]

14–6. Definition of a Security. In 1997, Scott and Sabrina Levine formed Friendly Power Co. (FPC) and Friendly Power Franchise Co. (FPC-Franchise). FPC obtained a license to operate as a utility company in California. FPC granted FPC-Franchise the right to pay commissions to "operators" who converted residential customers to FPC. Each operator paid for a "franchise"—a geographic area, determined by such factors as the number of households and competition from other utilities. In exchange for 50 percent of FPC's net profits on sales to residential customers in its territory, each franchise was required to maintain a 5 percent market share of power customers in that territory. Franchises were sold to telemarketing firms, which solicited customers. The telemarketers sold interests in each franchise to between fifty and ninety-four "partners," each of whom invested money. FPC began supplying electricity to its customers in May 1998. Less than three months later, the Securities and Exchange Commission (SEC) filed a suit in a federal district court against the Levines and others, alleging that the "franchises" were unregistered securities offered for sale to the public in violation of the Securities Act of 1933. What is the definition of a security? Should the court rule in favor of the SEC? Why or why not? [*SEC v. Friendly Power Co., LLC,* 49 F.Supp.2d 1363 (S.D.Fla. 1999)]

14–7. Securities Exchange Act. 2TheMart.com, Inc., was conceived in January 1999 to launch an auction Web site to compete with eBay, Inc. On January 19, 2TheMart announced that its Web site was in its "final development" stages and expected to be active by the end of July as a "preeminent" auction site, and that the company had "retained the services of leading Web site design and architecture consultants to design and construct" the site. Based on the announcement, investors rushed to buy 2TheMart's stock, causing a rapid increase in the price. On February 3, 2TheMart entered into an agreement with IBM to take preliminary steps to plan the site. Three weeks later, 2TheMart announced that the site was "currently in final development." On June 1, 2TheMart signed a contract with IBM to design, build, and test the site, with a target delivery date of October 8. When 2TheMart's site did not debut as announced, Mary Harrington and others who had bought the stock filed a suit in a federal district court against the firm's officers, alleging violations of the Securities Exchange Act of 1934. The defendants responded, in part, that any alleged misrepresentations were not material and asked the court to dismiss the suit. How should the court rule, and why? [*In re 2TheMart.com, Inc. Securities Litigation,* 114 F.Supp.2d 955 (C.D.Ca. 2000)]

WEB EXERCISES

Go to **http://lec.westbuslaw.com**, the Web site that accompanies this text. Select "Internet Applications," and then click on "Chapter 14." There you will find the following Internet research exercise that you can perform to learn more about the SEC:

Activity 14–1: The SEC's Role

Accounting/Taxation and E-Commerce

Contents

CHAPTER 15

Taxation in Cyberspace

Concepts Covered

After reading this chapter, you should be able to:

1. Describe the constitutional authority of state governments to levy sales taxes and the limits of that authority.
2. Summarize some of the taxation problems posed by mail-order transactions.
3. Indicate how the online environment has affected taxation.
4. State some of the pros and cons of Internet taxation.
5. Discuss recent innovations with respect to filing tax returns and some of the problems the government faces with respect to tax evasion.

"Taxes are what we pay for civilized society."

Oliver Wendell Holmes, Jr., 1841–1935 (American jurist)

SALES TAXES
Taxes levied by state and local governments on goods as they are sold. Merchants collect sales taxes from those who purchase their goods and forward the collected tax dollars to the relevant state or local government agencies.

State and local governments obtain over 30 percent of their tax receipts from sales taxes—taxes paid by those who purchase goods and forwarded to state or local governments by the sellers of those goods—and other types of taxes (such as gasoline taxes) on goods and services. Personal and corporate income taxes account for over 20 percent of state and local tax receipts. Which transactions are and are not taxable at the state and local levels is a critical question for the fiscal well-being of all such governments.

In this chapter we will examine from which legal source state and local jurisdictions derive their ability to tax transactions—whether they be purchases of goods or the earning of income—and the limitations that apply to the taxing actions of these governmental bodies. The advent of e-commerce and the ubiquitous nature of the World Wide Web have created ever-increasing problems for government tax collectors. The issues surrounding taxation in cyberspace are new, complex, and constantly evolving, as you shall see in the remainder of this chapter.

FEDERAL FORM OF GOVERNMENT
A system of government in which the states form a union and the sovereign power is divided between a central government and the member states.

SECTION 1 THE U.S. CONSTITUTION AND STATE POWERS

The U.S. Constitution established a federal form of government. A **federal form of government** is one in which the states form a union and the sovereign power is divided between a central governing authority and the member states. The

Constitution delegates certain powers to the national government, and the states retain all other powers. The relationship between the national government and the state governments is a partnership—neither partner is superior to the other except within the particular area of exclusive authority granted to it under the Constitution.

You can find a copy of the U.S. Constitution online, as well as information about the document, including its history, at **http://www.constitutioncenter.org**.

The Commerce Clause

Article I, Section 8, of the U.S. Constitution expressly permits Congress "[t]o regulate Commerce with foreign Nations, and among the several States, and with the Indian Tribes." This clause, referred to as the **commerce clause**, has had a greater impact on business than any other provision in the Constitution. This power was delegated to the federal government to ensure the uniformity of rules governing the movement of goods through the states.

COMMERCE CLAUSE
The provision in Article I, Section 8, of the U.S. Constitution that gives Congress the power to regulate interstate commerce.

One of the questions posed for the courts by the commerce clause is whether the word *among* in the phrase "among the several States" meant *between* the states or *between and within* the states. For some time, the federal government's power under the commerce clause was interpreted to apply only to commerce between the states (*interstate* commerce) and not commerce within the states (*intrastate* commerce). In 1824, however, in *Gibbons v. Ogden,*[1] the United States Supreme Court held that commerce within the states could also be regulated by the national government as long as the commerce concerned more than one state.

The Breadth of the Commerce Clause

As a result of the Supreme Court's interpretation of the commerce clause in *Gibbons v. Ogden,* the national government exercised increasing authority over all areas of economic affairs throughout the land. In a 1942 case, for example, the Court held that wheat production by an individual farmer intended wholly for consumption on his own farm was subject to federal regulation. The Court reasoned that the home consumption of wheat reduced the demand for wheat and thus could have a substantial effect on interstate commerce.[2] In *McLain v. Real Estate Board of New Orleans, Inc.,*[3] a 1980 case, the Supreme Court acknowledged that the commerce clause had "long been interpreted to extend beyond activities actually in interstate commerce to reach other activities, while wholly local in nature, which nevertheless substantially affect interstate commerce."

Today, at least theoretically, the power over commerce authorizes the national government to regulate every commercial enterprise in the United States. The breadth of the commerce clause permits the national government to legislate in areas in which there is no explicit grant of power to Congress. Only rarely has the Supreme Court limited the regulatory reach of the national government under the commerce authority. One of these occasions was in 1995, in *United States v. Lopez.*[4] In that case, the Court held—for the first time in sixty years—

1. 22 U.S. (9 Wheat.) 1, 6 L.Ed. 23 (1824).
2. *Wickard v. Filburn,* 317 U.S. 111, 63 S.Ct. 82, 87 L.Ed. 122 (1942).
3. 444 U.S. 232, 100 S.Ct. 502, 62 L.Ed.2d 441 (1980).
4. 514 U.S. 549, 115 S.Ct. 1624, 131 L.Ed.2d 626 (1995).

that Congress had exceeded its regulatory authority under the commerce power when it passed the Gun-Free School Zones Act in 1990. The Court stated that the act, which banned the possession of guns within one thousand feet of any school, was unconstitutional because it attempted to regulate an area that had "nothing to do with commerce, or any sort of economic enterprise."

Generally, today's Supreme Court has indicated a willingness to rein in the constitutional powers of the national government to a far greater extent than the Court has during the past six decades. The Court issued a number of decisions in the late 1990s and early 2000s that curbed Congress's powers under the commerce clause and significantly enhanced the sovereign powers of the states within the federal system.[5]

The Regulatory Powers of the States

POLICE POWERS
Powers possessed by states as part of their inherent sovereignty. These powers may be exercised to protect or promote the public order, health, safety, morals, and general welfare.

The Tenth Amendment to the U.S. Constitution states that the powers not delegated to the national government by the Constitution, nor prohibited by the Constitution to the states, are reserved to the states. As part of their inherent sovereignty, states possess **police powers**. The term does not relate solely to criminal law enforcement but rather refers to the broad right of state governments to enact laws to protect or promote the public order, health, safety, morals, and general welfare. Fire and building codes, antidiscrimination laws, parking regulations, zoning restrictions, licensing requirements, and thousands of other state statutes covering virtually every aspect of life have been enacted pursuant to states' police powers. Police powers also include the right of state governments to levy taxes on state residents to pay for the costs of implementing and enforcing such laws.

State Powers and the "Dormant" Commerce Clause

The Supreme Court has interpreted the commerce clause to mean that the national government has the *exclusive* authority to regulate commerce that substantially affects trade and commerce among the states. This express grant of authority to the national government, which is often referred to as the "positive" aspect of the commerce clause, implies a negative aspect of the clause—that the states do *not* have the authority to regulate interstate commerce. This negative aspect of the commerce clause is often referred to as the "dormant" (or implied) commerce clause.

The dormant commerce clause comes into play when state regulations impinge on interstate commerce. In such cases, the court usually will balance the state's interest in regulating a certain matter—such as the length of trucks or trains traveling on its highways—against the burden that the state's regulation places on interstate commerce. If a state law *substantially* burdens interstate commerce, then the law will be unconstitutional—in violation of the commerce clause.

---

5. See, for example, *Printz v. United States,* 521 U.S. 898, 117 S.Ct. 2365, 138 L.Ed.2d 914 (1997); *Alden v. Maine,* 527 U.S. 706, 119 S.Ct. 2240, 144 L.Ed.2d 636 (1999); *Kimel v. Florida Board of Regents,* 528 U.S. 62, 120 S.C. 631, 145 L.Ed.2d 522 (2000); *United States v. Morrison,* 529 U.S. 598, 120 S.Ct. 1740, 146 L.Ed.2d 658 (2000); and *Board of Trustees of the University of Alabama v. Garrett,* 531 U.S. 356, 121 S.Ct. 955, 148 L.Ed.2d 866 (2001).

In *Raymond Motor Transportation, Inc. v. Rice,*[6] for example, the United States Supreme Court invalidated Wisconsin administrative regulations limiting the length of trucks traveling on the state's highways. The Court weighed the burden on interstate commerce against the benefits of the regulations and concluded that the challenged regulations "place a substantial burden on interstate commerce and they cannot be said to make more than the most speculative contribution to highway safety."

State Jurisdictional Limits

The commerce clause clearly limits the regulatory powers of state governments to *instrastate* affairs. California laws, for example, apply only in the state of California; they do not apply in Oregon or in any other state. Exceptions are made to this general rule, however, when actions by out-of-state parties have a sufficient impact on, or connection with, the state. Recall from Chapter 2 that, under a state long arm statute, a court may exercise personal jurisdiction over nonresident defendants if the nonresident had sufficient contacts ("minimum contacts") with the state to justify the jurisdiction. If an out-of-state corporation sells its products within the state, a court may hold that the minimum-contacts test has been met.[7]

Similarly, the commerce clause limits the states' ability to impose sales taxes on out-of-state businesses. State and local governments may, of course, impose any nondiscriminatory sales taxes that are imposed on all purchases within their jurisdictions. A state sales tax, for example, can be imposed on all goods purchased within the geographic borders of the state. When state residents purchase goods from out-of-state merchants, however, a state or local government cannot require those merchants to collect taxes on the transactions and pay them to the state unless there is a sufficient **nexus**, or physical connection, with the jurisdiction in which the customer is located. This requirement may be met if an out-of-state business has sales representatives, retail outlets, or other facilities, such as warehouses, within the state.

NEXUS
A physical connection, or link. Before a state can impose taxes on an out-of-state resident, there must exist a sufficient nexus between the activities of the out-of-state resident and the taxing state.

For years, the nexus requirement has limited the ability of state and local governments to collect sales taxes from out-of-state merchants who sell goods via mail-order catalogues. Today, the same limitation exists with respect to the ability to tax goods sold via the Internet.

SECTION 2 MAIL-ORDER AND INTERNET SALES

Catalogue shoppers have known for a long time that they can avoid state and local sales taxes by purchasing from a catalogue company that is located in another state and that has no branch outlets or sales force in the customer's state. Catalogue sales represented a growing percentage of all retail sales until the Internet came along. Now, catalogue sales combined with Internet sales constitute an increasing part of retail sales that escape most state and local sales

6. 434 U.S. 429, 98 S.Ct. 787, 54 L.Ed.2d 664 (1978).

7. The minimum-contacts standard was established by the United States Supreme Court in *International Shoe Co. v. State of Washington,* 326 U.S. 310, 66 S.Ct. 154, 90 L.Ed. 95 (1945).

taxes. By the time you read this book, about $20 billion per year will be spent in retail transactions via the Web.[8]

What the Courts Have Ruled

Over the years, states have routinely attempted to collect sales taxes on catalogue sales. In numerous cases challenging such attempts, however, the courts have fairly consistently ruled against the states and in favor of the catalogue sales companies; that is, the courts have decided that collecting taxes from an out-of-state entity, when the entity has no physical presence or sales representatives in that state, is a violation of the commerce clause of the U.S. Constitution.

A leading case on this issue is *National Bellas Hess, Inc. v. Department of Revenue of the State of Illinois,*[9] which was decided by the United States Supreme Court in 1967. The case involved a Missouri mail-order company that sold goods in Illinois. The company had no physical presence or any sales representatives in Illinois, however. When the state of Illinois attempted to collect sales taxes, National Bellas Hess objected. The case eventually reached the Supreme Court, which ruled in favor of National Bellas Hess.

The Supreme Court again addressed this question in the following case.

---

8. While in absolute terms this may sound like a lot, in percentage terms it still only constitutes less than 2 percent of total annual retail sales in the United States, well below the 10 percent of retail sales predicted by the National Governors Association in 1998.
9. 386 U.S. 753, 87 S.Ct. 1389, 18 L.Ed.2d 505 (1967).

CASE 15.1 Quill Corp. v. North Dakota

Supreme Court of the United States, 1992.
504 U.S. 298,
112 S.Ct. 1904,
119 L.Ed.2d 91.
http://supct.law.cornell.edu/supct[a]

BACKGROUND AND FACTS Quill Corporation sells office equipment and supplies, soliciting orders through catalogues and flyers, ads in national periodicals, and telemarketing. Its annual sales exceed $200 million, of which almost $1 million are made to about three thousand customers in North Dakota. Quill is the sixth largest vendor of office supplies in that state. Quill delivers all of its merchandise to its North Dakota customers from out-of-state locations. None of its employees work or live in North Dakota, and its ownership of property in the state is insignificant. North Dakota requires mail-order companies to collect sales and use taxes from its North Dakota customers and remit the amounts to the state.[b] When Quill refused to pay the use tax, North Dakota filed a suit in a state court against the firm. Quill asserted that the state did not have the power to compel Quill to collect use taxes from its North Dakota customers. The court ruled in Quill's favor, the North Dakota Supreme Court reversed this ruling, and Quill appealed to the United States Supreme Court.

a. In the right-hand column, in the "Arrayed by party name" section, in the "1992" row, click on "1st party." On that page, scroll to the case name and click on it to access the opinion.

b. A *use tax* is a sales tax that is collectible by a seller when the buyer lives in a different state.

IN THE LANGUAGE OF THE COURT. . .
Justice *STEVENS* delivered the opinion of the Court.

* * * *

The [North Dakota] State Supreme Court reviewed our recent Commerce Clause decisions and concluded that those rulings signaled a "retreat from the formalistic constrictions of a stringent physical presence test in favor of a more flexible substantive approach" * * * . Although we agree with the state court's assessment of the evolution of our cases, we do not share its conclusion that this evolution indicates that the Commerce Clause ruling of *Bellas Hess* is no longer good law.

First, all of these cases involved taxpayers who had a physical presence in the taxing State and therefore do not directly conflict with the rule of *Bellas Hess* or compel that it be overruled. Second, and more importantly, although our Commerce Clause jurisprudence now favors more flexible balancing analyses, we have never intimated a desire to reject all established "bright-line" tests. * * *

* * * [T]he bright-line [clearly stated] rule of *Bellas Hess* furthers the ends of the dormant Commerce Clause. Undue burdens on interstate commerce may be avoided not only by a case-by-case evaluation of the actual burdens imposed by particular regulations or taxes, but also, in some situations, by the demarcation of a discrete realm of commercial activity that is free from interstate taxation. *Bellas Hess* followed the latter approach and created a safe harbor for vendors "whose only connection with customers in the [taxing] State is by common carrier or the United States mail." Under *Bellas Hess,* such vendors are free from state-imposed duties to collect sales and use taxes.

Like other bright-line tests, the *Bellas Hess* rule appears artificial at its edges: Whether or not a State may compel a vendor to collect a sales or use tax may turn on the presence in the taxing State of a small sales force, plant, or office. This artificiality, however, is more than offset by the benefits of a clear rule. Such a rule firmly establishes the boundaries of legitimate state authority to impose a duty to collect sales and use taxes and reduces litigation concerning those taxes. This benefit is important, for as we have so frequently noted, our law in this area is something of a quagmire and the application of constitutional principles to specific state statutes leaves much room for controversy and confusion and little in the way of precise guides to the States in the exercise of their indispensable power of taxation.

Moreover, a bright-line rule in the area of sales and use taxes also encourages settled expectations and, in doing so, fosters investment by businesses and individuals. Indeed, it is not unlikely that the mail-order industry's dramatic growth over the last quarter century is due in part to the bright-line exemption from state taxation created in *Bellas Hess.*

DECISION AND REMEDY The United States Supreme Court reversed the decision of the state supreme court and remanded the case for further proceedings. The United States Supreme Court reasoned that the value of a bright-line rule in the area of state use taxes and the doctrine of *stare decisis* indicated that the *Bellas Hess* rule was still good law.

FOR CRITICAL ANALYSIS–Technological Consideration *How might the reasoning in this case be reevaluated in light of the technological changes that have occurred since the decision was rendered?*

The Nexus Requirement in the Online Context

Until and unless federal legislation is passed that allows the states to tax all online transactions, every Web-based retailer must determine whether there exists an exposure to state and local sales taxes. In order to determine this issue, the many elements of the physical presence nexus test must be examined. Specifically, state taxing authorities may maintain that a Web-based retailer has a physical presence for the reasons discussed in the following subsections, some of which also apply to catalogue sales businesses.

HIRING SALES AGENTS Assume that a Boston-based online merchant believes that Los Angeles is a growing market for its goods. The merchant decides to hire several sales agents to canvas a certain geographic area within Los Angeles. That company has now established a physical presence in California. Such sales agents do not have to be employees of the company; they can be independent contractors. This e-retailer would more than likely be required to collect and remit California sales taxes.

In the following case, the issue was whether the physical presence nexus test required in the *Quill* case is still required under the commerce clause.

CASE 15.2 J. C. Penney National Bank v. Johnson

Tennessee Court of Appeals, 1999.
19 S.W.3d 831.

COMPANY PROFILE *J. C. Penney Company bought a national bank in 1983 and renamed it J. C. Penney National Bank (JCPNB). Through its offices in Delaware, JCPNB offers consumer banking services such as deposit accounts, home mortgage lending, consumer loans, and automated teller machine (ATM) services. JCPNB also engages in credit-card lending through the issuance of Visa and MasterCard credit cards.*[a] *JCPNB contracts with J. C. Penney, its parent company, to provide services such as credit-card solicitation, marketing, statement and payment processing, customer service, and collection.*

BACKGROUND AND FACTS J. C. Penney contracted with Maryland Bank National Association (MBNA), a corporation in Texas, to provide the data processing related to JCPNB's credit-card business. As transactions are received through the Visa or MasterCard network, MBNA posts them to the appropriate cardholder account. MBNA is also responsible for sending out account statements each month. Business Services, Inc. (BSI), provides general marketing and payment-processing services for JCPNB. Cardholders send their payments to a BSI payment-processing center in Texas. BSI also solicits credit-card accounts on behalf of JCPNB throughout the United States, including Tennessee. JCPNB charges an annual fee on most credit-card accounts and pays an income tax to the state of Delaware, but does not pay a similar tax in Tennessee. When Ruth Johnson, the Commissioner of Revenue for the state of Tennessee, assessed state franchise and excise taxes[b] on JCPNB on income generated by its credit-card activities in that state, the bank filed a suit in a state court against Johnson. JCPNB argued that taxing it violated the commerce clause. The court upheld the assessment, and the bank appealed to a state intermediate appellate court.

a. Visa and MasterCard are membership corporations that consist of member banks throughout the United States and the world. They were formed to facilitate the use of their respective brand-name credit cards.

b. A *franchise tax* is a tax on the privilege of doing business in a state. An *excise tax* is a tax on an occupation, an activity, or a privilege.

IN THE LANGUAGE OF THE COURT. . .

HIGHERS, J. [Judge.]

* * * *

* * * JCPNB relies on *Bellas Hess* and *Quill*[c] to argue that [its] physical presence [in Tennessee] is required [under the commerce clause]. Commissioner [Johnson], on the other hand, argues that physical presence is not a formal requirement * * * . The fundamental flaw in the Commissioner's argument is that [current case law] does not set a different standard than that contemplated in *Bellas Hess* and *Quill.* * * *

The only real issue is whether there is any reason to distinguish the present case from *Bellas Hess* and *Quill.* The Commissioner argues that those cases are distinguishable because they involved use taxes, whereas the present case involves franchise and excise taxes. We must reject the Commissioner's argument. While it is true that the *Bellas Hess* and *Quill* decisions focused on use taxes, we find no basis for concluding that the analysis should be different in the present case. In fact, the Commissioner is unable to provide any authority as to why the analysis should be different for franchise and excise taxes. * * * As such, we feel that the outcome of this case is governed by *Bellas Hess* and *Quill* * * * .

JCPNB argues that the present case is "almost identical" to the facts in *Quill.* In many respects, that assertion is correct. JCPNB is a Delaware corporation with no offices or agents in Tennessee, just as the taxpayer in Quill had no offices or employees in North Dakota. Also, JCPNB did not physically engage in any activities in Tennessee connected with its credit card business. Similarly, *Quill* solicited business in North Dakota through catalogs, flyers, and other advertisements and delivered those goods via mail or common-carrier, thereby having no physical presence in North Dakota.

* * * *

[Johnson argued in part that JCPNB had a physical presence in Tennessee] based on "the activities of the affiliates and third parties working on JCPNB's behalf." * * *

A review of the facts of the present case convinces this court that JCPNB did not have a physical presence in Tennessee through its affiliates. Neither BSI nor MBNA actually performed any services on behalf of JCPNB in the State of Tennessee. The solicitation, which was the most important function in allowing JCPNB to maintain its business, took place through the U.S. Mail, which, under the holding in *Quill,* does not allow a finding of [physical presence]. In short, the activities which allowed JCPNB to conduct its credit card operation did not occur in the State of Tennessee.

c. The court is referring to *National Bellas Hess, Inc. v. Department of Revenue of the State of Illinois,* which was discussed previously, and *Quill Corp. v. North Dakota,* which was presented as a case earlier in this chapter.

CASE 15.2—Continued

DECISION AND REMEDY The state intermediate appellate court reversed the decision of the lower court and dismissed the case. The appellate court held that because the bank did not have a physical presence in Tennessee, the state could not impose franchise and excise taxes on it.

FOR CRITICAL ANALYSIS—Economic Consideration *What effects would the imposition of taxes on business done through Web sites have on e-commerce?*

PHYSICAL INVENTORY Typically, all retailers have to carry an inventory somewhere. A Web retailer is not any different in this respect. If the Boston-based Web retailer mentioned above stores its inventory somewhere in Massachusetts, then no additional physical nexus has been created with another taxing jurisdiction. If, in contrast, the Boston-based firm holds some or all of its inventory in a building located in New York, then New York would have taxing authority over that firm. Assume that a New York resident purchases a product on the Web from the Boston-based Web retailer. That retailer would have to collect sales taxes and remit them to the New York state government.

Software is a special case. Many software companies carry almost no inventory, for the software is simply downloaded via the Internet. There is no physical delivery of a diskette or a CD-ROM. Nonetheless, nineteen states impose sales taxes on the sale of all intangible goods sold over the Internet. That means that if the reseller of downloadable software is located in one of those nineteen states, that business has to pay sales tax on all such sales no matter where those who purchased and downloaded the software were located.

A PHYSICAL PRESENCE AT E-COMMERCE TRADE SHOWS Routinely throughout the year, there are Internet trade shows. Often, Web-based companies send representatives to such trade shows. While they are at those shows, these employees or independent sales agents take orders. Most states require the collection of sales taxes on all such orders. Some states require that the sales personnel be at the trade show for a minimum number of days. Other states have a threshold revenue level before such sales taxes must be collected. Only a good tax adviser will be able to answer any questions about state tax liabilities at trade shows.

OFFICE AND STORAGE RENTALS As with all catalogue sales companies, whenever our Boston-based retailer rents a physical office or storage facility in another state, the physical presence nexus requirement has been met for tax purposes. It is not necessary that the office be used to generate sales. It is clear that until Congress passes legislation allowing states to tax all Web-based transactions, a prospective Web retailer might want to locate in one of the five states in which no sales taxes are assessed.

SOFTWARE LICENSING A Web-based company that has developed software (as opposed to a Web retailer) may choose to lease this software to others. If the licensees are in a state with a sales tax, then the licensor may be required to collect and remit sales taxes. At issue here, of course, is when and how a taxing authority could determine that such licensing arrangements are occurring. Most such arrangements are made via the Web and the software is downloaded. Of the myriad transactions of this type that take place, very few become public knowledge and come to the attention of taxing authorities.

What if a company that leases software sends technicians into a state to install the software and/or provide technical support? Do actions such as this constitute a sufficiently substantial physical presence to uphold imposing a state tax on the technicians' employer? This question was addressed by the court in the following case.

CASE 15.3 In re Appeal of Intercard, Inc.

Kansas Supreme Court, 2000.
14 P.3d 1111.

COMPANY PROFILE *Intercard, Inc. (***http://www.intercard.com***), makes and sells electronic data cards and card readers. The system allows a customer to use a card to buy photocopies. The electronic data cards are of two types, copy cards and store cards. Copy cards are either given or sold to the buyer's customers to pay for photocopies. The buyer can give the copy cards to its customers or sell the cards. Store cards are for in-store use only. Kinko's, Inc., is Intercard's largest customer and uses Intercard's card reading system exclusively. Intercard sells its products to over four hundred Kinko's stores nationwide.*

BACKGROUND AND FACTS Intercard's headquarters, offices, and manufacturing facility are in Missouri. United Parcel Service delivers Intercard's products to its customers. To perform the electronic wiring needed to install the card readers, Intercard sends technicians to its customers' locations. Between April 1992 and April 1996, Intercard technicians made eleven visits to Kinko's stores in Kansas, under the parties' "Master Contract," which had been negotiated in California. During this time, Intercard did not send any other representatives to, or otherwise solicit business in, Kansas. In May 1996, the Kansas Department of Revenue (KDR) assessed Intercard with the state's use and sales taxes, based on the amounts billed for the technicians' work plus the card readers and other supplies bought by Intercard's Kansas customers. Intercard appealed, and the Kansas Board of Tax Appeals (BOTA) reversed KDR's assessment. KDR appealed to the Kansas Supreme Court, claiming in part that Intercard's sending technicians into Kansas was a sufficiently substantial nexus to impose the tax.

IN THE LANGUAGE OF THE COURT. . .
LOCKETT, J [Justice]:

* * * *

The purpose of the Commerce Clause of the United States Constitution is to ensure a national economy free from unjustifiable local entanglements. * * *

It is well settled that under the Commerce Clause a state may not subject a business to tax unless the business has a substantial nexus within the state. * * *

* * * *

Some state courts have minimized the concept of substantial physical presence to uphold imposition of use tax collection and duties on out-of-state companies. KDR relies on such a case to support its argument that Intercard's contacts with Kansas constitute a substantial nexus.

CASE 15.3—Continued

* * * *

In summary, the Commerce Clause requires a taxing state to have substantial nexus with an out-of-state business to impose use tax collection and remittance duties. Substantial nexus requires a finding of physical presence in the taxing state. The continuous physical presence of offices and employees in a taxing state is sufficient to impose a use tax collection duty even though the in-state presence is unrelated to the transaction being taxed. Mail-order sales without more are a "safe harbor" for out-of-state vendors. A slightest presence is not sufficient to establish a substantial nexus, but some states have found that "more than a slightest presence" is sufficient. The physical presence requirement may turn on the presence in the taxing state of a small sales force, plant, or office.

The question is whether Intercard's installation activities in the state of Kansas constitute a physical presence sufficient to establish a substantial nexus with the state. The parties stipulated that Intercard was not incorporated * * * in Kansas; all contracts and sales occurred outside of Kansas; and Intercard had no offices or employees in Kansas. BOTA found that Intercard's 11 incursions to install card readers in Kansas were isolated, sporadic, and insufficient to establish a substantial nexus to Kansas. We agree and affirm BOTA's order abating the assessed sales and use tax.

DECISION AND REMEDY The Kansas Supreme Court affirmed the decision of BOTA. Sending technicians into the state was not, alone, a sufficiently substantial nexus to support imposing use and sales taxes on Intercard.

FOR CRITICAL ANALYSIS—Economic Consideration *Considering that the amount of taxes the state tried to collect from Intercard was small, what else might the state have gained from imposing such taxes on this type of company?*

SERVER LOCATION MAY BE IMPORTANT Sometimes, online businesses use the services of an application service provider (ASP) whose servers are located in another state. So far, there is no consistent law on whether the use of a server in another state passes the physical presence nexus test for taxing purposes. To the extent that a Web-based company's servers are also located in the same state in which orders are fulfilled, the physical presence nexus requirement may be met. In any event, the law on this issue remains unsettled.

SECTION 3 CONGRESS'S FIRST RESPONSE TO TAXATION IN CYBERSPACE

The National Governors Association includes its views on the taxation of Internet sales transactions on its Web site at **http://www.nga.org**.

In the *Quill* case discussed earlier in this chapter, the United States Supreme Court stated that Congress had the authority to pass laws allowing states to tax out-of-state merchants, whether they be catalogue companies or e-commerce companies. So far, however, Congress has not done so. In fact, Congress called for a moratorium on Internet sales taxation until the federal and state governments had time to thoroughly study the consequences of such an action.

The Internet Tax Freedom Act of 1998

In 1998, Congress passed the Internet Tax Freedom Act (ITFA) in an attempt to prevent the chaos that would result from all states and localities attempting to tax e-commerce transactions. Some states had already started taxing Internet service providers (ISPs). The ITFA allowed those states to continue to tax ISPs. No other state was allowed to impose any *new* taxes on Internet transactions for a period of three years, ending October 2001. (See Appendix H at the end of this text for excerpts from this act.)

The 1998 act created the Advisory Commission on Electronic Commerce. As of the writing of this text, the commission had yet to issue a recommendation supported by a simple majority of its members.

The Complexity of the Sales Tax Structure

One of the practical problems relating to the taxation of Internet sales is that there are approximately 6,500 separate sales tax rates in the various state and local jurisdictions within the United States. If Congress allows state and local governments to impose taxes on e-commerce transactions, e-tailers will face the challenging task of calculating, collecting, and remitting sales taxes on their Internet sales.

Obviously, with enough computing power and well-staffed software departments, large e-commerce companies as well as large mail-order companies could handle this onerous task. Smaller e-commerce businesses would not fare so well. If one could hear what is being said in the halls of Congress, one would probably find out that the largest e-commerce companies are not fighting so hard against the taxation of e-commerce transactions.

Other potential problems associated with Internet taxation continue to be debated. For a discussion of some of these problems, see this chapter's *Controversial Issues* feature on the next page.

Taxing ISPs

Interestingly, George W. Bush, while still governor of Texas, signed a Texas law in 1999 that clarified an earlier tax on information services. Since 1999, a Texas sales tax applies to all Internet fees above $25 per month. Some cities, such as Dallas, add on an extra 2 percent. This tax does not affect most dial-up Internet subscribers, who pay $22 or less a month. All subscribers to higher-priced services, however, including high-speed Internet access, will pay the tax.

There are numerous online organizations encouraging and discouraging e-commerce taxation. To view a site that is against Internet taxation, go to **http://nomorenettax.com**.

By the time you read this text, Congress may have allowed all the other states to do the same. If so, large national ISPs, such as America Online (AOL), EarthLink, Prodigy, and Cox Communications, will have to develop programming to comply with the act. Smaller ISPs, of which there are literally thousands, typically will only have to remit sales taxes for just one jurisdiction or only a few jurisdictions.

SECTION 4 ONLINE TRANSACTIONS AND INCOME TAXES

INCOME TAX
A tax on personal and corporate income. Income taxes are an important source of revenue for both state governments and the federal government.

Income taxes—taxes levied on personal and corporate income—constitute another source of revenue for both state governments and the national

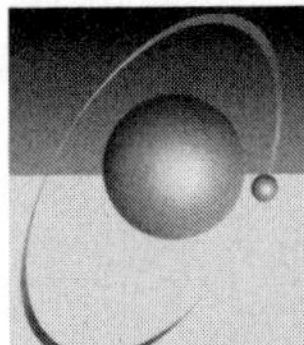

Controversial Issues in the Online World

The Ongoing Debate over Internet Taxation

The debate over the potential effects of Internet taxation on e-commerce has been taking place for some time. Today, Congress, the Advisory Commission on Electronic Commerce, state political leaders, and other groups continue to debate the pros and cons of Internet taxation.

Losses in State Revenues?

Many political leaders at the state level have pushed for Internet sales taxes to prevent revenue losses. They argue that the states are losing billions of dollars a year in taxes on mail-order and Internet purchases. The National Governors Association, for example, predicted that states are due to lose $20 billion a year in sales tax revenues as a result of the increase in Internet sales. The governors' dire predictions have yet to come true, however. Of course, to counter such an assertion, one can argue that virtually any retailer can open a Web store at very little cost.

Keep the Internet Growing, Say Others

Quite a few politicians at the federal level, however, have argued in favor of keeping the Internet tax free. For one thing, they claim, because of the complexity of the sales tax structure throughout the United States, taxing Internet sales would be extremely difficult. They also worry that excessive taxation in the online world will reduce the rate of growth of e-commerce. Finally, issues of fairness are involved.

Many coalitions of online companies share this view. They have lobbied in favor of keeping the moratorium on taxing Internet sales. Proponents of a tax-free Internet point out that, in spite of the National Governors Association's predictions, sales tax revenues went up, not down, in 2000; they increased by 7.3 percent. Personal income tax revenues for the states increased by 12.4 percent and corporate income tax revenues increased by 4 percent. In other words, there has been a positive correlation between the growth in e-retailing and the growth in state sales tax revenues.

Fairness Issues

Many, if not most, arguments in favor of imposing sales taxes on e-commerce revolve around issues of fairness. As discussed elsewhere, Internet taxation might unfairly discriminate against the welfare of small e-commerce companies that would find it more difficult than larger online businesses to calculate, collect, and submit the thousands and thousands of sales taxes in various jurisdictions. State governors claim that it is unfair not to allow them to tax e-commerce transactions, because they need to raise revenues if they are going to govern effectively.

Yet another important question is this: Is it fair to require retailers in a shopping mall to charge sales taxes and not require retailers on the Internet to do likewise? Clearly, looking at the price factor only, the differential final price of the same product gives a competitive advantage to Internet merchants. These and other fairness issues will likely continue to dominate the debate over whether to tax e-commerce.

FOR CRITICAL ANALYSIS

In determining whether to tax Internet sales, what factor should carry the most weight—practical concerns, fairness issues, or the policy encouraging e-commerce? What priority should each of these factors be given relative to the others?

government. These taxes are a greater source of revenue for governments, particularly the national government, than sales taxes. Yet governments must first know where income is earned before they can tax it. In addition, governments must have authority over activities in the locations where income is earned.

Even simple sales transactions are often hard to trace in the expanding world of e-commerce. If a U.S. customer orders a product from a Peruvian company with a Guatemalan factory and uses funds in an offshore bank to pay for the purchase, the transaction becomes difficult, if not impossible, to tax. Where did the transaction actually take place? Where was the product ordered? As more corporations spread to multiple locations throughout the world and as communications and encryption become increasingly sophisticated, multinational e-commerce transactions will become commonplace and even more complicated than they are now. Locating the point at which a transaction actually occurs or the source of corporate income will become more and more difficult as e-commerce continues to expand.

On the Web

You can find a state-by-state summary of Internet taxation at **http://www.vertexinc.com/taxcybrary20/CyberTax_Channel/taxchannel_70.asp**.

How to Source Income in the World of Cyberspace

As the above example points out, with the Internet it is difficult to use traditional sourcing rules to link income with a specific geographic location. Taxation based on a person's physical residence may be easier. The Internal Revenue Service (IRS), though, has not yet changed its income sourcing rules. Moreover, even if it does, the IRS will find it difficult to assess income taxes on those who are not U.S. citizens, permanent visa holders, or physically in the United States.

Can the Presence of a Server Create an Income Tax Nexus?

Some have argued that anyone in the world using a server located in the United States should be treated as generating income in the United States. The problem is that a server can be located anywhere on the globe. The user is indifferent to its location; it is simply an instrument for business. Any time U.S. tax authorities attempt to assess taxes on income generated by the use of servers within the United States, foreigners will simply use servers outside the United States. Clearly, foreigners can utilize U.S.-based servers without having any employees in the United States. Under the current federal tax code, facilities used solely for storage, display, or delivery of goods do not constitute a permanent business establishment in this country. Therefore, the use of servers would not alter this categorization.

Tax Havens and the Collection of Income Taxes

Web-based companies selling digitized photos, videos, software, and the like may locate in one of many offshore tax havens. These tax havens, by definition, have strict banking privacy laws and strong debtor protection laws. Many have more than adequate telecommunications systems. U.S. citizens, permanent residents, and others legally subject to U.S. income taxation may evade such income taxes by operating out of tax havens. Of course, the same can be said for those engaged in activities that do not involve e-commerce. Those using the Internet, however, have the ability to keep their income-producing activities more secret than if they were engaging in "old-economy" commerce.[10]

---

10. Income earned offshore is subject to the existing rules of subpart F of the Internal Revenue Code. Foreign-based income is defined in Internal Revenue Code Section 954. Internal Revenue Code Sections 951(a)(1) and 952(a)(2) imposed income taxes on the ratable portion of foreign-based company income for every U.S. shareholder, including corporations of a controlled foreign corporation.

Digital Money and Tax Evasion

Electronic payment systems, including digital cash and electronic money, are beginning to be used, and make the U.S. taxing authorities' jobs harder. By its very nature, electronic money clouds the identity of the parties to each transaction; that is, all transactions that take place outside normal banking channels are more difficult to trace than traditional transactions. Whenever electronic money is used as a way to deposit unreported income in offshore financial institutions, the IRS and the U.S. Treasury have an even harder time than usual collecting income taxes and catching tax evaders.

Already, it is possible to open an account online in a bank in a well-known tax haven, Antigua. Banks there offer numbered accounts, international wire transfers, time deposit accounts, and multicurrency accounts. Antigua has very strong bank secrecy and confidentiality laws.

All U.S. citizens and permanent residents are subject to income taxation on worldwide income. Nonetheless, given the existence of such tax havens as Antigua, along with the ease of using the Internet without such transactions being traceable, there now exists an increased potential for tax evasion. To the extent that *electronic* cash is used in an unaccounted manner—no records—it is equivalent to cash, for which there is no "paper trail."

Life for U.S. tax collectors is definitely going to become more difficult in the future.

SECTION 5 TAX FILING ONLINE

While the above discussion seems to indicate that state and federal taxing authorities are losing out because of the Internet, they are also gaining. At both the state and federal levels, taxpayers can now file their tax returns electronically. Almost half of the states offer e-filing.

Filing State Tax Returns Online

As of 2001, nineteen states had Web sites for tax filing. These states are listed in Exhibit 15–1. By the time you read this text, most of the forty-two states that levy income taxes will probably also provide free direct e-filing. It was only in 1998 that the first states began testing free, direct Internet filing. At first, a few required filing through private software companies. Today, in contrast, millions of Americans are filing their state income tax returns on the Web.

Prior to that, private software companies provided, for a fee, online filing for their customers. What has changed is that the states themselves are paying for the implicit software programs used for online filing.

Numerous online companies now provide, for a fee, electronic tax-filing services. One such site, hosted by USA Internet Tax Services, Inc., is online at **http://www.usaefile.com**.

Federal Income Tax Filing Online

In 2001, almost nine million self-preparers filed their federal income tax returns electronically. That represented an almost 100 percent increase from the previous year. The IRS has made the process more appealing by creating an electronic "signature" system. Online filers can select their own five-digit personal ID numbers and then "sign" their electronically filed returns. In order to authenti-

Exhibit 15–1 States Having Web Sites for Tax Filing as of 2001

Arkansas	Michigan
Colorado	Missouri
Delaware	Montana
Iowa	New Mexico
Illinois	Pennsylvania
Indiana	South Carolina
Louisiana	Vermont
Maine	Virginia
Maryland	Wisconsin
Massachusetts	

cate such online-filed returns, the filer has to provide adjusted gross income and a tax amount from the previous year's filed return. The filer must also pay a "tax payment convenience fee" to file tax returns electronically. Of course, some individuals do not wish to file electronically because they are worried about transmitting tax information over the Internet.

At one point, IRS Commissioner Charles Rossotti told Congress that the IRS should leave electronic preparation and the filing of federal returns to private software companies. In any event, there are a growing number of tax software programs that allow you to create your own returns and to file them electronically. These programs include KiplingerTaxCut, CompleteTax, H.D.Vest, PrepTax.com, TaxACT, and Quicken TurboTax.

TERMS AND CONCEPTS

commerce clause 363
federal form of government 362
income taxes 373
nexus 365
police powers 364
sales taxes 362

QUESTIONS AND CASE PROBLEMS

15–1. State Taxes. American Software Corporation has an office in Florida. American sells its products only through its Web site. Applied Business Systems, Inc., which is located in New York, buys an American product and, like all of American's customers, obtains the software by downloading it over the Internet. American provides technical support only over the phone. Once a year, American sends sale representatives to the Software Makers Trade Convention in New York City. Manhattan Services Company buys an American product from its representative at the convention. If the state of New York attempts to impose state taxes on American for the sale of the software to Applied Business Systems, what is American's best argument that it does not have to pay? What is New York's best argument that American has to pay tax on the sale to Manhattan Services?

15–2. Nexus. National Sporting Goods, Inc., sells its products to customers throughout the United States only through its Web site. National Sporting Goods owns a warehouse in Colorado, from which it ships its products, but

Omega Web Hosting Corporation, whose servers are located in California, maintains the Web site. Can California require National Sporting Goods to collect and pay taxes to California on all of its sales? Would it make any difference if National Sporting Goods's warehouse and Omega's servers were both located in California? Explain.

15–3. Independent Sales Representatives. Apex Networking Systems Corporation's headquarters, offices, and other facilities are located in California. Apex, which has sold its products exclusively through its Web site, believes that Texas would be a good market in which to begin in-person marketing. For this purpose, Apex hires independent sales representatives to "test the waters" for Apex's products in central Texas. Can Texas require Apex to collect and remit taxes on any of the representatives' sales in the state? Why or why not?

15–4. Software. B2B Management Products, Inc., markets software products only through its Web site. B2B leases the software to its customers, who download the programs from the site. B2B provides technical support only over the phone. B2B has no physical presence in Massachusetts, but many of B2B's customers are located there. Can Massachusetts successfully require B2B to collect and pay taxes on the transactions with its licensees located in that state?

15–5. Certificate of Authority. Bandag Licensing Corp. (BLC), which owns and licenses patents, is located in Iowa. The state of Texas has issued BLC a certificate of authority to do business in Texas, but the company does not own, possess, use, or maintain any property in that state. BLC does not have, and has never had, salespersons, employees, independent contractors, or any representatives in Texas. BLC does not have franchises in Texas, does not distribute goods or services in Texas, and does not transact any business in Texas. Based solely on the certificate of authority, Carolyn Rylander, the Texas Comptroller of Public Accounts, imposed a franchise tax on BLC. BLC paid the tax but filed a suit in a Texas state court against Rylander, asking for a refund. The court granted BLC's request, and Rylander appealed to a state intermediate appellate court. What are the respective parties' best arguments in favor of, and against, the refund? Explain fully. [*Rylander v. Bandag Licensing Corp.*, 18 S.W.3d 296 (Tex.App.—Austin 2000)]

15–6. Buyer's Location. TA Operating Corp. (TA) is a nationwide operator of truck stops, but does not own or operate any truck stops in Florida, does not have any personnel in that state, and has not made any sales there. A common carrier picked up diesel fuel in Jacksonville, Florida, for delivery to TA. Title to the fuel passed in Jacksonville. Amerada Hess, Inc., the Florida seller, collected a tax on the fuel of more than $1.3 million and remitted it to the Florida Department of Revenue (FDOR). In collecting the tax, Amerada passed the cost on to TA, which asked the FDOR for a refund. When the FDOR refused, TA filed a suit in a Florida state court against the state agency, arguing, among other things, that there was not a substantial nexus between TA and Florida. The court issued a summary judgment against TA, which appealed to a state intermediate appellate court. Will that court order a refund? Explain. [*TA Operating Corp. v. State, Dept. of Revenue,* 767 So.2d 1270 (Fla.App. 1 Dist. 2000)]

15–7. Delivery and Installation. Town Crier, Inc., is located in Lake Geneva, Wisconsin, where it sells furniture, carpeting, artwork, and window dressings. Lake Geneva is a resort community that is heavily populated by Illinois residents who maintain second homes there. Town Crier does not own property in Illinois, or have employees or independent contractors who solicit orders in Illinois. Over half of the firm's sales, however, consist of goods delivered in its trucks into Illinois. Town Crier also installs its window treatments in that state on request. When the Illinois Department of Revenue assessed Town Crier with use taxes covering those sales and installations, the firm filed a complaint in an Illinois state court against IDR, alleging that the firm did not have a nexus with the state. IDR filed a motion for summary judgment, which the court granted, and Town Crier appealed to a state intermediate appellate court. Should the court affirm the summary judgment? Why or why not? [*Town Crier, Inc. v. Department of Revenue,* 733 N.E.2d 780 (Ill.App. 1 Dist. 2000)]

WEB EXERCISES

Go to **http://lec.westbuslaw.com**, the Web site that accompanies this text. Select "Internet Applications," and then click on "Chapter 15." There you will find the following Internet research exercise that you can perform to learn more about taxation in cyberspace:

Exercise 15–1: Taxation in Cyberspace

CHAPTER 16

Auditing, Accounting, and Professional Liability

Concepts Covered

After reading this chapter, you should be able to:

1. Summarize areas in which professionals may be liable under the common law.
2. Outline the potential civil and criminal liability of accountants under various laws.
3. Identify professionals' privileges concerning working papers.
4. Explain what protection exists for professional-client communications.
5. Discuss professionals' responsibilities with respect to financial institutions' privacy obligations to their online customers.

> **"A member should observe the profession's technical and ethical standards, strive continually to improve competence and the quality of services, and discharge professional responsibility to the best of the member's ability."**
>
> Article V, *Code of Professional Conduct*, American Institute of Certified Public Accountants

Professionals such as accountants, attorneys, physicians, architects, and others are increasingly faced with the threat of liability. Perhaps the reason is a greater public awareness of the fact that professionals are required to deliver competent services and are obligated to adhere to standards of performance commonly accepted within their professions.

Considering the many potential sources of legal liability that may be imposed on them, accountants, attorneys, and other professionals should be well aware of their legal obligations. In the first part of this chapter, we look at the potential liability of professionals under the common law and then examine the potential liability of accountants under securities laws and the Internal Revenue Code. The chapter concludes with a brief examination of other topics of concern for professionals, including rights to working papers, professional-client privilege, and the increasing use of the limited liability partnership by accountants and other professionals to limit their tort liability.

SECTION 1 COMMON LAW LIABILITY

Under the common law, professionals may be held liable for breach of contract, negligence, or fraud.

For information on the accounting profession, including articles from the *Journal of Accountancy*, go to the Web site for the American Institute of Certified Public Accountants (AICPA) at **http://www.aicpa.org/index.htm**.

Liability for Breach of Contract

Accountants and other professionals face liability for any breach of contract under the common law. A professional owes a duty to his or her client to honor the terms of the contract and to perform the contract within the stated time period. If the professional fails to perform as agreed in the contract, then he or she has breached the contract, and the client has the right to recover damages from the professional. A professional may be held liable for expenses incurred by his or her client in securing another professional to provide the contracted-for services, for penalties imposed on the client for failure to meet time deadlines, and for any other reasonable and foreseeable monetary losses that arise from the professional's breach.

Liability for Negligence

Accountants and other professionals may also be held liable under the common law for negligence in the performance of their services. As with any negligence claim, the elements that must be proved to establish negligence on the part of a professional are as follows:

1. A duty of care existed.
2. That duty of care was breached.
3. The plaintiff suffered an injury.
4. The injury was proximately caused by the defendant's breach of the duty of care.

All professionals are subject to standards of conduct established by codes of professional standards and ethics, by state statutes, and by judicial decisions. They are also governed by the contracts into which they enter with their clients. In their performance of contracts, professionals must exercise the established standard of care, knowledge, and judgment generally accepted by members of their particular professional group. We now look at the duty of care owed by two groups of professionals that frequently perform services for business firms: accountants and attorneys.

ACCOUNTANT'S DUTY OF CARE Accountants play a major role in a business's financial system. Accountants have the necessary expertise and experience in establishing and maintaining accurate financial records to design, control, and audit record-keeping systems; to prepare reliable statements that reflect an individual's or a business's financial status; and to give tax advice and prepare tax returns.

An *audit* is a systematic inspection, by analyses and tests, of a business's financial records. The purpose of an audit is to provide the auditor with evidence to support an opinion on the fairness of the business's financial statements. A normal audit is not intended to uncover fraud or other misconduct. An accountant may be liable for failing to detect misconduct, however, if a normal audit would have revealed it or the auditor agreed to examine the records for evidence of fraud or other wrongdoing.

After performing an audit, the auditor issues an opinion letter stating whether, in his or her opinion, the financial statements fairly present the business's financial position. The opinion letter is said to certify the financial statements. Normally, an auditor issues an *unqualified opinion,* which means that the audit and the financial statements comply with the principles and standards discussed in the next section.

Standard of Care. Generally, an accountant must possess the skills that an ordinarily prudent accountant would have and must exercise the degree of care that an ordinarily prudent accountant would exercise. The level of skill expected of accountants and the degree of care that they should exercise in performing their services are reflected in what are known as **generally accepted accounting principles (GAAP)** and **generally accepted auditing standards (GAAS).** The Financial Accounting Standards Board (FASB, usually pronounced "faz-bee") determines what accounting conventions, rules, and procedures constitute GAAP at a given point in time. GAAS are standards concerning an auditor's professional qualities and the judgment that he or she exercises in auditing financial records. GAAS are established by the American Institute of Certified Public Accountants. GAAP and GAAS are also reflected in the rules established by the Securities and Exchange Commission.

As long as an accountant conforms to GAAP and acts in good faith, he or she normally will not be held liable for incorrect judgment. As mentioned above, an accountant is not required to discover every impropriety, **defalcation**[1] (embezzlement), or fraud in a client's books. If, however, the impropriety, defalcation, or fraud has gone undiscovered because of an accountant's negligence or failure to perform an express or implied duty, the accountant will be liable for any resulting losses suffered by the client and, in some cases, by third parties. Therefore, an accountant who uncovers suspicious financial transactions and fails to investigate the matter fully or to inform his or her client of the discovery can be held liable for the resulting loss.

A violation of GAAP and GAAS will be considered *prima facie* evidence of negligence on the part of the accountant. Compliance with GAAP and GAAS, however, does not necessarily relieve an accountant from potential legal liability. An accountant may be held to a higher standard of conduct established by state statute and by judicial decisions. If an accountant is found to have been negligent in the performance of accounting services, the client and, in some cases, third parties may collect damages for any losses that arose from the accountant's negligence.

Defenses to Negligence. Accountants have several defenses available. Possible defenses include the following allegations:

1. The accountant was not negligent.

2. If the accountant was negligent, this negligence was not the proximate cause of the client's losses.

3. The client was also negligent (depending on whether state law allows contributory negligence or comparative negligence as a defense—see Chapter 4).

GENERALLY ACCEPTED ACCOUNTING PRINCIPLES (GAAP)
The conventions, rules, and procedures necessary to define accepted accounting practices at a particular time. The source of the principles is the Federal Accounting Standards Board.

GENERALLY ACCEPTED AUDITING STANDARDS (GAAS)
Standards concerning an auditor's professional qualities and the judgment exercised by him or her in the performance of an examination and report. The source of the standards is the American Institute of Certified Public Accountants.

DEFALCATION
The misappropriation of funds or property.

On the Web

The mission of the Financial Accounting Standards Board is "to establish and improve standards of financial accounting and reporting for the guidance and education of the public, including issuers, auditors, and users of financial information," according to its Web site, which can be found at **http://www.rutgers.edu/Accounting/raw/fasb**.

1. This term, pronounced deh-ful-*kay*-shun, is derived from the Latin *de* ("off") and *falx* ("sickle"—a tool for cutting grain or tall grass). In law, the term refers to the act of a defaulter or of an embezzler. As used here, it means embezzlement.

In the following case, it was clear that the accountants had been less than accurate in their audits. The accountants' defense to a charge of negligent misrepresentation, however, was that their audits had not been the cause of the plaintiff investors' losses.

CASE 16.1 AUSA Life Insurance Co. v. Ernst and Young

United States Court of Appeals, Second Circuit, 2000.
206 F.3d 202.
https://www.tourolaw.edu/2ndCircuit/March00/[a]

HISTORICAL AND ECONOMIC SETTING *During the early 1990s, the retail computer market experienced a period of intense competition. The market was a battleground for what has been called the "PC price wars." Computer retailers relied on rapidly evolving product innovation, intuition as to which standard features customers would want, and cost-cutting marketing strategies to capture market share. Brick-and-mortar operations such as Businessland, Inc., and ComputerLand, Inc., found themselves losing ground to mail-order companies such as Dell Computer Corporation and Gateway 2000, Inc.*

BACKGROUND AND FACTS AUSA Life Insurance Company and others invested $149 million in notes issued by JWP, Inc. The notes were subject to "Note Agreements," which required JWP's independent auditor, the accounting firm of Ernst & Young (E&Y), to adhere to GAAP in auditing JWP's financial health. E&Y uncovered misrepresentations in the course of its audits, but JWP's chief executive officer, Ernest Grendi, persuaded or bullied E&Y into concealing them. Meanwhile, JWP expanded rapidly, using the investors' money to buy other firms. One of these firms was Businessland, Inc., a retailer of computers and a supplier of software. Businessland, which had lost an average of $10 million a month over the previous ten months, was a fatally costly acquisition. David Sokol, JWP's chief operating officer, hired Deloitte & Touche (D&T), another accounting firm, to review JWP's books and E&Y's audits. Based on this review, JWP's reports for the previous three years were restated to show losses of more than $500 million and a net worth of negative $176 million. JWP defaulted on the notes, and the investors lost about $100 million. AUSA and the others filed a suit in a federal district court against E&Y, claiming, in part, negligent misrepresentation. The court concluded that E&Y had been negligent but that the proximate cause of JWP's default on the notes was its acquisition of Businessland. The court issued a judgment in favor of E&Y, and the plaintiffs appealed to the U.S. Court of Appeals for the Second Circuit.

a. Touro College Jacob D. Fuchsberg Law Center in Huntington, New York, maintains this Web site for the U.S Court of Appeals for the Second Circuit. On this page, scroll to the title of the case and click on it to access the opinion.

IN THE LANGUAGE OF THE COURT. . .
OAKES, Senior Circuit Judge:

* * * *

* * * JWP was in default on its notes because it was in violation of the financial covenants in the Note Agreements. E&Y knew of these violations, but assisted in concealing them. This default could have allowed the plaintiffs to accelerate the due date on the notes. Accurate accounting, auditing, and reporting would have at least made the plaintiffs aware of the default and precarious financial position of JWP * * * . JWP was in default on its notes prior to its acquisition of Businessland, and the investors would have known of such had E&Y correctly performed [its] duties.

True, * * * JWP would not have defaulted on its debt obligations but for its acquisition of Businessland, which turned out to be a veritable sinkhole for cash. But had JWP's financial situation been accurately represented by E&Y, and had E&Y revealed the undisputed GAAP violations, JWP would have been in default on its notes prior to its acquisition of Businessland. Therefore, the acquisition of Businessland could not have taken place without a cure of the default or the investors' waivers of the default.

* * * *

* * * [T]he question is "did the fraud actually accomplish the result it was intended to achieve," [and] the answer is yes: E&Y certified financial statements that induced the investors not to abandon JWP. * * *

* * * *

The United States financial market is phenomenal. It can make poor people rich and rich people poor, it gives the United States international power, and it is a continual source of awe. While there is huge risk when dealing with the market, our legislators have consistently tried to at least ensure that the relevant information is conveyed accurately to those who want to assume the risk of jumping into the financial pool. Given that such a policy increases investor confidence, allows money to flow both in and out of the market in an honest way, and assists investors in maximizing their participation in the American economy, it is likely that this policy will endure. To this end, while we are far from holding auditors generally and absolutely liable to the investing public at large, the information publicly available to these market participants and certified as accurate needs to be just that.

DECISION AND REMEDY The U.S. Court of Appeals for the Second Circuit reversed the lower court's judgment and remanded the case. The appellate court reasoned that E&Y's concealment of JWP's true financial situation prevented the investors from taking appropriate action, ultimately causing the investors' losses.

FOR CRITICAL ANALYSIS–Economic Consideration *What might an accountant hope to gain by concealing a client's misrepresentation?*

Qualified Opinions and Disclaimers. In issuing an opinion letter, an auditor may qualify the opinion or include a disclaimer. An auditor will not be held liable for damages resulting from whatever is qualified or disclaimed. An opinion that disclaims any liability for false or misleading financial statements is too general, however. A qualified opinion or a disclaimer must be specific. For example, an auditor might qualify an opinion, in an audit of a corporation, by stating that there is uncertainty about how a lawsuit against the firm will be resolved. The auditor will not be liable if the result of the suit is bad for the firm. The auditor could still be liable, however, for failing to discover other problems that an audit in compliance with GAAS and GAAP would have revealed.

Unaudited Financial Statements. Sometimes accountants are hired to prepare unaudited financial statements. (A financial statement is considered unaudited if no auditing procedures have been used in its preparation or if insufficient procedures have been used to justify an opinion.) Accountants may be subject to liability for failing, in accordance with standard accounting procedures, to designate a balance sheet as "unaudited." An accountant will also be held liable for failure to disclose to a client facts or circumstances that create reason to believe that misstatements have been made or that a fraud has been committed.

ATTORNEY'S DUTY OF CARE The conduct of attorneys is governed by rules established by each state and by the American Bar Association's Model Rules of Professional Conduct. All attorneys owe a duty to provide competent and diligent representation. Attorneys are required to be familiar with well-settled principles of law applicable to a case and to discover law that can be found through a reasonable amount of research. The lawyer also must investigate and discover facts that could materially affect the client's legal rights.

Standard of Care. In judging an attorney's performance, the standard used will normally be that of a reasonably competent general practitioner of ordinary skill, experience, and capacity. If an attorney holds himself or herself out as having expertise in a special area of law (for example, domestic relations), the attorney's standard of care in that area is higher than for attorneys without such expertise.

Liability for Malpractice. When an attorney fails to exercise reasonable care and professional judgment, he or she breaches the duty of care and can be held liable for *malpractice* (professional negligence). In malpractice cases—as in all cases involving allegations of negligence—the plaintiff must prove that the attorney's breach of the duty of care actually caused the plaintiff to suffer some injury. For example, if the attorney allows the statute of limitations to lapse on a client's claim, he or she can be held liable for malpractice because the client can no longer file a cause of action in this case and has lost a potential award of damages.

Traditionally, to establish causation, the client normally had to show that "but for" the attorney's negligence, the client would not have suffered the injury. In recent years, however, several courts have held that plaintiffs in malpractice cases need only show that the defendant's negligence was a "substantial factor" in causing the plaintiff's injury. In the following case, the Supreme Court of New Jersey addressed the issue of what standard should be applied in determining whether an attorney's malpractice was the proximate cause of the plaintiffs' injuries.

CASE 16.2 Conklin v. Hannoch Weisman

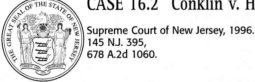

Supreme Court of New Jersey, 1996.
145 N.J. 395,
678 A.2d 1060.

BACKGROUND AND FACTS The Conklins hired the law firm of Hannoch Weisman, Professional Corporation, to represent them in a sale of one hundred acres of their farm to Longview Estates. The purchase price of the land was $12 million. Longview made a $3 million down payment and gave the Conklins a mortgage for the balance. The mortgage, however, was subordinate (second in priority) to a mortgage held by another lender: if Longview defaulted on its payments, the other lender would be paid first. When Longview defaulted, the other lender took the land, and the Conklins got nothing. They filed a suit in a New Jersey state court against Hannoch Weisman, claiming that the firm had not explained completely the risks of a subordinate mortgage. The jury was charged (instructed) to hold the firm liable only if the Conklins proved that their loss would not have occurred "but for" the firm's negligence. The jury issued a verdict in favor of the law firm, but the judge decided that the jury charge had been unclear and ordered a new trial. Hannoch Weisman appealed. The intermediate state appellate court affirmed the order of the trial judge (calling for a new trial), and the law firm appealed to the Supreme Court of New Jersey.

IN THE LANGUAGE OF THE COURT. . .
O'HERN, [Justice].

* * * *

In reality, there is usually no such thing as a risk-free deal. The best that a lawyer can do is to control the risks to help the clients to achieve their financial objectives. * * * Through advice and negotiating the terms of the contract, the parties and their lawyers control the risks of the deal. The Conklins wanted a specific price—twelve million dollars. They made a poor deal and sustained a grave loss. The question is whether the lack of adequate advice was a substantial factor in causing the Conklins' exposure to an unwanted risk of harm.

* * * *

* * * [T]he jury charge * * * could have confused the jury and led to an unjust result * * *. [T]he traditional jury charge [in which liability is subject to the "but for" test] * * * is inapt [inappropriate] for legal malpractice cases in which there are concurrent independent causes of harm and * * * a jury in such cases must be instructed to determine whether the negligence was a substantial factor in bringing about the ultimate harm.

DECISION AND REMEDY The Supreme Court of New Jersey affirmed the judgment of the lower court. A new trial should be held because the jury was given erroneous instructions in the applicable law. The law in New Jersey (and other states) provides that to recover in a legal malpractice case, a plaintiff needs to show only that the lawyer's negligence was a "substantial factor" in causing the harm.

FOR CRITICAL ANALYSIS–Social Consideration *Should lawyers be subject to higher legal and ethical standards than other professionals?*

Liability for Fraud

Fraud, or misrepresentation, consists of the following elements:

1. A misrepresentation of a material fact has occurred.
2. There exists an intent to deceive.
3. The innocent party has justifiably relied on the misrepresentation.
4. For damages, the innocent party must have been injured.

A professional may be held liable for *actual* fraud when he or she intentionally misstates a material fact to mislead his or her client and the client justifiably relies on the misstated fact to his or her injury. A material fact is one that a reasonable person would consider important in deciding whether to act.

In contrast, a professional may be held liable for *constructive* fraud whether or not he or she acted with fraudulent intent. For example, constructive fraud may be found when an accountant is grossly negligent in the performance of his or her duties. The intentional failure to perform a duty with reckless disregard of the consequences of such a failure would constitute gross negligence on the part of a professional.

The Privity Requirement

Traditionally, an accountant or other professional only owed a duty to those with whom he or she was in *privity of contract.* (Privity of contract refers to the relationship that exists between the promisor and the promisee of a contract.) In other words, a professional owed no duty to a third party outside the contractual relationship—a professional's duty was only to his or her client. Violations of statutory laws, fraud, and other intentional or reckless acts of wrongdoing were the only exceptions to this general rule.

Today, numerous third parties—including investors, shareholders, creditors, corporate managers and directors, regulatory agencies, and others—rely on the opinions of auditors (accountants) when making decisions. In view of this extensive reliance, many courts have all but abandoned the privity requirement in regard to accountants' liability to third parties. Like accountants, attorneys may be held liable under the common law to third parties who rely on legal opinions to their detriment. Generally, however, an attorney is not liable to a nonclient unless there is fraud (or malicious conduct) by the attorney. The liability principles stated in Section 552 of the *Restatement (Second) of Torts* (these principles will be discussed shortly), however, may apply to attorneys just as they apply to accountants.

Understanding an auditor's common law liability to third parties is critical, because when a business fails, its independent auditor may be one of the few potentially solvent defendants. The majority of courts now hold that auditors can be held liable to third parties for negligence, but the standard for the imposition of this liability varies. There are generally three different views of accountants' liability to third parties. These views, which we discuss next, can be summarized as follows:

1. Accountants should be liable only to those with whom they are in privity or "near privity" of contract (the *Ultramares* rule).

2. Accountants should be liable to foreseen, or known, users of their reports or financial statements (the *Restatement* rule).

3. Accountants should be liable to those whose use of their reports or financial statements is reasonably foreseeable.

THE *ULTRAMARES* RULE The traditional rule regarding an accountant's liability to third parties was enunciated by Chief Judge Benjamin Cardozo in *Ultramares Corp. v. Touche,*[2] a case decided in 1931. In *Ultramares,* Fred Stern & Company (Stern) hired the public accounting firm of Touche, Niven & Company (Touche) to review Stern's financial records and prepare a balance sheet for the year ending December 31, 1923.[3] Touche prepared the balance

2. 255 N.Y. 170, 174 N.E. 441 (1931).

3. Banks, creditors, stockholders, purchasers, and sellers often rely on balance sheets when making decisions relating to a company's business.

sheet and supplied Stern with thirty-two certified copies. According to the certified balance sheet, Stern had a net worth (assets less liabilities) of $1,070,715.26. In reality, however, Stern was insolvent—the company's records had been falsified by insiders at Stern to reflect a positive net worth. In reliance on the certified balance sheets, a lender, Ultramares Corporation, loaned substantial amounts to Stern. After Stern was declared bankrupt, Ultramares brought an action against Touche for negligence in an attempt to recover damages.

The New York Court of Appeals (that state's highest court) refused to impose liability on the accountants and concluded that they owed a duty of care only to those persons for whose "primary benefit" the statements were intended. In this case, Stern was the only one for whose primary benefit the statements were intended. The court held that in the absence of privity or a relationship "so close as to approach that of privity," a party could not recover from an accountant.

The court's requirement of privity has since been referred to as the *Ultramares* rule, or the New York rule. The rule was restated and somewhat modified in a 1985 New York case, *Credit Alliance Corp. v. Arthur Andersen & Co.*[4] In that case, the court held that if a third party has a sufficiently close relationship or nexus (link or connection) with an accountant, the *Ultramares* privity requirement may be satisfied without the establishment of an accountant-client relationship. The rule enunciated in *Credit Alliance* is often referred to as the "near privity" rule. Only a minority of states have adopted this rule of accountants' liability to third parties.

THE *RESTATEMENT* RULE Auditors perform much of their work for use by persons who are not parties to the contract; thus, it is asserted that they owe a duty to these third parties. Consequently, there has been an erosion of the *Ultramares* rule, and accountants have increasingly been exposed to potential liability to third parties.

The majority of courts have adopted the position taken by the *Restatement (Second) of Torts,* which states that accountants are subject to liability for negligence not only to their clients but also to foreseen, or *known,* users—or classes of users—of their reports or financial statements. Under Section 552(2) of the *Restatement (Second) of Torts,* an accountant's liability extends to those persons for whose benefit and guidance the accountant "intends to supply the information or knows that the recipient intends to supply it" and to those persons whom the accountant "intends the information to influence or knows that the recipient so intends." In other words, if an accountant prepares a financial statement for a client and knows that the client will submit that statement to a bank to secure a loan, the accountant may be held liable to the bank for negligent misstatements or omissions—because the accountant knew that the bank would rely on the accountant's work product when deciding whether to make the loan.

LIABILITY TO REASONABLY FORESEEABLE USERS A small minority of courts hold accountants liable to any users whose reliance on an accountant's statements or reports was *reasonably foreseeable.* This standard has been criticized as

4. 65 N.Y.2d 536, 483 N.E.2d 110 (1985): A "relationship sufficiently intimate to be equated with privity" is sufficient for a third party to sue another's accountant for negligence.

extending liability too far. In *Raritan River Steel Co. v. Cherry, Bekaert & Holland,*[5] for example, the North Carolina Supreme Court stated that "in fairness accountants should not be liable in circumstances where they are unaware of the use to which their opinions will be put. Instead, their liability should be commensurate with those persons or classes of persons whom they know will rely on their work. With such knowledge the auditor can, through purchase of liability insurance, setting fees, and adopting other protective measures appropriate to the risk, prepare accordingly."

The North Carolina court's statement echoes the view of the majority of the courts that the *Restatement's* approach is the more reasonable one because it allows accountants to control their exposure to liability. Liability is "fixed by the accountants' particular knowledge at the moment the audit is published," not by the foreseeability of the harm that might occur to a third party after the report is released.[6]

Even the California courts, which for years had relied on reasonable foreseeability as the standard for determining an auditor's liability to third parties, have changed their position. In a 1992 case, the California Supreme Court held that an accountant "owes no general duty of care regarding the conduct of an audit to persons other than the client." The court went on to say that if third parties rely on an auditor's opinion, "there is no liability even though the [auditor] should reasonably have foreseen such a possibility."[7]

SECTION 2 LIABILITY OF ACCOUNTANTS UNDER SECURITIES LAWS

Both civil and criminal liability may be imposed on accountants under the Securities Act of 1933, the Securities Exchange Act of 1934, and the Private Securities Litigation Reform Act of 1995.[8]

Liability under the Securities Act of 1933

The Securities Act of 1933 requires registration statements to be filed with the Securities and Exchange Commission (SEC) prior to an offering of securities.[9] Accountants frequently prepare and certify the issuer's financial statements that are included in the registration statement.

LIABILITY UNDER SECTION 11 Section 11 of the Securities Act of 1933 imposes civil liability on accountants for misstatements and omissions of material facts in registration statements. An accountant may be held liable if he or

5. 322 N.C. 200, 367 S.E.2d 609 (1988).

6. *Bethlehem Steel Corp. v. Ernst & Whinney,* 822 S.W.2d 592 (Tenn. 1991).

7. *Bily v. Arthur Young & Co.,* 3 Cal.4th 370, 834 P.2d 745, 11 Cal.Rptr.2d 51 (1992).

8. Civil and criminal liability may be imposed on accountants and other professionals under other statutes, including the Racketeer Influenced and Corrupt Organizations Act (RICO), 18 U.S.C. Sections 1961–1968.

9. Many securities and transactions are expressly exempted from the 1933 act.

she prepared any financial statements included in the registration statement that "contained an untrue statement of a material fact or omitted to state a material fact required to be stated therein or necessary to make the statements therein not misleading."[10]

Liability to Purchasers of Securities. An accountant may be liable to anyone who acquires a security covered by the registration statement. A purchaser of a security need only demonstrate that he or she has suffered a loss on the security. Proof of reliance on the materially false statement or misleading omission is not ordinarily required, nor is there a requirement of privity between the accountant and the security purchaser.

The Due Diligence Standard. Section 11 imposes a duty on accountants to use **due diligence** in the preparation of financial statements included in the filed registration statements. After the purchaser has proved the loss on the security, the accountant bears the burden of showing that he or she exercised due diligence in the preparation of the financial statements. To avoid liability, the accountant must show that he or she had, "after reasonable investigation, reasonable grounds to believe and did believe, at the time such part of the registration statement became effective, that the statements therein were true and that there was no omission of a material fact required to be stated therein or necessary to make the statements therein not misleading."[11] Further, the failure to follow GAAP and GAAS is also proof of a lack of due diligence.

DUE DILIGENCE
A required standard of care that certain professionals, such as accountants, must meet to avoid liability for securities violations.

In particular, the due diligence standard places a burden on accountants to verify information furnished by a corporation's officers and directors. The burden of proving due diligence requires an accountant to demonstrate that he or she did not commit negligence or fraud. The accountants in *Escott v. BarChris Construction Corp.*,[12] for example, were held liable for a failure to detect danger signals in materials that, under GAAS, required further investigation under the circumstances. Merely asking questions is not always sufficient to satisfy the requirement of due diligence.

Defenses to Liability. Besides proving that he or she has acted with due diligence, an accountant may raise the following defenses to Section 11 liability:

1. There were no misstatements or omissions.
2. The misstatements or omissions were not of material facts.
3. The misstatements or omissions had no causal connection to the plaintiff purchaser's loss.
4. The plaintiff purchaser invested in the securities knowing of the misstatements or omissions.

The following case involved a defense that combined the first two defenses listed above.

10. 15 U.S.C. Section 77k(a).
11. 15 U.S.C. Section 77k(b)(3).
12. 283 F.Supp. 643 (S.D.N.Y. 1968).

CASE 16.3 Danis v. USN Communications, Inc.

United States District Court,
Northern District of Illinois, 2000.
121 F.Supp.2d 1183.

BACKGROUND AND FACTS USN Communications, Inc., was a reseller of telecommunication services. USN bought local and long-distance service from regional Bell operating companies (RBOCs), such as Ameritech Corporation, bundled the services, and sold the packages by offering RBOC customers lower rates. USN grew rapidly, causing problems with the company's billing system. In February 1998, USN offered its stock to the public. The prospectus contained a certified 1996 audit report and uncertified 1997 interim financial statements. The statements were marked as unaudited. The prospectus included warnings about the accuracy of USN's billing system. Within ten months, the price of the stock dropped from $16 per share to less than $0.50 per share, and USN filed for bankruptcy. Deloitte & Touche, Limited Liability Partnership (D&T), had audited USN's financial statements from 1994 through 1997. USN shareholders filed a suit in a federal district court against USN, D&T, and others, charging in part violations of Section 11, as well as GAAP and GAAS. The plaintiffs alleged against D&T that the 1996 audit report in the prospectus contained material misrepresentations relating to the effects of USN's faulty billing system. D&T filed a motion for summary judgment.[a]

a. All of the other claims against USN and the other defendants were dismissed or settled.

IN THE LANGUAGE OF THE COURT. . .
CONLON, District Judge.

* * * *

Section 11 liability is triggered when (1) a prospectus contains false facts or misleading omissions; (2) the misrepresentations are material; and (3) the facts suggest preparation or certification by the defendant. * * * The information is deemed important to an investor if there is a substantial probability that the [false or] omitted fact would have been viewed by the reasonable investor as having significantly altered the "total mix" of information made available.

* * * *

Plaintiffs have not presented evidence of material misrepresentations in the 1996 financial statements or audit report. On August 24, 2000, plaintiffs' expert, Robert Berliner, testified that he was not of the opinion that the 1996 financial statements in the prospectus were materially misstated. He confirmed that he had no intention of testifying about the 1996 financial statements at trial. Berliner's expert report, dated July 7, 2000, supports his deposition testimony. * * *

* * * *

Plaintiffs advance evidence that as early as 1995, USN established a practice of billing customers for monthly recurring charges after those customers had left. This practice might have caused USN's 1996 revenue estimates to be inflated. However, plaintiffs have failed to offer any evidence that the alleged revenue inflation was material. Without any evidence as to the degree of alleged inflation, a trier of fact could not conclude that a reasonable investor's decisions would be affected by this information. Thus, this evidence is also insufficient for plaintiffs to withstand summary judgment.

Plaintiffs fail to present evidence to support their claims of material misrepresentations in regard to Deloitte's GAAP and GAAS certification. Violations of GAAP and GAAS standards are established through expert testimony. Plaintiffs' experts do not provide any evidence of material GAAP or GAAS violations. Berliner testified at his deposition that * * * he was not of the opinion that the 1996 financial statements were materially misstated as a result of the GAAP violations. * * * If the financial statements were not materially misstated as a result of alleged GAAP violations, Deloitte's assurance of compliance with GAAP was not materially misleading. Plaintiffs offer no other evidence of violations of GAAP or GAAS. Accordingly, there is no reasonable basis for a jury to find that the 1996 audit report violated [Section] 11.

DECISION AND REMEDY The court granted USN's motion for summary judgment. Regarding Section 11 liability, the plaintiffs failed to prove the required element of material misrepresentation. This same element was lacking in the plaintiffs' case for liability based on GAAP and GAAS violations.

FOR CRITICAL ANALYSIS–Technological Consideration *What do the facts in this case suggest about the relationship between technological capabilities and successful business expansion?*

LIABILITY UNDER SECTION 12(2) Section 12(2) of the Securities Act of 1933 imposes civil liability for fraud on anyone offering or selling a security to any purchaser of the security.[13] Liability is based on communication to an investor, whether orally or in the written prospectus,[14] of an untrue statement or omission of a material fact.

PENALTIES AND SANCTIONS FOR VIOLATIONS Those who purchase securities and suffer harm as a result of a false or omitted statement, or some other violation, may bring a suit in a federal court to recover their losses and other damages. The U.S. Department of Justice brings criminal actions against those who commit willful violations. The penalties include fines up to $10,000, imprisonment up to five years, or both. The SEC is authorized to seek, against a willful violator, an injunction against further violations. The SEC can also ask a court to grant other relief, such as an order to a violator to refund profits derived from an illegal transaction.

Liability under the Securities Exchange Act of 1934

Under Sections 18 and 10(b) of the Securities Exchange Act of 1934 and Rule 10b-5 of the Securities and Exchange Commission, an accountant may be found liable for fraud. A plaintiff has a substantially heavier burden of proof under the 1934 act than under the 1933 act. Unlike the 1933 act, which provides that an accountant must prove due diligence to escape liability, the 1934 act relieves an accountant from liability if the accountant acted in "good faith."

---

13. 15 U.S.C. Section 77*l*.

14. A *prospectus* contains financial disclosures about the corporation for the benefit of potential investors.

LIABILITY UNDER SECTION 18 Section 18 of the 1934 act imposes civil liability on an accountant who makes or causes to be made in any application, report, or document a statement that at the time and in light of the circumstances was false or misleading with respect to any material fact.[15]

Section 18 liability is narrow in that it applies only to applications, reports, documents, and registration statements filed with the SEC. This remedy is further limited in that it applies only to sellers and purchasers. Under Section 18, a seller or purchaser must prove one of the following:

1. That the false or misleading statement affected the price of the security.

2. That the purchaser or seller relied on the false or misleading statement in making the purchase or sale and was not aware of the inaccuracy of the statement.

Even if a purchaser or seller proves these two elements, an accountant can be exonerated of liability by proving good faith in the preparation of the financial statement. To demonstrate good faith, an accountant must show that he or she had no knowledge that the financial statement was false or misleading. Acting in good faith requires the total absence of an intention on the part of the accountant to seek an unfair advantage over, or to defraud, another party. Proving a lack of intent to deceive, manipulate, or defraud is frequently referred to as proving a lack of *scienter* (knowledge on the part of a misrepresenting party that material facts have been misrepresented or omitted with an intent to deceive).

The absence of good faith can be demonstrated not only by proof of *scienter* but also by the accountant's reckless conduct and gross negligence. (Note that "mere" negligence in the preparation of a financial statement does not constitute liability under the 1934 act. This differs from provisions of the 1933 act, under which an accountant is liable for all negligent actions.) In addition to the good faith defense, accountants have available as a defense the buyer's or seller's knowledge that the financial statement was false or misleading.

Under Section 18 of the 1934 act, a court also has the discretion to assess reasonable costs, including attorneys' fees, against accountants.[16] Sellers and purchasers may maintain a cause of action "within one year after the discovery of the facts constituting the cause of action and within three years after such cause of action accrued."[17]

LIABILITY UNDER SECTION 10(b) AND SEC RULE 10b-5 The Securities Exchange Act of 1934 further subjects accountants to potential legal liability in its antifraud provisions. Section 10(b) of the 1934 act and SEC Rule 10b-5 contain the antifraud provisions. As stated in *Herman & MacLean v. Huddleston,*[18] "a private right of action under Section 10(b) of the 1934 act and Rule 10b-5 has been consistently recognized for more than 35 years."

Section 10(b) makes it unlawful for any persons, including accountants, to use, in connection with the purchase or sale of any security, any manipulative

15. 15 U.S.C. Section 78r(a).
16. 15 U.S.C. Section 78r(a).
17. 15 U.S.C. Section 78r(c).
18. 459 U.S. 375, 103 S.Ct. 683, 74 L.Ed.2d 548 (1983).

or deceptive device or contrivance in contravention of SEC rules and regulations.[19] Rule 10b-5 further makes it unlawful for any person, by use of any means or instrumentality of interstate commerce, to do the following:

1. Employ any device, scheme, or artifice to defraud.
2. Make any untrue statement of a material fact or omit to state a material fact necessary to make the statements made, in light of the circumstances, not misleading.
3. Engage in any act, practice, or course of business that operates or would operate as a fraud or deceit on any person, in connection with the purchase or sale of any security.[20]

Accountants may be held liable only to sellers or purchasers under Section 10(b) and Rule 10b-5.[21] The scope of these antifraud provisions is extremely wide. Privity is not necessary for a recovery. Under these provisions, an accountant may be found liable not only for fraudulent misstatements of material facts in written material filed with the SEC but also for any fraudulent oral statements or omissions made in connection with the purchase or sale of any security.

For a plaintiff to recover from an accountant under the antifraud provisions of the 1934 act, he or she must, in addition to establishing status as a purchaser or seller, prove *scienter,*[22] a fraudulent action or deception, reliance, materiality, and causation. A plaintiff who fails to establish these elements cannot recover damages from an accountant under Section 10(b) or Rule 10b-5.

The Private Securities Litigation Reform Act of 1995

The Private Securities Litigation Reform Act (PSLRA) of 1995[23] made some changes to the potential liability of accountants and other professionals in securities fraud cases. Among other things, the act imposed a new statutory obligation on accountants. An auditor must use adequate procedures in an audit to detect any illegal acts of the company being audited. If something illegal is detected, the auditor must disclose it to the company's board of directors, the audit committee, or the SEC, depending on the circumstances.[24]

In terms of liability, the 1995 act provides that in most situations, a party is liable only for that proportion of damages for which he or she is responsible.[25] For example, if an accountant actually participated in defrauding investors, he or she could be liable for the entire loss. If the accountant was not aware of the fraud, however, his or her liability could be proportionately less.

The act also stated that aiding and abetting a violation of the Securities Exchange Act of 1934 is a violation in itself. The SEC can enforce this provision by seeking an injunction or money damages against any person who knowingly aids and abets primary violators of the securities law. An accountant aids and abets when he or she is generally aware that he or she is participating in an

19. 15 U.S.C. Section 78j(b).
20. 17 C.F.R. Section 240.10b-5.
21. See *Blue Chip Stamps v. Manor Drug Stores,* 421 U.S. 723, 95 S.Ct. 1917, 44 L.Ed.2d 539 (1975).
22. See *Ernst & Ernst v. Hochfelder,* 425 U.S. 185, 96 S.Ct. 1375, 47 L.Ed.2d 668 (1976).
23. 15 U.S.C. Sections 77z-1, 77z-2, 78j-1, 78u-4, and 78u-5.
24. 15 U.S.C. Section 78j-1.
25. 15 U.S.C. Section 78u-4(g).

activity that is improper and knowingly assists the activity. Silence may constitute aiding and abetting.

For example, Smith & Jones, an accounting firm, performs an audit for ABC Sales Company that is so inadequate as to constitute gross negligence. ABC uses the materials provided by Smith & Jones as part of a scheme to defraud investors. When the scheme is uncovered, the SEC can bring an action against Smith & Jones for aiding and abetting on the ground that the firm knew or should have known of the material misrepresentations that were in its audit and on which investors were likely to rely.

Under the PSLRA, *scienter* is required to impose liability in a securities fraud action. The issue in the following case was whether the facts as alleged gave rise to a sufficiently strong inference of *scienter.*

CASE 16.4 In re MicroStrategy, Inc., Securities Litigation

United States District Court, Eastern District of Virginia, 2000. 115 F.Supp.2d 620.

COMPANY PROFILE *MicroStrategy, Inc.* (**http://www.microstrategy.com**), *which was founded in 1989, is a developer and marketer of software and related services that facilitate business over electronic and wireless media. MicroStrategy software allows companies to retrieve raw data and turn it into useful information. The company also provides installation, maintenance, and consultation services. Since its inception, MicroStrategy's business has evolved from a focus on software licenses and maintenance to the provision of software products and services that often involve consulting work extended over long periods of time. MicroStrategy receives its revenue from product license fees, product support fees, and royalties.*

BACKGROUND AND FACTS In 1998, MicroStrategy announced a stock offering of four million shares of common stock. Over the next twenty-one months, MicroStrategy released financial statements showing as much as 400 percent annual increases in revenue, and issued more stock, which rose significantly in price. The company reported to the public that PwC, an independent accounting firm, had audited the statements in accord with generally accepted accounting principles (GAAP). Then, on March 20, 2000, after a two-week review of its records, MicroStrategy announced that its revenues for 1998 and 1999 had been overstated. By the end of the day, the price of its stock had fallen from $226.75 to $86.75. Later, the company also revised its financial statement for 1997. New statements showed that the firm had suffered net losses in each of the previous years. Shareholders filed a suit in a federal district court against, among others, PwC, claiming in part violations of GAAP and liability under Section 10(b) of the Securities Exchange Act of 1934 and SEC Rule 10b-5. PwC filed a motion to dismiss on this claim, contending that there was no *scienter,* as required under the PSLRA.

IN THE LANGUAGE OF THE COURT. . .
ELLIS, District Judge.

* * * *

* * * [T]he magnitude and pervasiveness of MicroStrategy's financial restatements and the relative simplicity of the accounting principles violated in this case lend * * * weight to Plaintiffs' allegations that the GAAP violations in this case raise a strong inference of *scienter.* * * *

First, Plaintiffs allege that PwC's failure to detect MicroStrategy's violations of GAAP or otherwise to abide by GAAS in conducting its audits of MicroStrategy's 1997, 1998, and 1999 financial reports and in assisting the Company in quarterly reports during the [same] period resulted in false reports of net income that aggregated to $18.9 million, when, in fact, the Company incurred net losses that aggregated to $36.8 million. In addition, these GAAP violations resulted in false reports of revenues that aggregated to an overstatement of $66 million. Second, the Complaint also alleges that the accounting principles violated in this case are so simple as to compel a stronger inference that PwC's failure to detect them resulted from either conscious fraud or severe recklessness. That these violations occurred consistently over the entire * * * period, resulted in such a large restatement, and involved the violation of relatively straightforward accounting principles is probative of *scienter.*

Also alleged is the celerity with which MicroStrategy and PwC were able to review the Company's financials, catch the accounting irregularities, and announce a restatement * * * . The alleged fact that MicroStrategy and PwC were able to conduct, within two weeks * * * , "a * * * detailed review of MicroStrategy's significant contracts" from the preceding two years further supports the inference of *scienter* stemming from the magnitude of the restatement and the simplicity of the GAAP principles violated in this case. This fact also effectively serves to rebut Defendants' contention that the complexity of the accounting principles at issue mitigate any inferences of *scienter.*

It is simply a matter of common sense and logic—particularly given the special expertise of accounting firms—that the less complex the rules violated, the greater the magnitude of the irregularities, and the more frequent the violations, the stronger is the inference that conscious fraud or recklessness is the explanation for the auditor's role in the violations. And, the fact that PwC was able quickly to identify and correct these violations from information accumulated for over two years weakens the inference that PwC acted with a nonculpable state of mind.

DECISION AND REMEDY The court denied the motion to dismiss. The court held that the shareholders' allegations concerning PwC's GAAP violations, and other circumstances, raised a strong inference that PwC's conduct of its audits was "so deficient that the audit amounted to no audit at all or that no reasonable accountant would have made the same decisions if confronted with the same facts." This met the PSLRA *scienter* requirement for a securities fraud claim.

FOR CRITICAL ANALYSIS—Economic Consideration *Why is* scienter *required in a securities fraud action?*

SECTION 3 POTENTIAL CRIMINAL LIABILITY OF ACCOUNTANTS

An accountant may be found criminally liable for violations of the Securities Act of 1933, the Securities Exchange Act of 1934, the Internal Revenue Code, and both state and federal criminal codes. Under both the 1933 act and the 1934 act, accountants may be subject to criminal penalties for *willful* violations—imprisonment for up to five years and/or a fine of up to $10,000 under the 1933 act and up to ten years and $100,000 under the 1934 act.

The Internal Revenue Code, Section 7206(2),[26] makes aiding or assisting in the preparation of a false tax return a felony punishable by a fine of $100,000 ($500,000 in the case of a corporation) and imprisonment for up to three years. Those who prepare tax returns for others also may face liability under the Internal Revenue Code. Note that one does not have to be an accountant to be subject to liability for tax-preparer penalties. The Internal Revenue Code defines a tax preparer as any person who prepares for compensation, or who employs one or more persons to prepare for compensation, all or a substantial portion of a tax return or a claim for a tax refund.[27]

Section 6694[28] of the Internal Revenue Code imposes on the tax preparer a penalty of $250 per return for negligent understatement of the client's tax liability and a penalty of $1,000 for willful understatement of tax liability or reckless or intentional disregard of rules or regulations. A tax preparer may also be subject to penalties under Section 6695[29] for failing to furnish the taxpayer with a copy of the return, failing to sign the return, or failing to furnish the appropriate tax identification numbers.

Section 6701[30] of the Internal Revenue Code imposes a penalty of $1,000 per document for aiding and abetting an individual's understatement of tax liability (the penalty is increased to $10,000 in corporate cases). The tax preparer's liability is limited to one penalty per taxpayer per tax year. If this penalty is imposed, no penalty can be imposed under Section 6694 with respect to the same document.

In most states, criminal penalties may be imposed for such actions as knowingly certifying false or fraudulent reports; falsifying, altering, or destroying books of account; and obtaining property or credit through the use of false financial statements.

SECTION 4 WORKING PAPERS

WORKING PAPERS
The various documents used and developed by an accountant during an audit. Working papers include notes, computations, memoranda, copies, and other papers that make up the work product of an accountant's services to a client.

Performing an audit for a client involves an accumulation of **working papers**—the various documents used and developed during the audit. These include notes, computations, memoranda, copies, and other papers that make up the work product of an accountant's services to a client. Under the common law, which in this instance has been codified in a number of states, working papers remain the accountant's property. It is important for accountants to retain such records in the event that they need to defend against lawsuits for negligence or other actions in which their competence is challenged. But because an accountant's working papers reflect the client's financial situation, the client has a right of access to them. (An accountant must return to his or her client any of the client's records or journals on the client's request, and failure to do so may result in liability.)

The client must give permission before working papers can be transferred to another accountant. Without the client's permission or a valid court order, the

26. 26 U.S.C. Section 7206(2).
27. 26 U.S.C. Section 7701(a)(36).
28. 26 U.S.C. Section 6694.
29. 26 U.S.C. Section 6695.
30. 26 U.S.C. Section 6701.

contents of working papers are not to be disclosed. Disclosure would constitute a breach of the accountant's fiduciary duty to the client. On the ground of unauthorized disclosure, the client could initiate a malpractice suit. The accountant's best defense would be that the client gave permission for the papers' release.

SECTION 5 CONFIDENTIALITY AND PRIVILEGE

Professionals are restrained by the ethical tenets of their professions to keep all communications with their clients confidential. The confidentiality of attorney-client communications is also protected by law, which confers a *privilege* on such communications. This privilege is granted because of the need for full disclosure to the attorney of the facts of a client's case.

To encourage frankness, confidential attorney-client communications relating to representation are normally held in strictest confidence and protected by law. The attorney and his or her employees may not discuss the client's case with anyone—even under court order—without the client's permission. The client holds the privilege, and only the client may waive it—by disclosing privileged information to a third party, for example. (One of the questions facing the legal profession in recent years is whether attorney-client e-mail communications can be considered "confidential." See this chapter's *Controversial Issues in the Online World* on the next page for a discussion of this topic.)

In a few states, accountant-client communications are privileged by state statute. In these states, accountant-client communications may not be revealed even in court or in court-sanctioned proceedings without the client's permission. The majority of states, however, abide by the common law, which provides that, if a court so orders, an accountant must disclose information about his or her client to the court. Physicians and other professionals may similarly be compelled to disclose in court information given to them in confidence by patients or clients.

Communications between professionals and their clients—other than those between an attorney and his or her client—are not privileged under federal law. In cases involving federal law, state-provided rights to confidentiality of accountant-client communications are not recognized. Thus, in those cases, in response to a court order, an accountant must provide the information sought.

SECTION 6 LIMITING PROFESSIONALS' LIABILITY

As mentioned earlier in this chapter, accountants (and other professionals) can limit their liability to some extent by disclaiming it. Depending on the circumstances, a disclaimer that does not meet certain requirements will not be effective, however; and in some situations, a disclaimer may have no effect at all.

Professionals may be able to limit their liability for the misconduct of other professionals with whom they work by organizing the business as a professional corporation (P.C.) or a limited liability partnership (LLP). In some states, a professional who is a member of a P.C. is not personally liable for a co-member's misconduct unless he or she participated in it or supervised the member who acted wrongly. The innocent professional is liable only to the extent of his or her interest in the assets of the firm. This is also true for professionals who are partners in an LLP.

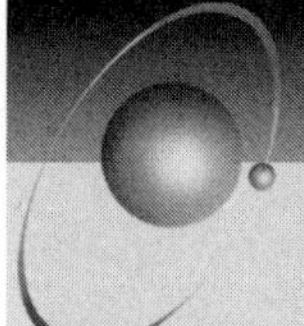

Controversial Issues in the Online World

The Confidentiality of E-Mail

The widespread use of the Internet by lawyers to communicate with their clients has raised a significant question: Does communicating with a client via e-mail violate the confidentiality rule discussed elsewhere in this chapter?

Although the courts have not yet addressed this question, bar associations in several states have rendered ethical opinions on the subject. Among the first to do so was South Carolina, which concluded in 1994 that lawyers should not use e-mail for sensitive client communications because it is possible for e-mail to be intercepted. For the next few years, there seemed to be a growing consensus that only encrypted communications (encoded messages, using encryption software) with clients could be considered confidential.

Since 1997, however, several states have reached the opposite conclusion. For example, when the Vermont state bar's ethics panel considered the issue, it reasoned that since "(a) e-mail privacy is no less to be expected than in ordinary phone calls, and (b) unauthorized interception is illegal, a lawyer does not violate [the confidentiality rule] by communicating with a client by e-mail . . . without encryption." The panel went on to say that in various instances "of a very sensitive nature, encryption might be prudent, in which case ordinary phone calls would obviously be deemed inadequate." This reasoning is typical of state bar ethics committees in about two dozen other states, including Illinois, Arizona, and even South Carolina—which reversed its earlier opinion when it revisited the issue later.

In 1999, the American Bar Association (ABA) issued an opinion on the matter. According to the ABA's Standing Committee on Ethics and Professional Responsibility, "a lawyer may transmit information relating to the representation of a client by unencrypted e-mail" without violating the ABA's rules governing attorney conduct. The committee went on to state that plain, unencrypted e-mail "affords a reasonable expectation of privacy from a technological and legal standpoint."[a] According to one commentator, when this announcement was made, the "sigh of relief" among attorneys was "almost audible."[b]

Nonetheless, attorneys remain concerned. Although the ABA's opinions wield considerable influence, it is entirely possible that a court may arrive at a different conclusion. Even the ABA opinion mentioned above cautioned that the opinion did not "diminish a lawyer's obligation to consider with her client the sensitivity of the communication, the cost of its disclosure, and the relative security of the contemplated medium of communication." For this reason, many attorneys remain cautious when communicating with clients over the Internet. Encrypting e-mail and files that are transmitted over the Internet is one way to avoid confidentiality problems. Another is to add disclaimers to e-mail indicating that the communications may not be secure. Finally, some legal ethicists suggest that lawyers should discuss the issue with their clients and let the clients decide on how sensitive information should be exchanged.

CHECKLIST

- ☑ An attorney who breaches his or her duty to preserve the confidentiality of client information may face serious consequences, including liability to the client for damages caused by the breach and the possibility of a disciplinary action by the state bar association. Because the law is not yet settled on the issue of e-mail as a confidential mode of communication, legal professionals should consider encrypting their e-mail messages to or about clients, using disclaimers, and discussing this issue with their clients.
- ☑ Businesspersons who communicate with their attorneys via the Internet should bring up the issue of confidentiality if their attorneys do not. Otherwise, the attorney-client privilege may be jeopardized.

a. American Bar Association Standing Committee on Ethics and Professional Responsibility, "Protecting the Confidentiality of Unencrypted E-Mail," Formal Opinion No. 99-413 (March 10, 1999).

b. Wendy R. Leibowitz, "E-Mail Ethics Evolving," *The National Law Journal*, May 17, 1999, p. A17.

CONCEPT SUMMARY 16.1 LIABILITY OF ACCOUNTANTS AND OTHER PROFESSIONALS

COMMON LAW LIABILITY	
Liability to Client	1. *Breach of contract*—An accountant or other professional who fails to perform according to his or her contractual obligations can be held liable for breach of contract and resulting damages. 2. *Negligence*—An accountant or other professional, in performance of his or her duties, must use the care, knowledge, and judgment generally used by professionals in the same or similar circumstances. Failure to do so is negligence. An accountant's violation of generally accepted accounting principles and generally accepted auditing standards is *prima facie* evidence of negligence. An accountant who reveals confidential information or the contents of working papers without the client's permission or a court order can be held liable for malpractice. 3. *Fraud*—Actual intent to misrepresent a material fact to a client, when the client relies on the misrepresentation, is fraud. Gross negligence in performance of duties is constructive fraud.
Liability to Third Parties	An accountant may be liable for negligence to any third person the accountant knows or should have known will benefit from the accountant's work. The standard for imposing this liability varies, but generally courts follow one of the following three rules: 1. *Ultramares rule*—Liability will be imposed only if the accountant is in privity, or near privity, with the third party. 2. *Restatement rule*—Liability will be imposed only if the third party's reliance is foreseen or known or if the third party is among a class of foreseeable or known users. The majority of courts adopt this rule. 3. *"Reasonably foreseeable user" rule*—Liability will be imposed if the third party's use was reasonably foreseeable.
STATUTORY LIABILITY	
Securities Act of 1933, Sections 11 and 12(2)	Under Section 11 of the 1933 Securities Act, an accountant who makes a false statement or omits a material fact in audited financial statements required for registration of securities under the law may be liable to anyone who acquires securities covered by the registration statement. The accountant's defense is basically the use of due diligence and the reasonable belief that the work was complete and correct. The burden of proof is on the accountant. Willful violations of this act may be subject to criminal penalties. Section 12(2) of the 1933 act imposes civil liability for fraud on anyone offering or selling a security to any purchaser of the security.
Securities Exchange Act of 1934, Sections 10(b) and 18	Under Sections 10(b) and 18 of the 1934 Securities Exchange Act, accountants are held liable for false and misleading applications, reports, and documents required under the act. The burden is on the plaintiff, and the accountant has numerous defenses, including good faith and lack of knowledge that what was submitted was false. Willful violations of this act may subject the violator to criminal penalties.
Internal Revenue Code	1. Aiding or assisting in the preparation of a false tax return is a felony. Aiding and abetting an individual's understatement of tax liability is a separate crime.

Concept Summary 16.1 (continued)

Statutory Liability (continued)	
Internal Revenue Code (continued)	2. Tax preparers who negligently or willfully understate a client's tax liability or who recklessly or intentionally disregard Internal Revenue rules or regulations are subject to criminal penalties. 3. Tax preparers who fail to provide a taxpayer with a copy of the return, fail to sign the return, or fail to furnish the appropriate tax identification numbers may also be subject to criminal penalties.

SECTION 7 WEB TRUST SEALS

Accountants (as well as attorneys) for banking institutions that have branched out into other areas are the "front line" for helping those companies comply with the privacy provisions of the Financial Services Modernization Act (FSMA)—also known as the Gramm-Leach-Bliley Act—of 1999,[31] as well as with other Internet-related privacy legislation. The 1999 act permits banks to acquire securities firms and insurance companies, and to engage in other activities that were previously prohibited by the Banking Act (Glass-Steagall Act) of 1933.[32]

As banks move into securities services and tax preparation, they can benefit economically by sharing information about their customers across these various divisions. The FSMA requires, though, that they must display and post their privacy policies on their Web sites. They must explain how they use "non-public personal information" and how they share information with their nonbanking affiliates.

When a financial institution passes a privacy audit, it obtains a Web Trust seal from the American Institution of Certified Public Accountants (AICPA). This Web Trust seal offers assurance—particularly to those in other countries that do business with a U.S. company—that the financial institution to which it was awarded is complying with each country's privacy laws. Indeed, accounting firms are seen as independent third party verifiers of banking institutions' privacy policies. Consumers have recourse against a company bearing the Web Trust seal, and an online arbitration system must be in place to settle disputes between consumers and companies posting the Web Trust seal.

SECTION 8 BOOKING REVENUES—ARE INTERNET COMPANIES DIFFERENT?

Until the Internet came along, the accountant's job of correctly booking revenues seemed relatively straightforward. But since the advent of large Web-based companies, some twists and changes have occurred in revenue recognition.

31. 12 U.S.C. Sections 24a, 248b, 1820a, 1828b, 1831v–1831y, 1848a, 2908, 4809; 15 U.S.C. Sections 80b-10a, 6701, 6711–6717, 6731–6735, 6751–6766, 6781, 6801–6809, 6821–6827, 6901–6910; and others.
32. 12 U.S.C. Section 277.

An Example—Priceline.Com

Consider a typical Web-based company, Priceline.com. Priceline.com is basically an electronic travel agency that allows you to "name your own price." Potential purchasers of airline tickets and hotel rooms offer to pay specified prices and no more for specific point-to-point travel and for hotel rooms on certain dates. Airline companies and hotel owners can then either accept or refuse these maximum prices.

An accountant for a conventional travel agency would never allow the agency to book revenues on anything other than the commissions it receives. Priceline.com, in contrast, treats all of the money that it collects for airline and hotel tickets as gross revenue. It has always argued that it owns the inventory of tickets for a nanosecond. If Priceline.com's accounting practices were similar to those of travel agencies not based on the Web, its gross revenues during its existence would have been less than one-eighth of those reported to the investing public.

The SEC Reacts

The Securities and Exchange Commission decided to develop guidelines for revenue recognition for online companies as well as film studios and biotechnology, telecommunications, and electronics companies. A staff bulletin issued by the SEC in December 1999[33] set forth, in 11,400 words, a new set of guidelines. In essence, the guidelines are much stricter on revenue recognition than they have been in the past.

For example, a manufacturer of large, expensive machines typically allows a customer to withhold 10 to 20 percent of the invoice price until the machine is fully installed. Because so few of these large machines are ever sent back, manufacturers of chip-making machines and similar large and expensive manufacturing equipment have booked the sales on the day the machines were shipped. The SEC is requesting that only when the entire amount is paid can the revenues be recognized. Sometimes, it takes a year for such a machine to be fully installed. That means that the machine's manufacturer would not be able to book revenues until twelve months after the machine was shipped, even though 80 to 90 percent of the revenues had already been obtained.

Clearly, the SEC's new guidelines will affect companies' reported gross profits. Consider what happened to Ultratech, a company making machines used to design and manufacture chips, when it decided to follow the new guidelines. It took an $18.9 million charge in the first quarter of 2000, contributing to most of its apparent $21.9 million first-quarter loss.

---

33. Staff Accounting Bulletin No. 101 (December 3, 1999); subsequently modified as to time of effectiveness in Staff Accounting Bulletin No. 101A (March 24, 2000) and Staff Accounting Bulletin No. 101B (June 26, 2000).

TERMS AND CONCEPTS

QUESTIONS AND CASE PROBLEMS

16–1. *Ultramares* Rule. Alpha Communications, Inc., a provider of Internet and other communications services, retains Bob, a certified public accountant, to manage its books and prepare its financial statements. Bob believes that with recent developments in technology, it is time for changes in the application of generally accepted accounting principles (GAAP), and Bob becomes creative in his accounting methods. Based on one of Bob's creative financial statements covering Alpha, Business Credit Corporation loans money to the firm. When Alpha defaults on the loan, Business Credit files a suit against Bob, alleging that he knew or should have known that Alpha's financial statements would be distributed to others. Furthermore, the creditor asserts that the statements were negligently prepared and are seriously inaccurate. What are the consequences of Bob's failure to adopt "traditional" GAAP? Under the *Ultramares* rule, can the lender recover damages from Bob? Explain.

16–2. Liability to Third Parties. The accounting firm of Goldman, Walters, Johnson & Co. prepared financial statements for Beta Webmasters, Inc. After reviewing the various financial statements, First Online Bank agreed to loan Beta $500,000 for expansion. When Beta declares bankruptcy six months later, First Online promptly files an action against Goldman, Walters, Johnson & Co., alleging negligent preparation of financial statements. Assuming that the court has abandoned the *Ultramares* approach, what might be the result? What are the policy reasons for holding accountants liable to third parties with whom they are not in privity?

16–3. SEC Rule 10b-5. In early 1998, B2B Application Services, Inc., offers a substantial number of new common shares to the public. Looking for investments, Carol obtains a prospectus prepared and distributed by B2B. Buoyed by the optimistic statements in the prospectus, which also includes realistic assessments of the market for the company's products and warnings about the potential for losses, Carol buys stock in the company. When the price of the stock falls dramatically and B2B later goes out of business, Carol files a suit against the firm's accountants, asserting that the prospectus was overly optimistic and contained materially misleading statements. Discuss fully how successful Carol would be in bringing a cause of action under SEC Rule 10b-5 against the accountants.

16–4. Securities Act of 1933. N2K, Inc., uses the Internet to market music and merchandise via its Web site, "Music Boulevard." On March 4, 1998, N2K filed a registration statement and prospectus with the Securities and Exchange Commission for a stock offering. The documents included financial reports prepared by N2K's accountants for 1994 through 1997, but did not include results for the period to end on March 31. The prospectus stated that N2K expected "significant" losses "on a quarterly and annual basis" for the "foreseeable future." The statement was declared effective on April 14, and sales of the stock were complete by April 15. Nine days later, N2K announced that for the period ending March 31, on revenues of about $7 million, its losses were almost $14 million. The price of N2K stock fell from more than $35 to less than $26 per share. When the price later fell below $14, those who had bought shares in April filed a suit against N2K and others. The investors charged in part that the failure to disclose financial results for the first three months of 1998 in the statement and prospectus made them misleading under Section 11 of the Securities Act of 1933. The defendants filed a motion to dismiss. How should the court rule, and why? [*In re N2K, Inc. Securities Litigation,* 82 F.Supp.2d 204 (S.D.N.Y. 2000), aff'd 202 F.3d 81 (2d Cir. 2000)]

16–5. Securities Exchange Act of 1934. Segue Software, Inc., supplies supporting software for e-commerce applications. Segue's publicized policy is to accept customer returns only occasionally and to maintain a reserve fund to offset the cost. In July 1998, Segue announced a contract of several million dollars with Universal Underwriters Group (UUG). The price of Segue's stock rose more than 20 percent. In February 1999, Segue reported that its 1998 profits were 3 cents per share, compared to 1997's loss of

21 cents per share. After UUG returned hundreds of thousands of dollars' worth of software, which was greater than the amount in Segue's reserve fund, Segue revised its 1998 report to reduce its revenues from $42.1 million to $41 million, resulting in a loss of 8 cents per share. Meanwhile, since July 1998, the price of Segue's stock had decreased by more than 65 percent. Segue shareholders filed a suit in a federal district court against the company and others, claiming in part improper accounting practices in violation of Section 10(b) of the Securities and Exchange Act of 1934 and SEC Rule 10b-5. Segue filed a motion to dismiss. What must the plaintiffs show to establish their claim? Should the court grant the motion to dismiss? Explain. [*In re Segue Software, Inc., Securities Litigation,* 106 F.Supp.2d 161 (D.Mass. 2000)]

16–6. Securities Exchange Act of 1934. Vantive Corp. sells and services customer-relationship management software (front-office software) that enables personnel to deliver customer service via the Internet, through a call center, or in person. Before 1998, Vantive publicized its revenue recognition policy as follows: "Sublicense fees are generally recognized as reported by the reseller in relicensing the Company's products to end users." In 1998, in a disclosure form filed with the Securities and Exchange Commission (SEC), Vantive added that "sublicense fees are recognized upon the initial sale" if certain conditions were met. In April 1997, the price of Vantive stock traded at up to $39 per share. By July 1998, the price had fallen to $11 per share. Vantive shareholders filed a suit in a federal district court against Vantive and others, claiming in part violations of Section 10(b) of the Securities and Exchange Act of 1934 and SEC Rule 10b-5. The plaintiffs claimed, among other things, that Vantive had secretly changed its revenue recognition policy in 1997 and that the change resulted in false financial reports. Vantive filed a motion to dismiss. Do the shareholders' allegations establish a securities fraud claim? Discuss. [*In re Vantive Corp. Securities Litigation,* 110 F.Supp.2d 1209 (N.D.Cal. 2000)]

16–7. Criminal Liability. Gregory and Deniene Ervasti owned and operated Corporate Financial Services, Inc. (CFS). CFS provided payroll services, including tax filing, to employers. The employers paid the amounts that they were required to withhold from their employees' pay to CFS. CFS would then prepare and file their clients' quarterly federal tax returns (Form 941) with the Internal Revenue Service (IRS) and make timely deposits with the IRS in the amounts due. To meet operating expenses, CFS began to borrow its clients' tax money without permission, which led to late payments to the IRS. Meanwhile, Deniene signed and submitted Forms 941 that claimed the amounts due were paid on time. Eventually, the amounts in arrears totaled more than $5.7 million for over one hundred employers. In a federal district court, Deniene admitted that she lied on the Forms 941 and that she had known it was wrong. The court convicted the Ervastis of numerous offenses, including aiding in the preparation of false tax returns. Deniene appealed her conviction to the U.S. Court of Appeals for the Eighth Circuit on the ground that she acted only in "good faith." Should the court reverse her conviction? Why or why not? [*United States v. Ervasti,* 201 F.3d 1029 (8th Cir. 2000)]

WEB EXERCISES

Go to **http://lec.westbuslaw.com**, the Web site that accompanies this text. Select "Internet Applications," and then click on "Chapter 16." There you will find the following Internet research exercise that you can perform to learn more about some of the steps professionals can take to avoid liability:

Activity 16–1: Avoiding Legal Liability

Economics and E-Commerce

Contents

CHAPTER 17

Cyberbanking and E-Money

Concepts Covered

After reading this chapter, you should be able to:

1. Describe the types of electronic fund transfers currently in use.
2. Indicate what a smart card is and how smart cards are used.
3. Discuss what e-signatures are and how they are verified.
4. Summarize the types of financial transactions that can be conducted online.
5. State some of the advantages and disadvantages of using digital cash as opposed to currency or checks.

"We've proven that the World Wide Web can draw a lot of people. Now we have to make some money at it."

Richard Pitt, 1943–
(Co-proprietor of Wimsey Information Services, Inc, 1993–1995)

The Treasury Department estimates that the total annual cost of handling physical cash throughout the United States is approximately $65 billion. This includes the costs of replacing worn-out currency, printing hard-to-counterfeit currency and minting new coins, and transporting boxes and bags full of currency and coins between banks and retailers. It also includes the cost of sorting and counting billions of coins every day.

Various forms of electronic payments have been with us for some time. What is new and different today is the potential to replace *physical* cash—coins and paper currency—with *virtual* cash in the form of electronic impulses. This is the unique promise of **digital cash,** which consist of funds stored on microchips and other computer devices. Digital cash will eventually reduce the nation's costs of transferring funds. The reason is that people can store and instantaneously transmit digital cash along preexisting electronic networks. People can keep digital cash on diskettes, compact disks, and hard drives. They can send digital cash payments along telephone lines, between cell phones, or over fiber-optic cables. Certainly, digital cash is in its early stages of experimentation and adoption. Nevertheless, the use of digital cash promises to change the nature of money and the world of banking.

DIGITAL CASH
Funds contained on computer software, in the form of secure programs stored on microchips and other computer devices.

SECTION 1 ELECTRONIC FUND TRANSFERS IN USE

The idea of electronic payments is not new. Most Americans use paper checks to pay for groceries and other items. The checks we write have magnetic ink encryptions that special machines use to sort and distribute checks automatically. Increasingly, the information on paper checks is transformed into digital information to permit computers to credit and debit accounts electronically. This large-scale automation of check sorting, accounting, and distribution has kept the per-check cost of clearing checks very low. Today, banking institutions clear millions of checks each day—a total of more than 72 billion per year.

Automated Teller Machines

In the twenty-first century, most U.S. consumers have used **automated teller machine (ATM)** networks. Many consumers regularly use ATM networks to make deposits, withdraw cash from their accounts, transfer funds among accounts, and pay bills. Even though all of these ATM functions are commonplace today, three decades ago about all an ATM could do was dispense cash. Furthermore, banks had to work hard to convince many skeptical customers to trust ATMs to handle even this simple function.

AUTOMATED TELLER MACHINE (ATM)
An electronic network, located at banks and other convenient locations such as airports and shopping centers, that receives deposits, dispenses funds from checking or savings accounts, makes credit-card advances, and accepts payments.

Automated Clearing Houses

Without knowing it, many of us have also used the services of **automated clearing house (ACH)** systems. Banks began to put ACH payment-clearing and settlement systems into place back in the days when the only computers were mainframes. Anyone who has received a direct deposit, such as an automatic payroll deposit, has taken advantage of the services of an ACH. So has a person who has arranged for a regular monthly insurance or mortgage payment to be debited automatically from a checking account. This is yet another example of an electronic means of payment that did not exist just a few years ago but that many of us commonly use today.

AUTOMATED CLEARING HOUSE (ACH)
An electronic banking system used to transfer payments and settle accounts.

THE FEDERAL RESERVE'S ACH TWO-DAY RULE Most electronic bill payment services use the Federal Reserve's Automatic Clearing House (ACH). Under ACH rules, a debit from a customer's bank account is reversible for up to forty-eight hours. For this reason, an electronic payment (e-payment) processing service must either hold debited funds for two days and run the risk of displeasing the customer, or immediately send the payment to the intended payee and run the risk that the transaction will be reversed because the customer's account has insufficient funds.

DEALING WITH THE ACH TWO-DAY RULE There are other ways of dealing with the ACH two-day rule. For example, one method is to send the payee a paper copy of the electronic transaction that is coded to the customer's bank account. The payee then negotiates (transfers) the paper and the transaction is completed through normal banking channels. The advantage of this method is that it lowers an e-payment provider's exposure to credit risk. The downside, however, is that the cost of sending a paper draft is almost ten times more than that of sending an e-payment.

One company's solution to the problem concerning debits in its customers' accounts is to use a multistep procedure that is designed to ensure the efficient, inexpensive remittance of e-payments while taking into account the ACH rules. A customer selects the "due date" on which the e-payment is to occur. The e-payment service initiates the credit side of the transaction in advance of that date and sends the payment to the payee. On the actual due date, the service electronically debits the customer's bank account.

There is still a credit risk in this solution, however. When the service initiates the e-payment, the service does not know whether the customer's account will contain sufficient funds to cover the amount of the payment. For this method to be cost effective, the service needs to know its customers' creditworthiness. This requirement led to the following case.

CASE 17.1 Kvalheim v. Checkfree Corp.

United States District Court,
Southern District of Alabama, 2000.
__ F.Supp.2d __.

COMPANY PROFILE *CheckFree Corporation (**http://www.checkfree.com**) designs, develops, and markets services that allow customers to conduct financial transactions over the Internet. CheckFree processes more than 12 million e-transactions per month on behalf of 3 million customers at over 350 banks and financial institutions. CheckFree's services are available through several Internet sites, including Yahoo!.com, Quicken.com, and WingSpanBank.com. CheckFree is also the exclusive provider of electronic bill payment services to individuals and financial institutions who use Quicken money management software.*

BACKGROUND AND FACTS Following a merger with Intuit Services Corporation (ISC), which was also in the business of providing electronic bill payment services, CheckFree set up procedures to permit customer payments originally initiated through the ISC system to be processed through the CheckFree system. As part of the process, CheckFree needed to assess the credit of the nearly 1.4 million former ISC customers. CheckFree obtained the credit scores of these individuals from Experian Information Solutions, Inc., a credit reporting agency.[a] Meanwhile, Kenneth Kvalheim applied for Compass Bank's online banking service.[b] Because Compass Bank had formerly used ISC's services, CheckFree obtained the credit score of every Compass Bank customer, including Kvalheim. After discovering this credit inquiry, Kvalheim requested information from CheckFree via a letter. When CheckFree did not respond, Kvalheim filed a suit in a federal district court against CheckFree, alleging in part that the firm had violated the Fair Credit Reporting Act (FCRA) when it obtained his credit report without permission and did not respond to his letter. CheckFree filed a motion for summary judgment.

a. A *credit score* is a way of assessing the likelihood that a debtor will repay a loan. The score is based on all credit-related data in a credit bureau's report, but it is not a measure of a borrower's income, assets, or bank accounts.

b. Compass Bank's service, CompassPC, allows customers to conduct their banking and pay bills at home through their personal computers.

IN THE LANGUAGE OF THE COURT. . .
VOLLMER, District J. [Judge.]

* * * *

Kvalheim first argues that CheckFree violated the FCRA by improperly obtaining his credit report from Experian without his permission. At the outset, the court notes that the [U.S. Court of Appeals for the] Eleventh Circuit has not directly addressed whether the FCRA imposes liability upon a party who obtains a consumer report from a consumer reporting agency for an impermissible purpose, and that the courts which have tackled this issue have reached conflicting results.[c]

However, the court need not resolve whether the FCRA imposes liability on a party who obtains a consumer report for an improper purpose, because the court concludes that CheckFree's purpose for obtaining Kvalheim's credit score is permitted under the statute. Specifically, the FCRA authorizes a party to obtain a consumer report when it "has a legitimate business need for the information—(i) in connection with a business transaction that is initiated by the consumer."

In this case, Kvalheim's credit score was obtained in connection with CheckFree's service of providing electronic payments to third-party creditors, a service which was initiated by Kvalheim when he enrolled in the CompassPC home computer banking service. Because the court concludes that this was a legitimate "business transaction" under [the FCRA] CheckFree is not subject to any liability under the FCRA for obtaining Kvalheim's credit score.

* * * *

* * * [Kvalheim also] alleges that CheckFree violated the FCRA when it failed to respond to his * * * letter because it had a statutory duty to respond. CheckFree counters that it has no duty under the FCRA to reply to such inquiries. In his response to CheckFree's summary judgment motion, Kvalheim concedes this point.

Based on Kvalheim's concession, the court will assume for purposes of this motion that the FCRA imposed no duty upon CheckFree to respond to Kvalheim's * * * letter concerning his credit report. * * *

* * * *

The FCRA imposes no liability for the allegations contained within Kvalheim's * * * complaint. Accordingly, the court GRANTS CheckFree's motion for summary judgment as it applies to Kvalheim's federal claims under the FCRA.

c. The U.S. District Court for the Southern District of Alabama, the court hearing this case, is bound by the decisions of the U.S. Court of Appeals for the Eleventh Circuit.

DECISION AND REMEDY The court granted CheckFree's motion. The court concluded that the FCRA does not impose liability for the actions alleged in Kvalheim's complaint.

FOR CRITICAL ANALYSIS–Social Consideration *Why would a person in Kvalheim's position object to CheckFree's investigation of his or her credit?*

Stored-Value Cards

According to the Bank for International Settlements, an international institution operated by major central banks, U.S. residents make more than 300 billion cash transactions (or nearly 1,100 per person) every year. Of these, 270 billion are in amounts of less than $2. It is easy to see why people use paper currency and coins to purchase a soft drink, a candy bar, or a magazine. Why would they use **e-money** instead of currency and coins?

E-MONEY
Prepaid funds recorded on a computer or a card (such as a *smart card*).

STORED-VALUE CARD
A card bearing magnetic stripes that holds magnetically encoded data, providing access to stored funds.

To understand why people might use e-money instead of physical cash, let's begin by thinking about the simplest kind of e-money system, one that uses **stored-value cards.** These are plastic cards embossed with magnetic stripes containing magnetically encoded data. Using a stored-value card, a person purchases specific goods and services offered by the card issuer. For example, a number of university libraries have copy machines that students operate by inserting a stored-value card. Each time a student makes copies, the copy machine deducts the per-copy fee. When the balance on the student's card runs low in the middle of copying a news article, the student can replenish the balance by placing the card in a separate machine and inserting physical cash. The machine stores the value of the cash on the card. Then the student can go back to the copy machine, reinsert the card, and finish copying the article.

Some stored-value cards are disposable. The cardholder throws the card away after the value stored on it has been depleted. In Europe, stored-value phone cards, often purchased at a corner newspaper store, are thrown away after their value is completely used up. Today, in the United States at least, most banks and other issuers prefer reusable stored-value cards. Bearers of these cards may use them to purchase goods and services offered by any participating merchant.

Debit Cards

DEBIT CARD
A plastic card that allows the bearer to transfer funds to a merchant's account, provided that the bearer authorizes the transfer by providing personal identification.

Plastic cards used in *open* funds transfer systems are called **debit cards.** These cards essentially adapt the technology of stored-value cards to permit authorization of direct funds transfers. People can use them to authorize transfers of funds from their accounts to those of merchants.

DEBIT CARDS AS ELECTRONIC CHECKING Exhibit 17–1 illustrates a sample transaction flow in a debit-card system. A card issuer, Bank X, provides cards to its customers, who use their cards to make purchases from retailers. The retailers' electronic cash registers record the value of the purchases and the routing numbers of the issuing banks. The retailers then submit the recorded data to their own bank, Bank Y. This bank forwards claims for funds to the system operator. The operator transmits these claims to each issuing bank, including Bank X. Once Bank X honors its obligations to Bank Y by debiting the customer's checking account, Bank Y credits the deposit accounts of the retailers. A fully electronic debit-card system is the equivalent of electronic checking. As with check clearing, behind-the-scenes interbank clearing must take place to finalize a transaction.

DEBIT-CARD EXPENSES TO THE BANKING SYSTEM The security features of debit-card systems make them somewhat cumbersome. When a cardholder presents a typical debit card to a retailer, the retailer's electronic cash register routes a request for authorization to the issuing bank. The bank's computer checks the cardholder's account number against a file of lost or stolen cards. It also verifies that funds are available in the customer's account. Then the bank sends confirmation of payment authorization.

This authorization system helps reduce the chance that the person using the card has stolen it. The thief would have to steal the customer's authorization codes as well as the card. Thus, the authorization procedure enhances the secu-

Exhibit 17–1 Sample Transaction Flow in a Debit-Card System

Holders of cards issued by Bank X can automatically authorize payments directly to retailers, who in turn transmit claims to Bank Y. This bank then transmits payment claims to the operator of the system, which then transmits the claims to Bank X.

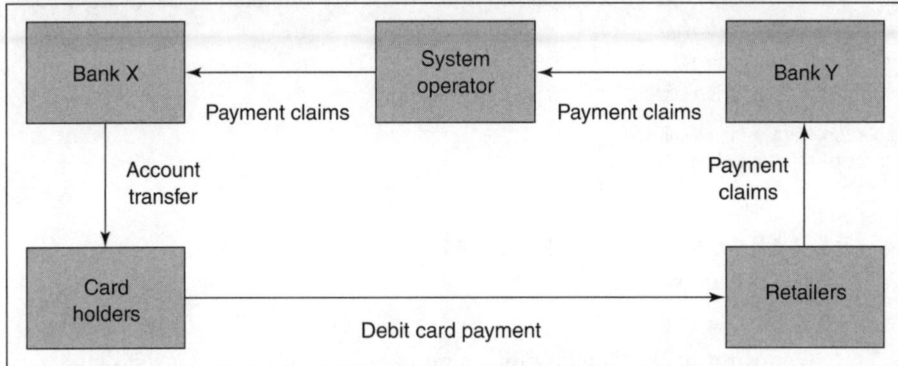

rity of the system for the legitimate cardholder. In addition, the system guarantees that the retailer will receive final payment. Nevertheless, the telecommunication costs of standard online authorizations range from 8 cents to 13 cents per transaction. This is typically much higher than the per-transaction cost of paper currency and coins. In addition, retailers such as fast-food restaurants are not enthusiastic about the slow speed of this kind of authorization system. Employees awaiting payment authorizations for customers they have already served cannot start serving customers waiting in line.

For these reasons, debit cards represent a purely technical innovation in retail payments. Unless debit-card systems become speedier and more cost effective, they are unlikely to fundamentally alter the nature of retail payments.

The following case, although it involves *offline* debit cards, illustrates the costs associated with the use of debit cards.

CASE 17.2 In re Visa Check/Mastermoney Antitrust Litigation

United States District Court,
Eastern District of New York, 2000.
192 F.R.D. 68.

HISTORICAL AND ECONOMIC SETTING *Visa U.S.A. (**http://www.visa.com**) and MasterCard International, Inc. (**http://www.mastercard.com**), dominate the credit-card market. Their share of this market exceeds 90 percent, and most retailers feel compelled to accept their credit cards. In 1979, Visa and MasterCard launched their offline point-of-service (POS) debit cards, VisaCheck and MasterMoney. Under both firms' "honor all cards" rules, any merchant accepting Visa or MasterCard credit cards was contractually obligated to accept VisaCheck and MasterMoney as well. In 1996, there were 1.2 billion annual retail transactions involving VisaCheck or MasterMoney, totaling $46 billion. The fees on these transactions amounted to $580 million, paid by the merchants who were required to accept the cards.*

BACKGROUND AND FACTS Offline debit-card fees are significantly higher than the fees for online debit cards. For example, the fee on a $100 retail transaction (excepting a supermarket) is $1.10 for a VisaCheck transaction or $1.31 for a MasterMoney transaction, but only $.05 for an online debit-card transaction. Also, the merchants that are required to accept the cards, under the firms' "honor all cards" rules, believe that these methods of payment are interchangeable with cash, checks, and traveler's checks, which means that the merchants would have lost virtually none of the sales if they had not accepted VisaCheck or

CASE 17.2–Continued

MasterMoney. The fees payable to Visa and MasterCard would have been as much as 85 percent less, however. Wal-Mart Stores, Inc., and others filed a suit in a federal district court against Visa and MasterCard, alleging in part that the "honor all cards" rules were illegal under the antitrust laws.[a] The plaintiffs asked the court to certify their case as a class action, with the proposed class including approximately 4 million businesses. To be certified as a class, potential members must have suffered a "classwide" injury.

a. Antitrust laws are discussed in the next chapter. Specifically, the plaintiffs charged that the "honor all cards" rule was an illegal tying arrangement.

IN THE LANGUAGE OF THE COURT. . .

GLEESON, District Judge.

* * * *

* * * According to the defendants, some members of the proposed class will not be able to show injury, and the injuries of the others will vary in ways not susceptible to resolution by a class-wide formula. Therefore, no plaintiff's claims will be "typical" of any others; there will be conflicts of interest within the proposed class; and individual issues of injury will predominate.

* * * *

The defendants' first challenge to [the plaintiffs' suit is that] * * * there could be no class-wide injury in fact because (1) even some named plaintiffs have testified that they would have continued to accept offline debit cards at current prices even absent the ["honor all cards" rule]; (2) some merchants have PIN pads, while others do not (for widely varying reasons), resulting in variation in their ability to process transactions on-line; (3) transactions formerly processed through offline debit would be replaced by other payment forms, whose mix and costs would vary merchant-by-merchant; and (4) the expense of those payment forms, when considered together with the incremental sales produced by accepting offline debit and the merchant's profit margin on those incremental sales, will determine whether a given merchant suffered any injury from the tie.

* * * [The plaintiffs argue that without the "honor all cards" rule] after large numbers of merchants refused off-line debit cards, Visa and MasterCard would have cut their interchange fees in order to preserve universal acceptance. That move, in turn, would have led merchants to accept the cards once again. [This] scenario is a complete answer to the defendants' attack * * * ; it posits class-wide injury resulting from every single class member's overpaying for off-line debit cards as a direct result of the ["honor all cards" rule]. * * *

* * * *

Second, the defendants contend that * * * [they likely would do] two things if the ["honor all cards" rule did not exist]: decrease the price of the [off-line debit card fees] and *increase* the price of the [credit-card fees]. * * *

* * * *

* * * [P]laintiffs contend that under the particular circumstances of the market at issue in this case, credit card interchange fees would not have increased [without the "honor all cards" rule]. * * * [I]n Canada, where banks do not issue

off-line debit cards * * * credit card interchange fees are *lower* than in the United States. In addition, * * * the dramatic increase in off-line debit transactions between 1991 and 1998 did not result in a corresponding decline in credit card interchange fees, as defendants' theory (all else being equal) would have predicted. Indeed, those fees generally stayed the same or increased (when adjusted for inflation). * * *

DECISION AND REMEDY The court held that the plaintiffs showed their injuries were susceptible to common proof. The court certified the plaintiffs as a class, concluding that without the "honor all cards" rules the defendants would have been compelled to lower their fees for offline debit cards and would not have raised the credit-card fees.

FOR CRITICAL ANALYSIS–Economic Consideration *Based on the facts of this case, what do you think might have caused the "dramatic increase in offline debit transactions" in the 1990s?*

SECTION 2 SMART CARDS AND DIGITAL CASH

A more dramatic innovation has been the development of **smart cards**—plastic cards containing minute computer microchips that can hold far more information than a magnetic stripe. Because of microchip technology, a smart card can do much more than maintain a running cash balance in its memory or authorize the transfer of funds.

SMART CARD
A card containing a microprocessor that permits storage of funds via security programming, can communicate with other computers, and does not require online authorization for fund transfers.

Smart Cards

A smart card carries and processes security programming. This capability of smart cards gives them a technical advantage over stored-value cards. Magnetic stripe cards fail to communicate a transaction correctly about 250 times in every million transactions. Smart cards fail to communicate properly less than 100 times per million transactions. Furthermore, smart cards are no more expensive to produce than standard stored-value cards or debit cards. Many smart cards are designed to be disposable.

On the Web

You can find a series of articles on smart cards at the following Web site: **http://www.cardshow.com/EN/Public/Welcome.html**.

The microprocessors on smart cards can also authenticate the validity of transactions. Retailers can program electronic cash registers to confirm the authenticity of the smart card by examining a unique "digital signature" stored on its microchip. The digital signature is created by software called a *cryptographic algorithm*. This is a secure program loaded onto the card's microchip. The digital signature guarantees to the retailer's electronic cash register that the information on the smart card's chip is genuine. Exhibit 17–2 on the next page shows how digital encryption helps guarantee the security of electronic payments.

In a smart-card–based system for **e-money transfers**, a smart-card user can remain anonymous. There is also no need for online authorization using expensive telecommunication services. Each time a cardholder uses a smart card, the amount of the purchase is deducted automatically and credited to a retailer. The

E-MONEY TRANSFER
A transfer of funds made through the use of a smart card.

Exhibit 17–2 Digital Encryption and the Security of Electronic Payments

An electronic payment instruction starts out in a form readable by a human being, called "plaintext." When this instruction is entered into a computer, it is secured, or encrypted, using an "encryption key," which is a software code. In computer-readable form, the payment instruction is called "ciphertext," which the computer transmits to another location. A computer at that location uses another software code, called a "decryption key," to read the data and turn it back into a plaintext form that a human operator can read.

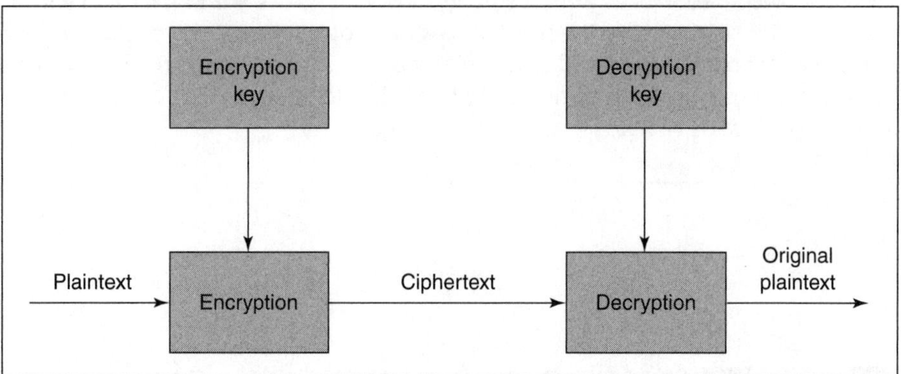

retailer, in turn, can store its electronic cash receipts in specially adapted point-of-sale terminals and transfer accumulated balances to its bank at the end of the day via telephone links. This permits payments to be completed within seconds. Effectively, smart cards can do anything that paper currency and coins can do.

Why Digital Cash May Become Popular

What does a smart card have that paper currency and coins do not? The answer is potentially greater convenience. Smart cards' microchips can communicate with any computing device equipped with the appropriate software. ATMs and retailers' electronic cash registers are examples, but so are desktop and laptop computers.

People cannot use paper currency and coins, checks, or stored-value cards to complete transactions over the Internet. Instead, they usually provide credit-card numbers and finalize payments to credit-card issuers when they pay their monthly bills. Using smart cards or other microchip-bearing devices, however, they can send cash directly across cyberspace and finalize a transaction instantly, just as they could by handing over physical cash in person.

For instance, it is now technologically feasible for someone to use smart-card technology to make a digital cash purchase of a service offered by an Internet-based retailer. Suppose that you like rap music and wish to hear the latest album from Eminem. You can do this by using a device that reads smart cards connected to your personal computer–hardware manufacturers began introducing these devices at retail prices between $80 and $140 in the late 1990s–or you can load digital cash onto a program located on the hard drive of your home computer. As long as the artist's recording company also has the necessary software, you can enter a designated location on the recording company's Web site, point, click, and download the music as a digital file. Your computer automatically sends digital cash as payment for this service. Then you can listen to the latest concert recording on your computer's speakers. (We are ignoring the illegal method of doing the same thing—by downloading a pirated version of the song using peer-to-peer file sharing through Napster, for example.)

Deposit Insurance for Smart-Card Balances

Normally, all depository institutions—including commercial banks, savings and loan associations, mutual savings banks, and savings and loan associations—offer $100,000 of federally backed insurance for deposits. The Federal Deposit Insurance Corporation (FDIC) is the largest organization offering this deposit insurance.

While the FDIC insures deposits in most bank accounts, does e-money qualify as a "deposit"? The FDIC has said that most forms of e-money do not qualify as deposits and thus are not covered by deposit insurance. If a bank becomes insolvent, an e-money holder would then be in the position of a general creditor. This means that he or she would be entitled to reimbursement only after nearly everyone else who is owed money is paid (except, of course, for other e-money holders and other general creditors). At that point, there may not be any funds left.

Legal Protection for Smart Cards

There are some existing laws that extend to e-money and e-money transactions. The Federal Trade Commission Act of 1914[1] prohibits unfair or deceptive practices in, or affecting, commerce. Under this law, e-money issuers who misrepresent the value of their products, or make other misrepresentations on which e-money consumers rely to their detriment, may be liable for engaging in deceptive practices.

General common law principles, discussed in Chapter 1, also apply. For example, the rights and liabilities of e-money issuers and consumers are subject to the common law of contracts. This means that the parties' relationships are affected by the terms of the contracts to which they agree. On the whole, however, it is unclear how existing laws will apply to e-money.

Even without legal protection, e-money payment systems could be safer than cash and checks. Encryption (discussed later in this chapter) may solve some of the problems associated with e-money and with unprotected online exchanges. For example, the theft of encrypted e-money would be a waste of time because without the code a thief could not use the money. The failure of a merchant to give a customer a receipt may not matter if the e-money payment system provides proof of a transaction. Digital signatures could eliminate the problems associated with forged and bounced checks. Digital signatures can also increase the enforceability of contracts entered into online.

1. 15 U.S.C. Sections 41–58.

Privacy Issues

Questions relating to privacy are certain to become important in the future. Are issuers of electronic cash subject to provisions of the Right to Financial Privacy Act of 1978?[2] Basically, before banks, savings and loan associations, credit unions, credit-card issuers, or other financial institutions may give financial information about you to a federal agency, you must explicitly consent that such financial records may be made available to the government. If you do not give your consent, a federal agency wishing to access your financial records must obtain a warrant or some other document entitling the financial institution to allow this.

Currently the Right to Financial Privacy Act applies to financial institutions, including credit-card issuers. Accordingly, a digital cash issuer may be subject to this act if that issuer is deemed to be (1) a bank by virtue of its holding customer funds or (2) any entity that issues a physical card similar to a credit or debit card.

Protection of Online Financial Information[3]

In 1999, Congress passed the Financial Services Modernization Act,[4] also known as the Gramm-Leach-Bliley Act, in an attempt to delineate how financial institutions can treat customer data. The Federal Trade Commission (FTC) determined the final rules[5] pursuant to the act. The final rules became mandatory on July 1, 2001. In general, the act and its implementing rules place restrictions and affirmative obligations on financial institutions to protect consumers' customer data and privacy. All financial institutions must provide their customers with information on their privacy policies and practices. No financial institution can now disclose nonpublic personal information about a consumer to an unaffiliated third party unless restrictive disclosure and opt-out requirements are met.

The FTC's implementing rule (which is found in a 159-page booklet) not only covers standard financial institutions, such as banks, but also online mortgage brokers, real estate brokers, and tax preparers. Interestingly, the rule covers data obtained through any cookies used to track consumers' actions on the Web. One business group that is bound to be hurt by the legislation is credit bureaus. These bureaus routinely sell information that contains names, addresses, Social Security numbers, and so on to help debt collectors and private investigators locate people. In the future, such information cannot be sold without the prior approval of each individual covered.

E-SIGNATURE
An electronic sound, symbol, or process attached to or logically associated with a record and executed or adopted by a person with the intent to sign the record, according to the Uniform Electronic Transactions Act.

SECTION 3 E-SIGNATURES[6]

The development of **e-signature** technology is an important part of the movement toward electronic payments systems as well as online commerce in gen-

2. 12 U.S.C. Sections 3401 *et seq.*

3 You may have been assigned this material in a previous chapter. If so, you may skip this section on the protection of online financial information.

4. 12 U.S.C. Sections 24a, 248b, 1820a, 1828b, 1831v–1831y, 1848a, 2908, 4809; 15 U.S.C. Sections 80b-10a, 6701, 6711–6717, 6731–6735, 6751–6766, 6781, 6801–6809, 6821–6827, 6901–6910; and others.

5. 12 C.F.R. Part 40.

6. You may have been assigned this material in a previous chapter. If so, you may skip this section on e-signatures, except for the case that concludes the section.

eral. Before the days when most people could write, they signed documents with an "X." Then came the handwritten signature, followed by typed signatures, printed signatures, and, most recently, digital signatures that are transmitted electronically. Throughout the evolution of signature technology, debates over what constitutes a valid signature have occurred, and with good reason—without some consensus on what constitutes a valid signature, little business or legal work could be accomplished.

E-Signature Technologies

Today, there are numerous technologies that allow electronic documents to be signed. These include digital signatures and alternative technologies.

The most prevalent e-signature technology is the *asymmetric cryptosystem,* which creates a digital signature using two different (asymmetric) cryptographic "keys." In such a system, a person attaches a digital signature to a document using a private key, or code. The key has a publicly available counterpart. Anyone can use it with the appropriate software to verify that the digital signature was made using the private key. A *cybernotary,* or legally recognized certificate authority (certificate authorities will be discussed shortly), issues the key pair, identifies the owner of the keys, and certifies the validity of the public key. The cybernotary also serves as a repository for public keys. Cybernotaries already are available, but they do not operate within any existing legal framework because they are so new.

Another type of signature technology, known as *signature dynamics,* involves capturing a sender's signature using a stylus and an electronic digitizer pad. A computer program takes the signature's measurements, the sender's identity, the time and date of the signature, and the identity of the hardware. This information is then placed in an encrypted *biometric token* attached to the document being transmitted. To verify the authenticity of the signature, the recipient of the document compares the measurements of the signature with the measurements in the token. When this type of e-signature is used, it is not necessary to have a third party verify the signatory's identity.

Other forms of e-signature have been—or are now being—developed as well. For example, smart cards, because they are embedded with code and other data, could be used to establish a person's identity as validly as a signature on a piece of paper. In addition, technological innovations now under way will allow an e-signature to be evidenced by an image of one's retina, fingerprint, or face that is scanned by a computer and then matched to a numeric code. The scanned image and the numeric code are filed with security companies that maintain files on an accessible server that can be used to authenticate a transaction.

State Laws Governing E-Signatures

Most states have laws governing e-signatures. The problem is that the state e-signature laws are not uniform. Some states—California is a notable example—provide that many types of documents cannot be signed with e-signatures, while other states are more permissive in this respect. Additionally, some states recognize the validity of only digital signatures, while others permit other types of e-signatures.

In an attempt to create more uniformity among the states, the National Conference of Commissioners on Uniform State Laws promulgated the Uniform Electronic Transactions Act (UETA) in 1999. The UETA defines an *e-signature* as "an electronic sound, symbol, or process attached to or logically associated with a record and executed or adopted by a person with the intent to sign the record."[7] A *record* is "information that is inscribed on a tangible medium or that is stored in an electronic or other medium and is retrievable in perceivable form."[8]

This definition of e-signature includes encrypted digital signatures, names (intended as signatures) at the ends of e-mail, and a click on a Web page if the click includes the identification of the person. The UETA also states, among other things, that a signature may not be denied legal effect or enforceability solely because it is in electronic form.

Federal Law on E-Signatures and E-Documents

In 2000, Congress enacted the Electronic Signatures in Global and National Commerce Act (E-SIGN Act)[9] to provide that no contract, record, or signature may be "denied legal effect" solely because it is in an electronic form. In other words, under this law, an electronic signature is as valid as a signature on paper, and an electronic document can be as enforceable as a paper one.

For an electronic signature to be enforceable, the contracting parties must have agreed to use electronic signatures. For an electronic document to be valid, it must be in a form that can be retained and accurately reproduced. Contracts and documents that are exempt include court papers, divorce decrees, evictions, foreclosures, health-insurance terminations, prenuptial agreements, and wills.

Despite these limitations, the E-SIGN Act expands enormously the possibilities for online banking and contracting. From a remote location, a businessperson might open an account with a financial institution, obtain a mortgage or other loan, buy insurance, and purchase real estate over the Internet. Payments and transfers of funds could be done entirely online. This can avoid the time and costs associated with producing, delivering, signing, and returning paper documents.

At issue in the following case was whether an electronic document constituted a "written" agreement under the Federal Arbitration Act of 1925 (FAA), which requires an agreement to arbitrate to be in "writing" to be enforceable. The court's opinion expresses the reason behind Congress's enactment of the E-SIGN Act.

7. UETA 102(8).
8. UETA 102(15).
9. 15 U.S.C. Sections 7001–7006, 7021, and 7031.

CASE 17.3 In re RealNetworks, Inc., Privacy Litigation

United States District Court,
Northern District of Illinois, 2000.
__ F.Supp.2d __.

BACKGROUND AND FACTS RealNetworks, Inc., (**http://www.realnetworks.com**), offers free basic versions of two products, RealPlayer and RealJukebox, for users to download from RealNetworks's Web site. These products allow users to see and hear audio and video available on the Internet and to download, record, and play music. Before a user can install either of these software packages, he or she must accept the terms of RealNetworks's "License Agreement," which appears on the user's screen. This agreement provides in part that "[a]ny and all unresolved disputes arising under this License Agreement shall be submitted to arbitration in the State of Washington." Michael Lieschke, a resident of Illinois, believed that RealNetworks's software products secretly allowed RealNetworks to access and intercept the users' electronic communications and stored information without their knowledge or consent. Lieschke and other Illinois residents filed a suit in a federal district court against RealNetworks, alleging, among other things, trespass to personal property. RealNetworks filed a motion to order the parties to arbitrate the dispute, under the License Agreement. David Keel, an intervenor,[a] argued in part that the License Agreement was unenforceable because it did not constitute a "writing."

a. An *intervenor* is a person who is not originally a party to a suit but who claims an interest in the matter and comes into the case to protect his or her right. The procedure by which this is done is known as *intervention*.

IN THE LANGUAGE OF THE COURT. . .

KOCORAS, J. [Judge.]

* * * *

Courts frequently look to dictionaries in order [to] determine the plain meaning of words and particularly examine how a word was defined at the time the statute was drafted and enacted. The FAA was enacted in 1925. * * * In relevant part, at the time, *Webster's Dictionary* defined "writing" as:

> 1. The act or art of forming letters or characters on paper, wood, stone, or other material, for the purpose of recording the ideas which characters and words express, or of communicating them to others by visible signs. * * *

A legal dictionary at the time provided that "The word 'written,' used in a statute, may include printing and any other mode of representing words and letters."[b] Thus, although the definition of a writing included a traditional paper document, it did not exclude representations of language on other media. Because electronic communications can be letters or characters formed on the screen to record or communicate ideas, can be visible signs and can be legible characters that represent words and letters as well as form the conveyance of meaning, it would seem that the plain meaning of the word "written" does not exclude all electronic communications. * * * [The] easily printable and storable nature [of the License Agreement] is sufficient to render it "written."

* * * *

* * * Intervenor points to Congress' present day discussions about electronic communications in arguing that the FAA's * * * writing requirement cannot be satisfied by an electronic communication. However, the modern congressional discussions that Intervenor points to do not serve as evidence of Congress' intent when it enacted the FAA in 1925. That Congress may now, with some hindsight on the advance of electronic communication, explicitly provide for written and electronic agreements in new legislation, does not mean that Congress in 1925 excluded electronic communications from the category of written communications by not explicitly providing for [them]. Rather, [n]ew words may be designed to fortify the current rule with a more precise text that

b. Here, the court cites Benjamin W. Pope, *Legal Definitions* (Deerfield, Ill.: Callaghan and Co., 1920).

CASE 17.3–Continued

curtails uncertainty. Modern Congress' discussions indicate that it was, in fact, the "uncertain" legal effect of an electronic record or an electronic signature that prompted Congress to consider the "Electronic Signatures in Global and National Commerce Act" * * * . Moreover, it seems that the License Agreement would, nevertheless, constitute a writing even for purposes of Congress' discussions today because the License Agreement may be printed and stored.

DECISION AND REMEDY The court concluded that the License Agreement was a written agreement and ordered the parties to submit their dispute to arbitration. The court held that an electronic communication qualifies as a writing if it satisfies the plain meaning of the word *writing.*

FOR CRITICAL ANALYSIS–Cultural Consideration *Why would anyone ever doubt that an electronic communication was a writing?*

SECTION 4 CYBERPAYMENT INTERMEDIARIES

Of course, the fact that a technology is available does not mean that people will actually adopt it. After all, the basic technology for stored-value cards has been available since the 1970s. Only recently, however, have people made widespread use of stored-value cards to purchase such items as telephone calls and gasoline.

Online Payment Usage Is Still in Its Infancy in the United States

Naturally, retailers do not want to install systems for reading smart cards and processing digital cash payments until additional customers are willing to use them. At the same time, customers have been unwilling to adopt cyberpayment technologies until they are convinced that their payments are secure from transmission errors, fraud, and theft. They also want to know that technologies such as smart cards will be accepted by many merchants before going to the trouble of learning to use them. Additionally, people would be more willing to use smart cards if they knew the cards would be accepted anywhere in the nation—or in the world.

The Standardization of Smart-Card Technology

Banks have traditionally served as payment intermediaries. Today, many banks have memberships in such credit-card industry groups as Visa International, MasterCard, and American Express. As a result, a number of banks are indirectly members of the Global Chipcard Alliance, an industry trade group that has promoted the standardization of smart-card technology. An example is so-called smart-card dial tones, which are sophisticated computer programs that allow any smart card to be accepted by any card-reading terminal.

Such standardization is necessary before widespread—indeed, worldwide—adoption of smart cards will be feasible. Today, U.S. videotapes cannot work on

European videocassette players. In future years, will U.S. residents who travel to Europe find that their smart cards do not work in European equipment or with European software? Will they find that their smart cards will not function in online systems installed in Japan, Hong Kong, or Dubai? Closer to home, will a San Francisco resident discover that her smart card does not work in Iowa City?

At present, every smart-card system has a digital cash **certificate authority.** This is a designated payment intermediary that administers and regulates the terms under which people legitimately engage in e-money transactions. A certificate authority's key job is to approve and implement standards for digital signatures of smart cards, thereby enabling smart-card systems to connect all users. Because the security of their funds and the unrestricted ability to spend them whenever they wish are so important to people, a lot of effort is currently being devoted to standardizing the functions and interactions among certificate authorities. Once this is accomplished, smart cards should work in most locales.

CERTIFICATE AUTHORITY
A group charged with supervising the terms governing how buyers and sellers can legitimately make digital cash transfers.

Digital Cash Use in the Future

It appears likely that there is an incentive for people to shift a portion of their paper-based transactions to exchanges using digital cash. No one can say for sure, however, if people will make this shift quickly or only gradually, perhaps over a period spanning a decade or more. We cannot estimate exactly what portion of retail transactions will ultimately be conducted using digital cash. One thing is certain, however: worldwide distribution of fund transfer cards, such as debit cards and smart cards, is growing rapidly. In 1989, there was one such card for every one hundred people in the world. In 2003, the ratio is estimated to be closer to one card for every seven people in the world.

SECTION 5 ONLINE BANKING

Banks were initially hesitant to jump into cyberspace. Now they recognize that they have an interest in seeing smart cards catch on. The reason is that widespread smart-card adoption holds the promise of significant profits. Funds stored on customers' bank-issued smart cards are still, technically speaking, on deposit with their banks. Thus, just as with traditional checking accounts, banks can earn profits by lending out unused balances on cards to other customers.

Banks also see the promise of fees that they will be able to charge retailers who accept the cards. In addition, they anticipate getting to keep any spare change that customers leave on a card if they decide to throw it away. For instance, suppose that a bank finds that during a given week, a "typical" customer using a disposable smart card has 19 cents in "spare change" left on the card that the customer does not think worth the effort to spend before throwing away the card. If 10,000 customers are "typical," then each week a bank will get to keep a total amount of $1,900. Over the course of a year, this "spare change" will accumulate to $98,800!

Before most people become comfortable about sending digital cash to retailers across cyberspace, they must be sure that they can have secure online dealings with their own banks. This process is further along than the development of digital cash.

E-Money Payment Information

REGULATION E
A set of rules issued by the Federal Reserve System's board of governors to protect users of elecronic fund transfer systems.

Presently, it is not clear which, if any, laws apply to the security of e-money payment information. The Federal Reserve has decided not to impose **Regulation E,** which governs certain electronic fund transfers, on e-money transactions. Federal laws prohibiting unauthorized access to electronic communications might apply, however. For example, the Electronic Communications Privacy Act of 1986[10] prohibits any person from knowingly divulging to any other person the contents of an electronic communication while that communication is in transmission or in electronic storage.

How Online Banking Has Developed

You can access the Federal Reserve Bank's home page as well as extensive information about "the Fed" at **http://woodrow.mpls.frb.fed.us/info/policy**.

Online banking began through the efforts of home financial management software developers, such as Quicken. These businesses wanted to include attractive features to induce people to buy their software, so they started offering to help software users consolidate bills and initiate payments over the Internet. Bill payments are typically issued from bank accounts, so ultimately the financial software companies formed alliances with banks.

Soon, banks realized that they might be able to earn fee income by providing these kinds of services themselves. By 2002, over one thousand U.S. banks offered online banking services via the Internet. Thousands of other banks are preparing to offer online banking services.

Most online bank customers use three kinds of services. One of the most popular is still bill consolidation and payment. Another is transferring funds among accounts. This online service eliminates the need to make trips to a bank branch or ATM. The third is applying for loans, which many banks now permit customers to do over the Internet. Customers typically must appear in person to finalize the terms of a loan. Nonetheless, they can save some time and effort by starting the process at home.

What Must Come First in Online Banking?

There are two important banking activities generally not available online: depositing and withdrawing funds. This, of course, is where smart cards can enter the picture. With smart cards, people could transfer funds on the Internet, thereby effectively transforming their personal computers into home ATMs. This, in turn, would give them more incentive to bank from home via the Internet. Many observers believe that online banking is the way to introduce people to e-money and to induce them to think about using smart cards.

This raises the potential for a chicken-or-egg problem to develop. Bank customers may wait for widespread acceptability of smart cards before exploring home banking options. At the same time, banks may wait for more customers to choose online banking before making big investments in smart-card technology.

Nevertheless, many bankers have decided that there are two very good reasons to promote online banking irrespective of smart cards. One is that, once in

10. 18 U.S.C. Sections 2510–2521.

place, online banking is less expensive for the bank. Banks require fewer employees to maintain automated systems, so online banking saves banks from incurring significant expenses associated with large networks of branch offices. The potential cost savings of online banking are hard to quantify. This has not stopped some banks from seeking to convert customers to Internet-based banking services, however. A number of banks have adopted explicit targets for segments of their customer bases that they wish to entice into online banking within the next few years. Many aim to convince more than half their customers to bank online by 2010.

Competitive Pressures for Online Banking

Another key rationale that bankers have for developing online services is the threat of competition. Many banks worry that if they do not figure out how to provide services online, someone else will—and steal away many of their best customers.

Since the late 1990s, several banks, such as Bank of Internet (**http://www.bofi.com**), have operated exclusively on the Internet. These "virtual banks" have no physical branch offices. Because few people are equipped to send virtual banks funds via smart-card technologies, the virtual banks have accepted deposits through physical delivery systems, such as the U.S. Postal Service or FedEx. This saves the expense of maintaining a costly branch network involving land, buildings, and tellers, which sharply reduces the costs that virtual banks incur relative to traditional banks. These Internet-only banks pass on part of the cost savings to customers in the form of lower banking fees and lower interest rates on loans. Some even offer free checking with very low minimum deposits, such as $100, and no-fee money market accounts with average monthly balances of $2,500 or more.

INTERNET LOAN BROKERS Virtual banks have not been the only online competition faced by traditional banks. Today, there are several Internet loan brokers, such as QuickenMortgage, E-Loan, GetSmart, Lending Tree, and Microsoft's HomeAdviser. Each of these broker systems uses software that matches consumers with appropriate loans. The consumer supplies information to the program. The program then searches among available loan products for the best fit. The loans are available from lenders with whom the broker has a contractual relationship.

INTERNET CREDIT-CARD BUSINESSES Internet loan brokers' biggest forays into banks' turf have been in the credit-card and mortgage markets. In the credit-card area, Internet brokers have been especially successful in providing credit-card debt-consolidation services. They do not always compete with banks; often, they act as marketers for traditional banks using credit cards. Credit-card issuers pay the brokers fees to match them with new customers. This saves the issuers from having to create lists of potential prospects and to develop and mail card offers.

INTERNET MORTGAGE MARKET In the mortgage market, however, the competition is more direct. When mortgage rates fell in the late 1990s, people who wished to refinance flooded the telephone lines of traditional banking institutions. Many experienced busy signals, long waits on hold, and slow responses from loan officers. This induced them to turn to the Internet. One Internet broker reported that visitors to its Web site increased from about 35,000 per month to over 500,000 per month. Some real estate experts estimate that within a few years, at least 10 percent of U.S. mortgage loan refinancings will be initiated through the Internet.

PROBLEMS WITH REGULATORY COMPLIANCE A traditional bank is required today to define its market area. It must provide information to regulators about deposits and loans. All of these compliance efforts are pursuant to the Home Mortgage Disclosure Act (HMDA).[11] In addition, these compliance efforts also fall under those required by the Community Reinvestment Act of 1977.[12]

One requirement under the Community Reinvestment Act is that all banks establish market areas contiguous to their branch offices. They must map them using existing boundaries, as defined by counties or standard metropolitan areas (SMAs) in which offices are located. This act also requires that after banks delineate the communities they serve, they must annually review the entire banking community using such maps to portray community delineations. All of this is done to prevent discrimination in lending practices.

A current issue has to do with how a successful "cyberbank" could delineate its community. If Bank of Internet becomes a tremendous success, does it really have any physical communities? Will the Federal Reserve Board simply allow a written description of a cybercommunity for Internet customers? Such regulatory issues are new, challenging, and certain to become more complicated as the scope of Internet banking widens internationally.

SECTION 6 SECURITY ISSUES LOOM LARGE

Electronic banking technologies make some people nervous. Often, people hesitate to adopt digital cash for the same kinds of reasons that have slowed adoption of other new technologies: until they have time to evaluate what's new, people often begin by assuming the worst.

The Security of Digital Cash

It remains to be seen whether people will find digital cash more convenient than other means of payment. A big issue in the minds of most potential users of smart cards or online banking services is the security of the e-money payments they make. For bank regulators, the security of digital cash is one of two key issues raised by electronic banking. The other concerns the potential for an upsurge of fraudulent banking practices.

Just because smart cards can be equipped with authentication software does not mean they are 100 percent secure. Criminals can be ingenious. There are a number of ways that one could imagine them stealing or otherwise interfering with digital cash. To thwart such efforts, banks and crime enforcement officials must anticipate them and develop ways to hinder potential criminals.

---

11. 12 U.S.C. Sections 2801–2810.

12. 12 U.S.C. Sections 2901–2908.

DIGITAL COUNTERFEITING One old-fashioned but potentially lucrative way that a crook could pilfer digital money is by **counterfeiting.** The most obvious way to counterfeit would be to produce smart cards that look, feel, and function just like legitimate smart cards.

COUNTERFEITING
Making a copy of currency (or a smart card containing digital cash) with the intent to defraud.

Issuers of smart cards have already undertaken a number of defensive measures aimed at preventing such counterfeiting efforts from succeeding. One is to make counterfeit smart cards easier to recognize. Smart-card issuers typically place holographic images on their own legitimate cards, just as credit-card issuers do. Issuers also include special features in the computer code on smart-card microprocessors that complicate efforts to access data stored in memory. They embed these features in a portion of the microprocessor's memory that can be changed only by altering its internal functions. Issuers also equip smart cards with physical barriers intended to inhibit optical or electrical analysis of the microprocessor's memory. Most smart-card chips are also coated with several layers of wiring, making it difficult to remove the chip without damaging it beyond repair.

STEALING DIGITAL CASH OFFLINE AND ONLINE One of the most common types of bank robbery today entails driving a pickup truck through the front window of a bank branch or supermarket containing an ATM. Two or three people quickly lift the ATM into the bed of the truck, drive to their hideout, and remove the cash from the machine. An *offline theft* of digital cash is only slightly more sophisticated. Thieves break into a merchant's establishment, physically remove electronic devices used to store value from customers' smart cards, and download these funds onto their own cards. The threat of this kind of offline theft is likely to be a bigger problem for small retailers that do not wish to incur the expense required to process all smart-card transactions immediately.

More sophisticated thieves might attempt to engage in *online thefts*. They could try to intercept payment messages as they are transmitted from smart cards and other electronic funds storage devices to host computers. For instance, thieves might learn the times of day that a large upscale department store transmits its receipts to a central computer. Then they could attempt to tap into the store's transmission line and steal the funds. These kinds of online theft are most likely to be "inside jobs," in which employees pilfer their own companies' funds using their knowledge of internal systems for transmitting digital cash.

MAKING E-MONEY "CATCH A COLD" A key feature of digital cash is its dependence on smoothly functioning microprocessors and software. This exposes electronic money to special security dangers, such as computer viruses that could damage the input-output mechanisms of smart-card microprocessors.

MALFUNCTIONING MONEY Paper currency can wear out. Magnetic-ink-scanning devices can misread checks. But people can still exchange physical units of money during electricity outages. Power failures or other equipment breakdowns can bring e-money transactions to a grinding halt.

Learn about the U.S. government's efforts to prevent money laundering at **http://www.ustreas.gov/fincen**.

The widespread use of digital cash could also contribute to a problem that is already well known to today's law enforcement officials. Many people try to move funds from place to place to avoid reporting the funds to tax authorities or to hide illegalities associated with the funds. These activities could become even more common in a world of digital cash. For a further discussion of this possibility, see this chapter's *Controversial Issues* feature.

SECTION 7 WHAT WILL DIGITAL CASH REPLACE, IF ANYTHING?

If people start to use smart cards, personal computers, and cellular phones to store and transmit digital cash, presumably they will have less of a desire to use other forms of money. To understand why, consider Exhibit 17–3 on page 428, which lists the key characteristics of checks, currency, and digital cash.

CHECKS VERSUS CURRENCY In comparing currency with checks, it is clear that people must trade off the various features offered by each type of money. Checks promise greater security, because if a thief steals a woman's handbag containing cash and checks, she can contact her depository institution to halt payment on all of the checks in the handbag. Currency payments are final, however, so the thief can spend all the cash he has taken from her. Checks can be sent through the mail, but the use of currency requires face-to-face contact. In addition, currency transactions are anonymous, which may be desirable under some circumstances. Nevertheless, not everyone will accept a check in payment for a transaction, and a check payment is not final until the check clears. Check transactions are also more expensive. After evaluating these features of currency and checks, people typically choose to hold both payment instruments.

DIGITAL CASH FEATURES People will likewise compare the features of digital cash with those currently offered by government-provided currency and checking accounts available from depository institutions. As Exhibit 17–3 indicates, the acceptability of digital cash is uncertain at present. Nonetheless, we are contemplating a future environment in which it would be widely accepted, and in such an environment, digital cash would be nearly as acceptable as government-provided currency. Digital cash held on smart cards without special security features, such as personal identification numbers, will be as susceptible to theft as government currency. Some digital cash, however, may be held on devices, such as laptop computers or even wristwatches (Swiss watch manufacturers have already developed watches with microchips for storing digital cash), that require an access code before a microchip containing digital cash can be accessed. Overall, therefore, digital cash is likely to be somewhat more secure than government-provided currency, although not as secure as check transactions.

Digital cash transactions are likely to be less costly to undertake, because people will not have to go to depository institution branches or automated teller machines to obtain digital cash (although they will be able to do this if they wish). They will also be able to access digital cash at home on their personal computers as well as send digital cash from remote locations using the Internet, and digital cash transactions will be instantaneously final. Unlike transactions using currency, therefore, digital cash transactions need not be conducted face-to-face. Like currency transactions, however, most digital cash transfers will be anonymous.

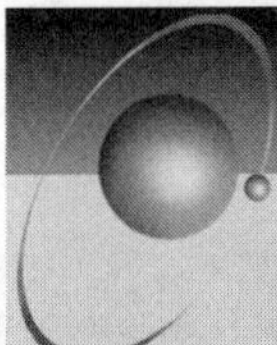

Controversial Issues in the Online World

E-Banking and Online Money Laundering

Tax evaders, drug traffickers, and others seek to "launder" money every day. That is, they try moving funds around the world without their actions being traced. Estimates are that about $500 billion is "laundered" worldwide every year. Congress has passed several laws aimed at minimizing money laundering, including the Money Laundering Control Act of 1986[a] and the Money Laundering Suppression Act of 1994.[b]

The Financial Crimes Enforcement Network

A U.S. Treasury Department division, the Financial Crimes Enforcement Network (FinCEN), seeks to fight money laundering. Every year, FinCEN receives 13 million reports covering everything from casino earnings to foreign bank accounts maintained by U.S. citizens. Money launderers today invest in bars, restaurants, travel agencies, jewelry stores, and construction companies—virtually any business through which they can channel cash earned illegally.

The Financial Action Taskforce, a group of twenty-six countries fighting money laundering, believes that the speed, security, and anonymity of new Internet payment systems will lead to massive additional money laundering. Drug traffickers in particular will no longer need to smuggle currency across borders—they will be able to move funds through the Internet. Technology will permit anonymous transactions outside the regulated banking sector. Consequently, all restrictions on the banking system to make money laundering riskier and costlier will be for naught. Even when digital cash enters the banking system, it will have already bounced among numerous intermediaries, making the funds hard to trace. By definition, e-cash will be heavily encrypted. Thus, law enforcement authorities will not be able to reconstruct transactions, nor will private providers of e-cash. DigiCash, a major European electronic money provider, indicates that it cannot track how its customers spend their money.

Online Banking and the Bank Secrecy Act

Under the Bank Secrecy Act of 1970,[c] all financial institutions have to monitor some financial transactions and file reports, particularly for "suspicious activity." When a bank accepts deposits through cyberpayments, its existing policies for customer identification may have to be changed in order to conform with the Bank Secrecy Act. After all, the type of information outlined above when we discussed FinCEN contemplates a face-to-face transaction including full name, address, date of birth, occupation, and some type of legally acceptable identification.

Whenever a financial institution accepts a cyberpayment, the information that it collects on the "client" will not be as reliable as in an in-person transaction. In order for financial institutions to comply with the Bank Secrecy Act's requirements, then, they have to require face-to-face transactions when an Internet bank account is first established. So far, no online banks have made this part of their account-opening procedure. After all, the main benefit of Internet banking is that the customer does not have to physically go to a building to open an account and to complete transactions.

FOR CRITICAL ANALYSIS

Imagine yourself as a FinCEN employee trying to hinder money-laundering activities. You know that banks that transfer cash into digital money systems have a limit of a few hundred dollars per transfer. How might money launderers overcome this constraint?

a. 18 U.S.C. Sections 981–982, and U.S.C. Section 5324.

b. 31 U.S.C. Section 5330.

c. Bank Secrecy Act, 12 U.S.C. 1951–1959, implemented by the Department of Treasury's Financial Record Keeping and Reporting of Currency and Foreign Transactions Regulation, 31 C.F.R. 103 *et seq.*

EXHIBIT 17–3 Characteristics of Various Types of Money

Here we compare various types of money with respect to six features. As you can see, digital cash offers many advantages. Its main drawback at the present time is its uncertain acceptability.

FEATURE	CHECKS	CURRENCY	DIGITAL CASH
Security	High	Low	Potentially high
Per-transfer cost	High	Medium	Low
Payment final, face to face	No	Yes	Yes
Payment final, non-face to face	No	No	Yes
Anonymity	No	Yes	Yes
Acceptability	Restricted	Wide	Uncertain at present

SOURCE: Aleksander Berentsen, "Monetary Policy Implications of Digital Money," *Kyklos*, 51 (1998), p. 92.

In most respects, therefore, digital cash looks like a better means of payment than government-provided currency. Certainly, for some time to come, a number of items—canned beverages and candy in vending machines, for example—will be easiest to purchase using government-provided currency. Many observers, however, believe that widespread adoption of privately issued digital cash will ultimately tend to crowd out government-provided currency. On many college campuses, vending machines already accept stored-value cards. Eventually, vending machines on street corners are likely to have smart-card readers.

SECTION 8 DIGITAL CASH, CENTRAL BANKERS, AND BANKING REGULATION

As long as regulated financial institutions are the main issuers of digital cash, central bankers worldwide and bank regulators do not have much to fear. The main concern will occur when (1) digital cash becomes significant as measured by its percentage of all liquid assets, and (2) the majority of digital cash is issued by nonbank entities that are not subject to banking regulations, deposit insurance requirements, and regulatory supervision.

All existing arrangements designed to protect consumers, such as federally backed deposit insurance, will not apply to digital cash created by nonbank entities. If there is a failure of certain nonbank issuers, the public could lose all confidence in any type of electronic cash system. This could cause runs on electronic cash systems, thereby endangering the soundness of financial systems in general.

There is also an issue with respect to regulating the rate of growth of the money supply. The Federal Reserve System is in charge of doing this. How much control will the "Fed" have over money supply growth when an increasing percentage of the money supply consists of digital cash issued by nonbank entities?

TERMS AND CONCEPTS

automated clearing house (ACH) 407
automated teller machine (ATM) 407
certificate authority 421
counterfeiting 425
debit card 410
digital cash 406
e-money 409
e-money transfer 413
e-signature 416
Regulation E 422
smart card 413
stored-value card 410

QUESTIONS AND CASE PROBLEMS

17–1. E-Payment Systems. First American Bank uses computer systems to credit and debit its customers' accounts. First American also uses automated teller machine networks and the services of automated clearing house systems. The bank is beginning to use stored-value cards and is considering the use of smart cards. What is the difference between the systems that the bank currently uses and the systems that it is beginning to use and is considering? What laws cover the newer methods of payment?

17–2. E-Signatures and E-Documents. Representatives of Omega Technologies Corp. in California and Gamma Investments, Inc, in New York negotiate the terms of a contract over the Internet. These representatives, who have never met face-to-face, want to enter into a binding contract. Is it possible, under federal law, to make these parties' e-signatures valid and their e-document enforceable? If so, what is required?

17–3. Online Banking. First Internet Bank operates exclusively on the Web with no physical branch offices. Although some of First Internet's business is transacted with smart-card technology, most of its business with its customers is conducted through the mail. First Internet offers free checking, no-fee money market accounts, and mortgage refinancing, among other services. With what regulation covering banks might First Internet find it difficult to comply, and what is the difficulty?

17–4. Stored-Value Cards and Smart Cards. The business of American Banknote Corp. (ABN) is security products and systems, including stored-value cards and smart cards. American Bank Note Holographics, Inc. (ABNH), was an ABN subsidiary that produced holographic images for use on those cards and other items. In July 1998, ABNH issued stock for sale to the public at $8.50 per share. At the time, ABNH stated, among other things, that it was more valuable than this price reflected. Six months later, when the share price was $18, ABNH announced that accounting "irregularities" had overstated its sales for the previous three years by more than 50 percent. The price of ABNH stock fell to $1.62. Investors who had bought the stock before the announcement, and others, filed a suit in a federal district court against ABNH and others, claiming violations of the securities laws. The defendants filed a motion to dismiss the suit, but the court largely denied it, in part because the statements about the value of ABNH had been false. How do stored-value cards and smart cards work? What is the market for these cards? How might that market have influenced the price of ABNH stock? [*In re American Bank Note Holographics, Inc. Securities Litigation,* 93 F.Supp.2d 424 (S.D.N.Y. 2000)]

17–5. Debit Cards. On April 20, 1999, while visiting her daughter and son-in-law Michael Dowdell, Carol Farrow asked Dowdell to fix her car. She gave him her car keys, attached to which was a small wallet containing her debit card. Dowdell repaired her car and returned the keys. Two days later, Farrow noticed that her debit card was missing and contacted Auburn Bank, which had issued the card. Farrow reviewed her automatic teller machine (ATM) transaction record and noticed that a large amount of cash had been withdrawn from her checking account on April 22 and April 23. When Farrow reviewed the photos taken by the ATM cameras at the time of the withdrawals, she recognized Dowdell as the person using her debit card. Dowdell was convicted in an Alabama state court of the crime of fraudulent use of a debit card. What are the steps in a debit-card transaction? What problems with debit-card transactions are apparent from the facts of this case? How might these problems be prevented? [*Dowdell v. State,* __ So.2d __ (Ala.Crim.App. 2000)]

17–6. Financial Services on the Web. Ford Motor Co. makes and markets motor vehicles and related products under the "Ford" trademark. The company also offers financial services under that mark and others, including

"Ford Financial," through, among other outlets, Ford Motor Credit Co. (FMC). FMC is one of the world's largest finance companies, providing services to more than 9 million individual and corporate customers. These services include investment opportunities, as well as individual and commercial lending. FMC has a Web site at **http://www.fordcredit.com**. In April 1998, Ford Financial Solutions (FFS) began using the mark "Ford" to offer financial services for individuals and small businesses. FFS has a Web site at **http://www.fordfinancialsolutions.com**. A survey of individuals seeking or planning to seek financial advice indicated that 54 percent believed Ford was responsible for the Web site at FFS's URL. Ford filed a suit in a federal district court against FFS to prevent its use of "Ford" in connection with financial services. The court ordered FFS to stop using the "Ford" mark. Would it have been as effective for the court to order FFS to simply include a disclaimer on its Web site? Why or why not? [*Ford Motor Co. v. Ford Financial Solutions, Inc.*, 103 F.Supp.2d 1126 (N.D. Iowa 2000)]

17–7. Smart Cards. Security Dynamics Technologies, Inc., a leading provider of data security solutions, markets products that help organizations conduct business securely and facilitate business-to-business and business-to-consumer e-commerce. Its products use a combination of smart-card technology, access control and management products, public key encryption technology, and security administration software. In July 1996, Security Dynamics acquired RSA, a leading provider of cryptographics technology. In July 1997, Security Dynamics acquired DynaSoft, another leading security company providing solutions for secure access to information. Between April and July 1998, the price of Security Dynamics's stock dropped more than 60 percent. Lori Fitzer and other investors filed a suit in a federal district court against Security Dynamics and its officers, alleging violations of the securities laws arising from their announcements about the firm and its prospects. The court dismissed the suit on the ground that the statements were, among other things, "puffing." What does the volatility of Security Dynamics's stock price, and the court's holding, indicate about the technology behind smart cards and similar financial security products? [*Fitzer v. Security Dynamics Technologies, Inc.*, 119 F.Supp.2d 12 (D.Mass. 2000)]

WEB EXERCISES

Go to **http://lec.westbuslaw.com**, the Web site that accompanies this text. Select "Internet Applications," and then click on "Chapter 17." There you will find the following Internet research exercise that you can perform to learn more about electronic payment systems:

Activity 17–1: Digital Cash versus E-Checks

CHAPTER 18
Antitrust

Concepts Covered

After reading this chapter, you should be able to:

1. **Explain the purpose of antitrust laws and identify the major federal antitrust statutes.**
2. **Summarize the types of activities prohibited by Sections 1 and 2 of the Sherman Act.**
3. **Discuss the potential for monopolization in a knowledge-based economy.**
4. **Indicate why the Clayton Act was passed and summarize the types of activities prohibited by this act.**
5. **Describe how the antitrust laws are enforced.**

"Free competition is worth more to society than it costs."

Oliver Wendell Holmes, Jr., 1841–1935
(Associate justice of the United States Supreme Court, 1902–1932)

Today's antitrust laws are the direct descendants of common law actions intended to limit **restraints on trade** (agreements between firms that have the effect of reducing competition in the marketplace). Concern over monopolistic practices arose following the Civil War with the growth of large corporate enterprises and their attempts to reduce or eliminate competition. They did this by legally tying themselves together in a *business trust,* a type of business entity. The participants in the most famous trust–the Standard Oil trust in the late 1800s–transferred their stock to a trustee and received trust certificates in exchange. The trustee then made decisions fixing prices, regulating production, and determining the control of exclusive geographic markets for all of the oil companies that were in the Standard Oil trust. It became apparent that the trust wielded so much economic power that corporations outside the trust could not compete effectively.

RESTRAINT ON TRADE
Any contract or combination that tends to eliminate or reduce competition, effect a monopoly, artificially maintain prices, or otherwise hamper the course of trade and commerce.

ANTITRUST LAW
The body of federal and state laws and statutes protecting trade and commerce from unlawful restraints, price discrimination, price fixing, and monopolies.

Many states attempted to control such monopolistic behavior by enacting statutes outlawing the use of trusts. That is why all of the laws that regulate economic competition today are referred to as **antitrust laws.** At the national level, the government recognized the problem in 1887 and passed the Interstate Commerce Act,[1] followed by the Sherman Antitrust Act in 1890.[2] In 1914,

1. 49 U.S.C. Sections 501–526.
2. 15 U.S.C. Sections 1–7.

Congress passed the Clayton Act[3] and the Federal Trade Commission Act[4] to further curb anticompetitive or unfair business practices. Since their passage, the 1914 acts have been amended by Congress to broaden and strengthen their coverage, and they continue to be an important element in the legal environment in which businesses operate.

To see the American Bar Association's Web page on antitrust law, go to **http://www.abanet.org/antitrust**.

This chapter examines these major antitrust statutes, focusing particularly on the Sherman Act and the Clayton Act, as amended, and the types of activities prohibited by those acts. Although antitrust laws are just beginning to be applied in the online environment, the potential for anticompetitive practices in that environment is significant. Remember in reading this chapter that the basis of antitrust legislation is the desire to foster competition. Antitrust legislation was initially created—and continues to be enforced—because of our belief that competition leads to lower prices, more product information, and a better distribution of wealth between consumers and producers.

SECTION 1 THE SHERMAN ANTITRUST ACT

In 1890, Congress passed "An Act to Protect Trade and Commerce against Unlawful Restraints and Monopolies"—more commonly referred to as the Sherman Antitrust Act, or simply the Sherman Act. The author of the 1890 act, Senator John Sherman, was the brother of the famed Civil War general and a recognized financial authority. He had been concerned for years about the diminishing competition within American industry. He told Congress that the Sherman Act "does not announce a new principle of law, but applies old and well-recognized principles of the common law."[5]

Major Provisions of the Sherman Act

Sections 1 and 2 contain the main provisions of the Sherman Act:

> 1: Every contract, combination in the form of trust or otherwise, or conspiracy, in restraint of trade or commerce among the several States, or with foreign nations, is hereby declared to be illegal [and is a felony punishable by fine and/or imprisonment].
>
> 2: Every person who shall monopolize, or attempt to monopolize, or combine or conspire with any other person or persons, to monopolize any part of the trade or commerce among the several States, or with foreign nations, shall be deemed guilty of a felony [and is similarly punishable].

These two sections of the Sherman Act are quite different. Section 1 requires two or more persons, as a person cannot contract, combine, or conspire alone. Thus, the essence of the illegal activity is *the act of joining together.* Section 2 applies both to an individual person and to several people, because it refers to "[e]very person." Thus, unilateral conduct can result in a violation of Section 2.

The cases brought to the courts under Section 1 of the Sherman Act differ from those brought under Section 2. Section 1 cases are often concerned with

3. 15 U.S.C. Sections 12–26a.
4. 15 U.S.C. Sections 45–48a.
5. 21 Congressional Record 2456 (1890).

finding an agreement (written or oral) that leads to a restraint of trade. Section 2 cases deal with the structure of a **monopoly** that exists in the marketplace. The term *monopoly* is generally used to describe a market in which there is a single seller. Whereas Section 1 focuses on agreements that are restrictive—that is, agreements that have a wrongful purpose—Section 2 looks at the so-called misuse of **monopoly power** in the marketplace. Monopoly power exists when a firm has an extreme amount of **market power**—the power to affect the market price of its product. Both Section 1 and Section 2 seek to curtail market industrial practices that result in undesired monopoly pricing and output behavior. Any case brought under Section 2, however, must be one in which the "threshold" or "necessary" amount of monopoly power already exists. We will return to a discussion of these two sections of the Sherman Act after we look at the act's jurisdictional requirements.

MONOPOLY
A term generally used to describe a market in which there is a single seller or a limited number of sellers.

MONOPOLY POWER
The ability of a monopoly to dictate what takes place in a given market.

MARKET POWER
The power of a firm to control the market price of its product. A monopoly has the greatest degree of market power.

Jurisdictional Requirements

The Sherman Act applies only to restraints that have a significant impact on interstate commerce. As will be discussed later in this chapter, the Sherman Act also extends to U.S. nationals abroad who are engaged in activities that have an effect on U.S. foreign commerce. State regulation of anticompetitive practices addresses purely local restraints on competition. Courts have generally held that any activity that substantially affects interstate commerce falls within the ambit of the Sherman Act. Courts have construed the meaning of *interstate commerce* more and more broadly over the years, bringing even local activities within the regulatory power of the national government.

SECTION 2 SECTION 1 OF THE SHERMAN ACT

The underlying assumption of Section 1 of the Sherman Act is that society's welfare is harmed if rival firms are permitted to join in an agreement that consolidates their market power or otherwise restrains competition. Not all agreements between rivals, however, *unreasonably* restrain trade or result in enhanced market power.

The Rule of Reason

Under what is called the **rule of reason,** anticompetitive agreements that allegedly violate Section 1 of the Sherman Act are analyzed with the view that they may, in fact, constitute reasonable restraints on trade. When applying this rule, the court considers the purpose of the arrangement, the powers of the parties, and the effect of their actions in restraining trade. If the court deems that legitimate competitive benefits outweigh the anticompetitive effects of the agreement, it will be held lawful.

RULE OF REASON
A test by which a court balances the positive effects (such as economic efficiency) of an agreement against its potentially anticompetitive effects. In antitrust litigation, many practices are analyzed under the rule of reason.

The need for a rule-of-reason analysis of some agreements in restraint of trade is obvious—if the rule of reason had not been developed, virtually any business agreement could conceivably violate the Sherman Act. Justice Louis D. Brandeis effectively phrased this sentiment in *Chicago Board of Trade v. United States,*[6] a case decided in 1918:

6. 246 U.S. 231, 38 S.Ct. 242, 62 L.Ed. 683 (1918).

> Every agreement concerning trade, every regulation of trade, restrains. To bind, to restrain, is of their very essence. The true test of legality is whether the restraint imposed is such as merely regulates and perhaps thereby promotes competition or whether it is such as may suppress or even destroy competition.

When analyzing an alleged Section 1 violation under the rule of reason, a court will consider several factors, including the purpose of the agreement, the parties' power to implement the agreement to achieve that purpose, and the effect or potential effect of the agreement on competition. Another factor that might be considered is whether the parties could have relied on less restrictive means to achieve their purpose.

Per Se Violations of Section 1

Some agreements are so blatantly and substantially anticompetitive that they are deemed illegal *per se* (on their faces, or inherently) under Section 1. If an agreement is found to be of a type that is deemed a **per se violation,** a court is precluded from determining whether the agreement's benefits outweigh its anticompetitive effects.

***PER SE* VIOLATION**
A type of anticompetitive agreement—such as a horizontal price-fixing agreement—that is considered to be so injurious to the public that there is no need to determine whether it actually injures market competition; rather, it is in itself (*per se*) a violation of the Sherman Act.

The dividing line between agreements that constitute *per se* violations and agreements that should be judged under a rule of reason is seldom clear. Moreover, in some cases, the United States Supreme Court has stated that it is applying a *per se* rule, and yet a careful reading of the Court's analysis suggests that the Court is weighing benefits against harms under a rule of reason. Perhaps the most that can be said with certainty is that although the distinction between the two rules seems clear in theory, in the actual application of antitrust laws, the distinction has not always been so obvious.

We turn now to the types of trade restraints prohibited by Section 1 of the Sherman Act. Generally, these restraints fall into two broad categories: *horizontal restraints* and *vertical restraints.* Some restraints are *per se* violations of Section 1, but others may be permissible; those that are not *per se* violations are tested under the rule of reason.

Horizontal Restraints

The term **horizontal restraint** is encountered frequently in antitrust law. A horizontal restraint is any agreement that in some way restrains competition between rival firms competing in the same market.

HORIZONTAL RESTRAINT
Any agreement that in some way restrains competition between rival firms competing in the same market.

PRICE FIXING Any agreement among competitors to fix prices, or price-fixing agreement, constitutes a *per se* violation of Section 1 of the Sherman Act. Perhaps the definitive case regarding **price-fixing agreements** remains the 1940 case of *United States v. Socony-Vacuum Oil Co.*[7] In that case, a group of independent oil producers in Texas and Louisiana were caught between falling demand due to the Great Depression of the 1930s and increasing supply from newly discovered oil fields in the region. In response to these conditions, a

PRICE-FIXING AGREEMENT
An agreement between competitors in which the competitors agree to fix the prices of products or services at a certain level; prohibited by the Sherman Act.

7. 310 U.S. 150, 60 S.Ct. 811, 84 L.E.2d 1129 (1940).

group of the major refining companies agreed to buy "distress" gasoline (excess supplies) from the independents so as to dispose of it in an "orderly manner."

Although there was no explicit agreement as to price, it was clear that the purpose of the agreement was to limit the supply of gasoline on the market and thereby raise prices. There may have been good reasons for the agreement. Nonetheless, the United States Supreme Court recognized the dangerous effects that such an agreement could have on open and free competition. The Court held that the reasonableness of a price-fixing agreement is never a defense; any agreement that restricts output or artificially fixes price is a *per se* violation of Section 1. The rationale of the *per se* rule was best stated in what is now the most famous portion of the Court's opinion. In footnote 59, Justice William O. Douglas compared a freely functioning price system to a body's central nervous system, condemning price-fixing agreements as threats to "the central nervous system of the economy."

GROUP BOYCOTTS A **group boycott** is an agreement by two or more sellers to refuse to deal with (boycott) a particular person or firm. Such group boycotts have been held to constitute *per se* violations of Section 1 of the Sherman Act. Section 1 has been violated if it can be demonstrated that the boycott or joint refusal to deal was undertaken with the intention of eliminating competition or preventing entry into a given market. Some boycotts, such as group boycotts against a supplier for political reasons, may be protected under the First Amendment right to freedom of expression.

GROUP BOYCOTT
The refusal to deal with a particular person or firm by a group of competitors; prohibited by the Sherman Act.

HORIZONTAL MARKET DIVISION It is a *per se* violation of Section 1 of the Sherman Act for competitors to divide up territories or customers. For example, manufacturers A, B, and C compete against one another in the states of Kansas, Nebraska, and Iowa. By agreement, A sells products only in Kansas, B sells only in Nebraska, and C sells only in Iowa. This concerted action reduces costs and allows each of the three (assuming there is no other competition) to raise the price of the goods sold in its own state. The same violation would take place if A, B, and C simply agreed that A would sell only to institutional purchasers (school districts, universities, state agencies and departments, cities, and so on) in the three states, B only to wholesalers, and C only to retailers.

TRADE ASSOCIATIONS Businesses in the same general industry or profession frequently organize trade associations to pursue common interests. Their joint activities may provide for exchanges of information, representation of the members' business interests before governmental bodies, advertising campaigns, and the setting of regulatory standards to govern their industry or profession. Generally, the rule of reason is applied to many of these horizontal actions. For example, if a court finds that a trade association practice or agreement that restrains trade is nonetheless sufficiently beneficial both to the association and to the public, it may deem the restraint reasonable.

Other trade association agreements may have such substantially anticompetitive effects that the court will consider them to be in violation of Section 1 of the Sherman Act. In *National Society of Professional Engineers v. United States*,[8]

8. 453 U.S. 679, 98 S.Ct. 1355, 55 L.Ed.2d 637 (1978).

for example, it was held that the society's code of ethics—which prohibited discussion of prices with a potential customer until after the customer had chosen an engineer—was a Section 1 violation. The United States Supreme Court found that this ban on competitive bidding was "nothing less than a frontal assault on the basic policy of the Sherman Act."

JOINT VENTURES Joint ventures undertaken by competitors are also subject to antitrust laws. A *joint venture* is an undertaking by two or more individuals or firms for a specific purpose. If a joint venture does not involve price fixing or market divisions, the agreement will be analyzed under the rule of reason. Whether the venture will then be upheld under Section 1 depends on an overall assessment of the purposes of the venture, a strict analysis of the potential benefits relative to the likely harms, and in some cases, an assessment of whether there are less restrictive alternatives for achieving the same goals.[9]

Vertical Restraints

VERTICAL RESTRAINT
Any restraint on trade created by agreements between firms at different levels in the manufacturing and distribution process.

VERTICALLY INTEGRATED FIRM
A firm that carries out two or more functional phases (manufacture, distribution, retailing, and so on) of a product.

A **vertical restraint** of trade is one that results from an agreement between firms at different levels in the manufacturing and distribution process. In contrast to horizontal relationships, which occur at the same level of operation, vertical relationships encompass the entire chain of production: the purchase of inputs, basic manufacturing, distribution to wholesalers, and eventual sale of a product at the retail level. For some products, these distinct phases are carried on by different firms. In other instances, a single firm carries out two or more of the separate functional phases. Such enterprises are considered to be **vertically integrated firms.**

Even though firms operating at different functional levels are not in direct competition with one another, they are in competition with other firms operating at their own respective levels of operation. Thus, agreements between firms standing in a vertical relationship do significantly affect competition. Some vertical restraints are *per se* violations of Section 1; others are judged under the rule of reason.

TERRITORIAL OR CUSTOMER RESTRICTIONS In arranging for the distribution of its products, a manufacturer often wishes to insulate dealers from direct competition with other dealers selling its products. In this endeavor, the manufacturer may institute territorial restrictions or may attempt to prohibit wholesalers or retailers from reselling the products to certain classes of buyers, such as competing retailers. There may be legitimate, procompetitive reasons for imposing such territorial or customer restrictions. For example, a manufacturer may wish to prevent a dealer from reducing costs and undercutting rivals by providing the product without promotion or customer service, while relying on a nearby dealer to provide these services. In this situation, the cost-cutting dealer reaps the benefits (sales of the product) paid for by other dealers who undertake promotion and arrange for customer service. This is an example of the "free rider"

9. See, for example, *United States v. Morgan*, 118 F.Supp. 621 (S.D.N.Y. 1953). This case is often cited as a classic example of how to judge joint ventures under the rule of reason.

problem.[10] The cost-cutting dealer, by not providing customer service, may also harm the manufacturer's reputation.

Territorial and customer restrictions are judged under a rule of reason. In the following case, *Continental T.V., Inc. v. GTE Sylvania, Inc.*, the United States Supreme Court overturned its earlier stance, which had been set out in *United States v. Arnold, Schwinn & Co.*[11] In *Schwinn,* the Court had held territorial and customer restrictions to be *per se* violations of Section 1 of the Sherman Act. The *Continental* case has been heralded as one of the most important antitrust cases since the 1940s. It marked a definite shift from rigid characterization of these kinds of vertical restraints to a more flexible, economic analysis of the restraints under the rule of reason.

10. For a discussion of the free rider problem in the context of sports telecasting, see *Chicago Professional Sports Limited Partnership v. National Basketball Association,* 961 F.2d 667 (7th Cir. 1993).
11. 388 U.S. 365, 87 S.Ct. 1856, 18 L.Ed.2d 1249 (1967).

CASE 18.1 Continental T.V., Inc. v. GTE Sylvania, Inc.

Supreme Court of the United States, 1977.
433 U.S. 36,
97 S.Ct. 2549,
53 L.Ed.2d 568.
http://www.findlaw.com/casecode/supreme.html[a]

HISTORICAL AND ECONOMIC SETTING *In determining what is or is not permitted under the antitrust laws, the trend has been to establish a flexible standard, rather than a rigid one, particularly in regard to conduct that is thought to have procompetitive benefits. Under a flexible standard, a business practice that is considered a criminal offense in one decade may be judged a corporate virtue in the next. In the mid-1970s, for example, the United States Supreme Court began to qualify or overrule many of its previous decisions that prohibited certain business practices as* per se *violations of the antitrust laws. The Court appeared to be focusing on economic considerations, such as consumer welfare,*[b] *economic efficiency,*[c] *and interbrand versus intrabrand competition.*

a. This page, which is part of a Web site maintained by FindLaw, contains links to opinions of the United States Supreme Court. In the "Citation Search" section, type "433" in the first box, type "36" in the second box, and click on "Get It" to access the case.
b. *Reiter v. Sonotone Corp.*, 442 U.S. 330, 99 S.Ct. 2326, 60 L.Ed.2d 931 (1979).

BACKGROUND AND FACTS GTE Sylvania, Inc., a manufacturer of television sets, adopted a franchise plan that limited the number of franchises granted in any given geographical area and that required each franchise to sell only Sylvania products from the location or locations at which it was franchised. Sylvania retained sole discretion to increase the number of retailers in an area, depending on the success or failure of existing retailers in developing their markets. Continental T.V., Inc., was a retailer under Sylvania's franchise plan. Shortly after Sylvania proposed a new franchise that would compete with Continental, Sylvania terminated Continental's franchise, and a suit was brought in a federal district court for money owed. Continental claimed that Sylvania's vertically restrictive franchise system violated Section 1 of the Sherman Act. The district court held for Continental, and Sylvania appealed. The appellate court reversed the trial court's decision. Continental appealed to the United States Supreme Court.

c. *Broadcast Music, Inc. v. Columbia Broadcasting System, Inc.,* 441 U.S. 1, 99 S.Ct. 1551, 60 L.Ed.2d 1 (1979).

IN THE LANGUAGE OF THE COURT. . .
Mr. Justice *POWELL* delivered the opinion of the Court.

* * * *

Vertical restrictions reduce intrabrand competition by limiting the number of sellers of a particular product competing for the business of a given group of buyers. * * *

CASE 18.1–Continued

Vertical restrictions promote interbrand competition by allowing the manufacturer to achieve certain efficiencies in the distribution of his products. * * * Established manufacturers can use them to induce retailers to engage in promotional activities or to provide service and repair facilities necessary to the efficient marketing of their products. * * * The availability and quality of such services affect a manufacturer's goodwill and the competitiveness of his product. * * * [Emphasis added.]

* * * *

* * * When anticompetitive effects are shown to result from particular vertical restrictions they can be adequately policed under the rule of reason * * * .

DECISION AND REMEDY The United States Supreme Court upheld the appellate court's reversal of the district court's decision. Sylvania's vertical system, which was not price restrictive, did not constitute a *per se* violation of Section 1 of the Sherman Act.

FOR CRITICAL ANALYSIS–Economic Consideration *Could the same argument made by the Court in this case (as to the effect of restrictions on market efficiency) be made in regard to resale price maintenance agreements (discussed next)?*

RESALE PRICE MAINTENANCE AGREEMENT An agreement between a manufacturer and a retailer in which the manufacturer specifies the minimum retail price of its products. Resale price maintenance agreements may be illegal *per se* under the Sherman Act.

RESALE PRICE MAINTENANCE AGREEMENTS An agreement between a manufacturer and a distributor or retailer in which the manufacturer specifies what the retail prices of its products must be is known as a **resale price maintenance agreement.** This type of agreement may violate Section 1 of the Sherman Act.

In a 1968 case, *Albrecht v. Herald Co.,*[12] the United States Supreme Court held that these vertical price-fixing agreements constituted *per se* violations of Section 1 of the Sherman Act. In the following case, which involved an agreement that set a maximum price for the resale of products supplied by a wholesaler to a dealer, the Supreme Court reevaluated its approach in *Albrecht.* At issue was whether such price-fixing arrangements should continue to be deemed *per se* violations of Section 1 of the Sherman Act or whether the rule of reason should be applied.

12. 390 U.S. 145, 88 S.Ct. 869, 19 L.Ed.2d 998 (1968).

CASE 18.2 State Oil Co. v. Kahn

Supreme Court of the United States, 1997.
522 U.S. 3,
118 S.Ct. 275,
139 L.Ed.2d 199.
http://www.findlaw.com/casecode/supreme.html[a]

BACKGROUND AND FACTS Barkat Khan leased a gas station under a contract with State Oil Company, which also agreed to supply gas to Khan for resale. Under the contract, State Oil would set a suggested retail price and sell gas to Khan for 3.25 cents per gallon less than that price. Khan could sell the gas at a higher price, but he would then be required to pay State Oil the difference (which would equal the entire profit Khan realized from raising the price). Khan failed to pay some of the rent due under the lease, and State Oil terminated the contract. Khan filed a suit in a federal district court against State Oil, alleging, among other things, price fixing in violation of the

a. This page, which is part of a Web site maintained by FindLaw, contains links to opinions of the United States Supreme Court. In the "Party Name Search" box, type "Khan" and click on "Search." When the results appear, click on the case name to access the opinion.

Sherman Act. The court granted summary judgment for State Oil. Khan appealed. The U.S. Court of Appeals for the Seventh Circuit reversed this judgment, and State Oil appealed to the United States Supreme Court.

IN THE LANGUAGE OF THE COURT. . .

Justice *O'CONNOR* delivered the opinion of the Court.

* * * *

* * * Our analysis is * * * guided by our general view that the primary purpose of the antitrust laws is to protect interbrand competition. * * * [C]ondemnation of practices resulting in lower prices to consumers is especially costly because cutting prices in order to increase business often is the very essence of competition.

* * * [W]e find it difficult to maintain that vertically-imposed maximum prices could harm consumers or competition to the extent necessary to justify their *per se* invalidation. * * *

* * * *

* * * [T]he *per se* rule * * * could in fact exacerbate problems related to the unrestrained exercise of market power by monopolist-dealers. Indeed, *both courts and antitrust scholars have noted that [the* per se*] rule may actually harm consumers and manufacturers.* * * * [Emphasis added.]

* * * *

* * * [V]ertical maximum price fixing, like the majority of commercial arrangements subject to the antitrust laws, should be evaluated under the rule of reason. In our view, rule-of-reason analysis can effectively identify those situations in which vertical maximum price fixing amounts to anticompetitive conduct.

DECISION AND REMEDY The United States Supreme Court vacated the decision of the appellate court and remanded the case. The Supreme Court held that vertical price fixing is not a *per se* violation of the Sherman Act but should be evaluated under the rule of reason.

FOR CRITICAL ANALYSIS–Economic Consideration *Should all "commercial arrangements subject to the antitrust laws" be evaluated under the rule of reason?*

REFUSALS TO DEAL As discussed previously, joint refusals to deal (group boycotts) are subject to close scrutiny under Section 1 of the Sherman Act. A single manufacturer acting unilaterally, however, is generally free to deal, or not to deal, with whomever it wishes. In vertical arrangements, however, a manufacturer can refuse to deal with retailers or dealers that cut prices to levels substantially below the manufacturer's suggested retail prices. In *United States v. Colgate & Co.,*[13] for example, the United States Supreme Court held that a manufacturer's advance announcement that it would not sell to price cutters was not a violation of the Sherman Act.

There are instances, however, in which a unilateral refusal to deal violates antitrust laws. These instances involve offenses proscribed under Section 2 of

13. 250 U.S. 300, 39 S.Ct. 465, 63 L.Ed. 992 (1919).

the Sherman Act and occur only if (1) the firm refusing to deal has—or is likely to acquire—monopoly power and (2) the refusal is likely to have an anticompetitive effect on a particular market.

SECTION 3 SECTION 2 OF THE SHERMAN ACT

PREDATORY PRICING
The pricing of a product below cost with the intent to drive competitors out of the market.

Section 1 of the Sherman Act proscribes certain concerted, or joint, activities that restrain trade. In contrast, Section 2 condemns "every person who shall monopolize, or attempt to monopolize." Thus, two distinct types of behavior are subject to sanction under Section 2: *monopolization* and *attempts to monopolize.* A tactic that may be involved in either offense is **predatory pricing.** Predatory pricing involves an attempt by one firm to drive its competitors from the market by selling its product at prices substantially *below* the normal costs of production; once the competitors are eliminated, the firm will attempt to recapture its losses and go on to earn very high profits by driving prices up far above their competitive levels.

Monopolization

MONOPOLIZATION
The possession of monopoly power in the relevant market and the willful acquisition or maintenance of the power, as distinguished from growth or development as a consequence of a superior product, business acumen, or historic accident.

In *United States v. Grinnell Corp.,*[14] the United States Supreme Court defined **monopolization** as involving the following two elements: "(1) the possession of monopoly power in the relevant market and (2) the willful acquisition or maintenance of the power as distinguished from growth or development as a consequence of a superior product, business acumen, or historic accident." A violation of Section 2 requires that both these elements—monopoly power and an *intent* to monopolize—be established.

MONOPOLY POWER The Sherman Act does not define *monopoly.* In economic parlance, monopoly refers to control by a single entity. It is well established in antitrust law, however, that a firm may be a monopolist even though it is not the sole seller in a market. Additionally, size alone does not determine whether a firm is a monopoly. For example, a "mom and pop" grocery located in an isolated desert town is a monopolist if it is the only grocery serving that particular market. Size in relation to the market is what matters, because monopoly involves the power to affect prices and output. *Monopoly power,* as mentioned earlier in this chapter, exists when a firm has sufficient market power to control prices and exclude competition.

MARKET SHARE TEST
The primary measure of monopoly power. A firm's market share is the percentage of a market that the firm controls.

As difficult as it is to define market power precisely, it is even more difficult to measure it. Courts often use the so-called **market-share test**[15]—a firm's percentage share of the "relevant market"—in determining the extent of the firm's market power. A firm generally is considered to have monopoly power if its share of the relevant market is 70 percent or more. This is merely a rule of

14. 384 U.S. 563, 86 S.Ct. 1698, 16 L.Ed.2d 778 (1966).

15. Other measures of market power have been devised, but the market-share test is the most widely used.

thumb, however; it is not a binding principle of law. In some cases, a smaller share may be held to constitute monopoly power.[16]

The relevant market consists of two elements: (1) a relevant product market and (2) a relevant geographic market. What should the relevant product market include? No doubt, it must include all products that, although produced by different firms, have identical attributes, such as sugar. Products that are not identical, however, may sometimes be substituted for one another. Coffee may be substituted for tea, for example. In defining the relevant product market, the key issue is the degree of interchangeability between products. If one product is a sufficient substitute for another, the two products are considered to be part of the same product market.

The second component of the relevant market is the geographic boundaries of the market. For products that are sold nationwide, the geographic boundaries of the market encompass the entire United States. If a producer and its competitors sell in only a limited area (one in which customers have no access to other sources of the product), then the geographic market is limited to that area. A national firm may thus compete in several distinct areas and have monopoly power in one area but not in another.

THE INTENT REQUIREMENT Monopoly power, in and of itself, does not constitute the offense of monopolization under Section 2 of the Sherman Act. The offense also requires an intent to monopolize. A dominant market share may be the result of business acumen or the development of a superior product. It may simply be the result of historical accident. In these situations, the acquisition of monopoly power is not an antitrust violation. Indeed, it would be counter to society's interest to condemn every firm that acquired a position of power because it was well managed, was efficient, and marketed a product desired by consumers. If, however, a firm possesses market power as a result of carrying out some purposeful act to acquire or maintain that power through anticompetitive means, it is in violation of Section 2. In most monopolization cases, intent may be inferred from evidence that the firm had monopoly power and engaged in anticompetitive behavior.

Attempts to Monopolize

Section 2 also prohibits **attempted monopolization** of a market. Any action challenged as an attempt to monopolize must have been specifically intended to exclude competitors and garner monopoly power. In addition, the attempt must have had a "dangerous" probability of success—only *serious* threats of monopolization are condemned as violations. The probability cannot be dangerous unless the alleged offender possesses some degree of market power.

ATTEMPTED MONOPOLIZATION Any actions by a firm to eliminate competition and gain monopoly power.

The following widely publicized case against Microsoft Corporation involved allegations of monopolization and attempted monopolization in violation of Section 2 of the Sherman Act. (For a further discussion of this case, see this chapter's *Controversial Issues* feature on page 444.)

16. This standard was first articulated by Judge Learned Hand in *United States v. Aluminum Co. of America,* 148 F.2d 416 (2d Cir. 1945). A 90 percent share was held to be clear evidence of monopoly power. Anything less than 64 percent, said Judge Hand, made monopoly power doubtful, and anything less than 30 percent was clearly not monopoly power.

CASE 18.3 United States v. Microsoft Corp.

United States District Court,
District of Columbia, 2000.
87 F.Supp.2d 30
http://www.usdoj.gov/atr/cases/ms_conclusions.htm[a]

HISTORICAL AND TECHNOLOGICAL SETTING *In 1981, Microsoft Corporation released the first version of its Microsoft Disk Operating System (MS-DOS). The system had a character-based interface that required the user to type specific instructions at a command prompt. When International Business Machines Corporation (IBM) selected MS-DOS for preinstallation on its first generation of personal computers (PCs), Microsoft's product became the dominant OS for Intel-compatible PCs.*[b] *In 1985, Microsoft began shipping a software package called Windows. This product included a graphical interface that enabled users to perform tasks by selecting icons and words on the screen using a mouse. Although originally just a user interface on top of MS-DOS, Windows took on more OS functionality over time.*

a. The U.S. Department of Justice maintains this Web site. On this page, to access the court's opinion, click on the link to "U.S. v. Microsoft Corporation: Conclusions of Law and Final Order."

b. An *Intel-compatible PC* is designed to function with Intel Corporation's 80x86/Pentium families of microprocessors or with compatible microprocessors.

Windows 95 was the first OS for Intel-compatible PCs that exhibited integrated features.

BACKGROUND AND FACTS Throughout the 1990s, Microsoft's share of the market for Intel-compatible OSs was more than 90 percent, and Microsoft did not even consider the prices of other OSs when it set the price of Windows 95's successor, Windows 98. In 1994, Netscape Communications Corporation began marketing Navigator, the first widely popular graphical browser distributed for profit. Navigator also began working with Sun Microsystems, Inc., in implementing Java technology. Java technology enables applications to run on a variety of platforms, which makes it easier to create software for OSs other than Windows. Microsoft perceived a threat to its dominance of the OS market and asked Netscape to refrain from distributing a platform-level browser for Windows. Netscape refused. Microsoft then withheld technical information that Netscape needed to make Navigator compatible with certain Internet service providers and developed a competing browser, Internet Explorer. Microsoft enlisted other firms in a campaign to increase Explorer's usage at Navigator's expense. The U.S. Department of Justice, and others, filed a suit in a federal district court against Microsoft, alleging in part that the firm had committed monopolization in violation of Section 2 of the Sherman Act.

IN THE LANGUAGE OF THE COURT. . .
JACKSON, District Judge.

* * * *

The plaintiffs proved at trial that Microsoft possesses a dominant, persistent, and increasing share of the relevant market. Microsoft's share of the worldwide market for Intel-compatible PC operating systems currently exceeds ninety-five percent * * * . The plaintiffs also proved that the applications barrier to entry protects Microsoft's dominant market share. This barrier ensures that no Intel-compatible PC operating system other than Windows can attract significant consumer demand, and the barrier would operate to the same effect even if Microsoft held its prices substantially above the competitive level for a protracted period of time. Together, the proof of dominant market share and the existence of a substantial barrier to effective entry create the presumption that Microsoft enjoys monopoly power.

* * * *

In a [Section] 2 case, once it is proved that the defendant possesses monopoly power in a relevant market, liability for monopolization depends on a showing that the defendant used anticompetitive methods to achieve or maintain its position. * * *

* * * *

In this case, Microsoft early on recognized middleware [non–OS software that relies on the interfaces of the underlying OS] as the Trojan horse[c] that, once having, in effect, infiltrated the applications barrier, could enable rival operating systems to enter the market for Intel-compatible PC operating systems unimpeded. Simply put, middleware threatened to demolish Microsoft's coveted monopoly power. Alerted to the threat, Microsoft strove over a period of approximately four years to prevent middleware technologies from fostering the development of enough full-featured, cross-platform applications to erode the applications barrier. In pursuit of this goal, Microsoft sought to convince developers to concentrate on Windows-specific APIs [application programming interfaces] and ignore interfaces exposed by the two incarnations of middleware that posed the greatest threat, namely, Netscape's Navigator Web browser and Sun's implementation of the Java technology. Microsoft's campaign succeeded in preventing—for several years, and perhaps permanently—Navigator and Java from fulfilling their potential to open the market for Intel-compatible PC operating systems to competition on the merits. Because Microsoft achieved this result through exclusionary acts that lacked procompetitive justification, the Court deems Microsoft's conduct the maintenance of monopoly power by anticompetitive means.

c. The *Trojan horse* was a hollow, wooden horse in which, according to legend, Greeks hid to gain entrance to the walled city of Troy, later opening the gates to the Greek army.

DECISION AND REMEDY The court held that Microsoft had monopoly power in the market for Intel-compatible PC OSs. Microsoft's anticompetitive acts to maintain that power resulted in liability for monopolization. The court ordered, among other things, a structural reorganization of Microsoft, including a separation of its OS and applications businesses.[d]

d. See *United States v. Microsoft,* 97 F.Supp.2d 59 (D.D.C. 2000). As of this writing, the case is on appeal.

FOR CRITICAL ANALYSIS–Economic Consideration *How did Microsoft's acts harm or benefit consumers and the economy?*

SECTION 4 THE KNOWLEDGE SOCIETY—ARE WE DESTINED FOR MORE MONOPOLIES?

WEIGHTLESS ECONOMY
That part of the economy that deals with information collection, transmission, analysis, and so on and that therefore has no physical weight. This also includes intellectual property and the financial sector.

DIMINISHING MARGINAL RETURNS
The point after which the additional benefit from engaging in some activity starts to decline, even though that marginal (additional) benefit remains positive.

Knowledge and information form the building bricks of the so-called new economy. Some observers believe that we will see an increasing number of monopolies similar to Microsoft because of this fact.

Knowledge is an intangible. It is part of the **weightless economy.** Even physical goods today embody increasing knowledge in the form of design and customer service. Knowledge does not appear to follow the standard laws of **diminishing marginal returns.** The reason is that once an idea is created, it can be reproduced and distributed via the Internet at a cost of almost zero; that is,

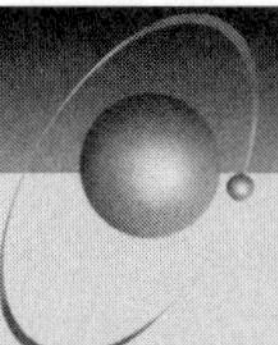

Controversial Issues in the Online World

Protecting Competition in Cyberspace

In the United States, competition among businesses is seen as a primary factor for the success of our economy. It is believed that those who violate laws protecting competition—antitrust laws—cause us to pay higher prices for products of lesser quality. Violations of antitrust laws can also block new advances in technology.

To date, there are very few cases involving the application of antitrust law in cyberspace. One court has held that it likely was *not* a violation of antitrust law for an Internet service provider, America Online, Inc. (AOL), to refuse to transmit free e-mail ads to its subscribers.[a]

The *Microsoft* Case

Currently, the most well-known instance involving cyberspace technology and antitrust law is the case brought by the U.S. Department of Justice and a number of state attorneys general against Microsoft Corporation. (This case was presented elsewhere in this chapter.) Microsoft has appealed the trial court's decision, so the final outcome of the case is undecided.

On appeal, Microsoft has argued, among other things, that the trial court judge, Judge Thomas Penfield Jackson, was biased against Microsoft from the outset. This claim, which some have described as a "wild card" in the case, was brought up in oral arguments before the U.S. Court of Appeals for the District of Columbia Circuit. At issue were various comments made by Judge Jackson in interviews with the press during the trial. In these interviews, Judge Jackson, among other things, referred to Microsoft executives as "depraved felons," compared Microsoft chair Bill Gates to Napoleon, and suggested that the company's officials were not "grown-ups."[b] Should the appellate court conclude that Judge Jackson's behavior amounted to judicial misconduct, the courts may have to start from scratch in evaluating the legality of Microsoft's actions.

What Sanctions against Microsoft Would Be Appropriate?

Even if Microsoft loses on appeal, what sanctions against Microsoft would be appropriate? Should the company be broken up into component parts? Should it—and all other software producers—be regulated by the government?

Professor Lawrence J. White, formerly chief economist at the Antitrust Division of the Justice Department, has suggested an alternative to breaking up Microsoft. He points out that the Bush administration needs a face-saving settlement. Such a settlement would be for the Justice Department to levy a large fine to settle the case—and then to move on. White argues for a $10 billion fine, which would make it the largest ever. Because Microsoft has about $20 billion in liquid assets, such a fine would not destroy the company. A fine this large, however, would deter anticompetitive behavior in the future not only by Microsoft but also by others.

The Browser Wars Still Exist

Although Microsoft initially lost the antitrust case against it, Netscape is not dead—far from it. In 2001, it came out with a new edition, Version 6.0. The new version allows for sidebar tabs, which are small mini-Web pages that appear to the left of the main browser window. One is viewed at a time, with the others stacked up with only their titles showing. You may have a list of your stocks, news from your hometown, and important sports scores in these sidebars, for example.

A newcomer to the browser wars since Microsoft supposedly squelched Navigator is Opera. Opera offers a choice of two versions—a free one, which shows small ads, and one that costs $39 with no ads. A key feature that distinguishes Opera from Microsoft Explorer and Netscape is that Opera opens a new window each time a user changes the URL that he or she wants to view. All of the other windows stay open in the background and keep updating themselves. A user can also tell Opera to remember the windows that were open and reopen the same pages the next time that he or she opens that Web browser.

FOR CRITICAL ANALYSIS

How is it possible to define the relevant market with respect to Internet products?

a. *Cyber Promotions, Inc. v. America Online, Inc.*, 948 F.Supp. 456 (E.D.Pa. 1996).
b. As cited in Leonard Orland, "A Judge Is Never off the Record," *The National Law Journal*, March 19, 2001, p. A53.

if knowledge can be transformed into a string of zeros and ones, which is the case for movies, books, financial services, and software, it is certainly cheap to reproduce. There are vast potential **economies of scale** with all knowledge-based products, mainly because of the Internet.

ECONOMIES OF SCALE
Decreases in long-run average costs resulting from increases in output.

Natural Monopolies and Increasing Returns

The concept of **increasing returns** is not new. The British economist Alfred Marshall discussed this concept in the 1890s. He used as his examples electricity and gas. At the time, the Standard Oil Trust in the United States was another real-world example of economies of scale. Note the difference between then and now, however. At the beginning of the twentieth century Standard Oil, which was twice the size of its rivals, saw average costs fall by about 10 percent. Compare that to a software firm today. A typical software firm that is twice as big as its rivals may have average costs that are 50 percent lower. This is the **natural monopoly** argument at its extreme–in the knowledge economy, it is becoming more and more difficult for new entrants to break into the market because existing firms have already taken advantage of increasing returns due to economies of scale.

INCREASING RETURNS
A production situation in which a doubling of all production inputs–for example, land, labor, machines, and so on–leads to more than a doubling of output.

NATURAL MONOPOLY
A monopoly that arises from the peculiar production characteristics in an industry. It usually arises when there are large economies of scale relative to the industry's demand such that one firm can produce at a lower average cost than can be achieved by multiple firms.

Switching Costs

Another factor that adds to the viability of monopolies in the knowledge economy is due to **switching costs**. Once someone has learned how to use the Windows operating system, for example, it is costly to switch to a new operating system. Consequently, potential rivals to Microsoft's Windows operating system are few and far between. They just cannot overcome the switching costs that hundreds of millions of computer users would have to incur.

SWITCHING COSTS
The costs associated with changing from one system of production to another–for example, the cost of switching from the Macintosh computer operating system to the Microsoft Windows operating system.

Comparing Traditional and Knowledge-Based Monopolists

The basis for all antitrust law is that monopoly leads to restricted output and hence higher prices for consumers. That is how a monopolist maximizes profits relative to a competitive firm. In the knowledge-based sector, in contrast, firms face economies of scale and will do the exact opposite–increase output and reduce prices. That is exactly what Microsoft has done over the years–the prices of its operating system and applications have fallen, particularly when corrected for inflation.

This may mean that antitrust authorities will have to have a greater tolerance for knowledge-based monopolies in order to allow them to benefit from the full economies of scale. After all, the ultimate beneficiary of such economies of scale is the consumer. In the early 1900s, economist Joseph Schumpeter argued in favor of allowing monopolies. He offered the theory of "creative destruction" in which monopolies stimulate innovation and economic growth because firms that capture monopoly profits have a greater incentive to innovate. Those that do not survive–those "destroyed"–leave room for more efficient firms, ones that will survive.

SECTION 5 THE CLAYTON ACT

In 1914, Congress attempted to strengthen federal antitrust laws by enacting the Clayton Act. The Clayton Act was aimed at specific anticompetitive or monopolistic practices that the Sherman Act did not cover. The substantive provisions of the act deal with four distinct forms of business behavior, which are declared illegal but not criminal. With regard to each of the four provisions, the act's prohibitions are qualified by the general condition that the behavior is illegal only if it tends to substantially lessen competition or to create monopoly power. The major offenses under the Clayton Act are set out in Sections 2, 3, 7, and 8 of the act.

Price Discrimination

PRICE DISCRIMINATION
Setting prices in such a way that two competing buyers pay two different prices for an identical product or service.

Price discrimination, which occurs when a seller charges different prices to competing buyers for identical goods, is prohibited by Section 2 of the Clayton Act. Because businesses frequently circumvented Section 2 of the act, Congress strengthened this section by amending it with the passage of the Robinson-Patman Act in 1936.

As amended, Section 2 prohibits price discrimination that cannot be justified by differences in production costs, transportation costs, or cost variations due to other reasons. To violate Section 2, the seller must be engaged in interstate commerce, and the effect of the price discrimination must be to substantially lessen competition or create a competitive injury.

In other words, a seller is prohibited from reducing a price to one buyer below the price charged to that buyer's competitor. An exception is made if the seller can justify the price reduction by demonstrating (1) that he or she charged the lower price temporarily and in good faith to meet another seller's equally low price to the buyer's competitor or (2) that a particular buyer's purchases saved the seller costs in producing and selling the goods (called *cost justification).* To violate the Clayton Act, a seller's pricing policies must also include a reasonable prospect of the seller's recouping its losses.[17]

Exclusionary Practices

Under Section 3 of the Clayton Act, sellers or lessors cannot sell or lease goods "on the condition, agreement or understanding that the . . . purchaser or lessee thereof shall not use or deal in the goods . . . of a competitor or competitors of the seller." In effect, this section prohibits two types of vertical agreements involving exclusionary practices—exclusive-dealing contracts and tying arrangements.

EXCLUSIVE-DEALING CONTRACT
An agreement under which a seller forbids a buyer to purchase products from the seller's competitors.

EXCLUSIVE-DEALING CONTRACTS A contract under which a seller forbids a buyer to purchase products from the seller's competitors is called an **exclusive-dealing contract.** A seller is prohibited from making an exclusive-dealing con-

17. See, for example, *Brooke Group, Ltd. v. Brown & Williamson Tobacco Corp.*, 509 U.S. 209, 113 S.Ct. 2578, 125 L.Ed.2d 168 (1993), in which the Supreme Court held that a seller's price-cutting policies could not be predatory "[g]iven the market's realities"—the size of the seller's market share, expanding output by other sellers, and additional factors.

tract under Section 3 if the effect of the contract is "to substantially lessen competition or tend to create a monopoly."

The leading exclusive-dealing decision was made by the Supreme Court in the case of *Standard Oil Co. of California v. United States.*[18] In this case, the then-largest gasoline seller in the nation made exclusive-dealing contracts with independent stations in seven western states. The contracts involved 16 percent of all retail outlets, whose sales were approximately 7 percent of all retail sales in that market. The Court noted that the market was substantially concentrated because the seven largest gasoline suppliers all used exclusive-dealing contracts with their independent retailers and together controlled 65 percent of the market. Looking at market conditions after the arrangements were instituted, the Court found that market shares were extremely stable, and entry into the market was apparently restricted. Thus, the Court held that Section 3 of the Clayton Act had been violated, because competition was "foreclosed in a substantial share" of the relevant market.

TYING ARRANGEMENTS When a seller conditions the sale of a product (the tying product) on the buyer's agreement to purchase another product (the tied product) produced or distributed by the same seller, a **tying arrangement**, or *tie-in sales agreement,* results. The legality of a tie-in agreement depends on many factors, particularly the purpose of the agreement and the agreement's likely effect on competition in the relevant markets (the market for the tying product and the market for the tied product). In 1936, for example, the United States Supreme Court held that International Business Machines and Remington Rand had violated Section 3 of the Clayton Act by requiring the purchase of their own machine cards (the tied product) as a condition to the leasing of their tabulation machines (the tying product). Because only these two firms sold completely automated tabulation machines, the Court concluded that each possessed market power sufficient to "substantially lessen competition" through the tying arrangements.[19]

TYING ARRANGEMENT
An agreement between a buyer and a seller in which the buyer, in order to purchase a specific product or service, must agree to purchase additional products or services from the seller.

Section 3 of the Clayton Act has been held to apply only to commodities, not to services. Tying arrangements, however, also can be considered agreements that restrain trade in violation of Section 1 of the Sherman Act. Thus, cases involving tying arrangements of services have been brought under Section 1 of the Sherman Act. Traditionally, the courts have held tying arrangements brought under the Sherman Act to be illegal *per se.* In recent years, however, courts have shown a willingness to look at factors that are important in a rule-of-reason analysis.

Mergers

Under Section 7 of the Clayton Act, a person or business organization cannot hold stock or assets in more than one business where "the effect . . . may be to substantially lessen competition." Section 7 is the statutory authority for preventing mergers that could result in monopoly power or a substantial

18. 37 U.S. 293, 69 S.Ct. 1051, 93 L.Ed. 1371 (1949).

19. *International Business Machines Corp. v. United States,* 298 U.S. 131, 56 S.Ct. 701, 80 L.Ed. 1085 (1936).

lessening of competition in the marketplace. Section 7 applies to three types of mergers: horizontal mergers, vertical mergers, and conglomerate mergers. We discuss each type of merger in the following subsections.

MARKET CONCENTRATION
A situation that exists when a small number of firms share the market for a particular good or service. For example, if the four largest grocery stores in Chicago accounted for 80 percent of all retail food sales, the market clearly would be concentrated in those four firms.

A crucial consideration in most merger cases is **market concentration.** Determining market concentration involves allocating percentage market shares among the various companies in the relevant market. When a small number of companies share a large part of the market, the market is concentrated. For example, if the four largest grocery stores in Chicago accounted for 80 percent of all retail food sales, the market clearly would be concentrated in those four firms. Competition, however, is not necessarily diminished solely as a result of market concentration, and other factors must be considered in determining whether a merger will violate Section 7. Another concept of particular importance in evaluating the effects of a merger is whether the merger will make it more difficult for potential competitors to enter the relevant market.

HORIZONTAL MERGER
A merger between two firms that are competing in the same market.

HORIZONTAL MERGERS Mergers between firms that compete with each other in the same market are called **horizontal mergers.** If a horizontal merger creates an entity with anything other than a small-percentage market share, the merger will be presumed illegal. This is because of the United States Supreme Court's interpretation that Congress, in amending Section 7 of the Clayton Act in 1950, intended to prevent mergers that increase market concentration.[20] Three other factors that the courts also consider in analyzing the legality of a horizontal merger are the overall concentration of the relevant market, the relevant market's history of tending toward concentration, and whether the merger is apparently designed to establish market power or restrict competition.

The Federal Trade Commission offers an abundance of information on antitrust law, including "A Plain English Guide to Antitrust Laws," at **http://www.ftc.gov/ftc/antitrust.htm**.

The Federal Trade Commission (FTC) and the U.S. Department of Justice (DOJ) have established guidelines indicating which mergers will be challenged. Under the guidelines, the first factor to be considered in determining whether a merger will be challenged is the degree of concentration in the relevant market. This is done by comparing the market concentration before the merger with the anticipated postmerger market concentration.

The guidelines stress that the determination of market share and market concentration is only the starting point in analyzing the potential anticompetitive effects of a merger. Before deciding to challenge a merger, the FTC and the DOJ will look at a number of other factors, including ease of entry into the relevant market, economic efficiency, the financial condition of the merging firms, the nature and price of the product or products involved, and so on. In the case of a leading firm—one having a market share that is at least 35 percent and is twice that of the next leading firm—any merger with a firm having as little as a 1 percent share will be challenged.

VERTICAL MERGER
The acquisition by a business at one stage of production of a business at a higher or lower stage of production (such as a business merging with one of its suppliers or retailers).

VERTICAL MERGERS A **vertical merger** occurs when a company at one stage of production acquires a company at a higher or lower stage of production. An example of a vertical merger is a company merging with one of its suppliers or retailers. Courts in the past have almost exclusively focused on "foreclosure" in assessing vertical mergers. Foreclosure occurs when competitors of the merging firms lose opportunities either to sell products to or buy products from the merging firms.

20. *Brown Shoe v. United States,* 370 U.S. 294, 82 S.Ct. 1502, 8 L.Ed.2d 510 (1962).

For example, in *United States v. E. I. du Pont de Nemours & Co.*,[21] du Pont was challenged for acquiring a considerable amount of General Motors (GM) stock. In holding that the transaction was illegal, the United States Supreme Court noted that stock acquisition would enable du Pont to foreclose other sellers of fabrics and finishes from selling to GM, which then accounted for 50 percent of all auto fabric and finishes purchases.

Today, whether a vertical merger will be deemed illegal generally depends on several factors, including market concentration, barriers to entry into the market, and the apparent intent of the merging parties. Mergers that do not prevent competitors of either of the merging firms from competing in a segment of the market will not be condemned as foreclosing competition and are legal.

CONGLOMERATE MERGERS There are three general types of **conglomerate mergers**: market-extension, product-extension, and diversification mergers. A market-extension merger occurs when a firm seeks to sell its product in a new market by merging with a firm already established in that market. A product-extension merger occurs when a firm seeks to add a closely related product to its existing line by merging with a firm already producing that product. For example, a manufacturer might seek to extend its line of household products to include floor wax by acquiring a leading manufacturer of floor wax. Diversification occurs when a firm merges with another firm that offers a product or service wholly unrelated to the first firm's existing activities. An example of a diversification merger is an automobile manufacturer's acquisition of a motel chain.

CONGLOMERATE MERGER
A merger between firms that do not compete with each other because they are in different markets (as opposed to horizontal and vertical mergers).

Interlocking Directorates

Section 8 of the Clayton Act deals with *interlocking directorates*—that is, the practice of having individuals serve as directors on the boards of two or more competing companies simultaneously. Specifically, no person may be a director in two or more competing corporations at the same time if either of the corporations has capital, surplus, or undivided profits aggregating more than $16,732,000 or competitive sales of $1,673,200 or more. The threshold amounts are adjusted each year by the Federal Trade Commission (FTC). (The amounts given here are those announced by the FTC in 2000.)

SECTION 6 THE FEDERAL TRADE COMMISSION ACT

The Federal Trade Commission Act was enacted in 1914, the same year the Clayton Act was written into law. Section 5 is the sole substantive provision of the act. It provides, in part, as follows: "Unfair methods of competition in or affecting commerce, and unfair or deceptive acts or practices in or affecting commerce are hereby declared illegal." Section 5 condemns all forms of anticompetitive behavior that are not covered under other federal antitrust laws. The act also created the Federal Trade Commission to implement the act's provisions.

21. 353 U.S. 586, 77 S.Ct. 872, 1 L.Ed.2d 1057 (1957).

SECTION 7 ENFORCEMENT OF ANTITRUST LAWS

The federal agencies that enforce the federal antitrust laws are the U.S. Department of Justice (DOJ) and the Federal Trade Commission (FTC). Only the DOJ can prosecute violations of the Sherman Act as either criminal or civil violations. Violations of the Clayton Act are not crimes, and the DOJ or the FTC can enforce that statute through civil proceedings. The various remedies that the DOJ or the FTC has asked the courts to impose include **divestiture** (making a company give up one or more of its operating functions) and dissolution. The DOJ or the FTC might force a group of meat packers, for example, to divest itself of control or ownership of butcher shops.

DIVESTITURE
The act of selling one or more of a company's parts, such as a subsidiary or plant; often mandated by the courts in merger or monopolization cases.

The FTC has sole authority to enforce violations of Section 5 of the Federal Trade Commission Act. FTC actions are effected through administrative orders, but if a firm violates an FTC order, the FTC can seek court sanctions for the violation.

You can access the Antitrust Division of the U.S. Department of Justice online at **http:// www. usdoj.gov**.

A private party can sue for treble damages and attorneys' fees if the party is injured as a result of a violation of the Sherman Act or the Clayton Act. In some instances, private parties may also seek injunctive relief to prevent antitrust violations. The courts have determined that the ability to sue depends on the directness of the injury suffered by the would-be plaintiff. Thus, a person wishing to sue under the Sherman Act must prove (1) that the antitrust violation either caused or was a substantial factor in causing the injury that was suffered, and (2) that the unlawful actions of the accused party affected business activities of the plaintiff that were protected by the antitrust laws.

In recent years, more than 90 percent of all antitrust actions have been brought by private plaintiffs. One reason for this is, of course, that successful plaintiffs may recover three times the damages that they have suffered as a result of the violation. Such recoveries by private plaintiffs for antitrust violations have been rationalized as encouraging people to act as "private attorneys general" who will vigorously pursue antitrust violators on their own initiative.

SECTION 8 U.S. ANTITRUST LAWS IN THE GLOBAL CONTEXT

U.S. antitrust laws have a broad application. They may subject persons in foreign nations to their provisions as well as protect foreign consumers and competitors from violations committed by U.S. business firms. Consequently, *foreign persons*, a term that by definition includes foreign governments, may sue under U.S. antitrust laws in U.S. courts.

Section 1 of the Sherman Act of 1890 provides for the extraterritorial effect of the U.S. antitrust laws. The United States is a major proponent of free competition in the global economy, and thus any conspiracy that has a substantial effect on U.S. commerce is within the reach of the Sherman Act. The violation may even occur outside the United States, and foreign governments as well as persons can be sued for violation of U.S. antitrust laws. Before U.S. courts will exercise jurisdiction and apply antitrust laws, it must be shown that the alleged violation had a *substantial effect* on U.S. commerce. U.S. jurisdiction is automatically invoked, however, when a *per se* violation occurs.

If a domestic firm, for example, joins a foreign cartel to control the production, price, or distribution of goods, and this cartel has a *substantial effect* on U.S. commerce, a *per se* violation may exist. Hence, both the domestic firm and the foreign cartel could be sued for violation of the U.S. antitrust laws. Likewise, if a foreign firm doing business in the United States enters into a price-fixing or other anticompetitive agreement to control a portion of U.S. markets, a *per se* violation may exist.

In 1982, Congress amended the Sherman Act and the Federal Trade Commission Act of 1914 to limit their application when unfair methods of competition are involved in U.S. export trade or commerce with foreign nations. The acts are not limited, however, when there is a "direct, substantial, and reasonably foreseeable effect" on U.S. domestic commerce that results in a claim for damages.

SECTION 9 EXEMPTIONS FROM ANTITRUST LAWS

There are many legislative and constitutional limitations on antitrust enforcement. Most statutory and judicially created exemptions to the antitrust laws apply to the following areas or activities:

1. *Labor.* Section 6 of the Clayton Act generally permits labor unions to organize and bargain without violating antitrust laws. Section 20 of the Clayton Act specifies that strikes and other labor activities are not violations of any law of the United States. A union can lose its exemption, however, if it combines with a nonlabor group rather than acting simply in its own self-interest.

2. *Agricultural associations and fisheries.* Section 6 of the Clayton Act (along with the Cooperative Marketing Associations Act of 1922[22]) exempts agricultural cooperatives from the antitrust laws. The Fisheries Cooperative Marketing Act of 1976 exempts from antitrust legislation individuals in the fishing industry who collectively catch, produce, and prepare their products for market. Both exemptions allow members of such co-ops to combine and set prices for a particular product, but they do not allow them to engage in exclusionary practices or restraints of trade directed at competitors.

3. *Insurance.* The McCarran-Ferguson Act of 1945[23] exempts the insurance business from the antitrust laws whenever state regulation exists. This exemption does not cover boycotts, coercion, or intimidation on the part of insurance companies.

4. *Foreign trade.* Under the provisions of the 1918 Webb-Pomerene Act,[24] U.S. exporters may engage in cooperative activity to compete with similar foreign associations. This type of cooperative activity may not, however, restrain trade within the United States or injure other U.S. exporters. The Export Trading Company Act of 1982[25] broadened the Webb-Pomerene Act by permitting the Department of Justice to certify properly qualified export trading companies.

---

22. 7 U.S.C. Sections 291–292.
23. 15 U.S.C. Sections 1011–1015.
24. 15 U.S.C. Sections 61–66.
25. 15 U.S.C. Sections 4001–4003.

Any activity within the scope described by the certificate is exempt from public prosecution under the antitrust laws.

5. *Professional baseball.* In 1922, the United States Supreme Court held that professional baseball was not within the reach of federal antitrust laws because it did not involve "interstate commerce."[26] Some of the effects of this decision, however, were modified by the Curt Flood Act of 1998. Essentially, the act allows players the option of suing team owners for anticompetitive practices if, for example, the owners collude to "blacklist" players, hold down players' salaries, or force players to play for specific teams.

6. *Oil marketing.* The 1935 Interstate Oil Compact allows states to determine quotas on oil that will be marketed in interstate commerce.

7. *Cooperative research and production.* Cooperative research among small business firms is exempt under the Small Business Act of 1958.[27] Research or production of a product, process, or service by joint ventures consisting of competitors is exempt under special federal legislation, including the National Cooperative Research Act of 1984,[28] as amended by the National Cooperative Research and Production Act of 1993.

8. *Joint efforts by businesspersons to obtain legislative or executive action.* This is often referred to as the Noerr-Pennington doctrine.[29] For example, video producers might jointly lobby Congress to change the copyright laws without being held liable for attempting to restrain trade. Though selfish rather than purely public-minded conduct is permitted, there is an exception: an action will not be protected if it is clear that the action is "objectively baseless in the sense that no reasonable [person] could reasonably expect success on the merits" and it is an attempt to make anticompetitive use of government processes.[30]

9. *Other exemptions.* Other activities exempt from antitrust laws include activities approved by the president in furtherance of the defense of our nation (under the Defense Production Act of 1950[31]); state actions, when the state policy is clearly articulated and the policy is actively supervised by the state;[32] and activities of regulated industries (such as the transportation, communication, and banking industries) when federal agencies (such as the Federal Communications Commission) have primary regulatory authority.

---

26. *Federal Baseball Club of Baltimore, Inc. v. National League of Professional Baseball Clubs,* 259 U.S. 200, 42 S.Ct. 465, 66 L.Ed. 898 (1922).
27. 15 U.S.C. Sections 631–657.
28. 15 U.S.C. Sections 4301–4306.
29. See *United Mine Workers of America v. Pennington,* 381 U.S. 657, 89 S.Ct. 1585, 14 L.Ed.2d 626 (1965); and *Eastern Railroad Presidents Conference v. Noerr Motor Freight, Inc.,* 365 U.S. 127, 81 S.Ct. 523, 5 L.Ed.2d 464 (1961).
30. *Professional Real Estate Investors, Inc. v. Columbia Pictures Industries, Inc.,* 508 U.S. 49, 113 S.Ct. 1920, 123 L.Ed.2d 611 (1993).
31. 50 App.U.S.C. 2061–2171.
32. See *Parker v. Brown,* 347 U.S. 341, 63 S.Ct. 307, 87 L.Ed. 315 (1943).

TERMS AND CONCEPTS

antitrust law 431
attempted monopolization 441
conglomerate merger 449
diminishing marginal returns 443
divestiture 450
economies of scale 445
exclusive-dealing contract 446
group boycott 435

horizontal merger 445
horizontal restraint 434
increasing returns 445
market concentration 448
market power 433
market-share test 440
monopolization 440
monopoly 433
monopoly power 433
natural monopoly 445
per se violation 434
predatory pricing 440
price discrimination 446
price-fixing agreement 434
resale price maintenance agreement 438
restraint on trade 431
rule of reason 433
switching costs 445
tying arrangement 447
vertical merger 448
vertical restraint 436
vertically integrated firm 436
weightless economy 443

QUESTIONS AND CASE PROBLEMS

18–1. Antitrust Laws. Allitron, Inc., and Donovan, Ltd., are interstate competitors selling similar appliances, principally in the states of Indiana, Kentucky, Illinois, and Ohio. Allitron and Donovan agree that Allitron will no longer sell in Ohio and Indiana and that Donovan will no longer sell in Kentucky and Illinois. Have Allitron and Donovan violated any antitrust law? If so, which law? Explain.

18–2. Antitrust Laws. The partnership of Alvaredo and Parish is engaged in the oil-wellhead service industry in the states of New Mexico and Colorado. The firm presently has about 40 percent of the market for this service. Webb Corp. competes with the Alvaredo-Parish partnership in the same state area. Webb has approximately 35 percent of the market. Alvaredo and Parish acquire the stock and assets of Webb Corp. Do the antitrust laws prohibit the type of action undertaken by Alvaredo and Parish? Discuss fully.

18–3. Horizontal Restraints. Jorge's Appliance Corp. was a new retail seller of appliances in Sunrise City. Because of its innovative sales techniques and financing, Jorge's caused a substantial loss of sales from the appliance department of No-Glow Department Store, a large chain store with a great deal of buying power. No-Glow told a number of appliance manufacturers from whom it made large-volume purchases that if they continued to sell to Jorge's, No-Glow would discontinue purchasing from them. The manufacturers immediately stopped selling appliances to Jorge's. Jorge's filed suit against No-Glow and the manufacturers, claiming that their actions constituted an antitrust violation. No-Glow and the manufacturers were able to prove that Jorge's was a small retailer with a small market share. They claimed that because the relevant market was not substantially affected, they were not guilty of restraint of trade. Discuss fully whether there was an antitrust violation.

18–4. Exclusionary Practices. Instant Foto Corp. is a manufacturer of photography film. At the present time, Instant Foto has approximately 50 percent of the market. Instant Foto advertises that the purchase price for Instant Foto film includes photo processing by Instant Foto Corp. Instant Foto claims that its film processing is specially designed to improve the quality of photos taken with Instant Foto film. Is Instant Foto's combination of film purchase and film processing an antitrust violation? Explain.

18–5. Restraint of Trade. The National Collegiate Athletic Association (NCAA) coordinates the intercollegiate athletic programs of its members by issuing rules and setting standards governing, among other things, the coaching staffs. The NCAA set up a "Cost Reduction Committee" to consider ways to cut the costs of intercollegiate athletics while maintaining competition. The committee included financial aid personnel, intercollegiate athletic administrators, college presidents, university faculty members, and a university chancellor. It was felt that "only a collaborative effort could reduce costs while maintaining a level playing field." The committee proposed a rule to restrict the annual compensation of certain coaches to $16,000. The NCAA adopted the rule. Basketball coaches affected by the rule filed a suit in a federal district court against the NCAA, alleging a violation of Section 1 of the Sherman Antitrust Act. Is the rule a *per se* violation of the Sherman Act, or should it be evaluated under the rule of reason? If it is subject to the rule of reason, is it an illegal restraint of trade? Discuss fully. [*Law v. National Collegiate Athletic Association,* 134 F.3d 1010 (10th Cir. 1998)]

18–6. Tying Arrangement. Public Interest Corp. (PIC) owned and operated television station WTMV-TV in Lakeland, Florida. MCA Television, Ltd., owns and licenses syndicated television programs. The parties entered into a licensing contract with respect to several television shows. MCA conditioned the license on PIC's agreeing to take another show, *Harry and the Hendersons.* PIC agreed to this arrangement, although it would not have chosen to license

Harry if it did not have to do so to secure the licenses for the other shows. More than two years into the contract, a dispute arose over PIC's payments, and negotiations failed to resolve the dispute. In a letter, MCA suspended PIC's broadcast rights for all of its shows and stated that "[a]ny telecasts of MCA programming by WTMV-TV . . . will be deemed unauthorized and shall constitute an infringement of MCA's copyrights." PIC nonetheless continued broadcasting MCA's programs, with the exception of *Harry.* MCA filed a suit in a federal district court against PIC, alleging breach of contract and copyright infringement. PIC filed a counterclaim, contending in part that MCA's deal was an illegal tying arrangement. Is PIC correct? Explain. [*MCA Television, Ltd. v. Public Interest Corp.,* 171 F.3d 1265 (11th Cir. 1999)]

18–7. Attempted Monopolization. To make personal computers (PCs) easier to use, Intel Corporation and other companies developed in 1995 a standard to enable the easy attachment of peripherals (printers and other hardware) to PCs called the Universal Serial Bus (USB) specification. Intel and others formed the Universal Serial Bus Implementers Forum (USB-IF) to promote USB technology and products. Intel, however, makes relatively few USB products and does not make any USB interconnect devices. Multivideo Labs, Inc. (MVL), designed and distributed Active Extension Cables (AECs) to connect peripheral devices to each other or to a PC. The AECs were not USB compliant, a fact that Intel employees told other USB-IF members. Asserting that this caused a "general cooling of the market" for AECs, MVL filed a suit in a federal district court against Intel, claiming in part attempted monopolization in violation of the Sherman Act. Intel filed a motion for summary judgment. How should the court rule, and why? [*Multivideo Labs, Inc. v. Intel Corp.,* __ F.Supp.2d __ (S.D.N.Y. 2000)]

WEB EXERCISES

Go to **http://lec.westbuslaw.com**, the Web site that accompanies this text. Select "Internet Applications," and then click on "Chapter 18." There you will find the following Internet research exercise that you can perform to learn more about the application of antitrust laws to vertical restraints:

Activity 18–1: Vertical Restraints and the Rule of Reason

APPENDIX A

Digital Millennium Copyright Act of 1998 (Excerpts)

Sec. 1201. Circumvention of copyright protection systems

(a) VIOLATIONS REGARDING CIRCUMVENTION OF TECHNOLOGICAL MEASURES—(1)(A) No person shall circumvent a technological measure that effectively controls access to a work protected under this title. * * *

* * * *

(b) ADDITIONAL VIOLATIONS—(1) No person shall manufacture, import, offer to the public, provide, or otherwise traffic in any technology, product, service, device, component, or part thereof, that—

(A) is primarily designed or produced for the purpose of circumventing protection afforded by a technological measure that effectively protects a right of a copyright owner under this title in a work or a portion thereof;

(B) has only limited commercially significant purpose or use other than to circumvent protection afforded by a technological measure that effectively protects a right of a copyright owner under this title in a work or a portion thereof; or

(C) is marketed by that person or another acting in concert with that person with that person's knowledge for use in circumventing protection afforded by a technological measure that effectively protects a right of a copyright owner under this title in a work or a portion thereof.

* * * *

Sec. 1202. Integrity of copyright management information

(a) FALSE COPYRIGHT MANAGEMENT INFORMATION—No person shall knowingly and with the intent to induce, enable, facilitate, or conceal infringement—

(1) provide copyright management information that is false, or

(2) distribute or import for distribution copyright management information that is false.

(b) REMOVAL OR ALTERATION OF COPYRIGHT MANAGEMENT INFORMATION—No person shall, without the authority of the copyright owner or the law—

(1) intentionally remove or alter any copyright management information,

(2) distribute or import for distribution copyright management information knowing that the copyright management information has been removed or altered without authority of the copyright owner or the law, or

(3) distribute, import for distribution, or publicly perform works, copies of works, or phonorecords, knowing that copyright management information has been removed or altered without authority of the copyright owner or the law, knowing, or, with respect to civil remedies under section 1203, having reasonable grounds to know, that it will induce, enable, facilitate, or conceal an infringement of any right under this title.

(c) DEFINITION—As used in this section, the term "copyright management information" means any of the following information conveyed in connection with copies or phonorecords of a work or performances or displays of a work, including in digital form, except that such term does not include any personally identifying information about a user of a work or of a copy, phonorecord, performance, or display of a work:

(1) The title and other information identifying the work, including the information set forth on a notice of copyright.

(2) The name of, and other identifying information about, the author of a work.

(3) The name of, and other identifying information about, the copyright owner of the work, including the information set forth in a notice of copyright.

(4) With the exception of public performances of works by radio and television broadcast stations, the name of, and other identifying information about, a performer whose performance is fixed in a work other than an audiovisual work.

(5) With the exception of public performances of works by radio and television broadcast stations, in the case of an audiovisual work, the name of, and other identifying information about, a writer, performer, or director who is credited in the audiovisual work.

(6) Terms and conditions for use of the work.

(7) Identifying numbers or symbols referring to such information or links to such information.

(8) Such other information as the Register of Copyrights may prescribe by regulation, except that the Register of Copyrights may not require the provision of any information concerning the user of a copyrighted work.

* * * *

Sec. 512. Limitations on liability relating to material online

(a) TRANSITORY DIGITAL NETWORK COMMUNICATIONS– A service provider shall not be liable for monetary relief, or, except as provided in subsection (j), for injunctive or other equitable relief, for infringement of copyright by reason of the provider's transmitting, routing, or providing connections for, material through a system or network controlled or operated by or for the service provider, or by reason of the intermediate and transient storage of that material in the course of such transmitting, routing, or providing connections, if–

(1) the transmission of the material was initiated by or at the direction of a person other than the service provider;

(2) the transmission, routing, provision of connections, or storage is carried out through an automatic technical process without selection of the material by the service provider;

(3) the service provider does not select the recipients of the material except as an automatic response to the request of another person;

(4) no copy of the material made by the service provider in the course of such intermediate or transient storage is maintained on the system or network in a manner ordinarily accessible to anyone other than anticipated recipients, and no such copy is maintained on the system or network in a manner ordinarily accessible to such anticipated recipients for a longer period than is reasonably necessary for the transmission, routing, or provision of connections; and

(5) the material is transmitted through the system or network without modification of its content.

APPENDIX B

ICANN's Uniform Domain Name Dispute-Resolution Policy (Excerpts)

* * * *

2. Your Representations. By applying to register a domain name, or by asking us to maintain or renew a domain name registration, you hereby represent and warrant to us that (a) the statements that you made in your Registration Agreement are complete and accurate; (b) to your knowledge, the registration of the domain name will not infringe upon or otherwise violate the rights of any third party; (c) you are not registering the domain name for an unlawful purpose; and (d) you will not knowingly use the domain name in violation of any applicable laws or regulations. It is your responsibility to determine whether your domain name registration infringes or violates someone else's rights.

* * * *

4. Mandatory Administrative Proceeding.

This Paragraph sets forth the type of disputes for which you are required to submit to a mandatory administrative proceeding. These proceedings will be conducted before one of the administrative-dispute-resolution service providers listed at http://www.icann.com/udrp/approved-providers.htm (each, a "Provider").

a. Applicable Disputes. You are required to submit to a mandatory administrative proceeding in the event that a third party (a "complainant") asserts to the applicable Provider, in compliance with the Rules of Procedure, that

(i) your domain name is identical or confusingly similar to a trademark or service mark in which the complainant has rights; and

(ii) you have no rights or legitimate interests in respect of the domain name; and

(iii) your domain name has been registered and is being used in bad faith.

In the administrative proceeding, the complainant must prove that each of these three elements are present.

b. Evidence of Registration and Use in Bad Faith. For the purposes of *Paragraph 4(a)(iii),* the following circumstances, in particular but without limitation, if found by the Panel to be present, shall be evidence of the registration and use of a domain name in bad faith:

(i) circumstances indicating that you have registered or you have acquired the domain name primarily for the purpose of selling, renting, or otherwise transferring the domain name registration to the complainant who is the owner of the trademark or service mark or to a competitor of that complainant, for valuable consideration in excess of your documented out-of-pocket costs directly related to the domain name; or

(ii) you have registered the domain name in order to prevent the owner of the trademark or service mark from reflecting the mark in a corresponding domain name, provided that you have engaged in a pattern of such conduct; or

(iii) you have registered the domain name primarily for the purpose of disrupting the business of a competitor; or

(iv) by using the domain name, you have intentionally attempted to attract, for commercial gain, Internet users to your web site or other on-line location, by creating a likelihood of confusion with the complainant's mark as to the source, sponsorship, affiliation, or endorsement of your web site or location or of a product or service on your web site or location.

c. How to Demonstrate Your Rights to and Legitimate Interests in the Domain Name in Responding to a Complaint. When you receive a complaint, you should refer to *Paragraph 5* of the Rules of Procedure in determining how your response should be prepared. Any of the following circumstances, in particular but without limitation, if found by the Panel to be proved based on its evaluation of all evidence presented, shall demonstrate your rights or legitimate interests to the domain name for purposes of *Paragraph 4(a)(ii):*

(i) before any notice to you of the dispute, your use of, or demonstrable preparations to use, the domain name or a name corresponding to the domain name in connection with a bona fide offering of goods or services; or

(ii) you (as an individual, business, or other organization) have been commonly known by the domain name, even if you have acquired no trademark or service mark rights; or

(iii) you are making a legitimate noncommercial or fair use of the domain name, without intent for commercial gain to misleadingly divert consumers or to tarnish the trademark or service mark at issue.

* * *

APPENDIX C

Anticybersquatting Consumer Protection Act of 1999 (Excerpts)

[15 U.S.C. Section 1114. Remedies; infringement; innocent infringement by printers and publishers

* * * *

[(2) Notwithstanding any other provision of this chapter, the remedies given to the owner of a right infringed under this chapter or to a person bringing an action under section 1125(a) or (d) of this title shall be limited as follows:]

* * * *

(D)(i)(I) A domain name registrar, a domain name registry, or other domain name registration authority that takes any action described under clause (ii) affecting a domain name shall not be liable for monetary relief or, except as provided in subclause (II), for injunctive relief, to any person for such action, regardless of whether the domain name is finally determined to infringe or dilute the mark.

(II) A domain name registrar, domain name registry, or other domain name registration authority described in subclause (I) may be subject to injunctive relief only if such registrar, registry, or other registration authority has–

(aa) not expeditiously deposited with a court, in which an action has been filed regarding the disposition of the domain name, documents sufficient for the court to establish the court's control and authority regarding the disposition of the registration and use of the domain name;

(bb) transferred, suspended, or otherwise modified the domain name during the pendency of the action, except upon order of the court; or

(cc) willfully failed to comply with any such court order.

(ii) An action referred to under clause (i)(I) is any action of refusing to register, removing from registration, transferring, temporarily disabling, or permanently canceling a domain name–

(I) in compliance with a court order under section 1125(d) of this title; or

(II) in the implementation of a reasonable policy by such registrar, registry, or authority prohibiting the registration of a domain name that is identical to, confusingly similar to, or dilutive of another's mark.

(iii) A domain name registrar, a domain name registry, or other domain name registration authority shall not be liable for damages under this section for the registration or maintenance of a domain name for another absent a showing of bad faith intent to profit from such registration or maintenance of the domain name.

(iv) If a registrar, registry, or other registration authority takes an action described under clause (ii) based on a knowing and material misrepresentation by any other person that a domain name is identical to, confusingly similar to, or dilutive of a mark, the person making the knowing and material misrepresentation shall be liable for any damages, including costs and attorney's fees, incurred by the domain name registrant as a result of such action. The court may also grant injunctive relief to the domain name registrant, including the reactivation of the domain name or the transfer of the domain name to the domain name registrant.

(v) A domain name registrant whose domain name has been suspended, disabled, or transferred under a policy described under clause (ii)(II) may, upon notice to the mark owner, file a civil action to establish that the registration or use of the domain name by such registrant is not unlawful under this chapter. The court may grant injunctive relief to the domain name registrant, including the reactivation of the domain name or transfer of the domain name to the domain name registrant.

[15 U.S.C. Section 1117. Recovery for violation of rights; profits, damages and costs; attorney fees; treble damages; election]

* * * *

(d) In a case involving a violation of section 1125(d)(1) of this title, the plaintiff may elect, at any time before final judgment is rendered by the trial court, to recover, instead of actual damages and profits, an award of statutory damages in the amount of not less than $1,000 and not more than $100,000 per domain name, as the court considers just.

[15 U.S.C. Section 1125. False designations of origin, false descriptions, and dilution forbidden]

* * * *

(d) Cyberpiracy prevention

(1)(A) A person shall be liable in a civil action by the owner of a mark, including a personal name which is protected as a mark under this section, if, without regard to the goods or services of the parties, that person

(i) has a bad faith intent to profit from that mark, including a personal name which is protected as a mark under this section; and

(ii) registers, traffics in, or uses a domain name that–

(I) in the case of a mark that is distinctive at the time of registration of the domain name, is identical or confusingly similar to that mark;

(II) in the case of a famous mark that is famous at the time of registration of the domain name, is identical or confusingly similar to or dilutive of that mark; or

(III) is a trademark, word, or name protected by reason of section 706 of Title 18 or section 220506 of Title 36.

(B)(i) In determining whether a person has a bad faith intent described under subparagraph (a), a court may consider factors such as, but not limited to

(I) the trademark or other intellectual property rights of the person, if any, in the domain name;

(II) the extent to which the domain name consists of the legal name of the person or a name that is otherwise commonly used to identify that person;

(III) the person's prior use, if any, of the domain name in connection with the bona fide offering of any goods or services;

(IV) the person's bona fide noncommercial or fair use of the mark in a site accessible under the domain name;

(V) the person's intent to divert consumers from the mark owner's online location to a site accessible under the domain name that could harm the goodwill represented by the mark, either for commercial gain or with the intent to tarnish or disparage the mark, by creating a likelihood of confusion as to the source, sponsorship, affiliation, or endorsement of the site;

(VI) the person's offer to transfer, sell, or otherwise assign the domain name to the mark owner or any third party for financial gain without having used, or having an intent to use, the domain name in the bona fide offering of any goods or services, or the person's prior conduct indicating a pattern of such conduct;

(VII) the person's provision of material and misleading false contact information when applying for the registration of the domain name, the person's intentional failure to maintain accurate contact information, or the person's prior conduct indicating a pattern of such conduct;

(VIII) the person's registration or acquisition of multiple domain names which the person knows are identical or confusingly similar to marks of others that are distinctive at the time of registration of such domain names, or dilutive of famous marks of others that are famous at the time of registration of such domain names, without regard to the goods or services of the parties; and

(IX) the extent to which the mark incorporated in the person's domain name registration is or is not distinctive and famous within the meaning of subsection (c)(1) of this section.

(ii) Bad faith intent described under subparagraph (A) shall not be found in any case in which the court determines that the person believed and had reasonable grounds to believe that the use of the domain name was a fair use or otherwise lawful.

(C) In any civil action involving the registration, trafficking, or use of a domain name under this paragraph, a court may order the forfeiture or cancellation of the domain name or the transfer of the domain name to the owner of the mark.

(D) A person shall be liable for using a domain name under subparagraph (A) only if that person is the domain name registrant or that registrant's authorized licensee.

(E) As used in this paragraph, the term "traffics in" refers to transactions that include, but are not limited to, sales, purchases, loans, pledges, licenses, exchanges of currency, and any other transfer for consideration or receipt in exchange for consideration.

(2)(A) The owner of a mark may file an in rem civil action against a domain name in the judicial district in which the domain name registrar, domain name registry, or other domain name authority that registered or assigned the domain name is located if

(i) the domain name violates any right of the owner of a mark registered in the Patent and Trademark Office, or protected under subsection (a) or (c); and

(ii) the court finds that the owner–

(I) is not able to obtain in personam jurisdiction over a person who would have been a defendant in a civil action under paragraph (1); or

(II) through due diligence was not able to find a person who would have been a defendant in a civil action under paragraph (1) by–

(aa) sending a notice of the alleged violation and intent to proceed under this paragraph to the registrant of the domain name at the postal and e-mail address provided by the registrant to the registrar; and

(bb) publishing notice of the action as the court may direct promptly after filing the action.

(B) The actions under subparagraph (A)(ii) shall constitute service of process.

(C) In an in rem action under this paragraph, a domain name shall be deemed to have its situs in the judicial district in which

(i) the domain name registrar, registry, or other domain name authority that registered or assigned the domain name is located; or

(ii) documents sufficient to establish control and authority regarding the disposition of the registration and use of the domain name are deposited with the court.

(D)(i) The remedies in an in rem action under this paragraph shall be limited to a court order for the forfeiture or cancellation of the domain name or the transfer of the domain name to the owner of the mark. upon receipt of written notification of a filed, stamped copy of a complaint filed by the owner of a mark in a United States district court under this paragraph, the domain name registrar, domain name registry, or other domain name authority shall

(I) expeditiously deposit with the court documents sufficient to establish the court's control and authority regarding the disposition of the registration and use of the domain name to the court; and

(II) not transfer, suspend, or otherwise modify the domain name during the pendency of the action, except upon order of the court.

(ii) The domain name registrar or registry or other domain name authority shall not be liable for injunctive or monetary relief under this paragraph except in the case of bad faith or reckless disregard, which includes a willful failure to comply with any such court order.

(3) The civil action established under paragraph (1) and the in rem action established under paragraph (2), and any remedy available under either such action, shall be in addition to any other civil action or remedy otherwise applicable.

(4) The in rem jurisdiction established under paragraph (2) shall be in addition to any other jurisdiction that otherwise exists, whether in rem or in personam.

[15 U.S.C. Section 1127. Construction and definitions; intent of chapter]

* * * *

The term "domain name" means any alphanumeric designation which is registered with or assigned by any domain name registrar, domain name registry, or other domain name registration authority as part of an electronic address on the Internet.

[15 U.S.C. Section 1129.] Cyberpiracy protections for individuals

(1) In general

(A) Civil liability

Any person who registers a domain name that consists of the name of another living person, or a name substantially and confusingly similar thereto, without that person's consent, with the specific intent to profit from such name by selling the domain name for financial gain to that person or any third party, shall be liable in a civil action by such person.

(B) Exception

A person who in good faith registers a domain name consisting of the name of another living person, or a name substantially and confusingly similar thereto, shall not be liable under this paragraph if such name is used in, affiliated with, or related to a work of authorship protected under Title 17, including a work made for hire as defined in section 101 of Title 17, and if the person registering the domain name is the copyright owner or licensee of the work, the person intends to sell the domain name in conjunction with the lawful exploitation of the work, and such registration is not prohibited by a contract between the registrant and the named person. The exception under this subparagraph shall apply only to a civil action brought under paragraph (1) and shall in no manner limit the protections afforded under the Trademark Act of 1946 (15 U.S.C. 1051 et seq.) or other provision of Federal or State law.

(2) Remedies

In any civil action brought under paragraph (1), a court may award injunctive relief, including the forfeiture or cancellation of the domain name or the transfer of the domain name to the plaintiff. The court may also, in its discretion, award costs and attorneys fees to the prevailing party.

(3) Definition

In this section, the term "domain name" has the meaning given that term in section 45 of the Trademark Act of 1946 (15 U.S.C. 1127).

(4) Effective date

This section shall apply to domain names registered on or after November 29, 1999.

APPENDIX D
Federal Trademark Dilution Act of 1995 (Excerpts)

[15 U.S.C. Section 1125. False designations of origin, false descriptions, and dilution forbidden]

* * * *

(c) Remedies for dilution of famous marks

(1) The owner of a famous mark shall be entitled, subject to the principles of equity and upon such terms as the court deems reasonable, to an injunction against another person's commercial use in commerce of a mark or trade name, if such use begins after the mark has become famous and causes dilution of the distinctive quality of the mark, and to obtain such other relief as is provided in this subsection. In determining whether a mark is distinctive and famous, a court may consider factors such as, but not limited to–

(A) the degree of inherent or acquired distinctiveness of the mark;

(B) the duration and extent of use of the mark in connection with the goods or services with which the mark is used;

(C) the duration and extent of advertising and publicity of the mark;

(D) the geographical extent of the trading area in which the mark is used;

(E) the channels of trade for the goods or services with which the mark is used;

(F) the degree of recognition of the mark in the trading areas and channels of trade used by the marks' owner and the person against whom the injunction is sought;

(G) the nature and extent of use of the same or similar marks by third parties; and

(H) whether the mark was registered under the Act of March 3, 1881, or the Act of February 20, 1905, or on the principal register.

(2) In an action brought under this subsection, the owner of the famous mark shall be entitled only to injunctive relief as set forth in section 1116 of this title unless the person against whom the injunction is sought willfully intended to trade on the owner's reputation or to cause dilution of the famous mark. If such willful intent is proven, the owner of the famous mark shall also be entitled to the remedies set forth in sections 1117(a) and 1118 of this title, subject to the discretion of the court and the principles of equity.

(3) The ownership by a person of a valid registration under the Act of March 3, 1881, or the Act of February 20, 1905, or on the principal register shall be a complete bar to an action against that person, with respect to that mark, that is brought by another person under the common law or a statute of a State and that seeks to prevent dilution of the distinctiveness of a mark, label, or form of advertisement.

(4) The following shall not be actionable under this section:

(A) Fair use of a famous mark by another person in comparative commercial advertising or promotion to identify the competing goods or services of the owner of the famous mark.

(B) Noncommercial use of a mark.

(C) All forms of news reporting and news commentary.

APPENDIX E
Uniform Electronic Transactions Act (Excerpts)

* * * *

Section 5. USE OF ELECTRONIC RECORDS AND ELECTRONIC SIGNATURES; VARIATION BY AGREEMENT.

(a) This [Act] does not require a record or signature to be created, generated, sent, communicated, received, stored, or otherwise processed or used by electronic means or in electronic form.

(b) This [Act] applies only to transactions between parties each of which has agreed to conduct transactions by electronic means. Whether the parties agree to conduct a transaction by electronic means is determined from the context and surrounding circumstances, including the parties' conduct.

(c) A party that agrees to conduct a transaction by electronic means may refuse to conduct other transactions by electronic means. The right granted by this subsection may not be waived by agreement.

(d) Except as otherwise provided in this [Act], the effect of any of its provisions may be varied by agreement. The presence in certain provisions of this [Act] of the words "unless otherwise agreed," or words of similar import, does not imply that the effect of other provisions may not be varied by agreement.

(e) Whether an electronic record or electronic signature has legal consequences is determined by this [Act] and other applicable law.

Section 6. CONSTRUCTION AND APPLICATION. This [Act] must be construed and applied:

(1) to facilitate electronic transactions consistent with other applicable law; (2) to be consistent with reasonable practices concerning electronic transactions and with the continued expansion of those practices; and

(3) to effectuate its general purpose to make uniform the law with respect to the subject of this [Act] among States enacting it.

Section 7. LEGAL RECOGNITION OF ELECTRONIC RECORDS, ELECTRONIC SIGNATURES, AND ELECTRONIC CONTRACTS.

(a) A record or signature may not be denied legal effect or enforceability solely because it is in electronic form.

(b) A contract may not be denied legal effect or enforceability solely because an electronic record was used in its formation.

(c) If a law requires a record to be in writing, an electronic record satisfies the law.

(d) If a law requires a signature, an electronic signature satisfies the law.

* * * *

Section 10. EFFECT OF CHANGE OR ERROR. If a change or error in an electronic record occurs in a transmission between parties to a transaction, the following rules apply:

(1) If the parties have agreed to use a security procedure to detect changes or errors and one party has conformed to the procedure, but the other party has not, and the nonconforming party would have detected the change or error had that party also conformed, the conforming party may avoid the effect of the changed or erroneous electronic record.

(2) In an automated transaction involving an individual, the individual may avoid the effect of an electronic record that resulted from an error made by the individual in dealing with the electronic agent of another person if the electronic agent did not provide an opportunity for the prevention or correction of the error and, at the time the individual learns of the error, the individual:

   (A) promptly notifies the other person of the error and that the individual did not intend to be bound by the electronic record received by the other person;

   (B) takes reasonable steps, including steps that conform to the other person's reasonable instructions, to return to the other person or, if instructed by the other person, to destroy the consideration received, if any, as a result of the erroneous electronic record; and

   (C) has not used or received any benefit or value from the consideration, if any, received from the other person.

(3) If neither paragraph (1) nor paragraph (2) applies, the change or error has the effect provided by other law, including the law of mistake, and the parties' contract, if any.

(4) Paragraphs (2) and (3) may not be varied by agreement.

APPENDIX F
Uniform Computer Information Transactions Act (Excerpts)

Section 104. MIXED TRANSACTIONS: AGREEMENT TO OPT-IN OR OPT-OUT. The parties may agree that this [Act], including contract-formation rules, governs the transaction, in whole or part, or that other law governs the transaction and this [Act] does not apply, if a material part of the subject matter to which the agreement applies is computer information or informational rights in it that are within the scope of this [Act], or is subject matter within this [Act] under Section 103(b), or is subject matter excluded by Section 103(d)(1) or (2). However, any agreement to do so is subject to the following rules:

(1) An agreement that this [Act] governs a transaction does not alter the applicability of any rule or procedure that may not be varied by agreement of the parties or that may be varied only in a manner specified by the rule or procedure, including a consumer protection statute [or administrative rule]. In addition, in a mass-market transaction, the agreement does not alter the applicability of a law applicable to a copy of information in printed form.

(2) An agreement that this [Act] does not govern a transaction:

  (A) does not alter the applicability of Section 214 or 816; and

  (B) in a mass-market transaction, does not alter the applicability under [this Act] of the doctrine of unconscionability or fundamental public policy or the obligation of good faith.

(3) In a mass-market transaction, any term under this section which changes the extent to which this [Act] governs the transaction must be conspicuous.

(4) A copy of a computer program contained in and sold or leased as part of goods and which is excluded from this [Act] by Section 103(b)(1) cannot provide the basis for an agreement under this section that this [Act] governs the transaction.

* * * *

Section 107. LEGAL RECOGNITION OF ELECTRONIC RECORD AND AUTHENTICATION; USE OF ELECTRONIC AGENTS.

(a) A record or authentication may not be denied legal effect or enforceability solely because it is in electronic form.

(b) This [Act] does not require that a record or authentication be generated, stored, sent, received, or otherwise processed by electronic means or in electronic form.

(c) In any transaction, a person may establish requirements regarding the type of authentication or record acceptable to it.

(d) A person that uses an electronic agent that it has selected for making an authentication, performance, or agreement, including manifestation of assent, is bound by the operations of the electronic agent, even if no individual was aware of or reviewed the agent's operations or the results of the operations.

* * * *

Section 202. FORMATION IN GENERAL.

(a) A contract may be formed in any manner sufficient to show agreement, including offer and acceptance or conduct of both parties or operations of electronic agents which recognize the existence of a contract.

(b) If the parties so intend, an agreement sufficient to constitute a contract may be found even if the time of its making is undetermined, one or more terms are left open or to be agreed on, the records of the parties do not otherwise establish a contract, or one party reserves the right to modify terms.

(c) Even if one or more terms are left open or to be agreed upon, a contract does not fail for indefiniteness if the parties intended to make a contract and there is a reasonably certain basis for giving an appropriate remedy.

(d) In the absence of conduct or performance by both parties to the contrary, a contract is not formed if there is a material disagreement about a material term, including a term concerning scope.

(e) If a term is to be adopted by later agreement and the parties intend not to be bound unless the term is so adopted, a contract is not formed if the parties do not agree to the term. In that case, each party shall deliver to the other party, or with the consent of the other party destroy, all copies of information, access materials, and other materials received or made, and each party is entitled to a return with respect to any contract fee paid for which performance has not been received, has not been accepted, or has been redelivered without any benefit being retained. The parties remain bound by any restriction in a contractual use term with respect to information or copies received or made from copies received pursuant to the agreement, but the contractual use term does not apply to information or copies properly received or obtained from another source.

Section 203. OFFER AND ACCEPTANCE IN GENERAL. Unless otherwise unambiguously indicated by the language or the circumstances:

(1) An offer to make a contract invites acceptance in any manner and by any medium reasonable under the circumstances.

(2) An order or other offer to acquire a copy for prompt or current delivery invites acceptance by either a prompt promise to ship or a prompt or current shipment of a conforming or nonconforming copy. However, a shipment of a nonconforming copy is not an acceptance if the licensor seasonably notifies the licensee that the shipment is offered only as an accommodation to the licensee.

(3) If the beginning of a requested performance is a reasonable mode of acceptance, an offeror that is not notified of acceptance or performance within a reasonable time may treat the offer as having lapsed before acceptance.

(4) If an offer in an electronic message evokes an electronic message accepting the offer, a contract is formed:

 (A) when an electronic acceptance is received; or

 (B) if the response consists of beginning performance, full performance, or giving access to information, when the performance is received or the access is enabled and necessary access materials are received.

* * * *

Section 209. MASS-MARKET LICENSE.

(a) A party adopts the terms of a mass-market license for purposes of Section 208 only if the party agrees to the license, such as by manifesting assent, before or during the party's initial performance or use of or access to the information. A term is not part of the license if:

(1) the term is unconscionable or is unenforceable under Section 105(a) or (b); or

(2) subject to Section 301, the term conflicts with a term to which the parties to the license have expressly agreed.

(b) If a mass-market license or a copy of the license is not available in a manner permitting an opportunity to review by the licensee before the licensee becomes obligated to pay and the licensee does not agree, such as by manifesting assent, to the license after having an opportunity to review, the licensee is entitled to a return under Section 112 and, in addition, to:

(1) reimbursement of any reasonable expenses incurred in complying with the licensor's instructions for returning or destroying the computer information or, in the absence of instructions, expenses incurred for return postage or similar reasonable expense in returning the computer information; and

(2) compensation for any reasonable and foreseeable costs of restoring the licensee's information processing system to reverse changes in the system caused by the installation, if:

 (A) the installation occurs because information must be installed to enable review of the license; and

 (B) the installation alters the system or information in it but does not restore the system or information after removal of the installed information because the licensee rejected the license.

(c) In a mass-market transaction, if the licensor does not have an opportunity to review a record containing proposed terms from the licensee before the licensor delivers or becomes obligated to deliver the information, and if the licensor does not agree, such as by manifesting assent, to those terms after having that opportunity, the licensor is entitled to a return.

* * * *

Section 211. PRETRANSACTION DISCLOSURES IN INTERNET-TYPE TRANSACTIONS. This section applies to a licensor that makes its computer information available to a licensee by electronic means from its Internet or similar electronic site. In such a case, the licensor affords an opportunity to review the terms of a standard form license which opportunity satisfies Section 112(e) with respect to a licensee that acquires the information from that site, if the licensor:

(1) makes the standard terms of the license readily available for review by the licensee before the information is delivered or the licensee becomes obligated to pay, whichever occurs first, by:

 (A) displaying prominently and in close proximity to a description of the computer information, or to instructions or steps for acquiring it, the standard terms or a reference to an electronic location from which they can be readily obtained; or

 (B) disclosing the availability of the standard terms in a prominent place on the site from which the computer information is offered and promptly furnishing a copy of the standard terms on request before the transfer of the computer information; and

(2) does not take affirmative acts to prevent printing or storage of the standard terms for archival or review purposes by the licensee.

APPENDIX G

Electronic Signatures in Global and National Commerce Act of 2000 (Excerpts)

SEC. 101. GENERAL RULE OF VALIDITY.

(a) IN GENERAL—Notwithstanding any statute, regulation, or other rule of law (other than this title and title II), with respect to any transaction in or affecting interstate or foreign commerce—

(1) a signature, contract, or other record relating to such transaction may not be denied legal effect, validity, or enforceability solely because it is in electronic form; and

(2) a contract relating to such transaction may not be denied legal effect, validity, or enforceability solely because an electronic signature or electronic record was used in its formation.

* * * *

(d) RETENTION OF CONTRACTS AND RECORDS—

(1) ACCURACY AND ACCESSIBILITY—If a statute, regulation, or other rule of law requires that a contract or other record relating to a transaction in or affecting interstate or foreign commerce be retained, that requirement is met by retaining an electronic record of the information in the contract or other record that—

(A) accurately reflects the information set forth in the contract or other record; and

(B) remains accessible to all persons who are entitled to access by statute, regulation, or rule of law, for the period required by such statute, regulation, or rule of law, in a form that is capable of being accurately reproduced for later reference, whether by transmission, printing, or otherwise.

(2) EXCEPTION—A requirement to retain a contract or other record in accordance with paragraph (1) does not apply to any information whose sole purpose is to enable the contract or other record to be sent, communicated, or received.

(3) ORIGINALS—If a statute, regulation, or other rule of law requires a contract or other record relating to a transaction in or affecting interstate or foreign commerce to be provided, available, or retained in its original form, or provides consequences if the contract or other record is not provided, available, or retained in its original form, that statute, regulation, or rule of law is satisfied by an electronic record that complies with paragraph (1).

(4) CHECKS—If a statute, regulation, or other rule of law requires the retention of a check, that requirement is satisfied by retention of an electronic record of the information on the front and back of the check in accordance with paragraph (1).

* * * *

(g) NOTARIZATION AND ACKNOWLEDGMENT—If a statute, regulation, or other rule of law requires a signature or record relating to a transaction in or affecting interstate or foreign commerce to be notarized, acknowledged, verified, or made under oath, that requirement is satisfied if the electronic signature of the person authorized to perform those acts, together with all other information required to be included by other applicable statute, regulation, or rule of law, is attached to or logically associated with the signature or record.

(h) ELECTRONIC AGENTS—A contract or other record relating to a transaction in or affecting interstate or foreign commerce may not be denied legal effect, validity, or enforceability solely because its formation, creation, or delivery involved the action of one or more electronic agents so long as the action of any such electronic agent is legally attributable to the person to be bound.

(i) INSURANCE—It is the specific intent of the Congress that this title and title II apply to the business of insurance.

(j) INSURANCE AGENTS AND BROKERS—An insurance agent or broker acting under the direction of a party that enters into a contract by means of an electronic record or electronic signature may not be held liable for any deficiency in the electronic procedures agreed to by the parties under that contract if—

(1) the agent or broker has not engaged in negligent, reckless, or intentional tortious conduct;

(2) the agent or broker was not involved in the development or establishment of such electronic procedures; and

(3) the agent or broker did not deviate from such procedures.

* * * *

SEC. 103. SPECIFIC EXCEPTIONS.

(a) EXCEPTED REQUIREMENTS–The provisions of section 101 shall not apply to a contract or other record to the extent it is governed by–

(1) a statute, regulation, or other rule of law governing the creation and execution of wills, codicils, or testamentary trusts;
(2) a State statute, regulation, or other rule of law governing adoption, divorce, or other matters of family law; or
(3) the Uniform Commercial Code, as in effect in any State, other than sections 1–107 and 1–206 and Articles 2 and 2A.

(b) ADDITIONAL EXCEPTIONS–The provisions of section 101 shall not apply to–

(1) court orders or notices, or official court documents (including briefs, pleadings, and other writings) required to be executed in connection with court proceedings;
(2) any notice of–
    (A) the cancellation or termination of utility services (including water, heat, and power);
    (B) default, acceleration, repossession, foreclosure, or eviction, or the right to cure, under a credit agreement secured by, or a rental agreement for, a primary residence of an individual;
    (C) the cancellation or termination of health insurance or benefits or life insurance benefits (excluding annuities); or
    (D) recall of a product, or material failure of a product, that risks endangering health or safety; or

APPENDIX H

Internet Tax Freedom Act of 1998 (Excerpts)

47 U.S.C. Section 151 [note]. * * *

* * * *

"[Section] 1101. Moratorium

"(a) Moratorium.—No State or political subdivision thereof shall impose any of the following taxes during the period beginning on October 1, 1998, and ending 3 years after the date of the enactment of this Act [Oct. 21, 1998]—

"(1) taxes on Internet access, unless such tax was generally imposed and actually enforced prior to October 1, 1998; and

"(2) multiple or discriminatory taxes on electronic commerce.

"(b) Preservation of state and local taxing authority.—Except as provided in this section, nothing in this title [this note] shall be construed to modify, impair, or supersede, or authorize the modification, impairment, or superseding of, any State or local law pertaining to taxation that is otherwise permissible by or under the Constitution of the United States or other Federal law and in effect on the date of enactment of this Act [Oct. 21, 1998].

"(c) Liabilities and pending cases.—Nothing in this title [this note] affects liability for taxes accrued and enforced before the date of enactment of this Act [Oct. 21, 1998], nor does this title [this note] affect ongoing litigation relating to such taxes.

"(d) Definition of generally imposed and actually enforced.—For purposes of this section, a tax has been generally imposed and actually enforced prior to October 1, 1998, if, before that date, the tax was authorized by statute and either—

"(1) a provider of Internet access services had a reasonable opportunity to know by virtue of a rule or other public proclamation made by the appropriate administrative agency of the State or political subdivision thereof, that such agency has interpreted and applied such tax to Internet access services; or

"(2) a State or political subdivision thereof generally collected such tax on charges for Internet access.

"(e) Exception to moratorium.—

"(1) In general.—Subsection (a) shall also not apply in the case of any person or entity who knowingly and with knowledge of the character of the material, in interstate or foreign commerce by means of the World Wide Web, makes any communication for commercial purposes that is available to any minor and that includes any material that is harmful to minors unless such person or entity has restricted access by minors to material that is harmful to minors—

"(A) by requiring use of a credit card, debit account, adult access code, or adult personal identification number;

"(B) by accepting a digital certificate that verifies age; or

"(C) by any other reasonable measures that are feasible under available technology.

"(2) Scope of exception.—For purposes of paragraph (1), a person shall not be considered to [be] making a communication for commercial purposes of material to the extent that the person is—

"(A) a telecommunications carrier engaged in the provision of a telecommunications service;

"(B) a person engaged in the business of providing an Internet access service;

"(C) a person engaged in the business of providing an Internet information location tool; or

"(D) similarly engaged in the transmission, storage, retrieval, hosting, formatting, or translation (or any combination thereof) of a communication made by another person, without selection or alteration of the communication.

"(3) Definitions.—In this subsection:

"(A) By means of the World Wide Web.—The term 'by means of the World Wide Web' means by placement of material in a computer server-based file archive so that it is publicly accessible, over the Internet, using hypertext transfer protocol, file transfer protocol, or other similar protocols.

"(B) Commercial purposes; engaged in the business.—

"(i) Commercial purposes.—A person shall be considered to make a communication for commercial purposes only if such person is engaged in the business of making such communications.

"(ii) Engaged in the business.—The term 'engaged in the business' means that the person who makes a communication, or offers to make a communication, by means of the World Wide Web, that includes any material that is harmful to minors, devotes time, attention, or labor to such activities, as a regular course of such person's trade or business, with the objective of earning a profit as a result of such activities (although it is not necessary that the person make a profit or that the making or offering to make such communications be the person's sole or principal business or source of income). A person may be considered to be engaged in the business of making, by means of the World Wide Web, communications for commercial purposes that include material that is harmful to minors, only if the person knowingly causes the material that is harmful to minors to be posted on the World Wide Web or knowingly solicits such material to be posted on the World Wide Web.

"(C) Internet.—The term 'Internet' means collectively the myriad of computer and telecommunications facilities, including equipment and operating software, which comprise the interconnected world-wide network of networks that employ the Transmission Control Protocol/Internet Protocol, or any predecessor or successor protocols to such protocol, to communicate information of all kinds by wire or radio.

"(D) Internet access service.—The term 'Internet access service' means a service that enables users to access content, information, electronic mail, or other services offered over the Internet and may also include access to proprietary content, information, and other services as part of a package of services offered to consumers. Such term does not include telecommunications services.

"(E) Internet information location tool.—The term 'Internet information location tool' means a service that refers or links users to an online location on the World Wide Web. Such term includes directories, indices, references, pointers, and hypertext links.

"(F) Material that is harmful to minors.—The term 'material that is harmful to minors' means any communication, picture, image, graphic image file, article, recording, writing, or other matter of any kind that is obscene or that—

"(i) the average person, applying contemporary community standards, would find, taking the material as a whole and with respect to minors, is designed to appeal to, or is designed to pander to, the prurient interest;

"(ii) depicts, describes, or represents, in a manner patently offensive with respect to minors, an actual or simulated sexual act or sexual contact, an actual or simulated normal or perverted sexual act, or a lewd exhibition of the genitals or post-pubescent female breast; and

"(iii) taken as a whole, lacks serious literary, artistic, political, or scientific value for minors.

"(G) Minor.—The term 'minor' means any person under 17 years of age.

"(H) Telecommunications carrier; telecommunications service.—The terms 'telecommunications carrier' and 'telecommunications service' have the meanings given such terms in section 3 of the Communications Act of 1934 (47 U.S.C. 153).

"(f) Additional exception to moratorium.—

"(1) In general.—Subsection (a) shall also not apply with respect to an Internet access provider, unless, at the time of entering into an agreement with a customer for the provision of Internet access services, such provider offers such customer (either for a fee or at no charge) screening software that is designed to permit the customer to limit access to material on the Internet that is harmful to minors.

"(2) Definitions.—In this subsection:

"(A) Internet access provider.—The term 'Internet access provider' means a person engaged in the business of providing a computer and communications facility through which a customer may obtain access to the Internet, but does not include a common carrier to the extent that it provides only telecommunications services.

"(B) Internet access services.—The term 'Internet access services' means the provision of computer and communications services through which a customer using a computer and a modem or other communications device may obtain access to the Internet, but does not include telecommunications services provided by a common carrier.

"(C) Screening software.—The term 'screening software' means software that is designed to permit a person to limit access to material on the Internet that is harmful to minors.

"(3) Applicability.—Paragraph (1) shall apply to agreements for the provision of Internet access services entered into on or after the date that is 6 months after the date of enactment of this Act [Oct. 21, 1998].

* * * *

"[Section] 1104. Definitions

"For the purposes of this title [this note]:

"(1) Bit tax.—The term 'bit tax' means any tax on electronic commerce expressly imposed on or measured by the volume of digital information transmitted electronically, or the volume of digital information per unit of time transmitted electronically, but does not include taxes imposed on the provision of telecommunications services.

"(2) Discriminatory tax.—The term 'discriminatory tax' means—

"(A) any tax imposed by a State or political subdivision thereof on electronic commerce that—

"(i) is not generally imposed and legally collectible by such State or such political subdivision on transactions involving similar property, goods, services, or information accomplished through other means;

"(ii) is not generally imposed and legally collectible at the same rate by such State or such political subdivision on transactions involving similar property, goods, services, or information accomplished through other means, unless the rate is lower as part of a phase-out of the tax over not more than a 5-year period;

"(iii) imposes an obligation to collect or pay the tax on a different person or entity than in the case of transactions involving similar property, goods, services, or information accomplished through other means;

"(iv) establishes a classification of Internet access service providers or online service providers for purposes of establishing a higher tax rate to be imposed on such providers than the tax rate generally applied to providers of similar information services delivered through other means; or

"(B) any tax imposed by a State or political subdivision thereof, if—

"(i) except with respect to a tax (on Internet access) that was generally imposed and actually enforced prior to October 1, 1998, the sole ability to access a site on a remote seller's out-of-State computer server is considered a factor in determining a remote seller's tax collection obligation; or

"(ii) a provider of Internet access service or online services is deemed to be the agent of a remote seller for determining tax collection obligations solely as a result of–

"(I) the display of a remote seller's information or content on the out-of- State computer server of a provider of Internet access service or online services; or

"(II) the processing of orders through the out-of-State computer server of a provider of Internet access service or online services.

"(3) Electronic commerce.–The term 'electronic commerce' means any transaction conducted over the Internet or through Internet access, comprising the sale, lease, license, offer, or delivery of property, goods, services, or information, whether or not for consideration, and includes the provision of Internet access.

"(4) Internet.–The term 'Internet' means collectively the myriad of computer and telecommunications facilities, including equipment and operating software, which comprise the interconnected world-wide network of networks that employ the Transmission Control Protocol/Internet Protocol, or any predecessor or successor protocols to such protocol, to communicate information of all kinds by wire or radio.

"(5) Internet access.–The term 'Internet access' means a service that enables users to access content, information, electronic mail, or other services offered over the Internet, and may also include access to proprietary content, information, and other services as part of a package of services offered to users. Such term does not include telecommunications services.

"(6) Multiple tax.–

"(A) In general.–The term 'multiple tax' means any tax that is imposed by one State or political subdivision thereof on the same or essentially the same electronic commerce that is also subject to another tax imposed by another State or political subdivision thereof (whether or not at the same rate or on the same basis), without a credit (for example, a resale exemption certificate) for taxes paid in other jurisdictions.

"(B) Exception.–Such term shall not include a sales or use tax imposed by a State and 1 or more political subdivisions thereof on the same electronic commerce or a tax on persons engaged in electronic commerce which also may have been subject to a sales or use tax thereon.

"(C) Sales or use tax.–For purposes of subparagraph (B), the term 'sales or use tax' means a tax that is imposed on or incident to the sale, purchase, storage, consumption, distribution, or other use of tangible personal property or services as may be defined by laws imposing such tax and which is measured by the amount of the sales price or other charge for such property or service.

"(7) State.–The term 'State' means any of the several States, the District of Columbia, or any commonwealth, territory, or possession of the United States.

"(8) Tax.–

"(A) In general.–The term 'tax' means–

"(i) any charge imposed by any governmental entity for the purpose of generating revenues for governmental purposes, and is not a fee imposed for a specific privilege, service, or benefit conferred; or

"(ii) the imposition on a seller of an obligation to collect and to remit to a governmental entity any sales or use tax imposed on a buyer by a governmental entity.

"(B) Exception.–Such term does not include any franchise fee or similar fee imposed by a State or local franchising authority, pursuant to section 622 or 653 of the Communications Act of 1934 (47 U.S.C. 542, 573), or any other fee related to obligations or telecommunications carriers under the Communications Act of 1934 (47 U.S.C. 151 et seq.).

"(9) Telecommunications service.–The term 'telecommunications service' has the meaning given such term in section 3(46) of the Communications Act of 1934 (47 U.S.C. 153(46)) and includes communications services (as defined in section 4251 of the Internal Revenue Code of 1986).

"(10) Tax on Internet access.–The term 'tax on Internet access' means a tax on Internet access, including the enforcement or application of any new or preexisting tax on the sale or use of Internet services unless such tax was generally imposed and actually enforced prior to October 1, 1998."

Glossary

A

ACCEPTANCE
In contract law, the offeree's notification to the offeror that the offeree agrees to be bound by the terms of the offeror's proposal. Although historically the terms of acceptance had to be the mirror image of the terms of the offer, the Uniform Commercial Code provides that even modified terms of the offer in a definite expression of acceptance constitute a contract.

ACCESS CONTRACT
Under the Uniform Computer Information Transactions Act (UCITA), "a contract to obtain by electronic means access to, or information from an information processing system of another person, or the equivalent of such access."

ACCREDITED INVESTORS
In the context of securities offerings, "sophisticated" investors, such as banks, insurance companies, investment companies, the issuer's executive officers and directors, and persons whose income or net worth exceeds certain limits.

ACTIONABLE
Capable of serving as the basis of a lawsuit.

ACTUAL MALICE
Real and demonstrable evil intent. In a defamation suit, a statement made about a public figure normally must be made with actual malice (with either knowledge of its falsity or a reckless disregard of the truth) for liability to be incurred.

ADMINISTRATIVE AGENCY
A federal or state government agency established to perform a specific function. Administrative agencies are authorized by legislative acts to make and enforce rules to administer and enforce the acts.

ADMINISTRATIVE LAW
The body of law created by administrative agencies (in the form of rules, regulations, orders, and decisions) in order to carry out their duties and responsibilities.

AGENCY
A relationship between two parties in which one party (the agent) agrees to represent or act for the other (the principal).

AGENT
A person who agrees to represent or act for another, called the principal.

AGREEMENT
A meeting of two or more minds in regard to the terms of a contract; usually broken down into two events—an offer by one party to form a contract, and an acceptance of the offer by the person to whom the offer is made.

ALLEGE
To state, recite, assert, or charge.

ALTERNATIVE DISPUTE RESOLUTION (ADR)
The resolution of disputes in ways other than those involved in the traditional judicial process. Negotiation, mediation, and arbitration are forms of ADR.

AMERICAN ARBITRATION ASSOCIATION (AAA)
The major organization offering arbitration services in the United States.

ANALOGY
In logical reasoning, an assumption that if two things are similar in some respects, they will be similar in other respects also. Often used in legal reasoning to infer the appropriate application of legal principles in a case being decided by referring to previous cases involving different facts but considered to come within the policy underlying the rule.

ANTITRUST LAW
The body of federal and state laws and statutes protecting trade and commerce from unlawful restraints, price discrimination, price fixing, and monopolies.

ARBITRATION
The settling of a dispute by submitting it to a disinterested third party (other than a court), who renders a decision. The decision may or may not be legally binding.

ARBITRATION CLAUSE
A clause in a contract that provides that, in the event of a dispute, the parties will submit the dispute to arbitration rather than litigate the dispute in court.

ARTICLES OF ORGANIZATION
The document filed with a designated state official by which a limited liability company is formed.

ASSAULT
Any word or action intended to make another person fearful of immediate physical harm; a reasonably believable threat.

ASSUMPTION OF RISK
A defense against negligence that can be used when the plaintiff is aware of a danger and voluntarily assumes the risk of injury from that danger.

ATTEMPTED MONOPOLIZATION
Any actions by a firm to eliminate competition and gain monopoly power.

AUTHENTICATE
To sign a record, or with the intent to sign a record, to execute or to adopt an electronic sound, symbol, or the like to link with the record.

AUTOMATED CLEARING HOUSE (ACH)
An electronic banking system used to transfer payments and settle accounts.

AUTOMATED TELLER MACHINE (ATM)
An electronic network, located at banks and other convenient locations such as airports and shopping centers, that receives deposits, dispenses funds from checking or savings accounts, makes credit-card advances, and accepts payments.

AWARD
In the context of arbitration, the arbitrator's decision.

B

BAIT-AND-SWITCH ADVERTISING
Advertising a product at a very attractive price (the "bait") and then informing the consumer, once he or she is in the store, that the advertised product is either not available or is of poor quality; the customer is then urged to purchase ("switched" to) a more expensive item.

BANKRUPTCY COURT
A federal court of limited jurisdiction that handles only bankruptcy proceedings. Bankruptcy proceedings are governed by federal bankruptcy law.

BATTERY
The unprivileged, intentional touching of another.

BINDER
A written, temporary insurance policy.

BINDING AUTHORITY
Any source of law that a court must follow when deciding a case. Binding authorities include constitutions, statutes, and regulations that govern the issue being decided, as well as court decisions that are controlling precedents within the jurisdiction.

BLUE SKY LAWS
State laws that regulate the offer and sale of securities.

BOUNTY PAYMENT
A reward (payment) given to a person or persons who perform a certain service—such as informing legal authorities of illegal actions.

BREACH
To violate a law, by an act or an omission, or to break a legal obligation that one owes to another person or to society.

BUSINESS INVITEES
Those people, such as customers or clients, who are invited onto business premises by the owner of those premises for business purposes.

BUSINESS TRUST
A voluntary form of business organization in which investors (trust beneficiaries) transfer cash or property to trustees in exchange for trust certificates that represent their investment shares. Management of the business and trust property is handled by the trustees for the use and benefit of the investors. The certificate holders have limited liability (are not responsible for the debts and obligations incurred by the trust) and share in the trust's profits.

C

CASE LAW
The rules of law announced in court decisions. Case law includes the aggregate of reported cases that interpret judicial precedents, statutes, regulations, and constitutional provisions.

CASE ON POINT
A previous case involving factual circumstances and issues that are similar to the case before the court.

CASH SURRENDER VALUE
The amount that the insurer has agreed to pay to the insured if a life insurance policy is canceled before the insured's death.

CAUSATION IN FACT
An act or omission without ("but for") which an event would not have occurred.

CEASE-AND-DESIST ORDER
An administrative or judicial order prohibiting a person or business firm from conducting activities that an agency or court has deemed illegal.

CERTIFICATE AUTHORITY
A group charged with supervising the terms governing how buyers and sellers can legitimately make digital cash transfers.

CERTIFICATE OF INCORPORATION
The primary document that evidences corporate existence (referred to as articles of incorporation in some states).

CERTIFICATE OF LIMITED PARTNERSHIP
The basic document filed with a designated state official by which a limited partnership is formed.

CERTIFICATION MARK
A mark used by one or more persons, other than the owner, to certify the region, materials, mode of manufacture, quality, or accuracy of the owner's goods or services. When used by members of a cooperative, association, or other organization, such a mark is referred to as a collective mark. Examples of certification marks include the "Good Housekeeping Seal of Approval" and "UL Tested."

CIVIL LAW
The branch of law dealing with the definition and enforcement of all private or public rights, as opposed to criminal matters.

CLICK-ON AGREEMENT
This occurs when a buyer, completing a transaction on a computer, is required to indicate his or her assent to be bound by the terms of an offer by clicking on a button that says, for example, "I agree." Sometimes referred to as a *click-on license* or a *click-wrap agreement.*

COLLECTIVE MARK
A mark used by members of a cooperative, association, or other organization to certify the region, materials, mode of manufacture, quality, or accuracy of the specific goods or services. Examples of collective marks include the labor union marks found on tags of certain products and the credits of movies, which indicate the various associations and organizations that participated in the making of the movies.

COMMERCE CLAUSE
The provision in Article I, Section 8, of the U.S. Constitution that gives Congress the power to regulate interstate commerce.

COMMON LAW
That body of law developed from custom or judicial decisions in English and U.S. courts, not attributable to a legislature.

COMPARATIVE NEGLIGENCE
A theory in tort law under which the liability for injuries resulting from negligent acts is shared by all parties who were negligent (including the injured party), on the basis of each person's proportionate negligence.

COMPUTER CRIME
Any wrongful act that is directed against computers and computer parts, or the wrongful use or abuse of computers or software.

COMPUTER INFORMATION
Information in electronic form obtained from or through the use of a computer, or that is in digital or an equivalent form capable of being processed by a computer.

CONCILIATION
A form of alternative dispute resolution in which the parties reach an agreement themselves with the help of a neutral third party, called a conciliator, who facilitates the negotiations.

CONCURRENT JURISDICTION
Jurisdiction that exists when two different courts have the power to hear a case. For example, some cases can be heard in either a federal or a state court.

CONGLOMERATE MERGER
A merger between firms that do not compete with each other because they are in different markets (as opposed to horizontal and vertical mergers).

CONSIDERATION
Generally, the value given in return for a promise. The consideration, which must be present to make the contract legally binding, must be something of legally sufficient value and bargained for and must result in a detriment to the promisee or a benefit to the promisor.

CONSTITUTIONAL LAW
Law that is based on the U.S. Constitution and the constitutions of the various states.

CONSUMER
One whose purchases are made primarily for personal, family, or household use.

CONSUMER LAW
The body of statutes, agency rules, and judicial decisions protecting consumers of goods and services from dangerous or mislabeled products, unfair credit practices, deceptive advertising, and so on.

CONTRACT
An agreement that can be enforced in court; formed by two or more parties, each of whom agrees to perform or to refrain from performing some act now or in the future.

CONTRACTUAL CAPACITY
The threshold mental capacity required by the law for a party who enters into a contract to be bound by that contract.

CONVERSION
The wrongful taking, using, or retaining possession of personal property that belongs to another.

COOPERATIVE
An association that is organized to provide an economic service to its members (or shareholders). An incorporated cooperative is a nonprofit corporation. It will make distributions of dividends, or profits, to its owners on the basis of their transactions with the cooperative rather than on the basis of the amount of capital they contributed. Examples of cooperatives are consumer purchasing cooperatives, credit cooperatives, and farmers' cooperatives.

COPYRIGHT
The exclusive right of authors to publish, print, or sell an intellectual production for a statutory period of time. A copyright has the same monopolistic nature as a patent or trademark, but it differs in that it applies exclusively to works of art, literature, and other works of authorship, including computer programs.

CORPORATION
A legal entity formed in compliance with statutory requirements. The entity is distinct from its shareholders-owners.

COUNTERADVERTISING
New advertising that is undertaken pursuant to a Federal Trade Commission order for the purpose of correcting earlier false claims that were made about a product.

COUNTERFEITING
Making a copy of currency (or a smart card containing digital cash) with the intent to defraud.

COURT OF EQUITY
A court that decides controversies and administers justice according to the rules, principles, and precedents of equity.

COURT OF LAW
A court in which the only remedies that could be granted were things of value, such as money damages. In the early English king's courts, courts of law were distinct from courts of equity.

COVENANT NOT TO COMPETE
A contractual promise to refrain from competing with another party for a certain period of time (not excessive in duration) and within a reasonable geographic area.

CRIME
A wrong against society proclaimed in a statute and, if committed, punishable by society through fines and/or imprisonment—and, in some cases, death.

CRIMINAL LAW
Law that defines and governs actions that constitute crimes. Generally, criminal law has to do with wrongful actions committed against society for which society demands redress.

CYBER CRIME
A crime that occurs online, in the virtual community of the Internet, as opposed to the physical world.

CYBER MARK
A trademark in cyberspace.

CYBER STALKER
A person who commits the crime of stalking in cyberspace. Generally, stalking consists of harassing a person and putting that person in reasonable fear for his or her safety or the safety of the person's immediate family.

CYBER TERRORIST
A hacker whose purpose is to exploit a target computer for a serious impact, such as the corruption of a program to sabotage a business.

CYBER TORT
A tort committed in cyberspace.

CYBERLAW
An informal term that refers to all laws governing electronic communications and transactions, particularly those conducted via the Internet.

CYBERNOTARY
A legally recognized certification authority that issues the keys for digital signatures, identifies their owners, certifies their validity, and serves as a repository for public keys.

CYBERSQUATTING
An act that occurs when a person registers for a domain name that is the same as, or confusingly similar to, the trademark of another and offers to sell the domain name back to the trademark owner.

D

DAMAGES
Money sought as a remedy by a party whose legal interests have been injured.

DEBIT CARD
A plastic card that allows the bearer to transfer funds to a merchant's account, provided that the bearer authorizes the transfer by providing personal identification.

DEFALCATION
The misappropriation of funds or property.

DEFAMATION
Any published or publicly spoken false statement that causes injury to another's good name, reputation, or character.

DEFAULT RULES
Rules that apply under the Uniform Computer Information Transactions Act only in the absence of an agreement between contracting parties to the contrary.

DEFENDANT
One against whom a lawsuit is brought; the accused person in a criminal proceeding.

DEFENSE
That which a defendant offers and alleges in an action or suit as a reason why the plaintiff should not recover or establish what he or she seeks.

DIGITAL CASH
Funds contained on computer software, in the form of secure programs stored on microchips and other computer devices.

DILUTION
With respect to trademarks, a doctrine under which distinctive or famous trademarks are protected from certain unauthorized uses of the marks regardless of a showing of competition or a likelihood of confusion. Congress created a federal cause of action for dilution in 1995 with the passage of the Federal Trademark Dilution Act.

DIMINISHING MARGINAL RETURNS
The point after which the additional benefit from engaging in some activity starts to decline, even though that marginal (additional) benefit remains positive.

DIRECT E-MAIL
Volume e-mailing via the Internet to customers and others to advertise goods or services; the online equivalent of direct mail.

DISCLOSED PRINCIPAL
A principal whose identity is known to a third party at the time the agent makes a contract with the third party.

DISPARAGEMENT OF PROPERTY
An economically injurious falsehood made about another's product or property. A general term for torts that are more specifically referred to as slander of quality or slander of title.

DISTRIBUTED NETWORK
A network that can be used by persons located (distributed) around the country or the globe to share computer files.

DIVERSITY OF CITIZENSHIP
Under Article III, Section 2, of the Constitution, a basis for federal court jurisdiction over a lawsuit between citizens of different states if the amount in controversy is more than $75,000.

DIVESTITURE
The act of selling one or more of a company's parts, such as a subsidiary or plant; often mandated by the courts in merger or monopolization cases.

DOMAIN NAME
The last part of an Internet address, such as "westlaw.com." The top level (the part of the name to the right of the period) represents the type of entity that operates the site ("com" is an abbreviation for "commercial"). The second level (the part of the name to the left of the period) is chosen by the entity.

DOUBLE JEOPARDY
A situation occurring when a person is tried twice for the same criminal offense; prohibited by the Fifth Amendment to the Constitution.

DUE DILIGENCE
A required standard of care that certain professionals, such as accountants, must meet to avoid liability for securities violations.

DUTY OF CARE
The duty of all persons, as established by tort law, to exercise a reasonable amount of care in their dealings with others. Failure to exercise due care, which is normally determined by the "reasonable person standard," constitutes the tort of negligence.

E

E-AGENT
A computer program, or electronic or other automated means used to independently initiate an action or to respond to electronic messages or performances without review by an individual, according to the Uniform Computer Information Transactions Act.

E-COMMERCE
A business transaction that occurs in cyberspace.

E-COMMERCE DISPUTE
A dispute that arises from business conducted in cyberspace.

E-CONTRACT
A contract that is entered into in cyberspace and is evidenced only by electronic impulses (such as those that make up a computer's memory), rather than, for example, a typewritten form.

E-MONEY
Prepaid funds recorded on a computer or a card (such as a *smart card*).

E-MONEY TRANSFER
A transfer of funds made through the use of a smart card.

E-SIGNATURE
An electronic sound, symbol, or process attached to or logically associated with a record and executed or adopted by a person with the intent to sign the record, according to the Uniform Electronic Transactions Act.

EARLY NEUTRAL CASE EVALUATION
A form of alternative dispute resolution in which a neutral third party evaluates the strengths and weakness of the disputing parties' positions; the evaluator's opinion forms the basis for negotiating a settlement.

ECONOMIES OF SCALE
Decreases in long-run average costs resulting from increases in output.

EMBEZZLEMENT
The fraudulent appropriation of money or other property by a person to whom the money or property has been entrusted.

EMPLOYMENT AT WILL
A common law doctrine under which either party may terminate an employment relationship at any time for any reason, unless a contract specifies otherwise.

EMPLOYMENT DISCRIMINATION
Treating employees or job applicants unequally on the basis of race, color, national origin, religion, gender, age, or disability; prohibited by federal statutes.

ENCRYPTION
The process by which a message (plaintext) is transformed into something (ciphertext) that the sender and receiver intend third parties not to understand.

ENDOWMENT INSURANCE
A type of insurance that combines life insurance with an investment so that if the insured outlives the policy, the face value is paid to him or her; if the insured does not outlive the policy, the face value is paid to his or her beneficiary.

ENTRAPMENT
In criminal law, a defense in which the defendant claims that he or she was induced by a public official—usually an undercover agent or police officer—to commit a crime that he or she would otherwise not have committed.

ENTREPRENEUR
One who initiates and assumes the financial risks of a new enterprise and who undertakes to provide or control its management.

EQUITABLE MAXIMS
General propositions or principles of law that have to do with fairness (equity).

EXCLUSIONARY RULE
In criminal procedure, a rule under which any evidence that is obtained in violation of the accused's constitutional rights guaranteed by the Fourth, Fifth, and Sixth Amendments, as well as any evidence derived from illegally obtained evidence, will not be admissible in court.

EXCLUSIVE-DEALING CONTRACT
An agreement under which a seller forbids a buyer to purchase products from the seller's competitors.

EXCLUSIVE JURISDICTION
Jurisdiction that exists when a case can be heard only in a particular court or type of court, such as a federal court or a state court.

EXECUTIVE AGENCY
An administrative agency within the executive branch of government. At the federal level, executive agencies are those within the cabinet departments.

F

FEDERAL FORM OF GOVERNMENT
A system of government in which the states form a union and the sovereign power is divided between a central government and the member states.

FEDERAL QUESTION
A question that pertains to the U.S. Constitution, acts of Congress, or treaties. A federal question provides a basis for federal jurisdiction.

FELONY
A crime—such as arson, murder, rape, or robbery—that carries the most severe sanctions, usually ranging from one year in a state or federal prison to the forfeiture of one's life.

FIDUCIARY DUTY
The duty, imposed on a person by virtue of his or her position, to act primarily for another's benefit.

FILTERING SOFTWARE
A computer program that includes a pattern through which data are passed. When designed to block access to certain Web sites, the pattern blocks the retrieval of a site whose URL or key words are on a list within the program.

FIREWALL
A barrier between networked computers and the network to which they are connected.

FLAME
An online message in which one party attacks another in harsh, often personal, terms.

FORGERY
The fraudulent making or altering of any writing in a way that changes the legal rights and liabilities of another.

FRANCHISE
Any arrangement in which the owner of a trademark, trade name, or copyright licenses another to use that trademark, trade name, or copyright, under specified conditions or limitations, in the selling of goods and services.

FRANCHISEE
One receiving a license to use another's (the franchisor's) trademark, trade name, or copyright in the sale of goods and services.

FRANCHISOR
One licensing another (the franchisee) to use his or her trademark, trade name, or copyright in the sale of goods or services.

FRAUDULENT MISREPRESENTATION (FRAUD)
Any misrepresentation, either by misstatement or omission of a material fact, knowingly made with the intention of deceiving another and on which a reasonable person would and does rely to his or her detriment.

G

GENERAL PARTNER
In a limited partnership, a partner who assumes responsibility for the management of the partnership and liability for all partnership debts.

GENERALLY ACCEPTED ACCOUNTING PRINCIPLES (GAAP)
The conventions, rules, and procedures necessary to define accepted accounting practices at a particular time. The source of the principles is the Federal Accounting Standards Board.

GENERALLY ACCEPTED AUDITING STANDARDS (GAAS)
Standards concerning an auditor's professional qualities and the judgment exercised by him or her in the performance of an examination and report. The source of the standards is the American Institute of Certified Public Accountants.

GENUINENESS OF ASSENT
Knowing and voluntary assent to the terms of a contract. If a contract is formed as a result of a mistake, misrepresentation, undue influence, or duress, genuineness of assent is lacking, and the contract will be voidable.

GROUP BOYCOTT
The refusal to deal with a particular person or firm by a group of competitors; prohibited by the Sherman Act.

H

HACKER
A person who uses one computer to break into another. Professional computer programmers refer to such persons as "crackers."

HORIZONTAL MERGER
A merger between two firms that are competing in the same market.

HORIZONTAL RESTRAINT
Any agreement that in some way restrains competition between rival firms competing in the same market.

HOSTILE-ENVIRONMENT HARASSMENT
According to the United States Supreme Court, a form of harassment that occurs when the workplace is "permeated with discriminatory intimidation, ridicule, and insult, that is sufficiently severe or pervasive to alter the conditions of the victim's employment and create an abusive working environment."

I

***IN PERSONAM* JURISDICTION**
Court jurisdiction over the "person" involved in a legal action; personal jurisdiction.

***IN REM* JURISDICTION**
Court jurisdiction over a defendant's property.

INCOME TAX
A tax on personal and corporate income. Income taxes are an important source of revenue for both state governments and the federal government.

INCREASING RETURNS
A production situation in which a doubling of all production inputs—for example, land, labor, machines, and so on—leads to more than a doubling of output.

INDEPENDENT CONTRACTOR
One who works for, and receives payment from, an employer but whose working conditions and methods are not controlled by the employer. An independent contractor is not an employee but may be an agent.

INDEPENDENT REGULATORY AGENCY
An administrative agency that is not considered part of the government's executive branch and is not subject to the authority of the president. Independent agency officials cannot be removed without cause.

INFORMATION SECURITY
The ability to control access to computer information.

INSIDER TRADING
The purchase or sale of securities on the basis of "inside information" (information that has not been made available to the public) in violation of a duty owed to the company whose stock is being traded.

INSURABLE INTEREST
An interest either in a person's life or well-being or in property that is sufficiently substantial that insuring against injury to (or the death of) the person or against damage to the property does not amount to a mere wagering (betting) contract.

INSURANCE
A contract in which, for a stipulated consideration, one party agrees to compensate the other for loss on a specific subject by a specified peril.

INTELLECTUAL PROPERTY
Property resulting from intellectual, creative processes. Patents, trademarks, and copyrights are examples of intellectual property.

INTENTIONAL TORT
A wrongful act knowingly committed.

INVESTMENT COMPANY
A company that acts on behalf of many smaller shareholder-owners by buying a large portfolio of securities and professionally managing that portfolio.

J

JAVASCRIPT
A programming language that enhances the capabilities of Web pages.

JOINT STOCK COMPANY
A hybrid form of business organization that combines characteristics of a corporation (shareholder-owners, management by directors and officers of the company, and perpetual existence) and a partnership (it is formed by agreement, not statute; property is usually held in the names of the members; and the shareholders have personal liability for business debts). Usually, the joint stock company is regarded as a partnership for tax and other legally related purposes.

JOINT VENTURE
A joint undertaking of a specific commercial enterprise by an association of persons. A joint venture is normally not a legal entity and is treated like a partnership for federal income tax purposes.

JUDICIAL REVIEW
The process by which courts decide on the constitutionality of legislative enactments and actions of the executive branch.

JURISDICTION
The authority of a court to hear and decide a specific action.

JUSTICIABLE CONTROVERSY
A controversy that is not hypothetical or academic but real and substantial; a requirement that must be satisfied before a court will hear a case.

L

LACHES
The equitable doctrine that bars a party's right to legal action if the party has neglected for an unreasonable length of time to act on his or her rights.

LARCENY
The wrongful taking and carrying away of another person's personal property with the intent to permanently deprive the owner of the property.

LAW
A body of enforceable rules governing relationships among individuals and between individuals and their society.

LEGAL REASONING
The process of reasoning by which a judge harmonizes his or her decision with the judicial decisions of previous cases.

LIBEL
Defamation in writing or other form (such as in a videotape) having the quality of permanence.

LIMITED LIABILITY COMPANY (LLC)
A hybrid form of business enterprise that offers the limited liability of the corporation but the tax advantages of a partnership.

LIMITED LIABILITY LIMITED PARTNERSHIP (LLLP)
A type of limited partnership. The difference between a limited partnership and an LLLP is that the liability of the general partner in an LLLP is the same as the liability of the limited partner. That is, the liability of all partners is limited to the amount of their investments in the firm.

LIMITED LIABILITY PARTNERSHIP (LLP)
A form of partnership that allows professionals to enjoy the tax benefits of a partnership while limiting their personal liability for the malpractice of other partners.

LIMITED PARTNER
In a limited partnership, a partner who contributes capital to the partnership but has no right to participate in the management and operation of the business. The limited partner assumes no liability for partnership debts beyond the capital contributed.

LIMITED-PAYMENT LIFE
A type of life insurance for which premiums are payable for a definite period, after which the policy is fully paid.

LITIGATION
The process of resolving a dispute through the court system.

LONG ARM STATUTE
A state statute that permits a state to obtain personal jurisdiction over nonresident defendants. A defendant must have "minimum contacts" with that state for the statute to apply.

M

MAILBOX RULE
A rule providing that an acceptance of an offer becomes effective on dispatch (on being placed in a mailbox), if mail is, expressly or impliedly, an authorized means of communication of acceptance to the offeror.

MARKET CONCENTRATION
A situation that exists when a small number of firms share the market for a particular good or service. For example, if the four largest grocery stores in Chicago accounted for 80 percent of all retail food sales, the market clearly would be concentrated in those four firms.

MARKET POWER
The power of a firm to control the market price of its product. A monopoly has the greatest degree of market power.

MARKET-SHARE TEST
The primary measure of monopoly power. A firm's market share is the percentage of a market that the firm controls.

MASS-MARKET LICENSE
An e-contract that is presented with a package of computer information in the form of a click-on license or a shrink-wrap license.

MEDIATION
A method of settling disputes outside of court by using the services of a neutral third party, called a mediator. The mediator acts as a communicating agent between the parties and suggests ways in which the parties can resolve their dispute.

MEMBER
The term used to designate a person who has an ownership interest in a limited liability company.

META TAGS
Words inserted into a Web site's key words field to increase the likelihood that the site will appear in search engine results.

MINI-TRIAL
A private proceeding in which each party to a dispute argues its position before the other side and vice versa. A neutral third party may be present and act as an adviser if the parties fail to reach an agreement.

MIRROR IMAGE RULE
A common law rule that requires, for a valid contractual agreement, that the terms of the offeree's acceptance adhere exactly to the terms of the offeror's offer.

MISDEMEANOR
A lesser crime than a felony, punishable by a fine or imprisonment for up to one year in other than a state or federal penitentiary.

MONOPOLIZATION
The possession of monopoly power in the relevant market and the willful acquisition or maintenance of the power, as distinguished from growth or development as a consequence of a superior product, business acumen, or historic accident.

MONOPOLY
A term generally used to describe a market in which there is a single seller or a limited number of sellers.

MONOPOLY POWER
The ability of a monopoly to dictate what takes place in a given market.

MULTIPLE PRODUCT ORDER
An order issued by the Federal Trade Commission to a firm that has engaged in deceptive advertising by which the firm is required to cease and desist from false advertising not only in regard to the product that was the subject of the action but also in regard to all of the firm's other products.

MUTUAL FUND
A specific type of investment company that continually buys or sells to investors shares of ownership in a portfolio.

N

NATURAL MONOPOLY
A monopoly that arises from the peculiar production characteristics in an industry. It usually arises when there are large economies of scale relative to the industry's demand such that one firm can produce at a lower average cost than can be achieved by multiple firms.

NEGLIGENCE
The failure to exercise the standard of care that a reasonable person would exercise in similar circumstances.

NEGOTIATION
A process in which parties attempt to settle their dispute without going to court, with or without attorneys to represent them.

NEWSGROUP
A discussion group operated according to certain Internet formats and rules. Like a bulletin board, a newsgroup is a location to which participants go to read and post messages.

NEXUS
A physical connection, or link. Before a state can impose taxes on an out-of-state resident, there must exist a sufficient nexus between the activities of the out-of-state resident and the taxing state.

OFFER
A promise or commitment to perform or refrain from performing some specified act in the future.

OFFEREE
A person to whom an offer is made.

OFFEROR
A person who makes an offer.

OMNIBUS CLAUSE
A provision in an automobile insurance policy that protects the vehicle owner who has taken out the insurance policy and anyone who drives the vehicle with the owner's permission.

ONLINE DISPUTE RESOLUTION (ODR)
The resolution of a dispute in cyberspace. Cyberspace is the online world within which computer-based networks operate.

OPERATING AGREEMENT
In a limited liability company, an agreement in which the members set forth the details of how the business will be managed and operated.

ORDINANCE
A law passed by a local governing unit, such as a municipality or a county.

PANEL
An arbitrator, or arbitrators, appointed to make a decision in a dispute-resolution proceeding.

PARTIALLY DISCLOSED PRINCIPAL
A principal whose identity is unknown by a third person, but the third person knows that the agent is or may be acting for a principal at the time the agent and the third person form a contract.

PARTNERING AGREEMENT
An agreement between a seller and a buyer who frequently do business with each other on the terms and conditions that will apply to all subsequently formed electronic contracts.

PARTNERSHIP
An agreement by two or more persons to carry on, as co-owners, a business for profit.

PATENT
A government grant that gives an inventor the exclusive right or privilege to make, use, or sell his or her invention for a limited time period. The word *patent* usually refers to some invention and designates either the instrument by which patent rights are evidenced or the patent itself.

PEER-TO-PEER (P2P) NETWORKING
A technology that allows Internet users to access files on other users' computers.

***PER SE* VIOLATION**
A type of anticompetitive agreement—such as a horizontal price-fixing agreement—that is considered to be so injurious to the public that there is no need to determine whether it actually injures market competition; rather, it is in itself (*per se*) a violation of the Sherman Act.

PERFORMANCE
In contract law, the fulfillment of one's duties arising under a contract with another; the normal way of discharging one's contractual obligations.

PETITIONER
In equity practice, a party that initiates a lawsuit.

PLAINTIFF
One who initiates a lawsuit.

POLICE POWERS
Powers possessed by states as part of their inherent sovereignty. These powers may be exercised to protect or promote the public order, health, safety, morals, and general welfare.

POLICY
In insurance law, a contract between the insurer and the insured in which, for a stipulated consideration, the insurer agrees to compensate the insured for loss on a specific subject by a specified peril.

PRECEDENT
A court decision that furnishes an example or authority for deciding subsequent cases involving identical or similar facts.

PREDATORY PRICING
The pricing of a product below cost with the intent to drive competitors out of the market.

PREMIUM
In insurance law, the price paid by the insured for insurance protection for a specified period of time.

PRICE DISCRIMINATION
Setting prices in such a way that two competing buyers pay two different prices for an identical product or service.

PRICE-FIXING AGREEMENT
An agreement between competitors in which the competitors agree to fix the prices of products or services at a certain level; prohibited by the Sherman Act.

PRINCIPAL
In agency law, a person who agrees to have another, called the agent, act on his or her behalf.

PRIVILEGE
In tort law, the ability to act contrary to another person's right without that person's having legal redress for such acts. Privilege may be raised as a defense to defamation.

PROBATE COURT
A state court of limited jurisdiction that conducts proceedings relating to the settlement of a deceased person's estate.

PROCEDURAL LAW
Rules that define the manner in which the rights and duties of individuals may be enforced.

PROMISE
A declaration that something either will or will not happen in the future.

PROMISSORY ESTOPPEL
A doctrine that applies when a promisor makes a clear and definite promise on which the promisee justifiably relies; such a promise is binding if justice will be better served by the enforcement of the promise.

PROSPECTUS
A document required by federal or state securities laws that describes the financial operations of the corporation, thus allowing investors to make informed decisions.

PROTECTED CLASS
A class of persons with identifiable characteristics who historically have been victimized by discriminatory treatment for certain purposes. Depending on the context, these characteristics include age, color, gender, national origin, race, and religion.

PROXIMATE CAUSE
Legal cause; exists when the connection between an act and an injury is strong enough to justify imposing liability.

PUBLIC FIGURES
Individuals who are thrust into the public limelight. Public figures include government officials and politicians, movie stars, well-known businesspersons, and generally anybody who becomes known to the public because of his or her position or activities.

PUBLIC POLICY
A government policy based on widely held societal values and (usually) expressed or implied in laws or regulations.

PUFFERY
A salesperson's often exaggerated claims concerning the quality of property offered for sale. Such claims involve opinions rather than facts and are not considered to be legally binding promises or warranties.

Q

QUESTION OF FACT
In a lawsuit, an issue involving a factual dispute that can only be decided by a judge (or, in a jury trial, a jury).

QUESTION OF LAW
In a lawsuit, an issue involving the application or interpretation of a law; therefore, the judge, and not the jury, decides the issue.

***QUID PRO QUO* HARASSMENT**
A form of sexual harassment that occurs when job opportunities, promotions, salary increases, and other benefits are given in return for sexual favors.

R

REASONABLE PERSON STANDARD
The standard of behavior expected of a hypothetical "reasonable person." The standard against which negligence is measured and that must be observed to avoid liability for negligence.

RECORD
Information that is either inscribed in a tangible medium or stored in an electronic or other medium and that is retrievable, according to the Uniform Electronic Transactions Act. The Uniform Computer Information Transactions Act uses *record* instead of *writing.*

REGULATION E
A set of rules issued by the Federal Reserve System's board of governors to protect users of elecronic fund transfer systems.

REMEDY
The relief given to an innocent party to enforce a right or compensate for the violation of a right.

REMEDY AT LAW
A remedy available in a court of law. Money damages are awarded as a remedy at law.

REMEDY IN EQUITY
A remedy allowed by courts in situations where remedies at law are not appropriate. Remedies in equity are based on settled rules of fairness, justice, and honesty, and include injunction, specific performance, rescission and restitution, and reformation.

REPORTER
A publication in which court cases are published, or reported.

RESALE PRICE MAINTENANCE AGREEMENT
An agreement between a manufacturer and a retailer in which the manufacturer specifies the minimum retail price of its products. Resale price maintenance agreements may be illegal *per se* under the Sherman Act.

RESCISSION
A remedy whereby a contract is canceled and the parties are returned to the positions they occupied before the contract was made; may be effected through the mutual consent of the parties, by their conduct, or by court decree.

RESPONDENT
In equity practice, the party who answers a bill or other proceeding.

RESPONDEAT SUPERIOR
In Latin, "Let the master respond." A doctrine under which a principal or an employer is held liable for the wrongful acts committed by agents or employees while acting within the course and scope of their agency or employment.

RESTRAINT ON TRADE
Any contract or combination that tends to eliminate or reduce competition, effect a monopoly, artificially maintain prices, or otherwise hamper the course of trade and commerce.

RISK
A prediction concerning potential loss based on known and unknown factors.

RISK MANAGEMENT
Planning that is undertaken to protect one's interest should some event threaten to undermine its security. In the context of insurance, risk management involves transferring certain risks from the insured to the insurance company.

ROBBERY
The act of forcefully and unlawfully taking personal property of any value from another; force or intimidation is usually necessary for an act of theft to be considered a robbery.

RULE OF FOUR
A rule of the United States Supreme Court under which the Court will not issue a writ of *certiorari* unless at least four justices approve of the decision to issue the writ.

RULE OF REASON

A test by which a court balances the positive effects (such as economic efficiency) of an agreement against its potentially anticompetitive effects. In antitrust litigation, many practices are analyzed under the rule of reason.

S

S CORPORATION

A relatively small business corporation that has met certain requirements as set out by the Internal Revenue Code and thus qualifies for special income tax treatment. Essentially, an S corporation is taxed the same as a partnership, but its owners enjoy the privilege of limited liability.

SALES CONTRACT

A contract for the sale of goods under which the ownership of goods is transferred from a seller to a buyer for a price.

SALES TAXES

Taxes levied by state and local governments on goods as they are sold. Merchants collect sales taxes from those who purchase their goods and forward the collected tax dollars to the relevant state or local government agencies.

SCIENTER

Knowledge by the misrepresenting party that material facts have been falsely represented or omitted with an intent to deceive.

SEC RULE 10b-5

A rule of the Securities and Exchange Commission that makes it unlawful, in connection with the purchase or sale of any security, to make any untrue statement of a material fact or to omit a material fact if such omission causes the statement to be misleading.

SECURITIES

Generally, corporate stocks and bonds. A security may also be a note, debenture, stock warrant, or any document given as evidence of an ownership interest in a corporation or as a promise of repayment by a corporation.

SERVICE MARK

A mark used in the sale or the advertising of services, such as to distinguish the services of one person from the services of others. Titles, character names, and other distinctive features of radio and television programs may be registered as service marks.

SEXUAL HARASSMENT

In the employment context, the granting of job promotions or other benefits in return for sexual favors or language or conduct that is so sexually offensive that it creates a hostile working environment.

SHRINK-WRAP AGREEMENT

An agreement whose terms are expressed inside a box in which goods are packaged; sometimes called a *shrink-wrap license.*

SLANDER

Defamation in oral form.

SMALL CLAIMS COURTS

Special courts in which parties may litigate small claims (usually, claims involving $5,000 or less). Attorneys are not required in small claims courts, and in many states attorneys are not allowed to represent the parties.

SMART CARD

A card containing a microprocessor that permits storage of funds via security programming, can communicate with other computers, and does not require online authorization for fund transfers.

SOLE PROPRIETORSHIP

The simplest form of business, in which the owner is the business; the owner reports business income on his or her personal income tax return and is legally responsible for all debts and obligations incurred by the business.

SPAM

Bulk, unsolicited ("junk") e-mail.

SPECIFIC PERFORMANCE

An equitable remedy requiring exactly the performance that was specified in a contract; usually granted only when money damages would be an inadequate remedy and the subject matter of the contract is unique (for example, real property).

STANDING TO SUE

The requirement that an individual must have a sufficient stake in a controversy before he or she can bring a lawsuit. The plaintiff must demonstrate that he or she either has been injured or threatened with injury.

STARE DECISIS

A common law doctrine under which judges are obligated to follow the precedents established in prior decisions.

STATUTE OF FRAUDS

A state statute under which certain types of contracts must be in writing to be enforceable.

STATUTE OF LIMITATIONS

A federal or state statute setting the maximum time period during which a certain action can be brought or certain rights enforced.

STATUTORY LAW

The body of law enacted by legislative bodies (as opposed to constitutional law, administrative law, or case law).

STORED-VALUE CARD

A card bearing magnetic stripes that holds magnetically encoded data, providing access to stored funds.

STRICT LIABILITY

Liability regardless of fault. In tort law, strict liability may be imposed on defendants in cases involving defective products, abnormally dangerous activities, or dangerous animals.

SUBSTANTIVE LAW

Law that defines the rights and duties of individuals with respect to each other, as opposed to procedural law, which defines the manner in which these rights and duties may be enforced.

SUMMARY JURY TRIAL (SJT)

A method of settling disputes in which a trial is held, but the jury's verdict is not binding. The verdict acts only as a guide to both sides in reaching an agreement during the mandatory negotiations that immediately follow the summary jury trial.

SWITCHING COSTS

The costs associated with changing from one system of production to another—for example, the cost of switching from the Macintosh computer operating system to the Microsoft Windows operating system.

SYLLOGISM
A form of deductive reasoning consisting of a major premise, a minor premise, and a conclusion.

SYNDICATE
An investment group of persons or firms brought together for the purpose of financing a project that they would not or could not undertake independently.

T

TARGETED MARKETING
Advertising directed to ("targeted" at) a specific group of consumers who, judging from their interests and past purchasing habits, would be the most likely purchasers of the product being marketed.

TERM INSURANCE
A type of life insurance policy for which premiums are paid for a specified term. Payment on the policy is due only if death occurs within the term period. Premiums are less expensive than for whole life or limited-payment life, and there is usually no cash surrender value.

TIPPEE
A person who receives inside information.

TOMBSTONE AD
An advertisement, historically in a format resembling a tombstone, of a securities offering. The ad informs potential investors of where and how they may obtain a prospectus.

TORT
A civil wrong not arising from a breach of contract. A breach of a legal duty that proximately causes harm or injury to another.

TORTFEASOR
One who commits a tort.

TRADE DRESS
The image and overall appearance of a product—for example, the distinctive decor, menu, layout, and style of service of a particular restaurant. Basically, trade dress is subject to the same protection as trademarks.

TRADE NAME
A term that is used to indicate part or all of a business's name and that is directly related to the business's reputation and goodwill. Trade names are protected under the common law (and under trademark law, if the name is the same as the firm's trademarked property).

TRADE SECRET
Information or a process that gives a business an advantage over competitors who do not know the information or process.

TRADEMARK
A distinctive mark, motto, device, or implement that a manufacturer stamps, prints, or otherwise affixes to the goods it produces so that they may be identified on the market and their origins made known. Once a trademark is established (under the common law or through registration), the owner is entitled to its exclusive use.

TRESPASS TO LAND
The entry onto, above, or below the surface of land owned by another without the owner's permission or legal authorization.

TRESPASS TO PERSONAL PROPERTY
The unlawful taking or harming of another's personal property; interference with another's right to the exclusive possession of his or her personal property.

TYING ARRANGEMENT
An agreement between a buyer and a seller in which the buyer, in order to purchase a specific product or service, must agree to purchase additional products or services from the seller.

U

UNDERWRITER
In insurance law, the insurer, or the one assuming a risk in return for the payment of a premium.

UNDISCLOSED PRINCIPAL
A principal whose identity is unknown by a third person, and the third person has no knowledge that the agent is acting for a principal at the time the agent and the third person form a contract.

UNIFORM LAW
A model law created by the National Conference of Commissioners on Uniform State Laws and/or the American Law Institute for the states to consider adopting. If the state adopts the law, it becomes statutory law in that state. Each state has the option of adopting or rejecting all or part of a uniform law.

UNIVERSAL LIFE
A type of insurance that combines some aspects of term insurance with some aspects of whole life insurance.

V

VENTURE CAPITAL
Funds that are invested in, or that are available for investment in, a new corporate enterprise.

VENTURE CAPITALIST
A person or entity that seeks out promising entrepreneurial ventures and funds them in exchange for equity stakes.

VENUE
The geographical district in which a trial is held and from which the jury is selected.

VERIFIABLE PARENTAL CONSENT
Under the Children's Online Privacy and Protection Act (COPPA) of 2000, a requirement that parental consent must be obtained by Web site operators before any information about children under the age of thirteen can access chat rooms and message boards of child-oriented Web sites.

VERTICAL MERGER
The acquisition by a business at one stage of production of a business at a higher or lower stage of production (such as a business merging with one of its suppliers or retailers).

VERTICAL RESTRAINT
Any restraint on trade created by agreements between firms at different levels in the manufacturing and distribution process.

VERTICALLY INTEGRATED FIRM
A firm that carries out two or more functional phases (manufacture, distribution, retailing, and so on) of a product.

VICARIOUS LIABILITY

Legal responsibility placed on one person for the acts of another.

W

WEIGHTLESS ECONOMY
That part of the economy that deals with information collection, transmission, analysis, and so on and that therefore has no physical weight. This also includes intellectual property and the financial sector.

WHISTLEBLOWING
An employee's disclosure to government, the press, or management authorities that the employer is engaged in unsafe or illegal activities.

WHITE-COLLAR CRIME
Nonviolent crime committed by individuals or corporations to obtain a personal or business advantage.

WHOLE LIFE
A life insurance policy in which the insured pays a level premium for his or her entire life and in which there is a constantly accumulating cash value that can be withdrawn or borrowed against by the borrower. Sometimes referred to as straight life insurance.

WORKING PAPERS
The various documents used and developed by an accountant dur-

Table of Cases

Index

B

C

E

J

K

V